DECISIONS FOR Teen HEALTH

HEALTHY LIVING

Mary Bronson Merki, Ph.D.

GLENCOE

Macmillan/McGraw-Hill

Lake Forest, Illinois
Columbus, Ohio
Mission Hills, California
Peoria, Illinois

Photo Credits

Page i: Stephen McBrady; page v, top: Comstock; page v, bottom: Richard Hutchings; page vi, top: Mark Snyder/Journalism Services; page vi, bottom: Bob Daemmrich/Stock, Boston; page vii, top: Don Smetzer/TSW/Click/Chicago; page vii, bottom: Janeart Ltd./The Image Bank;

page viii, top: Howard Sochurek/Medichrome; page viii, bottom: Courtesy of the American Lung Association; page ix, top: © 1985 Bobby Holland/Poster reprinted by permission of Reader's Digest Foundation; page ix, bottom: Tom Dunham; page x, top: Alvis Upitis/The Image Bank;

page x, bottom: Frank Cezus/FPG International; page xi, top: Alan Carey/Photo Researchers, Inc.; page xi, bottom: Tom Dunham; page xii: Spencer Swanger/Tom Stack & Associates; page xiii: Stephen McBrady; page xv: Stephen McBrady; page xvii: Stephen McBrady

photo credits continue on page A65

Production Services provided by Visual Education Corporation

Copyright © 1990 by Glencoe/McGraw-Hill Educational Division.

All rights reserved. Printed in the United States of America. Except as permitted under the United States Copyright Act, no part of this publication may be reproduced or distributed in any form or by any means, or stored in a database or retrieval system, without prior permission of the publisher.
Send all inquiries to:
GLENCOE DIVISION
Macmillan/McGraw-Hill
15319 Chatsworth Street
P.O. Box 9609
Mission Hills, CA 91346-9609
ISBN 0-02-652410-4 (Student Text)
ISBN 0-02-652411-2 (Teacher's Wraparound Edition)

5 6 7 8 9   93 92 91

Content Specialists

Medical and Dental Health

David Allen, M.D.
New York Hospital
Cornell Medical Center
New York, NY

Philip Cocuzza
Executive Director
New Jersey Dental Association
New Brunswick, NJ

Loraine Chammah
School nurse
Austin Independent
    School District

Mental and Social Health

Howard Shapiro, M.D.
Department of Psychiatry
University of Southern California
    Medical School
Los Angeles, CA

Food and Nutrition

Judy Alexander
Professor of Nutrition
Moorpark College
Moorpark, CA

Roberta Duyff
Nutrition education consultant
St. Louis, MO

Kitty Hester
Nutrition education consultant
Austin, TX

Tobacco, Alcohol, and Drugs

Robert Anastis
Executive Director
Students Against Driving Drunk

W. Robert Banks
Coordinator, Drug Education
    Unit
South Carolina State Department
    of Education
Columbia, SC

Beverly Barron
Texans' War on Drugs
Austin, TX

Ms. Gina Burnly
National Clearinghouse for
    Alcohol and Drug Information
Rockville, MD

Safety and First Aid

Diane Imhulse and others
Director, Community and
    Agricultural Safety Programs
    Group
National Safety Council

Health Educator

Richard L. Papenfuss, Ph.D.
Professor, Director of Health
    Promotion
University of New Mexico
Albuquerque, NM

Diseases and Disorders

**Ruth Donnelly Corcoran,
    Ed.D.**
Director of Youth Education
American Cancer Society
Atlanta, GA

D. Peter Drotman, M.D.
AIDS Program
Center for Infectious Diseases,
    Centers for Disease Control
Atlanta, GA

John R. Moore, Ph.D., R.N.
Division of Adolescent and
    School Health
Center for Chronic Disease
    Prevention and Health
    Promotion, Centers for
    Disease Control
Atlanta, GA

**Elizabeth Warren-Boulton,
    R.N., M.S.N.**
Director, Program Development
American Diabetes Association
Alexandria, VA

Mary Winston, Ed.D.
Senior Science Consultant
American Heart Association
Dallas, TX

Teacher Reviewers

Sandra Rae Badger
Department Head, Health
    Education
Thomas B. Doherty High School
Colorado Springs, Colorado

E. Lee Cook
Health Teacher
Markham Middle School
Portland, Oregon

Lynn Haley
Health Teacher
Mackenzie Junior High School
Lubbock, Texas

Thomas A. Hermanowski
Director of Health Education
Wayland Public Schools
Wayland, Massachusetts

Allen E. Petty
Coordinator, Science and Health
Carrollton-Farmers Branch
    Independent School District
Carrollton, Texas

Eileen M. Sake
Health and Physical Education
    Teacher
Northern Valley Regional High
    School
Demarest, New Jersey

Heidi R. Tyler
Health Teacher
Bay Trail Middle School
Penfield, New York

Earl Yost
Health and Physical Education
    Teacher
Camp Hill High School
Camp Hill, Pennsylvania

Drew F. Bolander
Assistant Principal and Health
    Curriculum Coordinator
Timpview High School
Orem, Utah

Lisa DeVeaux
Health Specialist
Dallas Independent School
    District
Dallas, Texas

Sonya Heckman
Health Teacher
Greencastle Antrim School
    District
Greencastle, Pennsylvania

Dorothy Oetter
Coordinator, Health and Physical
    Education
Anchorage School District
Anchorage, Alaska

Susan E. Polk
Health Teacher
Crabapple Middle School
Atlanta, Georgia

George Shackelford
Chief Consultant-Health
    Education
State Department of Public
    Instruction
Raleigh, North Carolina

Francis R. Veltri
Consultant for Secondary
    Science and Health
Corpus Christi Independent
    School District
Corpus Christi, Texas

Diane M. Bruckerhoff
Health Sciences Coordinator
Columbia Public Schools
Columbia, Missouri

Nell Fisher
Health Educator
Charlotte, North Carolina

Patricia Jo Helmers
Health Instructor
Sumner Junior-Senior High
    School
Sumner, Iowa

Odette Perkins
Health Teacher
Perkins Intermediate School
Brownsville, Texas

Valerie Pribnow
Health Resource Teacher
Renton School District
Renton, Washington

Shaune Troutman
Chairperson, Home and Family
    Life, Health Education
Lake Washington High School
Kirkland, Washington

Lynn Westberg
Health Teacher
Kearns High School
Salt Lake City, Utah

CONTENTS

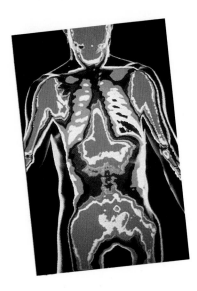

CHAPTER 13

Safety and Your Health

CHAPTER 14

Consumer and Public Health

CHAPTER 15

The Environment and Your Health

Health Handbook

Charts

Illustrations

Making Healthy Decisions

Teen Health Bulletin Boards

Wellness and Your Total Health

CHAPTER WARM-UP

Chapter Study Goals

After you have read this chapter, you will be able to

- explain the concept of wellness.
- explain the concept of total health.
- identify factors that play a role in your total health.
- identify key lifestyle factors.
- explain why fitness is important.
- tell what a person needs to know in planning an exercise program.

Be on the lookout for information in the chapter that will help you reach these goals.

Getting Started

"Health? Sure I know what health is. It's never being sick."
—Dom, age 14

"My brother's a weight lifter. You should see his muscles. Now that's what I call good health!"
—Chin, age 13

What is your definition of health? As you read this chapter, you will learn a good one. You will also learn a number of facts about healthy outlooks and how your attitudes lead to healthy living.

Study Tip

As you read this chapter, pay attention to the words in dark type. How do these words relate to your personal health and wellness?

Wellness and the Health Triangle

Words to Know
health
wellness

Life Skills
Many of the factors that relate to good mental and social health involve life skills. These skills include good *communication* skills, *decision-making* and *problem-solving* skills, and *goal-setting* skills. Like other skills you have learned in and out of school, these require practice. You will be learning more about these skills in later chapters. Chapter 3 has more on decisions and solving problems.

More About
People who have trouble **getting along** *with others often have needs that aren't being met. To find out more about this problem, see Chapter 3.*

This lesson contains a number of valuable facts and tips. Once you have studied them, you will be able to

- name the sides of the health triangle.
- define the term *wellness.*

Health and You

You make choices every day that affect your health. You decide what to eat, whom to have for friends, and how to spend your time. Do you know which choices lead to good health and which do not? This book will help you learn to recognize the right choices. It will also give you the chance to look at your health habits now. Then you can decide what you need to do to become a healthier person.

What Is Health?

Many people, like Dom in the Chapter Warm-Up, think that being healthy is not being sick. Or, like Chin, they think that if a person is in good physical shape, that person is healthy.

But there are problems with thinking of health in physical terms alone. Do you know students who are always getting into fights? Would you call these people healthy? And what about a person who never seems to feel happy no matter what he or she does? Being in good shape is important. Yet there is much more than that to good health.

"Total Health"

Besides physical health, your total health picture takes into account your *mental health* and your *social health.* In other words, being healthy also means feeling good about yourself and getting along with

others. **Health** is *a combination of physical, mental, and social well-being.* The meaning of each of the three sides of health is examined more fully in the chart that follows.

Learning from Photographs
Each of the three sides of health plays an important part in a person's overall well-being. Is one side more important than the other two?

The Three Sides of Health

Physical Health	Mental Health	Social Health
• Includes total care of your body and meeting the demands of life each day	• Includes liking who you are and accepting yourself	• Includes getting along with others
• Includes keeping your body fit	• Includes expressing your emotions in a healthy way	• Includes working well in a group
• Includes knowing and practicing good grooming habits	• Includes facing life's problems and dealing with its pressures, or stresses	• Includes making and keeping friends
• Includes eating a well-balanced diet		• Includes giving and getting support when it is needed

Your Health Triangle

The three sides of your health are connected, like the sides of a triangle. Each side affects the other two sides. For example, being physically tired can make you grouchy. Being depressed for a long time can make you feel weak and run-down.

To be healthy, you need to have a balanced health triangle. You can accomplish this by working to keep each side of your triangle healthy.

Learning from Drawings
By taking the self-inventory in Lesson 3, you can identify your own level of health. Which of the two triangles shown here reflects good health?

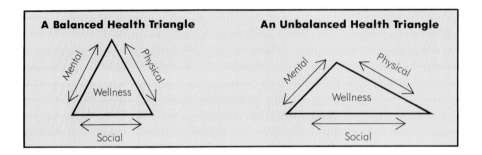

Wellness and Total Health

Thanks to modern research, we know more about health than ever before. We now know that many diseases and illnesses can be blamed at least partly on bad health habits. These bad habits include eating the wrong foods and using tobacco or alcohol or drugs. Other bad habits are getting too little exercise and handling stress poorly.

Practicing *good* health habits lessens our chances of illness and helps us stay well. Good health habits include the following.

- Choosing the right foods
- Avoiding tobacco, alcohol, and drugs
- Taking part in a regular program of exercise
- Learning ways of handling stress

Learning from Drawings
A person's level of health falls somewhere on a line, or continuum, from a high level to a low level. Why do you think most people are below the midpoint on the continuum?

Health and Wellness Continuum

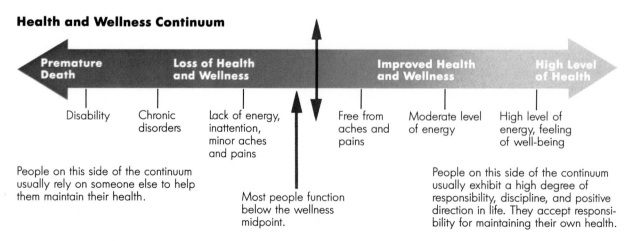

Learning from Photographs
Keeping up with health news can help you make healthy decisions. Where can you get information on health?

This knowledge has led health educators to add a word to our language. That word is **wellness.** Wellness is *actively making choices and decisions that promote good health.* Wellness is more than just the absence of illness. It is a way of living. It is taking an active role in trying to reach and stay at a high level of health. When you practice wellness, you work at having a balanced health triangle. You also stay on the alert for ways to protect and improve your health.

Check Your Understanding

Conclusion Health has three sides—a physical side, a mental side, and a social side. By making the right choices, you can balance the three sides of your health triangle.

1. **Vocabulary** Find meanings for the words *healthful* and *healthy* in a dictionary. In your own words, explain the difference in meanings.
2. **Recall** What are the three sides of total health?
3. **Recall** What is wellness?
4. **Synthesize** What are some rules in your school that promote wellness?

DID **YOU** KNOW?

The Mind-Body Connection
So strongly do the three sides of total health affect one another that some physicians have begun to "prescribe" the following medicine to people scheduled to have major surgery.

- Think one happy thought every hour, or as needed, for each of the three days leading up to the operation.
- Take an extra-large dose of visits from family and close friends the day before the surgery.

As a rule, when people follow this prescription the surgery goes more smoothly and the period of recovery is shorter.

You Control Your Health

Words to Know
heredity
environment
behavior
attitudes

This lesson contains a number of valuable facts and tips. Once you have studied them, you will be able to

- name three factors that affect your health.
- define the term *behavior*.

Factors That Affect Your Health

The health choices that you make every day are a major factor in your total health. Other factors affect your health as well. Several of these factors are *heredity*, *environment*, and *available health care*.

Heredity

Heredity (huh·RED·uh·tee) is *the passing on of traits from your parents*. Your heredity includes your eye color, your body build, and your patterns of growth.

Your heredity may also include a tendency to get certain diseases. Heart disease is one disease that may be passed down through generations of a family. The presence of such diseases in past generations of your family is a factor in your health.

Environment

Environment (in·VY·ruhn·muhnt) is *the sum total of your surroundings*. Your environment includes the place where you live and the school you attend. Your environment also includes your friends, family, and all the other people whom you see often. Each part of your environment is a factor in your wellness and health.

- **The people in your environment.** What the people around you do and say can affect your health choices. These effects can be both positive and negative. If you see many of your friends trying out for sports teams at school, you may become interested in trying out as well. If your family snacks a lot on foods like potato chips and candy, you may do the same.

Health Minute

Gifts of Heredity
Compare your hair color and eye color with those of family members. Which features do you have in common with a parent, grandparent, brother or sister? Whom do you resemble most?

More About
*For more information about **heredity** and **environment** and how they affect the mental side of your health triangle, see Chapter 3.*

Learning from Photographs
Heredity and environment are important factors in health. How would you describe this child's environment?

- **Where you live.** Is your home in the suburbs? Do you live on a farm? The answer can be very important. Living in a big city, for example, can expose you to smog. This may be a health risk that is not present in areas where the air is cleaner.

Available Health Care

The place where you live also determines what health care is available to you. This, in turn, is a third factor in your total health. A person living in a small town will probably have fewer doctors and clinics to choose from than a person in a major city. Yet a person living in a major city with hundreds of health care outlets may be confused over where to turn for treatment.

Behavior and Choices

Heredity, environment, and available health care are factors over which you have little or no control. Your **behavior,** on the other hand, is a factor over which you have complete control. Behavior is *the way you act in the many different situations and events in life.* Your behavior includes the health choices you make every day. When you behave responsibly, you make the right health choices. This, in turn, increases your chances of reaching and maintaining a high level of health.

It's Up to You
Your friends do influence you, but in the end, your health choices are yours alone. You alone have the power to decide whether you will develop good or bad health habits.

More About
*For more information on how to go about **making decisions** and solving problems, see Chapter 3.*

*T*een *I*ssue

Responsibility

As you get older, you probably want adults to give you more responsibilities. One way to get responsibility is to demonstrate that you are ready for it. Here are some ways to do this.

- If you see something that needs doing, do it without waiting to be told.
- Get your schoolwork done and turned in on time.
- Do your household chores without having to be reminded.
- Follow through on things that you promise to do.
- Show up on time.
- Finish tasks that you start, and clean up after yourself.

Making the right health choices means taking into account all factors in your total health.

- **Behavior and heredity.** Knowing about your family's history of disease can help you behave in a way that will reduce your risk. People whose parents or grandparents have high blood pressure or have had heart attacks, for example, can reduce their own risk of heart disease. They can do this by exercising regularly and eating foods low in fat.

- **Behavior and environment.** Knowing which foods are healthful and which are not can help you behave responsibly and choose the right ones. Suppose your family stocks up on foods high in salt and sugar. You can still select healthy snacks from among the many other foods in your home.

- **Behavior and available health care.** Keeping up on current events can help you choose ways to promote and protect your health. This is true regardless of where you live and of the kinds of health care available to you.

Behavior and Attitudes

Developing responsible health habits depends on more than just recognizing healthy choices. Your personal **attitudes** (AT·uh·toodz)—your *feelings and beliefs*—also play a role in how well you take care of yourself. Some people believe that the choices they make will not affect their health one way or the other. People with this sort of negative attitude seldom make good choices or develop good health habits. They fail to understand how important personal responsibility is to health.

Your attitude also includes the way you feel about yourself. If you like who you are and feel liked by others, you will want to take care of yourself. You will want to be at your best in all areas. To reach these goals, you will make choices that protect and promote your health.

Behavior and Your Future

The habits that you form right now will affect your future health. As a teenager, you may not care that much about health. Like most teenagers, you are probably fairly healthy and strong. When you get sick, you probably bounce right back.

In order to want to develop healthy habits, you may need to see some personal rewards. The rest of this book will describe some of the rewards of developing good health habits.

Form Bad Habits Now, Pay Later

The next few years are an especially important time for you to begin developing good health habits if you aren't already doing so. To understand why, think about this: With no changes in diet or exercise patterns after the age of 18, an inactive person may gain 1 pound of body fat and lose the use of about ½ pound of muscle each year.

Check Your Understanding

Conclusion A number of factors play a role in your total health. Heredity, environment, and the health care available to you are beyond your control. You have complete control over your behavior, which is yet another factor in your health.

1. **Vocabulary** Use the words *heredity* and *environment* together in an original sentence.
2. **Recall** Name three factors that affect your health.
3. **Recall** Define behavior and explain how it relates to good health.
4. **Interpret** What kinds of health habits would you expect in a person whose motto is "I live just for the here and now"? Explain why you feel as you do.

Teen Issue

Feeling Low Lately?
Have there been times lately when you find yourself suddenly feeling moody or sad but don't know why? Do not worry. This is all part of being a teenager and a sign of certain changes that are taking place in your body. To learn more about these changes, see Chapter 6.

Teen Health
BULLETIN BOARD

Sports and Recreation

A Full Head of Steam

If vigorous exercise makes you hot under the collar—that is, if you perspire a lot after sports—you may be doing your body more good than you know. That's the latest word from researchers at the University of Michigan Medical School. Early studies reveal that the slight rise in body temperature following exercise may be caused by the same chemical in the blood that leads to fever when you get a cold. It has been proven that cold-related fevers help the body fight off serious infection. So working up a sweat during exercise may be a way of keeping well. Think about that the next time you head for the showers.

CAREERS

Wanted
Fitness Director

Specifics
Set up or run fitness programs for groups, schools, or companies; train employees to practice better fitness.

Qualifications
Need to be able to take charge and work well with people. Must be good at planning and have some knowledge of sports and exercise. Must be willing to keep up-to-date on new breakthroughs in sports and fitness.

Preparation
A four-year college education is needed. Some courses in the workings of the human body are essential.

Contact
President's Council on Physical Fitness and Sports
450 Fifth Street NW
Washington, DC 20001

Sports and Recreation

The Sky's the Limit

People who wonder whether birth defects set limits on the kinds of things a person can do should ask Jim Abbott. Abbott was born with only part of his right hand. That hasn't stopped him, however, from becoming an important talent in baseball.

As a pitcher, Abbott throws a mean fastball. But as a fielder, he is even more remarkable. Catching the ball with his left hand, Abbott tosses the ball in the air and quickly flips his glove to his right in order to complete the play. Sports writers have nicknamed the technique the "Abbott Switch."

Many people tell Jim Abbott that he is an inspiration to them. But the words Abbott always dreamed of hearing—and, now that his dream has become a reality, does hear—are these: "Play ball!"

Jim Abbott, the one-handed pitcher, was a starting pitcher for the 1988 U.S. Olympic team.

TEEN Q & A

Q: I'm trying to lose weight, but I'm afraid that if I exercise my appetite will get bigger and I will eat more. What should I do?

A: You should stop worrying and start exercising. Experts agree that exercise *helps* people with weight problems. While exercise can increase your appetite, it also increases the rate at which you "burn up" the food your body takes in as energy. The key is to exercise up to your *aerobic* rate. You can find out your aerobic rate in the Health Handbook at the back of this book.

Lifestyle

Let a Smile Be Your Health's Umbrella

Have you ever heard the expression "Look on the bright side"? Recent studies show that people who do this tend to lead healthier lives than people who don't. The findings suggest that smiling protects and promotes your health on all three sides of your wellness triangle. People who smile recover more quickly from illness and even from surgery. They are also better able to cope with such life pressures as getting homework done on time, taking tests, and getting along with friends. So the next time someone says, "Smile!" try it. You may find that it's good for what ails you.

Word to Know
lifestyle factors

Building Healthy Habits

This lesson contains a number of valuable facts and tips. Once you have studied them, you will be able to

- name three steps you can take toward more responsible health habits.
- identify health habits that make a difference in your level of health.

Learning from Photographs
Everyone has ups and downs. Being healthy means that although there are times when you feel low, you usually have ways of bouncing back. Does being healthy mean you always have to feel on top of the world?

Being Responsible for Your Health

Your health varies from day to day. Some days you may feel "on top of the world." On other days, you may feel "down in the dumps." For this reason, you need to examine your health closely from time to time. Doing so allows you to see whether there are areas that need work. It also means that you have begun to take responsibility for your health.

Learning from Photographs
Taking control of your health helps ensure good health. How is this teen taking responsibility for his own health?

DID **YOU** KNOW?

Blood Speed
During vigorous exercise, blood can travel as fast as 450 feet (135 meters) per minute.

Steps to Responsible Health

Taking care of your health is mainly your own responsibility. There are three basic steps you take in accepting responsibility for your health.

1. *Find out how much you know about your health.* This means knowing at any time your health level on each of the three sides of your health triangle. You can determine this by taking a self-health inventory such as the one on page 14.

2. *Get good information on how to stay healthy or improve your health.* Breakthroughs in health are happening all the time. By reading special magazines or newspapers, you can keep up-to-date on events that could affect your health.

3. *Take action.* This means setting realistic goals for yourself. If you decide you want to lose weight, do it gradually, under a doctor's care—don't starve yourself. Taking action also means becoming actively involved in your total health. Eating a bowl of high-fiber cereal each morning isn't enough if you are going to snack on sweets the rest of the day. Working at your health is a full-time job.

Know Yourself
A first step toward improving yourself is knowing yourself. This means taking a frank look at your strengths and weaknesses. Since you are changing all the time, one look is not enough. Make a habit of examining your pluses and minuses often. Take the self-inventory "Your Health Habits" every month or so.

Your Health Habits

Is your health triangle balanced? The following survey will help you find out how healthy you are in each of the three sides. On a separate sheet of paper, write *yes* or *no* for each statement.

Physical Health

1. I eat breakfast every day.
2. I eat what I believe to be a well-balanced diet.
3. I choose healthy snacks that are low in sugar and salt.
4. I get at least 8 hours of sleep each night.
5. I exercise regularly.
6. I do not use tobacco.
7. I do not use alcohol or nonmedicine drugs.
8. I brush and floss my teeth daily.
9. I am within 5 pounds of my ideal weight.
10. I usually feel good and have plenty of energy.

Mental Health

1. I have a variety of interests and enjoy learning new things.
2. I can laugh easily.
3. I like to be alone sometimes.
4. I can name several things I do well.
5. I can name at least two reasons why people like me.
6. I can say *no* to other people without feeling guilty.
7. I can express my thoughts and feelings to others.
8. I feel satisfied with my effort if I've done my best.
9. I ask for help if I need it.
10. I try to work through my problems and take responsibility for my actions.

Social Health

1. I meet people easily.
2. I have several close friends.
3. If I have a problem with someone, I try to talk about it and work it out with him or her.
4. When working with a group, I can accept other people's ideas or suggestions.
5. I say *no* to my friends if they are doing something I do not want to do.
6. I do not talk about others behind their backs.
7. I get along well with several different groups.
8. I continue to take part in an activity after I've lost an argument.
9. I accept the differences in my friends and classmates.
10. I enjoy going to different places and having new social experiences.

To rate yourself, give yourself 1 point for a *yes*. A score of 9–10 in any area is *very good*. A score of 6–8 in an area is *good*. A score of 4–5 is *fair*. If you score below 4 in any area, that side of your triangle *needs work*.

Learning from Photographs
Getting enough sleep is important to good health. How much sleep do you get?

Health Habits That Make a Difference

What habits affect your health? After studying many different types of people over the years, health experts have identified certain habits that can make a difference in people's lives. Those who practice these *life-related habits,* or **lifestyle factors,** appear to live longer and stay happier. These habits include the following.

- Eating three meals a day, each at a regular time
- Never missing breakfast
- Getting 8 to 9 hours of sleep each night
- Avoiding tobacco, drugs, and alcohol
- Staying at a recommended level of weight
- Doing vigorous exercise at least 3 to 4 hours each week

Check Your Understanding

Conclusion   Taking care of your health is mainly your responsibility. When you decide to take responsibility, you recognize and practice health habits that make a difference in the quality of your life.

1. **Vocabulary** What is a term that means "habit or activity that relates to life"?
2. **Recall** Name three steps you can take toward more responsible health habits.
3. **Recall** Identify six health habits that make a difference in your level of health.
4. **Analyze** Choose two of the good habits presented in this lesson. Explain how each relates to a person's social and mental health.

Health May Be Habit-Forming

Look at the list of lifestyle factors on this page. Are any not part of your present daily routine? Then do the following.

- Identify a habit you want to start. On a piece of paper, write it down four times. Next to the habit, write at least two benefits you could gain from making it part of your routine.

- Practice the habit at least four times in the next week. Each time, circle one of the times you wrote it on your list. Also circle the benefits you got from practicing the habit.

If, at the end of the week, every item on your paper has been circled, you are well on your way to mastering a new health behavior.

Fitness and Your Health

Words to Know

fit
flexibility
muscle strength
muscle endurance
heart and lung
   endurance
aerobic exercises
lifetime sports
warming up
target pulse rate
cooling down

How Much?

Do you get enough exercise? Here are some questions that will help you decide whether you need more exercise to improve your fitness.

- Do you get tired easily from physical activities?
- Do you get tired easily from mental activities?
- Do you have low endurance of the muscles, heart, or lungs?
- Do you have poor posture?

If your answer to any of these questions is yes, then you need to work on your fitness level!

This lesson contains a number of valuable facts and tips. Once you have studied them, you will be able to

- name the factors that determine fitness.
- identify two ingredients of any good workout.

Fitness and You

Many people think of fitness, like health, in purely physical terms. They think fitness means being in good shape or being able to play a sport well. But fitness has more than just a physical side. When you are **fit,** you are *ready to handle whatever comes your way from day to day.*

Being fit carries many benefits. Some are listed in the box below.

Benefits of Fitness

Being fit . . .

- helps you be at ease with yourself and sure of yourself.
- gives you more energy and helps you keep your weight down.
- prepares you mentally, physically, emotionally, and socially for the ups and downs of life.
- increases your chances of succeeding in whatever tasks you take on and helps you feel confident.
- helps you to manage stress and have more fun.

Factors Affecting Fitness

How a person lives is a factor affecting that person's fitness. People who lead active lives are as a rule more fit than people who do not. Active people are often less at risk for certain diseases such as heart disease. They are usually better able to deal with the pressures of life. Unfortunately, we live in an age where machines do much of our work for us. Cars and other twentieth-century inventions have removed the need to do even the smallest amount of physical activity.

Determining Fitness

Are you fit? To determine whether you are, you need to be honest with yourself about your own level of activity. Ask yourself, for example, whether you prefer to be driven to places where you could walk or ride your bike.

You also need to test yourself in several areas that are factors in fitness.

- **Flexibility.** *Your ability to move your body joints in certain ways is called* **flexibility** (flek·suh·BIL·uht·ee).

- **Muscle strength and endurance.** *The most work your muscles can do at any given time is* **muscle strength.** *How well a muscle group can perform over a given time without becoming overly tired is* **muscle endurance** (in·DER·uhns).

- **Heart and lung endurance. Heart and lung endurance** is *how well the heart and lungs get oxygen to the body during exercise and how quickly they return to normal.*

Tests for each of these areas may be found in the Health Handbook at the back of this book.

DID **YOU** KNOW?

A Heartbeat Away
A strong heart does not have to do as much work as a weaker one. Through regular aerobic exercise, you can lower your heart rate by 10 to 15 beats per minute. That saves your heart 15,000 to 20,000 beats each day. In a year, that amounts to over 7 million beats!

Learning from Photographs
Being fit means being ready. How might fitness help you get ahead in life?

Some teens have learned the pleasures of "sport walking," or walking for fitness. This type of very brisk walking carries none of the risks of injury to the knees or ankles suffered by some runners. If you plan to walk for fitness, you'll want to have the right shoes. Experts recommend the following features.

- Plenty of room in the "toe box."
- "Uppers" that let your foot breathe.
- A padded, snug-fitting "heel collar."
- A good firm heel counter.
- A slightly elevated heel.
- Soles that curve up slightly at the heel and toe.

Exercise—A Key to Fitness

An important key to fitness is exercise. Regular exercise gives you added energy and helps you fight disease and illness. It also makes you look and feel better. In general, it improves your sense of well-being.

In recent years, many Americans have discovered this key to fitness. **Aerobic** (ehr·OH·bik) **exercises**—*rhythmic, nonstop, vigorous activities that aid the heart*—have become very popular. So have programs involving weight training. More and more people are turning to **lifetime sports** to maintain fitness. These are *physical activities that can be enjoyed throughout life.* Swimming and tennis are two lifetime sports.

You can improve your own level of fitness by starting an exercise program of your own.

Developing an Exercise Program

In planning a program of exercise, you need to have a plan and start out slowly. You also need to ask yourself several questions. Having answers to these questions will increase your chances of success with your program.

- **What are my goals? Are they realistic?** Deciding to ride your bicycle 20 miles each day is not a realistic starting goal. If you use bicycling as an exercise, start with a distance you can manage.
- **What do I like doing?** Pick an activity that you think you will enjoy and can do reasonably well. Remember, this is going to become a regular part of your life.
- **What do I hope to accomplish?** Your body has its own fitness needs and limits. Your purpose in exercising should be to become the best *you* possible. Don't start an activity just to beat someone else's record.

Learning from Photographs
Among the good aerobic exercises are swimming, bicycling, soccer, running, and hiking uphill. Which aerobic exercises do you enjoy?

Which Exercise?

Different exercises offer different fitness benefits. Some exercises help increase your flexibility. Others build muscle strength. Still others build endurance. The sport or activity you choose should reflect your abilities and interests. To check on how fit you are, take the four tests of fitness in the Health Handbook.

The following table shows how various sports rate in the different areas of fitness. Each number shows the benefits of a sport when played for 30 minutes or longer. The highest score in any category is 21.

DID **YOU** KNOW?

5,000 Miles
A person who is 5 pounds overweight has nearly 5,000 extra miles of blood vessels.

Fitness Ratings for Different Sports				
Exercise	Flexibility	Muscle Strength and Endurance	Heart and Lung Endurance	Total
Handball	16	15	19	50
Swimming	15	14	21	50
Jogging	9	17	21	47
Roller skating	13	15	18	46
Bicycling	9	16	19	44
Tennis	14	14	16	44
Walking	7	11	13	31
Softball	9	7	6	22

Two Important Ingredients of Your Workout

You have chosen an exercise program. Now you are ready to take action. Two important parts of any workout are *warming up* at the beginning and *cooling down* at the end.

Warming Up
If you have ever had a muscle cramp after a game or other vigorous activity, you know how painful cramps can be. If you have had a cramp, it is probably because you didn't warm up. Warming up gets your muscles ready for action.

More About

*For examples of **warm up** and **cool down** exercises, see the Health Handbook.*

Health Minute

Taking Your Pulse
To take your pulse, do the following.

1. Sit down.
2. Press the first two fingers of one hand against one side of your neck just under your jaw. (Do not use your thumb, which has its own pulse.)
3. Find the pulse (it is a mild throbbing feeling).
4. While someone times you with a clock, count the number of throbs, or "beats," over a period of 1 minute.

The number you end up with is your *pulse,* or heart rate. The average heart rate is 70–80 beats per minute.

Warming up is *doing activities and movements that stretch your muscles.* Warming up helps your muscles to be more elastic during the vigorous activity to follow. This helps prevent injury. Warming up also allows your pulse rate to rise slowly to its **target pulse rate.** This is *the level at which your heart and lungs receive the most benefit from a workout.* The chart "Finding Your Target Pulse Rate" in the Health Handbook explains how to find your target pulse rate.

Cooling down is *slowly winding down an activity.* Cooling down allows the heart to slow down by degrees. It also allows blood flow to return to normal. The best way to cool down after exercise is to slow down the activity for 5 minutes. Then stretch for another 5 minutes.

Check Your Understanding

Conclusion Being fit has many benefits. The most important one is that you feel good about yourself. When you feel good about yourself, you are more likely to make healthy choices.

1. **Vocabulary** Which of the following terms from the lesson names a state or condition of the body rather than an activity? *warming up, aerobic exercise, fit, cooling down*
2. **Recall** What is fitness?
3. **Recall** Name the three tests that determine fitness.
4. **Recall** What are two questions you should ask yourself when planning an exercise program?
5. **Recall** Name two ingredients of any good workout.
6. **Interpret** What advice might you give a friend who said he or she was running late and didn't have time to warm up before exercising?

Developing a Fitness Program

Do you get out of breath running for the bus? Begin a personal fitness program! You can make your life healthier through the right exercise program—one that follows a plan.

How to Develop a Personal Fitness Program

An effective fitness program requires thoughtful planning and careful thinking. Here are seven steps to follow in developing your own program:

1. *Choose an activity that you enjoy.* Don't begin an activity because you believe "it's the thing to do."
2. *Identify the best time of day to exercise.* Instead of watching TV for a half hour, exercise!
3. *Set realistic goals.* You might build your bicycle-riding skills so that you can bike a certain distance by the end of the first month of your program.
4. *Don't exercise too much at one time.* Start slow, and work up little by little. Allow time for improvement. Don't expect results immediately.
5. *Reward yourself.* Feeling and looking better are their own rewards. But consider celebrating in some way when you reach a goal.
6. *Don't exercise just for now—make your fitness program a part of your future, too.* You will get long-term health benefits from a fitness program.
7. *Make friends with others who exercise.* Give each other advice. Help each other stick to your programs.

Using the Skill

Read the following stories. They are about problems faced by teens trying to decide on programs of fitness that are right for them.

Case One

Maria has tried exercising before. The last time, she tried rowing on the lake. The first day she rowed a half mile. Her shoulders hurt for three whole days. She would like to try running, but she doesn't want to cause herself more pain. She's not sure what to do.

Case Two

Joey loves to walk in the park behind his house. Sometimes, when he walks really fast for a long time, he feels as though he could walk forever. The only thing is, his closest friends are really into volleyball. For Joey, volleyball is boring. But he figures he has to go along with the crowd.

Case Three

Miyo knows exactly what she wants out of her fitness program! Or does she? She has watched Olympic high-divers on T.V. Starting tomorrow, she plans to be a high-diver herself. She is going to go off the highest diving board at the community pool. She has never tried it before. But she figures the best place to start is at the top.

Divide a separate sheet of paper into three columns. Label one column "Maria," one "Joey," and one "Miyo." For each teen, write the following: (1) a sentence stating the problem, (2) the possible choices facing the teen, (3) the best choice, and (4) the step in "How to Develop a Personal Fitness Program" that helped you reach your answer.

Chapter 1 Review

Summary

- Your total health has a physical side, a mental side, and a social side. Wellness is actively making choices that promote each side of total health.
- Heredity, environment, and availability of health care are factors in your health. Your behavior, which includes your daily health choices, is the most important factor.
- Taking care of your health is mainly your responsibility. When you accept responsibility, you develop healthy habits. These include a balanced diet, plenty of rest, being fit, and avoiding harmful substances.
- Being fit makes you feel good about yourself. A regular program of exercise helps you stay fit. A good workout includes warming up and cooling down.

Reviewing Vocabulary and Concepts

On a separate sheet of paper, write the numbers 1–15. After each number, write the letter of the answer that best completes each of the following statements.

Lesson 1

1. Total health is made up of mental, social, and physical
   a. well-being   **b.** stress   **c.** weaknesses   **d.** support

2. Liking who you are and knowing how to express your emotions are part of your
   a. physical health   **b.** wellness   **c.** social health   **d.** mental health

3. Actively making decisions that promote good health is called
   a. exercise   **b.** wellness   **c.** total health   **d.** knowledge

Lesson 2

4. Traits passed on to you from your parents make up your
   a. heredity   **b.** family   **c.** environment   **d.** wellness

5. Your friends and all the other people you come into contact with are part of your
   a. heredity   **b.** family   **c.** environment   **d.** wellness

6. In addition to heredity, available health care, and environment, your total health is shaped by your
   a. friends   **b.** family   **c.** behavior   **d.** family medical history

7. Another term for feelings and beliefs is
   a. wellness   **b.** environment   **c.** health care   **d.** attitudes

Lesson 3

8. Knowing your level of health at any given time is part of taking
   - **a.** responsibility for your health
   - **b.** your pulse
   - **c.** your temperature
   - **d.** time to think about life

9. Daily habits, such as getting enough sleep, are grouped together by experts as
   - **a.** total health
   - **b.** unbreakable habits
   - **c.** lifestyle factors
   - **d.** breakable habits

10. Healthy habits include all of the following *except*
   - **a.** eating breakfast each day
   - **b.** eating three meals a day
   - **c.** exercising often
   - **d.** dieting once a month

Lesson 4

11. The importance of fitness is that it prepares you to
   - **a.** handle whatever comes your way
   - **b.** be a top athlete
   - **c.** run long races
   - **d.** study wellness

12. Your ability to move your body joints in certain ways is
   - **a.** muscle strength
   - **b.** flexibility
   - **c.** muscle endurance
   - **d.** surprising

13. A vigorous nonstop activity that aids the heart is called
   - **a.** warming up
   - **b.** target pulse rate
   - **c.** an aerobic exercise
   - **d.** endurance

14. In planning an exercise program, you need to
   - **a.** get plenty of sleep
   - **b.** set realistic goals
   - **c.** find a partner
   - **d.** see a doctor

15. Performing activities that stretch your muscles before a workout is
   - **a.** endurance
   - **b.** target pulse rate
   - **c.** aerobic exercising
   - **d.** warming up

Thinking Critically About the Facts

Write your answers to the following questions on a separate sheet of paper.

16. **Compare and contrast** Explain the difference between wellness and total health.

17. **Interpret** How would you explain the idea of the health triangle to a brother or sister two years younger than you? What examples would you use?

18. **Synthesize** Imagine you live in a location that has lots of hills. Give an example of two health habits—one good, one bad—that you might develop on the basis of this environment.

19. **Analyze** A friend of yours is about to begin bicycling to keep fit. How might you answer this friend if he or she tells you it is important to have another bicyclist to race against "to make the exercise more interesting"?

20. **Analyze** Suppose you have a friend who stays up each night until midnight and must wake up at 6:00 A.M. He is tired every afternoon. What health habit does your friend need to work on?

Applying the Facts

21. Make a list of all the people in your environment who are at least partly responsible for good health choices you have made. Identify the health habits. Then make a list of your own behaviors that may have led to good health habits in others. Share your lists with your class.

22. Write down a health goal you want to achieve in the next week or two. Prepare a plan of action that will help you reach your goal. Think about what information you need to put your plan into effect. Decide where you can find the information. Start your plan, and keep records of your progress.

23

Wellness and Your Appearance

CHAPTER WARM-UP

Chapter Study Goals

After you have read this chapter, you will be able to

- name the jobs of the skin and mouth.

- explain how you see and hear.

- explain how you can care for your skin, hair, nails, mouth, eyes, ears, and feet.

- identify common problems of the skin, hair, nails, mouth, eyes, ears, and feet.

- state why good posture is important.

- identify treatments for problems of the skin, hair, nails, mouth, eyes, ears, and feet.

Be on the lookout for information in the chapter that will help you reach these goals.

Getting Started

Have you ever heard the saying "Put your best foot forward"? Your appearance says a lot about you. When you take care of your skin, hair, nails, mouth, eyes, and ears, you are telling other people that you have decided to be the best "you" possible. As a bonus, taking responsibility for your appearance helps you feel good about yourself.

As you read the chapter on wellness and your appearance, you will learn facts about *grooming*, or taking care of your appearance.

Study Tip

As you read this chapter, pay attention to the labeled drawings in many of the lessons. These drawings will allow you to "see" the parts being described.

24

Healthy Skin

This lesson contains a number of valuable facts and tips. Once you have studied them, you will be able to

- identify four jobs of the skin.
- name the main layers of the skin.
- name two things you can do to protect your skin from the sun.
- identify the most common skin problems among teenagers.

What Is Skin?

You probably never thought of your skin as a body organ like your heart or brain, but it is one. In fact, it is the largest organ of all. Unlike most organs, however, your skin is on view to everyone you meet. That is why it plays such an important role in your appearance.

Words to Know

nerve endings
epidermis
melanin
dermis
oil glands
sweat glands
pores
acne
hormones
sebum
whitehead
blackhead
pimple
dermatologist
warts
boils
herpes simplex I

DID YOU KNOW?

New Skin
Millions of dead skin cells flake off your body daily. The outer layer of skin is replaced every 28 days.

Learning from Photographs
Your skin does many jobs for you. How many can you name before reading on?

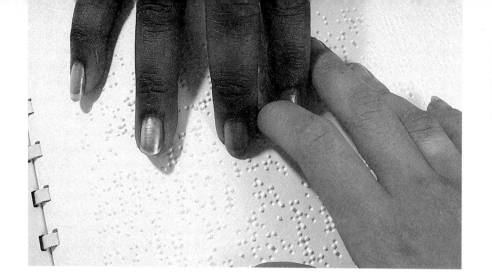

The Many Jobs of the Skin

Your skin performs several important jobs for your body.

- **It is a protective shield against water.** Your skin acts like a form-fitting raincoat. It keeps out water when you swim or take a bath.

- **It is a defense against germs.** That is why people badly burned in fires have such a high risk of infection. That is also why you need to administer first aid for open cuts.

- **It helps control your body temperature.** Your skin prevents your internal organs from being overheated by the sun or frozen by the cold.

- **It works as a sense organ.** Your skin is full of **nerve endings,** which are *sensitive areas that react to forces outside yourself.* These nerve endings let you know when someone or something touches your body. They let you feel differences in the textures of different objects, and they warn you when you might come into contact with something that could cause pain.

The Parts of the Skin

Your skin has two main layers, an outer layer and an inner layer. The *outermost layer of skin* is called the **epidermis** (ep·uh·DER·muhs). The epidermis is made up of many layers of cells. As new cells are manufactured deep down, old ones at the surface are wiped away. This process of making and replacing cells is continuous.

The cells in the deepest part of the epidermis produce **melanin** (MEL·uh·nuhn). Melanin is *an agent that gives the skin most of its color. Freckles* and *moles* are both spots of melanin. Most moles are harmless, though when one changes shape, size, or color, or bleeds you should see your doctor.

Buying Clothes
The clothes you wear are part of your overall physical appearance. You can choose to wear the latest styles as long as your clothes fit you comfortably. It is especially important to avoid tight clothes that might prevent your skin from "breathing."

More About

For more information on nerve endings and what they do, see Chapter 7.

Lesson 1: Healthy Skin   **27**

Learning from Drawings

Skin is made up of two layers, the epidermis and the dermis. Below the dermis is a layer of fat tissue called the *subcutaneous* (suhb·kyoo·TAY·nee·uhs) layer. In which layer is melanin found?

The Skin

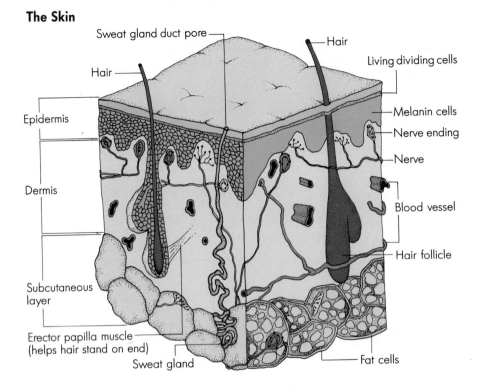

- Sweat gland duct pore
- Hair
- Hair
- Epidermis
- Dermis
- Subcutaneous layer
- Erector papilla muscle (helps hair stand on end)
- Sweat gland
- Living dividing cells
- Melanin cells
- Nerve ending
- Nerve
- Blood vessel
- Hair follicle
- Fat cells

SKILLS FOR LIVING

Shaving

Some teenage boys begin shaving early. If you think you may start shaving soon and suffer from acne, use extra care not to disturb any pimples.

The *broad inner layer of skin* is called the **dermis** (DER·muhs). The dermis contains the skin's most important structures. These include the blood vessels, nerve endings, and hair roots. The dermis also contains two types of glands.

- **Oil glands,** or *glands which produce oils that keep the skin soft and waterproof.*
- **Sweat glands,** or *pouches in the skin that hold body wastes and water.* This combination is called *perspiration.* It is released through **pores,** *tiny holes in the skin.* When it reaches the surface, the perspiration cools on contact with the air. Since you perspire when you are hot, you might think of the sweat glands as your body's built-in air-conditioning system.

Taking Care of Your Skin

The best way you can care for your skin is by keeping it clean. Daily bathing or showering with soap will rid your skin of bacteria and any excess oils.

The regular use of soap and water is an especially important habit for people in your age-group to develop. During the early teen years, there is increased activity in the sweat glands. When sweat accumulates in certain areas, such as under the arms and around the feet, it feeds bacteria. The bacteria then give off an unpleasant odor. This *body odor* can be controlled partly by the use of *deodorants* or *antiperspirants*. These are products that cover up the odor with a pleasant scent. Antiperspirants additionally contain chemicals that help the area remain dry. The best way to combat the smell, however, is through daily baths or showers.

Your Skin and the Sun

Many people used to think that plenty of sunshine was good for you. Individuals with deep tans were thought to be "the picture of health." Recent research has shown otherwise. Medical authorities now understand that prolonged exposure to the sun can do serious damage to the skin. Early aging of the skin and certain forms of skin cancer are just two risks you take when you spend too much time in the sun.

If you are planning to spend time in the sun, play it safe.

- **Limit your exposure to the sun.** Spend no more than about 30 minutes per day in direct sunlight. Also, arrange to be in the sun when the harmful rays are at their weakest. These times are early in the morning and late in the afternoon.

- **Wear protection.** *Sun-blocking agents* contain chemicals that prevent the harmful sun rays from reaching your skin. Almost as good are *sunscreens*, which at least slow down the tanning process. If you insist on using *suntan lotions*, choose ones with the highest *sun protection factors, or SPFs.* These are numbers from 2 to 40 that tell you how many times your body's natural protection from the sun they provide. A lotion with an SPF of 10, for example, gives you 10 times your body's natural protection.

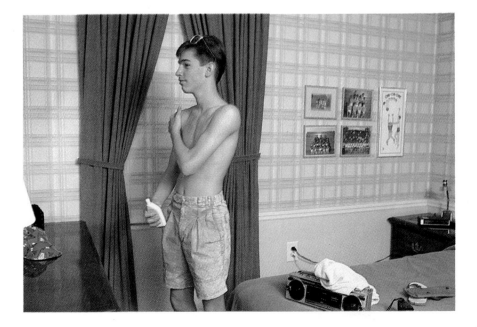

Sun and Clouds

It is possible to get a sunburn even on a cloudy day. That is because the harmful *ultraviolet rays* are present even when bright sunlight is not.

The Truth About SPFs

While many people are aware that the higher the SPF, the better the protection from the sun, few are aware that SPFs block only one of *two* types of harmful sun rays. If you really want protection, look for products that have high SPFs *and* one of the following ingredients listed on the bottle: oxybenzone, methoxybenzone, or sulisobenzone.

Learning from Photographs

Prolonged exposure to the sun can harm the skin. How can you protect yourself from this problem?

More About

*For more about **hormones** and the changes they bring about in your body, see Chapter 6.*

Acne

No matter how much care you take, some skin problems that affect people your age are hard to avoid entirely. The most common of these is **acne** (AK·nee), *a clogging of the pores with oil.*

At the beginning of the teen years, many body changes are caused by **hormones** (HOR·mohnz), which are *chemicals produced in the body.* One of these hormones causes the oil glands to become larger. Greater quantities of an *oily substance* called **sebum** (SEE·buhm) are made. Eventually, sebum clogs the pores, creating the condition known as acne.

Technically speaking there are three types of acne. The first type, the **whitehead,** is *the result of oil becoming trapped in a pore.* Type two, the **blackhead,** is *an oil-plugged pore that is exposed to the air and darkens.* The third type of acne, the **pimple,** is the most severe. A pimple is *a clogged pore that has become infected and filled with pus.*

Treating Acne

The worst thing you can do when you have a pimple is squeeze it. This can spread the infection and also result in a scar. If the condition is serious you may want to see a **dermatologist** (DER·muh·TAHL·uh·juhst), *a doctor who treats skin disorders.* You can also practice the following *do's* and *don'ts:*

DID **YOU** KNOW?

Skin Wrinkles
The skin on the palms of your hands and soles of your feet contains no oil glands to keep water out. That is why your fingers and toes become "pruny" after a bath or swim.

More About

*For more on how a **well-balanced diet** affects your health, see Chapter 5.*

DO	DON'T
• Wash at least twice a day, morning and night, with mild soap and warm water.	• Use heavy or greasy creams or makeup.
• Blot dry with a clean towel.	• Rub affected areas hard with a towel when drying off.
• Use acne-fighting preparations recommended or prescribed by your doctor.	• Pick at infected areas.
• Get lots of exercise and rest.	
• Eat a **well-balanced diet.**	

Learning from Drawings
In blackheads, whiteheads, and pimples, a pore is blocked by wax. What happens to the skin at the site of a pimple which does not occur with the other two types of acne?

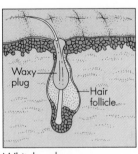

Whitehead

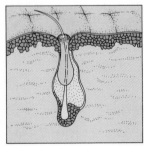

Blackhead

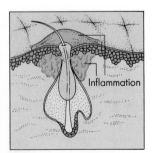

Pimple

Skin experts recommend washing acne-affected areas with warm water. The warm water opens the pores, ridding them of excess oils, and softens the outer layer of skin for better cleaning.

Other Skin Problems

Other skin problems that may occur include *warts, boils,* and *herpes simplex I.*

Warts are *small growths on the skin caused by a virus.* These usually appear as raised areas on the surface of the skin. Warts as a rule are painless and harmless. You should, however, check warts on your body from time to time for possible changes in color or size. Report any such changes to your doctor.

Boils are *infections of the skin accompanied by swelling, redness, and a buildup of pus.* Unlike warts, boils are caused by bacteria, which can damage skin tissue and spread. If you think you have a boil, you need to see your doctor.

Herpes simplex I (HER·peez SIM·pleks) can cause *a cold sore or fever blister.* It appears as *a small sore on or near the lips* that usually clears up in 10 to 14 days. Such blisters can spread if scratched or broken. Certain people seem more prone to getting these sores than others. If you are one of them, you should take care that the infection does not spread.

Check Your Understanding

Conclusion   Your skin is a vital organ of your body. It is also one of the first things other people notice about you. Good grooming, along with other good health habits, promotes healthy skin.

1. **Vocabulary** Use a dictionary to find the meanings of the words *porous, dermatologic,* and *hormonal.* (*Hint:* All are related to words you learned in this lesson.) Use each in an original sentence.
2. **Recall** Identify four jobs of the skin.
3. **Recall** Name the two main layers of the skin.
4. **Recall** Name two things that you can do to protect your skin from the sun.
5. **Recall** Identify the most common skin problem among teenagers.
6. **Analyze** Which of the parts of the skin helps control body temperature?

Wart Removers
Some wart removers sold in pharmacies and other stores can be dangerous when not used correctly. These products contain acids that can damage the skin. For more information on being a smart shopper when it comes to health care products, see Chapter 14.

Teen Issue

This, Too, Shall Pass
Despite regular cleansing of the face, some teens end up with pimples anyway. At your age acne is common. The next time you look in the mirror and see those unsightly red dots, don't "throw in the towel." Look beyond the skin you have now to the skin you will have some day. Keep reminding yourself that this, too, shall pass.

DID **YOU** KNOW?

Your Skin
Your skin weighs almost twice as much as your brain. One square inch of skin on your hand contains 72 feet of nerve fiber.

CAREERS

Wanted:
Cosmetologist

Specifics:
Work as a hairdresser or beauty operator in a barbershop, beauty salon, or styling shop. Responsibilities include cutting, washing, and styling hair. Tasks also include caring for hands and clipping and polishing nails. A cosmetologist also helps people learn to apply makeup and take proper care of the skin.

Qualifications:
Must enjoy working with people and have interest in good grooming habits.

Preparation:
Must take special courses at a business or other professional school and pass licensing exam.

Contact:
Associated Master Barbers and Beauticians of America
219 Greenwich Road
P.O. Box 220782
Charlotte, NC 28222

HEALTH IN THE NEWS

A Chart of a Different Color

The eye chart that doctors have been using for years may soon be replaced by a new chart. That's the word from researchers at the National Eye Institute. They are currently experimenting with a new eye chart developed by two researchers—one British and one American—that not only tests for vision problems but also helps detect some eye diseases.

The top three lines of the Pelli-Robson eye chart, which is a new tool for testing vision.

O H D N S
S N V O S
R K C H D

The old chart, invented by Hermann Snellen of the Netherlands in 1862, is made up entirely of black letters that get gradually smaller. The new chart contains letters of the same size that get gradually lighter in color. According to Denis Pelli, who with John Robson created the new chart, eye doctors will now be able to spot problems in patients' eyes that once would have gone unnoticed.

The Pelli-Robson chart has not yet gained total acceptance by eye-care specialists. If and when it does, however, we all may be seeing eye tests in a new light.

Sports and Recreation

If the Shoe Fits (and Only Then!), Wear It

Are you "into" sports? If you are, you need to be careful about the shoes you wear. Recent research has shown that close to three-fourths of all foot problems are caused by the wrong shoe being worn.

So how do you go about choosing the *right* shoes? First, make sure your shoes fit properly. Your shoes should be wide enough so that you can wiggle all of your toes when you are standing. Second, select a shoe that is right for the sport you play. Runners, for example, need a soft sole while cyclists need a hard one. Finally, keep in mind that a pair of shoes is not forever. Even top-quality running shoes lose their protective quality after about 400 miles of wear.

TEEN
Q & A

Q: I'm embarassed when I wear a bathing suit because I have a large birthmark on my right shoulder. Will it ever go away? What is a birthmark, anyway?

A: No, birthmarks don't go away. They are often there at birth or appear early in life. They are blotches of *melanin*, the substance that gives skin its color.

There are several basic kinds of birthmarks. Some are reddish in color. Others are dark brown and stand out slightly from the surface of the skin. All might be thought of as a special mark, like a tattoo. In a way, your birthmark is part of what makes you *you*.

Lifestyle
Shades of Blue

Are "blue-blocking" sunglasses the rage in your school? If not, they may be soon, now that some manufacturers have put out claims that "blue is better." Their theory goes like this: Light from the blue end of the color spectrum, or rainbow, can harm your eyes over long periods. (This light, which doesn't necessarily appear blue to the eye, is present in sunlight.) Blue-blocking lenses cut out much of this blue light.

While the harmful effects of blue light have been demonstrated with laboratory animals, no one has yet shown that humans are at risk. Since blue-blocking glasses are costly, you might be better off investing in a pair of good wraparounds. These have been proven beneficial in cutting out some of the sun's *ultraviolet* rays. These are the more harmful rays from the sun.

Healthy Hair and Nails

Words to Know
follicles
dandruff
head lice
cuticle
keratin
hangnails
ingrown toenail

This lesson contains a number of valuable facts and tips. Once you have studied them, you will be able to

- identify two sensible habits of daily hair care.
- tell what dandruff is.
- name two problems of the nails.

Teen Issue

Hair and Style
Hairstyle fashions come and go so often these days that some people change their hairstyles almost as often as they change clothes. There is nothing wrong with being stylish, but try to find a cut and style that fits your features. If you wear bangs, remember also that the hair covering your forehead may irritate the skin and make it oilier. This could increase your chances of developing acne there.

DID YOU KNOW?

Eyelashes
You shed 1,600 eyelashes every year.

Hair and Nails

Perhaps no other features of your entire body make a stronger or more personal statement about you than your hair and fingernails. Do you wear your hair long or short? Do you bite your nails, or are you careful about trimming them? These are just a couple of the many questions that you and everyone else faces when it comes to hair and nail grooming and care.

Your Hair

The hair that you see on your body is made of dead cells. Its roots are in the deepest layer of skin, the dermis, housed in *small pockets* called **follicles** (FAHL·i·kuhlz). As new hair cells are formed, old ones are forced outward through the surface of the skin and die.

Like living skin, hair takes its color from melanin. The color of your hair is *inherited*, or passed along to you by your parents. The shape of the hair shaft determines whether your hair is wavy, curly, or straight.

Hair Care

Sensible care of your hair will help you look your best. Proper daily care includes the following.

- **Brushing.** This will prevent dirt from building up as well as move the oils down the hair shaft. The oils make your hair shine

Learning from Photographs
Hair color is inherited from parents (or grandparents). What makes hair the color it is?

and look attractive. Occasionally massaging your scalp with your fingers is also good for your hair. Brushing too much can pull the hair out or break it. Brushing once a day is enough.

- **Washing.** Use a gentle soap or shampoo. If possible, let your hair dry by itself. The heat from electric blow-dryers can rob your hair of much-needed oils. This makes the hair ends rough and dry.

Problems of the Hair and Scalp

Have you ever seen white, scaly flakes on your shoulders? They may have been **dandruff,** a very common scalp problem. Dandruff is a *flaking of the outer layer of dead skin cells.* It is usually caused by a dry scalp. Often, a person your age can control dandruff through washing. Sometimes a special dandruff shampoo is needed. If the problem persists even then, you may want to talk to a nurse or doctor. What you think is dandruff may be a skin infection.

At times, an itchy scalp is caused by **head lice,** *insects that live in the hair.* Head lice are very common and very easy to catch from someone else. You can control head lice by using a medicated shampoo. Also be sure to wash all bedding, towels, and clothing that have come into contact with the scalp. If left untreated, head lice can lead to infection.

Your Nails

Your fingernails and toenails are, like your hair, dead cells. The nails are also similar to hair in that they grow out of living tissue located in the dermis. Around the nail is *a nonliving band of epidermis* called the **cuticle** (KYOOT·i·kuhl).

DID **YOU** KNOW?

What Your Hair Reveals
Scientists can determine a person's sex, age, and race by examining a single strand of hair. In most cases, finding a hair for this purpose is not difficult. The average head contains between 100,000 and 200,000 hairs.

DID **YOU** KNOW?

Your Hair's Strength
Hair is as strong as aluminum. If you could make a rope out of strands of hair, it could lift a 1-ton car.

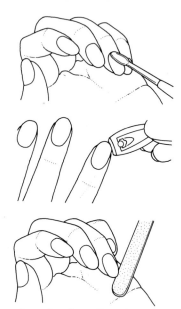

Learning from Drawings
The tools for nail care are a cuticle stick, nail clippers, and emery board. Why is good nail care important?

Teen Issue

Fingernail Length

How long is *too* long? That is a question you may already have asked yourself if you are a girl just beginning to grow long nails. Keep in mind that the longer your nails are, the more care they will require. Remember, too, that longer nails tend to chip and break more easily than shorter ones. In general, if your fingernails interfere with such simple tasks as dialing a telephone or holding a pencil, chances are they are too long for your own good.

Nail Care

Caring for your nails means more than just trimming them when they get too long, though that is certainly important. Good nail grooming also includes using plenty of soap when you wash to clean underneath the nails. If your hands are especially dirty, use a gentle brush to get at the dirt and grease under the nails and around the cuticles.

When trimming your nails, remember the following.

● Fingernails should be slightly rounded at the ends. The best way to accomplish this is with a nail file or emery board, though many people prefer to use a fingernail clipper or small scissors.

● Toenails should be cut straight across, with the nail at or slightly above skin level. If you cut the nail any shorter than this, you risk infection.

Problems of the Nails

The nails on your fingers and toes contain **keratin** (KEHR·uh·tuhn), *a substance that makes them hard.* Daily routines, however, sometimes cause minor problems.

● **Hangnails** are *splits in the cuticle along the edge of the nail.* They can be painful if left untrimmed. Once you have cut away the splintered edge, the nail will grow back in several days.

● **Ingrown toenail** is *a condition in which the nail pushes into the skin on the side of the toe.* This sometimes happens when you cut your toenails too short. If the toe becomes red and inflamed, that may be a sign that infection has set in. This is your cue to see your doctor.

Check Your Understanding

Conclusion Your hair and nails say a great deal about who you are. Knowing how to care for and correct problems in them is an important part of a sound program of wellness.

1. **Vocabulary** From the following list, select the *two* vocabulary words that name problems, and describe each. *follicles, keratin, dandruff, cuticle, head lice*
2. **Recall** Identify two sensible habits of daily hair care.
3. **Recall** What is dandruff?
4. **Recall** Name two problems of the nails.
5. **Analyze** How might cutting your toenails too short lead to ingrown toenails?

Healthy Mouth and Teeth

Words to Know
taste buds
periodontium
crown
root
neck
tissue
pulp
dentin
cementum
enamel
incisors
canines
premolars
molars
plaque
calculus
tartar
abscess
gingivitis
malocclusion
orthodontist

This lesson contains a number of valuable facts and tips. Once you have studied them, you will be able to

- list the jobs of the mouth.
- name the three main parts of a tooth.
- name the steps in sensible dental care.

Mouth and Teeth

Did you know that your mouth speaks even when you aren't talking? Strange as that sounds, it is true. Your mouth and teeth can communicate many things to other people, and all of what they say is about you! Clean teeth and gums and a fresh breath are a signal to others that you know about and practice good health habits. What silent message do your mouth and teeth give out? Make tooth care a part of your daily grooming. This lesson will tell you how.

Learning from Photographs
A smile can tell many things about you. What does a smile tell others about your health habits?

Health Minute

Under Your Tongue
A good place to observe living blood vessels is under your tongue. Use a mirror, a magnifying glass, and a strong light to look at the underside of your tongue. Locate thick blue lines. These are veins. The thick pink lines are arteries. The tiny, hair-thin lines are capillaries.

More About

For more about **digestion,** *see Chapter 7.*

DID **YOU** KNOW?

Your Teeth
The outer layer of your teeth, enamel, is the hardest part of your body.

The Jobs of the Mouth

Your mouth, teeth, and tongue together form a complex body system. This system is responsible for some very important jobs.

- **Tasting.** You taste by means of *sensitive areas of the tongue* called **taste buds.** When food touches the taste buds, a signal is sent to the brain, identifying the food as sweet, sour, salty, or bitter.

- **Digestion.** Your teeth and saliva work together to break down food. The teeth tear and crush the food and then the saliva dissolves it. The food is then ready to pass into the stomach.

- **Speech.** All the consonant and vowel sounds you make are determined by precise placements of the tongue, lips, teeth, and other parts of the mouth. In order to see just how important these placements are, try saying the word *teeth* without letting your tongue touch your teeth.

Your Teeth

In addition to helping you chew food, your teeth help shape and structure your mouth. They also work with muscles in your face to help form your smile.

The teeth are supported by the **periodontium** (pehr·ee·oh·DAHN·shee·um). This is *a structure made up of the jawbone, the gums, and connectors called ligaments.* Each tooth is divided into three parts: the **crown,** *the part visible to the eye;* the **root,** *the part inside the gum;* and the **neck,** *the part between the crown and the root.*

The Tooth

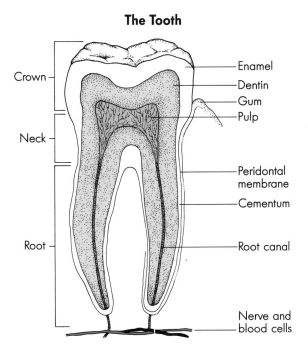

Crown

Neck

Root

Enamel

Dentin

Gum

Pulp

Peridontal membrane

Cementum

Root canal

Nerve and blood cells

Learning from Drawings
Tooth decay occurs when acid eats away the enamel and reaches the dentin. Why do you think this causes pain?

Each of your teeth also contains the following types of **tissue,** or *groups of cells.*

- **Pulp** is *soft sensitive tissue containing nerves and blood vessels deep within the root of a tooth.*

- **Dentin** (DEN·tuhn) is *bonelike material surrounding the pulp of a tooth.*

- **Cementum** (si·MEN·tuhm) is *thin bonelike material covering the root of a tooth.*

- **Enamel** (ee·NAM·uhl) is *the hard material that covers the crown of a tooth.*

Within each tooth are nerve and blood cells. The blood brings the tooth the food particles and oxygen it needs to grow and stay healthy.

Types of Teeth

You have a total of 32 teeth, each with a specific name and function. **Incisors** (in·SY·serz) are the main, *front or center teeth.* They cut into and tear the food for chewing. Incisors are located on the top and bottom of the mouth. **Canines** (KAY·nynz) are the *four pointed teeth next to the incisors.* They are for grasping and tearing food. **Premolars** (PREE·moh·lerz) and **molars** (MOH·lerz) are the *shorter, stubbier teeth to the sides and back of the mouth.* They do the major work of chewing and grinding down the food.

Double Teeth
Everyone really has two sets of teeth. Your first set is your *baby teeth.* These teeth begin to come in late in the first year of life. By the fifth year, your baby teeth begin to be pushed out by the teeth you have now—your *permanent teeth.* In spite of the name, some people lose their permanent teeth later in life. By taking good care of your permanent teeth now, they can last you a lifetime.

Tartar Check

Use a mirror to examine the back of your bottom teeth for deposits of tartar. If you see a great deal of this hard material, it is time for a tooth cleaning by a health professional.

Toothbrushes

It is a good idea to change toothbrushes regularly. Experts have found that bacteria in toothbrushes can cause certain illnesses and may prolong them.

How Do Teeth Decay?

Teeth are always exposed to the air, food, and bacteria. Because of these factors, your teeth are easy targets for decay.

A sticky film called **plaque** (PLAK) is *constantly forming on your teeth.* Plaque is a soft, sticky, see-through layer of bacteria that live in your mouth. Plaque combines with sugar in the foods you eat to form an acid. This acid destroys tooth enamel and irritates gums.

Normal brushing will help fight plaque. If left on the teeth for a day or longer, plaque hardens into a *hard material* called **calculus** or **tartar** (TAR·ter). Once tartar has formed, brushing alone isn't enough.

Decay starts when the acid under the plaque or tartar eats a hole, or *cavity*, through the enamel. The decay spreads to the dentin and finally to the pulp, where it infects and exposes a nerve. Air hitting the exposed nerve causes your tooth to ache. If the decay goes untreated by a dentist, *pus collects in the bone sockets around the tooth.* This very painful condition is known as an **abscess** (AB·sess).

Other Mouth Problems

Bacteria can also attack your gums. **Gingivitis** (JIN·juh·VY·tuhs) is *a gum disease.* It may be *caused by plaque or decaying food caught between the teeth.* Gums may swell and bleed. A dentist can spot gingivitis during a patient's regular checkup.

Gingivitis can also be caused by **malocclusion** (MAL·uh·KLOO·zhuhn). This is *a condition in which teeth fail to line up properly.* Many

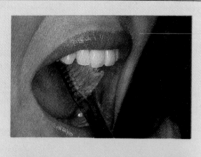

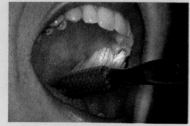

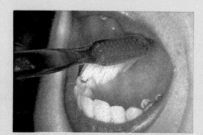

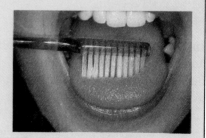

Learning from Photographs
Proper Brushing Technique
To brush teeth, hold the brush at a 45° angle facing into the gum. Move the brush in short strokes across the tooth. Then brush the inside of the teeth and the chewing surfaces, top and bottom. You can brush your tongue when you're done to freshen your breath. How often do you brush?

Learning from Photographs
Proper Flossing Technique
Wrap 18 inches of floss around your two middle fingers. Hold the floss tightly between your thumb and forefinger. Move the floss down the side of a tooth. When it reaches the gumline, curve it below the tooth until you feel pressure. Gently scrape the side of the tooth. Repeat on all teeth—and don't forget the back teeth. Have you ever flossed?

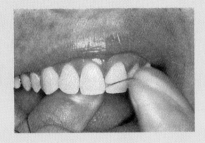
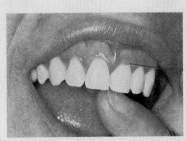

people are born with malocclusion. When it interferes with speaking or eating, small wires, or *braces*, can be applied to the teeth. An **orthodontist** (OR·thuh·DAHNT·ist) is *a dentist who specializes in treating malocclusion.*

Taking Care of Your Teeth

Dentists in the United States have recently reported a sharp decline in tooth decay among young people. Some even predict that tooth decay will disappear in the United States in the next 20 years. You can be a part of those encouraging statistics by following sensible dental care.

- **Brushing.** Use a soft or medium-soft toothbrush to remove plaque. As often as you can, brush after eating.
- **Fluoride.** Fluoride has been found effective in fighting plaque and tooth decay. More than 90 percent of all toothpastes now have fluoride. Many communities add fluoride to the water supply.
- **Flossing.** Use a special string called floss to clean between your teeth. Dental floss can reach food particles that a toothbrush can't. Try always to floss after eating.
- **Mouth rinses.** If you use a mouth rinse, choose one that has been shown to reduce plaque or kill bacteria.
- **Diet.** What you eat plays an important role in the health of your teeth. A diet rich in sugar promotes the buildup of plaque. If you eat candy or other sweets, brush and floss afterwards.

Teen **Issue**
. . . .

Teeth and Your Individual Smile
It's nice to have straight, even teeth. But it's better to have teeth that are strong and healthy. While some models, actors, and other celebrities have "million dollar" smiles, less than perfect smiles appear to be more common now than before. Teeth that have spaces between them or that slightly overlap should be accepted as part of a person's uniqueness.
. . . .

Lesson 3: Healthy Mouth and Teeth   **41**

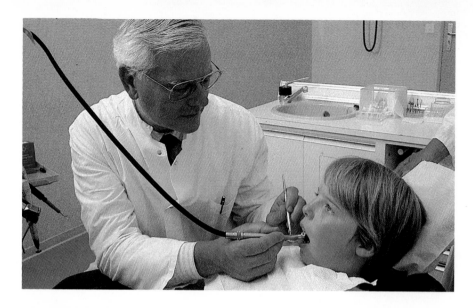

Water, Water Everywhere

Brushing your teeth is not always convenient. When brushing is impossible, rinse your mouth out with water. This will help rid your teeth of at least some of the food particles that build up when you eat.

The Role of the Dentist

You and your dentist are partners in the care of your teeth. While you should do your part to brush and floss your teeth and maintain a good diet, the dentist can help in other, specialized ways. Through regular checkups, a dentist can look for any signs of tooth decay or gum disease. He or she will *scale,* or scrape, your teeth to remove any tartar buildup. X rays of the teeth help dentists find any unseen problems. In addition, a dental hygienist can thoroughly clean your teeth and show you how to brush and floss properly.

Check Your Understanding

Conclusion A healthy smile adds to your overall appearance and feeling of self-esteem. You can achieve and maintain a healthy mouth, teeth, and gums while you are young. By following a good diet and the basic rules of dental hygiene, you can have strong, healthy teeth for the rest of your life.

1. **Vocabulary** Copy the following words onto a separate sheet of paper. Put a *C* next to any word naming a condition of the teeth and a *D* next to any word naming a disease of the gums. *malocclusion, gingivitis, plaque, cavity*

2. **Recall** List three jobs of the mouth.

3. **Recall** Name the three main parts of a tooth.

4. **Recall** Name three steps in sensible dental care.

5. **Synthesize** What kinds of food should you eat to keep your teeth healthy? Explain your answers.

Healthy Eyes

Words to Know
sclera
cornea
iris
pupil
lens
retina
optic nerve
rods
cones
farsightedness
nearsightedness
astigmatism

This lesson contains a number of valuable facts and tips. Once you have studied them, you will be able to

- name the parts of the eye.
- name the parts of a standard eye exam.
- list common eye problems.

Windows to the World

Your eyes are your windows to the world. People with full vision gather about 80 percent of their knowledge through their eyes. Your eyes can distinguish shapes, colors, movements, darkness, and light. Taking care of your eyes and protecting them are important to your total health and well-being.

The Structure of the Eye

In humans, the eye is similar to a camera. It has an opening to let in light and can focus depending on what is being viewed. Your eye is nearly round and rests in a bony socket in your skull. Each eye is made of several parts. These include the following.

- The **sclera** (SKLEHR·uh), *the tough outer covering.* This is the white of the eye. It covers all of the eye except the front. As a result, it protects the inner eye.
- The **cornea** (KOR·nee·uh), *a clear, almost round structure that serves as the window of the eye.* The cornea lets in light.
- The **iris** (EYE·ruhs), *the color of the eye that is seen from the outside.*
- The **pupil** (PYOO·puhl), *the dark opening in the center of the iris.* The pupil controls the amount of light that enters the eye. If the light is dim, the pupil grows larger to let in more light. If the light is bright, the pupil becomes smaller to keep out some of the light.

Health Minute

Your Pupil
You can actually observe your pupil growing smaller by doing the following. Position yourself before a mirror in a darkened room. Have someone turn on the light. As you look on, you will see your pupil "shrinking" to block out the increased light.

The Eye

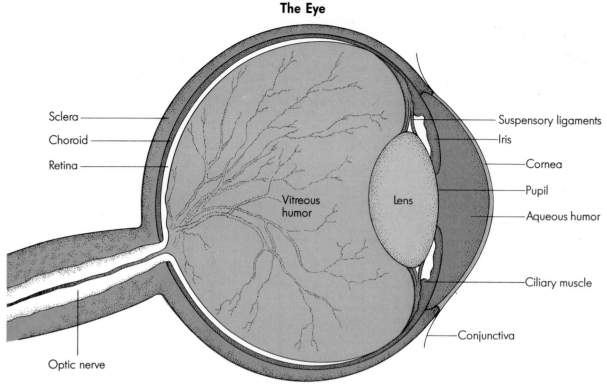

Sclera
Choroid
Retina
Vitreous humor
Lens
Suspensory ligaments
Iris
Cornea
Pupil
Aqueous humor
Ciliary muscle
Conjunctiva
Optic nerve

Learning from Drawings
Light enters through the pupil, is focused by the lens to the retina, which changes it to electrical messages sent to the brain. How does the pupil move?

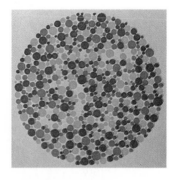

Learning from Drawings
Can you see the number in this circle? If so, your color vision is fine. If not, you may be red/green color blind.

- The **lens** (LENZ), *a structure behind the pupil that allows the light to come together in the inner part of the eye.*
- The **retina** (RET·uh·nuh), *a network of nerves that absorbs the light rays after they pass through the lens.* The retina is responsible for vision. It changes the light rays into an electrical message to create images or pictures in the brain.
- The **optic** (AHP·tik) **nerve,** *a cord of nerve fibers that carries electrical messages to the brain.* The brain interprets these messages and arranges them so that vision matches the object viewed.

How Does the Eye See Color?

Within the retina are millions of nerve endings that contain pigments or colors. These pigments change when light comes into the eye. Some of these *nerve endings distinguish objects in shades of black, white, and gray.* These are known as **rods,** and they are used by your eye in dim light. Other *nerve endings,* the **cones,** *distinguish the colors red, blue, and green and their different shadings.* Your eyes mix these colors just as you would adjust the color on a television set.

Taking Care of Your Eyes

Your eyes are a vital part of your body. For this reason, you should be aware of some ways to care for them.

Read and watch television in a well-lighted room. Set up your reading lamp so the light shines on what you are reading and not in your eyes. While viewing television, sit a comfortable distance from the set. Take breaks from using your eyes for long periods of time. Just close your eyes for a short time. In addition, avoid rubbing your eyes and exposing them to direct sun or other bright light. Naturally, you know to keep sharp objects away from your eyes. Finally, wear protective goggles or glasses when engaging in an activity that could cause an eye injury. The chart titled "Eye Injuries Related to Sports" on this page shows specific sports that put you at risk.

A Vision Checkup

An eye checkup by a trained doctor also helps you to maintain healthy eyes. If you wear glasses, you should have your eyes checked once a year. If not, an eye examination every two years is sufficient.

During an eye checkup, the doctor will usually do the following.

- **Examine each eye.** The doctor checks the cornea, pupil, and lens, to see if they are clear.

Teen Issue

Which Kind of Shades

Do you wear sunglasses? If you do, you are probably aware of the many different types that are sold—ones with special lenses, ones with colored lenses ... the list goes on and on. But not all of the sunglasses sold are safe. Some cause the pupil of your eye to get larger, which actually lets in more of the sun's harmful rays. The safest sunglasses available are the ones that wrap around and that have special no-glare lenses.

Learning from Photographs
Many eye injuries are related to sports accidents. What can be done to protect the eye from injuries?

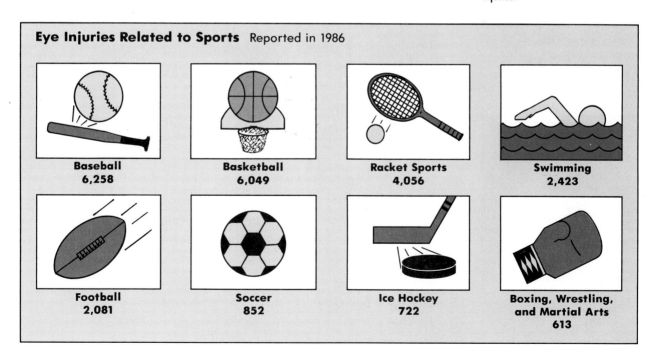

Eye Injuries Related to Sports Reported in 1986

Baseball 6,258

Basketball 6,049

Racket Sports 4,056

Swimming 2,423

Football 2,081

Soccer 852

Ice Hockey 722

Boxing, Wrestling, and Martial Arts 613

Eye Care

Make sure any towels or washcloths you wipe your eyes with are clean. Diseases such as pink eye can be spread easily by soiled or dirty towels.

Teen Issue

Glasses or Contacts?

Most people can wear contact lenses. However, some individuals cannot stand contacts for one reason or another. Wearing glasses is a "must" for them. This should be no cause for alarm. Attractive eyeglass frames of many styles are available everywhere.

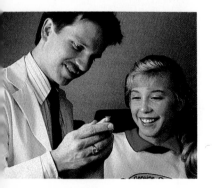

- **Check for glaucoma.** The doctor checks the pressure of the eye for early detection of this eye disease.
- **Check for cataracts.** Cataracts are a clouding of the lens that may cause some loss of vision. If one is found, an operation is done to fix the problem.
- **Check vision.** Your vision will be determined by the size of the letters you are able to read on the eye chart. If you have 20/20 vision, you will not need corrective lenses.

Some Common Eye Problems

The main job of the eye is to focus images for you. Many people have vision problems because their eyes do not focus perfectly. Following are some common eye problems that involve focusing.

- **Farsightedness,** *a condition in which* you can see far objects clearly, but *close objects appear blurred.*
- **Nearsightedness,** *a condition in which* you can see close objects clearly, but *distant objects appear blurred.*
- **Astigmatism** (uh·STIG·muh·tiz·uhm), *a condition in which images are distorted* because of an irregularly shaped cornea or lens.

Correcting Eye Problems

There are many ways doctors can correct eye problems. Nearsightedness, farsightedness, and astigmatism can be corrected with eyeglasses or contact lenses. The type of lenses suggested by a doctor depend on the condition of your eyes. Today, many people can wear contact lenses to correct a vision problem. These lenses float on the cornea and may be hard or soft. An eye doctor can tell you whether or not you can wear contact lenses.

Check Your Understanding

Conclusion   Your eyes are very complex organs. They help you to receive information about your world. Protecting your eyes is an important part of maintaining good health.

1. **Vocabulary** From the following list, select two structures of the eye and tell what each does. *sclera, cornea, iris, pupil, lens, retina, optic nerve*
2. **Recall** Name the three parts of a standard eye exam.
3. **Recall** List three common eye problems.
4. **Analyze** What advice would you have for a friend who wears sunglasses indoors?

Healthy Ears

This lesson contains a number of valuable facts and tips. Once you have studied them, you will be able to

- name the main parts of the ear.
- define balance.
- list ways of taking care of your ears.
- name some common ear problems.

Your Ears

Imagine listening to your favorite music, or recognizing the bark of your dog as you walk into your home. Your ears are the organs that allow you to experience the sounds of everyday life. Do you know that they also help your body keep its balance? Good health care is needed to protect this important body organ.

Words to Know
outer ear
middle ear
eardrum
Eustachian tube
inner ear
vestibule
semicircular canals
cochlea
auditory nerve
sound waves
oval window
balance
deafness

Learning from Photographs
Do you know how this skater's ears help him keep his balance? If not you will find out in this lesson.

The Parts of the Ear

Your ears go deep into your skull. Each has three main parts.

- **The outer ear.** The outer ear is the fleshy, curved part attached to each side of the head. It is shaped like a cup.

- **The middle ear.** The middle ear contains the **eardrum,** a thin piece of tissue that separates the outer ear from the middle ear. Behind the eardrum are three small bones: the *hammer, anvil,* and *stirrup.* These small bones link together to connect the eardrum with the inner ear. The **Eustachian** (yoo·STAY·shuhn) **tube,** while not actually part of the middle ear, stretches from the back of the nose to your middle ear. This tube *allows air to pass from the nose to the middle ear.*

- **The inner ear.** The inner ear is made up of three parts. The **vestibule** (VES·tuh·byuhl) is in the center of the inner ear. It is *a baglike structure lined with hair cells that are essential to your hearing.* The **semicircular** (SEM·i·SER·kyuh·ler) **canals** connect with the vestibule. These canals also *have hair cells and nerve fibers.* This part is *responsible for your balance.* Finally, the

Learning from Drawings
The bones in the middle ear are often called the *malleus, incus,* and *stapes,* from the Latin words for *hammer, anvil,* and *stirrup.* Why do you think they were named after these objects?

The Ear

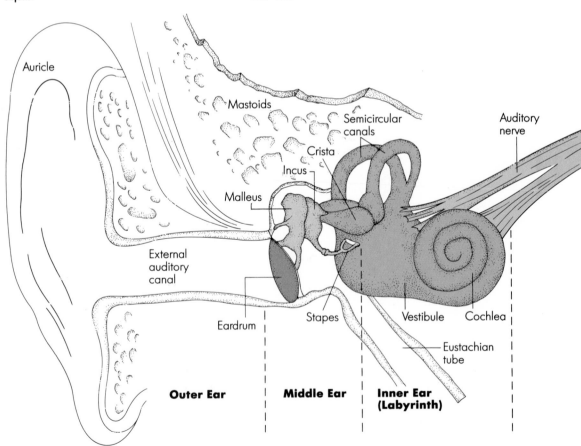

Auricle · Mastoids · Semicircular canals · Crista · Incus · Malleus · Auditory nerve · External auditory canal · Eardrum · Stapes · Vestibule · Cochlea · Eustachian tube

Outer Ear · **Middle Ear** · **Inner Ear (Labyrinth)**

cochlea (KOK·lee·uh), a snail-like *structure*, is *made up of three ducts filled with fluid and more than 15,000 hair cells*. The *nerves in the cochlea carry messages to the brain.* These nerves *form a network* called the **auditory** (AWD·uh·tor·ee) **nerve.**

How You Hear

Hearing is a complex process that takes place in a very few seconds. The steps are these.

Steps in Hearing

1. **In the outer ear.** The outer ear collects **sound waves.** These are *vibrations in the air caused by anything that moves.*

2. **In the middle ear.** The sound waves cause the eardrum to vibrate, which makes the hammer, anvil, and stirrup move. The stirrup carries the vibrations to the **oval window,** *an opening between the middle and inner ear.* The plunger-like movement of the stirrup causes fluid in the cochlea to move.

3. **In the inner ear.** Tiny hairs inside the cochlea are set into motion. As they move, the hairs produce electrical messages in the nerves deep in the inner ear. The messages pass along the auditory nerves to the brain, which identifies the messages as music, squeaks, or some other sound.

What Is Balance?

When you learned to ride a bike or roller skate, you also had to learn to balance yourself. **Balance** is *the feeling of stability and control over your body.* As noted, balance is controlled by the semicircular canals in the inner ear. These canals are filled with fluid and tiny hairs. The hairs are connected to nerve cells. When you move or change positions, the fluid and hairs move, sending messages to the brain. The brain receives the messages and tells your body how to adjust or change to meet the new situation. Your brain does this every time you walk, stand, run, or simply lift your foot off the ground.

Action in the semicircular canals is also responsible for *motion sickness.* This is the uncomfortable feeling of dizziness or nausea some people have when riding in a car, boat, or airplane. In motion sickness, constant motion causes continuous movement of the fluid in the canals. As a result, many different messages are sent to the brain at once. After a while, the brain becomes confused and sends distress signals to the body. Motion sickness can be controlled by medications, but these often make the user sleepy. Other solutions include sitting in the front seat, sitting near a window, or focusing on the horizon.

DID **YOU** KNOW?

At the Sound of the Tone
Your ear can hear more than 300,000 tones.

A Healthy Balance
Try practicing your balance. Find a crack or line in the sidewalk and see how long you can walk that crack or line without wavering. You will find that relaxed breathing will help you keep your balance.

Learning from Photographs
How is this teen caring for her ears?

Health Minute

"Signing"
Learn some basic signs in sign language. For example, what are the signs for "please" and "thank you"?

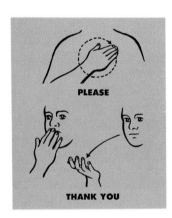

PLEASE

THANK YOU

Taking Care of Your Ears

You can take care of your hearing by avoiding very loud sounds. Loud noise may damage the nerve cells in your ears. You can prevent permanent hearing loss by turning down the volume on your radio, stereo, television, and so on. Wear hearing protection if you work with an object that makes a very loud noise. Cover your ears with your hands when you are exposed to loud noises.

Naturally, you should keep all sharp objects out of your ears. When cleaning the outside of your ears, use a cotton swab. Make sure not to push the swab into your ear when cleaning. Ear muffs or a hat that covers your ears can often prevent ear infections in cold weather.

Some Ear Problems

Ear infections are the most common ear problems. Any infection of the nose, throat, or Eustachian tube can lead to pain in the ear, known as *earache*. Cold weather or sudden changes in temperature can also cause earaches.

Deafness, or *the loss of hearing,* is the most serious ear problem. It can be either partial or complete. Partial hearing loss is called *hearing impairment*, which can be caused by ear infections, nerve damage, or a buildup of wax in the ear. A total loss of hearing can be caused by injury to the ear, birth defects, or diseases.

People who have hearing disorders can lead normal lives through the use of hearing aids, sign language, and lip reading.

Check Your Understanding

Conclusion Your ears are very important body organs. They help you to hear and also maintain your balance. Protecting your ears and hearing should be part of your personal health care.

1. **Vocabulary** Copy the following words on a separate sheet of paper. Write *E* next to words that describe parts of the ear and *H* next to words that relate to the process of hearing. *anvil, eardrum, sound waves, vibrations, auditory nerve*

2. **Recall** Name the three main parts of the ear.

3. **Recall** Define balance.

4. **Recall** List three ways of taking care of your ears.

5. **Recall** Name the two most common ear problems.

6. **Interpret** Why might a person living near an airport need to take special care of his or her ears?

Healthy Feet and Posture

Words to Know
callus
corn
blister
bunion
athlete's foot
fallen arches
posture

This lesson contains a number of valuable facts and tips. Once you have studied them, you will be able to

- name the jobs the feet perform.
- list four problems that can be lessened by good foot care.
- give some reasons for having good posture.
- state ways you can improve your posture.

Your Feet and Posture

Have you ever worn shoes that hurt your feet? How did that affect your mood? Your feet are really engineering marvels! They support your weight, act as shock absorbers, and help you to maintain good posture. Feet and posture go together to make you feel and look good.

Taking Care of Your Feet

Most foot problems are caused by ill-fitting shoes and socks. A simple rule to follow for foot care is to wear shoes and socks that fit your feet comfortably.

Learning from Photographs
Athletes like these are careful about their shoes. Why should you be also?

Swollen Feet

During the hot summer months and after exercise, your feet are likely to be warm and swollen. Place them under cool running water and allow the water to run through your toes and around your ankles. Then rub your feet with some rubbing alcohol.

Comfortable shoes...
- fit without being too tight or too loose.
- never bind or pinch.
- are roomy enough that you can wiggle your toes.
- give good support to the heel and ball of your foot.

Your feet are enclosed inside shoes most of the day, so they perspire. This perspiration can cause the buildup of bacteria. To prevent this buildup, wash between your toes and scrub away dead skin from the heel and ball of your foot. Then be sure to dry your feet thoroughly.

Feet swell during the day. As a result, shoes that fit in the morning may be too tight in the afternoon. If possible, switch to another pair of shoes during the day to relax your feet.

Some Foot Problems

Many of the foot problems described below can be reduced by good foot care.

- A **callus** is *a hard, thickened part of the skin on the foot.* It results from your foot rubbing against the inside of a shoe. Calluses are often found on the heel or back of the foot.

- A **corn** is *an overgrowth of the skin at some point on a toe.* It usually appears where the toe rubs against a shoe. Corns can be painful. If they thicken too much, they must be cut away by a foot doctor.

- A **blister** is *a fluid-filled pouch on the skin.* Again, a blister is formed by an ill-fitting shoe. Blisters are painful and can lead to corns.

- A **bunion** (BUHN·yuhn) is *a swelling in the first joint of the big toe.* It is caused by tight shoes.

- **Athlete's foot** is *a problem caused by fungi growing in the warm, damp areas of the foot.* Redness and itching usually appear between the toes. Athlete's foot can be treated with powder or medications. It is important to wear clean socks if you have athlete's foot. Since athlete's foot is contagious, you should always wear some kind of foot covering in showers and locker rooms.

- **Fallen arches** is another name for *flatness in the bottom of the feet.* This condition, also known as flat feet, happens when the muscles and connective tissues in the arches weaken. The best protection against flat feet is walking for exercise and wearing shoes that fit comfortably.

Learning from Photographs
Keeping feet dry is a good way to care for them. What problem is this teen preventing by using powder?

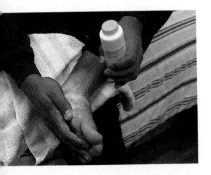

What Is Posture?

Posture is *the way you carry yourself.* Posture can tell as much about you as the appearance of your hair and skin. You can work to improve your posture. Some reasons for having good posture are listed in the box below.

> Good posture...
>
> - helps you move, stand, and sit with ease.
> - helps you save energy because you can move more easily.
> - allows your internal organs to function properly.
> - helps your bones and muscles grow properly.
> - makes your figure and body build look good.

Building Good Posture

Posture involves standing, sitting, and walking. Your feet are the key to good posture. When you stand, your head, upper body, and lower body should be balanced on the balls of your feet.

When you sit, your head and shoulders should be balanced directly over your hips. Make sure your feet are flat on the floor and your back is straight against the chair. Doing this can also help you stay alert.

Check how you walk by making sure your body is balanced over the balls of your feet. Hold your shoulders back in a natural way, and tuck in your stomach. Allow your arms to hang freely at your sides. Use your upper legs to move your body forward.

SKILLS FOR LIVING

Good Posture
Practice good posture by doing a simple exercise. Stand with your back to a wall or a door. Your head, backside, and heels should be touching the wall. Stretch your hands out over your head along the wall. Then push off on your toes so that your heels are off the floor. You will improve your balance and muscle coordination.

Learning from Drawings
Good posture is based on the head and shoulders being balanced over the hips. Posture can reflect a person's mood. Someone sad or tired may have poorer posture than normally. Why do you think this is so?

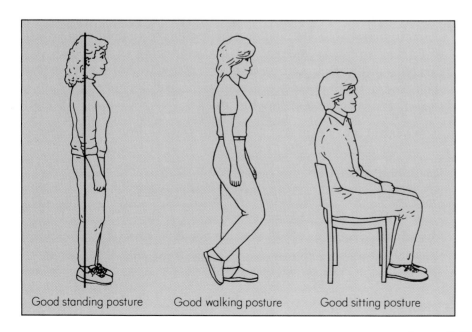

Good standing posture   Good walking posture   Good sitting posture

The proper way to lift is to keep the buttocks low and the back straight. This method keeps strain off the back and uses the strong leg muscles to lift. The method shown in the photo at right is incorrect. What problems might be caused by lifting incorrectly?

Correct   Incorrect

Teen Issue

Stand Up and Be Counted

Tall teens are sometimes uncomfortable or self-conscious about their height. Because of this, they lean over or slouch, which can harm their posture. Everyone grows at a different rate. If you are a tall teen, stand up and be counted as the special person you are.

DID YOU KNOW?

Feet, Don't Fail Me

In a single lifetime, a pair of feet carries several million tons and covers enough distance to circle the earth four times.

Here are some easy ways to improve your walking posture.

- Keep your back straight when rising from a chair.
- Keep your feet parallel to each other. Your toes should not point in or out.
- Wear comfortable walking shoes. Walking shoes should be almost flat. High-heeled shoes throw off your balance, creating stress on your ankles and the arches of your feet.

Check Your Understanding

Conclusion Your feet and posture are linked to grooming. The care and attention you give to the well-being of your feet—keeping them clean and wearing comfortable shoes—can also help you achieve good posture. Correct, well-balanced posture can increase your energy and alertness.

1. **Vocabulary** Which of the following terms *do not* name foot problems? *ball of the foot, blisters, heel, corns, calluses*
2. **Recall** Name three jobs the feet perform.
3. **Recall** List four problems that can be lessened by good foot care.
4. **Recall** Give five reasons for having good posture.
5. **Recall** State three ways you can improve your posture.
6. **Synthesize** What advice might you give a friend who stoops because he or she is self-conscious about being tall?

Who Is at Risk from the Sun?

Many people think that a suntan looks healthy. The facts tell otherwise. The sun can dry out and damage skin, causing early aging. The ultraviolet (UV) rays of the sun can lead to skin cancer. In fact, *one* blistering sunburn can double the chances of getting skin cancer. *Everyone* is at risk from the sun.

Knowing Sun Safety

Some people insist on tanning no matter what the dangers. If you are one of these people, you can reduce your risk by following these tips.

1. Work on a tan little by little. Stay out in the sun for only short periods over several weeks.
2. Stay out of the sun between 10 A.M. and 2 P.M. Your skin will burn the fastest during these hours.
3. Use sunscreens for protection, not lotions and especially not oils. A good sunscreen contains the substance PABA.
4. Stay away from tanning parlors. The "safe" sunlamps they use can be just as dangerous as the sun.

The sun is especially dangerous to people in high-risk groups.

- People with light-colored skin, light hair, or freckles.
- People who burn easily.
- People with relatives who have had skin cancer.

These people should limit their time in the sun. When in the sun, they should wear brimmed hats and long sleeves and pants to protect their faces, arms, and legs.

Using the Skill

Read the following story. Then, on a separate sheet of paper, answer the questions that follow it.

Case

Tod, Jana, Karen, and Barry had been at the beach since 9 o'clock this morning. It was now 1:30. The sun felt hot.

"I think I'm starting to burn," Barry said. "Hey, Karen, how about rubbing some of this on my shoulders?" He handed her a bottle of oil.

Stacey came over. She was wearing a big floppy beach hat, jeans, and a long-sleeve shirt. "Aren't you hot?" Barry asked, looking up at her. "Come on, get into your bathing suit. You don't want to be the only pale face in the crowd, do you?"

"I don't think I better," Stacey said, brushing back her long blond hair. "I burn pretty easily."

"I do, too," Karen said. "But the way I feel about it is you have to get one good burn. Then you're okay for the rest of the summer."

"Besides," Tod added, "you can put some of this on. It's got PABA."

1. Which sun safety tip do Tod, Jana, Karen, and Barry not follow in the first paragraph of the story?
2. Which safety tip does Barry not follow in the second paragraph?
3. On the next-to-the-last paragraph of the story, it is revealed that Karen has not followed a safety tip. Which one is it?
4. What healthy decision has Stacey made before coming to the beach? Explain your answer.
5. What decision is Stacey faced with now? What are her choices?
6. Would Stacey be wise in taking Tod's advice? Why or why not?

Chapter 2 Review

Summary

- Your skin does three important jobs. Washing can help prevent a serious acne problem.
- Hair and nail care are an important part of your appearance.
- Teeth allow you to chew food; they also form the shape of your mouth. Brushing and flossing help prevent tooth decay.
- Your eyes receive light and help create images. Caring for your eyes includes reading with good light.
- Your ears enable you to hear sounds and maintain body balance.
- Foot care is essential to healthy feet and good posture.

Reviewing Vocabulary and Concepts

On a separate sheet of paper, write the numbers 1–16. After each number, write the letter of the word or phrase in Column B that best matches the phrase in Column A.

Column A

Lesson 1

1. A job of the skin
2. The agent that gives the skin most of its color
3. An important part of skin care
4. The most common skin problem among teens

Lesson 2

5. One of two parts of sensible hair care
6. A common problem of the scalp
7. A part of toenail care
8. Splits in the cuticle along the edge of the nail

Lesson 3

9. A job of the mouth
10. The hard material covering the crown of every tooth
11. With brushing, a way of caring for your teeth
12. Sticky film that builds up on teeth
13. A common treatment for malocclusion

Lesson 4

14. The opening at the center of the eye, which controls the amount of light coming in
15. An eye problem in which distant objects are blurred
16. A way of correcting many eye problems

Column B

a. tasting food
b. brushing
c. showering daily
d. provides waterproof covering for the body
e. hangnails
f. nearsightedness
g. enamel
h. dandruff
i. melanin
j. pupil
k. braces
l. wearing eyeglasses
m. keeping the nails cut straight across
n. acne
o. plaque
p. flossing

Write the numbers 17–23 on your paper. After each number, write the letter of the answer that best completes each of the following statements.

Lesson 5

17. Vibrations made by moving objects and essential to our ability to hear are called
    a. sound waves   **b.** electrical messages   **c.** cochlea   **d.** oval windows
18. The feeling of stability and control you have over your body is
    a. wellness   **b.** balance   **c.** impairment   **d.** total health
19. Two common problems of the ear are earaches and
    a. infections   **b.** itches   **c.** rashes   **d.** none of these
20. Sign language is a form of communication used
    a. by doctors only   **b.** by deaf people   **c.** before 1940   **d.** none of these

Lesson 6

21. An important way of caring for your feet is
    a. stretching your toes   **b.** wearing comfortable shoes   **c.** running often   **d.** wearing sandals
22. A hard, thickened part of the skin on the foot is called a
    a. bunion   **b.** wart   **c.** callus   **d.** athlete's foot
23. Keeping your back straight when rising from a chair is a
    a. bad posture habit   **b.** cause of back strain   **c.** good posture habit   **d.** none of these

Thinking Critically About the Facts

Write your answers to the following questions on a separate sheet of paper.

24. **Synthesize** Imagine that you are in a park and see your best friend using a sun reflector—a mirrorlike device that concentrates the sun's rays. What advice might you give your friend? What facts would you use to back up that advice?
25. **Identify** Suppose you worked in a pharmacy and a customer asked you to recommend a shampoo. What information about the customer's hair would you need before making a recommendation?
26. **Organize** Plan a menu for healthy teeth.
27. **Understand** Think of ways to improve the lighting in your home. Where should reading lamps be positioned? What is good overhead lighting and where should it be located?
28. **Summarize** Name at least three examples of harmful noise levels in your environment. What can you do to correct these high levels?
29. **Analyze** Imagine shopping with a friend for a pair of walking shoes. What shoe features would you recommend to your friend? Why?

Applying the Facts

30. Read the labels of six different acne creams. What do they advertise? What are the ingredients found in each? Do they all claim to treat acne? Show your findings in a chart.
31. Research the latest inventions in hearing devices. Choose one and draw an illustration to show how it helps a person to hear.
32. Prepare several questions you would ask a physical therapist about techniques that can be used to improve posture. Then interview a physical therapist. Write his or her responses to your questions. Present your findings in an oral report.

Wellness and Your Mental Health

CHAPTER WARM-UP

Chapter Study Goals

After you have read this chapter, you will be able to

- identify the traits of good mental health and the benefits of a positive self-concept.
- identify healthy ways of meeting your emotional needs and communicating.
- explain how to make responsible decisions.
- identify ways of dealing with stress.
- identify major mental disorders and factors that may lead to teen suicide.
- identify where to go for help.

Be on the lookout for information in the chapter that will help you reach these goals.

Getting Started

"Alexandra is great. She's always there to help. She's always cheerful, too."
—Lissa, age 12

What do these comments tell you about Alexandra? Do you see these qualities in yourself? If not, are they qualities you would like to have? This chapter will give you some ideas on how to improve your level of mental health.

Study Tip

As you read, note that the captions show ways of improving your mental health.

What Is Mental Health?

Words to Know

mental health
personality
heredity
environment
behavior

This lesson contains a number of valuable facts and tips. Once you have studied them, you will be able to

- define the term *mental health.*
- name some qualities shared by people with good mental health.
- identify three factors that shape your personality.

Mental Health

The three important parts of good health form a triangle. Two sides of the triangle are physical health and social health. Another side of the triangle is mental health. **Mental health** is *your ability to like yourself and to accept yourself as you are.* When you have good mental health, you feel good about yourself and are comfortable around other people. You are also able to take charge of your life and meet its demands.

The box below contains some other qualities that are true of people with good mental health.

People with good mental health...

- can take a disappointment every now and then and know how to accept their limitations.
- are happy and active most of the time and have a positive outlook on life.
- are aware of their thoughts and feelings and can usually express them in a healthy way.
- work well in a group.
- know how to accept criticism and don't get angry when they can't have their way.
- are not afraid to face problems and look forward to new challenges.
- give their best at whatever they do and set realistic goals for themselves.

Aim High

Do you realize there are lots of people walking around who could have been great—great singers, great teachers, great ball players, great chefs, great friends? The biggest waste we know of is people who never reached their highest potential. Don't let this happen to you. Get into the practice of achieving by doing your best at everything. Make it a habit. Aim high!

Learning from Photographs
Being mentally healthy means accepting people for who they are. Why is this important?

Naturally, this is the ideal picture of mental health. Like physical health, there are many different levels of mental health, and everyone's mental health has its ups and downs. But just as you can work at improving your physical health, you can also develop good mental health habits.

Developing Good Mental Health Habits

A first step toward developing good mental health habits is understanding yourself. This means focusing on your strengths. It also means accepting things about yourself that you cannot change and working at changing those that you can. Rather than be miserable over the fact that you are too slow for the track team or too tall for a lead part in the class play, find another sport or activity at which you excel. Try also to learn from past mistakes. Once you can learn from these mistakes, you stand a much better chance of not repeating them.

Another important step toward improving your mental health is learning to accept other people for who they are. Everyone has faults. But everyone also has qualities to be admired. Making a habit of looking for those qualities will lead to a healthier you.

Personality and Mental Health

Just as no two snowflakes are alike, no two people are exactly the same. Rather, every person is a special individual with a unique set of feelings, attitudes, and habits. The *sum total of these feelings, attitudes, and habits* is the person's **personality.** Your personality is the thing that makes you *you.* You cannot be separated from it.

Teen Issue

"Pegging" Others
How good are you at evaluating the personality of someone you have just met? Here are some common mistakes or snap judgments people make in evaluating new acquaintances.

- **They place too much value on surface traits.** Some people are considered to have a good personality simply because they are good-looking.

- **They stereotype people.** They assume that someone who comes from a certain group, race, nationality, or religion will act in a certain way. This is what is known as prejudice.

You can't really tell what an individual is like until you get to know that person. Some people use **magazine personality tests** to figure out what a person is like. These tests are very limited and not at all accurate.

Your Message Here
Your mental well-being is strongly affected by your surroundings. So use your creativity to improve your personal environment, your surroundings. Decorate your room with things that mean a lot to you. Those personal belongings will inspire you when times are tough.

DID **YOU** KNOW?

Mental Health
Your mental health can affect your physical health. So strong is the mind-body connection that people have made themselves physically ill through worry.

Factors That Shape Your Personality

Your personality is shaped by a number of factors. The three most important of these are identified below.

- **Heredity** (huh·RED·uh·tee), or *the passing on of traits from your parents.* Your hair color and intelligence are part of your heredity. Parts of your personality such as talents, sense of humor, and interests may also be picked up or learned from your parents.

- **Environment** (in·VY·ruhn·muhnt), or *the sum total of your surroundings.* Your environment includes where you grew up, who your family and friends are, and all the experiences you have had. A person who grows up surrounded by love is apt to have a happier outlook than someone who does not. Similarly, a person whose childhood was complicated by illness may have a less positive outlook than one who enjoyed good physical health.

- **Behavior,** or *the way you act in the many different situations and events in your life.* Behavior is the factor of your personality over which you have the most control. It is based on your system of *values,* or guides as to what you hold important in life. Most of your values are learned from your family and, to a lesser extent, friends. How you behave reflects these values. If you have learned the value that health is precious, then you will behave in a way that reflects this.

Learning from Photographs
This teen enjoys taking pictures. How does a hobby or pastime reflect a person's interests and talents?

Learning from Photographs
The family and home are part of a person's environment. How might you describe this teen's growing up environment?

Your heredity, environment, and behavior have all come together to help shape the person you are at this very moment. To some extent, they will continue to shape your personality throughout your life.

Your behavior is the factor that you control. The choices you make can lead to good health.

Check Your Understanding

Conclusion Your physical, social, and mental health are equal parts of your health triangle. Good mental health habits can be learned. These good habits can positively affect your personality and the ways in which you get along with yourself and others.

1. **Vocabulary** *Synonyms* are words that have the same meaning. In a good dictionary, find synonyms for the words *personality* and *environment*.

2. **Recall** Define mental health.

3. **Recall** Name two qualities shared by people with good mental health.

4. **Recall** Identify three factors that shape your personality.

5. **Interpret** Imagine a boy with a gift for playing the piano who keeps his talent a secret because he is afraid others will tease him. What might you say about his mental health?

Dear Diary
Keep a diary or notebook. Put anything at all in it. Write down your hopes, plans, daydreams, and concerns. Writing these down can help you achieve your goals and make important changes in your life. Reviewing what you have written will give you some insights into how you've grown.

Words to Know
self-concept
reinforce

Your Self-Concept and Mental Health

This lesson contains a number of valuable facts and tips. Once you have studied them, you will be able to

● define the term *self-concept.*

● list ways of developing a positive self-concept.

Self-Concept and Your Health

Have you ever wondered what other people see when they look at you? *The picture you have of yourself and the way you believe you are seen by others* is your **self-concept.** Your self-concept always plays an important role in your behavior and in how well you get along with others.

Learning from Photographs
By focusing on your successes, you can build your self-concept. What are you good at?

Your self-concept begins to take shape in your earliest years of life. It is influenced by how your parents and others treat you and by what they say to you. If, as an infant, a person is given support and encouragement, that person will most likely start out with a positive self-concept. If, on the other hand, the person is neglected or spoken to harshly, he or she may begin early on to develop a negative self-concept.

As you grow older and begin school, your friends and teachers become important forces in the development of your self-concept. Remarks that people make and ways that they act toward you **reinforce,** or *back up*, the view you have of yourself. Having a teacher praise your class work can build up a self-image you have of being a good student. In the same way, not being invited to a party or being ignored by classmates might simply add fuel to an already low self-opinion. All of the spoken—and unspoken—"messages" you get from people are factors in how you see yourself.

Throughout your teens, you grow and change. Your self-concept will change with you. These changes may be confusing, but they are part of growing up. You will gain more confidence as you grow more sure of your new self.

SKILLS FOR LIVING

What Goes Around Comes Around

Everyone has a self-concept of some kind. It is also important to people you know. Learn to be aware of things you say and do that might help friends and relatives improve their self-concept. Some examples follow.

- When you find a meal especially enjoyable, tell the family member who cooked it what a good cook he or she is.
- When someone you know looks particularly nice, tell the person.

Who knows—saying and doing nice things *could* catch on!

SELF-INVENTORY

A Look at Myself

Do you have some or all of the qualities you admire in others? To find out, take this survey. On a separate sheet of paper, write *yes*, *no*, or *sometimes* for each statement. Be honest in your answers. When you have finished, think about what you can do to change any *no's* and *sometimes* to *yeses*.

- I am really interested in what other people say and do.
- It is fun for me to be part of a group.
- I get along well with most people.
- Other people can count on me.
- I care about other people's feelings.
- I'm a good listener.
- I cooperate.
- I try to be on time.
- I have good manners.
- I set realistic goals for myself.
- I usually bounce back from a setback.

Learning from Photographs
A person's self-concept has great impact on his or her health. How can you help someone else develop a positive self-concept?

A Story That Can Help
Copy the following story onto a piece of paper, and hang it in your room to read whenever you feel down on yourself.

He was a school dropout. He failed at business. His marriage was unhappy. He lost four elections. He was attacked by newspapers and hated by half the country. But, in spite of all this, he managed to do so much good in his lifetime that he is considered one of the greatest Americans who ever lived. His name was Abraham Lincoln.

Having a Good Self-Concept

Probably no single factor has a greater impact on your total health than your self-concept. When your self-concept is good, you are at your best mentally, physically, morally, emotionally, and socially. You are usually happy with yourself and get along well with others. You are able to bounce back quickly after a loss, and you take pride in your appearance.

For these reasons, having a good self-concept is an important goal to work toward. There are a number of ways of reaching this goal. Here are three.

- **Focus on your successes.** Congratulate yourself when you succeed at something, and work at increasing your chances for future success. Remember, success builds confidence, and confidence is part of a good self-concept.

- **Pay attention to the messages you give yourself.** Negative messages come not only from other people but, sometimes, from ourselves. When you find that you are giving yourself a negative message, find a more positive way of putting it. Don't tell yourself, for example, that you are slow because it takes you a long time to finish your homework. Instead, tell yourself that you are careful and thorough.

- **Turn to people you are close to for help when you need it.** Everyone needs help now and again. People who care about you will be more likely to give support in a way that builds, rather than breaks down, your self-concept.

When you build a positive self-concept, you give yourself the power and confidence to take on life's challenges.

Check Your Understanding

Conclusion Your self-concept is the way you see yourself and think other people see you. Your self-concept begins to develop early in life and is supported by messages you get throughout life. You can work at improving your self-concept.

1. **Vocabulary** Use the word *reinforce* in an original sentence.
2. **Recall** Define self-concept.
3. **Recall** List three ways of developing a positive self-concept.
4. **Analyze** Name a common problem among people your age that affects self-concept. What can people with this problem do to feel better about themselves?

Emotional Needs and Mental Health

This lesson contains a number of valuable facts and tips. Once you have studied them, you will be able to

- identify three basic emotional needs of every human being.
- name ways of meeting your emotional needs.
- list rules of good communication.

What Are Emotional Needs?

As a human being, you have a number of basic physical needs. These include the need for food, the need for water, and the need for sleep. You also have emotional needs. **Emotional needs** are *needs that affect your feelings and sense of well-being.* These emotional needs play an important role in your mental health.

Words to Know
emotional needs
emotions
hormones

Health Minute

A Healthy Hug
Make hugging a part of your life. A healthy dose of hugs from friends and family can help you make it through.

Learning from Photographs
We all have three main emotional needs. Before reading on, can you say which of these teens' emotional needs you think are being met?

The ways of expressing emotions differ from culture to culture. Some cultures allow people to freely show fear, joy, sorrow. In other cultures, it is required that those emotions be hidden.

Having a Good Day

Make a list like the one below. Look at the list before you go to bed. See how many things you accomplished that day.

- Did I get up on time?
- Did I eat a good breakfast?
- Did I brush my teeth and wash up?
- Did I learn something new today?
- Did I do something kind for a friend?
- Did I do a kind deed for a family member?
- Did I complete all of my schoolwork?
- Did I earn some money to pay my expenses?
- Did I do something to make myself feel proud?

Every human being has three basic emotional needs.

- **The need to love and be loved.** You need to feel that you are cared for and that in someone's eyes you are a special individual. You also have a need to care for others. Loving others helps you to feel better about yourself.

- **The need to belong.** You need to know that others like you and accept you as a part of a group. For most people, the first group to satisfy the basic need to belong is the family. As you grow up, other groups that may satisfy this need include circles of friends, teams, and social clubs.

- **The need to feel worthwhile.** You need to feel that you make a difference in the world—that you are making a contribution. When you help another person do something or come up with a useful idea you are contributing. There are many other ways of contributing, but all of them have one thing in common. They all add to your feeling of self-worth.

Good and Bad Ways of Meeting Emotional Needs

We are constantly striving to have our emotional needs met. Much of the time, we are not even aware of doing this. People who have not had these needs met may find unhealthy ways to meet them.

Have you ever wondered why some people tease or make fun of others when there is an audience? Or why some people bully or pick on others? These people may be trying to have their emotional needs met, but they are going about it in the wrong way. Perhaps the "comic" showoff and bully are seeking recognition. Perhaps they believe that acting as they do is the only way they can get it.

When you are mentally healthy, you seek out positive, healthy ways of satisfying your emotional needs. The need to feel worthwhile, for example, could be satisfied by helping someone in need. The need to love and be loved could be met by adopting a homeless pet from a shelter. Here are some other possibilities you can try.

Healthy Ways to Satisfy Emotional Needs

- Offer to help out with chores around the house that are usually someone else's responsibility.
- Help with the care of a younger brother or sister at home.
- Become a pen pal with someone your age.
- Form an action group to pick up litter around school.
- Volunteer time to help out at a local nursing home or hospital.

Learning from Photographs
By helping a younger sister, this teen is helping herself feel worthwhile. What other ways are there for making yourself feel worthwhile?

Emotions

Another factor influencing your mental health is your **emotions,** or *feelings.* Emotions are a natural part of being alive. Your emotions protect you from danger. They also help you achieve goals. There are many different emotions, including anger, happiness, and sadness. Everyone has emotions.

During your teen years, changes in your body cause your emotions to shift suddenly. Have you noticed on occasion lately that one minute you feel happy and the next minute you feel blue? These sudden emotional swings "go with the territory" of being a teen. They are related to the body's making of **hormones** (HOR·mohnz), *chemicals produced in the body that are responsible for rapid growth.* These shifts are quite normal in people your age and are no cause for alarm.

Expressing Emotions

Some people believe that certain emotions are "wrong" or "unhealthy." This is not true. In themselves, emotions are neither healthy nor unhealthy. How they are *expressed* is another matter. A person with good mental health seeks out healthy, responsible ways of expressing his or her emotions.

An important step in learning to express your emotions is becoming aware of them. This is not always as easy as it sounds. Sometimes we confuse one emotion with another. This is especially true of the

Teen Issue

Beating the Blues

It is natural for someone your age to feel down in the dumps sometimes for no apparent reason. Still, it's no fun to feel this way. So the next time it happens try the following.

- Stop thinking any negative thoughts that might be on your mind, and concentrate on a happy memory or good joke.

- Do something active. Take a walk, exercise, or try to get a game going with friends.

- Get your mind into high gear. Start a new project you've been meaning to take on, write a letter you've been putting off writing, or phone a friend you haven't spoken to in a long time.

One or all of these tips should help chase away the blues.

When You Are Angry...

When you are angry, go off by yourself where no one can hear you and scream as loudly as you can. Get your whole body into it. You'll see. You'll feel better. Moving to music alone in your room can help, too.

Health Minute

You Don't Say!
To get an idea of how much your tone of voice can change a message, read the following sentence five different times. Each time put the stress on a different word. Start by stressing the first word first.

Did Sylvia finally call Miguel?

Which of the readings simply sounded like questions? Which sounded angry or emotional?

emotion anger. People may at times say things like "I hate you!" and "I never want to see you again!" when what they mean is "I'm angry with you." When you are feeling angry, try to take the following steps.

- Pause for a moment and take a deep breath.
- Try to focus on what it is that has made you angry.
- Try to think of the words that will express your true feelings.
- Tell the other person how you feel.

Learning to Communicate

Everyone responds to situations and shows feelings differently. Have you ever worried that a friend was hurt over something you did only to find out that the person wasn't hurt? Have you ever caught yourself denying that you were angry just as you were slamming a door? Because human feelings are complex, it is important to learn how to communicate them effectively.

Problems in Communication

Experts have found that, when people communicate their feelings, only about 10 percent of the communication is through words. Much of the message, the experts say, comes through the *way* the words are said—through the speaker's *tone of voice*. And most of the message—over half—is passed along through movements of the body, or *body language*. Problems in communication arise when your words send one message and your body language or tone of voice sends a different message. These "mixed messages" can be a source of confusion.

Rules of Good Communication

Communication is not an easy skill to learn, but it is a vital one. With practice you can become better at understanding what other people are feeling and at letting others know what you are feeling. Here are three rules of good communication.

Rules of Good Communication

- **Think about the words you are using.** Start your sentences with "I" and avoid saying "you." Doing this helps you to focus on *your* part in the situation or disagreement.
- **Tell the other person what has happened and state your feelings.** Pay attention to your own body language. Are you sending the same message as the one you are stating?
- **Listen to what the other person has to say.** Don't tune the person out. Instead, pay attention to his or her words. You might see the problem in an entirely new light.

Using these rules is no guarantee that the problem will be solved. Communication is a two-way street. If the other person refuses to listen or to express his or her own real feelings, there is nothing else you can do. Still, you will feel good about yourself for having communicated your feelings in a healthy fashion.

Check Your Understanding

Conclusion Every human being has the need to love and be loved, the need to belong, and the need to feel worthwhile. People with good mental health find ways to have their emotional needs met. Expressing and communicating feelings is a vital skill.

1. **Vocabulary** Which of the following terms is a chemical produced by the body? *emotional need, emotion, hormone*

2. **Recall** Identify three basic emotional needs of every human being.

3. **Recall** Name two ways of meeting your emotional needs.

4. **Recall** List three rules of good communication.

5. **Synthesize** Imagine that you have been asked to speak to a group of fifth-graders about having a good self-concept. Describe an activity you could do with them to promote a good self-concept.

Idle Chatter

Have you ever repeated a story about someone that you weren't sure was true? If so, you have gossiped. Nothing can damage a person's reputation faster or more completely than a piece of gossip.

Before you repeat something you have heard, ask yourself these questions.

- Who will gain if I pass along this story?
- Who will lose if I pass along this story?
- Will the story accomplish some good?
- Would I want this story told about me?

Answering these questions may keep you from saying something you'll be sorry for later.

Teen Health ▲▲ BULLETIN BOARD

CAREERS

Wanted:
Counselor—someone to talk with students about teen concerns.

Needed:
A genuine fondness for people and especially young people; a desire to help teens work out problems with school and schoolwork and plan for their future.

Education:
A degree from a four-year college.

Write to:
American School Counselor Association
22 Skyline Place, Suite 400
5203 Leesburg Pike
Falls Church, VA 22041

TEEN Q & A

Q: Two of my friends at school are kind of bad influences on me. They're always trying to get me to do things I don't want to do. How can I say *no* without losing their respect?

A: A more important question you might ask is how good are these friends if they want you to do things you think you shouldn't do? Is their "respect" worth having? If, after thinking about this last question, your answer is *yes*, then you might do this. Find out as much as you can about whatever it is your friends are involved in, whether it's drugs, alcohol, or tobacco. Suggest doing something else. Tip your friends off to the dangers of their habits. Encourage them to get help—to discuss their habits with a grown-up. If that doesn't earn their respect, then it's time to find new friends.

L ifestyle

A Friend Indeed

Have you heard the expression "You can be your own best friend"? There is something to it. Taking care of your physical and emotional health is a good way to be a friend to yourself. Start treating yourself like a friend today by doing the following.

- *Give up self put-downs.* If the criticism is helpful, that's fine. But if it is simply being hard on yourself, get rid of it.
- *Show yourself a good time.* When was the last time you bought yourself a present? Or took yourself to the movies? There's no time like the present to start.
- *Make a list of the things you like about you.* You may surprise yourself by finding that you're just the sort of person you enjoy spending time with.

L ifestyle
Old Feelings?

You've heard it all before. Life is hard. Life, especially as you are growing up, can be a disaster. Well, that simply is not true. You don't have to feel terrible emotional pain in order to grow up. If you have any of the following signs of distress, you may need some help to work it out.

- Feelings that you don't want friends
- Feelings that everybody hates you
- Becoming terrified because of shyness
- Feelings that you want to withdraw from family and friends
- Feelings that you need to quit school

If you find that you have feelings such as those above, you can try the following remedies.

- Talk to a trusted adult immediately.
- Don't hope people will guess how bad you feel. You have to tell them.
- Check out hot lines listed through city or county medical facilities.

Sports and Recreation
What You See Is What You Get

The batter stands at the plate, scraping his cleats in the dirt. The pitcher winds up and releases the ball. The batter takes a mighty swing, hears the crack of wood against horsehide, and watches as the ball sails deep into the stands—a home run! At least that is what the batter sees in his mind just before the game. This baseball player, like so many athletes today, is using a process called *mental imaging*. In mental imaging, the athlete pictures himself or herself going through all the moves necessary to success. Many people have described the process as similar to watching a movie of themselves in slow-motion.

HEALTH IN THE NEWS
Do You Have the Blahs?

Do you find yourself feeling depressed when the thermometer rises in summertime? How about when the skies cloud over and turn dreary on a winter's day?

If your answer to either of these questions is *yes*, you are not alone. Recent research shows that many people suffer from a form of depression related to certain seasons. It is called *seasonal affective disorder*, or *SAD* for short. Victims of summer SAD often feel moody and uncomfortable and have trouble sleeping. Victims of winter SAD are troubled by the darkness of shorter days. They tend to sleep more and crave starchy foods, such as bread and macaroni.

The treatment? For summer SAD sufferers, the solution seems to be cool baths and staying in air-conditioned rooms. For winter SAD sufferers, the answer is staying near a source of light that imitates daylight.

Making Decisions

Word to Know

decision making

This lesson contains a number of valuable facts and tips. Once you have studied them, you will be able to

- name the five steps in decision making.
- identify the advantage of handling personal problems one step at a time.

Problems and Decisions

One important part of good mental health is being able to face problems and work on finding solutions to them. We all have problems, some of them big, some of them small. To solve many of these problems requires making decisions. For this reason *problem solving* is often called **decision making.** Knowing how to handle problems and make decisions is an important skill to develop.

SKILLS FOR LIVING

Seeking Advice

Don't be afraid to ask for advice. Ask friends and trusted adults to help you make tough decisions.

Learning from Photographs
Important decisions require careful thought. Why might it help to write down your choices when faced with a decision?

Do you know people who sit and worry when they are faced with a problem or called upon to make a decision? Perhaps you know people who run away from problems. Neither of these approaches is healthy or sensible. A much better approach to solving problems is to break a problem into steps, the way you would solve a math problem. When personal problems are handled in this fashion—one step at a time— they become more manageable.

Steps to Solving Problems

Here are the five key steps in solving a problem or making a decision.

Steps in Decision Making

1. *Identify the problem.* Be sure that you understand exactly what the problem is. This sounds easy, but in fact it is the most difficult step.

2. *Make a list of all the choices available to you.* Try to form a mental picture of how things would look if the problem were solved. Think of as many different ways as you can to solve it. Get the help of family members as you make a list of possible solutions.

3. *Carefully examine the consequences of each possible solution.* Ask yourself in each case what would happen if the solution were acted on. Again, ask for the opinion of an adult.

4. *Determine which solution seems to be the best and act on it.* Keep in mind the consequences of your solution. Ask how it will affect you, both now and later on. Ask also how it will affect others.

5. *Check the results.* Determine whether your solution worked or whether the problem still exists. If the problem has not been solved, go back over your list of possible solutions and try again.

Not every problem needs to be worked out in such a careful step-by-step fashion. Deciding, for example, whether to brush your teeth or wash your face first in the morning would never need this much thought. By practicing this skill on easier problems, however, you will be more likely to use it when more serious problems arise.

Try your hand at solving Li's problem, which is described on page 76. Use the steps listed in the box above to reach a solution.

Health Minute

Decisions, Decisions
Make a list of all the decisions you made today. Then rank them in the order of importance to you. Are you getting to be a good decision maker?

More About

Each chapter of your textbook has a page devoted to giving you practice in "Making Healthy Decisions."

Learning from Photographs
This boy and his grandfather are making fishing lures. Why does success in making or planning things boost confidence?

Saying "No"

Many of the decisions you will face as a teen are important to your well-being. Some of these decisions may be hard. Resisting the pressure of other teens to do unsafe or unhealthy things is a skill you will need. You will find help in building this skill in Chapters 4, 6, 8, 9, and 10.

Li's Problem

Tomorrow, Saturday, Li is going to the movies with her best friend, Marguerite. Tonight, Marcus calls. He is a boy that Li likes but thought never even noticed her. Marcus wants to know if Li would like to go to the park with him tomorrow afternoon. Li has been dreaming about this day for months. She would love to go! But if she does, she will be letting Marguerite down.

If you were Li, how would you decide what to do?

Check Your Understanding

Conclusion Knowing how to solve problems and make decisions is an extremely important skill. Solving problems is a part of life that everyone must face.

1. **Vocabulary** Write what you believe is the meaning of the word *decisive*. Check your guess in a good dictionary.

2. **Recall** Name the five steps in decision making.

3. **Recall** What is the advantage of handling personal problems one step at a time?

4. **Synthesize** Look at "Li's Problem" above. Imagine that Li has broken her date with Marguerite. Imagine a problem that might arise for Marguerite as a result. Then describe how Marguerite might solve her problem.

Stress

This lesson contains a number of valuable facts and tips. Once you have studied them, you will be able to

- define the term *stress*.
- name the two basic types of stress.
- name ways of managing stress.

Stress in Your Life

You've probably heard of stress, and you've felt stress. You may feel stress when you meet someone new, try out for a school play, or get ready to go to a party. **Stress** is *your body's response to changes around you.*

Words to Know
stress
distress
stressors
adrenaline
fatigue
physical fatigue
psychological fatigue

SKILLS FOR LIVING

Making Positive Stress Work for You
Some people do better under pressure. Many teens, for example, find they are able to concentrate better on their schoolwork when a big test is coming up. You can make this positive stress pay off for you in a big way by "setting your clock forward." If you have a test on Wednesday, tell yourself the test is on Tuesday. After a while, you will find that you can control those helpful energy bursts.

Learning from Photographs
Stress can be positive or negative. What good thing can come out of positive stress?

Lesson 5: Stress   **77**

Controlling Stress

Can you control any of these life changes? Can you plan ahead for any of these events? By being ready for changes and planning for them whenever possible, you can reduce stress and the chance of becoming sick. Just realizing that it's impossible to avoid change often helps to lessen stress.

Deep Breathing

When you are feeling tense do the following.

1. Close your eyes.
2. Rid your mind of all thoughts, good and bad. Think about nothing.
3. Take five deep breaths. Let the air out slowly each time.

When you do this, you can almost feel the tension draining out of your body.

Life Changes and Stress

Change is stressful, sometimes so much so that a person can become ill. Researchers have given values in "stress points" to the life changes listed below. The experts have determined that a person who accumulates between 150 and 299 stress points in one year has a 50 percent chance of getting sick.

Rank	Event	Stress Points
1.	Death of a parent	98
2.	Death of a sister or brother	95
3.	Death of a friend	92
4.	Divorce or separation of parents	86
5.	Failure in one or more school subjects	86
6.	Getting arrested	85
7.	Repeating a grade in school	84
8.	Family member's alcohol or drug problem	79
9.	Starting to use alcohol or drugs	77
10.	Loss or death of a pet	77
11.	Family member's serious illness	77
12.	Losing money you've saved	74
13.	Breaking up with your girlfriend or boyfriend	74
14.	Quitting or being suspended from school	73
15.	Pregnancy of a close friend	69
16.	Father or mother losing a job	69
17.	Being seriously sick or hurt	64
18.	Arguing with parents	64
19.	School troubles with teacher or principal	63
20.	Discomfort and problems with weight, height, acne	63
21.	Going to a new school	57
22.	Moving to a new home	51
23.	Change in physical appearance because of braces, glasses	47
24.	Arguing with sisters or brothers	46
25.	Beginning to menstruate (for girls)	45
26.	Having someone, such as a grandparent, move in	35
27.	Mother's pregnancy	31
28.	Beginning to go out on dates	31
29.	Making new friends	27
30.	Marriage for sister or brother	26

Learning from Photographs
Whether the stressor is a concert or a test, the body's response is the same. What is part of "fight or flight" response?

There are two basic types of stress, positive stress and negative stress.

- **Positive stress.** Positive stress is stress that helps you to accomplish and reach goals. When you feel excited or challenged by an activity, you are experiencing positive stress. Positive stress can make you alert and focused on a task. This helps you get the task done.

- **Negative stress.** Negative stress, also known as **distress,** is *stress that can hold you back.* When people talk about being under a lot of stress, they usually mean negative stress. Too much negative stress can be unhealthy.

Stress and Stressors

In order to function, your body needs a certain amount of stress. Stress is natural, and is triggered by many different types of things. These *triggers of stress* are called **stressors.** The loud blast of a car horn is a possible stressor. Another is oversleeping and missing your school bus. Still another is winning a spelling bee. Stressors can take the form of events, people, places, and objects.

"Fight or Flight"

When you come into contact with a stressor, your body begins to produce *a chemical* called **adrenaline** (uh·DREN·uhl·uhn). Adrenaline *makes your heart beat faster and speeds up blood flow* to your brain and muscles. It also sends more oxygen through your body by causing you to breathe faster. Adrenaline gives your body extra strength to protect itself from harm and added speed to flee from danger. This sudden burst of energy is sometimes called the "fight or flight" response. Once a stressor has been removed or dealt with, your body stops making adrenaline and returns to normal.

DID **YOU** KNOW?

Amazing Acts
At times of extreme stress, adrenaline helps the body perform amazing acts, such as lifting automobiles to rescue people trapped under them.

More About
To learn more about **adrenaline** *and the work it does for the body, see Chapter 7.*

Stress and Fatigue

Sometimes a stressor continues to operate over a long period of time. Stress over school or personal problems at home, for example, can be long-lasting. When this happens, the body continues to operate at a high energy level. After a time, the body becomes exhausted. **Fatigue,** or *extreme tiredness,* sets in. Fatigue takes a toll on all levels of your health. It can get in the way of your schoolwork and dealings with friends.

There are actually two types of fatigue.

- **Physical fatigue** is *extreme tiredness of the body as a whole.* It usually occurs after vigorous activity. Muscles may be overworked and sore, and your body feels tired all over. The solution to this kind of fatigue is rest.

- **Psychological** (SY·kuh·LAW·uh·kuhl) **fatigue** is *extreme tiredness caused by your mental state.* This is the type of fatigue brought on by stress. It can also be caused by worry and by feelings of *depression* and boredom. Unlike physical fatigue, the remedy for psychological fatigue is activity. Exercise or getting involved in a project can be helpful.

You need to know which kind of fatigue you are feeling before you can treat it. It is thus important to try to pinpoint the source of your fatigue.

More About

For more on depression and where to get help for serious emotional problems, see Lesson 6 of this chapter.

Coping with Stress

Everyone feels stress from time to time but not for the same reasons. You might feel stress over not being asked to join a new club at school. Your friend might not give it a second thought. On the other hand, your friend may feel stress in not wearing the clothes "everyone

Learning from Photographs
What positive outlets for energy can you find to counter stress?

80

else" is wearing, while you may prefer to stand apart from the crowd. It is important to know what is stressful for you. It is just as important to know how to handle that stress. Here are some rules for managing stress effectively.

- **Plan.** Learn how to budget your time. Thinking ahead can help you avoid the stresses of cramming for tests, turning in homework late or poorly done, and dealing with mountains of chores at home. Planning your time can result in accomplishments that will build on your self-concept.

- **Talk.** Discuss your problems with a friend, a teacher, or a family member. This can help relieve stress. People with some distance from your problems can often see solutions more clearly.

- **Redirect.** Your body reacts the same way to positive and negative stress—by making adrenaline, which raises your energy level. Rechannel all that added energy into something worthwhile. Clean your room, wash the family car, or help out with a younger brother or sister. Any of these activities can turn a bad situation into a good one.

- **Relax.** Lie down or sit down and try to empty your mind of troubling thoughts. This can ease stress. Listen to soothing music, which can also help. So can imagining yourself in a quiet and peaceful place, such as under a tree by a lake.

- **Laugh.** Spend time with people who make you laugh. This is a good way to relax. If you are planning to go to the movies after an especially stressful day, choose a funny movie. You will most likely feel better after you laugh.

Learning from Photographs
A great way to relieve stress is to have a good laugh. What do you find funny?

Knowing Stress
When you are feeling very stressed, ask yourself some of these questions to help you feel better.
1. What am I feeling?
2. What happened to make me feel this way?
3. When I had this feeling before, how long did it last?
4. What can I do to feel better?
5. Should I talk to someone? To whom?

Check Your Understanding

Conclusion Some stress is necessary. Too much negative stress, or distress, can lead to fatigue and physical illness. Being aware of the stress in your life is the first step in managing it.

1. **Vocabulary** Write the words from the following list that name responses of the body to change. *stressor, distress, stress*

2. **Recall** Name the two basic types of stress.

3. **Recall** Name four ways of managing stress.

4. **Interpret** What advice might you give an athlete on managing stress? Name a sport you are familiar with, and describe specific suggestions you might make to a player of that sport.

Mental Disorders

Words to Know
defense mechanisms
neurosis
psychosis
schizophrenia
depression

This lesson contains a number of valuable facts and tips. Once you have studied them, you will be able to

- identify types of defense mechanisms.
- name some important mental disorders.
- list the warning signs of suicide.

Facing Problems

Life is filled with events and changes that can lead to stressful problems. Your father's company transfers him to another city, and you are faced with the fears of going to a new school. Your family moves to an apartment building that doesn't allow pets, and you are faced with the problem of having to give up your cat.

When you encounter a problem, an important part of good mental health is to meet the problem head on. This includes talking about it with someone you trust and using the stress management rules you have learned. When you don't take the right action promptly, problems can grow and affect your total health. Some of the situations that can arise are described on the next few pages.

Learning from Photographs
By talking with her parent, this adopted girl can solve her problems. What other sources of help can you think of?

82   Chapter 3: Wellness and Your Mental Health

Learning from Photographs
Choosing a positive outlet when you have a problem is a healthy approach to take. But you cannot avoid a problem completely. Why?

Defense Mechanisms

Defense mechanisms (duh·FENS MEK·uh·nizmz) are *ways by which people temporarily escape from their problems*. People who develop defense mechanisms are not usually aware that they have them. The following are some common ones.

- **Denial,** or an inability to see reality
- **Fantasy,** or imagining through daydreaming that a problem has been solved
- **Suppression** (suh·PRESH·uhn), or the blocking out of unpleasant thoughts
- **Displacement,** or having bad feelings toward someone not really related to the cause of the problem
- **Projection,** or unknowingly blaming someone else for a problem

Though getting distance from a problem often helps to solve it, defense mechanisms are not the best answer. A person who has difficulty coping with a stressful problem should talk to someone who can help.

Neurosis

Everyone has, at some time in life, felt fear or been anxious about something. When *a fear gets in the way of a person's ability to function in daily life,* that person may suffer from *a condition* known as **neurosis** (noo·ROH·sis). Neurosis can cause physical symptoms, including uneven breathing, a speeding up of the heart, muscle pain, and sweating.

One type of neurosis is *obsessive-compulsive* (uhb·SES·iv·kuhm·PUL·siv) behavior. People who are obsessive-compulsive may spend a great deal of time washing their hands or making sure doors are locked. Professional counseling can help people with different types of neurosis.

The *Whole* Truth
When people first read about mental disorders, they usually assume they have every disorder they read about. If that is what you have been assuming during your reading of this lesson, then you might want to keep the following *absolutes* uppermost in your mind.

- *No one* is successful at dealing with stress *all* of the time.
- *Everyone* needs to escape the pressures of life every now and then.
- *Everyone* is depressed once in a while.
- *Everyone* feels uncomfortable at some time in his or her life. Difficulty in meeting new people or adjusting to new surroundings does not make a person anti-social.
- *Everyone* is afraid of something. Having fears is normal and does not mean you suffer from a phobia.

Psychosis

Sometimes problems are so severe that the victim's view of the world becomes distorted. When this happens, the person is said to suffer from **psychosis** (sy·KOH·sis). This is *a condition in which a person is not able to function in the real world.* A person with psychosis may hear voices or speak in a way that is meaningless to others.

There are many types of psychosis. The most common type is **schizophrenia** (skit·zoh·FREE·nee·uh), which means "split mind." Schizophrenia is *a serious disorder in which people turn inward and often lose touch with reality completely.* Some experts believe that schizophrenia is caused by an imbalance of brain chemistry.

Depression

Everyone feels sad or lonely from time to time. At such times, some people will say that they "feel depressed." **Depression** (di·PRESH·uhn) is also the name of *a medical condition in which the sufferer feels extreme sadness and a lack of energy.* Medical depression is usually brought on by a serious disappointment.

Victims of medical depression will often suffer from a variety of symptoms, including the following.

- Not being able to sleep
- Having no appetite
- Feeling bored
- Losing interest in day-to-day affairs of life

Some sad or blue periods in life are normal. But it is also normal for unhappy feelings and tension from a letdown to begin to lift after a reasonable time. When depression lingers for weeks or longer, the victim may be in need of help.

SKILLS FOR LIVING

Depression

At times when you are depressed, remember that other people feel depressed too. It isn't only you. During your darkest moments, someone may be thinking your life is wonderful compared to his or hers. When you feel down, make a list of things someone else might be wishing for and admiring about your life.

Learning from Photographs
Psychologists and psychiatrists are trained to help someone who has a serious problem. How can someone get in touch with such a professional?

84

Learning from Photographs
Having a friend to talk to may help handle day-to-day troubles. Is it helpful simply to know that someone cares?

Other Mental Disorders

Neurosis, psychosis, and depression are disorders with clear symptoms that are present all or most of the time. Other mental disorders exist where the symptoms surface only sometimes.

- **Personality disorders.** A person with a *personality disorder* has trouble getting along with others or getting along in certain situations.

- **Phobias.** Phobias are forms of neurosis in which the fear of an object or idea is so great that it interferes with reasonable action. A victim of acrophobia (fear of heights), for example, might have great trouble looking out of a second-floor window.

- **Anorexia and bulimia.** These two serious *eating disorders* are often lumped together. Victims of both suffer from an unreasonable fear of being overweight. People with these disorders see themselves as fat no matter how little they weigh.

More About

You can learn more about **anorexia** *and* **bulimia** *by reading Chapter 5.*

Seriously Troubled Teens

The teen years can be an especially stressful time. Many teens find themselves going through changes they don't always understand. Friendships seem to have become more complicated, and so have dealings with parents and other family members. The pressure to succeed may seem greater than ever. On top of these stresses, teens must continue to deal with the stress brought on by other changes that are a part of life. Many teens find it difficult to cope.

Suicide

Suicide is the second leading cause of death among teenagers. The events most responsible for teen suicides may include breaking up with a boyfriend or girlfriend, competition, and feeling pressure to get ahead. To some teens, such problems seem to have no solution.

Learning from Photographs
Everyone feels down from time to time. What are some things you can do to cheer up when you feel down?

Teen Issue
. . . .

Getting Help
In the next lesson, you will read about where you can go for help when someone you know is troubled by thoughts of suicide or less serious forms of depression.

. . . .

The experts have pinpointed some of the warning signs of suicide. These include the following.

The Warning Signs of Suicide

- Statements such as "I want to die" and "When I'm gone they'll all be sorry"
- Shying away from activities involving friends or family
- Changes in sleeping and eating patterns
- A low level of energy
- Giving away prized personal possessions
- Taking greater risks than usual
- A past history of suicide attempts

The Meaning Behind the Numbers

Every year about 25,000 teen suicides occur. Nearly ten times as many teenagers attempt suicide. What makes these numbers especially chilling is that *almost none* of these teenagers really want to die. Almost all are really pleading for help. What these troubled teens are doing, without realizing it, is acting on a permanent solution to a temporary problem.

Check Your Understanding

Conclusion Life is filled with stresses that can affect our total health. Some stress is positive and can help us achieve good things. Some mental disorders can result from negative stress. Severe depression causes some teenagers to take their own lives or to think about doing so.

1. **Vocabulary** The word *neurosis* consists of two parts, *neur-* and *-osis*. The second of these parts means "condition of." In a good dictionary, find three other words that begin with *neur-*. Then write a definition of *neurosis* based exactly on the sum of its parts.

2. **Recall** Identify four types of defense mechanisms.

3. **Recall** What are three important mental disorders?

4. **Recall** List four warning signs of suicide.

5. **Interpret** What advice might you give to a friend who seems to spend almost all of his or her time daydreaming?

Help for the Troubled Teen

Word to Know
teen hot lines

This lesson contains a number of valuable facts and tips. Once you have studied them, you will be able to

- name some signs that point to a need for help with emotional problems.
- list places where a person with an emotional problem can turn for help.

Knowing When to Go for Help

Everyone needs help at one time or another in solving problems. Knowing when to ask for help is a sign that you are growing up. It shows that you are capable of thinking through a problem and deciding which parts of the problem you can—and can't—solve by yourself.

With mental health problems, knowing when to seek help is largely a matter of paying attention to warning signs. Heeding these signs in yourself and in people you are close to could actually save a life. When you experience—or see in another person—any of the following symptoms over a period of days or weeks, something may be seriously wrong.

- Anger over the belief that everyone is against you
- Sadness over a particular event or over nothing at all
- Great or sudden swings in mood
- Trouble concentrating or reaching decisions
- Aches and pains that seem to have no medical cause
- The feeling that everything is hopeless
- Trouble sleeping or constant bad dreams
- Unusually reckless behavior

Teen Issue

Say "When"!
One of the most important things to learn is when to say "when"! When you are faced with a problem that seems to have no answer, that is probably a good time. If you're in that situation, you need to talk to somebody. The person can help just by listening. In fact, you will often find the answer yourself as you talk the problem out. Getting help is not a sign of weakness. It shows you're smart enough to go for a solution.

Learning from Photographs
A support "group" can be one person, such as a teacher, counselor, or coach. What kind of relationship is needed between someone giving and someone getting help?

Naturally, no one warning signal is a sure sign of a mental disorder. On the other hand, any one signal may be a symptom of an unhealthy buildup of stress.

Knowing Who Can Help

There are a number of people you can turn to when you or someone you know has a serious emotional problem. Here are just a few of them.

- **A parent or other relative.** Families are like built-in support systems. A parent, an older brother or sister, an aunt, or an uncle can be a great source of help. These people know you best and care about you most.

- **A school counselor or school nurse.** These professionals are specially trained to understand and deal with the problems of teenagers. Counselors and nurses can give you comforting advice and will hold what you tell them in strict confidence.

Who, When, Where?

To talk out your problems, find somebody you feel comfortable with. Adults can be very helpful with problems because many times they faced the same problem themselves. But even a teen can help. Find a time to talk when you and the other person won't be interrupted. And pick a quiet spot so that noise or other people won't disturb you.

- **A priest, minister, rabbi, or other clergy member.** The leader of your church or synagogue may be a good person to see. Members of the clergy are educated in counseling people with emotional problems.

- **A teacher.** Is there a teacher that you particularly like and trust? Such a person could be a friend in need and give you understanding and guidance.

- **A hot line.** Some communities have **teen hot lines,** or *special telephone services that teens can call when feeling stress.* The people who answer these calls are trained to listen and help teens experiencing a crisis.

Talking out your problems with someone will not make them vanish instantly. It will, however, reassure you that you are not alone. Knowing this is often the first step in conquering depression.

Troubled Friends

If you suspect that someone you know is thinking about suicide, immediate action is needed. A teenager thinking about suicide feels no one cares or understands his or her troubles.

Try to get your friend to go to see an adult who can help. Insist that you come along to make sure the friend actually seeks help. If the friend refuses to come along, see someone yourself. Your friend may be in serious danger.

Teen Issue

No Promises!
If you talk to a friend who is thinking about suicide, don't promise to keep it a secret. Your friend needs help. Perhaps that help must come from a counselor or perhaps from a parent. Either way, your friend can only get that help if someone else knows. Share what you know with someone else. This isn't blabbing or gossiping. It's helping in the best way.

Learning from Photographs
Hot lines provide help over the phone. Where could you find out about hot lines for troubled teens in your community?

Learning from Photographs
Everyone needs someone they can turn to for help because no one can solve all problems alone. What benefits come from getting help?

In an emergency, you may be able to help the friend yourself by doing the following.

- **Listen.** At the very least this lets your friend know that someone is there. Your staying calm can also be a source of comfort to your friend. Don't, however, let yourself be sworn to secrecy.

- **Talk.** Tell your friend you are on her or his side. Point out that this bad time will pass. Emphasize that there are alternatives to such an extreme act.

Check Your Understanding

Conclusion We all need help from time to time in solving problems. Looking for warning signs helps us know when to seek help. There are many people around us who are willing and eager to listen when we have emotional problems.

1. **Vocabulary** Find a definition for the term *hot line* in a dictionary. In what ways is this definition similar to the meaning of *hot line* as it is used in this lesson? In what ways is it different?

2. **Recall** Name three signs that point to a need for help with emotional problems.

3. **Recall** List five places where a person with an emotional problem can turn for help.

4. **Synthesize** Imagine that a friend who is usually very cheerful has been quiet most of the time lately. What action might you take if the friend, when asked, claims to be "perfectly OK"?

Being a Good Listener

If you have ever listened to someone explaining a personal problem, you know that people sometimes get carried away. They express their troubles in a way that is "colored," or distorted, by their feelings. Rather than say, "I'm angry at her," a person might say, "I hate her!"

Being a good listener is a skill that can help you to help someone in this type of situation. When you listen carefully, you sometimes hear the message *behind* the emotional words. This can be a first step in helping the person get back on track and decide what to do next.

Steps in Being a Good Listener

- **Pay close attention to all that the person has to say.** Don't begin to form your answer while the person is still speaking.
- **Pay attention to the person's tone of voice.** Often the *way* the person says something tells you as much or more than his or her words.
- **Pay close attention to body language.** If the person is there in the room with you, observe his or her hand gestures. Look for other important clues to feelings, such as clenched fists or teeth.
- **Think for a moment before speaking.** Give yourself a chance to think of the best way of stating your answer.
- **Speak calmly.** Give the person assurance. Let the person know that you care about his or her problem.

You won't always be able to help a person solve a problem. By being a good listener, however, you might at least be able to tell the person where to turn for help.

Using the Skill

Read the following emotional descriptions of problems, including the "stage directions" in parentheses.

Case One
(Angrily, exaggerating the words *stupid* and *dumb*), "Ms. Franti has assigned me a stupid part in the play. I'm sorry now that I ever wasted my time rehearsing for tryouts. I never wanted to be in that dumb play anyway."

Case Two
(Frantically, arms flying, eyes wide), "I'm not going to the dance in the gym. I don't have anything to wear. My face is all broken out! My hair is just a clump of strings! I'll just die if Kent sees me. He'll never ask me out on a date!"

Case Three
(Quietly), "I can't ask her over to my house. She lives in a great house. She won't like me when she sees the way I live."

Case Four
(Grumpily, staring at the ground), "I'm not trying out for the team. I didn't make it last year, so why should I bother?"

Now number a sheet of paper from 1 through 4. For each of the above descriptions, answer the following questions.
  a. What is the speaker feeling?
  b. What words or other clues reveal these feelings?
  c. What problem is the speaker facing?
  d. What are the speaker's choices?

Chapter 3 Review

Summary

- Good mental health habits can positively affect your personality and how you get along with others. With positive messages, you can improve your self-concept.
- All humans have the need to love and be loved, to belong, and to feel worthwhile. Learning how to express your feelings is important.
- Solving problems is a part of life everyone faces. Practice can make you good at it.
- Stress is a part of life. Some stress is necessary to function well. Recognizing sources of stress can help you to manage it.
- Some people suffer mental disorders. Very deep depression may lead some teenagers to suicide.
- Everyone needs help with problems now and then. There are people around you who care when you have a problem, and they are eager to help.

Reviewing Vocabulary and Concepts

On a separate sheet of paper, write the numbers 1–9. After each number, write the term from the list on the right that best completes the statement.

Lesson 1

1. People with good _____ are happy and active most of the time and have a positive outlook on life.
2. Your _____ is the sum total of your attitudes, habits, and feelings.
3. Your _____ is the way you act in situations.

Lesson 2

4. Your mental picture of yourself and the way in which you believe others see you is your _____ .
5. Ways people act toward you _____ , or back up, your self-concept.
6. When your image of yourself is positive, you are at your best physically, morally, emotionally, socially, and _____ .

Lesson 3

7. The need to love and be loved, the need to feel worthwhile, and the need to _____ are basic to every human being.
8. Learning to express _____ , or feelings, is an important part of mental health.
9. Much of what people communicate comes not through words but through tone of voice and _____ .

behavior

belong

body language

emotions

mental health

mentally

personality

reinforce

self-concept

Write the numbers 10–21 on your paper. After each number, write the letter of the word or phrase in Column B that best matches the phrase in Column A.

Column A

Lesson 4

10. Another name for decision making
11. The second step in decision making is identifying
12. What to check after making a decision

Lesson 5

13. Your body's response to changes
14. Another name for negative stress
15. A way of dealing with stress

Lesson 6

16. Ways of temporarily escaping from a problem
17. A fear that prevents a person from being able to function
18. A warning sign of suicide

Lesson 7

19. A phone service to call for help
20. Someone who can help teens with problems
21. What a troubled teen should do

Column B

a. choices
b. stress
c. member of clergy
d. defense mechanisms
e. results
f. planning
g. hot line
h. talk to an adult
i. problem solving
j. distress
k. taking risks
l. psychosis

Thinking Critically About the Facts

Write your answers to the following questions on a separate sheet of paper.

22. **Synthesize** Suppose a short friend told you that he was planning to use a new pill or health food he had heard of because it will make him taller. Would you advise your friend to take the pill or eat the health food? Explain your answer.

23. **Compare and contrast** Identify two healthy ways of meeting your emotional needs. Identify two unhealthy ways.

24. **Interpret** Tell which sentences show good communication. Explain why.
    (1) "You don't know what you're talking about!"
    (2) "Please calm down and tell me what the problem is. I'm willing to listen."
    (3) "Why do I have to *tell* you why I'm mad? You're supposed to be my friend. *You* figure it out."

Applying the Facts

25. Make a poster titled "My Strengths." Begin by finding pictures in old magazines or newspapers that illustrate strengths that you feel you have. Clip the pictures out and paste them on a large piece of cardboard. Under each picture, write what strength of yours it shows. Bring your poster to class, or hang it up at home in a place where you can look at it often.

26. Create a "Teen Help" bulletin board in your classroom. The board should contain names, addresses, and phone numbers of places and people teens can turn to in times of need. You might look in the telephone directory under the words *mental*, *emotional*, *youth*, and *crisis*. Your school librarian or teacher may also be able to help you locate names of sources.

Wellness and Your Social Health

CHAPTER WARM-UP

Chapter Study Goals

After you have read this chapter, you will be able to

- identify the traits of good social health.
- identify skills necessary to build healthy relationships.
- explain the importance of friends.
- identify positive and negative peer pressure.
- identify several types of families and list some changes in modern families today.
- define various types of abuse and name places to go for help.
- explain why many teen marriages fail.
- identify ways to be a good parent.

Be on the lookout for information in the chapter that will help you reach these goals.

Getting Started

What do you think people need most to survive in the world? Food? Clothing? Shelter? Medical care? These are all basic needs, but humans have other needs that are just as important. One of these is the need for other people. These needs are met by members of our families and by our friends.

After reading this chapter, you will recognize the many ways in which the people around us make a difference in our lives.

Study Tip

As you read, use the main headings and subheadings to make an outline of the information in this chapter.

Words to Know
social health
relationships
communication
cooperation
compromise

Building Healthy Relationships

This lesson contains a number of valuable facts and tips. Once you have studied them, you will be able to

- define the term *social health.*
- name some qualities that people with good social health share.
- name three skills that help build healthy relationships.

What Is Social Health?

Two sides of your health triangle are physical health and mental health. The third side is social health. **Social health** is *your ability to get along with the people around you.* When you have good social health, you work well as a member of a group. You also know how to make and keep friends and how to offer and get help when it is needed. The box shows some other qualities of good social health.

People with good social health...

- are able to accept differences in other people.
- meet people easily.
- have at least one or two close friends.
- can accept other people's ideas and suggestions when working in a group.
- are usually successful at making friends with people of both sexes.
- continue to take part in an activity even when they don't get their way in an argument.

SKILLS FOR LIVING

It's All Relative
Do you worry that you act differently with different people? Do you think you're putting up a false front? Stop worrying. It's natural to relate to different people in different ways. This may be true even of relationships involving people of the same "type," such as friends. With some friends, you may be quiet and serious. With others, you may be louder and joke a lot. All that means is that you have many sides to your personality and much to offer. Isn't that something worth smiling about?

Learning from Photographs
We all have many different relationships. What relationships are there in your life?

Social Health and Relationships

Your social health is tied directly to your relationships with other people. **Relationships** (rih·LAY·shuhn·ships) are *the connections you have with other people and groups in your life.* These connections are based on how you relate to, or act toward, others. Your life is full of relationships. You have a relationship with your family and with each family member. You have a relationship with every one of your friends and teachers and with each of those groups as a whole.

Building Healthy Relationships

Most people do not relate to everyone in their lives in exactly the same way. How you relate to a younger brother or sister, for example, may be very different from how you relate to an older brother or sister. You may relate to one of your teachers as a friend and to another one almost in the way you would act with a parent. What is important about all of your relationships is that they be as healthy as possible.

You can build healthy relationships by learning three social health skills. They are *communication, cooperation,* and *compromise.*

**Tele-
Communication?**

Have you ever tried to work out a problem over the telephone? it works for some people. The trouble is when you are talking to someone over the phone, you can hear them but you cannot *see* them. So much of what we have to "say" is communicated through *body language,* how we move and express ourselves with our bodies. On the phone, you might miss an important part of the message. For more on body language see Chapter 3.

Communication

Communication is *the exchange of thoughts, ideas, and beliefs between two or more people.* You have probably had the experience of trying to settle an argument with a friend who just did not seem to hear your side. You may have learned later that your friend saw the situation in a totally different way. Communication is a two-way street. When you communicate well, you not only *give* messages. You also *get* them. Rules of good communication include the following.

- **Stay calm.** Although it sounds odd, the louder you speak, the less likely the other person is to hear you. Few people ever settled an argument by screaming or slamming a door.

- **Choose the right time and place.** There is a time and place for everything, including solving a problem. Find a time when the other person is not in a hurry or busy with something else. Find a quiet place where there is little chance of outside interruption.

- **Stick to the point.** Think your ideas through before you begin to speak. If a friend returns a borrowed sweater with a tear in the sleeve, let the friend know you are disappointed and upset. Then offer a fair solution, such as your friend's paying the cost of the repair. Name-calling or attacking your friend will get you nowhere.

- **Listen.** There are at least two sides to every issue. After you have had your turn to speak, give the other person a chance. Pay attention to what she or he has to say. You may see things in a new light.

Learning from Photographs
Good listening habits are very important in a group. Is thinking about what you are going to say while someone is talking a good listening skill?

Learning from Photographs
We relate to different people differently. What are some differences between how you relate to an old friend and to someone you have just met?

Cooperation

Cooperation is *working together for the good of all.* Another name for cooperation is *teamwork.* Suppose that you get a part in the school play and then find that the rehearsals take place on afternoons when you have agreed to look after your little brother. By cooperating with family members, you might be able to reach a solution. You might, for example, arrange to trade your baby-sitting task for a chore that can be done earlier in the day. For instance, you could make the beds before you go to school.

Working as a team builds strong relationships. The main thing you need to be a good team player is an open mind.

Compromise

Have there ever been times when you wanted to see a movie and your friend wanted pizza but there was not enough money for both? Do you remember how you handled the problem? At such times, compromise is the answer. **Compromise** (KAHM·pruh·myz) is *the result of each person's giving up something in order to reach a solution that satisfies everyone.* Compromise is also known as "give and take."

Compromise can take many forms. In the above example, the compromise might be that your friend gets to choose the activity this time and you get to choose next time. It may be that the two of you

Teen Issue

Nothing Doing!
It is important to learn to compromise, but it is just as important to learn *never* to compromise about things that you believe in strongly. Suppose someone tries to get you to do something you believe is wrong or bad for you. When you are faced with this situation, the right answer is not to compromise. The right answer is to say, "Nothing doing!"

How Many Groups?

On a sheet of paper, list the different groups to which you belong. Start by listing your family and your class at school. Then add all your other groups. Include clubs, religious groups, sports teams, and any others you can think of.

Friends and Acquaintances

Most people you know are acquaintances. People you care about and are especially close to are friends. Do you think you have trouble making friends? If you have one or two good friends, you are doing very well.

decide to do a completely different activity. Whatever form the compromise takes, it helps a relationship to run smoothly. It also accomplishes something that arguing never will: it leads to *action*.

Working in a Group

Have you ever stopped to think about the number of groups to which you belong? You belong to your family and to your class at school. You belong to your circle of friends. You may belong to clubs, teams, or religious groups. Certainly, you are a member of the very, very large group known as *society*.

The health of each of those groups depends on the social health of each of its members. Each member shares an equal responsibility for maintaining the health of the group. By the same token, the health of every member is affected by the overall health of the group. It is thus the responsibility of every member to make sure the group looks out for and balances the individual needs, interests, and abilities of all of its members.

In the following lessons, you will see how every group, large and small, to which you belong is shaped by what you contribute as well as by what every other member contributes.

Check Your Understanding

Conclusion Social health is part of the health triangle. Relationships are important to your growth and happiness. Good social health is based on communication, cooperation, and compromise. The welfare of the group is the responsibility of all of its members.

1. **Vocabulary** The words *cooperate* and *communicate* are forms of two words in this lesson. Use *cooperate* and *communicate* in an original sentence.

2. **Recall** Define social health.

3. **Recall** Name four qualities that people with good social health share.

4. **Recall** Name three social health skills that help build healthy relationships.

5. **Recall** List three rules of good communication.

6. **Synthesize** Suppose that at a family dinner three people wanted turkey drumsticks and there were only two. What sort of compromise might you suggest?

Social Health and Friends

This lesson contains a number of valuable facts and tips. Once you have studied them, you will be able to

- name qualities of good friends.
- explain the difference between negative and positive peer pressure.
- list strategies for dealing with negative peer pressure.

Friends

Everyone needs friends. Friends provide us with companionship, and they can be a source of help when we have a problem. Friends are people with whom we can share a common interest or hobby. We cooperate with our friends to get jobs done better and faster. In short, good friendships are important to our social health.

Teen Issue

Learning to Relax
Many teens feel nervous or uncomfortable when meeting new people. Much of this nervousness has to do with self-doubts. The teen imagines that the new person is finding him or her too short or too tall, too thin or too fat. It might help to remember that the other person may be feeling the same way you are. Try to relax and put the other person at ease. This will help both of you feel more comfortable.

Learning from Photographs
Being a good friend is a way to build solid friendships. What are some of the qualities of being a good friend?

Health Minute

Best Friends

Think for a moment about your best friend. Then, on a sheet of paper, answer the following questions.

1. What things do you like about your best friend?

2. How would you describe your best friend to other people?

3. In what ways does your best friend help you to feel good about yourself?

Teen Issue

Making Friends

Making new friends is sometimes hard. But it is not impossible—not as long as you remember that making friends is a skill that gets better with practice. To make friends, first be around people. Then try the following two tips.

- *Start a conversation with someone in your class.* At the very least, you'll have class work to talk about.

- *Join a club.* Meeting someone with similar interests is a good start toward making a new friend. If you like to collect things, join a stamp-collecting club. If you like singing, join a chorus.

Qualities of Good Friends

Think of all the people you consider to be your friends. You may have known some of your friends for as long as you can remember. Others may have entered your life just this year. You see some of your friends every day. You may see others only once in a great while. No matter how you met your friends or how long you have known them, four qualities are true of all good friends. The following box explains these qualities.

Qualities of Good Friends

- **Loyalty.** Good friends stick by you. They like you for who you are, not for what you have. They are there when you need them.

- **Reliability.** Good friends are **reliable**—*able to be counted on.* Have you ever stood outside a movie theater after the picture started waiting for a friend to show up? A good friend will do his or her best to keep dates and promises.

- **Sympathy.** Good friends are usually **sympathetic** (sim·puh·THET·ik), or *aware of how you are feeling at a given moment.* Any friend will share your happy times, but only a *good* friend will share your bad ones. Have you ever had a classmate comfort you after you were turned down for the school band or after your pet cat ran away? If so, then someone you know is a good friend.

- **Caring.** Good friends care for and about each other. A friend who cares can accept the other person's weaknesses as well as strengths. Caring friends will value each other's feelings as much as they do their own.

Remember, good friendship points in both directions. It is important to have good friends. But it is just as important to *be* a good friend to others.

Peers and Peer Pressure

During your teen years, your friendships take on a special role. As **peers,** or *people your age who are similar to you in many ways,* your friends and classmates as a group may come to stand for certain attitudes and beliefs. *Influence to go along with these beliefs and to try new things* may come from the group, either directly or indirectly. This **peer pressure** can be hard to resist.

Learning from Photographs
These teens are working in a food drive. What good habits can be picked up through peer pressure?

There are two types of peer pressure, *positive peer pressure* and *negative peer pressure.*

- **Positive peer pressure.** This is what you feel when others your age inspire you to do something worthwhile. If you see your friends working hard at a team sport, their enthusiasm may be catching. You may find yourself exercising more often and practicing a sport in which you are interested.

- **Negative peer pressure.** This is what you feel when others your age try to persuade you to try something you don't want to do. This might be using tobacco or other drugs, including alcohol. It can also be pressure to try something you feel you are not ready for.

Dealing with Negative Peer Pressure

As you grow into a young adult, it is important for you to develop your own identity, one that is separate from the group. When someone challenges what you believe in, it is important for you to know how to stand your ground and resist negative peer pressure. You can use a number of strategies.

- **Avoid situations that could mean trouble.** Think ahead. Ask: "Am I being asked to go somewhere that it is unwise to go?" Learn the answers to such questions, if you do not already know them.

- **Think about what is right for you.** Ask yourself: "Do I really need this, or am I better off with other people or alone?"

- **Think about your values.** We all pick up values and beliefs from our families. Some of these are religious. Ask yourself: "Does what I am being asked to do go against the things I really believe in?"

Teen Issue

I Said, "No!"

When it comes to peer pressure, the only person you owe an answer to is you. If, in a given situation, you have decided that your answer is no, do the following.

- Get out of the situation as quickly as you can; there is no need to stand around and defend your position.

- Don't agree to "meet the person halfway." It is your right to say no. Besides, giving in even a little is saying yes a little.

- If the person persists in trying to persuade you, make up an excuse—anything that will end the conversation.

- Suggest some alternatives to the behavior the other person is suggesting; see if you can create a little positive peer pressure of your own.

- If all else fails, walk away. That's a surefire way to put an end to the "debate."

Learning from Photographs
When someone pressures you to do something against your values, you need to resist. How many ways of saying "no" can you think of?

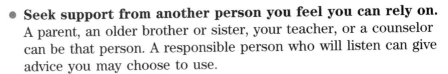

More About

For more about resisting peer pressure to use **tobacco, alcohol,** *and* **drugs,** *see Chapter 8, Chapter 9, and Chapter 10.*

SKILLS FOR LIVING

Keeping Friends
Some friendships are easy to form. Some take work to develop. The important thing to remember is that once a friendship starts, it needs to be looked after and cared for like any living thing. Protect your friendships. Never take your friends for granted.

- **Seek support from another person you feel you can rely on.** A parent, an older brother or sister, your teacher, or a counselor can be that person. A responsible person who will listen can give advice you may choose to use.

- **Plan ahead.** Think about pressure that peers might put on you. Plan how you will respond.

- **Get a "buddy."** Find a friend like yourself who does not want to give in to pressure to use drugs, tobacco, or alcohol, for example. Stick together. Support each other when other teens turn on the pressure.

- **Walk away.** If the pressure is too great, leave.

Check Your Understanding

Conclusion We all need other people. Friends fill some of that need and can contribute to good social health. Pressure from friends, or peers, can be useful or hurtful, depending on the kind of pressure. You can resist hurtful pressure by deciding what is right for you and sticking to your decision.

1. **Vocabulary** Look up the words *friend* and *peer* in a dictionary. In what ways are peers and friends similar? In what ways are they different?

2. **Recall** Name four qualities of good friends.

3. **Recall** What is the difference between negative and positive peer pressure?

4. **Recall** List six strategies for dealing with negative peer pressure.

5. **Interpret** Think about the following saying, "One rotten apple spoils the bunch." What do you think this saying means? How might it apply to peer pressure?

Social Health and Family

This lesson contains a number of valuable facts and tips. Once you have studied them, you will be able to

- name some types of families in our society.
- identify some changes in the modern family.
- identify several types of family abuse.
- list places where troubled families can get help.

The Need To Belong

Humans are social beings. Each of us needs to feel that he or she belongs. Most of the time, this need to belong is satisfied by *groups*.

In your lifetime, you will belong to many groups. Some of those groups will be large, and some will be small. For some, such as clubs, you will make an active choice about whether or not to belong. For others, such as your class at school, membership will be decided for you. Regardless of how you become part of a group, if your social health is good, you will relate well and work well with other members of the group.

Words to Know

family
nuclear family
single-parent family
extended family
blended family
stepparent
abuse
spouse abuse
relative abuse
child abuse
sexual abuse

Learning from Photographs
Families have changed over the years. What part of family health shown in this picture is as true today as it was fifty years ago?

More About

For more about how family living can affect the health of children, see Chapter 6.

Family

The first group to which we belong is the **family.** This is *the basic unit of society.* All societies in the world are made up of families.

In a way, the family is like a testing ground for all the other groups to which we later belong. In your family you begin to develop social skills. Through your family you form a sense of who you are. Through your family you also learn to care for and share with others.

Family Roles

In most societies, different family members have different roles, or jobs. In our society, it is the job of the adults of the family to supply food, clothing, shelter, and medical care for the rest of the family. The adults are also responsible for teaching the children right from wrong and helping them to grow. Children, in turn, take on more responsibilities as they grow older. They learn how to succeed as adults.

There are many different kinds of families in our society. These kinds include the following.

Teen Issue

"Step"-ing on Toes

More teens than ever before in our country have a stepparent or half-brother or half-sister living in their home. At first, it seems awkward to have "strangers" in the house. A solution that occurs to some teens in this situation is to try to avoid their new relatives. A better solution might be to search for interests and hobbies shared in common with members of the blended family. Teens in blended homes do much better when they keep in mind that *everyone* in the house has to adjust to the new living arrangement—not just themselves.

Kinds of Families

- **Nuclear family.** A family made up of *a mother, a father, and children* is called a **nuclear** (NOO·klee·er) **family.** About one-third of all families in the United States are nuclear families.

- **Single-parent family.** A type of *family in which only one parent lives with the child or children* is called a **single-parent family.** The parent may be unmarried, divorced, or widowed.

- **Extended family.** *A nuclear family plus other relatives* is an **extended family.** Grandparents, aunts, uncles, cousins, and grown-up children living at home may all be part of an extended family.

- **Blended family.** When a parent remarries, a **blended family** is formed. This family is made up of *a parent, a stepparent, and the children of one or both parents.* A **stepparent** is *someone who marries a child's mother or father.*

The Healthy Family

Living in a family presents certain challenges. It also presents certain opportunities. In an extended or blended family, for example, there are more people to get along with. But, at the same time, there

Learning from Photographs
There are many types of
families. What type of family do
you think this is?

are also more people to know and enjoy. Older people such as
grandparents can be a special source of enrichment in the lives of
younger family members.

For a family to succeed and be healthy, it must respond well to the
challenges it faces. This, in turn, is possible only when the social
health of every family member is taken into account. If one member of
the family is troubled or does not get along with another member, the
family as a whole can suffer. Only when there is caring and respect
among all members of a family can that family be at its healthiest.

Changing Families

Many major changes have taken place in family lifestyles in recent
years. Because of today's faster pace, children spend far less time in
family activities than children did earlier in the century. Through
television, children today are exposed to a variety of family types and
situations. The values and beliefs they see on television may have little
to do with what actually takes place in their own homes.

These and other changes of modern times have affected the idea of
"family" in our society. These other changes include the following.

- **More smaller families.** Married couples these days are having
  fewer children. Many people lead busy lives. Some of them feel
  they can be better parents by devoting what time they have to
  one or two children. Other reasons for smaller families include
  the expense of raising a family and concerns about overcrowding
  the earth.

Teen Issue

Divorce

Some teens whose parents get divorced turn inward. They don't feel like
talking to anyone or being with anyone. These teens might be better off
talking about their feelings. They could
talk to any or all of the following
people:

- a parent;
- another family member;
- friends who have divorced parents.

Talking would help these teens realize
that divorce is not the end of the
world. It would also help them understand that the divorce is *not their fault*
—a mistaken belief that many children of divorced parents have. They
would learn that parents divorce because they cannot continue to live
together happily.

Learning from Photographs
More women work outside the home now than in the past. What factors have led to this trend?

- **More single-parent families.** One-fifth of the families in the country now have one parent, usually the mother. The single parent now does the job of two parents.
- **More working mothers.** More and more mothers are working outside the home. One reason for this is the rise in the number of single mothers. Another is the expense of supporting a family. Still another reason is that some women like their jobs and want to keep working after they begin families.

Changes—Good or Bad?

Even though these changes affect the family, they are not necessarily bad. Many young people are now taking a more responsible role in the day-to-day affairs of the family. Their parents are asking them to share in housekeeping tasks or to look after younger brothers and sisters while their mothers work. These changes give these teens an opportunity to develop responsibility earlier. This gives them a way of earning the trust of adults and of sharing more directly in family decisions.

Dealing with Problems

All families have problems from time to time. One key to dealing with these problems is communication within the family. In a healthy family, members feel free to express their thoughts and feelings. Children and adults each listen to what the other has to say.

Some families discuss important issues at family meetings. At these meetings, each member is encouraged to speak up.

No Problem!
Does your family have problems every now and then? If it does, you are not alone. Almost every family has problems at one time or another. Problems are nearly impossible to avoid when two or more people with different needs and wants live under the same roof. The important thing to do when a problem arises in your family is to deal with it. Discuss it with other family members and try to reach a solution. Ignoring a problem will usually only make it worse.

Troubled Families

Sometimes family problems are too serious to be worked out within the family. At such times, a family needs outside help. A serious problem that goes unsolved can threaten the health of the family and the personal well-being of each family member.

Abuse in the Family

Some members of a family in trouble turn to unhealthy acts. One of these, **abuse** (uh·BYOOS), is *physical or mental mistreatment of another person*. There are several types of abuse within the family.

- **Spouse abuse.** As its name suggests, **spouse** (SPOWS) **abuse** is *the mistreatment of a husband or wife*. Most victims of spouse abuse are women married to men who easily lose control. Many men who commit spouse abuse become violent after drinking.

- **Relative abuse.** As the name tells us, **relative abuse** is *the mistreatment of a brother, sister, parent, or other family member*. Being cruel to a grandparent can be a form of abuse. Brothers and sisters may abuse each other because of jealousy or a desire to get more attention from a parent.

- **Child abuse.** *The mistreatment of a child* is called **child abuse.** No one knows for sure how many children are victims of such abuse. A child who is beaten may show signs of physical abuse. A child who is neglected or emotionally abused carries emotional scars.

More About

Many cases of abuse are related to **alcohol** *or* **drug abuse.** *See Chapters 9 and 10 for more on where to get help if someone in the family has these problems.*

Teen Issue

Lending a Hand

Anyone who suspects that someone is being abused should help that person out. The best step is to call the local child welfare authorities. This is so important that doctors are required by law to report suspected cases of child abuse.

Learning from Photographs

Doing things with other family members is a way to keep lines of communication open. What are some recreational activities family members can share?

- **Sexual abuse.** Another type of child abuse, **sexual abuse** is *any sexual act between an adult and a child.* Many victims are young, teenage girls, although boys can also be victims. The abuser is often a parent, a stepparent, an uncle or aunt, or an older brother or sister. No matter who the abuser is, sexual abuse is *never the child's fault*—it is always the adult's. The adult who commits sexual abuse badly needs help. The only way the adult can get that help is for the child to talk about what has happened to someone he or she can trust.

Teen Issue

Talk, Don't Run

When pressure at home gets great, some teens think the solution to the problem is to leave home. But running away doesn't *solve* problems; it *creates* them. If you are having trouble, a better solution is to talk about it—to a parent or other grown-up you feel you can trust.

Running Away

Some teens try to get away from a problem by leaving home. Running away, however, often leads to other problems. Runaways usually have no way to support themselves. They have no place to live and no money for food. Life on the street is rough. Some runaways turn to crime. Many runaways become the victims of crime.

Getting Help

The key to getting help is talking about the problem. If someone has been abused or is in danger of being abused, it is important for that person to tell someone. That could be a family member, teacher, doctor, or other adult he or she trusts. If a friend is being abused, it is important to get help for her or him.

What kind of help is available for abused children and troubled families? There are programs in the community to deal with and prevent problems. These include the following.

- **Crisis hot lines.** These are telephone services that parents or children in trouble can call to get help. Two national hot lines are the National Child Abuse Hotline (1-800-442-4453) and the Runaway Hotline (1-800-448-4663). These are toll-free numbers.

- **Family violence shelters.** These are places where families in danger of abuse can stay while they figure out what to do. Counselors at these shelters will help families get help in working out problems.

- **Family counseling programs.** These programs help family members identify their problems and work together to solve them. School counselors, youth counselors, and hospital social workers may also provide support to family members separately or as a group.

- **Support groups.** These are groups in which people have a chance to talk with and listen to others with problems like their own. Some support groups are made up of victims of abuse. Some are made up of abusers. Parents Anonymous, for example, is a group for parents who have abused their children or who are afraid that they might. Members encourage each other as they learn to understand and change their behavior.

The Kindness of Strangers

Some people, teens and adults alike, feel funny or embarrassed talking about their problems to people on hot lines or at shelters. They feel as though they are opening their private lives to strangers. But the people who work in these places are kind and caring. They have special training to help people in trouble. They know what to do.

Check Your Understanding

Conclusion A healthy family is one in which the members get along, fulfill their responsibilities to one another, and care about each other. A socially healthy family can find ways to deal with stresses brought about by change. A family unable to work out its problems should seek outside help.

1. **Vocabulary** From the following list, select the *two* vocabulary words that name types of families, and describe each: *nuclear, abuse, extended, stepparent.*

2. **Recall** Identify three changes in the modern family.

3. **Recall** Identify four types of family abuse.

4. **Recall** List four places or services from which troubled families can get help.

5. **Synthesize** Suppose a friend is complaining about having to spend a week at the home of his or her aunt, uncle, and three cousins. What could you tell your friend about the benefits of visiting his or her family?

"Nights" of the Round Table

Some families work out their problems after dinner some nights or on weekends in a "round-table" discussion. In this kind of discussion, no one is boss. Everyone is given a chance to speak his or her mind. Everyone has an equal voice.

Teen Health
BULLETIN BOARD

TEEN
Q & A

Q: Cal has been my friend since kindergarten. Lately, he's started pulling all these dumb jokes, like tripping kids in the hall so they'll drop their books. He thinks he's pretty funny. I think he's become a jerk. Should I tell him I don't want to be his friend anymore?

A: What's happening to you and Cal is common among teens. It's known as growing up.

As we grow, we change. Often, this happens at different rates. That is part of the reason for your feelings about Cal—he doesn't seem to be maturing as fast as you. One thing you might try is patience. Let Cal know you don't approve of his jokes. That may help the problem. But the real solution to the problem is time. As Cal matures, he may grow out of his childish pranks, and the two of you can go on being good friends.

CAREERS

Wanted
Day-Care Worker

Specifics
Work at day-care center to help preschool children learn and develop socially.

Qualifications
Must enjoy children and know how to give them a feeling of security. Must be able to work as part of a team to develop effective programs.

Preparation
At least a high school education is needed. An associate degree from a 2-year college is available. On-the-job experience may be required. Education courses are helpful.

Contact
National Association for Child Care Management
1800 M Street, NW
Washington, DC 20036
or
National Association for the Education of Young Children
1834 Connecticut Avenue, NW
Washington, DC 20009

HEALTH IN THE NEWS

Latchkey Kids

Many parents put their "latchkey kids" in programs that provide extra learning experiences.

Mark is ten years old. His parents work. Mark lets himself into his house after school. Sometimes he watches television. Sometimes he goes to a friend's house. Mark is one of the millions of "latchkey kids" in America today. These are children whose parents or guardians are not home when the children get home from school.

Some concerned parents have made sure that there are activities for their kids to go to after school. There are programs such as day care. There are clubs at school. Some parents arrange for a neighbor to watch their children. Sometimes, however, parents are unable to provide after-school care for their children.

Children who care for themselves after school must learn how to handle many situations that grown-ups do. Concerned parents, doctors, and family health experts are searching for solutions to this problem.

Do you have a suggestion?

Sports and Recreation

Families Who Play Together

What's that you see in the park? Could that be your best friend's mom swinging the softball bat? Is that your neighbor from across the street tagging his daughter out at third? You bet it is!

All across the nation, scenes such as these are becoming common as more and more adults decide that what's fun for their kids can be fun for them, too. Part of the reason for this rise in family sports is the new interest in exercise and fitness. But an equally large part is a desire to get the family back together. Among the sports and activities that some families are taking part in are cross-country skiing, downhill skiing, volleyball, badminton, and camping. Can you think of an activity that might be right for you and your family?

Lifestyle

Group Daters

Rod has a date tonight with Shelley. He also has a date with Kaity, Luisa, Sara, Tom, Alphonse, and Dale. Rod and his friends are "group daters," teens who have discovered the fun of group dating. The four couples got together in the first place after reports of crime in their community. They all found that they liked going out in a group and each other's company so much that they started doing it often. Now, when one couple cannot make it for a date, the rest feel disappointed.

Tonight's date is going to start off with records at Luisa's house. Then it's off to the movies and after that to the neighborhood pizza parlor, where the eight teens will meet some other group daters.

Dating, Marriage, and Parenthood

Words to Know

adolescence
socializing
group dating
going steady
date rape
commitment
love

This lesson contains a number of valuable facts and tips. Once you have studied them, you will be able to

- define the term *adolescence.*
- identify defining traits of emotional maturity.
- state reasons why teenage marriages do not usually work out.
- name some of the jobs and responsibilities that are part of being a good parent.

Adjusting to Adolescence

The time of life between childhood and adulthood is known as **adolescence** (ad·uhl·ES·uhns). Adolescence is not an easy time.

As you begin your adolescent years, you are probably becoming more aware of both the need to belong and the need to be yourself. You may spend some time trying to figure out who you are and where you fit into the scheme of things. Having a healthy relationship with your family and your friends helps. Knowing that parents and friends will accept you for who you are also helps. They will give you room to grow into the best person you can be.

Dating

During adolescence you begin to develop an interest in members of the opposite sex. Dating can help you learn more about yourself and about relating to people of both sexes. By going out with different people, you practice your skill at **socializing** (SOH·shuh·ly·zing), *getting along and communicating with other people.* You learn your strengths and weaknesses. You learn how to express yourself and how to work out differences of opinion.

Teen Issue

Having a Successful Date

There are right ways and wrong ways to do everything, including dating. The following tips will increase your chances of a successful date.

- Make the date well in advance.
- Pick an activity that you will both enjoy.
- Get there on time. Don't keep your date waiting.
- Ask questions to keep the conversation going smoothly.

A last tip you might think about is dating in a group. This certainly takes pressure off you. What's more, going out with "the gang" can be a lot of fun.

Learning from Photographs
These teens are enjoying a group date. What are some of the advantages of dating in groups?

To Date, or Not to Date

While dating often begins during adolescence, not all teens feel ready to date. Some teens have other interests that they would rather follow for the time being. Others are simply shy. **Group dating,** or *going out with a group of friends of both sexes*, is a good way to ease into dating. Many young people are most comfortable going to parties, movies, and dances in groups.

Going Steady

After dating for a while, many teenagers decide to *go steady*. **Going steady** is *dating only one other person*. While couples who go steady can develop a very special relationship, they can also run into problems. People who go steady at a young age may miss the chance to meet other people and have new experiences.

Going steady can also lead to pressure to have sex. Sexual relations can lead to many problems. Some teenage boys feel that persuading a girl to have sex makes them grown-up. Some teenage girls feel that saying "no" will make them unpopular. Both of these ideas are wrong.

There are good reasons why teens of both sexes should say "no" to sexual relations. These include the following.

- **The risk of pregnancy.** A smart teen will ask himself or herself: "Am I ready to take on the responsibility of being a parent?"

- **The risk of disease.** Certain diseases can be passed along through sexual relations. If untreated, some of these diseases can be deadly.

Teen Issue

First Date

Many teens, when they think about beginning to date, get nervous. Their underarms sweat and they're jittery. The idea of dating can be scary. Boys find themselves wondering: "How do I ask her? What if she says no?" Girls wonder: "What if I don't get asked out? Is it okay to ask the boy first?" If you are one of these teens, it may help you to know that you are not the first person to have these fears. Here are some rules for dating.

1. Start by being straightforward—just go ahead and ask.

2. If the person says no, don't figure that there is something wrong with you. Instead, find someone else you would like to date and ask that person. You could even try again another time with the person you asked first.

3. Don't get upset if the date doesn't turn out as you had hoped. You and your date may not have been right for each other.

Finally, keep in mind that dating is a skill. You will get better with practice.

Not everyone chooses to marry. Some people like their lives as single people and prefer to remain that way. Some people choose to concentrate on their careers or other life goals. People have different reasons for remaining single, just as they have different reasons for getting married. Whatever the reason, remaining single is the right choice for some people.

A Riddle

Here is a riddle for you: Who's perfect? The answer is "no one." Remember this when you are taking note of your strengths and weaknesses. Everyone has weak points, and everyone makes mistakes. Instead of feeling bad about your weak points, work at making them strong points. Become a better you!

Date Rape

When sex becomes an issue in a relationship, there is a danger of date rape. **Date rape** is *the act of forcing a person to have sexual relations with a date or someone else he or she knows.* Date rape is against the law, and it is wrong. No one has a right to force you to do anything you do not want to do. You can avoid date rape by making sure that you always go out as part of a group. You can protect yourself, too, by never being someplace with a date all alone.

Marriage

"I do" are words most American adults say at some time in their lives. At least nine out of ten Americans marry. In doing so, they make a lifetime commitment to live with and care for another person. A **commitment** (kuh·MIT·muhnt) is *a pledge or promise.* Making a commitment means

- accepting responsibility and acting in a trustworthy way.
- sharing yourself with another person.
- having respect for the other person's needs and desires.
- working at all times to make the relationship stronger.

Most people claim they get married because they are "in love." **Love** is *a strong emotional attachment to another person.* While love is important in a marriage, it is often not enough to keep a relationship going. Many other factors affect whether a marriage will work. One of the most important of these is being *emotionally mature.* Two emotionally mature people can make a marriage work.

> Being emotionally mature means…
> - knowing yourself and accepting your strengths and weaknesses.
> - knowing what is important to you and what is not.
> - setting goals and having plans for reaching those goals.
> - understanding someone else's needs and feelings.
> - being able at times to put the other person's needs ahead of your own.

Teen Marriage

Teenage marriage, as a rule, does not work. Only one out of four teenage marriages lasts. Why do the other three fail? Here are several reasons.

Learning from Photographs
These teens are going steady.
How might their lives change if
they were to marry at too young
an age?

- **Most people are simply not ready to get married during their teen years.** Teenagers are just beginning to learn about themselves and to figure out what they want from life. Most do not yet know enough about themselves to choose a partner for life. Most are not mature enough to make a lasting commitment to someone else.

- **Most teenagers are not ready to be parents.** Many teenagers get married because of an unplanned pregnancy. The responsibility of a baby is often more than the couple can handle.

- **Most teenage couples do not have enough money.** Teenage couples are likely to have a hard time supporting themselves. Stress from money problems often breaks up a marriage.

Divorce

A marriage that does not work is likely to end in divorce. Divorce involves splitting up a household and breaking up a family. For a child, it means one parent leaving. At some point, it may also mean getting used to a new stepparent and new brothers and sisters.

Divorce can be stressful. But it is not hopeless. Many families go on after a divorce to live more happily and healthfully than ever. The key is communication. By talking out their feelings, either among themselves or with an outside professional, many families are able to adjust well to their new lives. By communicating, the divorced parent is able to comfort his or her child, who may be frightened and unsure of the future. The child, in turn, learns through communication that she or he is not to blame for the divorce. Divorces happen because adults are no longer able to live together.

Teen Issue

Just Say: "I Don't"
Many teens think that when they say, "I do," they will be rid of problems like bossy parents who tell them how late they can stay out. But marrying and starting a family can create another set of problems. Not the least of those problems is being tied down to an infant, a responsibility that makes it hard to go out at all!

Learning from Photographs
Our need for others begins at birth. Who is responsible for meeting a baby's needs?

Parenthood

Most people assume that at some point in their lives, they will be parents. But being a good parent takes work. Raising a family means providing food, clothing, and shelter. It also means helping children grow up to be happy and healthy. At the same time, parenthood can offer enormous rewards.

To be a good parent, a person must be able to fill many roles and juggle many responsibilities.

- **Setting fair limits.** All people in society must learn to follow rules. Children especially need to know what they can and cannot do. A good parent sets fair rules.

- **Giving encouragement.** Parents are their children's teachers from birth. From watching or listening to their parents, children learn how to eat, how to walk, and how to talk. Parents must therefore set good examples. They need to teach their children life skills and pass on values. They must do their best to help their children grow socially and emotionally.

- **Looking after themselves.** Parents are people too. They have their own needs and feelings. They must take time for themselves and their partners. They must look out for their own social, emotional, and physical well-being.

Parents who can balance their own needs and their children's needs are likely to raise healthy children who can later succeed as adults in our society.

Health Minute

Being a Parent Is a Full-Time Job

Have a brother or sister set an alarm clock to go off at different times without telling you the times. When the alarm goes off, stop *whatever* you are doing, whether it is eating, watching a favorite television show, or talking to a friend on the telephone. Spend the next ten minutes doing household chores, such as washing dishes. This is part of what it means to be the parent of a new baby.

Check Your Understanding

Conclusion   As children grow up, they learn to accept responsibility and to make commitments. Adolescence is a time that prepares people for adulthood. Only mature adults are ready for the full commitment of marriage and the responsibility of parenthood.

1. **Vocabulary** Use the terms *group dating* and *going steady* in an original sentence.

2. **Recall** Define adolescence.

3. **Recall** Identify five defining traits of emotional maturity.

4. **Recall** State three reasons why teen marriages often fail.

5. **Recall** Name three jobs and responsibilities that are part of being a good parent.

6. **Synthesize** What skill might be lacking in people who walk away angry when they cannot have their way?

Recognizing Faulty Thinking

When you have good social health, you are able to deal well with groups and other individuals. Since most of people's dealings with others are through words, what people say to each other can often have a great effect on their social health.

Sometimes, people say things to each other that show signs of *faulty thinking*. This means approaching an event or situation without thinking through all the possible consequences. Telling someone that it is best to drive a car during rainstorms because there are fewer cars on the road is using faulty thinking.

Being able to recognize statements based on faulty thinking is especially important during the teen years. This is a time when you are developing a sense of *who* you are and *what* you believe in. It is also a time when friends or peers might try to pressure you into doing something you do not want to do. Knowing when their statements are based on faulty thinking can help you avoid situations that might be dangerous.

Identifying Faulty Thinking

Statements based on faulty thinking often fit one of two patterns.

- **The "it-only-happens-to-others" pattern.** People, and especially teens, use statements such as "It won't happen to me" when they are about to do something they shouldn't. The "it" in the statement refers to a danger that the speaker is aware of.

- **The "everybody's-doing-it" pattern.** This sort of statement is another way of saying, "Even if it's not good for you, it's popular." Teens often use this pattern to pressure other teens. It preys on the teen's desire to be popular and well liked. It can be more important, though, to protect oneself from possible harm.

Using the Skill

Read the story that follows. Then, on a separate sheet of paper, answer the questions that follow.

Case

It was Sunday night. Juan had a math test the next morning. He was about to begin studying when the doorbell rang. It was his friend Roy. Roy said that some of the kids were getting together at Kim's house to listen to records. When Juan mentioned that they had a math test the next day, Roy pointed out that everyone was going to be at Kim's. Juan thought for a moment. He knew it was risky to put off preparing till the last minute. He remembered the time when his brother planned to study the morning of a test and ended up oversleeping. But the same thing wouldn't happen to him, Juan figured. He went to the front closet to get his coat.

1. What problem is Juan faced with?

2. What are his choices?

3. What is the consequence of each choice?

4. What type of faulty thinking is Roy guilty of? What statement of his shows this?

5. What type of faulty thinking is Juan guilty of? What statement of his shows this?

6. On the basis of Juan's choices, do you think he made the right decision? Why or why not?

Chapter 4 Review

Summary

- The health of our relationships with other people is a factor in our total health. Good relationships are based on communication, cooperation, and compromise.
- Peer pressure can be both positive and negative. Teens can control negative peer pressure by planning and by getting support.
- The first group to which we belong is the family. Modern times have brought about certain changes in the idea of "family."
- Part of growing up is learning to accept responsibility and make commitments. Teens are not ready for the responsibilities of marriage and parenthood.

Reviewing Vocabulary and Concepts

On a separate sheet of paper, write the numbers 1–8. After each number, write the letter of the answer that best describes each of the following statements.

Lesson 1

1. Having good social health includes having all of the following qualities *except*
   a. being liked by everybody
   b. having at least one close friend
   c. meeting people easily
   d. getting along with others

2. A word that means working together for the good of all is
   a. communication
   b. compromise
   c. cooperation
   d. caring

3. Picking the right time and place to talk is one rule of good
   a. communication
   b. compromise
   c. cooperation
   d. caring

4. The give-and-take often needed to get a job done is
   a. communication
   b. compromise
   c. cooperation
   d. caring

Lesson 2

5. The qualities of good friends include all of the following *except*
   a. reliability
   b. loyalty
   c. giving gifts
   d. sympathy

6. A friend who is aware of how you are feeling at a particular moment is
   a. reliable
   b. sympathetic
   c. loyal
   d. caring

7. Pressure to go along with beliefs of people your age is
   a. always positive
   b. always negative
   c. peer pressure
   d. a form of abuse

8. Ways of coping with negative peer pressure include all of the following *except*
   a. avoiding
   b. fighting back
   c. walking away
   d. getting a "buddy"

Write the numbers 9–19 on your paper. After each number, write the letter of the word or phrase in Column B that matches the phrase in Column A.

Column A

Lesson 3

9. A family made up of a father, mother, and children
10. A family that includes a stepparent
11. A change in modern families
12. One reason more women work outside the home
13. Abuse of a husband
14. Places where families in danger of abuse can go

Lesson 4

15. The period of life between childhood and adulthood
16. Going out with a group of friends of both sexes
17. A danger of going steady
18. A reason teen marriages fail
19. A part of being a good parent

Column B

a. spouse abuse
b. adolescence
c. to have a career
d. setting limits
e. blended family
f. lack of money
g. pressure to have sex
h. single-parent families
i. family violence shelters
j. group dating
k. nuclear family

Thinking Critically About the Facts

Write your answers to the following questions on a separate sheet of paper.

20. **Interpret** Why might a noisy after-school hangout not be a good place to discuss a problem you are having with a friend?
21. **Interpret** Write down the qualities that your "perfect friend" would have. Which of these qualities do you see in others? Which do you see in yourself? Explain your choices.
22. **Analyze** Fairy tales sometimes include a "wicked stepmother." What effect do you think this idea of stepparents might have on children who are about to become part of a blended family?
23. **Synthesize** What are three benefits of being a member of a small family? What are three benefits of being a member of a large family?
24. **Analyze** What problems for the family as a whole might arise out of a parent's never looking out for his or her own needs?

Applying the Facts

25. Write a two-page play with parts for at least three actors. The first page of the play should contain a scene in which two of the characters are using negative peer pressure on the third character. The second page should contain a scene illustrating positive peer pressure. Ask two friends to study two of the parts, and take the third part yourself. Then stage the play for your class.

26. Interview a grandparent or another person of that generation. Ask the person what family life was like when he or she was your age. In particular, find out what sorts of things the person did for amusement, how the family worked out problems, and how much time family members spent together. Bring your findings to class for a discussion on how family life has changed in two generations.

Meeting Your Nutritional Needs

| Lesson 1 | **Building a Balanced Diet** | Lesson 3 | **Using Calories for Weight Control** |
| Lesson 2 | **Making Healthy Food Choices** | Lesson 4 | **Eating Disorders** |

CHAPTER WARM-UP

Chapter Study Goals

After you have read this chapter, you will be able to

- describe the role of each type of nutrient and identify food sources for each type.
- explain the meaning of RDA.
- describe how to use the food groups to build a healthy diet.
- list some healthy snack foods.
- explain the relationship of fiber, sugar, fat, cholesterol, and salt to overall health.
- identify the principles of healthy weight-loss and weight-gain diets.
- describe key eating disorders and explain how to get help.

Be on the lookout for information in the chapter that will help you reach these goals.

Getting Started

Raymond watches his diet carefully to make sure that he eats healthy food. Today's lunch, for instance, is a sandwich, a glass of milk, and fresh fruit. His friend Ling is trying to lose weight, but feels frustrated. Ling went on a crash diet and lost 10 pounds, but gained it all back in a few weeks. What and how you eat play a major role in how you look, feel, and act.

This chapter will explain how healthy food choices will also help you look, feel, and perform at your best.

Study Tip

This chapter contains charts concerning food and health. Use the charts to find the facts that relate to you.

Building a Balanced Diet

Words to Know

nutrition
diet
nutrients
carbohydrates
fats
proteins
amino acids
vitamins
minerals
water
Recommended Dietary
  Allowances (RDA)

This lesson contains a number of valuable facts and tips. Once you have studied them, you will be able to

- explain the benefits of good nutrition.
- say what the word *diet* means.
- name the factors that influence what and how you eat.
- name the nutrients you need to be healthy.
- tell what the RDA is and how to use it.

Food for Life

Food, along with air and water, is one of life's basic needs. When you go without food for a long time, you feel hungry. This is your body's signal that it needs more food. After you eat, the hunger disappears. Your body has received the fuel it needs to keep going.

By eating healthful foods in recommended amounts, you make sure that you will grow and that you will be healthy. *Eating the foods the body needs to grow, to develop, and to work properly* is called **nutrition** (noo·TRISH·uhn). Good nutrition is one of the main factors in good health. Because you eat food every day, good nutrition can have a powerful impact on your health.

Good nutrition is especially important in your teenage years. In these years you are growing more than at any other time after early childhood. You can give your body what it needs for growth by eating well.

DID **YOU** KNOW?

Tasty, Too
There's another reason that people eat—food that tastes good makes people feel good. Taste buds on your tongue help you taste. You can read more about taste buds in Chapter 2.

Health Minute

What's Your Diet?
Write down everything you ate for the last three days. Compare your diet with the suggestions in this chapter. Is your diet nutritious?

Are You on a Diet?

What do you think of when you hear the word *diet*? Most people think of eating less to lose weight. But that is only one type of diet—a weight-loss diet. A **diet** is something we all follow; *it is the food and drink that we regularly eat.* Think of the foods that you eat each day, each week. Think of the beverages you drink. You will begin to get a picture of the diet you follow. Many factors affect your diet.

Learning from Photographs
Family backgrounds can be a strong influence on your food choices. What two backgrounds are shown here?

- **Where you live.** Some foods may be available in your area and others not.
- **Family.** Your family may eat chicken and potatoes for dinner often. Your friend's family may prefer tortillas and beans.
- **Convenience** (kuhn·VEE·nyuhns). You may prefer some foods because they can be prepared more quickly than others.
- **Cost.** The price of food may play a role in the kinds and amounts of food your family eats.
- **Advertisements.** Commercials and newspaper ads may persuade you to try a new food.
- **Friends.** You may enjoy eating out at certain restaurants with your friends. Or a friend may introduce you to a new food.

Another factor is personal taste. You may like some foods and dislike others. Many of the eating habits you had as a young child affect the choice of foods in your present diet.

The Balanced Diet

Though you have a diet, you may not have a healthy one. A healthy diet provides the nutrients you need for proper growth and development. **Nutrients** (NOO·tree·uhnts) are *substances in foods that your body needs.* There are six types of nutrients. A healthy diet contains the right amount, or balance, of specific nutrients of each type. That is where the term *balanced diet* comes from.

Learning from Photographs
Foods from all over the world are now available year round. Where does the produce sold at your supermarket come from?

Learning from Photographs
Healthy foods help you grow. How much have you grown in the last year?

Teen Issue

The Vegetarian Diet

Some teens choose to be *vegetarians,* meaning they will not eat meat. While meat is a good source of protein, it isn't the only source. Some vegetarians eat fish and eggs for protein. Some drink milk. Others combine grains and beans to make complete proteins. A vegetarian diet can be healthy—but it must be properly planned.

DID **YOU** KNOW?

Vita-myths

Vitamins are important nutrients, but they *don't* provide energy. Fruits, vegetables, breads, and cereals are the best energy foods.

The Six Types of Nutrients

Scientists have found some 50 nutrients that you need to grow and function. These nutrients can be grouped into six main types. These are shown below. To learn what foods contain these nutrients and what jobs they perform, see the chart "Nutrients You Need."

- **Carbohydrates.** *Sugars and starches give you energy.* These are the simple and complex **carbohydrates** (kar·boh·HY·drayts).

- **Fats.** *Fatty acids also provide energy.* Some of these **fats** are called *essential* (i·SEN·chuhl) *fatty acids* because you must have them in your diet. *Essential* means "needed."

- **Proteins** (PROH·teens). The nutrients that *help to build cells and make them work properly* are **proteins.** They are made up of *chains of building blocks* called **amino** (uh·MEE·noh) **acids.** Your body can make 14 of the 22 amino acids. The other eight, called *essential amino acids*, must come from the foods you eat. There are two kinds of protein foods. *Complete proteins* contain all eight of the essential amino acids. They are found in such foods as meat, fish, eggs, and milk. *Incomplete proteins*, found in foods such as grains and beans, do not have all eight essential amino acids. But grains and beans can be eaten together to make complete proteins. Peanut butter on bread also makes a complete protein.

- **Vitamins.** Some *substances the body needs in small amounts to work properly.* There are two types of these **vitamins** (VYT·uh·muhns). *Water-soluble* (SAHL·yuh·buhl) *vitamins* dissolve in water. They may be lost in cooking. They must be replaced in the body every day because the body does not store them. Examples are vitamin C and the many B vitamins. *Fat-soluble vitamins* can be stored in the body. Examples are vitamins A, D, E, and K.

- **Minerals.** *The body needs some nonliving substances in small amounts to work properly.* These are called **minerals** (MIN·uh·ruhls). *Iron, calcium,* and *potassium* are important minerals.

- **Water.** *The most common nutrient* is **water.** The body needs water for many tasks. About 60 percent of your body is made up of water. You must constantly replace the water your body loses.

Good health comes partly from eating enough of each of these nutrients. Eating too much of some may cause health problems. Too much fat in the diet, for instance, may lead to heart disease. Eating too little of these nutrients causes health problems, too. Someone who does not eat enough protein may not grow normally. The lack of certain vitamins or minerals can cause other health problems.

DID **YOU** KNOW?

Are Foods in Ads Nutritious?
Almost two-thirds of the television ads for food try to convince viewers to buy sugars, desserts, snacks, and soft drinks. These are the foods lowest in nutrients.

Nutrients You Need

Type of Nutrient	Food Source	Effect
Carbohydrates	Foods from plant sources, milk	Provide energy
Simple	Fruits, milk, table sugar	Provide energy
Complex	Starchy foods (bread, pasta, potatoes, rice), vegetables, milk	Provide energy, provide fiber to aid digestion
Fats	Butter, margarine, salad oil, chocolate, animal foods (fish, meat, poultry, milk, eggs)	Provide stored energy, insulate body from temperature changes, cushion body organs, carry fat-soluble vitamins
Proteins	Foods from animal and plant sources	Build, repair, and maintain body tissue; help body grow; provide energy
Complete protein foods	Foods from animals (fish, meat, poultry, milk, cheese, eggs)	
Incomplete protein foods	Foods from plant sources (grains, dry beans, seeds, peas)	
Vitamins	Variety of foods	Help body process other nutrients so it can grow and function
Water-soluble	Variety of foods	Help body fight infection
Fat-soluble	Variety of foods	Many functions such as helping eyes adjust to darkness
Minerals	Variety of foods	Many functions such as strengthening bones (calcium), helping body process other nutrients
Water	All foods, beverages	Carries other nutrients through body, helps digestion, removes wastes from body, lubricates body joints, keeps body from overheating

How Much of the Nutrients?

You know that you need each nutrient. But two big questions remain.

- How much of each nutrient should you eat?
- Which foods contain which nutrients, and how much do they have?

Scientists have studied how the body uses nutrients. As a result, they have written *guidelines for the amount of each nutrient to be eaten each day.* These are called the **Recommended (rek·uh·MEND·uhd) Dietary Allowances,** or RDA. The RDA is reviewed and put out again every five years or so.

The RDA plays an important part in good nutrition. Labels on food packages state how much of the U.S. Recommended Daily Allowances (U.S. RDA) for certain key nutrients the food contains. The U.S. RDA is based on the RDA. Federal school-lunch programs are planned to provide one-third of the students' RDA.

More About

*See the **RDA table** in the Health Handbook.*

R Is for Recommended

Keep in mind that the RDA guidelines are suggestions for all people. Your needs may be different. If you are not sure, you could talk to your family doctor or the school dietitian.

Learning from Photographs
The amount of physical activity you do affects your need for nutrients. What kinds of exercise do you enjoy?

Of course, people's nutrition needs differ. Age, sex, weight and height, general health, and amount of exercise all affect how much of each nutrient we each need. The RDA takes these factors into account when setting guidelines. The RDA calcium level for teens, for instance, is higher than that for adults. This is because teens need more calcium to build growing bones. The RDA table in the Health Handbook shows the differences for each group.

As a rule, the RDA nutrient levels are set fairly high. That way, scientists are sure that a diet that meets the RDA will be healthy for 95 out of every 100 Americans. By following the RDA, most people get enough of the nutrients they need.

Scientists also studied hundreds of foods. They made up tables stating how much of each nutrient each food contains. You can see some of what they learned in the "Table of Food Values" in the Health Handbook. The nutrients shown in these tables include carbohydrates, proteins, fats, and all vitamins and minerals. The tables in the Health Handbook focus on such key vitamins as Vitamins A and C and important minerals such as iron and calcium.

Teen Issue

Iron Ladies
Pregnant women need so much more iron that nutritionists say their diet cannot supply enough. They suggest that pregnant women take iron supplement pills.

More About
*See the **Table of Food Values** in the Health Handbook.*

Check Your Understanding

Conclusion   All six types of nutrients are necessary for good nutrition. Understanding nutrients and the ways they help your body function is the first step in developing a healthy, well-balanced diet. Such a diet will help you look and feel good and perform at your best.

1. **Vocabulary** Write an original sentence defining the word *diet.*

2. **Recall** What are the three benefits of good nutrition?

3. **Recall** Name three influences on your food choices.

4. **Recall** What six groups of nutrients do you need to be healthy?

5. **Recall** What factors make a difference in your nutritional needs?

6. **Analyze** Sharon's diet includes no meat. She eats oatmeal plus orange juice and milk for breakfast. She has salad, cheese and crackers, a hard-cooked egg, and fruit juice for lunch. She snacks on yogurt. Her dinner includes rice and beans, a green vegetable, and milk. Her friend Tasha says she doesn't eat any protein. What do you think?

Now You're Cooking!
If you learn to cook, you can add to the variety of foods you enjoy. You can learn from one or both of your parents or in a home economics class. Many cookbooks are written for beginners.

Making Healthy Food Choices

Words to Know
basic food groups
leader nutrients
fiber
cholesterol
caffeine

This lesson contains a number of valuable facts and tips. Once you have studied them, you will be able to

- discuss how to have a balanced diet using the food groups.
- name several healthy snacks.
- give examples of foods from each food group.
- name some foods that are unhealthy if eaten in large amounts.

The Food Groups

Putting together a diet by using the RDA tables and food tables would take lots of time. An easier way to ensure a balanced diet is to eat foods from each of four **basic food groups.** The *foods within each group supply similar nutrients.* By eating the suggested number of servings from each group, you eat a balanced diet.

The food-group plan has another benefit. Each group has a variety of foods. This makes it easy for each person to find a number of healthy choices that appeal to his or her taste.

The box on the next page lists the four food groups. It tells *the main nutrients each group supplies.* These are called the **leader nutrients.** The box also tells the minimum number of servings a teen should have from each group and gives examples of what makes a serving.

The "Other" Group

There is a fifth food group known as the "other" group. This group has many different foods that are filling, but give few or no nutrients. Examples are butter, sugar, jams and jellies, candy, dips, soft drinks, and doughnuts. Many of these foods contain large amounts of fat or sugar. They may be eaten from time to time, but in small amounts. They should not be eaten in place of more nutritious foods.

Teen Issue

Megavitamins
Stores have shelves full of multivitamins and megavitamins. Are they helpful? Some people may need extra amounts of some vitamins and minerals. But most people can get enough from a balanced diet. Besides, what tastes better—a frosty-cold glass of orange juice or a vitamin C pill?

DID YOU KNOW?

How It's Cooked Counts
Many people say potatoes aren't healthy. Not true. They're great sources of carbohydrates, vitamin C, and fiber. But two-thirds of the vitamin C in a raw potato is cooked away in frying. Baked or boiled potatoes are more nutritious than fries or chips.

The Milk and Milk Products Group

Leader nutrients: protein, calcium, and vitamin B_2 (riboflavin)
Daily servings: 4
Examples: milk (8-ounce glass)
                 cheese (1 ounce)
                 yogurt (1 cup)
Note: It is most healthful to choose low- and nonfat milk products.

The Meat, Fish, Poultry, Eggs, and Bean Group

Leader nutrients: protein, iron, niacin, and vitamins B_1 (thiamine)
                 and B_{12}
Daily servings: 2
Examples: beef, fish, or poultry (3 ounces)
                 dry beans (1½ cups)
Note: It is most healthful to choose low-fat meats and cook them with little added fat.

The Fruit and Vegetable Group

Leader nutrients: vitamins A and C, folic acid
Daily servings: 4
Examples: apples (1)
                 carrots (½ cup)
                 broccoli (½ cup)
Note: Vitamins A and C are important. For Vitamin A, eat a deep yellow or dark green vegetable every day. For Vitamin C, eat a citrus fruit or drink citrus fruit juice every day.

The Breads and Cereal Group

Leader nutrients: complex carbohydrates, iron, niacin, and vitamin B_1
                 (thiamine)
Daily servings: 4
Examples: bread (1 slice)
                 tortilla (1)
                 cereal (¾ cup)
Note: Whole-grain breads and cereals provide nutrients and fiber.

Learning from Photographs
Grain products like pasta come in a variety of shapes and sizes. What nutritional benefit do grain products supply?

Using the Food Groups

To use the food groups properly, you need to keep a few points in mind.

Hints for Using the Food Groups

- **Serving sizes are important.** The food groups recommend four servings from the milk and milk products group. A serving of milk is 8 ounces—not less.
- **Meats should be lean.** The less fat on the meat, the healthier it is for you. Fish and poultry cooked without added fat are good lean sources of protein.
- **Grain products should be whole grain or enriched.** Labels on bread and pasta packages will say if these foods were made with whole-wheat or enriched flour. Whole-grain products provide the most nutrients. They also contain more fiber than enriched foods.
- **How food is prepared matters.** Broiled foods are healthier than fried foods because broiled foods have less fat. Vegetables steamed to crispness give more vitamins than vegetables cooked in water until they are mushy.

Planning—The Way to Health

A key to having a balanced diet is to plan your meals in advance. Think each day about what you will eat tomorrow. Ask the person who does the cooking in your family what dinner will be. Then plan to get the additional servings you need from the four food groups during breakfast and lunch. By thinking ahead, you can make sure that you don't miss any food-group servings. You can also be sure not to eat too much.

Are Snacks Bad?

Snacks can be fun. Snacks can also be healthy. As an energy booster in midafternoon, a snack can help you perform better and feel better. It's desirable to snack as long as you follow two rules.

- **Follow the food-group suggestions.** Snacks can be part of your daily meal plan. Simply include them as part of the suggested daily servings from each food group.
- **Snack on healthy foods.** Most snacks from the "other" group give fat and sugar, but few nutrients. Eat healthy snacks from the four basic food groups. See the chart "Healthy Snacks" for some ideas.

Teen **Issue**
....

Are Natural Foods Better?
Many snack foods claim to be healthy because they are "natural." Are they? Maybe—it depends on what's in the food. A "natural" candy bar made of fruit sugar, honey, and carob is no more healthy than a regular candy bar. You want a healthy snack? Eat a banana.
....

Learning from Photographs
Whole-grain crackers can be a healthy snack, especially if they are low in sodium and fat. Nutritional labels list ingredients from the largest proportion to the smallest. What food additive that contains sodium should you look for on the label?

Healthy Snacks

Milk and Milk Products Group—yogurt, cottage cheese

Meat, Fish, Poultry, Eggs, and Beans Group—slice of boiled ham, cup of tuna fish in water (but no mayonnaise)

Fruit and Vegetable Group—any raw fruit, carrot or celery sticks, cut-up tomato, popcorn (but no butter)

Breads and Cereal Group—cup of oatmeal, whole-wheat crackers, air-popped popcorn (without butter)

Combination Foods—fruit and milk shake (made with low- or nonfat milk), pizza with vegetables, raw vegetables and yogurt dip

Healthy Food Choices

People who study nutrition have found that we should pay special attention to a number of foods. Their suggestions can be summed up in a list.

- Eat plenty of fiber.
- Reduce the amount of fat, cholesterol, sugar, and salt that you eat.
- Limit your intake of caffeine.

Following these guidelines will produce a diet that is not only balanced but also healthy.

Fiber and Your Diet

One part of certain foods that is very good for you is fiber. **Fiber** (FY·ber) is *the part of fruits, vegetables, grains, and beans that your body cannot digest.* Fiber is not a nutrient, but it is very important to digestion. While other parts of food are broken down in your stomach

Learning from Photographs
Vegetables can increase the amount of fiber in your diet. Can you name a source of fiber other than vegetables?

More About

*To learn more about the process of **digestion** and its role in the body's health, see Chapter 7.*

and small intestine, fiber just passes through. Fiber helps carry the other food particles through your digestive system. Some scientists believe that diets with lots of fiber can lower people's chances of getting cancer of the colon.

People who study nutrition believe that most Americans do not get enough fiber in their diets. You should eat about a third of an ounce (6 to 10 grams) of fiber each day. Whole-grain bread, raw fruits and vegetables, and beans are high in fiber.

Hidden Fats

Like sugar, the foods you eat probably have more fat than you think. You can see some fats, such as butter on toast or the fat on steak. But most fats are hidden. Cheese, soups, nuts, and eggs, for example, all contain hidden fats.

You need some fat for good health. Too much, however, can lead to heart disease and other health problems. It is easy to cut down on the fats you can see. For instance, do not put butter on your baked potato, and avoid fried foods. It's harder to cut down on hidden fats, but it can be done. Read the labels on cans and packages and avoid buying foods high in fat. Learn which fresh foods are high in fat and avoid them.

Cholesterol

Cholesterol (kuh·LES·tuh·rawl) is found in every cell of your body. It is *a fatty, waxlike substance that helps your body produce substances it needs.* It also helps protect nerve fibers.

Your body makes its own cholesterol, and you get even more from the foods you eat. Though your body needs cholesterol, too much of some types can be unhealthy. Large amounts of cholesterol can build up on the walls of blood vessels. This makes it harder for blood to pass through and can lead to heart disease. To keep your cholesterol levels low, avoid eating too many eggs and too much animal fat.

Trim That Meat!
Take a minute at the beginning of your meal to trim the fat from meat and remove the skin from poultry. Your meat will be leaner—and you will be healthier.

Learning from Photographs
Drinking low-fat or nonfat milk helps keep down the amount of fat you drink. Can you name any types of low-fat milk?

Sodium

Although salt contains a nutrient called *sodium* (SOHD·ee·uhm) that the body needs, most Americans eat far more salt than is healthy. If you check the label on a can or box of prepared food, you will probably discover that the food has added sodium. Salt is often added when food is prepared, and many people add extra salt to foods from a saltshaker. You can get all the sodium you need by eating less than one-third of an ounce of salt (3 to 8 grams) a day. But the average American eats double or triple that amount. Read the chart "Sodium in Foods" to see that less-processed foods often have less sodium than many highly processed foods.

Eating too much sodium can be unhealthy. It can make your body hold more fluid than it should. It can also promote high blood pressure, which is dangerous. Read the food labels, and control the number of foods you eat that contain added sodium or salt. Stop yourself from adding salt to your meals.

Less Salt

To eat less salt, cut down on salty snacks and processed meats, such as sausage or bologna. Flavor foods with herbs like sage or spices like pepper. They'll be so tasty you won't miss the salt.

Sodium in Foods

Less-Processed Food	Milligrams of Sodium	Processed Food	Milligrams of Sodium
Potato (1 baked)	6	Potato chips (14 chips)	133
Corn (1 cooked ear)	1	Canned sweet corn (1 cup)	389
Peach (1 fresh)	1	Canned peaches (1 cup)	5
Whole-wheat flour (1 cup)	4	Whole-wheat bread (1 slice)	132
Turkey (8 ounces, roasted)	130	Turkey roll (3½ ounces)	690
Pork chop (1 broiled)	47	Ham lunch meat (2 ounces)	508

Sugar

If you are like most Americans, you probably eat much more sugar than is healthy for you. Sugar is added to many of the foods you eat. In fact, the average American eats about 100 pounds of sugar a year. Almost three-fourths of that is sugar hidden in prepared foods. Some people believe that honey is more nutritious than sugar. Like sugar, honey has only the tiniest amount of nutrients.

Is sugar healthy? It contains no important nutrients. Is sugar harmful? Sugar can promote tooth decay. You shouldn't eat too many foods high in sugar, especially if you eat them in place of foods with more nutrients.

Spotting Sugar

Sugar comes in many forms. Among the most common are *sucrose* (SOO·krohs), *lactose* (LAK·tohs), *galactose* (guh·LAK·tohs), *fructose* (FRUHK·tohs), *dextrose* (DEK·strohs), and *maltose* (MAWL·tohs). Look for these words on food package labels. Look, too, for *sugar, brown sugar, honey, corn syrup, corn sweeteners,* and *concentrated fruit juice.*

Pick Me Up?

Do you drink a cola in midafternoon to perk yourself up? The need for that caffeine may be a sign—you might need more rest or more food in the early part of the day. Getting a good rest the night before is a healthy way to get through the afternoon.

Teen Issue

Too Busy to Eat?

Many teens skip breakfast or lunch, then find themselves tired and without energy. You'll be able to do more by taking a few minutes to eat a good meal. Your stomach will be happier, too!

Caffeine

You may already know that caffeine is a substance found in coffee. But did you know that tea and many soft drinks also contain caffeine? **Caffeine** (ka·FEEN) is *a chemical found in some plants that can make your heart beat faster.* Caffeine can "perk up" a person who uses it. Many people drink beverages with caffeine to help them remain more alert.

Caffeine can also be abused. If you take in too much of it, it can make you tense and hard to get along with. It can also make it hard for you to fall asleep. Like some drugs, caffeine can be habit-forming. For these reasons, you should be aware of how much of it you drink. You may decide to drink fewer beverages containing caffeine. Many soft drink makers now offer caffeine-free products.

The amount of caffeine in coffee is greater than that in tea or soft drinks. Doctors recommend drinking no more than 5 cups of black coffee a day. Weak coffee, coffee with milk, and instant coffee contain less caffeine than does brewed black coffee.

Check Your Understanding

Conclusion   The key to a balanced diet is to eat the recommended number of servings from each of the food groups. Doing so will give you the nutrients you need to grow and be healthy. Planning your meals — even planning healthy snacks — helps, too. You can also make healthy food choices about fiber, sugar, fat, cholesterol, sodium, and caffeine. The result of this healthy eating is that you will look better, feel better, and work and play better.

1. **Vocabulary** Write an original sentence using the terms *fiber* and *cholesterol.*

2. **Recall** Give examples of two foods from each food group.

3. **Recall** How many servings do you need from each of the four food groups each day?

4. **Recall** What is the advantage of planning meals?

5. **Recall** Name three foods that need special attention.

6. **Classify** Which of the foods listed below are nutritious snacks?

fresh broccoli	air-popped popcorn	cantaloupe half
potato chips	without butter	cheese puffs
candy	cupcake	fruit milk shake
an orange	soft drink	

Using Calories for Weight Control

Words to Know
weight control
desired weight
overweight
obesity
calorie
nutrient density

This lesson contains a number of valuable facts and tips. Once you have studied them, you will be able to

- name the three factors that determine a person's ideal weight.
- tell how to lose weight healthfully.
- tell how to gain weight healthfully.
- name several eating behaviors that can help you maintain your weight.

What Is Weight Control?

Many people go through their lives gaining weight and then trying to lose it. These people are struggling with weight control. **Weight control** is *reaching the weight that is best for you and then staying there. The weight that is best for you* is known as your **desired weight.** It is based on your sex, height, and body frame (small, medium, or large). A person who stays at his or her desired weight stands a better chance of being healthier than someone who is overweight or underweight.

Take a look at the chart "Finding Your Desired Weight" in the Health Handbook. It will give you an idea of the best weight for you based on your sex, height, and body frame.

The Pressure to Be Thin

Many of us feel a strong pressure to be thin. The stars we see in movies and television and the models we see in ads usually tell us that "thin is beautiful." But most young people don't need to lose weight. Their bodies are in a state of change. Unwise dieting might get in the way of normal growth and development.

Teen Issue
. . . .

Balanced Weight Loss

The urge to eat less is great for some people. But any diet—even a weight-loss diet—must be *balanced.* Skipping meals or eating only one food is not the answer. You'll read in this lesson how to devise a healthy weight-reduction diet.
. . . .

DID YOU KNOW?

Is Thin Beautiful?

In past centuries, heaviness was seen as beautiful. Plumpness was a sign that the person could afford food. The truth is, neither thin nor heavy is beautiful. *Healthy* is beautiful.

Check It Out

Don't start on a diet without seeing a doctor. Get good advice on how much you really need to lose and how to do it.

DID **YOU** KNOW?

Obesity

Scientists estimate that 10 to 25 percent of all teens are obese.

More About

For more information on **diabetes** *and how diet affects it, see Chapter 12.*

Still, there are people, young and old, who have a desire or need to lose weight. There are both healthy and unhealthy ways to do so. A healthy weight-loss diet must take into account all the principles of good nutrition you have already learned.

Overweight or Obese?

A person who needs to lose weight is either overweight or obese. A person who is **overweight** weighs *more than the desired weight for his or her sex, height, and frame size.* Some athletes may seem overweight. But if their bodies have a lot of muscle, they are probably healthy even if they are above their desired weight.

Obesity is more dangerous than overweight. **Obesity** (oh·BEE·suh·tee) is *having too much fat in the body.* It is a serious health problem, and it is common in America. When the body has too much fat, it does not function as well as it would otherwise. Here are some of the results of obesity.

- The body frame has to bear more weight than it should, putting stress on bones and muscles.
- The heart has to work harder to make blood circulate.
- It becomes more difficult to exercise. Calories do not get burned off, and weight gain continues.

Many serious diseases are related to obesity. These include heart disease, high blood pressure, and diabetes, among others.

Overweight people can lose their extra weight. People who are more than 20 percent over their desired body weight are obese. They need a weight-loss diet, too. It may be best for them to start that diet under a doctor's care.

Calories

Calories need to be considered in any diet. A **calorie** (KAL·uh·ree) is *a unit of heat that measures the energy available in different foods.* The more calories in a food, the more available energy it has. Calories also measure the energy your body uses.

Whenever you eat, you take in calories. Those calories give you energy throughout the day. The more active you are, the more calories you burn up. When you take in more calories than you burn up, however, your body stores the extra calories as fat. You gain about one pound of fat for every 3,500 calories you eat but do not burn up.

The calories in food should be looked at along with nutrients. Eating a high-calorie food that is low in nutrients is not a good idea. You should avoid foods that are high in sugar or fat, such as those in the "other" food group. It is better to eat foods that have *a large number of nutrients compared with the calories they provide.* The following foods have **nutrient density** (DEN·suht·ee).

- **Meats.** Chicken and tuna.
- **Milk group.** Low-fat and nonfat milk, yogurt, and cheese.
- **Grains.** Whole-wheat pasta, whole-grain breads, and rice.
- **Fruits and vegetables.** Almost all fruits and vegetables.

Managing Weight Gain or Loss

Someone who is overweight or obese needs to lose weight. Someone who weighs more than 15 percent below his or her desired weight may need to gain weight.

You can control your weight by following two principles.

- **Calorie control.** To lose weight, you must take in *fewer* calories than you normally do. To gain weight, you must take in *more* calories than you normally do.

- **Exercise.** You can exercise to burn up calories at a faster rate than normal. This can help a weight-loss diet. You should also exercise when trying to gain weight to be sure that the weight you add is muscle and not fat.

Whichever kind of diet you follow, the foods you eat should be foods that are high in nutrient density. Even on a weight-gain diet, the calories you eat should not be empty calories.

There is another rule to remember before starting either a weight-loss or a weight-gain diet. See a doctor or dietitian to be sure that your goals are healthful and that the diet you plan is nutritious. Keep in mind that it is not healthy to lose or gain more than 2 pounds a week.

DID **YOU** KNOW?

Cookies and Cola

To burn off the calories of just one chocolate chip cookie, you would need to walk for ten minutes or jog for three. To burn off one 12-ounce cola, you would need to walk for 29 minutes or run for eight.

The Tasty Diet

Choose low-calorie foods that you *like.* That makes staying on the diet easier.

Just a Pinch

For a quick check on whether you are overweight, try the pinch test. Pinch a fold of your skin on the back of your upper arm or at your hipbone. If the skin is more than one inch thick, you may be overweight. See a doctor to know for sure.

Reducing Calorie Intake

To lower the number of calories you take in, you can eat less food than you normally do or eat foods with fewer calories.

For example, a dinner might include only half the chicken you would normally eat and two servings of low-calorie vegetables (such as plain carrots and green beans). Or you might switch from fried chicken to broiled chicken or fish. Be creative in planning low-calorie meals. It will make dieting easier to follow and more fun. Above all, be smart. Never eat so little food that you are always hungry.

Increasing Calorie Intake

An underweight person can gain weight by taking in more calories. Eating more complex carbohydrates such as bread and pasta, for example, can boost calorie intake. An underweight person should eat healthy between-meal snacks, but not too close to mealtimes.

Exercising

The fastest way to burn up calories is to exercise. The more you exercise, the more calories you burn. One way to get more exercise is by changing your daily activities. For example, walk to school instead of riding the bus, and you will burn up more calories.

Eating to Gain
A weight-gain diet must follow the principles of good nutrition. Add healthy foods like grains, fruits, and vegetables to your diet. Stay away from sugars, fats, and empty calories.

Learning from Drawings
This drawing shows the number of calories burned in one hour of doing a few physical activities. Which burns up the most? Which the least?

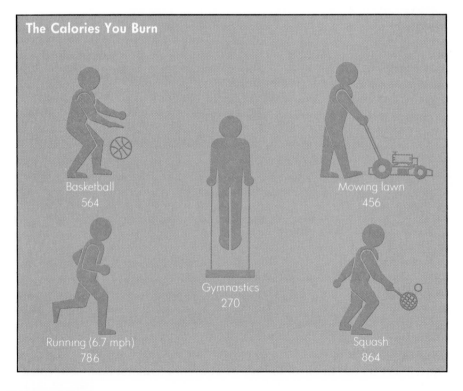

The Calories You Burn

Basketball
564

Gymnastics
270

Mowing lawn
456

Running (6.7 mph)
786

Squash
864

Exercise does more than help you burn calories.

- Exercise helps tone your muscles and burn off fat.
- Exercise often makes you feel less hungry, so it is easier to avoid overeating.
- Exercise makes you feel good, and when you feel good, you look good.

Daily exercise is also important for a person on a weight-gain diet. Exercise will allow for the gained weight to be added in the form of muscle, not fat.

Staying at Your Desired Weight

To maintain your weight, plan your meals and snacks so you will take in the same number of calories as you burn up. The idea is to make this part of your lifestyle, something you do every day. The habits you develop now will keep you healthy later.

If you find your weight rising, start to keep track of the calories you eat. Some days, of course, you will take in more calories than usual. When this happens, you may eat less the next day or increase your exercise. This is all right once in a while, but don't let it become a habit.

Check Your Understanding

Conclusion Controlling weight is a difficult process for many people. But understanding the connection between calories and exercise can help. Whether you need a weight-loss or a weight-gain diet, the secret is to combine good nutrition with exercise. If you do, you will feel better—and look better too.

1. **Vocabulary** What is the difference between being overweight and obese?
2. **Recall** What three factors determine a person's desired weight?
3. **Recall** What two things help someone lose weight in a healthy way? Gain weight in a healthy way?
4. **Recall** Name at least three eating behaviors that can help you maintain your weight.
5. **Analyze** Kevin went to a fast-food restaurant for lunch. He ordered a cola drink; a taco with chicken, shredded lettuce, and tomato; and ice cream. Which of these foods has high nutrient density, and which has low nutrient density?

Eating Behaviors

Weight control is determined not only by what you eat but by how you eat.

- **Sit down and slow down.** Eating quickly or "on the run" is unhealthy and can make you gain weight. Try to make your meal last at least 20 minutes.
- **Chew well.** Chew your food completely rather than swallowing large chunks.
- **Drink lots of water.** Water will help you feel full, aids digestion, and has no calories!
- **Avoid high-sugar foods.** These foods usually don't provide many nutrients. They can leave you feeling hungry again in a short time.
- **Eat breakfast.** Eating in the morning is important. If you eat in the morning, you won't be tempted to eat unplanned snacks or overeat at lunch.

Teen Health
BULLETIN BOARD

CAREERS

Wanted:
Registered Dietitian

Specifics:
Work in hospitals, clinics, businesses, or nursing homes or on a one-to-one basis with people who need special diets. Help people learn to eat healthy diets.

Qualifications:
Ability to talk to people. Must be up-to-date on nutrition information and trends.

Preparation:
A degree from a four-year college, a one-year internship in a hospital, and passing a licensing exam.

Contact:
American Dietetic Association
430 N. Michigan Avenue
Chicago, IL 60611

TEEN Q & A

Q: Why does my stomach sometimes growl when I skip a meal?

A: After you eat, your stomach starts to digest the food. Stomach muscles and liquids called *gastric juices* churn the food to break it down.
Your stomach gets used to working at certain times. Come mealtime, it may go to work even if you haven't eaten anything. Sometimes your empty, churning stomach can get pretty noisy!

Sports and Recreation

What's the best food to eat before an athletic event? Is it a thick steak that provides protein? What about a couple of candy bars for energy? Or maybe a slice of pizza?

None of these foods will help you perform at your best. The protein in steak takes a long time to digest. Candy bars provide energy, but sweets eaten just before exercise actually *reduce* the energy the body can use by 25 percent. Pizza dough is good for athletes, but the cheese takes time to digest.

The best pregame meal is high in complex carbohydrates and low in protein and fat. Look at the training tables at the Olympics. They are full of pasta, breads, rices, potatoes, and unsweetened fruit juices. The best time to eat is two to three hours before the event. That gives the body plenty of time to digest the food and leaves the blood ready to carry oxygen to the exercising muscles. If you want a snack just before the event, drink water, juice, or diet sodas. You'll need the fluids to compete at your best!

Eating to Win

Fluids like water, fruit juice, or diet soda are excellent snacks before events.

HEALTH IN THE NEWS

Food as a Cure?

A bowl of spaghetti as a cure for depression? Not quite, but researchers at the Massachusetts Institute of Technology and elsewhere have discovered that *pure* forms of certain food substances can be used to treat some disorders of the brain. The carbohydrates in spaghetti, for instance, actually cause the brain to produce more of a chemical that helps the body fight against depression. Researchers hope to apply this discovery to the treatment of other illnesses such as insomnia and bulimia.

TEEN Q & A

Q: What makes me burp?

A: Burping is a way of getting rid of gas in your stomach. When you eat, you sometimes swallow a lot of air. If your stomach begins to feel uncomfortable, it will try to force the air back out through your mouth. Soft drinks that are filled with bubbles make you burp for the same reason. Of course, it is not polite to burp, but try telling that to your stomach!

Eating Disorders

Words to Know
eating disorders
anorexia nervosa
malnutrition
bulimia

This lesson contains a number of valuable facts and tips. Once you have studied them, you will be able to

- discuss the fear that causes common eating problems among teenagers.
- talk about the health risks of serious eating problems such as anorexia nervosa and bulimia.
- tell where a person with eating problems can get help.

Taking Weight Loss to Extremes

In the previous lesson, you read about our nation's concern with being thin. Most Americans want to be slim, and an army of doctors and thousands of diet books are ready to guide them.

Some people, however, get carried away with losing weight and obtaining that ideal figure. This can lead to **eating disorders,** which are *extreme and damaging eating behaviors that can lead to sickness and even death.*

Learning from Photographs
Weight loss is necessary sometimes. What are the rules of healthy weight loss?

Anorexia Nervosa

Life is full of all kinds of pressures and stress. Some people feel the stress more strongly than others. For some, the pressure is too much. They begin to look at things such as dieting in an odd way. These pressures can result in a person becoming overly concerned with being thin. If so, they may lead to an eating disorder known as **anorexia nervosa** (an·uh·REK·see·uh ner·VOH·suh). It is *a severe fear of becoming overweight that often leads to extreme weight loss from self-starvation.*

Anorexia means "without appetite," and *nervosa* means "of a nervous origin." Most of the people who suffer from it are female. Most of them are young women or teenage girls. But men and boys can also have the disorder. Anorexia lowers the level of important hormones. That makes it very dangerous for teens.

Anorexia nervosa is a disorder of both the mind and the body. People with it are so afraid of becoming fat that they do not eat much. This usually results in **malnutrition** (mal·noo·TRISH·uhn). With this condition, *the body does not get the nutrients it needs to grow and function well.* People with anorexia nervosa view themselves as fat, even if they are wasting away from not eating. Many people with the disorder wind up in the hospital. There they are fed nutrients and given counseling. And some die when the condition goes unchecked.

Bulimia

Bulimia (byoo·LIM·ee·uh) is *a condition in which people repeatedly eat large amounts of food and then try to get rid of the food.* Bulimia also grows out of a person's need for control of his or her body. Like anorexia nervosa, bulimia is more common among young women and teenage girls than it is among men or boys.

Many people with bulimia have a desire to be beautiful, to have a perfect shape. After they eat a lot of food, they panic that they are losing control of their bodies. They may force themselves to vomit the food, believing that this will put them back in control. They may also take *laxatives* (LAK·suht·ivs). These medicines make foods speed through the digestive system with little time to release their nutrients. Someone with bulimia may go on a crash diet to make up for overeating. The result of any of these steps is that the person does not get enough nutrients to be healthy.

The behavior of someone with bulimia can do much damage to the body.

- Vomiting and abusing laxatives can lead to serious *dehydration* (dee·hy·DRAY·shuhn), or drying out of the body.

Teen Issue

Anorexia Strikes
About 1 of every 100 women has anorexia nervosa. Nineteen out of 20 people with anorexia are young women.

Learning from Photographs
People who suffer from anorexia see themselves as fat even when they are thin. What kind of help do they need?

Bulimia is more common than anorexia. In some studies, ten percent of the people interviewed had a history of bulimia. Bulimia is more common in males than anorexia is.

Teen **Issue**

How Can You Tell?

How do you know if someone around you has anorexia or bulimia? You don't. You don't have the background or training to know. But if you think you know someone who *might* be suffering from one of these disorders, try to get help for that person. Speak to an adult you can trust.

● The acids from frequent vomiting can damage teeth and injure the mouth and throat.

● Emptying the body of nutrients can cause malnutrition.

● If the starvation continues, it can cause damage to the heart and other organs.

Help for People with Eating Disorders

People with anorexia nervosa and bulimia can rarely cure themselves. This is because they do not have a realistic view of themselves. They need support and understanding, but friends and relatives often find it impossible to get through to them. Eating disorders have deep psychological roots. It usually takes a professional counselor to help.

If you suspect that someone you know is suffering from an eating disorder, you should notify the school nurse, a counselor, or that person's parent. Try to talk the person into getting help, too. Many psychologists are trained to help people with eating disorders. Most towns have clinics and groups such as Overeaters Anonymous that can help people with eating disorders.

People who are treated for eating disorders may need to return to see the doctor again. This step helps make sure that the person does not experience the problem again.

Check Your Understanding

Conclusion Sometimes our society seems to be saying "the thinner the better." This is not only a false statement, but it can be a deadly one. Both anorexia nervosa and bulimia can be cured, but they first must be brought to the attention of a professional counselor.

1. **Vocabulary** From what you have read in this lesson, write your own definitions of *anorexia nervosa* and *bulimia.*

2. **Recall** What are people with anorexia nervosa and bulimia most afraid of?

3. **Recall** What are the health risks of anorexia nervosa and bulimia?

4. **Recall** Where can a person with eating problems get help?

5. **Synthesize** You discover that a friend has been making herself vomit after eating large meals. When you talk to her, she says that everything is under control. What will you do next?

Reading a Nutrition Label

Supermarket shelves are full of hundreds of products. It can be hard to decide which to buy. By learning to read and understand a nutrition label, you can make the right choices for a healthful diet.

What to Look for on a Nutrition Label

Before you decide what product to buy, read its label carefully. Every packaged food is required by law to include certain facts. The package must give the name of the product, the kind of food it is, and the name and address of the company that made it. The label also tells what form the food is in and how much food the package contains.

The nutrition information on the package is very important. It includes a number of facts.

- The serving size and the number of servings per package
- The number of calories in a serving
- The amount of carbohydrate, fat, and protein in one serving
- The percentage of the U.S. RDA for certain key nutrients that a serving provides

Food packages also list the ingredients. These are listed by weight, from highest to lowest.

Using the Skill

Suppose that you are shopping for a breakfast cereal. Study the nutrition label to the right. Then, on a separate sheet of paper, answer the questions that follow.

1. Would this box of cereal be enough to serve a family of four at three breakfasts?

2. How can you double the amount of protein when you eat this cereal?

3. This cereal lists sugar as its second ingredient. Is there more or less sugar than oat bran in it?

4. Look at the list of vitamins and minerals under U.S. RDA. This cereal provides nearly half of the U.S. RDA for which nutrient?

BRIGHT MORNING OATIES

Serving size: 1 cup
Servings per box: 10

	1 cup cereal	With ½ cup skim milk
Calories	110	150
Protein, grams	4	8
Carbohydrates, grams	20	26
Fat, grams	2	2
% of U.S. Recommended Daily Allowances (U.S. RDA)		
Protein	6	15
Vitamin A	25	30
Vitamin C	25	25
Calcium	4	20
Iron	45	45

Ingredients:
Oats, sugar, oat bran, malted barley, vitamin C, artificial coloring.

Note:
This cereal provides 1.3 g of fiber per serving.

5. A serving of whole-grain oats contains 7 grams of fiber and has no sugar. Does *this* cereal provide more or less fiber than the whole-grain oats?

6. Suppose the whole-grain oats provide the same vitamins and minerals as this cereal. Which would you decide to buy, this cereal or a box of whole-grain oats? Explain your decision.

Chapter 5: Meeting Your Nutritional Needs   **147**

Chapter 5 Review

Summary

- Good nutrition helps the body grow, develop, and work properly.
- Food provides six important groups of nutrients that your body needs. To get all those nutrients, you need a balanced diet.
- Your diet needs to be high in fiber while avoiding too much added sugar, fats and cholesterol, and sodium.
- Maintaining weight is a matter of achieving the right balance of wise food choices and exercise.
- Some people suffer from eating disorders. These practices can lead to serious health problems. People with eating disorders need professional help.

Reviewing Vocabulary and Concepts

On a separate sheet of paper, write the numbers 1–12. After each number, write the letter of the word or phrase in Column B that best matches the phrase in Column A.

Column A

Column B

Lesson 1

1. Important nutrients often found in fruits and vegetables
2. Calcium, iron, and potassium
3. Fats, proteins, and carbohydrates
4. Sources like starches, sugars, and fats; give energy
5. Eating healthy foods in the amount the body needs
6. Chart showing how much of each nutrient you need each day

a. minerals
b. carbohydrates
c. protein
d. vitamins
e. fiber
f. four food groups
g. salt
h. healthy snacks
i. nutrients
j. cholesterol
k. RDA
l. balanced diet

Lesson 2

7. Classifies food according to common nutrients
8. An aid to digestion that most people need in greater amounts
9. A kind of fat that can contribute to heart disease
10. A flavoring added to food that can contribute to high blood pressure
11. Low-fat sources of this nutrient are beans, fish, and chicken
12. Examples are yogurt, whole-wheat crackers, and fresh fruit

Write the numbers 13–19 on your paper. After each number, write the letter of the answer that best completes each of the following statements.

Lesson 3

13. Being more than 20 percent above desired weight is called
    a. overweight   b. underweight   c. obesity   d. acceptable

14. A healthy way to lower the number of calories that you eat and thereby to lose weight is to

   a. skip meals

   b. eat low-calorie foods that are also low in nutrient density

   c. cut out protein

   d. eat low-calorie foods that are also high in nutrient density

15. A diet can be created to

   a. lose weight

   b. gain weight

   c. maintain weight

   d. all of these

16. An important part of any weight-control program is

   a. exercise

   b. eliminating caffeine

   c. cutting out carbohydrates

   d. eliminating fat

Lesson 4

17. The eating disorder that involves self-starvation is called

   a. bulimia

   b. anorexia nervosa

   c. obesity

   d. none of these

18. Eating disorders relate to society's overemphasis on

   a. thinness

   b. exercise

   c. protein

   d. sugar

19. People often trained to help others with an eating disorder are

   a. teachers

   b. friends

   c. psychologists

   d. none of these

Thinking Critically About the Facts

Write your answer to the following questions on a separate sheet of paper.

20. Classify Write down the names of the basic food groups plus the "other" group. List each of these foods in the correct group.

   spinach   kidney beans
   roast beef   cake
   candy   a bagel
   yogurt   an egg
   a peach   salad
   spaghetti   skim milk

21. Compare and contrast What are two similarities and two differences between anorexia nervosa and bulimia?

22. Analyze You read an ad that calls for eating grapefruit three times a day, with a slice of bread in the morning, two pieces of cheese at midday, and a cup of tuna with lemon juice at dinner. Is this a healthy diet? Explain your answer.

23. Interpret Answer these questions about the RDA table in the Health Handbook.

   a. Who needs more protein, males between 11 and 14 or between 15 and 18?

   b. Who needs more iron, adult females or adult males?

   c. At what age do the RDA for males and females begin to differ?

   d. Who needs more calcium, teens or adults?

Applying the Facts

24. Make a chart with columns for the four basic food groups. Through a day or weekend, write the foods you eat under the appropriate columns. Use the chart to see whether your diet is balanced.

25. Use the phone book or library to find the names and numbers of groups that help someone with an eating disorder. Call to ask for any information they have. Bring whatever you obtain to class to show.

Your Growth and Development

CHAPTER WARM-UP

Chapter Study Goals

After you have read this chapter, you will be able to

- explain fertilization.
- identify the key factors that influence the health of the developing baby.
- identify the stages of life from birth through adolescence.
- describe how a person changes in puberty.
- list the developmental tasks of a teen.
- identify the changes caused by aging.
- identify the stages of death and grief.

Be on the lookout for information in the chapter that will help you reach these goals.

Getting Started

There are few miracles as great as the one that has led to the person you are at this very moment. That miracle began with a tiny speck of matter—a single cell. And it continues even as you read these words. The miracle is life. In this chapter, read about the stages of life. You will learn about the changes that take place in adolescence and what you can look forward to in the future.

Study Tip

On a sheet of paper, write the chapter study goals. As you read, write the numbers of the pages with information toward reaching each goal.

The Beginning of Life

Words to Know

cells
tissues
organs
systems
fertilization
egg cell
sperm cell
uterus
placenta
umbilical cord
contractions
cervix

This lesson contains a number of valuable facts and tips. Once you have studied them, you will be able to

- define the term *fertilization.*
- tell where the developing baby gets its food and oxygen.
- say how a baby is born.

Growth

Growth is a process that goes on throughout life. Everyone grows at a different rate. However, there are stages of growth that each person goes through.

The Building Blocks of Life

All living things are made of cells, bits of matter so small they can be seen only through a microscope. **Cells** are the *basic units, or building blocks, of life.* We are each made up of billions of cells.

Every cell in your body does a specific job. *Cells that do similar jobs* form **tissues.** Your body is made up of several kinds of tissue. Nerve tissue and muscle tissue are just two of those types.

Like cells, tissues are combined into larger structures. These **organs** are *body parts* such as the brain, the heart, and the lungs. *Groups of organs that work together* are called **systems.** Your body has several systems. The *digestive system* and the *nervous system* are two of them.

A Single Cell

The body begins with a single cell. This cell comes about through a process known as fertilization. **Fertilization** (fert·uhl·uh·ZAY·shuhn) is *the joining together of two special cells, one from each parent.* The *cell from the mother that plays a part in fertilization* is called an **egg cell.** The *cell from the male that joins with the female egg* is called a **sperm cell.** The sperm cell is said to *fertilize* the egg cell. Fertilization takes place inside the female's body.

DID **YOU** KNOW?

Skin
Skin is an organ. In fact, it is your body's largest organ.

More About

For more about the digestive system, nervous system, and other body systems, see Chapter 7.

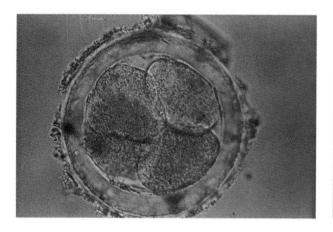
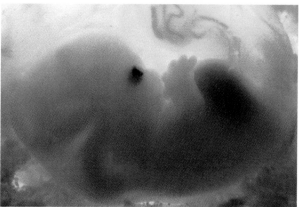

Learning from Photographs
The photo on the left shows a cell shortly after fertilization. The photo on the right shows an embryo in the seventh week of development. What structure do you see to the right of center in the embryo picture?

Growth During Pregnancy

The newly fertilized cell attaches itself to the wall of a *pear-shaped organ inside the mother's body*. This organ is the **uterus** (YOOT·uh·ruhs). Here, in the uterus, the fertilized egg cell divides over and over. This dividing happens millions of times. As time goes on, some cells join to make tissues, organs, and systems. Gradually, the cells become a developing baby. At the end of about nine months, the baby is ready to be born.

The chart "Development Before Birth" on the next page shows how the unborn baby grows over time.

Growth Inside the Uterus

From the start, the developing baby needs food to help it grow. It gets this food from *a thick, rich lining of tissue that builds up along the walls of the uterus and connects the mother to the baby*. This tissue is called the **placenta** (pluh·SENT·uh). The placenta also gives the baby oxygen to breathe. The food and oxygen reach the baby through *a cord that grows out of the placenta*. This tube, called an **umbilical** (uhm·BIL·i·kuhl) **cord,** attaches to what will become the baby's navel. The baby's waste travels through the umbilical cord as well. The waste is carried away in the mother's bloodstream.

Birth

By the ninth month, the now fully developed baby is ready to be born. Birth happens in three stages.

- **Stage one.** The first stage begins with labor pains. These pains are caused by **contractions** (kuhn·TRAK·shuhns), or *sudden tightenings in the muscles of the uterus*. These contractions cause the muscles of the uterus to shorten. This forces the **cervix** (SER·viks), which is the *neck of the uterus*, to open.

DID **YOU** KNOW?

Two of a Kind
Sometimes a newly fertilized egg splits into two complete fertilized eggs, which then copy themselves. When this happens, the result at birth is identical twins. If two eggs are fertilized at the same time, twins are also born. But these *fraternal* (fruh·TERN·uhl) twins are not identical.

Development Before Birth

End of First Month
Length is one-quarter inch (0.6 cm).
Heart, brain, and lungs are forming.
Heart begins to beat.

End of Second Month
Length is 1.5 inches (3.8 cm).
Skin and other organs are developing.
Arms, fingers, legs, and toes are forming.

End of Third Month
Length is 3 inches (7.6 cm).
Weight is 1 ounce (28.3 g).
Baby begins to move around.

End of Fourth Month
Length is 8 to 10 inches (20 to 25 cm).
Weight is 6 ounces (169.8 g).

End of Fifth Month
Length is about 12 inches (30 cm).
Weight is 1 pound (453.6 g).
Eyelashes and nails appear.
Heartbeat can be heard.

End of Sixth Month
Baby develops abilities to kick, cry, and
    maybe even hiccup.
Baby has ability to hear sounds.
Footprint appears.

End of Seventh Month
Weight is 2 to 2.5 pounds (907.2 to 1,134 g).
Arms and legs can move freely.
Eyes open.

End of Eighth Month
Length is 16.5 inches (41.25 cm).
Weight is 4 pounds (1,814.4 g).
Hair gets longer.
Skin becomes smoother.

End of Ninth Month
Length is 18 to 20 inches (45 to 50 cm).
Weight is 7 to 9 pounds (3,175.2 to 4,082.4 g).
Body organs have developed enough to
    work on their own.

- **Stage two.** By the beginning of the second stage, the cervix has opened to a width of about 4 inches (10 cm). Contractions are now quite strong. They push the baby through the cervix and out of the mother.

- **Stage three.** In this final stage of birth, several more contractions of the uterus help push out the placenta. If any part of the placenta remains inside the mother, she could become ill.

DID YOU KNOW?

Who's Got the Button?
Your belly button is where your umbilical cord was attached.

Check Your Understanding

Conclusion Growth is a lifelong process that starts with a single cell. The cell is created by the joining together of one special cell from each parent. The newly formed cell divides over and over, developing finally into a baby.

1. **Vocabulary** What is meant by the word *fertilization*?
2. **Recall** How does the developing baby get its food and oxygen?
3. **Recall** What are the three stages of birth?
4. **Analyze** Why do you suppose a pregnant woman is told to be careful about what she eats and drinks?

Factors in Your Development

Words to Know
heredity
chromosomes
genes
genetic disorder
environment
prenatal care
obstetrician
birth defects
addiction
fetal alcohol
   syndrome
rubella

This lesson contains a number of valuable facts and tips. Once you have studied them, you will be able to

- name two main structures within cells that are involved in heredity.
- name four steps a pregnant woman can take to protect the health of her unborn baby.
- list four causes of birth defects that are from the baby's environment.

The Making of an Individual

Have you ever wondered what makes you *you*? You are a one-of-a-kind person with your own special looks, mannerisms, and personality.

A number of factors shape who each of us is at birth. These factors affect how we look and how healthy we are. The two most important of these factors are *heredity* and *environment*.

Learning from Photographs
Traits such as hair color and hair shape are passed on from parent to child. What other traits do parent and child share?

Do you have a little brother or sister? If you do, you can make a difference in the development of a child. Older brother and sisters are important people in the lives of small children. They are the people in the family that little ones often look up to most. Try, when you can, to teach your brother or sister right from wrong. Help out when they have a problem. Your help will be appreciated by everyone in the family, now *and* later.

. . . .

DID **YOU** KNOW?

Genetic Disorders
Less than 1 percent of all babies born in the United States today suffer from genetic disorders. What's more, some of these disorders, such as cleft palate and clubfoot, can be corrected through surgery.

Heredity

Heredity (huh·RED·uh·tee) is *the passing on of traits from your parents.* The color of your eyes, the shape of your face, and your body build are all controlled by heredity.

Two structures within cells shape your heredity.

- **Chromosomes.** *The tiny structures found within cells that determine the specific type of creature you turn out to be* are **chromosomes** (KROH·muh·sohms). It is because of chromosomes that humans give birth only to other humans, dogs only to other dogs, and so on.
- **Genes.** Inside chromosomes are **genes** (JEENS). They are *tiny bits of matter that control which traits of your parents get passed along to you.* Genes control whether you will have straight or wavy hair, or whether your skin will be dark or light. You get genes from each of your parents.

Heredity and Genetic Disorders

Most of the time the genes that both parents pass on to children will produce a healthy, normal baby. Sometimes, however, the genes carried by one parent or the other will lead to unexpected results. When this happens, the baby may be born with a **genetic** (juh·NET·ik) **disorder.** This is *a disease or condition in which the body does not work normally because of a problem with genes.*

Several hundred thousand babies are born each year with genetic disorders. These disorders can seriously affect their health. Some of these disorders can be seen at birth. Others do not show up until later in life.

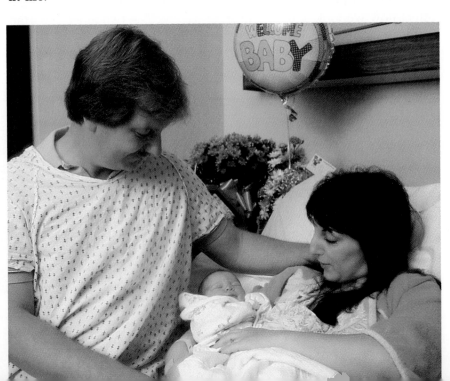

Learning from Photographs
Good prenatal care helps women have healthy babies. What do you think would be five keys to good prenatal care?

The cause of over half of all genetic disorders remains a mystery. But scientists have made many breakthroughs in the past 20 years. Research continues to find ways of preventing and treating many of these disorders.

Environment

The second major factor in the health of the developing baby and the newborn child is *environment.* **Environment** (in·VY·ruhn·muhnt) is *the sum total of a person's surroundings.* The environment of the developing baby is the uterus. The baby's health, then, is affected directly by the actions and total health of the pregnant woman.

Care of the Pregnant Woman

Healthy babies are born of healthy mothers. That is why it is important for a woman to begin a program of *prenatal care* as soon as she finds out that she is pregnant. **Prenatal** (pree·NAYT·uhl) **care** includes *a number of steps taken to provide for the health of a pregnant woman and her unborn baby.* It includes regular visits by the woman to an **obstetrician** (ahb·stuh·TRISH·uhn). This *doctor specializes in the care of a woman and her baby.* The obstetrician will make sure that the pregnant woman stays healthy and that her child is developing as it should.

Good prenatal care also includes...

- eating right.
- getting enough rest.
- getting enough of the proper type of exercise.
- avoiding the use of tobacco, alcohol, and all drugs that have not been allowed by the obstetrician.

When the mother takes good care of her own health, she is giving her baby the best possible start in life.

Birth Defects

When a pregnant woman fails to give her baby good prenatal care, the baby may be born with one or more birth defects. **Birth defects** (DEE·fekts) are *disorders of the developing and newborn baby.* They are present in the baby from birth.

Some of the causes of birth defects are the following.

- **Poor diet.** The baby gets its food from the mother. When a woman fails to eat the right foods during pregnancy, the baby

Drugs and Pregnancy

A pregnant woman should never take *any* drug—including a medicine—without the approval of an obstetrician or her family doctor. Even drugs that seem harmless, such as over-the-counter cold pills, can affect the developing baby. For more on medicines, see Chapter 10.

Teen **Issue**

Teen Pregnancies

Teen pregnancies cause problems for more than just the mother and father of the baby. The baby can have problems, too. Babies born to very young mothers often have a lower than normal weight when born. In general, the younger the mother, the greater the risks to the baby's health.

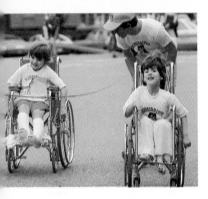

Learning from Photographs
Despite being born with a physical disability, these children lead active and happy lives. What kind of attitude do you think these teens have?

DID **YOU** KNOW?

Inherited Traits
Some of the traits you have may be shown by your mother, some may be shown by your father—and some may be shown by *neither one*. Some traits are carried by a parent's genes, but do not show themselves. If you have blond hair but neither of your parents does, that is probably why.

may be born too early or have a low birth weight. Babies with low birth weight have a greater chance of having mental or physical problems.

- **Certain drugs.** Some drugs taken by the mother during pregnancy may interfere with the development of her baby. Drugs may also cause the baby to be born too early. Certain drugs can lead to an **addiction** (uh·DIK·shuhn), *a physical or mental need for a drug or other substance.* When such substances are taken by a pregnant woman, her baby may be born with an addiction to drugs.

- **Alcohol.** When a pregnant woman drinks alcohol, it enters the baby's body. This can cause **fetal** (FEET·uhl) **alcohol syndrome** (SIN·drohm) in the baby. This is *a group of physical and mental problems caused by the mother-to-be drinking alcohol.* The problems include cleft palate, speech problems, and slow body growth.

- **Smoking.** Babies born to women who smoke usually weigh less than babies of nonsmoking mothers. The baby of a smoker may also form an addiction to *nicotine* (NIK·uh·teen), a drug found in tobacco.

- **Certain infections.** If a mother-to-be has **rubella** (roo·BEL·uh), *the disease called German measles,* her baby may be born deaf. Rubella also causes eye and heart problems and mental retardation. Some sexually transmitted diseases may also pass from the mother to the baby. These can cause such problems as brain damage, blindness, or even death.

Check Your Understanding

Conclusion Heredity and environment are important to the development of the unborn and newborn child. Proper health care of the mother-to-be can help make sure that a healthy baby is born. Sometimes a problem in the baby's genes or environment can lead to a birth defect.

1. **Vocabulary** Which two of the following terms name structures within cells that are involved in heredity? *chromosomes, fetal alcohol syndrome, environment, addiction, genes*

2. **Recall** Name four steps a pregnant woman can take to protect the health of her unborn baby.

3. **Recall** List four environmental causes of birth defects.

4. **Synthesize** What advice might you give a pregnant woman who says that smoking calms her worries over giving birth?

From Childhood to Adolescence

Words to Know
infancy
adolescence
hormones
puberty
developmental tasks

This lesson contains a number of valuable facts and tips. Once you have studied them, you will be able to

- name the stages of development during the growth years.
- name the three types of growth that occur during adolescence.
- tell which developmental tasks you face as an adolescent.

The Growth Years

The period of life from the first years through the teen years is a time of great growth. During these growth years, we learn many skills and form many habits. We also go through many physical, emotional, and social changes.

Researchers have studied these changes, often breaking the growth years down into stages of development. One important view of these stages of growth is that of scientist Erik Erikson. In Erikson's view, all humans go through eight stages in their lifetimes. The first five of these stages cover the period from birth through the teen years.

Infancy

The first year of life is when the fastest physical growth takes place. The weight of the child triples and the height doubles. During **infancy** (IN·fuhn·see), as this *first year of life* is called, trust develops. If a young child's needs are met in a loving way, he or she learns to trust and feel safe. The child sees other people as dependable. If important needs go unmet, children learn to be fearful of people and the world around them.

Early Childhood

Between the ages of one and three, children learn to walk and talk. They also learn how to climb, pull, and push, and how to control the

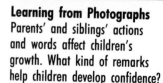

Learning from Photographs
Parents' and siblings' actions and words affect children's growth. What kind of remarks help children develop confidence?

Erikson's Stages of Life

Infancy
(birth to age one)

Developmental task: Trust—a sense that others will be there to help
If not mastered: Mistrust—the sense that one is alone

Early Childhood
(2 to 3 years)

Developmental task: Autonomy—confidence in one's ability
If not mastered: Shame and doubt—a lack of confidence

Middle Childhood
(4 to 5 years)

Developmental task: Initiative—ability to create one's own play
If not mastered: Guilt—feeling about the actions one creates

Late Childhood
(6 to 11 years)

Developmental task: Industry—interest in making things
If not mastered: Inferiority—feeling that one is unable to make things

Adolescence
(12 to 18 years)

Developmental task: Identity—a sense of who one is
If not mastered: Role confusion—being mixed up over the many roles one plays.

Young Adulthood
(19 to 30 years)

Developmental task: Intimacy—forming a strong relationship with another person
If not mastered: Isolation—being alone

Middle Adulthood
(31 to 60 years)

Developmental task: Generativity—helping young people learn
If not mastered: Self-Absorption—being concerned only with one's own needs

Old Age
(61 years to death)

Developmental task: Integrity—feeling satisfied with one's life
If not mastered: Despair—feeling that one's life has not been satisfying

removal of wastes from the body. Children feel proud of their achievements and eager to do more things for and by themselves. Sometimes, a child will fail when trying something new, but that is part of learning and growing.

How adults treat the child helps him or her to grow. If adults accept these failures and permit the child to develop freely, she or he gains self-confidence. Parents may be critical or insist on doing everything for a child. Then the youngster learns to have doubts about his or her abilities.

Childhood

Between the ages of three and five, children are able to begin to play on their own rather than just go along with what they see other children do. They enjoy playing make believe, copying adults. They also begin to ask many questions. Once again, the way adults handle these changes is important. Parents may approve of these new abilities and encourage questions. If so, the child learns to be creative. On the other hand, parents may be impatient with questions, making the child feel that creativity is wrong. Then the child begins to feel guilty about starting up new activities.

Later Childhood

From ages six through eleven, children develop new skills and spend a good deal of time making things. Some children make model airplanes. Others write stories or poems. If the child's creative efforts are appreciated and rewarded, pride in her or his work increases.

Learning from Photographs
Infants depend on parents to survive. Preschool children enjoy making puzzles and building. School-age children spend a lot of time playing with friends. How does success at these things make a difference to children?

Learning from Photographs
Adolescence is a time of great change and growth. Before reading on, can you name one change that takes place in adolescence?

Teen Issue

A Declaration of Teen Independence

Becoming more independent is an important task of adolescence. But trying to gain more independence can also be a source of trouble between a teen and a parent. There is a solution to this problem. It is called *communication*. For more on communication and its role in family and social health, see Chapter 4.

Teen Issue

Your Time Will Come

Some teens have a rough time when everyone around them seems suddenly to be taller and more grown-up looking. Boys may notice other boys their age beginning to have beards. Girls may notice other girls their age beginning to have breasts. If you have been seeing yourself lately as not blending in, stop worrying. Everyone grows at a different rate. You'll catch up—and soon!

Children who are scolded for getting in the way or creating a mess may begin to feel worthless.

A person's success or failure in any of these stages of growth affects his or her development at that stage. However, by succeeding at later stages we can overcome our failures in earlier stages. For example, a small child who lives with very critical adults might feel worthless. But if that same child is praised for his or her drawings in later years, he or she can still develop pride.

Adolescence

Next to infancy, the second fastest period of growth is adolescence. **Adolescence** (ad·uhl·ES·uhns) is *the time of life between childhood and adulthood.* It usually begins somewhere between the ages of 12 and 15. Girls often show the physical changes of adolescence earlier than boys.

Perhaps at the start of this school year you noticed that certain of your classmates had grown much taller over the summer, while others looked the same. You may be aware of some changes in yourself as well. Maybe some new hair has begun to appear on your face or other parts of your body. These changes are all part of a growth spurt that happens during adolescence. They are related to the release of **hormones** (HOR·mohnz), *chemicals produced in the body that cause the body to react in certain ways.* These hormones and the changes they bring about are preparing you for adulthood.

Growth during adolescence takes place in all three of the areas of your health triangle. You grow *physically, mentally,* and *socially.*

Physical Growth

Adolescence begins with **puberty** (PYOO·bert·ee), *the time when you begin to develop certain traits of adults of your sex.* The exact

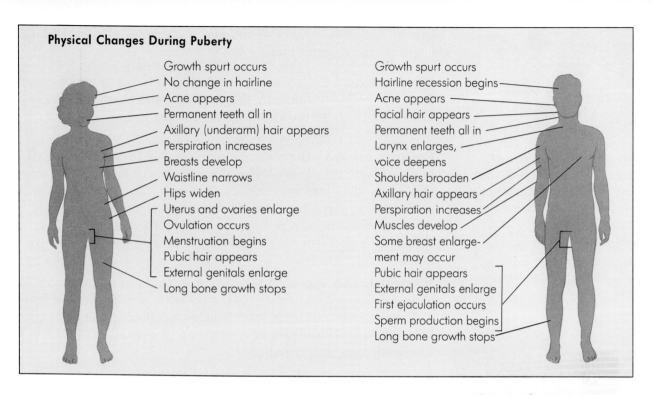

Physical Changes During Puberty

Growth spurt occurs
No change in hairline
Acne appears
Permanent teeth all in
Axillary (underarm) hair appears
Perspiration increases
Breasts develop
Waistline narrows
Hips widen
Uterus and ovaries enlarge
Ovulation occurs
Menstruation begins
Pubic hair appears
External genitals enlarge
Long bone growth stops

Growth spurt occurs
Hairline recession begins
Acne appears
Facial hair appears
Permanent teeth all in
Larynx enlarges, voice deepens
Shoulders broaden
Axillary hair appears
Perspiration increases
Muscles develop
Some breast enlargement may occur
Pubic hair appears
External genitals enlarge
First ejaculation occurs
Sperm production begins
Long bone growth stops

Learning from Drawings
The drawing shows many of the changes that occur in puberty. What brings these changes on?

age at which puberty begins is different in different people. No two people grow in exactly the same way.

During puberty, many changes take place. Boys may find their voices growing deeper. Girls may find that their figures are developing. Some of the other changes are shown in the illustration above.

Physical growth during puberty is rapid but uneven. Your hands and feet may suddenly seem too large for the rest of your body. You may feel awkward. Some young people feel unhappy or self-conscious about their bodies during this stage. These changes, however, are perfectly normal.

Mental Growth

Thinking skills develop during adolescence. As a child, you were able to solve only very basic kinds of problems. You saw most situations in an "either-or" way—as either true or false, good or bad. As an adolescent, you are now able to solve more complex problems. You are able to see *degrees* in situations and understand other points of view. You can now think ahead to what might happen if you act in a certain way, and to understand that you often have choices. When friends dare you to walk into an old boarded-up house, you are able to weigh the consequences of accepting or refusing the dare.

More About
For more about hormones and the many ways in which they affect your mental and emotional health, see Chapter 4.

Here's to Your Health

True, hormones have a lot to say about the sort of person you will grow into. But you have some say over your development as well. How? By practicing healthy habits, such as

- eating the right foods.
- getting enough exercise.
- getting enough rest.

During adolescence, your *emotions,* or feelings, also go through changes. These changes include the following.

- **Mood swings.** Lately, you may be feeling very happy one minute and very moody or unhappy the next. Like the physical changes in your body, these mood swings are related to the release of hormones.

- **Feelings toward others.** You may be seeing family and friends in a new way. People around you are no longer just "givers," as they were when you were a child. You now see these people as having needs, just like yourself. Sometimes you are able to help meet the needs of others. You can listen, for example, when a friend has a problem. Or you can help out with tasks around the house.

- **Interest in the opposite sex.** You may begin to feel a desire to spend time with members of the opposite sex. These new feelings can be confusing, even frightening. Having them, however, is a normal part of growing up. It is healthy to have both male and female friends.

SELF-INVENTORY

Your Developmental Rate

How successful are you at the nine developmental tasks at this point in your life? The following quiz will help you find out. For each statement, write *true* or *false* on a separate sheet of paper.

1. I try to think through problems, looking at all possible solutions.
2. There are several jobs I think I would do well as an adult.
3. I have more adult discussions with my parents or other grown-ups than I used to have.
4. I am able to list my four most important beliefs.
5. I act in a way that goes along with my beliefs.
6. I can describe at least two ways that my life would be different if I were a parent.
7. I am successful most of the time at making male and female friends.
8. I do some things alone or with friends that I used to do with my family.
9. The choices I make promote my overall health and well-being.
10. I know and accept my physical strengths and weaknesses.
11. I listen to other people's ideas even when they are different from mine.
12. I am concerned about local and national problems in the news today.
13. I have one or two close friends whom I can talk to about almost anything.
14. I have an idea of what kind of man or woman I want to be as an adult.

Look at all the statements for which you wrote *false.* Find the developmental task on page 165 that each one relates to. Which tasks do you need to work on?

Social Growth

During adolescence your friends and their views become more important than ever. You begin looking, often without knowing it, for an answer to the question, "Who am I?" This search for yourself is one of many **developmental** (di·vel·uhp·MENT·uhl) **tasks** that you take on in adolescence. These tasks are *things that need to happen in order for you to continue growing toward becoming a healthy, mature adult*. These tasks are shown in the following box.

Learning from Photographs
What developmental task do you think is being shown here?

Developmental Tasks of Adolescence

- Accept your body and its characteristics.
- Become more independent of parents and other adults for your emotional health.
- Gain a *masculine* (MAS·kyuh·luhn) or *feminine* (FEM·uh·nuhn) view of yourself.
- Form more mature relationships with people of both sexes.
- Learn more about who you are.
- Develop a set of your own values.
- Get ready for marriage and family life as an adult.
- Learn how to solve problems in an adult way.
- Develop an interest in and a concern for your community.

The choices you make over the next few years will affect your success in these tasks. But you will grow throughout your life. The choices that you make shape how healthy that growth will be.

Check Your Understanding

Conclusion Early childhood through adolescence is a time of growth. During adolescence, you change physically, mentally, and socially. How you respond to the challenges of growing will affect your success in adulthood.

1. **Vocabulary** Which of the following is not a period of growth? *adolescence, hormone, puberty*
2. **Recall** List the four stages of development during the growth years.
3. **Recall** Name the three types of growth that occur during adolescence.
4. **Analyze** Which of the developmental tasks would seem to be the most difficult one? Explain your opinion.

Health Minute

Truth About Consequences
On a sheet of paper, write down at least four goals and plans that you have for the next two months. The possibilities can include getting accepted to a club, attending a rock concert, or being able to buy a sweater you have had your eye on. Next to each goal or plan, describe how it would change or be affected if you were (1) married, (2) pregnant, or a father-to-be, or (3) a parent.

Teen Health
BULLETIN BOARD

Q: Can one twin really tell what the other is thinking?

A: No one knows for sure. Researchers are studying identical twins to find answers to the ways in which twins develop and relate to each other. One set of identical male twins that was studied had been separated at birth. Neither twin knew about the other until they were reunited at the age of 39. Here's what researchers found out.

- In school both had disliked math and spelling.
- Both of their first wives were named Linda.
- Both had remarried and their second wives' names were the same.
- Both had a son named James Allen (one spelled Alan).
- Both had gained weight at the same age and had had the same kind of surgery.
- Both had a white seat around a tree in his yard.

CAREERS

Wanted:
Obstetrician/Gynecologist (OB/GYN)

Specifics:
OB provides care for pregnant women. GYN provides health maintenance care for females and treats diseases of the reproductive system.

Qualifications:
Like other physicians, OB/GYN should have good interpersonal skills. Stamina is also needed because an OB/GYN must work long and unpredictable hours.

Preparation:
In addition to medical degree, four years of postdoctoral training, plus one year of clinical practice, teaching, or research to be certified.

Contact:
American Board of Obstetricians
100 Meadow Road
Buffalo, NY 14216

HEALTH IN THE NEWS

America Is Getting Gray

America is getting older. In fact, it is becoming gray. Older people are now beginning to outnumber younger people in our population. People who study changes in population have projected that by the late 1990s, people aged 40 to 64 will outnumber those aged 20 to 39. Already, by the mid-1960s, the over-65 people far outnumbered children under 5. In the mid-1980s, the number of older people shot way ahead of the number of teenagers in our population. Part of the reason for this change is that people are living longer. More than a hundred years ago only 30 percent of babies could expect to live to age 60. Today, 83 percent will live that long. The average life span in the United States is now 73 years.

Lifestyle
Reaching Out to the Elderly

Have you ever volunteered to visit an elderly person who is shut in? Or maybe you have worked in a senior citizen center. A family in Boston went further than that. They adopted a woman of 87. Each week the whole family visits her. They talk and laugh with her. They take her shopping. They drive her to the beauty parlor. She has become a part of their family. Helping the elderly is not just a way of doing a good deed. It is a rewarding experience. There are many places that will help you get in touch with seniors who might need your help. The Little Brothers—Friends of the Elderly is one such agency. Nursing homes in your community have many older people who need someone to visit them. And you might even have a neighbor who would welcome your company and help.

HEALTH IN THE NEWS

Retirement Doesn't Mean Not Working

You may know an older person who has retired but would still like to contribute his or her skills and business experience to the workplace. SCORE has found a way. Through the Service Corps of Retired Executives, some 12,000 volunteers give free advice and direction to small businesses just starting out. For instance, a retired marketing director in North Carolina helped a young woman open a cake-decorating shop. She had good ideas and an excellent product, but she didn't know about pricing and advertising. He showed her how to do a marketing survey, and her business began to flourish. SCORE is sponsored by the government's Small Business Administration and has 480 chapters around the nation. If you know anyone who would like to know more about SCORE, you can check your telephone book under "SCORE" or "Small Business Administration."

Retired executives from SCORE give advice to owners of small businesses.

Adulthood and Aging

Words to Know
chronological age
biological age
social age
dementia
Alzheimer's disease

This lesson contains a number of valuable facts and tips. Once you have studied them, you will be able to

- name the stages of adulthood.
- list some physical and mental changes that take place as a person gets older.
- pinpoint the basic needs of older people.

DID YOU KNOW?

Life Span
One hundred and fifty years ago, less than a third of all babies born could be expected to live to age 60.

From Adolescence On

Adolescence prepares you to become a young adult able to be independent and responsible for yourself. As you look to the future, you may think of adulthood as the time when growth finally ends. Adulthood, however, is just a beginning. This is even more true now that humans are living longer than ever before. Today, 83 percent of all people are expected to reach the age of 60. The average life span is 73, and it is getting longer all the time.

Learning from Photographs
If this girl leads a healthy life, what is her possible life span?

The Adult Years

Like the early years of life, the adult years—the period from our twenties on—are made up of stages.

The Stages of Adulthood

- **Early adulthood.** In their twenties, most people strongly feel the need to share their lives with another person. For many, that need is met by marrying and beginning one's own family. The twenties is also a time when most people begin a career.
- **Middle adulthood.** Advancing in their jobs is a key goal for many people in their thirties, forties, and fifties. People in their middle adult years often gain satisfaction from helping young people. Doing so adds to their feelings of self-worth. Raising one's own children is a common way many people get this satisfaction.
- **Late adulthood.** People in their mid-sixties and beyond often look forward to retirement. They also look backward on their lives as a whole. If they can feel they have made a contribution, they enter these years feeling content and at peace.

While this is the pattern most people in our society follow, not everyone does. Some people choose to marry later on. Some never marry at all. Some begin new careers well into their middle adult years. Others choose not to retire. Each person must do what is best for him or her. It is only then that that person can feel the sense of well-being that comes from living a full and healthy life.

Age

You have heard the expression, "Act your age." You may also have heard certain people described as "looking younger than their years." Actually, age is measured in three different ways.

- **Chronological age.** *Age measured in years* is called **chronological** (krahn·uhl·AHJ·i·kuhl) **age.** This is the number of your most recent birthday.
- **Biological age.** *How well various body parts are working* determines your **biological** (by·uh·LAHJ·i·kuhl) **age.** This age is affected by heredity and by your health habits, exercise, and diet.
- **Social age.** *A person's lifestyle* is his or her **social age.** Social age has to do with the things that society expects you to do at a particular point in life. As a teen, you are expected to be in school learning. Later, you will be expected to be working.

Lesson 4: Adulthood and Aging   **169**

Teen Issue

There Is No Time Like the Present

The teens years are a time to enjoy. There is no reason, however, why you can't enjoy yourself *and* prepare for the future. Remember, your decisions now will affect the person you become as an adult. You can invest in your future by thinking maturely when you are faced with tough choices.

Learning from Photographs
This teen and his father are preparing for a fishing trip. What stage of adulthood is this man probably in? Why do you think so?

Learning from Photographs
These runners are all using exercise to stay fit. What is the effect on your future of building healthy habits today?

*T*een *I*ssue

Charity Begins at Home
If you are looking to get involved in helping senior citizens but don't know where to turn in your community, think *family* first, and not just grandparents. Are there older people in your family such as aunts and uncles who could use some company?

DID **YOU** KNOW?

Life Begins at 65
Many companies that used to force their employees to retire at 65 have raised the age. And not a minute too soon! Many senior citizens have plenty of energy *plus* the experience and wisdom that come with growing older.

Physical Aging

When you think of aging, you may think of wrinkled skin and white or gray hair. Actually, physical aging begins when we are still in our twenties. Starting in this period and going on through later adulthood, the body cells divide and replace themselves more slowly. Other signs of aging include

- a slow weakening of the five senses.
- a slow loss of calcium in the bones, which causes them to become more brittle.
- a stiffening of the joints and weakening of the muscles.

Although aging is a part of life, the signs differ from person to person. The signs also have much to do with a person's lifestyle. A person who makes healthy choices in diet, rest, and exercise throughout life may show fewer signs of aging.

Mental Aging

Mental aging also depends on the person. Many people have active and alert minds well into old age.

Some, however, suffer from **dementia** (di·MEN·chuh). This *disease interferes with the normal working of the mind*. Dementia is often caused by a series of small strokes, which damage the brain. The disorder often touches people in their sixties or seventies. Victims lose memory and may be unable to carry on their usual activities.

Another *form of mental slowdown is* **Alzheimer's** (AHLTS·hy·merz) **disease.** This problem may strike people in their forties and fifties, but most victims are over 65. People with Alzheimer's lose their memories over a period of time. They may also lose the power of speech and control of body movement. The cause of Alzheimer's disease is not yet known, though some researchers believe it is linked to heredity.

Meeting the Needs of the Elderly

Older people have the same emotional needs that younger people have. These include the need to love and be loved, to feel worthwhile, and to feel they are making a contribution.

A number of factors can help to make old age a rewarding, productive stage of life.

- **Having dealt with changes effectively throughout life.** People who learn early in life to accept change often have less difficulty accepting the changes that are part of growing old.

- **Maintaining contact with family and close friends.** Older people who have their loved ones close by tend to adjust much better than those who live alone.

- **Getting involved with younger people.** Some communities keep their older people involved through programs like Adopt a Grandparent. Such programs keep the elderly active and, at the same time, make them feel useful and needed.

Learning from Photographs
Older people still have the need to stay active and involved. What can you do to help an elderly person lead a happy, active life?

Check Your Understanding

Conclusion Adolescence prepares you for the responsibilities and challenges of adulthood. Good health habits and an active lifestyle can help lessen the effects of aging. There are steps we can all take to help the elderly use their skills and energies to serve themselves and society.

1. **Vocabulary** What are the differences between *chronological age, biological age,* and *social age*?

2. **Recall** Name the three stages of adulthood.

3. **Recall** Identify two physical changes that take place as a person gets older.

4. **Recall** What three basic emotional needs of people are shared by the elderly?

5. **Synthesize** What possible benefits await young people who take part in the Adopt a Grandparent program?

Words to Know
clinical death
brain death
grief
coping strategies

Facing Death and Grief

This lesson contains a number of valuable facts and tips. Once you have studied them, you will be able to

- give two definitions of *death*.
- list the five stages of dying.
- name the five stages of grieving.

The End of Life

Of all the creatures on earth, humans alone go through life knowing that someday they will die. This is not a fact that healthy people spend a great deal of time thinking about. Yet, healthy people learn to accept the reality of death as a natural part of the cycle of life. Learning to face this reality becomes a little easier when we better understand the nature of death.

Two Meanings of Death

There is no single clear definition of death. In **clinical** (KLIN·i·kuhl) **death,** *a person's body systems shut down.* Sometimes people who are declared clinically dead can be brought back to life. This is the case when a person who dies on the operating table is saved through the efforts of doctors. Another case is when a drowning victim is revived with CPR.

Brain death occurs when *oxygen is cut off from all of the brain cells.* If the damage is not too great, the person who is brain dead can be kept alive with machines. The part of the brain that controls the heart and lungs may die. If so, there is no chance for the brain to recover its ability to work.

Accepting Death

For some people the end of life comes peacefully, while they are asleep. For others, death comes after a long struggle with a disease or illness. For still others, it is sudden and unexpected.

More About
For more about CPR and its role in saving lives, see Chapter 13 and the Health Handbook.

More About
*For more on the parts of the body that each section of the **brain** controls, see Chapter 7.*

Elisabeth Kübler-Ross, a noted doctor, has studied the experiences of dying people and their families. She identified five stages that people go through in facing death. These stages are not the same for all people. Rather, they are general guidelines we can use to understand how people experience dying.

The Stages of Dying

- **Stage 1: Denial.** Many dying people refuse to accept that they are dying. They tell themselves that "it is all a mistake" and hope they will awaken from this "nightmare."

- **Stage 2: Anger.** The dying person begins angrily to ask, "Why me?" The anger may be directed at anyone close by— at friends and family, doctors and nurses.

- **Stage 3: Bargaining.** The dying person looks for ways to prolong life. Some patients begin to hope for a medical miracle. Many turn to prayer, promising to become a better person if spared.

- **Stage 4: Depression.** The anger and bitterness are gone. The dying person realizes that he or she will not live to keep certain promises or meet certain goals. Deep sadness sets in.

- **Stage 5: Acceptance.** The dying person finally accepts the reality of death. He or she makes peace with the world.

The family of a dying person often finds a great strength and comfort in the dying person's acceptance of death. In this way, the dying sometimes teach the living about life.

As a teen, you can understand death. Children do not see death as final, but adolescents do. Because you now understand death, the death of someone close to you may hurt even more. Knowing how to grieve can help you handle that hurt.

The Grief Process

The death of someone we care deeply about brings out many different feelings. The *sum total of feelings caused by the death of a loved one* is known as **grief.**

Some experts have observed that grief has several stages similar to Kübler-Ross's stages of dying. As with dying, grief reactions vary from person to person. But five reactions are common.

- **Shock.** Shortly after the death of a loved one, people tend to feel separated from their emotions. They are often numb. If they have any feeling at all, it is an emptiness.

Learning from Photographs
Sometimes someone who is dying can comfort the people who will survive. Which stage of dying is such a person probably in?

Learning from Photographs
People follow rituals such as funerals to handle the sense of loss that death brings on. How might it be healthy to go to a funeral?

Teen Issue

Shedding a Tear
Some people think that if they haven't cried over a death or loss, they haven't been hurt by it. That isn't true. Grieving can take many forms. When you or someone you know suffers a loss, the important thing is to let the feelings come. It is only when the hurt has a chance to be expressed that healing can begin.

- **Anger.** Sometimes, the survivors will feel anger. This anger may even be directed at the dead person for having died.
- **Yearning.** The survivors ache. The loss of the loved one has left a great emptiness in their lives. They wish that the loved one could come back, if just for a moment.
- **Depression.** The survivors accept the reality of their loss. The person who has died will not be coming back.
- **Moving on.** The survivors are able to go forward with their lives. They have not forgotten the one who died, but the deep pain over the loss has lessened.

Dealing with the Death of a Loved One

Everyone, at one time or another, loses a loved one to death. Regardless of whether the one to die is a friend, a relative, or a pet, the death of someone close can be terribly painful.

Mental health experts have come up with a number of **coping strategies.** These are *ways of dealing with the sense of loss people feel at the death of someone close.* They include the following.

- **Remember good things about the person.** Focusing on happy times and on ways in which the person was special can help ease the pain.
- **Don't run away from your feelings.** The hurt from the loss is there and cannot be denied. It is best to let the feelings out.
- **Share your feelings with others.** If nothing else, telling someone about the hurt you are feeling will remind you that you are not alone.

Check Your Understanding

Conclusion   Death is loss. The dying person and grieving person each go through several stages as they learn to accept death. Talking about death and expressing your feelings about it can help you accept it as a natural part of the life cycle.

1. **Vocabulary** Write two definitions of death.
2. **Recall** Identify the five stages in dying.
3. **Recall** List the five stages of grieving.
4. **Synthesize** How might you help a younger brother or sister whose pet hamster has died?

Helping Another Person Cope with Loss

Have you ever had a serious disappointment or lost something that meant a lot to you? Maybe you lost a favorite ring. Perhaps you lost the friendship of someone close after the two of you had a big argument. You may have felt very sad when a good friend moved away. Possibly you were depressed because you did not make the basketball team. If you have had such an experience, do you remember how you felt?

The feelings people have after a loss or disappointment are often similar to grief. When someone you care about suffers a loss, you can do some things to help that person cope.

How You Can Help

There are three main ways to help a friend in need.

- **Let the person set the speed of recovery.** Everyone handles these feelings differently. Some people get over losses quickly. Others do not.
- **Let the person decide how you can be the most helpful.** Some people simply need to feel the presence of someone close. Don't insist on talking or giving the person advice when he or she just wants to sit quietly.
- **Respect the person's right to feel sad.** Don't tell the person she or he is wrong or silly to feel bad or that the loss isn't important. To her or him, the loss may be *very* important. The best help is to deal with the grief, not to pretend it will go away.

Using the Skill

Read the statements from teens below. Then, on a separate sheet of paper, answer the questions that follow.

Case One

Stan: "Ted's girlfriend broke up with him over a week ago. And he's still not totally over it. Can you believe it? Maybe I should go have a talk with him. He needs to snap out of it."

Case Two

Curtis: "Wayne's dog died, and he's acting like it's the end of the world. I don't get Wayne. It was only a dog, after all. Don't you think somebody should tell him?"

Case Three

Denise: "I feel bad for Felicia. She didn't get a part in the Christmas program after working so hard. I'm going to go and see if there's anything I can do — anything she needs."

Case Four

Patty: "I heard that Trish lost the watch she had gotten for her birthday. What she needs now is somebody to help her snap out of it. I'm going to go joke with her, to get her mind off it. If that doesn't work, I have some great ideas about what she should do next."

1. Which of the speakers seem not to understand that
   a. people who have suffered a loss need to recover at their own speed?
   b. people who have suffered a loss should be the ones to decide how others can be of help?
   c. people who have suffered a loss have a right to feel as they do?
2. Which of the speakers have made a healthy choice? Which have not? Explain your answers.

Chapter 6 Review

Summary

- Heredity and environment affect the development of the unborn child. Proper health care in the mother-to-be helps the unborn child grow in a healthy way.
- The period from birth through adolescence is one of great growth. Your success with the developmental tasks of adolescence will affect your life as an adult.
- Practicing good health habits during adulthood can lessen the effects of aging. Older people can use their skills and energies to make the most of their later years.
- Dying people and their loved ones go through five stages as death approaches. Grieving people go through five similar stages in learning to accept the death of a loved one.

Reviewing Vocabulary and Concepts

Number a separate sheet of paper from 1–11. After each number, write the letter of the word or phrase in Column B that best matches the phrase in Column A.

Column A

Lesson 1

1. Groups of cells that do similar kinds of jobs
2. The joining together of a sperm cell from the father and an egg cell from the mother
3. A rich lining of tissue along the wall of the uterus that provides nourishment to the developing baby
4. A tube through which nourishment and oxygen reach the developing baby

Lesson 2

5. Tiny bits of matter that control exactly which traits of your parents get passed along to you
6. One of two factors that influence the health of the unborn and newborn baby
7. Care that a pregnant woman should take to help ensure the health of her unborn baby

Lesson 3

8. The time of life between childhood and adulthood
9. Chemicals produced in the body that are responsible for rapid growth
10. The time when you begin to develop traits of adults of your sex
11. A developmental task you face in adolescence

Column B

a. umbilical cord
b. hormones
c. genes
d. prenatal care
e. adolescence
f. tissues
g. environment
h. learning who you are
i. placenta
j. fertilization
k. puberty

Write the numbers 12–17 on your paper. After each number, write the letter of the answer that best completes each statement.

Lesson 4

12. The time of life when most people strongly feel the need to share their lives with another person and begin a career is
    a. middle adulthood
    b. early adulthood
    c. puberty
    d. late adulthood

13. A gradual weakening of the five senses is one of several signs of
    a. mental aging
    b. middle adulthood
    c. social age
    d. physical aging

14. Keeping up contacts with friends and family is one way elderly people can
    a. pay their bills
    b. complain when they need to
    c. meet new people
    d. meet their emotional needs

Lesson 5

15. The term used to describe what happens when a person's body systems shut down is
    a. clinical death
    b. brain death
    c. biological aging
    d. denial

16. The stages in the acceptance of death include all of the following except
    a. denial
    b. anger
    c. clinical death
    d. acceptance

17. Remembering good things about a person who has died is one of several
    a. forms of depression
    b. types of aging
    c. coping strategies
    d. none of these

Thinking Critically About the Facts

Write your answers to the following questions on a separate sheet of paper.

18. **Summarize** In which of the three stages of the birth process does the mother first have contractions? In which stage does the cervix open to a width of about 4 inches (10 cm)?

19. **Synthesize** What factor in the development of a human being accounts for the person's having red hair and blue eyes?

20. **Classify** Troy just turned 13. He feels proud of how his body is becoming more muscular. His character seems to be changing, too. Every day Troy feels that he learns something new about himself. He has grown interested in talking to some of the girls in his class. Last month, he joined the community health center as a volunteer. What developmental tasks is Troy working on?

21. **Summarize** What are some of the changes that take place in a person due to physical aging? What can a person do to slow down the aging process?

Applying the Facts

22. Create a poster titled "The Tasks Ahead" using pictures and articles from magazines and newspapers that show teens successfully meeting the developmental tasks of adolescence. Include a sentence describing each picture.

23. Interview a senior citizen in your community who appears to be in very good health. Ask this individual how eating habits and exercise helped him or her live a long and healthy life. Report your findings to your class.

177

Wellness and Your Body Systems

CHAPTER WARM-UP

Study Goals

After reading this chapter, you will be able to

- name the nine major body systems and explain the function of each.
- describe the parts and tasks of the nine major body systems.
- explain how to care for the nine major body systems.
- identify problems that affect the nine major body systems and explain how they are treated.

Be on the lookout for information in the chapter that will help you reach these goals.

Getting Started

New technology has shown us new ways of looking at the body. The pictures they provide are marvelous. But even more of a marvel is the body itself. Your brain stores memories of events that happened when you were 2 or 3. Your heart beats about 100,000 times a day. The other systems of the body do equally wonderful things. In this chapter, you will see how each system works.

Study Tip

As you read this chapter, use the drawings to learn the how the parts work together.

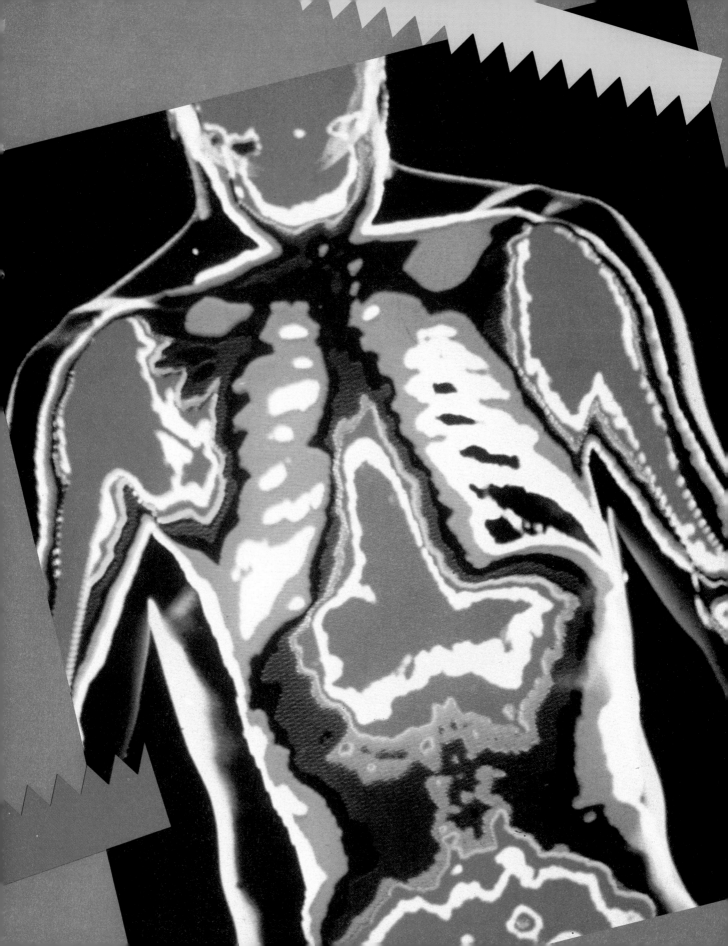

Your Nervous System

Words to Know

nervous system

central nervous system (CNS)

peripheral nervous system (PNS)

neurons

spinal cord

brain

stroke

pinched nerve

polio

rabies

epilepsy

cerebral palsy

multiple sclerosis (MS)

This lesson contains a number of valuable facts and tips. Once you have studied them, you will be able to

- name the parts of the nervous system.
- tell what each part of the nervous system does.
- tell how to care for your nervous system.
- list some problems that affect the nervous system.

The Control Center

What happens when you sit down to eat a hamburger? Your eyes — and your nose — tell you that food is on your plate. Your hands reach for the burger. They lift it to your mouth, which opens at just the right time. Your hands put the burger in your mouth, which takes a bite. As you begin chewing, your teeth and saliva begin to digest the food.

All these actions are the result of messages sent to and from your brain. You are aware of some of these messages, but others happen without your even thinking about them. All these messages are handled by your **nervous system.** This is *the group of body parts that makes and sends the commands that control all your actions.*

Parts of the Nervous System

The nervous system is divided into two main sections.

- **The central nervous system (CNS).** This includes the brain and the spinal cord. It is the body's main control center.
- **The peripheral nervous system (PNS).** This includes the nerves that connect the CNS to all parts of the body. It carries messages to and from the CNS.

Both parts of the nervous system are made up of *special nerve cells* called **neurons** (NOO·rahns). Neurons are not like other cells in your body. They cannot repair or replace themselves. Once damaged, these cells no longer work.

Teen Issue

Caring for Your Neurons
The fact that neurons cannot replace themselves makes caring for them very important. Accidents, disease, and drugs can all damage neurons. And the damage is permanent. You can protect neurons by staying away from the things that hurt them.

Neurons Do the Work

Neurons are more sensitive than other cells. They respond to small electrical charges. Each of these charges is like a message, which the neuron then sends on to another neuron. Neurons work very quickly. They send their messages as fast as 248 miles an hour.

Your body has three kinds of neurons to do this work. They are shown in the illustration "How Neurons Work" on the next page. The caption explains how they work.

Even as simple an action as patting a cat's fur requires the work of many neurons. Yet the action takes place in a few seconds.

DID **YOU** KNOW?

Your Nerves
Nearly 45 miles of nerves run through your body. They receive and send the signals that control all your body's movements and processes.

The Nervous System

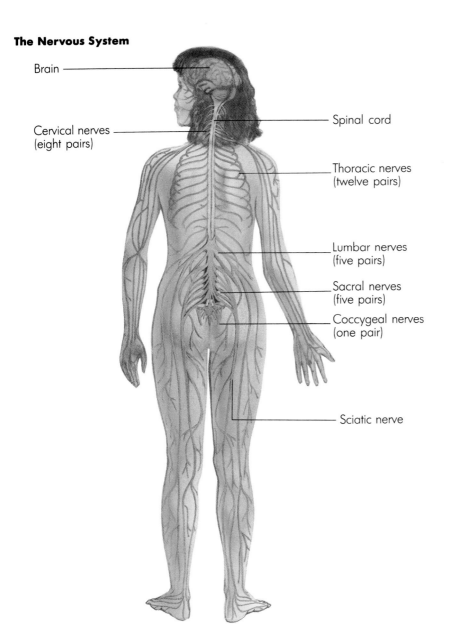

Brain

Cervical nerves (eight pairs)

Spinal cord

Thoracic nerves (twelve pairs)

Lumbar nerves (five pairs)

Sacral nerves (five pairs)

Coccygeal nerves (one pair)

Sciatic nerve

Health Minute

Are You Ticklish?
With a feather, tickle the palm of your hand or bare foot. Where you are ticklish, you have nerve endings.

Learning from Drawings
Branching out from the spinal cord are 31 pairs of nerves that reach the trunk of the body. Other nerves reach down the arms and legs. What organ controls these nerves?

Learning from Drawings

When you touch a cat, a receptor (ri-SEP-ter) at the end of a *sensory* (SENS-ree) *neuron* feels something. It passes the information to a *connecting neuron* in the brain, which decides to stroke the cat's fur. The connecting neuron sends this message to a *motor neuron,* which tells the muscle to move. What kind of messages are passed along?

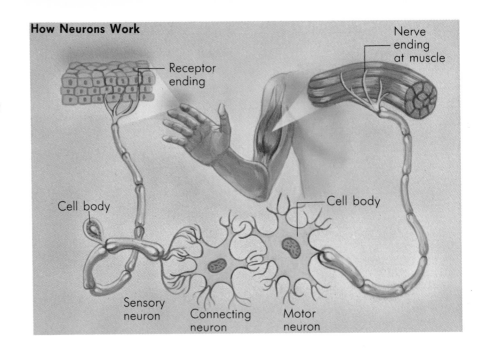

How Neurons Work

Receptor ending

Nerve ending at muscle

Cell body

Cell body

Sensory neuron

Connecting neuron

Motor neuron

DID **YOU** KNOW?

The CNS at Work

The CNS not only tells the muscles what to do. It continues to receive messages to make sure that the action was done correctly. If not, it sends another order to make the movement right.

Posture and Your Spine

Good posture is good for your nervous system. It can prevent problems with your spinal cord. For more on good posture, see Chapter 2.

The Central Nervous System

The **central nervous system (CNS)** is the key to your body's actions. The CNS is *the control center of your body. It tells all body parts what to do.* Its two main parts are the *spinal cord* and the *brain.*

The Spinal Cord. The **spinal** (SPYN·uhl) **cord** is a long stalk that runs nearly the whole length of your back. It *carries messages from the body to the brain and from the brain to the body.* This bundle of nerves sits inside the backbone, which protects it.

The Brain. *The organ that commands all your body's actions and allows you to think* is the **brain.** The brain is a grayish-pink ball that weighs about 3 pounds. All your brain cells are present when you are born. They simply grow larger as you get older.

The brain is covered by blood vessels, which carry the food and oxygen the brain needs to work. Like the spinal cord, the brain sits in a wash of fluids that protect it from damage. The brain and the fluids are encased in bone.

The brain has three main parts, each with many jobs. The *cerebrum* (suh·REE·bruhm) controls the five senses; senses pain, heat, and cold; controls the movement of muscles; and controls thinking and speech. The *cerebellum* (ser·uh·BEL·uhm) controls balance, posture and coordination. The *brain stem* controls such body actions as breathing, the heartbeat, and digestion.

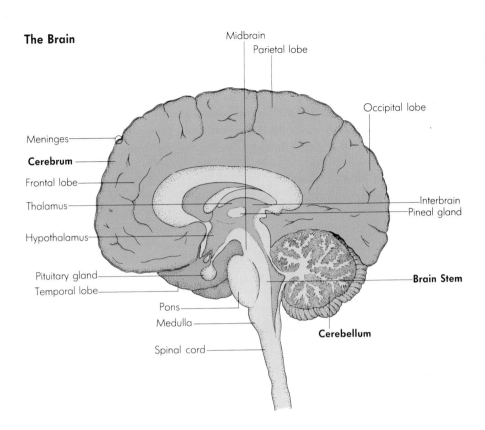

The Brain

Midbrain
Parietal lobe
Occipital lobe
Meninges
Cerebrum
Frontal lobe
Thalamus
Interbrain
Pineal gland
Hypothalamus
Pituitary gland
Temporal lobe
Brain Stem
Pons
Medulla
Cerebellum
Spinal cord

Learning from Drawings
The brain is divided into four sections called *lobes*. The three main parts are the cerebrum, the cerebellum, and the brain stem. It includes: the *thalamus* (THAL-uh-muhs), *hypothalamus* (hy-poh-THAL-uh-muhs), the *pituitary* (puh-TOO-uh-tehr-ee) gland, and the *pineal* (PI-nee-uhl) gland. What part of the nervous system connects to the brain?

The Peripheral Nervous System

The brain would not be able to control your body if you did not have a **peripheral** (puh·RIF·uh·ruhl) **nervous system (PNS).** This *system is made up of many nerves that connect your CNS to all parts of your body.* Some of them take messages to and from your muscles. Others take messages to and from your body organs.

Most of these nerves connect to the CNS through the spinal cord. Some connect directly to the brain.

Caring for Your Nervous System

Because nerve cells cannot replace themselves, damage to them is permanent. As a result, it is very important to protect your nervous system. You can do this by making good health choices and by acting safely.

Making Healthy Choices

There are three main kinds of choices that will protect your nervous system. The first is to get plenty of rest. The nervous system needs sleep.

DID **YOU** KNOW?

Taking Sides
The brain is divided into two halves, or *hemispheres* (HEM·uh·sfirs). The right side of the brain controls the left side of your body. The left side of the brain controls the right side of your body. For right-handed people, the left side of the brain is strongest.

Got a Headache?
Many headaches are caused by tension. You could take medicine for a headache. Safe choices include products that have *acetaminophin* (uh·SEET·uh·MIN·uh·fuhn). Or you could try relaxing.

More About

Chapter 10 has advice on how to stay away from **drugs.**

The second is to take good care of your circulatory system. High blood pressure raises the chance of having a **stroke.** This *occurs when the blood supply to part of the brain is cut off.* Strokes damage brain cells, making them unable to do their jobs. Someone who has a stroke may become unable to speak or move part of the body afterward. The person may learn to speak or move again by training another part of the brain to do the job. The chances of having a stroke can be lowered by eating the right foods and by exercising.

The last way to help your nervous system is to stay away from drugs. Drugs, including alcohol, can damage or destroy brain cells, and the damage cannot be undone.

Avoiding Injuries

Injuries are the most common cause of damage to the nervous system. Blows to the head can damage the brain. Other injuries can result in a **pinched nerve.** This *happens when one part of the spine becomes displaced after a sudden movement or blow.* Pinched nerves are painful.

More About

For more on **staying safe,** *see Chapter 13.*

These injuries result from accidents. You can prevent them from happening by acting safely.

Preventing Head Injuries

- **Wear a helmet.** When you are bicycling, skateboarding, or playing a contact sport, always wear a helmet.
- **Wear a safety belt.** Whenever you are in a car, fasten your seat belt.
- **Obey all traffic safety rules.** Whether you are on a bike or in a car, obey all traffic laws.
- **Lift objects properly.** Bend your knees when you lift heavy objects, and do not lift more than you can carry.
- **Avoid head blows.** Stay away from situations where you could get a blow to the head.

Problems of the Nervous System

Some diseases and disorders can affect your nervous system. You can prevent some of them. Others cannot be prevented, but people who have them can often be helped with therapy.

Infections

When germs enter your body, they can cause an *infection* (in·FEK·shuhn). Some infections damage the nervous system.

Teen Issue

Boxing Your Brains Out

Boxing can cause brain damage. Some boxers have had blood vessels in their brain explode. Even if that doesn't happen, boxers may suffer long-term damage from the frequent blows to the head. The results can be slurred speech, loss of memory, and clumsiness.

Learning from Photographs
While people have fun with pets, a problem can occur if a pet bites a person. If the animal has rabies, the person could get sick. What should someone who is bitten by a pet do?

Polio (POH·lee·oh) is *a serious disease that can make the victim unable to move the legs.* The polio germ may also attack the nerves that control breathing. Polio was once a common deadly disease. Luckily, we now have a *vaccine* (vak·SEEN) that can prevent polio. You were probably given this vaccine when you were younger.

Rabies (RAY·bees) is *a disease that enters the nervous system from a bite by an infected animal.* Rabies is serious. It can choke the victim or make him or her unable to breathe. Someone who is bitten by an animal with rabies can be helped with a series of shots. Wild animals like squirrels and raccoons can carry rabies. So can some pet dogs and cats. Pets should regularly have shots to prevent rabies.

Other Conditions

Some problems of the nervous system are caused by injury or damage to cells. *Brain tumors* (TOO·mers) are masses of cells in the brain that grow out of control. Tumors can damage the brain cells near them. They can be removed with surgery. If the tumor is a sign of cancer, other treatment is also needed.

Epilepsy (EP·uh·lep·see) is *a brain disorder that results from a sudden burst of nerve action.* When this occurs, the person has a *seizure* (SEE·zher). This is a physical reaction that can be mild or severe. Some seizures last as long as 5 minutes. The victim may fall, shake, and lose awareness of what is happening. Other seizures are much milder. The person may only stare blankly for a few seconds or feel faint or dizzy.

Doctors have found some medicines that can control seizures. People with epilepsy can live normal, healthy lives.

Health Minute

Are You Protected?
Ask your parents if you have had the polio vaccine. It could have been a shot, or you might have taken it by mouth.

Helping Someone with Epilepsy

If someone has an epileptic seizure, he or she needs help. If the person falls, try to break the fall. Keep the person as quiet as possible, and cushion his or her head. The seizure will pass.

Cerebral palsy (suh·REE·bruhl PAWL·zee) is *a condition in which the cerebrum is damaged.* Injury to the brain at birth or in an accident causes this condition. Lead poisoning can also cause it. The effect of cerebral palsy depends on what part of the cerebrum is damaged. It can cause muscle spasms, poor balance, or problems with seeing, hearing, and talking. Some children with cerebral palsy are mentally retarded, but some are highly intelligent.

There is no cure for cerebral palsy, but people with it can lead healthy, active lives. They get help from *therapy* (THEHR·uh·pee), which is training to make the body work. Some people with cerebral palsy use braces to help them walk.

Multiple sclerosis (skluh·ROH·suhs) **(MS)** is *a disease in which the outer coating that protects some nerves is destroyed.* When this happens, the nerves cannot send their signals. This makes it impossible for the brain to control the body's muscles. The effects of this disease depend on which nerves are damaged. Some people lose balance and control over movement. Others have problems speaking and hearing.

MS is hard to treat because it can come and go over many years. Some medicines and therapy can help people who have MS, but as with cerebral palsy, there is no cure.

Check Your Understanding

Conclusion Your nervous system tells your muscles what to do, tells you what is going on in the world, and controls your other body systems. You use it to think, remember, and plan. The cells that make up your nervous system cannot repair themselves if they are damaged. For that reason, healthy choices are an important part of having a healthy nervous system.

1. **Vocabulary** Which of the following problems that affect the nervous system can be prevented with a vaccine? *cerebral palsy, polio, epilepsy*

2. **Recall** Name the three kinds of neurons.

3. **Recall** What are the two sections of the nervous system?

4. **Recall** What are three ways you can take care of your nervous system?

5. **Classify** Which part of the brain—the cerebrum, the cerebellum, or the brain stem—controls each of the following actions? memory, breathing, speaking, balance, posture, digesting food

Your Circulatory System

This lesson contains a number of valuable facts and tips. Once you have studied them, you will be able to

- list the parts and jobs of the circulatory system.
- tell how to care for the heart and blood.
- name some common problems that affect the heart and blood.

Words to Know

circulatory system
heart
blood vessels
arteries
veins
capillaries
blood pressure
leukemia
hemophilia
arteriosclerosis

The Transport System

The nervous system is your body's control center. The **circulatory** (SER·kyuh·luh·tohr·ee) **system** is its transport system. This system is *the group of body parts that carries the blood throughout the body to keep the body working well.* It has four main jobs.

- **The transportation of fuel.** The circulatory system carries food and oxygen to all the body's cells so they can work properly.

- **The transportation of wastes.** After the cells use this fuel, the system carries waste products to the liver and kidneys so that the wastes can be removed.

- **The transportation of disease fighters.** The system carries cells that fight disease.

- **The transportation of hormones.** The system carries hormones throughout the body.

DID **YOU** KNOW?

Your Blood Vessels
Your body has about 100,000 miles of blood vessels.

What Is in the Circulatory System?

The circulatory system includes your heart, your blood vessels, and your blood.

The Muscle That Pumps

Your **heart** is the muscle that drives the circulatory system. It *pumps blood throughout your body.* Your heart began beating before you were born, and it has gone on beating every minute of your life.

Health Minute

Feel It Work
Put your hand on the left side of your chest. You can feel your heartbeat. Close your hand and make a fist. That's about the size of your heart.

Learning from Drawings

The arteries, in red, take blood from the heart. The veins, in blue, return blood to the heart. Diseases of the circulatory system cause more than half of all deaths in the United States. Why are these diseases so serious?

Health Minute

Putting on the Squeeze

With one hand, squeeze the tip of a finger on your other hand. Notice that the fingertip turns white. This is because you are cutting off the flow of blood to your fingertip. After you release the finger, watch it turn color.

The Circulatory System

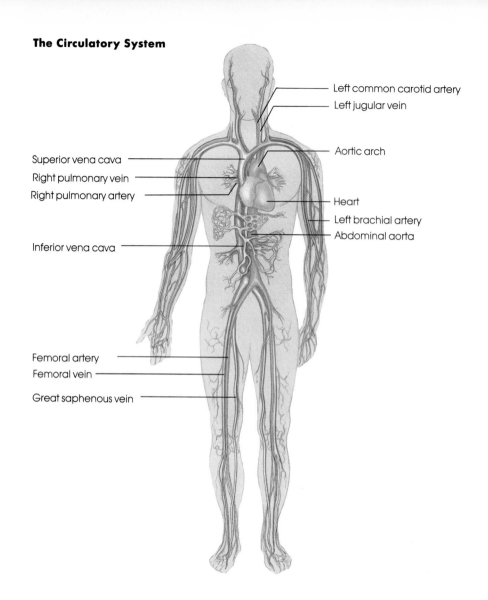

- Left common carotid artery
- Left jugular vein
- Aortic arch
- Superior vena cava
- Right pulmonary vein
- Right pulmonary artery
- Heart
- Left brachial artery
- Abdominal aorta
- Inferior vena cava
- Femoral artery
- Femoral vein
- Great saphenous vein

Your heart is split into two sides, each with two hollow chambers. Each side has a pump. See the drawing "How the Heart Pumps Blood." It shows the parts of the heart and describes how the heart works.

Your heart pumps blood, or beats, about 60 to 80 times a minute. The number of beats per minute is called your *pulse.*

Blood Vessels: The Roadways of the Body

Your heart pumps blood into your **blood vessels** (VES·uhls). These are *tubes that carry blood throughout your body.* There are three main types of blood vessels.

- **Arteries.** The largest blood vessels are the **arteries** (AR·tuh·rees). These *take blood away from the heart.*

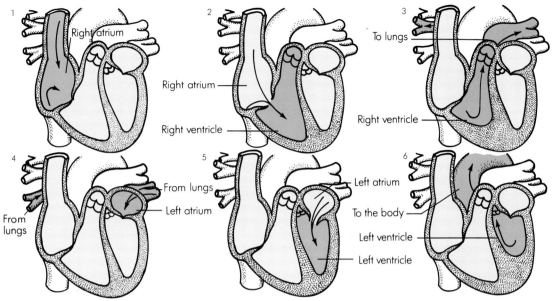

- **Veins.** The *blood vessels that take blood from the body back to the heart* are the **veins** (VAYNS).
- **Capillaries.** The smallest blood vessels are the **capillaries** (KAP·uh·lehr·ees). These tiny tubes *carry blood from the arteries to the body's cells and from those cells to the veins.*

Blood moves through the arteries because of the force of the heart's pumping. Veins are thinner than arteries, though. Muscles must be used to move blood along the veins. Veins also have valves that direct the flow of blood back to the heart.

Blood Pressure

As the blood moves around the body, it puts *a force on the inside walls of the blood vessels.* This force is called **blood pressure.** Blood pressure is measured by how much force the blood applies. Two numbers are used for blood pressure. The high number measures the force at its greatest, which occurs at the moment the heart pumps. The lower number shows the force at its least, when the heart is between beats.

Normal blood pressure is between 110 and 140 for the high number and between 70 and 90 for the low number. Blood pressure higher than this may be a health problem.

You can have your blood pressure checked in a clinic or a doctor's office. Many drugstores have machines that check blood pressure. If your pressure seems high, see a doctor.

Learning from Drawings
The top chamber on each side of the heart is called an *atrium* (AY-tree-uhm). The two bottom chambers are called *ventricles* (VEN-tri-kuhls). Blood from the body (1) enters the right atrium. It collects there until (2) it is squeezed into the right ventricle. (3) There, it is pumped out of the heart and toward the lungs. Once the blood picks up oxygen in the lungs, it returns to the heart. (4) It enters the left atrium this time. This chamber (5) squeezes the blood into the left ventricle. (6) Then, the pump on the left side pushes the blood into the arteries, which carry it to all parts of the body. Which pump do you think is the stronger of the two?

What Is in the Blood?

Blood has liquid and solid parts. The chart "The Parts of Your Blood" tells what each of the four main substances in your blood does.

Teen **Issue**

Self-Transfusions

People who know they will need a transfusion because they have surgery coming up can donate their own blood for use when the operation takes place.

The Parts of Your Blood

Name	What It Is and Does
Plasma (PLAS·muh)	Liquid that carries all other parts along
Red blood cell	Solid that carries oxygen to all cells
White blood cell	Solid that fights disease
Platelet (PLAYT·luht)	Solid that helps blood to clot, or thicken, when cuts happen

Sharing Blood

Blood is so important to life that someone who loses too much blood dies. Doctors can put one person's blood into the body of another in a process called a *blood transfusion* (trans·FYOO·zhuhn). Transfusions are often used in surgery. Sometimes they are needed by a person who has had an accident.

To give someone's blood to another person, doctors must be sure that the two people's blood is of the same type. There are two ways of looking at blood type—the ABO system and the Rh system. The ABO system has four different groups. Blood can either be type A, type B, type AB, or type O. The Rh system has two groups, called Rh-positive and Rh-negative.

Someone with Rh-positive blood can receive only that type of blood. The same is true of Rh-negative blood. People with type O blood can give blood to anyone with the same Rh factor. People with AB blood can receive blood from anyone with the same Rh factor. Those with type A or B blood can receive blood from people with either the same blood type or type O, as long as the blood has the same Rh factor.

Someone with the right type of blood need not be on hand for a transfusion. Blood can be given at any time, then frozen and stored for a long time. The places where blood is given and stored are called *blood banks*.

Many people are worried that the blood supply is infected with the virus that causes AIDS. There is no cure for this disease, which leads to death. At this time, though, the blood supply is safe. All blood that is donated is tested to make sure that the AIDS virus is not present. Because new needles are used when taking the blood and when giving it to someone else, there is no risk of getting AIDS from needles used in transfusions.

DID **YOU** KNOW?

Everybody Loves an *O*

Because people with blood type O can give blood to people with all other types, they are called *universal donors*. People with type AB blood are called *universal recipients*.

Know Your Blood Type

You can find out your blood type by checking your birth records. Keep this information in your wallet or purse at all times.

Caring for Your Circulatory System

Many problems with the circulatory system are linked to the way we live. Poor diet, lack of exercise, smoking, and being overweight all increase the chances of getting heart disease or high blood pressure. Good health habits can give you a healthy circulatory system.

More About
*For more on **heart disease**, see Chapter 12.*

Habits for a Healthy Circulatory System

- **Eat a balanced diet.** Choose foods from each of the four food groups. Be sure your diet is high in fiber and low in fat, cholesterol, and salt.
- **Exercise regularly.** Regular vigorous exercise strengthens the heart and helps it do its job better.
- **Maintain your ideal weight.** Keep your weight at the level normal for your height and body frame.
- **Stay away from smoking.** Smoke puts carbon monoxide into the blood and prevents it from carrying the oxygen the body needs.
- **Lower your stress.** Reduce the amount of stress that you feel by avoiding stressful situations when you can. Try to think and plan ahead, and learn to relax.

Problems of the Circulatory System

Some problems of the circulatory system affect the blood. Others affect the heart or blood vessels.

Problems of the Blood

A person who does not have enough red blood cells suffers from *anemia* (uh·NEE·mee·uh). This can be caused by a loss of blood or because the body does not make enough red blood cells. The treatment depends on the cause of the problem. Females need to be sure to get enough iron in their diet to avoid anemia.

Leukemia (loo·KEE·mee·uh) is *a disease of both the bones and the blood.* It occurs when a person has too many white blood cells. These cells crowd out the red cells. Doctors do not understand why this takes place. Some kinds of leukemia cannot be cured, but medicines and radiation can slow it down.

Hemophilia (hee·muh·FIL·ee·uh) is *a disease in which the blood clots little or not at all.* Only males can have this disease. Females can carry it and pass it along to their children, though. Someone with hemophilia must be careful not to be injured. He could bleed to death. A person with hemophilia can take medicine that allows the blood to clot.

DID **YOU** KNOW?

Sickle-cell Anemia

One type of anemia is called *sickle-cell anemia*. It is a condition passed on from parents that results in red blood cells that are not correctly shaped. People with roots in Africa, some Mediterranean countries, and India are almost the only people with this disease. The round cells in this photo are normal red blood cells. The flatter, slightly curved cells are sickle cells.

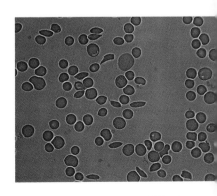

Problems of the Heart and Blood Vessels

Many people have the problem called **arteriosclerosis** (ar·tir·ee·oh·skluh·ROH·suhs). This means *hardening of the arteries*. It includes anything that causes the artery walls to become thick. The main cause of arteriosclerosis is that fats moving through the blood attach to the walls of the arteries. As more and more fat attaches, the flow of blood can slow or even stop. One cause of this problem is a diet high in cholesterol.

If the flow of blood to the heart is cut off, the heart stops working. This is called a *heart attack*. Heart attacks can also be caused by problems with the valves or muscles in the heart. If someone has a high chance of having a heart attack, a doctor may recommend surgery to correct the problem.

Sometimes a *clot*, or lump of blood, forms in an artery. When this happens, the lump often attaches to the artery wall. If it becomes too large, a clot can block the flow of blood. If a clot becomes detached, it can travel through the bloodstream and block a smaller blood vessel somewhere else. When this happens to one of the blood vessels leading to the brain, a *stroke* occurs.

Another condition of the circulatory system is *high blood pressure*. Like heart disease, this can be prevented in many cases by living in a healthy way.

Learning from Photographs
In the stress test shown here, a person is made to exercise while doctors measure breathing and heart rate. Doctors use the information to see how healthy the person's circulatory system is. Why is it necessary to test the circulatory system in this way?

Check Your Understanding

Conclusion Your circulatory system is a key to your health. It fuels all your other body systems. By practicing good health habits now, you not only give yourself a healthy heart today. You will improve your chances of having a healthy future.

1. **Vocabulary** Label the words that are a kind of blood vessel with a *V*. Label the parts of the blood with a *P. arteries, platelets, veins, capillaries, red blood cells, plasma*

2. **Recall** Name two jobs of the circulatory system.

3. **Recall** What does the heart do?

4. **Recall** What are two things you can do to give yourself a healthy circulatory system?

5. **Recall** Name one health problem that affects the blood and one that affects the heart or blood vessels.

6. **Analyze** Could someone with blood type A that is Rh-positive accept a transfusion from someone with blood type O that is Rh-positive? Could he or she accept type B, Rh-positive blood?

Your Respiratory System

Words to Know
respiratory system
trachea
epiglottis
bronchi
lungs
alveoli
diaphragm
pneumonia
bronchitis
asthma
emphysema

This lesson contains a number of valuable facts and tips. Once you have studied them, you will be able to

- name the main parts and jobs of the respiratory system.
- list ways to take care of your respiratory system.
- talk about common diseases of the lungs.

The Breath of Life

You probably never thought of your body as running on gas, but in a way it does. Every time you breathe in, your body takes in the gas oxygen. Oxygen is "fuel" that turns the food you eat into energy. Every time you breathe out, your body puts out the gas carbon dioxide.

Both of these jobs are done by the respiratory system. The **respiratory** (res·puh·ruh·TOHR·ee) **system** is *the group of body parts that changes gases in order for the body to work properly.*

How Does Breathing Work?

The respiratory system has two sections. The upper area includes your nose, mouth, and **trachea** (TRAY·kee·uh), or *windpipe.* The lower section includes the lungs and two structures within the lungs, the bronchi and the alveoli.

The Beginning of Breathing

Air enters the body through the nose or mouth. The nose is lined with hairs that help clean this air. These hairs filter out dirt and other particles. The nose is also lined with *mucous membranes* (MYOO·kuhs MEM·brayns) that keep the inside of the nose moist. These membranes also trap dirt. Every so often, you swallow a packet of dirt-filled mucus. Then you cough it out.

The air passes through your throat to the trachea. Food moves along part of this path as well, but in the neck the throat splits in two.

DID **YOU** KNOW?

Just the Opposite
Plants breathe in the opposite way to humans. They take in carbon dioxide to produce energy. They send out oxygen.

DID **YOU** KNOW?

Cool It!
At one time, people thought that the purpose of breathing was to cool the blood.

DID **YOU** KNOW?

Take a Deep Breath
In an average lifetime, a person will breathe in about 13 million cubic feet of air.

Learning from Drawings

The *pulmonary* (PUL-muh-nehr-ee) *artery* carries blood from the heart to the lung. The *pulmonary vein* carries blood full of oxygen back from the lung to the heart. Each lung is connected to the heart by both a vein and an artery. How do these veins and arteries play a role in breathing?

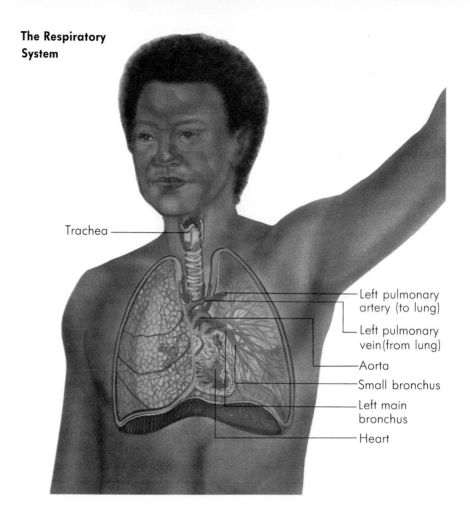

The Respiratory System

Trachea

Left pulmonary artery (to lung)

Left pulmonary vein (from lung)

Aorta

Small bronchus

Left main bronchus

Heart

The Wrong Pipe

Ever hear people say that a piece of food "went down the wrong pipe"? They mean that the epiglottis didn't close properly and the food entered the trachea. More often than not, the food is coughed out. When it cannot be, though, the person may choke. Chapter 13 tells what to do to save someone who is choking.

The front part becomes the trachea and carries air to the lungs. The back part becomes the *esophagus* (i-SAHF-uh-guhs) and takes food and drink to the stomach. *A small flap of skin* called the **epiglottis** (ep-uh-GLAHT-uhs) *closes over the top of the trachea to make sure that no food enters there.*

The trachea, like the nose, is lined with hairs and mucous membranes. It, too, filters the air to help keep dust and dirt out of the lungs. In your chest, the trachea divides into *two passages through which air enters the lungs.* These are the **bronchi** (BRAHN-ky). (Each one is called a *bronchus*.) When they enter your lungs, the bronchi split many times into smaller tubes so that air can enter all parts of each lung.

What Happens in the Lungs?

Your two **lungs** are *the main organs of breathing.* They are large elastic bodies, one on each side of the heart. They are filled with millions of *tiny air sacs* called **alveoli** (al-vee-OH-ly). The alveoli are at the ends of the bronchi.

The alveoli do the main work of trading gases with the blood. They send the oxygen you breathe into the vein that leads to the heart. They also take the carbon dioxide carried by the blood coming *from* the heart and send it up the trachea and out the body.

One other part of the body is important to breathing. The **diaphragm** (DY·uh·fram) is *a large muscle that separates the chest from the abdomen.*

DID YOU KNOW?

Tennis, Anyone?
The lungs hold millions of air sacs. If the walls of all those sacs were stretched out, they would cover a tennis court.

How Breathing Works

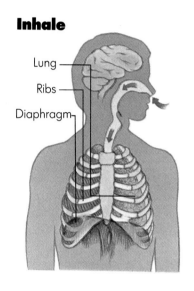

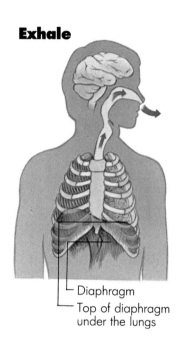

Inhale

Lung
Ribs
Diaphragm

Exhale

Diaphragm
Top of diaphragm under the lungs

Learning from Drawings
When you *inhale,* or breathe in, the diaphragm pulls down into the abdomen. This allows the lungs to fill with air. When the alveoli are done trading oxygen and carbon dioxide with the blood, the body is ready to rid itself of the carbon dioxide. The diaphragm relaxes, pushing on the chest. This forces the air out of the lungs. You have *exhaled,* or breathed out. What kind of tissue is the diaphragm?

Caring for Your Respiratory System

To care for your respiratory system and to keep it healthy, you can take the following steps.

- **Get regular exercise.** To help keep your lungs working well exercise regularly.

- **Use good posture.** Standing, sitting, and walking straight helps your respiratory system work as it should. Stooping or slouching makes breathing more difficult.

- **Take deep breaths.** Breathe deeply to keep your lungs strong.

- **Say "no" to smoking.** The hot smoke from cigarettes harms the membranes of the nose and throat. Harmful gases and sticky tars from cigarettes settle in the lungs. They make it harder for your lungs to work well. They can even lead to cancer.

Teen Issue

Smokers Aren't Winners
If you play a sport, you have another great reason not to smoke. Since smoking makes the lungs work less well, you'll get less air with each breath. That means you'll need to use more energy to breathe. And *that* means you'll have less energy left for your muscles. Stay away from cigarettes and you'll have that extra step!

Learning from Photographs
Covering your nose and mouth protects you from breathing in harmful dirt and gases. This helps your respiratory system. Can you name other ways to help this system?

DID **YOU** KNOW?

The Nose Knows
The mouth doesn't have the hairs and mucous membranes that the nose has. It can't filter the air that comes in, which the nose can do. That's why it's better to breathe in through the nose.

Teen **I**ssue

Bad News, Good News
The bad news is that children and teens suffer more colds than do adults. The good news is that when you're an adult, you'll have fewer colds!

- **Try to avoid breathing in dirty air.** Wear a mask if you are doing something that will cause you to breathe in dirt and harmful substances. Protect yourself if you will be mowing the lawn, painting, or using strong chemicals to clean.

- **If you have a cold or a cough, try to keep the airways in your nose and throat open.** Blow your nose, though not too hard, and don't hold back a sneeze or a cough. They work to get rid of harmful substances. Do remember, though, to cover your mouth and nose!

Disorders of the Respiratory System

The most common disease of the respiratory system is the cold. It is caused by germs called *viruses* (VY·ruhs·uhs). There are over a hundred different cold viruses. Once you have one kind, you will never have it again. But there are so many different types that there is always a new one that you can catch.

There are no cures for the cold, although there are medicines that you can take to relieve the symptoms. Colds bring on fever, aching body, running nose, and itchy eyes. They make it hard to breathe. On average, each of us suffers two or three colds a year. Fortunately, they don't last long.

A more serious disease that can affect this system is **pneumonia** (noo·MOH·nyuh). This is *an infection of the lungs.* A person with pneumonia has a hard time breathing. Some kinds of pneumonia can be treated with medicines. Those that are caused by a virus have no treatment.

Some people suffer from **bronchitis** (brahn·KYT·uhs). This disease is *a swelling of the bronchi.* They become red and painful. Someone with bronchitis usually has a fever and may cough often. It can last several weeks.

Asthma (AS·muh) is not a disease but *a condition in which the bronchi swell and close up.* Someone with asthma could be affected by an allergy to dirt in the air. Cigarette smoke nearby can also cause an attack of asthma. The person who has asthma finds it very hard to breathe and may cough often.

Emphysema (em·fuh·SEE·muh) is *a severe disease of the alveoli.* Breathing in smoke and dirty air are the main causes. The smoke and dirt destroy the alveoli. As a result, air cannot easily pass in and out of the lungs. People with emphysema may use up to 80 percent of their energy to breathe. A person with healthy lungs only uses 5 percent of his or her energy for this purpose. The damage caused by this disease cannot be undone. Emphysema can be deadly.

Lung cancer is another very serious disease. Cancer cells grow out of control and destroy the alveoli. This disease is treated with radiation or chemicals. Sometimes it is necessary to remove a diseased lung. The biggest cause of lung cancer is smoking.

Say "No" to Emphysema

The main cause of emphysema is breathing in smoke. Many people who suffer from emphysema are cigarette smokers. Avoid this disease—don't smoke. Learn how to protect yourself from the smoke of other peoples' cigarettes in Chapter 8.

Check Your Understanding

Conclusion Your nose, throat, and lungs combine to make a system that does an important job. It brings in the oxygen you need for your cells to work and takes out the carbon dioxide they produce as waste from that work. You can take steps to make sure that your respiratory system is as healthy as possible. If you do, you will feel healthy and be able to perform at your peak.

1. **Vocabulary** Which of the following is the name of the muscle that is an important part of breathing? *lungs, alveoli, diaphragm, bronchi*

2. **Recall** Name two parts of the upper section of the respiratory system and two parts of the lower section.

3. **Recall** What are three things you can do to have a healthy respiratory system?

4. **Recall** What is the most common respiratory disease? What is the cure for it?

5. **Sequence** Write down the following parts of the respiratory system in the order that they receive air when a person inhales. *bronchi, nose, alveoli, throat, trachea*

Health Minute

Take a Breather
Put your hand on your chest and breathe in slowly and deeply. You can feel your chest rise as your lungs expand.

Words to Know

skeletal system
cartilage
joints
ligaments
fractures
dislocation
sprain
arthritis
osteomyelitis
osteoporosis

Your Skeletal System

This lesson contains a number of valuable facts and tips. Once you have studied them, you will be able to

- name the jobs the bones do and name the three different kinds of bones.
- tell how you can care for your bones.
- name the types of fractures.
- talk about some problems that affect the bones.

The Body's Framework

Have you ever seen a house being built? Before the builders put in the walls and the roof, they make a framework of boards and beams. The bones in your body are a framework, too.

Together with the joints and connecting tissues, the bones form the **skeletal** (SKEL·uht·uhl) **system.** The skeletal system works closely with the muscular system.

Learning from Photographs
Milk products are an excellent source of the calcium that bones need to be healthy. What vitamin is often added to milk?

The Bones

Even though bones are hard, they are living tissue. They need food to grow and repair themselves. They get this food from your blood, just like other cells in the body. And, just like other cells of your body, you need to care for them if they are to work properly.

Your bones do a number of important jobs.

- **Movement.** Bones make it possible for you to move.
- **Protection.** Bones help protect the organs inside your body from injury.
- **Sites of cell making.** Bones are where red blood cells and most white blood cells are made.
- **Storage.** Bones store important minerals and protein for use when your body needs them.

The Skeletal System

Learning from Drawings
The *axial* (AK-see-uhl) *skeleton* is the skull and spine. The *appendicular* (ap-uhn-DIK-yuh-ler) *skeleton* includes the shoulder, arms, hips, and legs. What two sections make up the backbone?

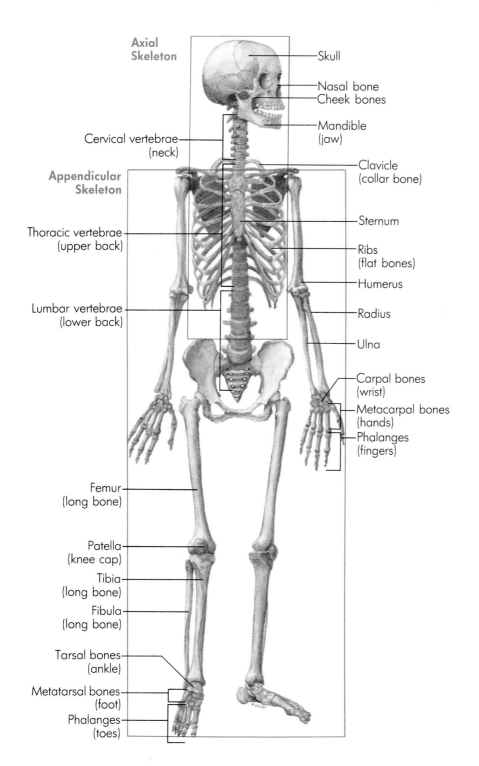

Axial Skeleton

Skull

Nasal bone
Cheek bones

Mandible (jaw)

Cervical vertebrae (neck)

Clavicle (collar bone)

Appendicular Skeleton

Sternum

Thoracic vertebrae (upper back)

Ribs (flat bones)

Humerus

Radius

Lumbar vertebrae (lower back)

Ulna

Carpal bones (wrist)

Metacarpal bones (hands)

Phalanges (fingers)

Femur (long bone)

Patella (knee cap)

Tibia (long bone)

Fibula (long bone)

Tarsal bones (ankle)

Metatarsal bones (foot)

Phalanges (toes)

DID **YOU** KNOW?

Numbers of Bones
One person in every 20 has 13 pairs of rib bones. Most people have 12.

DID **YOU** KNOW?

Kinds of Bones
The skull has 29 bones, the backbone 26, the ribs 24, each arm 32, and each leg 30.

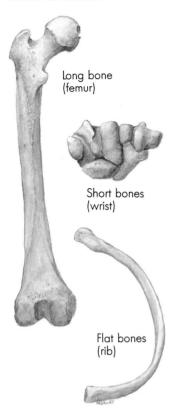

Long bone
(femur)

Short bones
(wrist)

Flat bones
(rib)

Learning from Drawings
Locate these bones on the drawing of the whole skeletal system.

Health Minute

Jaws
Move your jaw. The ligaments allow you to move the lower jaw sideways, forward and back, and up and down. These movements are important to eating and talking.

Kinds of Bones

Your body has three kinds of bones.

- **Long bones.** These are long and shaped like a cylinder. Examples are the bones in your leg that connect your hip to your knee. Their ends are thick and shaped to fit the bones they connect with.
- **Short bones.** Some bones are just short. They are the bones in your wrists and ankles. They have a soft material inside that is covered by harder bone.
- **Flat bones.** Ribs and the bones of the skull are flat bones. They have two layers of hard bone with soft matter between. Flat bones protect body organs.

The center of a bone is hollow. It is filled either with *yellow bone marrow* (MAR·oh), which is mostly fat, or with *red bone marrow*. The red marrow is made of blood vessels, connecting tissues, and cells. This is where some blood cells are made. The outside of bones is covered with a strong membrane. This tissue is full of blood vessels that carry food to the bones.

The Connectors

Three kinds of tissue are where bones connect. They are *cartilage, joints,* and *ligaments.*

Bones have *a strong, elastic material on their ends.* This matter is called **cartilage** (KAHRT·uhl·ij). A layer of cartilage is on the ends of bones. As a bone grows, the cartilage becomes harder and turns into bone. For this reason, adults' bones are more brittle than children's.

Bones that connect have cartilage between them. This cartilage cushions each bone from damage.

The **joints** are *the points where two bones meet.* Some joints do not move. Your skull joints are an example. But most joints allow the bones to move. It is their action—along with the muscles—that allows you to run, jump, play the piano, write, build a model, eat, and do thousands of other things. A fluid keeps the joints moist and slippery, much as oil works on the moving parts of a car engine.

There are three kinds of joints. What makes them different from one another is the kind of movement they allow. The drawing "The Joints" shows each kind.

The joints that allow the most movement are helped by another tissue that is a connector. The **ligaments** (LIG·uh·muhnts) are *cords of tissue that join bones or keep organs in place.*

Caring for Your Skeletal System

You could not move your body without a healthy skeletal system. For this reason, it is important to take care of your skeletal system. Exercise and plenty of rest help build strong bones. But the three best steps for having strong bones are these.

Ways to Care for the Skeletal System

- **Have good posture.** Good posture will help your skeleton take the shape it should. That way it can do its job best. Lifting heavy things in the right way helps, too. To lift, bend the legs and keep the back straight.
- **Have a good diet.** Calcium and phosphorus are important to bones. Be sure that you get enough of these minerals. For calcium, eat or drink milk products. Good sources of phosphorus are beans, peas, meat, milk products, and whole grains.
- **Play carefully.** Playing it safe will protect your bones from possible accidents. This includes wearing a helmet and padding when you go skateboarding. You can also be sure not to take dares that can lead to the danger of an injury.

Problems of the Skeletal System

The problems of the skeletal system are caused by accident, disease, or other conditions. They can affect bones or connectors.

Accidents That Need Not Happen

Bones can break. There are six different kinds of **fractures,** or *breaks in a bone.* All breaks can be treated and can heal. The person with the break must get medical help, however, so that a doctor can set the bone correctly. Then the bone can heal properly. Many broken bones must be put in a cast during the healing time.

Sometimes *the end of a bone is pushed out of its joint.* This is called a **dislocation** (dis·loh·KAY·shuhn). The bone must be pushed back in place and kept there until it heals. As with setting a broken bone, a doctor should do this.

Joints can be injured also. A **sprain** is *the sudden and violent stretching of a joint.* The result is pain and swelling. Putting cold packs on the sprained joint can keep the swelling down. With time, the sprain will heal. Sometimes ligaments can be stretched or even torn. A doctor should examine these injuries.

The Joints

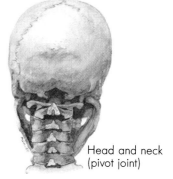

Skull
(immoveable joint)

Head and neck
(pivot joint)

Shoulder
(ball-and-socket joint)

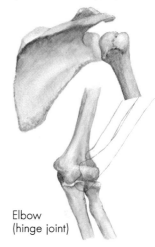

Elbow
(hinge joint)

Learning from Drawings
Immovable joints like those in the skull allow no movement at all. Where the head meets the spine and where the arm meets the shoulder, are *freely movable joints.* They allow movement in all directions. Hinge joints, like the elbow, are *partially movable joints.* Movement is allowed only in one or two directions. Move your head and elbows to see the difference.

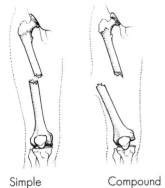

Simple   Compound

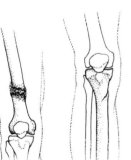

Incomplete   Chip

Nonunion   Stress

Learning from Drawings
A stress fracture is not a complete break, but a weakening of the bone. What do broken bones need to heal properly?

Diseases and Disorders of the Skeletal System

One of the most common problems of the skeletal system is the disorder known as **arthritis** (ar·THRYT·uhs). This condition is *a swelling in the joints caused by the breakdown of bones or connective tissue.* Arthritis often happens in the hands and feet, fingers and toes, and wrists and ankles. It is a painful condition. For many types of arthritis, there is no cure.

Osteomyelitis (ahs·tee·oh·my·uh·LYT·uhs) is *an infection of the bone caused by a germ.* The bone becomes swollen and painful. Doctors can give medicines to cure this disease.

Many older people have **osteoporosis** (ahs·tee·oh·puh·ROH·suhs). In this condition, *the body does not have enough calcium for bones to stay strong and flexible.* A person can usually prevent it by having a good diet, getting exercise, and keeping the right level of a special hormone. In fact, getting enough calcium today can help you make sure that you will not have this problem in the future. A person with osteoporosis has very brittle bones. Those bones are likely to break if the person falls.

You can help a grandparent or older neighbor prevent the damage that a fall could cause. Volunteer to do chores that may be dangerous. Examples are changing ceiling lightbulbs or cleaning high places.

Check Your Understanding

Conclusion   Your skeletal system does many important jobs. It provides a structure for your body and allows movement. You can care for your skeletal system by having a good diet and acting safely. The result will be a body that can perform at its best.

1. **Vocabulary** Which of the following are problems caused by an accident and which are the result of a disease or disorder? *arthritis, sprain, fracture, osteoporosis*

2. **Recall** Name two jobs of the bones.

3. **Recall** What are the three types of bones?

4. **Recall** What three kinds of tissues appear where bones connect?

5. **Recall** Name three kinds of fractures of a bone.

6. **Analyze** Robin is about to go skateboarding in the park. What can she do to make sure that she is acting safely?

Your Muscular System

Words to Know
muscular system
contract
extend
smooth muscles
skeletal muscles
tendons
cardiac muscle
aerobic exercise
muscle tone
muscular dystrophy

This lesson contains a number of valuable facts and tips. Once you have studied them, you will be able to

● name the different types of muscles and tell what jobs they do.

● tell how to care for your muscles.

● define the terms *aerobic exercise* and *muscle tone.*

● list some problems that occur with muscles and tell how to treat them.

The Magicians of Motion

Your body's muscles can do wonderful things. They hold you up when you sit, move you when you walk, chew your food, and help you talk. Skilled athletes have trained their muscles to run fast and far and to jump high and long. Eye surgeons have trained their muscles to be able to do delicate operations using tiny tools.

Your bones give your body a framework like the boards and beams of a house being built. Your muscles allow you to move that framework. Your **muscular** (MUHS·kyuh·ler) **system,** then, is *the group of tough tissues that makes body parts move.* This system includes more than the muscles that move your bones. Many of your internal organs, like the stomach and the intestines, are muscles that move without your being aware of them. Your heart may be the most important muscle of all.

DID **YOU** KNOW?

Muscle Records
The record for the 100-yard dash is just over 9 seconds. The record long jump is over 29 feet. The best marathon time is close to 2 hours.

All About Muscles

Like the brain, all your muscle cells are present when you are born. They simply grow larger as you get older. The body has over 600 major muscles, and they all work the same way. They **contract,** or *shorten,* and they **extend,** or *stretch.* By making these motions, muscles keep you moving.

DID **YOU** KNOW?

Muscle Numbers
You use 17 muscles to smile and 43 to frown.

The Muscular System

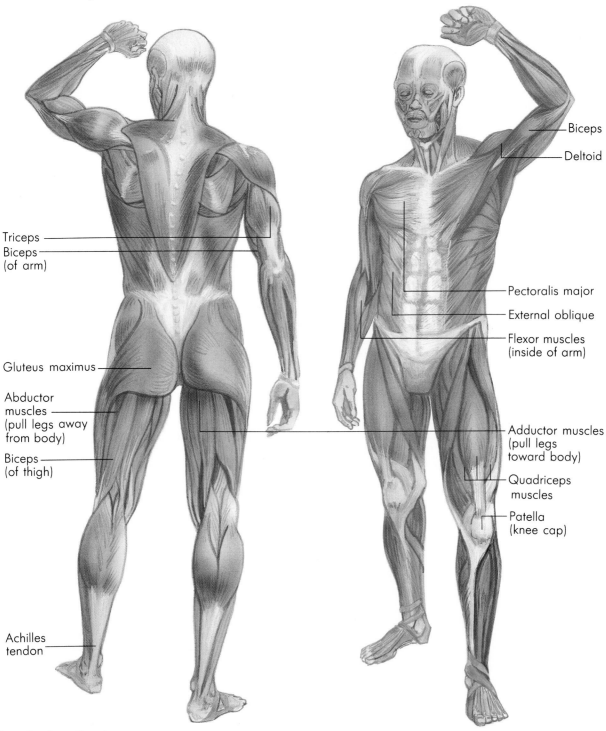

Triceps

Biceps
(of arm)

Gluteus maximus

Abductor
muscles
(pull legs away
from body)

Biceps
(of thigh)

Achilles
tendon

Biceps

Deltoid

Pectoralis major

External oblique

Flexor muscles
(inside of arm)

Adductor muscles
(pull legs
toward body)

Quadriceps
muscles

Patella
(knee cap)

Learning from Drawings
The drawings show the main
skeletal muscles. What muscle
that is important to breathing is
not shown?

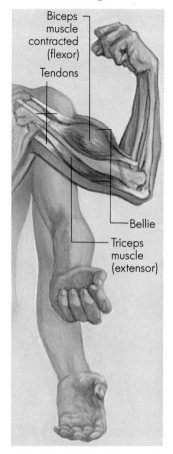

How Muscles Work Together

Biceps muscle contracted (flexor)

Tendons

Bellie

Triceps muscle (extensor)

Kinds of Muscle

- **Smooth muscles.** *The muscles in your digestive system and your blood vessels* are **smooth muscles.** They are found in your throat, stomach, intestines, arteries, and veins. The diaphragm is one of these muscles as well.
- **Skeletal muscles.** *The muscles that make your body move* are the **skeletal** (SKEL·uht·uhl) **muscles.** They attach to the bones and joints or, like the muscles of the face, attach directly to the skin. *The strong fibers that join skeletal muscles to other parts of the body* are called **tendons.** Skeletal muscles come in different sizes. Those in your legs, for instance, are quite long. The muscles in your face that make you smile are much shorter.
- **Cardiac muscle.** *The muscle that makes your heart work is* **cardiac** (KAHRD·ee·ak) **muscle.** This kind of muscle is in the heart only.

The work of smooth muscles and cardiac muscle is controlled by the brain stem. Both types are kept working without your being aware of it. For that reason, these muscles are called *involuntary* (in·VAHL·uhn·tehr·ee) *muscles.* The skeletal muscles are moved in a *voluntary* way. You control their movement.

All muscles need energy to do their work. They are covered with arteries that bring them food and oxygen so they can move.

How Muscles Work

All muscles work the same way. Each muscle is connected to the nervous system by a neuron. When the brain sends a signal, the muscle contracts. With another signal, the muscle extends.

Skeletal muscles often work in pairs. When one muscle contracts, its partner extends. When the other muscle contracts, the first extends. The muscles that bend an arm or a leg are called *flexors* (FLEK·sers). The muscles that straighten an arm or a leg are called *extensors* (ik·STEN·sers).

Caring for Your Muscles

Following the two general rules of good health helps your muscular system. Good nutrition supplies the right mix of food that your muscles need. This includes protein to build muscle and carbohydrates to supply energy. Another rule of good health that is important to muscles is rest.

Learning from Drawings
When the biceps (BY-seps) muscle contracts, the triceps (TRY-seps) extends. This pulls the forearm up toward the shoulder. When the triceps contracts, the biceps extends. This motion straightens the arm. Do you think each of these muscles connects to the same bone?

More About
*For more on **nutrition**, see Chapter 5.*

Caring for your muscles also means helping them to do their jobs well. You can do that in the following ways.

More About

For more on how to make a good exercise program and on warming up and cooling down, see Chapter 1.

- **Exercise regularly.** To keep muscles fit, make regular exercise a lifelong activity.
- **Build up slowly to a high level of activity.** Don't try to do too much too fast when you exercise.
- **Warm up and cool down.** Start each exercise session with a good warm-up to get the muscles ready. End each period with a cool-down to help the muscles get rid of the waste products that build up during exercise.
- **Include aerobic exercise in your program.** An important and healthy part of any exercise program is **aerobic** (ehr·OH·bik) **exercise.** This is *nonstop vigorous activity.*

Aerobic Exercise and Muscle Tone

Skeletal muscles grow better able to produce energy when you do aerobic exercise, such as running or swimming, about 30 minutes each day.

Working Out Works Out

Muscles contract with greater force when they have already contracted a few times. That's why warming up helps muscles work better.

When you exercise for a short time, your muscles use a kind of sugar stored in the muscles and liver as the source of energy. If you exercise without stopping for 15 minutes or more, though, your muscles also use another source of energy. They call on fat stored in your body and, using oxygen to break it down, produce energy.

Aerobic exercise is good for the muscles because it trains them to work at peak level. It helps the lungs because large amounts of oxygen are needed for the muscles to work. It is good for the heart because that muscle is also made to work more efficiently.

Learning from Photographs
With practice and training, muscles can develop strength, endurance, and flexibility. Which of those three abilities is shown here?

Muscle tone is *the firmness that muscles have at all times.* If you exercise regularly, your muscles become more firm. Some of your muscle cells contract at all times, even when you are asleep. The better your muscle tone, the more cells are always contracted.

Problems of the Muscular System

The most common muscle problems are caused by injury.

Common Muscle Problems		
Problem	**Cause**	**Treatment**
Bruise	Strong blow	Cold pack
Strain	Overwork	Rest and heat
Cramp	Muscle does not relax	Heat
Pulled or torn muscle	Muscle torn from bone	Medical help
Tendinitis	Stretched or torn tendon	Rest and medicines

The disease known as **muscular dystrophy** (DIS·truh·fee) is *a wasting away of skeletal muscle tissue.* Muscles are replaced by fat cells. The problems caused by this disease depend on which muscles are affected. Muscular dystrophy is passed on from parent to child. Most victims are males. There is no cure, but the amount of damage caused by the disease can be slowed by therapy.

Check Your Understanding

Conclusion Your muscles are the parts of your body that cause movement. You can give yourself a healthy muscular system by having a good diet, getting plenty of rest, and exercising regularly. With these steps, you can work and play at your best.

1. **Vocabulary** What happens to someone who has muscular dystrophy?
2. **Recall** Name the three types of muscle and tell what each does.
3. **Recall** Explain how skeletal muscles make the body move.
4. **Recall** What two general rules of good health can you follow to care for your muscular system?
5. **Recall** What can you do to build good muscle tone?
6. **Classify** Which of the following muscle problems are treated with heat and which is treated with an ice pack? strain, cramp, bruise

Take It Easy
Muscle strain shows up when you feel sore the day after you used your muscles. If you do feel sore, you did more the day before than your muscles were ready for. Get them up to the level you want by taking one step at a time.

Take Your Time
One way to prevent stomach cramps is to take a break between eating and working out. Give your stomach time to do its work. Give your blood time to deliver the nutrients from food throughout the body. *Then* work out!

DID **YOU** KNOW?

Biggest and Smallest
The largest muscles in your body are the two *gluteus maximus* muscles that cover your buttocks. The smallest are the eye muscles.

Teen Health
BULLETIN BOARD

CAREERS

Wanted:

Registered Nurse

Specifics:

Judge patients' condition and assist in recovery; keep records; give medicine. Settings include hospitals, doctor's offices, clinics, schools.

Qualifications:

Must be in good health and be well-balanced emotionally in order to handle close contact with patients. Attention to details a prime concern.

Preparation:

High school, then either a nursing program at a community college or nursing school, or a 4- or 5-year college program. All states require licensing.

Contact:

American Nurses Association
2420 Pershing Road
Kansas City, MO 64108
or

National League for Nursing
10 Columbus Circle
New York, NY 10019

HEALTH IN THE NEWS

A Man Who Loves Physics and Life

Stephen Hawking has a warm, friendly smile. He has a wife and three kids. He loves to travel. His busy schedule as a professor, writer, and lecturer keeps him on the go every day. Stephen Hawking is also the most brilliant physicist alive. There is one other noteworthy fact about Stephen Hawking. He has lost the ability to walk and to speak.

Physicist Stephen Hawking has reached out of his wheelchair to help us understand more about the complexities of the universe.

Stephen Hawking has ALS, also called "Lou Gehrig's disease." ALS causes the nervous system to break down. Muscles stop working. Hawking gets around in an electric wheelchair. He uses a computer with a voice to help him speak. He has much to learn and to teach.

Stephen Hawking expects to win the Nobel Prize for physics one day. ALS has not stopped him from doing his life's work.

Sports and Recreation

It's a Pain in the Knees!

One day you have a tough workout on the basketball court. Later, your knees *really* hurt. When you look closer, you see a lump below each kneecap. You don't know what to do next. Should you be scared?

It's possible that you have Osgood-Schlatter's disease, or OS. OS is a disease that appears in kids between the ages of 9 and 13. OS is not a serious disease. The pain usually goes away when you stop growing.

If you have OS, see a doctor. You may have to cut back on running and jumping for a while. But don't worry. The better you follow your doctor's instructions, the sooner you will be back to your old athletic self again.

TEEN Q & A

Q: I just turned 13. All the other boys in my class sound okay, but when I speak my voice cracks. Why?

A: Most boys' voices crack once in a while at your age. Your larynx has grown and your body has started making more testosterone, or male hormone. This makes your voice deepen. However, the hormones in your body are not flowing smoothly yet. So sometimes you still sound like you did when you were a kid. It can be embarrassing, but at least it's normal. In fact, listen to the other boys in your class. Are you sure they all sound "okay"?

HEALTH IN THE NEWS

A Balloon That Saves Lives

In 1977, someone invented an exciting new use for balloons. These are not, however, the kind of balloons you'd see at a party. They are thin, long balloons that are placed inside a clogged artery. Such a balloon is blown up to make the passage in the arteries wider. This allows more blood to flow through it.

This invention is used for the arteries near the heart. It helps people live longer. It helps them to live better, more active lives. And that is a great reason for a party, with or without balloons.

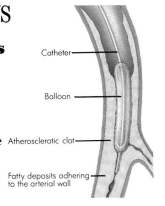

Catheter

Balloon

Atherosclerotic clot

Fatty deposits adhering to the arterial wall

Doctors insert a balloon into blocked coronary arteries, then inflate it to push aside fatty deposits and clear a path for blood.

Your Digestive and Excretory Systems

Words to Know

digestive system
excretory system
digestion
saliva
stomach
small intestine
liver
colon
kidneys

This lesson contains a number of valuable facts and tips. Once you have studied them, you will be able to

- name the parts of the digestive system and tell what jobs they do.
- name the parts of the excretory system and tell what jobs they do.
- tell what you can do to have healthy digestive and excretory systems.
- list some problems that affect these systems.

The Body's Engine

The **digestive** (dy·JES·tiv) **system** is like the engine of a car. It is *the group of body parts that takes in food and puts it in a form that can be used to create energy.* Food is the body's fuel. As part of this work, the body produces solid and liquid waste products. The **excretory** (EK·skruh·tohr·ee) **system** is *the group of body parts that removes these wastes from the body.* It is like the car's exhaust pipe.

The main tasks of these two systems, then, are three.

- They break food down into smaller substances that can be used by the body to work.
- They move these useful particles into the bloodstream.
- They remove solid and liquid wastes from the body.

Breaking Down Food

As food moves through the digestive system, it is changed. *The food is broken down into small particles that can pass through the bloodstream.* The breaking down of food is **digestion** (dy·JES·chuhn). Many parts of the body help in digestion.

Teen Issue

Skipping and Snacking
Many teens lead busy lives. They are always on the go, and fitting in meals seems very difficult. But taking the time for a proper meal pays off. It gives you the energy to keep going. It prevents the tiredness caused by hunger. And it means you won't be tempted to stuff yourself when you finally do eat. Give your stomach a break. Take it out to lunch.

The Digestive and Excretory Systems

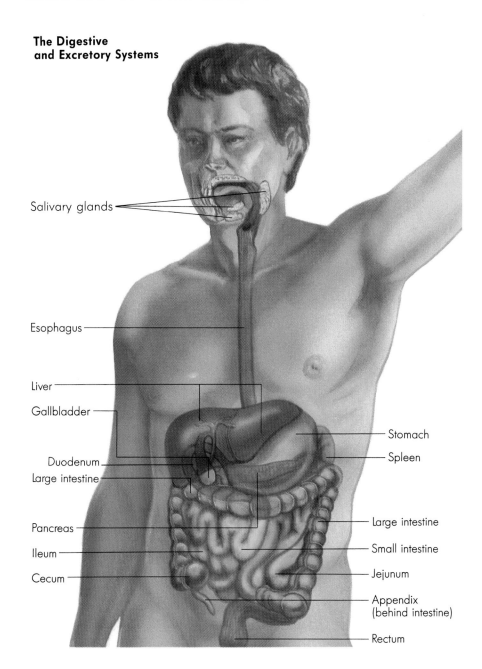

Salivary glands

Esophagus

Liver

Gallbladder

Duodenum

Large intestine

Pancreas

Ileum

Cecum

Stomach

Spleen

Large intestine

Small intestine

Jejunum

Appendix (behind intestine)

Rectum

Learning from Drawings
The kidneys cannot be seen because they are behind the upper intestine, one on each side of the body. Do you know what the kidneys do?

DID **YOU** KNOW?

Saliva
Saliva is at work even when you are not eating. It keeps the mouth moist and easy to move, which helps with speaking.

Learning from Drawings
The tongue has about 9,000 taste buds that can detect four tastes: sweet, salty, sour, and bitter. What liquid plays a role in taste?

The Taste Buds

Bitterness

Sour

Saltiness

Sweetness

Sour

Mouth and Teeth

The teeth begin digestion by breaking the food into smaller bits. As the teeth chew, three bodies in the mouth called *salivary* (SAL·uh·ver·ee) *glands* send out **saliva** (suh·LY·vuh). This *liquid is used to soften food so that it can be swallowed.* Saliva is 99 percent water. It has some chemicals that also break down food.

When the food is chewed down, it is time to swallow. What happens next is shown in "The First Stage of Swallowing" and "The Second Stage of Swallowing."

Lesson 6: Your Digestive and Excretory Systems   **211**

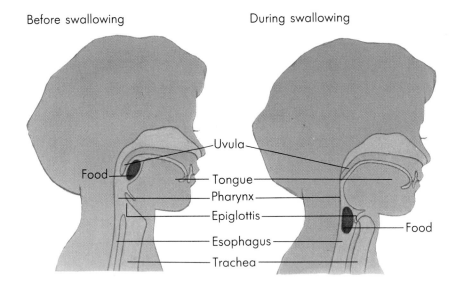

Before swallowing   During swallowing

Uvula
Food
Tongue
Pharynx
Epiglottis
Esophagus
Trachea
Food

Learning from Drawings
The First Stage. As food enters the back of the throat, two flaps of skin close off the air passages. The *uvula* (YOO-vyuh-luh) closes the airway to the nose. The *epiglottis* (ep-uh-GLAHT-uhs) shuts the trachea.
The Second Stage. When food enters the esophagus, the muscles there contract and relax, pushing the food along. What kind of muscles are these?

The Second Stage of Swallowing

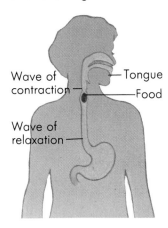

Wave of contraction
Tongue
Food
Wave of relaxation

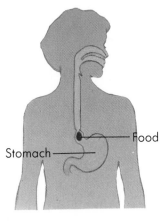

Food
Stomach

The Stomach and the Small Intestine

The stomach and small intestine do most of the work of digesting food. The **stomach** is *a j-shaped organ with many layers of muscle.*

- **Storage.** The stomach stores food before sending it along to the small intestine.
- **Regulation.** The stomach controls how quickly food moves into the small intestine.
- **Mixing.** The stomach mixes food and stomach juices and continues the process of digestion.

The food that leaves the stomach is not yet fully digested. In fact, the stomach only digests about 10–15 percent of protein and 30–50 percent of starch. Fat is hardly broken down at all. The **small intestine** (in·TES·tuhn) is *where most of digestion occurs.* This organ is a 20-foot-long tube that is folded many times over. Inside are millions of *villi.* Food passes through these fingerlike points into the bloodstream.

The Liver, Gallbladder, and Pancreas

Helping the small intestine are the liver, gallbladder, and pancreas. The **liver** is *the largest gland in the body.* Among the more than 500 jobs it does, six are the most important. They are shown in the chart "Some Jobs of the Liver."

The *gallbladder* (GAWL·blad·er) stores the bile that the liver produces. When the small intestine is ready for the bile, the gallbladder releases it. The *pancreas* (PAN·kree·uhs) also releases chemicals. They enter the small intestine to break down nutrients in food.

Some Jobs of the Liver

1. To produce *bile*, which helps to digest fat
2. To change sugar into either a form useful for storage or a form that can be used by the cells for energy
3. To maintain the correct level of blood sugar
4. To convert carbohydrates, proteins, and fats into energy
5. To change poisonous wastes into harmless substances
6. To store fat-soluble vitamins

Once these organs have all done their work, the food is completely digested. The villi in the small intestine absorb the digested food and transfer it to the bloodstream, which carries it throughout the body to fuel the work of the cells.

Removing Wastes

The body has two kinds of wastes that need to be removed. Solid wastes are what remains after digestion. Liquid wastes remove some products formed by the activity of the body's cells.

The Large Intestine

All food cannot be used by the body. The parts the body cannot use pass into the *large intestine.* Another name for this organ is the **colon** (KOH·luhn). It absorbs nearly all the water from this food. This action turns the food into an almost solid waste called *feces* (FEE·sees). When the large intestine is full, nerves signal the muscles to contract. As a result, the feces pass out of the body through the *anus* (AY·nuhs).

The Kidneys and Bladder

As the body's cells use food, they produce waste products. Water and salt are removed through sweat glands in the skin. Some water and carbon dioxide are sent out of the body through the lungs. *Removing the waste products that can be dissolved in water* is the job of the **kidneys.** These two bean-shaped organs are very important to the body. In fact, without a working kidney, you would die. The kidneys also keep the water and salt in the body at the right level.

The wastes made by the body's cells enter the bloodstream. The blood carries them to the kidneys, which filter out the wastes. The kidneys return the blood to the bloodstream and send the wastes to the *bladder* in the form of *urine* (YUR·uhn). The urine is stored there until the bladder is full. Then it is pushed out of the body.

DID **YOU** KNOW?
How Long It Takes
The digestive system takes about 24 hours to digest a meal. Food is in the stomach from 1 to 8 hours. The small intestine works on it for about 4 hours. Then it spends 10 to 15 hours in the large intestine.

DID **YOU** KNOW?
Kidney Machines
People who have lost both kidneys are helped by the use of machines that do the work of the kidneys for them.

Caring for These Systems

The main way to care for the digestive and excretory systems is to practice good eating habits.

- **Eat a balanced diet.** This means eating foods from the four food groups. It also means making sure your diet is low in fats and high in fiber.

- **Eat regular meals.** Eat complete meals well spaced apart during the day.

- **Make meals a relaxing time.** Do not hurry through your meals. Relax and enjoy them.

- **Eat enough but not too much.** Eat enough food to satisfy your hunger, but not so much as to stuff yourself.

- **Drink plenty of water.** Your digestive and excretory systems need a lot of water to do their jobs properly.

Problems of These Systems

Like the other body systems, the digestive and excretory systems sometimes have problems. Some are shown in the chart "Common Problems of the Digestive and Excretory Systems."

Food Poisoning

You can prevent food poisoning from hurting you by taking a few simple steps.

- Don't eat any canned foods if the can is bulging.
- Don't eat any food that has not been stored properly.
- Don't eat any food that has changed color or gives off an odor that shows it isn't fresh.
- Be careful to cook chicken, pork, and eggs thoroughly before eating them.

Common Problems of the Digestive and Excretory Systems		
Problem	**What It Is**	**What Causes It**
Indigestion	Food not digested completely	Eating too much; eating too fast; drinking too much alcohol
Heartburn	Stomach acid enters esophagus	Sphincter muscle does not close
Nausea	Ill feeling in stomach	Motion; germs; drugs; something eaten
Vomiting	Expelling food from stomach	Nausea; indigestion; food poisoning
Flatulence	Gas in stomach or intestine	Eating too quickly; eating food filled with air; action of bacteria in intestine
Diarrhea	Feces are liquid and passed often	Change in diet; food poisoning; germs
Constipation	Feces are hard and difficult to pass	Low-fiber diet; lack of water; poor eating habits; overuse of laxatives; lack of physical activity

More Serious Problems

Some problems that affect these two systems are more serious. Different problems affect different parts of these systems.

- **Stomach and small intestine.** These two organs are lined with mucous membranes. This soft material protects the organs from being harmed by their own juices. If this tissue breaks down, an *ulcer*, or sore, can develop. Ulcers can be treated with medicines.

- **Liver.** The liver can be badly damaged if a person drinks too much alcohol over a long time. Because the liver must break down the alcohol, fat builds up. This buildup may destroy liver cells, and lead to a disease called *cirrhosis* (suh·ROH·suhs).

- **Gallbladder.** The bile can harden into small crystals. These solids can block the passage to the small intestine, causing pain. Doctors remove the *gallstones*, as these solids are called. Sometimes doctors must remove the entire gallbladder.

- **Kidneys.** Kidneys can also develop stones. Smaller ones can pass out with the urine. Larger ones can block the exit. Doctors now use sound waves directed at the kidney to break the larger stones into smaller bits.

Don't Be Sore

The number of cases of ulcers is declining. Doctors are not sure why this is true, but it may be that people are avoiding the risk factors for developing an ulcer. By taking these steps, you can lower your risk for this condition.

- Avoid tobacco and alcohol.
- Avoid taking large amounts of painkillers that contain aspirin.
- Eat regular meals in a relaxed way.

Check Your Understanding

Conclusion   Your digestive system provides the fuel you need to work and play. The excretory system removes the body's waste products. The best way to maintain the health of these systems is to practice good eating habits.

1. **Vocabulary** Which of the following are parts of the digestive system and which are parts of the excretory system? *stomach, liver, kidneys, colon, teeth, small intestine*

2. **Recall** Where does most of digestion take place — in the stomach or in the small intestine?

3. **Recall** What are three common problems that affect the digestive or excretory system?

4. **Analyze** Andrea starts each day with a glass of juice, but then eats only one meal and one snack. Her snack is usually a candy bar or a bag of chips. Her meal is dinner, which is usually lots of meat, potatoes or noodles, and a glass of milk. She fills up afterward on ice cream and cookies until she's too full to move. Is Andrea following healthy eating habits? Why or why not?

DID **YOU** KNOW?

How Sweet It Is!

Chew a piece of soda cracker several times, but don't swallow it. As you hold the chewed cracker in your mouth, you will begin to notice a sweet taste. This is caused by your saliva's digesting of the cracker.

Words to Know
endocrine system
hormones
gland
pituitary gland
thyroid gland
adrenal glands
islets of Langerhans
ovaries
testes
diabetes
adrenaline

Your Endocrine System

This lesson contains a number of valuable facts and tips. Once you have studied them, you will be able to

- name the main parts of the endocrine system and tell what they do.
- tell how to have a healthy endocrine system.
- name some problems that affect the endocrine system.

More About
For more about the nervous system, see Lesson 1 of this chapter.

The Regulator

The **endocrine** (EN·duh·kruhn) **system** is the body's regulator. It is *the group of body parts that uses chemicals to control some of the body's actions.* The nervous system sends electrical messages to many parts of the body. They direct the arms and legs to move, the heart to pump blood, and the stomach to help digest food. The endocrine system sends out messages, too. But its messages are *chemicals produced in the body* called **hormones** (HOR·mohnz).

The hormones of the endocrine system work in the background. When your nervous system makes your arms move or your head turn, you know that this is the action you want to happen. Hormone action, though, takes place without your being aware of it. It also happens without your being able to control it.

The Glands of the Endocrine System

The workers of the endocrine system are eight glands. A **gland** is *a part of the body that releases a substance.*

The **pituitary** (puh·TOO·uh·tehr·ee) **gland** may be the most important gland in the endocrine system. It *does many jobs to control body actions.* It does so many, in fact, that it is often called the "master gland." The pituitary is controlled in part by the brain stem.

The **thyroid** (THY·royd) **gland** is found in the throat. It *releases the hormone that controls how fast the body uses food for energy.* The thyroid is controlled by the pituitary.

DID YOU KNOW?

The Pituitary Gland
The pituitary is about the size of an acorn.

The Endocrine System

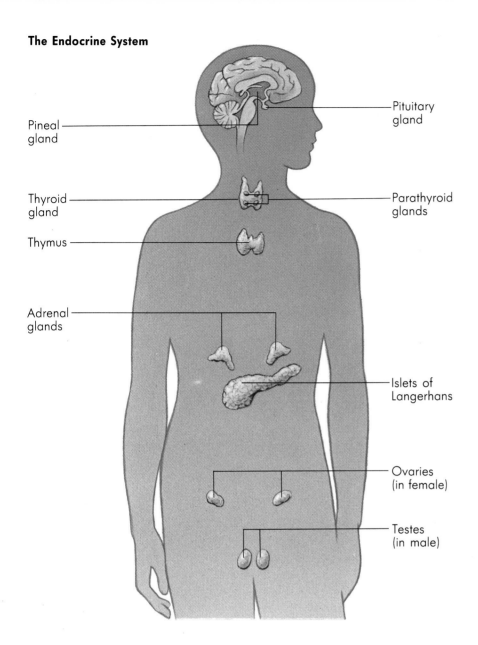

Pineal gland

Thyroid gland

Thymus

Adrenal glands

Pituitary gland

Parathyroid glands

Islets of Langerhans

Ovaries (in female)

Testes (in male)

Learning from Drawings
The glands of the endocrine system all release hormones. The body contains other glands as well. These release substances, but not hormones. Can you name one of these glands?

The **adrenal** (uh·DREEN·uhl) **glands** sit on top of the kidneys. They are important because they *control the stress response and the amount of salt and water in the body.*

The **islets of Langerhans** (EYE·luhts uhv LAHNG·er·hahnz) are in the pancreas. There are many of these groups of cells throughout that organ. They are *important in the control of sugar in the blood.*

The **ovaries** (OHV·uh·rees) are *the glands in the female reproductive system.* The **testes** (TES·tees) are *the glands in the male reproductive system.* These glands release hormones that cause the secondary sex traits to develop during puberty.

The jobs of these glands are shown in a chart on the next page.

Islets of Langerhans
There are hundreds of these bodies in the pancreas.

The Glands in the Endocrine System	
Gland	**What It Does**
Pineal	Unknown; may be involved in sexual development
Pituitary	Controls growth Controls working of thyroid and adrenal glands Tells kidney to retain water when needed Controls movement of smooth muscle
Thyroid	Controls how fast food is used for energy
Parathyroid	Regulates amount of calcium and phosphorus
Thymus	Unknown; may be involved in starting immune system
Adrenals	Controls body's water balance Controls body's use of carbohydrates, proteins, and fats Starts the stress response
Islet(s) of Langerhans	Regulates amount of blood sugar
Ovary, testis	Controls the appearance and maintenance of secondary sex characteristics

More About

For more on the male and female reproductive systems, see Lesson 8 of this chapter.

These glands work as a team. The brain tracks the presence of substances in the blood. For example, when the brain senses too little thyroid hormone in the blood, the pituitary signals the thyroid to release more of the hormone.

Getting Iodine

Many salts have iodine added to them. If you do use salt, be sure to use a salt that says it is *iodized*.

Caring for Your Endocrine System

The way to care for your endocrine system is to have overall good health. Eating a balanced diet is very important. Some glands in this system need to get enough of certain nutrients to work correctly. The hormone released by the thyroid, for instance, needs iodine. This mineral, then, must be part of your diet.

This kind of care is especially important in the teen years because the body is growing and changing so much.

Problems of the Endocrine System

The glands in the endocrine system can cause problems when they do not work correctly.

- **The pituitary gland.** If it releases too much growth hormone, a condition called *gigantism* (jy·GAN·tis·uhm) occurs. The person becomes very tall. If the pituitary releases too little growth hormone, the person will be very small.

- **Thyroid.** A lack of hormone from the thyroid during the growth years causes *cretinism* (KREET·uhn·is·uhm). The person grows little and may have some mental retardation. If the diet does not have enough iodine, the thyroid enlarges and the throat swells. This produces the condition known as *goiter* (GOYT·er).

- The most common problem with hormones is **diabetes** (dy·uh·BEET·eez). This is *a condition in which the body cannot properly use food to make energy.* Either the islets of Langerhans do not make enough insulin or insulin is released but is not used properly. Someone with diabetes must watch his or her diet carefully and may need a daily dose of insulin.

The Stress Response

The hormone **adrenaline** (uh·DREN·uhl·uhn) *controls the body's response to stress.* The body faces stress by readying itself for physical action in four ways.

- The rate of the heart and breathing rise.
- More blood goes to the muscles.
- The digestive system slows down.
- More usable sugar enters the blood.

This "fight or flight" response ends in one of two ways. It stops once whatever caused the stress is no longer present. Or the response ends when the body simply cannot keep itself going at this high level of activity any longer.

The stress response can harm the body if it goes on too long or happens too often. It is a heightened level of readiness for action, but not the normal state of the body. People can keep down the harm caused by this response by managing stress.

Learning from Photographs
Learning to relax is one way to control stress. What gland of the endocrine system is involved in the stress response?

Check Your Understanding

Conclusion The hormones of the endocrine system control growth, sexual maturity, and the use of food for energy. Eating a healthy diet ensures that these hormones work as they should.

1. **Vocabulary** Define the words *glands* and *hormones* and explain their relation to each other.
2. **Recall** What can you do to care for your endocrine system?
3. **Recall** Name two problems that can arise with the endocrine system and tell which gland is involved.
4. **Analyze** Why is caring for your endocrine system especially important in the teen years?

Words to Know

reproductive system
sperm
testes
penis
inguinal hernia
ovaries
fertilization
menstruation
menstrual cycle
gynecologist
premenstrual
 syndrome (PMS)
vaginitis

Your Reproductive System

This lesson contains a number of facts and tips. Once you have studied them, you will be able to

- name the parts of the male reproductive system and tell how to care for them.
- name some problems that affect the male reproductive system.
- name the parts of the female reproductive system and tell how to care for them.
- name some problems that affect the female reproductive system.

The Producer of New Life

All plants and animals produce new plants and animals. Animals produce eggs that must be fertilized. The human **reproductive** (ree·pruh·DUHK·tiv) **system** is *the group of body parts that is used to produce children.* The male and the female systems differ.

The Male Reproductive System

The purpose of the male reproductive system is to produce **sperm.** This is *the male cell that joins with the female egg to start a new life.* Males become able to produce sperm when they reach *puberty* (PYOO·bert·ee). This happens between the ages of 12 and 15.

The Parts of the Male Reproductive System

A major part of the male reproductive system is the **testes** (TES·tees). These are *the glands that produce sperm.* They sit in a bag called the *scrotum* (SKROHT·uhm) that hangs outside the male body between the legs. The scrotum is just below the **penis** (PEE·nuhs). This *organ is like a tube that hangs outside the body.* It is used in urination and reproduction.

The scrotum is sensitive to temperature. It pulls the testes closer to the body when cold. It moves the testes away from the body when warm. This keeps sperm at the right temperature.

DID **YOU** KNOW?

Sperm
The sperm cell is shaped like a tadpole. The head contains the genes needed for reproduction. The tail is used for moving.

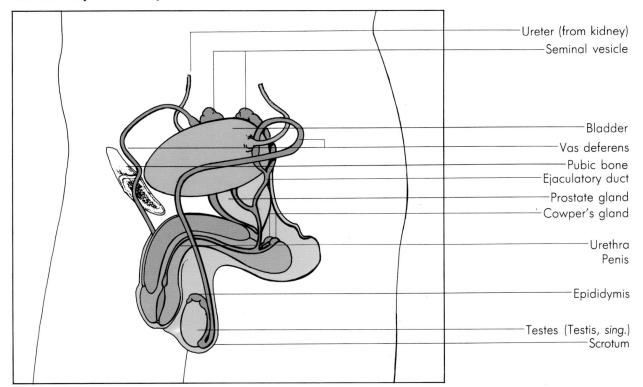

Ureter (from kidney)
Seminal vesicle
Bladder
Vas deferens
Pubic bone
Ejaculatory duct
Prostate gland
Cowper's gland
Urethra
Penis
Epididymis
Testes (Testis, *sing.*)
Scrotum

Caring for the Male Reproductive System

The main way to care for the male reproductive system is to keep it clean. A daily shower that includes washing the penis and scrotum will be enough. It can be helpful, too, to avoid clothing that is too tight.

Another way to care for the reproductive organs is to protect them. This is important during athletic games. Any male who plays a contact sport should use a protector or supporter.

Problems of the Male Reproductive System

Some males develop a cancer in the testes. This is a fairly common disease in males between 15 and 34. It can be detected by feeling a hard lump or swelling in the testes. Pain in that area may also be a sign. Anyone with these signs should see a doctor. The problem can be cured if it is treated early.

Some males are affected by an **inguinal hernia** (IN·gwuhn·uhl HER·nee·uh). This happens when *a hole opens in the abdominal wall through which a piece of intestine pushes into the scrotum.* The hole can be opened by putting too much strain on the muscles of the abdomen. Lifting heavy objects incorrectly can cause this problem. It helps, then, to avoid lifting more than you can manage.

Learning from Drawings
The sperm are stored in the *epididymis* (ep·uh·DID·uh·muhs). They leave the body in a process called *ejaculation* (i·jak·yuh·LAY·shuhn). They pass through the *urethra* (yoo·REE·thruh) in a mixture of liquids called *semen* (SEE·men). Semen includes liquids produced by the seminal vesicles, the prostate gland, and Cowper's gland. How does the sperm pass from the epididymis to the urethra?

More About
*For how to do a **testicular self-exam**, see Chapter 12.*

The Female Reproductive System

The female reproductive organs are inside the body. They have three tasks. One is to store eggs that can be fertilized. The second is to provide a place for the fertilized egg to grow into a baby. The third is to give birth to the baby.

Parts of the Female Reproductive System

The egg cells are stored in the organs called the **ovaries** (OHV·uh·rees). One ovary is on either side of the body. Each holds many thousands of egg cells, which are present even at birth. When puberty takes place, the egg cells begin to mature. They are then released by the ovaries one at a time every month or so. This release is called *ovulation* (ahv·yuh·LAY·shuhn).

The released egg travels to a *Fallopian* (fuh·LOH·pee·uhn) *tube*. If a sperm reaches it there, **fertilization** (fert·uhl·uh·ZAY·shuhn) can take place. This is *the joining together of a sperm and an egg*.

Learning from Drawings
Once fertilized, the egg enters the *uterus* (YOOT·uh·ruhs), a pear-shaped organ where the baby will develop until it is ready to be born. When fully developed, the baby is pushed out of the female body through the *vagina* (vuh·JY·nuh). Does the uterus change as the baby grows?

The Female Reproductive System

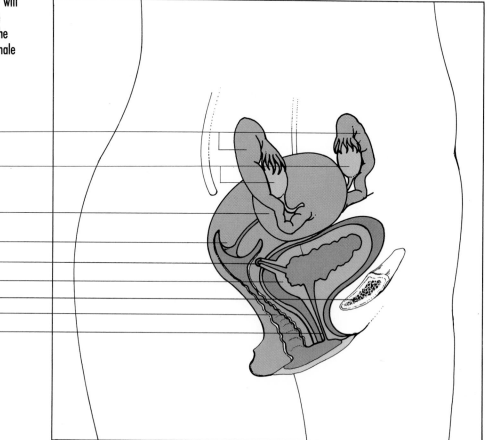

Fallopian tube

Ovary

Uterus

Cervix

Ureter (from kidney)

Bladder

Pubic bone

Vagina

Urethra

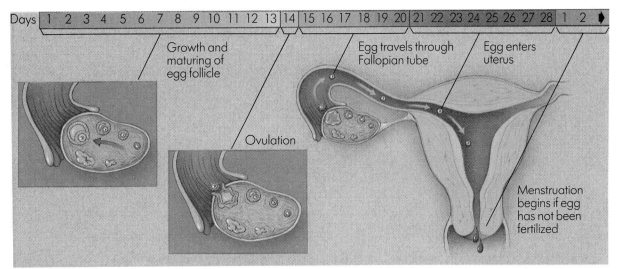

Days | 1 2 3 4 5 6 7 8 9 10 11 12 13 | 14 | 15 16 17 18 19 20 | 21 22 23 24 25 26 27 28 | 1 2 ▶

Growth and maturing of egg follicle

Ovulation

Egg travels through Fallopian tube

Egg enters uterus

Menstruation begins if egg has not been fertilized

The Menstrual Cycle

Just before the ovaries release their eggs, the lining of the uterus walls begin to thicken with blood. This is to prepare the uterus in case fertilization does take place. When it does not, *the lining breaks down and passes out of the body.* This action is called **menstruation** (men•struh•WAY•shuhn). At this time, very little actual blood—only 2 or 3 tablespoons—and other tissue leaves the body. It occurs over 5 to 7 days. The amount of bleeding and length of time vary greatly.

When all the tissue is gone, the ovaries release another egg. The **menstrual** (MEN•struhl) **cycle** is *the time from one menstruation to the next.* The time this takes also differs greatly from one female to another. But in general it lasts about 28 days.

Menstruation varies greatly from person to person. Some females have much blood and others have little. Some feel cramps and some do not. Some always have cycles that are the same length of time, and others have cycles that vary in length. Most girls begin menstruation between the ages of 10 and 15. In these years, the body is just beginning to get used to this new event. Cycles can differ from one time to the next. It is impossible to predict exactly when fertilization will take place.

Caring for the Female Reproductive System

The key to caring for the female reproductive system is to keep it clean. Sanitary pads can be used to catch the flow during menstruation, but they need to be changed often. A shower or bath every day can keep the genital area clean. This should also be enough to remove any mild odors. Odor can be a sign of a problem. If it lasts a long time, however, the person should talk to a doctor.

Learning from Drawings
The *menstrual cycle* is the time from one menstruation to the next. What takes place halfway through the cycle?

Teen Issue

Toxic Shock Syndrome
Some females use tampons rather than sanitary pads to collect the menstrual flow. Doctors now feel that tampons may be related to a serious condition called *toxic shock syndrome.* They suggest that females who do use tampons stay away from the super-absorbent types and make sure to change them frequently.

More About

For how to do a breast self-exam, see Chapter 12.

Females should also have regular medical checkups. These may be given by a family doctor or by a **gynecologist** (gyn·uh·KAHL·uh·juhst). This is *a doctor who specializes in health care of the female reproductive system.* A checkup at least once a year is a good idea.

Problems of the Female Reproductive System

Some women have **premenstrual syndrome** (pree·MEN·struhl SIN·drohm) or *PMS*. PMS is not a disease but *a set of symptoms that some females feel just before menstruation.* Among them are feeling tired, nervous, worried, or depressed. Most women with PMS are in their 30s, but many women never have such problems. A change in diet and lifestyle can help women with PMS.

Another common problem is **vaginitis** (vaj·uh·NYT·uhs). This is simply *an infection of the vagina.* There are three types, each with a different cause. Signs of this problem are itching, and a burning feeling during urination. The appearance of a thick liquid in the vagina may also be a sign. Vaginitis can be treated.

Women can suffer cancer of the cervix or of the breast. The *cervix* (SER·viks) is part of the uterus. Both of these cancers can be treated if they are found early. Cancer of the cervix is found with a test called a *Pap smear.* The American Cancer Society says that all women over 20 should have a Pap smear regularly. Females can use *breast self-examination* to test themselves for breast cancer.

Dealing with Cramps
Those who suffer cramps can take some steps to relieve the discomfort. Mild exercise, massage, and gentle heat can help.

Check Your Understanding

Conclusion   The reproductive system is the part of the body that produces children. The key to caring for the organs in the male and female systems is to keep them clean.

1. **Vocabulary** A *gynecologist* is what kind of doctor?
2. **Recall** What are two things a male can do to care for his reproductive organs?
3. **Recall** What part of the male reproductive system may develop cancer?
4. **Recall** Describe what happens in menstruation.
5. **Recall** What are two exams a female can have to detect cancer?
6. **Classify** Which of the following organs are part of the male and which are part of the female reproductive systems? ovaries, testes, scrotum, penis, uterus, vagina

Recognizing When Your Body Says "Stop"

ave you ever heard the saying "no pain, no gain"? The idea is that only if exercise actually hurts is it effective. Nothing could be further from the truth.

There are many ways to tell that an exercise program is effective. Pain is not one of them. In fact, pain is a sign that the exercise has gone wrong. When done properly, activities like running, biking, or swimming help you. They make your muscles, lungs, and heart work better. If you feel pain, you should stop.

How to Tell When Your Body Should Stop

To protect your body from pain and injury, watch for the following signs of harm. If you feel any of these problems often after you exercise, it's time for a decision. You need to cut back.

- Your heart beats rapidly minutes after you stop exercising.
- You cannot sleep well.
- You feel extremely tired after exercising.

- You must struggle to catch your breath each time you exercise.

If you feel any of these problems *during* your exercise, you need to stop right away.

- You feel nauseated.
- You feel pain in your calf muscles.
- You feel pain in the sides or front of your lower legs.

Using the Skill

Write the name of the three teens described below on a

separate sheet of paper. For each situation, write *stop!* if the teen described should stop the activity. Then tell what that person could decide to do that would be different—and healthier. If the teen described has made a healthy decision already, just write *OK*.

Case One
Juan has begun training for the swim team. He gets up every morning and swims for 2 hours before his classes start. He swims again in the afternoon for 2 hours and often puts in an extra couple of hours at night. Juan has been restless at night lately and is not sleeping well.

Case Two
Sandra is on the school track team. She runs the distance races. She trains every day by running for about 3 hours after her warm-up. When she is done with each day's training, she feels tired but pleased with her work.

Case Three
Beth wants to take up weight training to go along with her aerobics. She worked very hard at the weight machines the first week. But she found that when she finished at the machines, she felt sick and her heart was pounding.

Chapter 7 Review

Summary

- You have nine body systems, each with an important role in your health and well-being.
- Your nervous system is your control center. It reads messages from other parts of your body and tells the body what to do.
- Your circulatory system is the transport system. Blood carries food, oxygen, and waste products to and from the body's cells.
- Your respiratory system supplies the oxygen to your cells and takes away the carbon dioxide you do not need.
- Your skeletal system is the framework of your body. It provides the structure for the body and protects some of the body's organs.
- Your muscular system moves your body and helps you breathe, digest food, and pump blood.
- Your digestive system provides the fuel that your body needs. Your excretory system removes the body's waste products.
- Your endocrine system controls how you grow, how fast you use food for energy, and other important body actions.
- Your reproductive system is changing now to give you the ability to produce new life.
- You must care for all these systems so that they can work properly. Some basic health practices are good for all of these systems. They include eating a good diet, getting plenty of rest, exercising, avoiding tobacco, alcohol, and drugs, and acting safely to avoid injury.

Reviewing Vocabulary and Concepts

On a separate sheet of paper, write the numbers 1–39. After each number, write the letter of the answer that best completes each of the following statements.

Lesson 1

1. The most common damage to the nervous system comes from
   a. polio   **b.** injuries   **c.** cerebral palsy   **d.** stroke

2. The part of the nervous system that controls thinking, remembering, and speaking is the
   a. cerebellum   **b.** spinal cord   **c.** brain stem   **d.** cerebrum

3. Which of the following is true of neuron cells?
   a. They can be repaired but not replaced.
   b. They cannot be repaired or replaced.
   c. They can be replaced but not repaired.
   d. They can be repaired and replaced.

4. Each of the following is a way to care for the nervous system *except*
   a. wearing a helmet when necessary
   b. staying away from drugs
   c. riding in a car without a safety belt
   d. getting rest

5. Which of the following parts of the nervous system controls breathing, the heartbeat, digestion, and hormone levels?
   a. cerebellum   **b.** cerebrum   **c.** spinal cord   **d.** brain stem

226

Lesson 2

6. Each of the following is a job of the circulatory system *except*
   a. fighting disease
   b. carrying food and oxygen to the body's cells
   c. making new blood cells
   d. carrying hormones

7. The blood vessel that carries blood to the heart is the
   a. vein
   b. artery
   c. capillary
   d. plasma

8. When arteries harden with the buildup of fats, the condition is called
   a. heart attack
   b. arteriosclerosis
   c. stroke
   d. hemophilia

9. Someone with the blood type A negative can give blood to someone with the blood type
   a. A positive
   b. AB negative
   c. B positive
   d. B negative

10. The part of the blood that carries oxygen is called
    a. plasma
    b. white-blood cells
    c. red-blood cells
    d. platelets

11. The organ that pumps blood to the lungs to get oxygen and from the lungs to all parts of the body is the
    a. artery
    b. vein
    c. capillary
    d. heart

Lesson 3

12. The muscle that helps in the process of breathing is the
    a. trachea
    b. epiglottis
    c. alveoli
    d. diaphragm

13. The air sacs that trade gases in the lungs are the
    a. tracheas
    b. epiglottises
    c. alveoli
    d. diaphragms

14. Each of the following is a way to care for your respiratory system *except*
    a. having good posture
    b. painting without a mask on
    c. exercising
    d. saying "no" to smoking

15. The most common respiratory problem is
    a. the cold
    b. emphysema
    c. lung cancer
    d. asthma

16. Each of the following respiratory problems is related to smoking *except*
    a. the cold
    b. emphysema
    c. lung cancer
    d. asthma

17. The main organs of breathing are the
    a. trachea
    b. diaphragm
    c. lungs
    d. bronchi

Lesson 4

18. Each of the following is a job of the skeletal system *except*
    a. making blood cells
    b. making food into energy
    c. storing some nutrients
    d. protecting internal organs from injury

19. All of the following are found where bones connect *except*
    a. joints
    b. cartilage
    c. ligaments
    d. tendons

20. Which of the following nutrients are important for bones?
    a. simple and complex sugars
    b. iron and potassium
    c. calcium and phosphorus
    d. protein and carbohydrates

21. Each of the following is a problem that affects joints *except*
    a. fracture
    b. arthritis
    c. sprain
    d. dislocation

22. The kind of bones found in your wrists and ankles are
    a. long bones
    b. cartilage
    c. flat bones
    d. short bones

(continued on page 228)

Lesson 5

23. The muscles in your leg are

    a. smooth muscles   **b.** skeletal muscles   **c.** heart muscle   **d.** involuntary muscles

24. The muscles in your digestive system are

    a. smooth muscles   **b.** skeletal muscles   **c.** heart muscle   **d.** voluntary muscles

25. Each of the following is a muscle problem caused by injury *except*

    a. torn muscle   **b.** strained muscle   **c.** muscular cramp   **d.** muscular dystrophy

26. Aerobic exercise directly helps the muscular system and the

    a. skeletal system   **b.** circulatory system   **c.** digestive system   **d.** endocrine system

27. Two important rules for exercising are to start off by warming up and to

    a. stop before you reach your peak level   **b.** avoid working the muscles too hard   **c.** cool down before stopping   **d.** stop once you reach your peak level

Lesson 6

28. The main work of the digestive system is done by the

    a. small intestine   **b.** stomach   **c.** liver   **d.** mouth

29. The organ that removes solid wastes is the

    a. small intestine   **b.** liver   **c.** large intestine   **d.** kidney

30. The organ that removes liquid wastes is the

    a. small intestine   **b.** liver   **c.** large intestine   **d.** kidney

31. To maintain a good diet and help the digestive and excretory systems, you need to get plenty of

    a. protein and carbohydrates   **b.** fiber and water   **c.** protein and fiber   **d.** carbohydrates and water

Lesson 7

32. All of the following are part of the endocrine system *except* the

    a. pituitary gland   **b.** salivary glands   **c.** thyroid glands   **d.** adrenal glands

33. The pituitary gland controls growth and the action of what other glands?

    a. thyroid and islets of Langerhans   **b.** adrenal and islets of Langerhans   **c.** parathyroid and adrenal   **d.** thyroid and adrenal

34. Good diet and plenty of rest are keys to caring for the endocrine system. These are especially important in

    a. childhood   **b.** adulthood   **c.** the teen years   **d.** infancy

35. Diabetes is a problem that results when the body does not produce enough

    a. growth hormone   **b.** insulin   **c.** iodine   **d.** adrenaline

Lesson 8

36. Eggs are produced in the female's

    a. ovaries   **b.** Fallopian tubes   **c.** uterus   **d.** vagina

37. The basic way to care for both the male and female reproductive systems is
    a. to have a good diet   **b.** to get plenty of rest   **c.** to protect them from injury   **d.** to keep them clean

38. The male's sperm are produced in the
    a. penis   **b.** urethra   **c.** testes   **d.** epididymis

39. The menstrual cycle varies in length from female to female, but it tends to average every
    a. 25 days   **b.** 28 days   **c.** 30 days   **d.** 32 days

Thinking Critically About the Facts

Write your answers to these questions on a separate sheet of paper.

40. Synthesize Give one basic rule for caring for your body systems in each of the following areas: diet, rest, exercise, safety.

41. Analyze Which body systems are involved when you eat and digest food? Explain how each one helps in this action.

42. Classify Name the body system that each of these parts of the body belongs to.
    a. brain
    b. pituitary gland
    c. liver
    d. lung
    e. hip
    f. artery
    g. pancreas
    h. uterus
    i. bicep
    j. neuron
    k. tricep
    l. kidney

43. Sequence Write the letters of the following steps in the right order to make this description of breathing correct.
    a. The alveoli pass carbon dioxide to the blood coming from the heart.
    b. The lungs fill with incoming air.
    c. The diaphragm relaxes, pushing on the chest.
    d. The lungs expel air.
    e. The alveoli send oxygen to blood headed to the heart.
    f. The diaphragm pulls down into the abdomen.

44. Analyze What body systems does aerobic exercise help? How does this type of exercise help them?

45. Analyze Which body systems are harmed by a diet that is not balanced and is high in salt and fat and low in fiber? How are they harmed? What can you do to help them?

Applying the Facts

46. Do some research on the part of the brain that controls movement. Find out what sections control which part of the body. What does the amount of space given to each of these sections tell you about the part of the body controlled? Report what you find to the class.

47. Keep a body systems scrapbook. Clip articles from magazines or newspapers that talk about some part of one of the body systems. The stories can be about feats of athletic skill or creativity, new discoveries in medicine, or people with diseases or disorders who lead active lives. Share your scrapbook with the class.

48. Read about organ transplants. Which organs have been transplanted successfully? What steps do doctors have to take to make the operations a success?

Tobacco and Your Health

Lesson 1	**What's in Tobacco?**	Lesson 2	**Staying Away from Tobacco**

CHAPTER WARM-UP

Chapter Study Goals

After you have read this chapter, you will be able to

- explain how tobacco harms the body.
- explain why many teens use tobacco.
- explain how to say "no" when offered tobacco.
- describe ways of breaking the tobacco habit.
- describe the effects of cigarette smoke on nonsmokers.
- identify steps the government has taken to reduce tobacco use.

Be on the lookout for information in the chapter that will help you reach these goals.

Getting Started

Some people wrongly think that smoking makes them look cool. The truth is, smoking is a habit. A smoker depends on the cigarette to feel good. A habit like this is not "cool." It's just unhealthy.

In this chapter, you will learn the truth about tobacco. You will also learn techniques for saying "no."

Study Tip

As you read this chapter, learn the meanings of the words in dark type. Doing this will help you understand the dangers of smoking.

Words to Know

nicotine
tar
carbon monoxide
bronchi
cancer
alveoli
emphysema
addiction
snuff
leukoplakia

What's in Tobacco?

This lesson contains a number of valuable facts and tips. Once you have studied them, you will be able to

- name the three substances in tobacco that cause health problems.
- tell how smoking harms various parts of the body.
- explain why smokeless tobacco is dangerous.
- tell what the government has done to convince people to avoid using tobacco.

Warnings About Tobacco

In 1964, a report from the surgeon general of the United States linked smoking to lung cancer and heart disease. Soon after this report came out, the federal government took a tough stand against smoking. A law required cigarette makers to label all cigarette packages with warnings about the dangers of smoking. Congress passed a law that banned cigarette ads from television and radio. More

Learning from Photographs
To be able to live and play at your best, you must stay away from harmful substances such as tobacco. Before reading on, can you name any dangers of tobacco?

recent government reports have clearly stated that smoking is the single most preventable cause of lung disease and of death. The warnings on cigarette packages are even stronger now. They speak of the dangers to an unborn baby if a pregnant woman smokes.

People are catching on. Because of such warnings, many people's ideas about smoking have changed. The number of smokers has gone down. Fewer young people are beginning to smoke.

More research was done on tobacco. Studies showed that smoke also harms the health of nonsmokers. As a result, many cities passed tough antismoking laws. These laws ban or limit smoking in restaurants and other public places. The federal government joined in by forbidding smoking on some airplane flights.

What Is in Tobacco?

A single puff of cigarette smoke exposes the body to over 3,000 chemicals. Some are deadly. Almost all make the body unable to work properly. There are three main harmful substances in tobacco smoke.

Harmful Substances in Tobacco Smoke

- **Nicotine.** *A drug in tobacco speeds up the heartbeat.* Called **nicotine** (NIK·uh·teen), this drug also makes tobacco users crave more tobacco. It can cause the dizziness and upset stomach that many beginning smokers feel.

- **Tar.** *A thick, dark liquid is formed when tobacco burns.* This **tar** covers the linings of the lungs, where it can cause disease.

- **Carbon monoxide.** *A poisonous gas is produced when tobacco burns.* This gas, **carbon monoxide** (KAR·buhn muh·NAHK·syd), is what makes the exhaust fumes of cars dangerous.

All three of these poisons are in tobacco smoke, whether the user is smoking a cigarette, a cigar, or a pipe. Tar and carbon monoxide are not in smokeless tobacco. But nicotine is, and that drug creates serious health problems.

What Tobacco Does to the Body

The drugs in tobacco are powerful. They affect the body in many ways, all unhealthy. Worse, smokers have a greater chance than nonsmokers of getting lung disease and heart disease. Smokeless tobacco, too, raises the chances of the user getting certain diseases.

Hop on the Bandwagon

Every year, fewer and fewer people are smoking cigarettes. In 1976, the American Cancer Society said that roughly 37 percent of all American adults smoked. Ten years later, only 30 percent did. The number of teen smokers is also dropping. Join the growing number of nonsmokers. If you never start smoking, you won't have to quit.

DID **YOU** KNOW?

Nicotine: A Deadly Poison
Nicotine is used in making many insecticides. It is used because it kills.

Health Minute

Smoking and Breathing
Take a few seconds to fill your lungs with fresh, clean air. Feel your lungs expand. Then slowly breathe out. What could be easier? Because their lungs are damaged, heavy smokers cannot do what you just did.

What Tobacco Does to the Lungs

You need food, water, and air to live. The air you breathe moves down your windpipe to your lungs. The tar and other chemicals in smoke damage the **bronchi** (BRAHN·kee). These are *the passages through which air enters the lungs.* These tubes can become clogged, then *infected*, or sore and swollen.

The infections may lead to **cancer.** This is *a serious disease caused by the uncontrolled growth of cells.* This cancer is often not found until it has spread to other parts of the body. Once it has done so, it is usually fatal. Lung cancer is the leading cause of death for men in the United States among all cancers. It is now a leading cause of cancer deaths for women.

Cancer is not the only lung disease caused by smoking. Your lungs contain thousands of **alveoli** (al·VEE·oh·ly), or *tiny air sacs.* The alveoli fill with air, then pass oxygen to the blood. Once in the blood, the oxygen is carried throughout the body. The disease called **emphysema** (em·fuh·SEE·muh) occurs when *the alveoli are damaged or destroyed.* This disease forces the lungs to work much harder to take in air. The tar in smoke is one cause of emphysema.

Starting Young, Dying Early

Men who begin smoking cigarettes before the age of 15 are five times more likely to die from lung cancer than are those who begin to smoke after age 25.

Learning from Drawings

The illustration and labels detail how smoking harms the body. Which part of the body do you think is harmed the most?

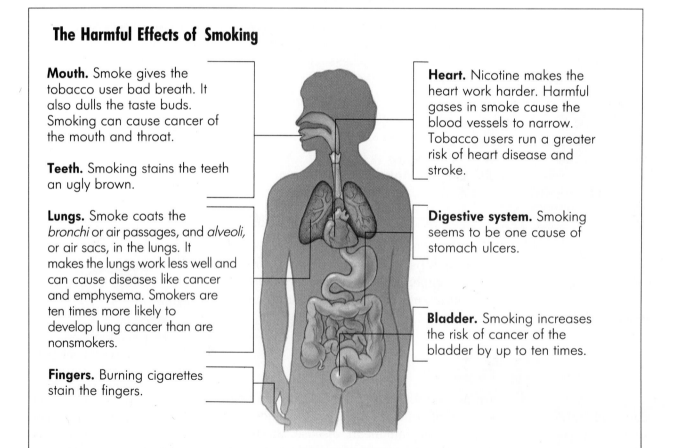

The Harmful Effects of Smoking

Mouth. Smoke gives the tobacco user bad breath. It also dulls the taste buds. Smoking can cause cancer of the mouth and throat.

Teeth. Smoking stains the teeth an ugly brown.

Lungs. Smoke coats the *bronchi* or air passages, and *alveoli,* or air sacs, in the lungs. It makes the lungs work less well and can cause diseases like cancer and emphysema. Smokers are ten times more likely to develop lung cancer than are nonsmokers.

Fingers. Burning cigarettes stain the fingers.

Heart. Nicotine makes the heart work harder. Harmful gases in smoke cause the blood vessels to narrow. Tobacco users run a greater risk of heart disease and stroke.

Digestive system. Smoking seems to be one cause of stomach ulcers.

Bladder. Smoking increases the risk of cancer of the bladder by up to ten times.

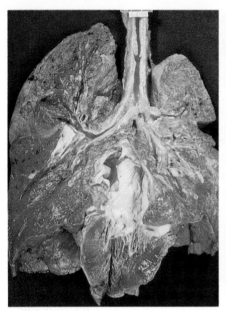
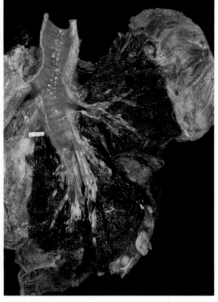

Learning from Photographs
The two pictures show two pairs of lungs. Which do you think are the lungs of the smoker? How would you describe them?

What Tobacco Does to the Heart

Smoking affects the heart also. Nicotine makes the heart beat faster. It also causes the dizziness and upset stomach that many beginning smokers feel. Carbon monoxide passes from the lungs into the blood. Once in the blood, it works to stop the flow of oxygen to all parts of the body. The lack of oxygen causes the smoker to feel tired. Other chemicals in smoke clog the vessels that carry blood to and from the heart.

These effects may give the smoker one of many deadly heart diseases. In fact, doctors say that over 100,000 people die every year from heart disease brought on by smoking.

Other Effects of Tobacco

Tobacco harms a number of other parts of the body. Smoke can cause diseases of the stomach and bladder. It even affects the mouth. Smoke dulls the taste buds, which means that smokers are less able to enjoy the flavor of food than nonsmokers. Smoking can cause cancer in the mouth as well.

Tobacco can make the user less attractive. It stains the teeth and fingernails. Smokers' clothes smell bad, too, because the smoke clings to them.

Smoking is a serious health problem for unborn babies. The babies of pregnant women who smoke might be killed by the effects of smoking. Those who live are more likely to be small and have low birth weight. This raises the chances that they will be ill when they are first born. It also slows their growth throughout childhood.

DID **YOU** KNOW?

Smoking and Heart Attacks
Smoking causes over two thirds of the heart attacks suffered by women under 50.

Not So Nice to Look At
Studies have shown that regular smoking ages the skin, giving it a wrinkled look. One way to keep your skin looking and feeling healthy, then, is to stay away from cigarettes.

Teen Issue

Spare Yourself the Pain
When a smoker quits smoking, he or she may be easy to bother, quick to anger, and all-around unpleasant. Do you want to be unfriendly to your friends? Do you want to be grouchy? You don't? Then don't start smoking—you'll never have to quit!

Why Tobacco Has People Hooked

Worst of all, perhaps, the tobacco user forms an **addiction** (uh·DIK·shuhn). This is *a physical or mental need for a drug or other substance.* Not only does tobacco poison the user. The nicotine actually makes the user *want* the poison! Using tobacco becomes a habit—a very unhealthy habit.

This need for more nicotine is strong. The tobacco user does not feel normal until he or she has another dose of the drug. Only by smoking another cigarette is this need met. The smoker feels better after smoking, but the feeling does not last long. Soon the smoker must smoke again. As the smoker's body becomes more accustomed to the drug, he or she needs it more often to feel its effect.

Smokeless Tobacco

You may know people who use smokeless tobacco. They may chew a wad of tobacco. Or they may use a packet of **snuff** (SNUHF), or *finely ground tobacco.* The user places the snuff between the cheek and gum.

Learning from Photographs
Smokeless tobacco is harmful, just as cigarettes are. What substance in all tobacco products affects the heart?

Smokeless tobacco may seem like a safe thing to use. The user feels that he or she is staying away from the harmful tar and carbon monoxide in smoke. While that may be true, smokeless tobacco is just as dangerous as smoking tobacco. Like cigarettes, smokeless tobacco has nicotine. It, too, is addictive. Like tobacco that is smoked, smokeless tobacco can cause serious diseases.

People who use smokeless tobacco are much more likely to develop mouth and gum cancer than are nonusers. The juice made by chewing may cause *white spots on the gums and on the inside of the cheeks.* These are called **leukoplakia** (loo·koh·PLAY·kee·uh). They often become cancerous.

Chewing tobacco also harms the stomach, intestines, and bladder. Chewing raises the amount of watery saliva in the mouth. When people who chew tobacco swallow this saliva, the poisons that were in the tobacco enter the body. These poisons can cause *ulcers,* or sores, in the stomach. They can also damage the small intestine by harming its inner lining. They may also affect the bladder.

Like cigarettes, smokeless tobacco causes bad breath and stains the teeth. In time, chewing makes it harder for the user to smell and taste certain foods. Because the tobacco leaf has dirt and grit, chewing wears down the teeth and damages the gums.

More About

For more information on how to care for your mouth and teeth, see Chapter 2.

Teen Issue

One Practice That Is Not So "Cool"

Spitting in public is not a cool or classy thing to do. Have you ever seen your favorite movie star spit? But people who chew tobacco have to spit out the tobacco juice that forms in the mouth. Keep this in mind when you think about chewing tobacco. Having to spit often is not going to win you any popularity awards.

Check Your Understanding

Conclusion Using tobacco products, even in smokeless forms, is dangerous. It can lead to cancer and heart disease. By avoiding tobacco products, you are likely to remain much healthier and more attractive and to live longer.

1. **Vocabulary** Copy the following words on a separate sheet of paper. Write *H* next to each word that names a harmful product of tobacco use. Write *D* next to each word that names a disease. *cancer, emphysema, nicotine, carbon monoxide, leukoplakia, tar*

2. **Recall** Name two things the federal government has done to try to influence people not to use tobacco.

3. **Recall** Explain how smoking harms the lungs, heart, stomach, and bladder.

4. **Recall** Give two harmful effects of smokeless tobacco.

5. **Analyze** Why do you think it is difficult to quit smoking?

Teen Health
BULLETIN BOARD

CAREERS

Wanted:
Health Educator

Specifics:
Run public health programs to teach people about how to stay away from tobacco; create brochures and posters.

Qualifications:
Need to be able to communicate well and work well with people. Need to be creative. Must be able to speak to groups.

Preparation:
A four-year college degree is required; a master's degree is helpful.

Contact:
American Public Health Association
1015 Fifteenth Street, NW
Washington, DC 20005

Lifestyle

A Dangerous Fad

Some young people are smoking clove cigarettes because they think these cigarettes are safer than pure tobacco. The truth is that clove cigarettes are dangerous, too. They can cause allergies and can make already existing lung diseases worse. In 1984, a 17-year-old student died from smoking clove cigarettes.

Teen STARS

If you want to see stars in Richardson, Texas, you don't have to look up in the sky. You can look in the schools, which have their own STARS. These are "Students Teaching About the Risks of Smoking," and they are young people eager to spread the word to other young people about the dangers of tobacco use. STARS was founded on the idea that the time to reach students was at the fifth-grade level. As a result, volunteers visit classrooms of fifth-graders, armed with information about decision-making and the risks of smoking. Because of its STARS, Richardson, Texas, is a much brighter place.

TEEN
Q & A

Q: I really like this guy in my science class, but he chews tobacco. It makes me sick. His breath smells terrible! Besides, I know the dangers of using the stuff. What can I do besides just forgetting him?

A: You can begin by pointing out what the chewing does to his breath. Try telling him in a friendly way. You may even try to let him know how you feel in an amusing way. If you need to, tell him the other, more serious effects of smokeless tobacco. They are pretty hard to ignore. That may persuade him to quit using it.

HEALTH IN THE NEWS
Hiding the Dangers

People's ideas about smoking are changing, but the tobacco industry is not taking this change lying down. Recently, several companies have come out with a "smoke-free" cigarette. Of course, the tobacco companies do not claim that the smokeless cigarettes are safer than regular cigarettes. How could they? Though the gases given off may be invisible, the burning tobacco still gives off the same poisons. It exposes both smoker and nonsmoker to the same harmful effects. The truth is that these new smoke-free cigarettes are just as deadly as smoking ones.

HEALTH IN THE NEWS
Save Money on Your Next Prescription— Don't Smoke

Picture a druggist in the pharmacy. He types out a prescription label. It reads, "Take two pills two times a day if you don't smoke. Take *four* pills *four* times a day if you *do* smoke." These labels do not exist yet, but the statement seems to be true.

New studies at the National Cancer Institute show that smokers need bigger doses of some kinds of medicine than do nonsmokers. The reason for this is that chemicals in cigarette smoke cause the liver to release certain substances. These substances make the medicine weaker. Smoking also makes some illnesses worse. You might need new medicine then, too.

Smokers and prescription drugs don't mix well. In fact, smoking and good health don't mix well. The choice is yours. Do you want to smoke or do you want to be healthy?

Word to Know
sidestream smoke

Staying Away from Tobacco

This lesson contains a number of valuable facts and tips. Once you have studied them, you will be able to

- say why teenagers use tobacco.
- tell how to say "no" to using tobacco.
- name some ways of breaking the tobacco habit.
- tell how nonsmokers can defend their rights.

Refusing to Use Tobacco

Now that you have entered your teens, you probably feel that you are no longer a child and that you are ready to be an adult. Unfortunately, many teenagers believe wrongly that using tobacco makes them more adult. They may also think that it helps them look and feel "cool," or in control.

SKILLS FOR LIVING

The Pressure Is On
Understanding the pressures to use tobacco now can help you later on. You will probably feel these pressures more in the years to come.

Learning from Photographs
Smoking damages the lungs' ability to work. What difference would that make to someone trying out for this team?

Other young people try a cigarette just to find out what smoking is like. As many have discovered, the result may not be pleasant. That first cigarette can cause dizziness, a headache, and an upset stomach. Their bodies are sending them a message—smoking is not good.

Pressure from other young people is a reason that some teenagers use tobacco. If some teens you know smoke or chew tobacco, you may get the wrong idea that you have to do the same thing. Some teens may even make fun of you if you don't try tobacco. You may be tempted to give in to this pressure.

There are some very good reasons *not* to use tobacco. It might be easier for you to stay away from tobacco if you remember some of these reasons. Here are a few.

Reasons Not to Use Tobacco

- Tobacco use can cause many serious diseases.
- Smoking makes your hair and clothes smell bad.
- Tobacco use causes bad breath and dulls your senses of smell and taste.
- Smoking or chewing stains your teeth. Smoking stains your fingers.
- Using tobacco can be expensive.
- Tobacco use is no longer considered "cool."
- New laws limit or ban tobacco use in schools and workplaces. In most states it is illegal for persons under 16 years of age to purchase tobacco products.
- Tobacco can be addictive.

DID **YOU** KNOW?

Smoking Is Not Cheap
People who smoke one pack of cigarettes each day could spend over $500 in a year. Can you think of better things they might do with the money?

Saying "No" to Tobacco

Saying "no" is not easy. When friends or peers put the pressure on, it can be hard to resist. But you *can* resist—just as tens of thousands of teens have done.

Begin by being prepared. The time might come when someone will ask you to use tobacco. It is better to know ahead of time what you will say. A well-prepared answer will get better results.

If the pressure seems light, just refuse. Say you are not interested. If the pressure is greater—if, for example, other people ask you what you are afraid of—use one of the reasons listed in the box above. Or give a reason of your own. Say you want to keep your breathing healthy for basketball or swimming. Say the smoke you smelled from a relative's cigarette always made you sick.

DID **YOU** KNOW?

TV Is Helping
Television networks are doing their part to change the public's ideas about cigarette smoking. Talk-show hosts and actors in series rarely smoke. By staying away from cigarettes, they show that smoking is not cool.

Learning from Photographs
None of these teens smoke. How does being with friends who don't smoke help you resist the pressure to smoke?

Healthy Snacks

Many people who quit smoking gain weight because they eat instead of smoking. Choosing healthy snacks will make this less likely. For some ideas for healthy snacks, see Chapter 5.

Teen Issue

Not Just Teens and Adults

When smokers hear the word *nonsmokers,* many of them do not think of children. But an infant's lungs are easily damaged by harsh side-stream smoke. You might point this out to smokers.

Sometimes the pressure can be very strong. Other people might try to shame you into using tobacco by calling you names like "coward" or "chicken." When this happens, you need to stand your ground. Ask why it is so important to them that you share their habit. Point to all the teens who do not smoke. Tell them that you respect their decision, but they should respect yours. If nothing else works, walk away.

One way to help yourself resist pressure is by choosing friends who do not smoke. Stick together when the pressure is on. You will find it easier for each of you to say no.

Breaking the Tobacco Habit

A recent study found that almost three quarters of all smokers wanted to quit. They knew that smoking was unhealthy, but they weren't sure how to stop. The best way for many is to stop quickly and completely. Slowly cutting back simply does not work for some people. Others, though, find that quitting in stages is the best way.

TOBACCO QUIZ

The True and False About Smoking

These questions deal with some of people's ideas about tobacco. How would you answer each? After you have finished, look at the answers on page 247 of this chapter.

1. Can smoking for a few years as a teen hurt me?
2. If I don't breathe in the smoke, can smoking still hurt me?
3. Can I smoke only a few cigarettes now and then without getting the "habit"?
4. Are filtered cigarettes much safer than nonfiltered ones?
5. If I quit smoking now, will my risk of getting lung disease become less?
6. Is it easier for a teen to quit smoking than it is for a person who has smoked for many years?

Tactics That May Help

Someone who is trying to kick the tobacco habit can do a number of things. Exercising regularly and eating healthy snacks are two things that can help a person avoid tobacco. As a bonus, these activities are healthy in and of themselves. The box has some other suggestions.

Tips for Someone Quitting Smoking

- List the reasons to quit and read the list when he or she wants to smoke.

- When he or she feels the urge to smoke, delay lighting up for a few minutes. In that time, think about the benefits of not smoking.

- Set small goals. He or she could try to quit for one day, then another, then another.

- Get rid of all reminders of smoking such as ashtrays and lighters.

- At the beginning, he or she should try to avoid people who smoke.

- Change habits that are linked to smoking. Someone who always has a cigarette after dinner, for instance, could get up from the table right after eating.

- Invent a reward. He or she could find some way to give himself or herself a treat for *not* lighting a cigarette.

Learning from Photographs
Every year, the American Cancer Society sponsors the "Great American Smokeout," calling for all smokers to avoid smoking for one day. How might this help a smoker quit?

People who succeed at quitting keep in mind how they will benefit. And they always remember that it is within their power to quit.

Programs That May Help

Many groups offer programs to help people quit smoking. The American Lung Association, the American Heart Association, and the American Cancer Society offer several of these programs. Anyone can contact these groups by telephone or mail to get more information.

People who do not use tobacco can help someone trying to quit. If you know someone who is kicking the habit, be encouraging. Praise the person each day that he or she stays away from smoking.

Smoking and the Nonsmoker

Cigarette smoke does not harm just smokers. *The smoke coming from the burning tip of another person's cigarette* is called **sidestream smoke.** Sidestream smoke contains twice as much tar and nicotine as does the smoke that the smoker breathes in. This is because the sidestream smoke has not passed through the length of the cigarette and cigarette filter.

Helping Out
If you know someone who is trying to quit smoking, make it easier for him or her. Remind others not to smoke nearby. Give support by pointing out how much you admire the step he or she is taking.

Health Minute

You're Not Alone

Next time you're in a restaurant, compare the numbers of people sitting in the nonsmoking and smoking sections. Nonsmoking sections are getting more popular every day.

DID YOU KNOW?

Clean Airplanes

The government now bans smoking on any airplane flight that is shorter than two hours. On longer flights, smoking is allowed, but smokers must sit in the rear of the plane.

Though you may not smoke cigarettes, you may often find yourself around people who do. Some of your friends may smoke at parties. In restaurants, people sitting near you may smoke. At these times, you are likely to breathe in sidestream smoke.

A New Bill of Rights

A group called the National Interagency Council on Smoking and Health is letting nonsmokers know that they have choices about sidestream smoke. This group has written a Nonsmoker's Bill of Rights.

The Nonsmoker's Bill of Rights

- The right to breathe clean air
- The right to speak out
- The right to act

If someone around you smokes, you can ask that person not to smoke or to put out the cigarette. Nowadays, most smokers do what nonsmokers ask of them. If a smoker refuses to put out the cigarette, you can move farther away.

Nonsmokers can make use of their right to act by working to get laws that ban smoking or limit it to certain places. Nonsmokers have had much success in many cities and counties. Most restaurants now have separate nonsmoking sections. Some do not allow smoking at all. Perhaps in the future you will help to make a smoke-free America.

Check Your Understanding

Conclusion   It is important to understand why people use tobacco, how it affects them, and how they can break the tobacco habit. Making use of your rights as a nonsmoker can protect your health and the health of those around you.

1. **Vocabulary** Define the term *sidestream smoke*.
2. **Recall**   Give two reasons why some teens begin to smoke.
3. **Recall** State four reasons why no one should use tobacco.
4. **Recall** List three hints for someone trying to break the tobacco habit.
5. **Analyze** Miguel went to a party with his friend Sam. A group offered them a cigarette, but Miguel did not want to smoke. What could he have done?

Seeing Through the Tobacco "Smoke Screen"

What do you think when you see a cigarette ad that shows a group of smokers having fun? Do you believe that smoking is a way to make friends and share a good time? This is the hidden message that the cigarette makers want you to get.

They send this message to influence your decision about smoking. They show appealing pictures to make you feel good about smoking. They try to persuade you to decide to smoke. The ad is concerned with "image," the way things appear. But this image is a "smoke screen" that hides the truth about smoking.

How to Spot the Hidden Messages

You can avoid being confused by this smoke screen. You can make your *own* decision. Just analyze the ad to see the hidden messages.

■ **Look for the hidden message in the picture.** Does the ad show attractive, healthy-looking people enjoying a smoke together? The image is that smokers

look and feel great. The reality is that smokers are at much greater risk of getting lung cancer, heart disease, and emphysema than are nonsmokers.

■ **Look for the hidden message in the words.** Does the ad say "Be in on the action" or "Join the crowd"? The image is that smokers are popular. The reality is that smokers are becoming more and more left out because nonsmokers don't want to

breathe their smoke. Do the words say "Fresh," "Satisfying"? The image is that smoking refreshes your mouth. The reality is that smoking gives you a dry mouth and bad breath.

Using the Skill

Look carefully at the cigarette ad on this page. Then, on a separate sheet of paper, answer the questions that follow.

1. What is the hidden message in the picture?
2. What things are you *not* told about smoking in this ad?
3. What is the hidden message in the words at the bottom of the ad?
4. After analyzing this ad, what decision about smoking would you make? Explain your choice.

Chapter 8 Review

Summary

- People are responding to the warnings about the dangers of using tobacco. Cigarette smoke can cause lung cancer, heart disease, and other illnesses. It also makes the user look unattractive.
- Chewing smokeless tobacco is as dangerous to the health of the user as is smoking. It can lead to diseases of the mouth, gums, stomach, small intestine, and bladder.
- There are many good reasons to not use tobacco. Teens who want to be healthy and attractive can say "no" to tobacco use.
- Breaking the tobacco habit is not easy. However, every user has the power to do so.
- The sidestream smoke from other people's cigarettes is dangerous. Nonsmokers have the right to ask others not to smoke.

Reviewing Vocabulary and Concepts

Lesson 1

On a separate sheet of paper, write the numbers 1–9. After each number, write the term from the list on the right that best completes each statement.

1. One of the major health hazards of smoking is lung _____ .
2. Chewing smokeless tobacco is just as _____ as smoking.
3. Both smoking and chewing tobacco are unattractive. They cause bad breath and _____ the teeth.
4. The government has put a _____ on all radio and television advertising of tobacco products.
5. Tobacco contains the powerful drug _____ , which causes the user to become addicted.
6. Smoking can damage the _____ by making it beat faster.
7. Chewing tobacco can cause sores in the stomach that are called _____ .
8. Cigarette packages contain _____ about the health hazards that smoking can cause.
9. Tar coats the alveoli in the lungs, where it can cause the disease _____ .

ban
cancer
dangerous
emphysema
heart
nicotine
stain
ulcers
warnings

Lesson 2

On a separate sheet of paper, write the numbers 10–15. After each number, write the letter of the answer that best completes each of the following statements.

10. Among the reasons for *not* smoking is the fact that tobacco use is
    a. cool
    b. unattractive
    c. popular
    d. a cheap habit
11. A smoker who wants to quit smoking can
    a. quit
    b. *not* quit
    c. only cut down
    d. only change to chewing tobacco

12. Each of the following is a reason that teens begin to use tobacco *except*
    a. to look better
    b. to go along with the crowd
    c. to be more adult
    d. to know what smoking is like
13. Each of the following is a group that helps people who want to quit smoking *except* the
    a. American Heart Association
    b. American Lung Association
    c. American Cancer Society
    d. National Interagency Council on Smoking and Health
14. Each of the following is a method used by a person who wants to quit smoking *except*
    a. exercising regularly
    b. keeping all habits
    c. eating healthy snacks
    d. inventing rewards
15. Sidestream smoke
    a. is less dangerous than firsthand smoke
    b. is not dangerous at all
    c. is more dangerous than firsthand smoke
    d. dissolves in the air

Thinking Critically About the Facts

Write your answers to the following questions on a separate sheet of paper.

16. **Synthesize** Explain what you would say to a friend who tells you that he has decided to try using smokeless tobacco.
17. **Cause and effect** Write the words *nicotine* and *tar* on your paper. Then read the following list and copy down the names of the conditions or diseases caused by each of these substances.
lung cancer	addiction to tobacco
heart works harder	emphysema
18. **Draw conclusions** Someone you know is trying to kick the smoking habit. List three things she could do when she feels the urge to have a cigarette.
19. **Synthesize** You are in a subway station waiting for a train. You are with your grandmother, who has emphysema and is bothered by smoke. Someone standing next to you lights a cigarette. Name two things you could do.

Applying the Facts

20. Action for Smoking and Health, or *ASH*, is a national organization working for a smoke-free America. Write a letter to ASH at its headquarters: Action for Smoking and Health, 2013 H Street NW, Washington, DC 20006. Ask how you can fight smoking in your community. Find out whether your community has a local chapter of ASH. Discuss your findings with the class.
21. Make a list of interview questions. For ex-smokers, ask why and how they stopped smoking. For people who have never smoked, ask whether they ever wanted to smoke, and what kinds of pressures they felt to smoke. Then interview several people. Write down their answers. Share your findings with the class.

Answers to Tobacco Quiz (page 242)

1. Yes. Smoking damages the throat and lungs and affects your appearance.
2. Yes. Even if you do not inhale, some smoke will enter your lungs.
3. Yes. But it is risky; most people who begin smoking become addicted to tobacco.
4. No. Some filter cigarettes contain more nicotine and tar than do nonfilter brands.
5. Yes. If you quit now, damaged lungs can heal themselves.
6. Yes. The longer you smoke, the worse your addiction becomes.

Alcohol and Your Health

CHAPTER WARM-UP

Chapter Study Goals

After you have read this chapter, you will be able to

- describe a variety of health risks for teens who drink.
- explain how you can help someone with a drinking problem.
- state some reasons teens give for using alcohol.
- state some reasons teens give for not using alcohol.
- identify healthy alternatives to alcohol use.

Be on the lookout for information in the chapter that will help you reach these goals.

Getting Started

"I don't want to drink. Why risk being caught?"
—Shari, age 12

"Drinking? No way! Alcohol just means trouble."
—Marcus, age 13

Which of these beliefs about alcohol matches what the poster with Stevie Wonder says? In this chapter, you will learn some hard facts about alcohol.

Study Tip

As you read this chapter, pay special attention to the numbers and percentages given. They will help you understand the dangers of using alcohol.

"Before I'll ride with a drunk, I'll drive myself." —Stevie Wonder

Driving after drinking, or riding with a driver who's been drinking, is a big mistake. Anyone can see that.

What Alcohol Does to Your Body

Words to Know
alcohol
depressant
oxidize
cirrhosis
fetal alcohol
    syndrome
blood alcohol level
    (BAL)
addiction

This lesson contains a number of valuable facts and tips. Once you have studied them, you will be able to

- tell how alcohol affects the body.
- list the factors that determine alcohol's effects on a person.
- name dangers that exist for teens who drink.
- define the term *addiction*.

DID **YOU** KNOW?

Drinking Makes People Sick
Over one third of patients in hospitals in this country have problems related to alcohol. About a fifth of the total money spent on hospital care is spent on alcohol-related problems.

Alcohol: Fact and Fiction

Over 14 million Americans have problems that are related to alcohol use. Some of these people are teens. Yet people's beliefs about alcohol are clouded in myth. Some of these myths are stated by teens in the Chapter Warm-Up. Eduardo believes that drinking alcohol is not as harmful as taking drugs. The truth is that **alcohol** (AL·kuh·hawl) *is a drug*. It is *a drug that is produced by a chemical reaction in some foods and that has powerful effects on the body.*

Shari knows that drinking alcohol is illegal for teens. That's a good reason to stay away from alcohol. But Shari does not mention that alcohol also can do serious damage to your body.

Learning from Photographs
Staying away from alcohol helps keep you mentally and physically healthy. How does saying "no" to alcohol help teens prevent legal problems?

Alcohol and Your Body

Alcohol is a **depressant** (di·PRES·uhnt), *a drug that tends to slow down the working of the brain and other parts of the nervous system.* When a person takes a drink, the alcohol enters the person's stomach the way food does. About 20 percent of the alcohol passes through the lining of the stomach and into the bloodstream. The rest moves to the small intestine, where it then enters the bloodstream.

Once in the blood, the alcohol begins to affect the brain. The brain becomes less able to control the body. This is why a person who drinks alcohol is likely to do things he or she would not normally do. A quiet person, for example, may suddenly become loud. Other common results of alcohol include clumsiness, trouble seeing straight, and trouble speaking clearly. Alcohol causes problems for other parts of the body as well.

More About

To learn more about **depressant drugs** *and how they affect the body, see Chapter 10.*

Problems Created by Alcohol

Body Part	Problem
Bloodstream	As it passes through the bloodstream, alcohol widens the blood vessels. This allows more blood to flow through them. The drinker feels warmer because more blood flows near the surface of the skin. But this warmth is misleading. Since blood close to the surface of the body loses its heat quickly, body temperature actually drops. The false sense of warmth produced by alcohol can be dangerous. It can lead a person not to dress warmly enough or to stay out too long in cold weather.
Liver	Nearly all the alcohol taken into the body passes through the liver. The liver is a gland that does hundreds of jobs for the body. When alcohol is present, the liver **oxidizes** (AHK·suh·DYZ·uhs) it, or *changes it into water and the gas carbon dioxide.* However, the liver can oxidize only one-half ounce of alcohol each hour. When forced to oxidize alcohol, a condition known as **cirrhosis** (suh·ROH·suhs), or *scarring of the liver,* results. Cirrhosis can be deadly.
Kidneys	Alcohol tricks the kidneys into making more urine. The drinker urinates often. *Dehydration* (dee·hy·DRAY·shuhn), or a loss of needed body fluids, can result.
Stomach	Alcohol causes the stomach to make acids. This can lead to an upset stomach. Drinking over a long period can cause *ulcers.* These open sores are caused by the acids breaking down the lining of the stomach.
Lungs	Alcohol can be smelled on a person's breath because small amounts are breathed out through the lungs.

DID **YOU** KNOW?

More Than Just a Depressant
Drinking alcohol over a long period of time destroys millions of brain cells. Unlike other body cells, brain cells cannot be repaired or replaced.

DID **YOU** KNOW?

To Be Sober, Stay Sober
One popular myth is that caffeine or a cold shower can make someone less drunk. They *can* work to make someone who has been drinking less tired. But they *cannot* give the drinker's brain more control over his or her body. The result of drinking coffee, then, isn't a person who is no longer drunk, but a more awake drunk. There is no way to speed up the process of ridding the body of alcohol.

Learning from Photographs
This baby was born in excellent health, partly because the mother took care of herself. Why does alcohol that a pregnant female drinks affect the developing baby?

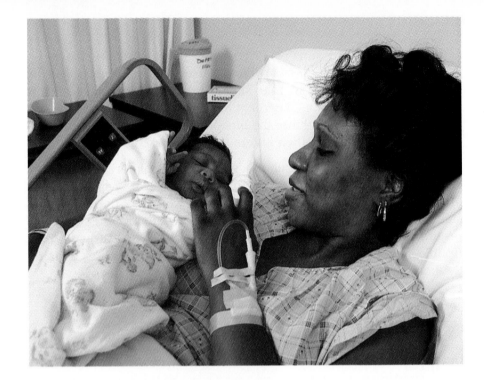

DID **YOU** KNOW?

Chemistry Lesson
Everyone's body is made up of different amounts of many different chemicals. Which chemicals your body contains is a factor in how alcohol affects you.

Teen Issue
. . . .

No Safe Drinks
Some teens believe that wine coolers — blends of fruit juice and wine — are safe. These teens are wrong. Coolers contain alcohol, which means they can have harmful effects on the body. Also, because coolers are made to taste sweet, people tend to drink large amounts. That makes coolers even more dangerous.
. . . .

Fetal Alcohol Syndrome

When a pregnant woman drinks alcohol, another person may be harmed. Such women may pass along to their unborn babies a condition called **fetal** (FEET·uhl) **alcohol syndrome** (SIN·drohm). Babies with this condition *have a group of physical and mental problems caused by the mother-to-be drinking alcohol.* These babies may weigh less than normal at birth, be weak, and be mentally retarded. Some babies show all these effects, others only a few. There can be other effects as well.

The most tragic part of fetal alcohol syndrome is that the unborn baby has no control over what enters its body. The choice to drink or not drink is the mother's. Research has not yet shown how much alcohol, if any, is safe for a pregnant woman to drink.

Alcohol and the Individual

Six factors shape how alcohol affects the person who drinks.

- **Speed.** Drinking a lot in a short period of time causes the alcohol to remain in the bloodstream longer.
- **Quantity.** The amount a person drinks plays an important part in how his or her body reacts.

- **Food.** A person who has eaten recently has food in the stomach. This slows down the passing of the alcohol into the bloodstream.

- **Weight.** A lighter person feels the effects of alcohol sooner than a heavier person. Heavier people have more blood and water in the body to "thin out" the effects of the alcohol.

- **Mood.** How a person feels before drinking affects how she or he feels afterward. A drinker who starts off depressed usually ends up more depressed.

- **Other drugs.** Mixing alcohol with other drugs increases the effects of the alcohol or of the other drug. Even aspirin makes a difference in how alcohol affects the body.

The amount of alcohol in the blood is measured using a number called the **blood alcohol level (BAL).** This is *the percentage of alcohol in the blood.* The figure is found by comparing the weight of alcohol in the blood to the weight of the blood itself. In most states, driving with a BAL of 0.1 percent or more is defined as drunk driving. Notice in the chart "Alcohol in the Blood" that this level is reached after drinking just 3 ounces of liquor.

More About

To learn more about the dangers of mixing alcohol with other drugs, see Chapter 10.

Alcohol in the Blood

BAL	Approximate amount of alcohol drunk in two hours	Effect on a 100-pound person
0.05%	1–2 ounces of liquor or 1–2 12-ounce beers	Small decrease in reaction time and judgment; carelessness; some loss of coordination and self-control.
0.1%	3–4 ounces of liquor or 3–4 12-ounce beers	Large decrease in coordination, ability to see, and judgment; relaxing of self-control.
0.2%	5–6 ounces of liquor or 5–6 12-ounce beers	Great loss of self-control, ability to think clearly, and memory; emotional behavior is unusual; muscle control is difficult.
0.3%	7–8 ounces of liquor or 7–8 12-ounce beers	Senses—sight, hearing, ability to judge distances—very poor; very difficult to move.
0.4%	9–10 ounces of liquor or 9–10 12-ounce beers	Brain can barely work; may be uncontrolled vomiting or urination; unable to move.
0.5%	Over 10 ounces of liquor or over 10 12-ounce beers	Body enters coma; brain unable to control body temperature or breathing, which may cause death.

DID **YOU** KNOW?

A Drink Is a Drink
A 12-ounce beer, a 5-ounce glass of wine, and 1½ ounces of 80 proof liquor all have the same amount of alcohol.

Teen Issue

The Winner Is the Loser
Recently, members of a college fraternity were charged with contributing to the death of a new member. He died after "chug-a-lugging"—swallowing many drinks in single gulps. Drinking games can cause the heart and respiration to shut down. That, in turn, can cause death—which is no game.

The penalties for driving while drunk are severe. People convicted of this crime can lose their driver's license, pay a big fine, and spend time in jail. Another penalty is living with the knowledge that they might have caused someone to become crippled or caused another person's death.

Helping Out

Many adults choose a "designated driver" before a party. That person promises not to drink and is responsible for driving the others home.

Teen Issue

Is Jail Fun?

You might be offered a drink at a party, after a sporting event, or while just hanging out with others. Remember that drinking is against the law for teens. Jail is not worth taking that drink. Say "no" to breaking the law.

Drinking and Driving

Alcohol harms a person's ability to think and to make responsible decisions. When people who have been drinking alcohol get behind the wheel of a car, they are turning the car into a dangerous weapon.

Some people claim that they drive better after drinking. Others insist that alcohol makes them think more clearly. Both of these beliefs are wrong. In fact, the opposite is true.

Alcohol causes other accidents as well. The following facts paint an unpleasant picture.

Alcohol's Safety Record

- The National Highway Traffic Administration reports that someone dies every 27 minutes in a car accident that involves alcohol.
- More than half of all people who die from drowning had been drinking.
- About half of all deaths by fire involve drinking.

Alcohol and Teens

Drinking alcohol is against the law for people your age. Have you ever wondered why this is so? Laws that forbid the use of alcohol by young people are not meant to punish you. They are there to *protect* you.

Right now, your body is going through some very important changes that will continue over the next few years. These changes will partly affect how you turn out as an adult. Alcohol interferes with these changes.

In addition, the use of alcohol by young people leads to some "sobering" statistics.

Alcohol's Danger for Teens

- About 12,000 young people die in this country each year in accidents that involve alcohol.
- Almost two thirds of all traffic deaths involving a young person are related to alcohol.
- Nearly 50 percent of all suicide victims had been drinking alcohol at the time of their death.

Alcohol Can Be Habit-Forming

People who drink alcohol regularly come to need more and more alcohol to feel a desired effect. After a while, this increased use causes the drinker to form an addiction to alcohol. An **addiction** (uh•DIK•shuhn) is *a physical or mental need for a drug or other substance*. Studies show that people who begin drinking at an early age have a greater chance of becoming addicted. This raises the risk of family problems, losing jobs, and poor health.

Learning from Photographs
These teens are enjoying themselves *without* alcohol. How might alcohol get in the way of having fun?

Check Your Understanding

Conclusion Alcohol can do serious harm to the body. It is against the law for teens to use alcohol. Teens are at great risk of serious harm or death when they use alcohol. Alcohol can cause a person to come to rely on it.

1. **Vocabulary** Two of the following terms from the lesson name an illness or condition: *depressant, cirrhosis, fetal alcohol syndrome, oxidizes*. Which terms are they?

2. **Recall** List at least three factors that determine alcohol's effects on a person.

3. **Recall** Name four dangers that exist for teens who drink alcohol.

4. **Recall** What is an addiction?

5. **Synthesize** Suppose a friend told you it is okay to drink as long as you only drink beer. How might you respond?

DID **YOU** KNOW?

The Two Faces of Addiction
Some habit-forming substances lead to *psychological addiction*. This is addiction where the mind sends the body the message that it needs more and more of the drug. Other substances lead to *physical addiction*. This is addiction where the body itself feels a direct need for the drug. Either type of addiction—and some substances can cause *both*—can only be overcome through great mental and physical pain.

Teen Health
BULLETIN BOARD

Q: A friend of mine tells me beer drinking is OK. He says only the "harder" stuff can get you in trouble. Is he right?

A: No, he is absolutely wrong, as any of the many alcoholics who drink only beer can tell you. Like other forms of liquor, beer contains alcohol, about an ounce per 12-ounce can or bottle. When a person who weighs 100 pounds drinks one or two beers over a period of 2 hours, that person's judgment becomes flawed. Objects may appear closer or farther away than they really are. When the same person has twice as many beers over the same period, the situation is twice as serious. The person, in fact, is now drunk—which is probably what your friend means by "getting in trouble."

Lifestyle

Are you S.A.D.D.?

If the thought of someone driving drunk makes your blood boil, don't get mad—get S.A.D.D. A high school teacher and coach in a town in Massachusetts founded S.A.D.D. He did this after two of his hockey players died in alcohol-related accidents. Now S.A.D.D. runs two programs. The junior high school program is called Students Against Doing Drugs. The high school and college program is Students Against Driving Drunk.

Student members of S.A.D.D. sign "contracts" with their parents. In the contract, the teen promises to call home at any hour when a "sober" ride is not available. In return, the parent agrees to come and pick up his or her child at any hour—*no questions asked at the time*. Both teen and parent agree that the issue of drinking will be talked about at another time.

Since S.A.D.D. began in 1981, it has grown. It is now in more than 15,000 schools across the country. If you would like to learn about membership in S.A.D.D. or about starting a local chapter, send a stamped, self-addressed envelope to S.A.D.D., P.O. Box 800, Marlboro, MA 01752.

CAREERS

Wanted:

Alcohol Counselor

Specifics:

Works with alcoholics and families of alcoholics.

Qualifications:

Must relate well with people and have ability to put people at ease. Must have desire to help people deal with personal problems and improve their personal lives.

Preparation:

A degree in psychology, social work, nursing, or counseling is good preparation. Some colleges offer training programs. Laws concerning licensing vary from state to state.

Contact:

A university or college department of counseling, social work, or psychology.

L ifestyle

"Teen"-der Loving Care

Yvonne, who is 15, has been feeling upset lately over her father's drinking problem. Today, she has an appointment with her counselor, Leslie. Leslie seems to know just how to talk to someone Yvonne's age. Maybe that's partly because Leslie *is* Yvonne's age.

Leslie is a "peer helper," a participant in a program for teens who want to help out other teens. Volunteers for the program are usually very good listeners. They learn to help people their age deal with many different kinds of problems, ranging from trouble at school to alcohol and drug abuse. Often peer helpers are teens who have been through serious problems themselves.

So far, the program has caught on in a dozen states around the country. Thanks to peer helpers, teens are finding that other teens not only care about their problems but often have answers.

HEALTH IN THE NEWS

Mothers Who Are M.A.D.D.

On May 3, 1980, Cari Lightner, a 13-year-old from Fair Oaks, California, was killed when a car hit her from behind. The driver, who was drunk at the time of the accident, had been arrested twice before for drunk driving. In fact, his last arrest had been just two days before this crime.

When Cari's mother, Candy, learned that the man would probably not go to jail for her daughter's senseless death, she was outraged. She quit her job and formed M.A.D.D.—Mothers Against Drunk Driving. The goals of M.A.D.D. are to work toward harsher penalties for drunk drivers and to offer assistance to victims and families of drunk-driver crimes. M.A.D.D. also sponsors school programs to educate young people about the dangers of driving drunk. You can obtain more information on M.A.D.D.'s school programs by writing to the organization headquarters: M.A.D.D., 669 Airport Freeway, Suite 310, Hurst, TX 76053

What Is Alcoholism?

Words to Know

alcoholism
Alcoholics
    Anonymous (AA)
Alateen
Al-Anon

This lesson contains a number of valuable facts and tips. Once you have studied them, you will be able to

- define *alcoholism.*
- list the stages of alcoholism.
- name some groups that can help people with drinking problems and their families.

Alcoholism: Problems and Disease

Alcohol can become addictive. In some cases, this *physical and mental need for alcohol turns into a disease* called **alcoholism.** People with this disease are called *alcoholics.* They cannot keep from drinking. They cannot stop drinking once they have started. They drink even when they know they are harming their own health.

Researchers are looking for reasons why people become alcoholics. Some feel the disease may run in families. Scientists do not believe, however, that children of alcoholic parents will automatically become alcoholics themselves.

DID **YOU** KNOW?

Beyond Addiction
The average life expectancy of a heavy drinker is 10 to 12 years less than that of a nondrinker.

Stages of Alcoholism

Experts say that alcoholism develops in three stages. These stages happen over a period of time.

- **Stage One.** Some adults in our society drink alcohol on occasion. Trouble begins when the person begins to use alcohol to relieve stress or to relax. Soon the person needs alcohol to cope with the day-to-day pressures of life. The drinker begins to make excuses to family and friends about his or her drinking habits. The person may become drunk often.

- **Stage Two.** As the person continues to drink, the body develops a need for more and more alcohol. Drinking becomes the most important part of the person's life. The drinker spends much time and energy figuring out where and when the next drink will be.

Learning from Photographs
Scientists do not know for sure, but children *may* be more likely to become alcoholics if their parents are alcoholics. What can be done to prevent this disease?

The person is often absent from school or work. All the while, the person continues to deny that there is a problem.

- **Stage Three.** In the final stage of alcoholism, the problem is clear to other people. The drinking is now totally out of control. The drinker's body is strongly addicted. Without alcohol, he or she feels strong mental and physical pain. The person often drifts away from family and friends.

Help for the Victim

Alcoholism *can* be treated. With proper care, more than 60 percent of all alcoholics who try to stop drinking succeed. After stopping, however, the person must never drink alcohol. Otherwise, he or she has a very high chance of becoming addicted again.

One group that has had success in helping alcoholics beat their addiction is **Alcoholics Anonymous** (uh·NAHN·uh·muhs). Also known as **AA,** this is *a support group for alcoholics.* AA has local chapters across the country. These chapters are listed in the telephone book. At AA meetings, people who are recovering from alcoholism help other drinkers to stop.

Do You Want to Be Like This?

Consider these facts before you take that first drink.

- Alcohol causes many drinkers to become nervous and hostile.
- Alcohol damages the brain and other body organs.
- One alcohol-related accident can ruin your life and the lives of other innocent people.

Learning from Photographs
Alateen offers support to the children of alcoholics. How could a group meeting like this help?

DID **YOU** KNOW?

The "Don't List" for Recovering Alcoholics
Many medicines such as cough syrups and mouthwashes contain small percentages of alcohol. Since recovering alcoholics must stay away from alcohol to continue their recovery, they must avoid these products.

Help for the Victim's Family

The harmful effects of alcohol do not stop with the drinker. Family members and friends of heavy drinkers suffer, too. If the alcoholic has health or job problems because of drinking, the family must live with these problems. Most cases of spouse and child abuse involve people who have been drinking.

One in four families in the United States is touched by alcoholism. This means that a growing number of young people are living with or are friends with a person addicted to alcohol.

What can be done? Some groups help friends and family cope.

- **Alateen.** *One group helps children of alcoholic parents.* Called **Alateen,** it suggests ways children can help the drinking parent. It also helps them learn how to cope with the problems of having a parent who suffers from alcoholism.

- **Al-Anon.** Another *group helps the husbands, wives, and friends of alcoholics.* This group is called **Al-Anon.** Local chapters of both Alateen and Al-Anon are listed in the telephone book. Al-Anon has a toll-free phone number. This number is 1–800–356–9956.

How Can You Help?

If a friend or family member has a drinking problem, you can do several things to help.

More About

Sometimes alcoholic parents may abuse their children. For ideas on where to go for help with child abuse, see Chapter 4.

How to Help Someone with an Alcohol Problem

- Talk calmly with the person about the harm that alcohol does. Talk to the person when he or she has *not* just been drinking.
- Tell the person how concerned you are and offer to help.
- Help the drinker to feel good about quitting.
- Give the drinker information about groups that can help.
- Encourage the person to get help.

Someone who has a drinking problem needs help. You can talk honestly but with sympathy to a problem drinker. However, there are some things you should *not* do.

What *Not* to Do with Someone with an Alcohol Problem

- Never drive with a person who has been drinking.
- Do not argue with someone who is drunk.
- Avoid using an "I'm-better-than-you" tone of voice when talking about the person's drinking problem.
- Do not make excuses to others for the drinker's behavior.
- Do not feel that you are responsible for the drinker's actions.

Teen Issue

Who Is a Problem Drinker?
A problem drinker is someone who
- likes to get high
- cannot manage tension without drinking
- cannot stop drinking once he or she has begun.

Check Your Understanding

Conclusion Regular drinking develops over time into alcoholism. Several groups help alcoholics to recover. Other groups help the families and friends of alcoholics.

1. **Vocabulary** Use the word *alcoholism* in an original sentence that shows your feelings about this disease.
2. **Recall** Define alcoholism.
3. **Recall** List the stages of alcoholism.
4. **Recall** Identify three groups that can help people with drinking problems and their families.
5. **Synthesize** What problems might children of alcoholics have at home and at school?

Word to Know
alternatives

Choosing to Be Alcohol Free

This lesson contains a number of valuable facts and tips. Once you have studied them, you will be able to

- list some of the reasons why some teens begin to drink.
- state ways you can say no when offered a drink.
- list some healthy alternatives to drinking.

Why Some Young People Drink

There are many reasons not to drink. In spite of them, many young people still experiment with alcohol. At present, about 1,300,000 teenagers in the United States have drinking problems. Of these, about 750,000 are alcoholics. Some of the reasons young people give for drinking include the following.

- **They give in to pressure from friends who drink.** You are at an age when friendship counts a lot. Sometimes, teens choose to go along with the crowd, even if the crowd's actions include drinking.
- **They want to appear grown up.** Some young people, especially boys, want to show they are mature. They think drinking makes them look more mature.
- **They try to escape problems.** Like adults, many teens believe that alcohol will help them leave their problems behind.
- **They want to relax.** The teen years are a hectic, action-packed time. Some young people think alcohol helps them relax or "unwind."
- **They see family members drink.** Some young people feel tempted to take their first drink after seeing a parent or older brother or sister drink. They may be curious to know what it is like to drink.

Teen **Issue**

Shocking Statistics
In a recent survey of 9- to 12-year-olds, almost half reported pressure from friends to drink.

Some Reasons Not to Drink

One third of the people in the United States do not drink. Many people who did drink have stopped. As people become aware of the physical and emotional damage that drinking can cause, fewer and fewer want to drink.

More and more young people are choosing not to drink. Here are some of the reasons they are giving.

- **It's illegal.** Drinking is against the law for anyone under 21 in every state. Obeying the law makes your life and the lives of others around you safer.

- **It gets in the way.** Think of the challenges you face every day. As a teen, your life is full of activities. You study, take tests, play sports, try to be your best around your friends and family. By choosing not to drink, many teens know they will be alert to meet these challenges.

- **It's not fun.** Drinking can give people a bad headache and make them sick at the stomach. It can also cause them to do something that may embarrass them. Many young people have decided that they can do without that kind of "fun."

- **It's not smart.** Many teens know that they do not need to drink to be popular. They know that drinking *definitely* does not make a person more mature.

Health Minute

The High Cost of Alcoholism
Think about how much money can be saved by not taking on the alcohol habit. The average cost of a beer is 68.4 cents. Figure out how much is saved by *not drinking* four beers a week. How much is saved in a month? In a year?

- **It doesn't taste good.** Many teens know that beer and liquor have unpleasant odors. Knowing this, they are simply not eager to find out what these beverages taste like.

- **It's no solution to problems.** Many teens understand that drinking does not solve problems but creates them.

- **It disappoints others and makes the user feel guilty.** Teens who drink alcohol live a lie because they must hide their habit. Many prefer to stay away from drinking so they can be honest about their lives.

Teen Issue

Shame, Shame!

Some teens try to pressure others into taking a drink of alcohol by using shame tactics. These include calling the person a "baby" or a "chicken" or trying in some other way to make the person feel bad about refusing. If this happens to you, you might want to give these bullies a dose of their own medicine.

- When you are called a baby, you can say: "I'm a baby? You're the one holding the bottle!"

- When they say you are no fun, ask: "What's so much fun about not being able to stand up straight?"

Saying "No" to Alcohol

If you do not want to drink, don't. It's your body, and it's your decision. No one has the right to pressure you to do something you really do not want to do.

One popular way of saying "no" is simply saying, "I don't need it." Here are some other ways.

Ways to Say "No"

- "No way!"
- "It's dumb! Who needs it?"
- "Are you kidding? I hear it tastes *disgusting*."
- "I can have a good time *without* booze."
- "I don't want to get in trouble."
- "I'd rather dance instead."

Can you think of still other ways of saying "no"?

There are other ways of avoiding the pressure to drink alcohol. One good technique is to stay away from situations where there may be alcohol. If you suspect alcohol will be used at a party, you can decide not to go to that party. You can always get together with other friends who, like you, don't want to drink. Give a party of your own.

Another useful idea is to work out a plan with your parents in case a party gets out of hand. A ride home should only be a phone call away.

Remember to use your friends for support in your decision not to drink. You can give support to them, too. When more than one person says "no," the message is stronger.

If the pressure ever gets too great, you have a solution. Just walk away. No one can force you to drink if you don't want to.

Things to Do Instead of Drinking

When tempted or pressured to try alcohol, some teens simply give in. That is partly because they have not thought about alternatives. **Alternatives** (ahl·TER·nuht·ivs) are *other ways of thinking or acting.* People who want to do alternatives can try the following.

What to Do at a Party
Many adults who don't drink alcohol feel pressure to drink, too. At a party, they may hold a glass with a soft drink or mixer at all times. With glasses in their hands, they are not offered any alcohol.

Learning from Photographs
Volunteering at a local hospital or nursing home is a good alternative to drinking. So is learning a new sport. Can you name two others?

More About

*For more on **saying "no,"** see Chapter 3.*

Raising Money
You and other teens could hold a bake sale, car wash, or rummage sale to raise money for a "no alcohol" publicity fund. Then you could use the money for posters, brochures, and other effective ways of getting your message to other teens.

- **Get good at something that requires a very steady hand.** They can practice building castles out of playing cards, or make tiny houses out of toothpicks. They can remind themselves that a person whose senses are dulled by alcohol could not perform this skill.

- **Start a no-alcohol fund.** Every time people say "no" to alcohol or other harmful things, they can put a small sum of money aside in a special place. They can call it their "no-alcohol fund." At the end of a few months, they can treat themselves to a present with the money.

- **Join with other teens for alcohol-free fun.** They could have an alcohol-free dance. Or they could have a baseball or soccer game, keeping in mind that they will play better if they stay away from drinking.

- **Volunteer to help others.** Teens trying to show that they are mature can show it by helping others. They can give time to a worthwhile program like the Special Olympics or a school cleanup campaign. Or they could work at a hospital or nursing home helping sick or elderly people.

- **Spread the word.** Teens could volunteer to teach younger children the dangers of alcohol and the benefits of saying "no."

- **Learn a sport or join a team.** Teens could get instruction in a sport they have never tried before, such as swimming or golf. They could also practice their skills until they try out for a team.

Check Your Understanding

Conclusion The best way to deal with the dangers of alcohol is not to start drinking in the first place. Not giving in to the pressures or temptations to drink can make you feel better and live better.

1. **Vocabulary** *Synonyms* are words with the same meaning. Find at least one synonym for *alternative*. You may use a dictionary for help.

2. **Recall** List three reasons why some teens begin to drink.

3. **Recall** State four ways you can say "no" when offered a drink.

4. **Recall** List three healthy alternatives to drinking.

5. **Synthesize** What personal reasons can you give for saying "no" to drinking alcohol?

Knowing the Truth About Alcohol

Perhaps no drug is more misunderstood than alcohol. When abused, alcohol can damage a person's body and lead to addiction. It can even kill. Yet, according to at least one study, alcohol is the most widely abused drug among young people in this country.

Part of the confusion over alcohol stems from certain myths about the drug. When you understand the truth about alcohol's dangers, you can make healthy decisions about its use. You can also help others to do the same.

Telling the Myths from the Facts

Here are some of the more commonly believed myths, plus the facts, about alcohol.

- **Myth one.** Only middle-aged and older people can develop drinking problems. **Fact.** Alcohol is an addictive drug. *Anyone* who uses it can develop a drinking problem.

- **Myth two.** Drinking beer cannot make a person an alcoholic. **Fact.** Any alcoholic beverage, including beer, can become habit-forming. Drinking beer *can* lead to alcoholism.

- **Myth three.** A person who has been drinking can drive just as carefully as a person who has not. **Fact.** Alcohol slows down reactions and interferes with judgment. A person who has been drinking is a threat to his or her own safety and to the safety of everyone else on the road.

- **Myth four.** People with drinking problems always drink alone. **Fact.** Many "social drinkers" have serious drinking problems.

- **Myth five.** In order for a person to have a drinking problem, that person must drink every day. **Fact.** Some people with drinking problems drink only every other day. Some drink only on weekends. What all problem drinkers share is a *need* for alcohol.

Using the Skill

Read the story and answer the questions that follow.

Case

Sabrina walked into the basement and found her older brother with a can of beer. When she acted surprised, her brother told her everything was all right. "It's only beer," Mark said. "Beer can't cause problems."

A few days later, Sabrina saw Mark on the street after school. He didn't see her. When she got close to him, she noticed he smelled like beer. That night after dinner, she talked to Mark. "Listen," he said to her. "It's not like I'm a drunk. Only older people are drunks."

That Saturday night, Mark had a date. When he came into the kitchen, he was wearing a lot of after-shave lotion. Sabrina figured that he had been drinking again. She walked out to his car with him. "Stop worrying about me," Mark said. "If it will make you feel better, I know for a fact that people drive better after they've had a couple of beers to calm them down."

Mark came home safely that night, but Sabrina was upset. She didn't know what to do.

1. What is Sabrina's problem?
2. What are her choices?
3. What myths about alcohol does Mark seem to believe?
4. What would you decide to do if you were Sabrina?

Chapter 9 Review

Summary

- Alcohol is a dangerous drug that can become habit-forming. Alcohol poses a health threat to the brain, bloodstream, liver, kidneys, and other body organs. Use of alcohol by teens is against the law.
- Alcohol contributes to many fatal accidents, especially on the highways. Someone who has drunk alcohol is unable to control a car safely.
- Alcohol can lead to the disease of alcoholism. For the alcoholic, alcohol becomes the central focus of life. The addiction to alcohol is so strong that other aspects of the alcoholic's life suffer.

- Alcoholism can be overcome, but it is difficult. Groups like Alcoholics Anonymous, Alateen, and Al-Anon can help alcoholics and their families. Friends and family members can help alcoholics by caring about them and assisting them in finding help.
- Teens give many reasons for trying alcohol. There are many more reasons not to drink. There are a number of ways to say "no" when offered alcohol. A teen can be healthier when he or she finds alternatives to using alcohol.

Reviewing Vocabulary and Concepts

On a separate sheet of paper, write the numbers 1–11. After each number, write the letter of the word or phrase in Column B that best matches the phrase in Column A.

Column A

Lesson 1

1. Any drug that slows the working of the brain and nervous system
2. To change alcohol into water and the gas carbon dioxide
3. Two of the factors that determine how alcohol will affect an individual
4. The effect that alcohol has on a teen's normal body development
5. A condition in which a baby is born with alcohol-related birth defects
6. A physical or mental need for a drug

Lesson 2

7. A disease caused by an addiction to alcohol
8. A part of the first stage of alcoholism
9. A support group for alcoholics
10. An organization that helps the children of alcoholic parents
11. One of the ways you can help a person with a drinking problem

Column B

a. interferes with it
b. alcoholism
c. Alcoholics Anonymous
d. social drinking
e. mood and body weight
f. addiction
g. oxidize
h. depressant
i. fetal alcohol syndrome
j. by giving information about support groups
k. Alateen

Lesson 3

Write the numbers 12–16 on your paper. After each number, write the letter of the answer that best completes each of the following statements.

12. Which of the following is a reason that some teens give for using alcohol?
    - **a.** they want to look grown up
    - **b.** it tastes bad
    - **c.** it is illegal
    - **d.** they want to be in control

13. Each of the following is a reason teens give for *not* using alcohol *except*
    - **a.** it is illegal
    - **b.** it takes away control
    - **c.** it is inexpensive
    - **d.** it's not smart

14. If someone has a problem, what affect would using alcohol have?
    - **a.** it would solve the problem
    - **b.** it would make the person forget the problem
    - **c.** it would create new problems
    - **d.** it would have no effect at all

15. Other ways of thinking or acting are called
    - **a.** options
    - **b.** choices
    - **c.** maturity
    - **d.** alternatives

16. Each of the following is a healthy alternative to using alcohol *except*
    - **a.** starting a no-alcohol club
    - **b.** drinking beer
    - **c.** learning a new skill
    - **d.** volunteering to help others

Thinking Critically About the Facts

Write your answers to the following questions on a separate sheet of paper.

17. **Synthesize** What might you say to a friend who tells you that because she has just finished a big meal, she will not get drunk on a few beers?

18. **Synthesize** You are preparing to leave a friend's home after studying all evening for a test. You notice that it is too late to go out on the streets by yourself. Your friend's older brother offers to drive you home. However, you believe you smell alcohol on his breath. What do you do?

19. **Analyze** Imagine that you had to prepare an oral report for a fifth-grade health class on the dangers of alcohol. How would you relate what you have learned in this chapter to the idea of total health?

20. **Interpret** Think of some of the factors that might lead the child of a parent who abuses alcohol to abuse alcohol himself or herself.

21. **Synthesize** You are at a party and someone offers you a drink in a glass with ice. You don't recognize the drink and suspect that it may contain alcohol. What do you do?

Applying the Facts

22. Write a one-act play about two teens who attend a school where hardly any alcohol is used by students. The teens' names are Paul and Quentin. Paul is thinking of trying alcohol, but Quentin is not. Pay close attention to what Quentin might say to change Paul's mind. With a classmate, act out your play for the class.

23. Make a poster that shows healthy alternatives to using alcohol. Find or draw pictures that show young people taking part in worthwhile activities. At the top or bottom of your poster, write a headline that will persuade others of the importance of alternatives. Bring your finished poster to class.

Drugs and Your Health

CHAPTER WARM-UP

Chapter Study Goals

After you have read this chapter, you will be able to

- describe some of the uses of medicines.
- tell what the Food and Drug Administration does.
- describe ways in which drugs can harm the body.
- describe the health risks related to the use of stimulants, depressants, marijuana, hallucinogens, and inhalants.
- identify ways of saying "no" when offered drugs.
- identify healthy alternatives to using drugs.

Be on the lookout for information in the chapter that will help you reach these goals.

Getting Started

The drugs we have today can work wonders. But they can also do great harm when taken incorrectly or for the wrong reasons. There are many ways to take a stand against drugs—to just say "no." In this chapter, you will learn about the many different types of drugs in our society. You will learn about how to use medicines safely. You will also learn about drugs that are never safe and never should be taken.

Study Tip

As you read this chapter, pay attention to the charts and boxes. They will help you learn which drugs are used as medicines and which are not.

Drugs as Medicine

Words to Know

drugs
medicines
vaccines
antibiotics
sulfa drugs
side effect
tolerance
prescription drugs
over-the-counter
(OTC) drugs

This lesson contains a number of valuable facts and tips. Once you have studied them, you will be able to

• define the terms *drug* and *medicine*.

• name the main groups of medicines.

• name some unhealthy reactions the body can have to medicines.

• tell the difference between prescription and OTC drugs.

More About

Tobacco and alcohol are drugs. To learn more about these drugs, see Chapters 8 and 9.

Drugs and Health

In this century, drugs have changed the overall health of the American people. Many drugs have been discovered that prevent or cure diseases. These drugs have helped us to live longer.

Not all of the changes brought about by modern drugs have been healthful, however. When drugs are not used the way they are supposed to be used, they can do great harm.

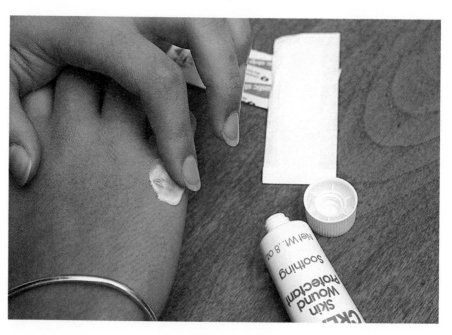

Learning from Photographs
Many drugs are medicines. What do you think this cream is being used for?

What Are Drugs?

Drugs are *substances other than food that change the structure or function of the body or mind.* Much of the time, we use the term *drug* to mean "medicine." **Medicines** are *drugs meant to cure or prevent diseases and other conditions.* Medicines can be divided into many groups. Four of those groups are listed in the following box.

Four Kinds of Medicine

- Drugs that prevent disease.
- Drugs that fight germs that cause disease.
- Drugs that affect the heart and blood.
- Drugs that affect the nervous system.

Drugs That Prevent Diseases

Many drugs that prevent disease are vaccines. **Vaccines** (vak·SEENS) are *drugs made of dead or weak germ cells that are put in the body so it will produce antibodies.* The antibodies allow the body to fight off the disease. A person who is vaccinated for measles, then, will never get the measles.

Drugs That Fight Germs

The medicines used to fight the germs that produce disease are an important and familiar group.

Antibiotics (an·ti·by·AHT·iks) are *drugs produced by tiny living organisms that are used to fight germs. Penicillin* (pen·uh·SIL·uhn) is one antibiotic you have probably heard of. It can destroy germs that cause infections like strep throat. Most antibiotics are given in pills or in shots. Others are rubbed on the skin. These are used mainly to protect cuts and burns while they heal.

Sulfa (SUHL·fuh) **drugs** are *a family of germ killers made from certain chemicals.* These drugs are not made from living organisms. Rather, they are produced in a laboratory. Sulfa drugs were the first disease-fighting drugs found. Today they are used less often than antibiotics because those drugs are more effective.

Drugs for the Heart and Blood

Drugs for the heart and blood do a number of different jobs. Some of them cause a weak heart to beat more strongly. Others make narrow or slightly blocked blood vessels larger. Still others prevent high blood pressure.

DID **YOU** KNOW?

Drugs and Mold
An English physician named Alexander Fleming accidentally discovered the antibiotic penicillin. The drug occurs in the kind of mold you sometimes see on bread.

More About
To learn more about vaccines, see Chapter 11.

Don't Be Rash
Penicillin is often the first antibiotic that doctors use for a patient. But about 10 percent of Americans are allergic to penicillin. If you have this allergy, let the doctor know before he or she treats you.

Drugs for the Nervous System

Many drugs work on the body's nervous system. Some calm the nerves or ease anxious feelings. Some help a person to sleep. Others, like aspirin, stop or dull pain. Another type treats emotional problems such as depression.

A number of drugs do several of these jobs. Since these drugs change moods and feelings, they are sometimes *abused*. This means they are used by people who do not need them as medicine. You will read more about the abuse of these and other drugs in Lessons 2 and 3 of this chapter.

Drugs in the Body

When a drug is swallowed, it usually dissolves in the stomach. A small amount may pass into the intestines. The dissolved drug is then absorbed by the walls of the stomach and intestines. It next passes into the bloodstream.

Drugs given by needle go right to the bloodstream. They do not enter the stomach or intestines. Because of this, drugs given by needle act more quickly than drugs that are swallowed.

Your Body's Reaction to Drugs

Every person's body contains different amounts of certain chemicals. Because of these differences, drugs affect each person in a different way. For some people, a drug takes a longer time to begin working. Some body reactions to drugs are unhealthy.

Unhealthy Reactions to Drugs

- **Side effects.** *Any reaction to a drug other than the one intended* is called a **side effect.** Side effects include upset stomach, dizziness, and drowsiness. One cause of side effects is an allergy to a drug. Sometimes an allergic reaction is severe enough to cause serious illness and even death. When a doctor prescribes a drug, he or she will tell what side effects to look for.

- **Tolerance.** When used over a period of time, certain drugs can cause a *person's body to become used to the drug's effect.* This **tolerance** (TAHL·uh·ruhns) to a drug can cause the person to need greater and greater amounts of it.

- **Problems related to mixing drugs.** When two or more drugs are taken at the same time, the effects may be dangerous. Each drug may have a stronger effect than if it were taken alone. Or the drugs may combine to do damage to the body.

DID **YOU** KNOW?

Pain Relief
Americans take almost 600 bushels of pain relievers each day. Included in that number are at least 52 million aspirin.

Learning from Photographs
Many medicines are sold only by a pharmacist who must have a doctor's written order. The pharmacist passes along any warnings the doctor may have about a drug's effects. What unhealthy reactions might a doctor be concerned about?

Help with Drug Safety

In our country, the safety of drugs is a concern of the government. The Food and Drug Administration (FDA) makes sure that all drugs sold to the public are safe. Before a new drug can be sold, the FDA requires the drugmaker to state the following facts.

- What the drug is
- What medical use the drug has
- Any possible side effects the drugmaker knows of

The drug is then tested, sometimes for many years, before it is released for sale.

Prescription Drugs

The FDA takes other steps to make sure that medicines are safe when used according to directions. One step is to allow certain *drugs to be sold only with a written order from a doctor.* These **prescription** (pri·SKRIP·shuhn) **drugs** come with instructions from the doctor. The instructions are typewritten on the container. These directions tell you the following.

- How to take the medicine
- How often to take it
- How much of it to take each time
- Whether the medicine needs to be taken in a special way (for example, with food or with a milk product)

An Ounce of Prevention

Whenever a drug is prescribed for you, take time to ask your doctor these questions.

- Does the drug cause side effects?
- Is there any food, such as a milk product, that I should avoid eating while taking this drug?
- Are there any other medications I should avoid while taking this drug?

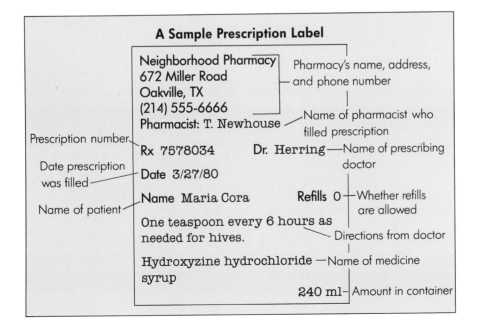

A Sample Prescription Label

Neighborhood Pharmacy
672 Miller Road
Oakville, TX
(214) 555-6666
Pharmacist: T. Newhouse — Pharmacy's name, address, and phone number

Name of pharmacist who filled prescription

Prescription number — Rx 7578034   Dr. Herring — Name of prescribing doctor

Date prescription was filled — Date 3/27/80

Name of patient — Name Maria Cora   Refills 0 — Whether refills are allowed

One teaspoon every 6 hours as needed for hives. — Directions from doctor

Hydroxyzine hydrochloride — Name of medicine syrup

240 ml — Amount in container

Learning from Drawings

A prescription label must contain the basic information shown here. Some labels also include cautions about how to use the medicine. There may even be an expiration date, after which the medicine is not effective. When using prescription medicines, follow the doctor's orders exactly. Why was this medicine prescribed?

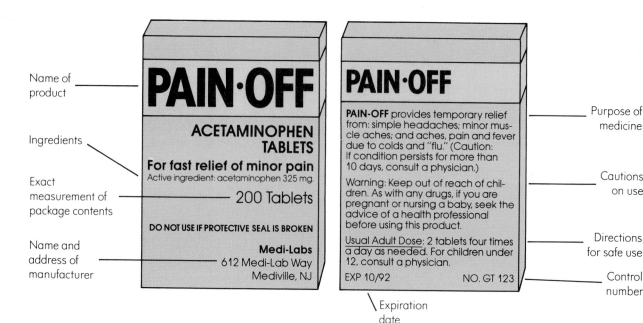

Name of product

Ingredients

Exact measurement of package contents

Name and address of manufacturer

PAIN·OFF

ACETAMINOPHEN TABLETS

For fast relief of minor pain
Active ingredient: acetaminophen 325 mg.

200 Tablets

DO NOT USE IF PROTECTIVE SEAL IS BROKEN

Medi-Labs
612 Medi-Lab Way
Mediville, NJ

PAIN·OFF

PAIN-OFF provides temporary relief from: simple headaches; minor muscle aches; and aches, pain and fever due to colds and "flu." (Caution: If condition persists for more than 10 days, consult a physician.)

Warning: Keep out of reach of children. As with any drugs, if you are pregnant or nursing a baby, seek the advice of a health professional before using this product.

Usual Adult Dose: 2 tablets four times a day as needed. For children under 12, consult a physician.

EXP 10/92   NO. GT 123

Purpose of medicine

Cautions on use

Directions for safe use

Control number

Expiration date

Learning from Drawings
Labels for all over-the-counter drugs must carry the kinds of information shown here. That way, people are able to use the drug safely. What should someone using this medicine do if he or she cannot get rid of a headache after more than 10 days? Why?

DID **YOU** KNOW?

But No Soda Fountain
The first drugstore was not on the main street of a small American town. It was in Baghdad in A.D. 754. The medicines sold included camphor, cloves, and fruit syrups. At the time, these items seemed pretty modern compared with other popular medicines of the day: lizard blood, antelope droppings, and frog toes.

Over-the-Counter (OTC) Drugs

The FDA sometimes decides that *a drug* is *safe enough to be taken without a written order from a doctor.* Such drugs are called **over-the-counter** (or **OTC**) **drugs.**

OTC drugs can be bought at a drugstore or other store that sells medicines. Aspirin and cold pills are examples of OTC drugs. Every OTC drug has a label that carries the following important information.

- The name of the drug
- What the drug is to be used for
- How much of the drug is in the package
- Directions for using the drug
- Warnings about the use and possible side effects
- The date after which it is no longer safe to use the contents of the package

The illustration above shows you how this information appears on an actual OTC drug label.

Using Medicine Safely

Sometimes medicines are not used properly. Some people take too much of a medicine. They may take four aspirin pills instead of two, hoping to get relief twice as fast. Or a teen may use a medicine prescribed for a parent, brother, or sister.

These practices are not safe. Medicines have powerful effects on the body. When the FDA approves a drug, it says that the drug is "safe and effective when used as directed." That means that using the drug without following directions may *not* be safe.

Some tips for using medicines follow.

- Use OTC drugs as specified on the label. If you are ill and an OTC drug does not help you, you may need a stronger medicine. Call a doctor.
- Remember that prescription drugs are only meant for the person for whom they were prescribed. These drugs should not be shared.
- Destroy drugs that have passed their expiration date.
- Keep drugs safely sealed in childproof containers, and keep them out of the reach of children.
- Drugs should never be mixed with alcohol.
- Never mix medicines without your doctor's approval.

By using prescription and OTC drugs safely, you can enhance your health. If you are not sure how to use a medicine, ask the pharmacist or call your doctor.

Health Minute

Label Check
Read the label of any drug you might be taking at the moment. Are you following the directions exactly?

More About

*For more information on how to be a wise **consumer**, see Chapter 14.*

Check Your Understanding

Conclusion Medicines are useful in preventing and curing diseases and other disorders. Since every person's body reacts differently to a drug, it is important to use care when taking any drug, even a medicine. Part of drug safety is making sure you read the label and take the drug as instructed.

1. **Vocabulary** Tell which of the following are terms used by the FDA to classify drugs. Then define each term. *prescription drug, sulfa drug, OTC drug*

2. **Recall** Define the words *drug* and *medicine.*

3. **Recall** Name the four main groupings of medicines.

4. **Recall** What are three unhealthy reactions the body can have to medicine?

5. **Recall** What is the difference between prescription and OTC drugs?

6. **Analyze** Suppose you went to your local pharmacy to buy nose spray and the label was torn off the only bottle left. Would you buy the spray? Why or why not?

SKILLS FOR LIVING

Keep Alert
Do you, or does someone in your family, have a serious allergy to a drug such as aspirin? People with allergies should have a Medi-Alert bracelet or necklace. Such bracelets and necklaces have saved the lives of people with allergies who have had an accident that left them unconscious. Workers in emergency rooms are trained to look for the Medi-Alert symbol before ordering a drug for a patient.

Stimulants and Depressants

Words to Know

drug misuse
drug abuse
stimulants
addiction
amphetamines
cocaine
crack
depressants
coma
narcotics
heroin

This lesson contains a number of valuable facts and tips. Once you have studied them, you will be able to

- define the term *addiction*.
- name the stimulants that are most often misused and abused.
- name some of the dangers of misusing and abusing depressants.
- name some of the dangers of misusing and abusing narcotics.

Drug Misuse and Abuse

Medicines are meant to do good. Yet each year thousands of people do serious harm to their bodies by taking medicines or other drugs they have no business taking. In a recent year, over 4,000 people died as a result of drug abuse. Some of those people were teenagers.

Teen Issue

Public Enemy Number 1
A group of 13- to 18-year-olds were asked to name the most serious problem facing teens today. The answer that came up most often was "drugs." More and more teens are coming to recognize drug misuse and abuse as Public Enemy Number 1.

Learning from Photographs
Many teens are joining the campaign to say "no" to drugs. Why is it healthy to avoid drugs?

People who hurt themselves with drugs belong to one or two groups, *drug misusers* and *drug abusers.*

- **Drug misuse.** *Using a drug in a way other than how it is supposed to be used* is **drug misuse.**

- **Drug abuse.** *Using substances that are against the law or not supposed to be taken into the human body* is **drug abuse.** Some drugs that are abused have no medical purpose at all.

The box shows some forms of drug misuse and drug abuse.

Drug Misuse	Drug Abuse
• Using a drug without following directions	• Using a drug for purposes other than medical use (such as to get "high")
• Changing the amount of a drug taken without first getting a doctor's approval	• Taking a substance that was not meant to enter the body
• Using a drug prescribed for someone else	• Using a drug in a way that hurts the user's mental, emotional, or social well-being
• Using a drug for longer than a doctor advises	

Which Drugs Are Misused and Abused Most?

Among the drugs most often misused and abused are two groups. One group is called *stimulants*. The other is called *depressants*. These are drugs that affect the nervous system.

Stimulants

Stimulants (STIM·yuh·luhnts) are *drugs that speed up the body's functions*. Stimulants cause the blood pressure to rise. They make breathing speed up and the heart beat faster. A person using a stimulant feels excited and may be jittery. Some stimulants are prescription drugs. They are given by doctors to patients with physical or emotional problems. Stimulants might be given to a person with too little energy, for instance, to make him or her more alert and lively.

When stimulants are misused or abused, they can do serious damage to the body. They can even cause death. Another danger of stimulants is that they can become habit-forming. The more of them a person uses, the more the person needs. After a while the person can develop an addiction to the drug. An **addiction** (uh·DIK·shuhn) is *a physical or mental need for a drug or other substance.*

Time Out

One common form of drug misuse is using a drug after its *expiration date*—the last day that it is safe to use. Make a habit of checking this date each time you use an OTC or prescription drug. If the date has passed, dump the medicine into the toilet and flush.

Teen Issue

Hands Off!

Many teens may wrongly believe that by taking twice as many diet pills, they can lose weight faster. This belief is false. Use the recommended dosage. Or better yet, follow the suggestions for a weight-loss plan in Chapter 5.

Stimulant Fact Sheet

Drug	What It's Called	How It Looks	How It's Taken	What It Can Do to You
Amphetamine(s)	Speed Crank Uppers Pep pills Footballs Bumblebees Black beauties Hearts Benzedrineties Dexedrine Biphetamine	Pills Tablets Capsules	Swallowed By needle Inhaled	• Interferes with muscle control • Causes uneven heartbeat, rapid rise in blood pressure, physical collapse, high fever • Leads to stroke, heart attack, and death
Cocaine	Coke Snow White Blow Flake Lady Snowbirds Big C Nose candy	White powder	Inhaled By needle Smoked	• Interferes with workings of brain • Causes nervousness and malnutrition • Damages nose lining, liver, and heart • Causes heart failure and death
Crack (a form of cocaine)	Rock Freebase rocks	Light-brown crystals	Smoked	• Causes increase in pulse rate, blood pressure, sleeplessness • Causes loss of appetite • Leads to seizure, heart attack, and death

Abused Stimulants

Some stimulants are so mild that people are unaware that they are using a drug. One such stimulant is *caffeine* (ka·FEEN). It is found in cocoa, coffee, tea, and certain sodas. Too much caffeine can make a person edgy. Unlike caffeine, however, most dangerous stimulants are abused on purpose. The abuser is trying to get "high." Two stimulants that are often abused are amphetamines and cocaine.

Amphetamines

Amphetamines (am·FET·uh·meenz) are *drugs prescribed to stimulate the central nervous system.* They are usually taken as pills, tablets, or capsules. They can also be taken by needle. Abusers of amphetamines have nicknames for them such as "speed" and "uppers." A better nickname for these drugs might be "killers."

Amphetamines are highly addictive. They make the user mentally dependent. When misused or abused, amphetamines can cause the

DID **YOU** KNOW?

Chocolate Lovers Beware!

Many smart teens have learned that sodas with caffeine can make a person tense and moody. Not nearly as many realize that chocolate also contains caffeine. The next time you are looking for something to "hold you" until dinner, try an apple or a pear—both are 100 percent caffeine free!

damage listed in the "Stimulant Fact Sheet." When taken in large quantities, they can even lead to collapse. Amphetamines taken by needle cause the blood pressure to rise rapidly. This, in turn, can lead to a stroke or to a heart attack.

Cocaine

Cocaine (koh·KAYN), *an illegal stimulant,* is destroying many lives in our society. Some users of this deadly but very addictive drug are very young. In a recent year, over 15 percent of all high school seniors admitted to using cocaine.

"Coke," as the drug is commonly called, usually takes the form of a white powder. The powder is inhaled, or "snorted," through the nose. It then enters the bloodstream and is carried to the brain. In the brain, cocaine changes eating and sleeping habits and damages memory. Its other serious effects on the body are listed in the "Stimulant Fact Sheet."

Users of cocaine boast that the drug gives them a "rush," or short burst of high energy. What users seldom mention is that this energy is quickly followed by a letdown or feeling of sadness that makes them crave more of the drug. In this way, users become mentally addicted.

Studies are showing that cocaine can also be physically addictive. The drug makes the user dependent in this way when it is taken in its most powerful forms. These forms include injecting cocaine into the bloodstream and smoking it. Smoking cocaine is called *freebasing.*

Crack

Crack is *a more pure and very powerful form of cocaine.* It is one of the most addictive and dangerous drugs in the United States today. Many of its users are teens. Since crack is so pure, it reaches the brain within seconds after it is taken. A person can become addicted to crack after only one use!

Teen Issue
. . . .

It's no crank!
Use of a new and highly dangerous form of amphetamine, called *crank,* is a growing problem that has law enforcement and health officials very concerned. The drug, which is an off-white or brownish chunky powder, stimulates the nervous system. It is a highly habit-forming drug and can lead to psychotic episodes, terrifying hallucinations, and death.
. . . .

Teen Issue
. . . .

The First and Last Time?
Cocaine can kill. And someone doesn't have to be a long-term user to suffer this death. A few years ago, Len Bias had everything he wanted. He was leaving college with a multimillion dollar contract from a pro basketball team. But Len used cocaine one night—for the first time. He also died that night.
. . . .

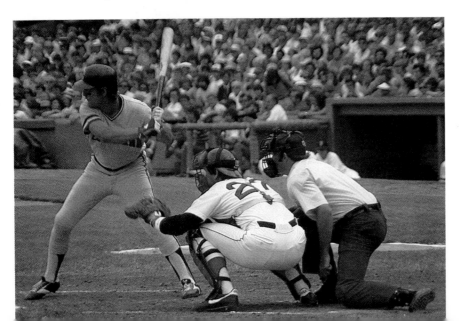

Learning from Photographs
Players of professional sports know that they'll perform at their best by staying free of drugs. Why is that true?

Using crack is like riding on a roller coaster that is speeding out of control. At the start of the crack "trip," everything happens very quickly. Heart rate, blood pressure, and body temperature all soar. Pupils widen. The user may be confused about how close or far away nearby objects really are. Concentrating is hard. Then, just as suddenly, the user plunges into a valley of deep depression. To get out of this valley, the user takes more crack, and the "ride" begins again.

The rapid ups and downs that go along with crack put great stress on the user's heart. Many users have suffered heart attack and died.

A dangerous side effect of crack is that it may lead to violence and crime. Users need the drug so badly that they will do anything to get the money for another dose.

Depressants

Depressants (di·PRES·uhnts) are *drugs that tend to slow down the body's functions and reactions.* Depressants lower the heart rate and blood pressure. They cause breathing to slow. A person using a depressant feels drowsy and may have a hard time focusing. Like stimulants, many depressants are prescription drugs. Also like stimulants, many depressants can be addictive.

> ## Main Groups of Depressants
>
> - **Tranquilizers** (tran·kwuh·LY·zers). When taken in small amounts, tranquilizers can calm a person without making the person less alert.
> - **Barbiturates** (bahr·BICH·uh·ruhts). Barbiturates are meant to help a person relax. They are sometimes given to people who have trouble sleeping.
> - **Hypnotics** (hip·NAHT·iks). Hypnotics are very strong drugs that bring on sleep.

All depressants should be taken *only* when a person is under the care of a doctor.

Abuse of Depressants

Depressants can also cause harm. Taking these drugs can cause nausea, headaches, and nosebleeds. When combined with alcohol, depressants become deadly. The mixing of the two drugs causes breathing to slow. After a time, the brain becomes starved for oxygen. The user lapses into a **coma** (KOH·muh), *a deep unconscious state.* Many times, the user suffers permanent brain damage.

More About

*To learn more about the dangers of mixing **alcohol** and other drugs, see Chapter 9.*

Narcotics

Narcotics (nahr·KAHT·iks) are *drugs meant to bring on sleep or a loss of feeling.* Doctors may prescribe the narcotic *morphine* (MOR·feen) to control extreme pain. *Codeine* (KOH·deen) is prescribed to stop a severe cough. *Paregoric* (pehr·uh·GAWR·ik) is used to stop diarrhea and to relieve teething pain.

Because these three drugs are so strongly addictive, their sale and use is controlled by law. Doctors must give extra information when prescribing them. Pharmacists must keep records of all such drugs sold.

Heroin

A very powerful and dangerous narcotic is **heroin** (HEHR·uh·wuhn). This is *an illegal narcotic that is strongly addictive.* Heroin was first used to help people overcome their addiction to morphine. Then it was found that the addiction they developed to heroin was worse!

Heroin is sold as a white powder. But the drug is often mixed with other substances. They include powdered milk and even *strychnine* (STRIK·nyn), which is a poison. One danger of heroin, then, is that the user doesn't know what he or she is getting.

Heroin also has dangerous effects on the body. It lowers the user's feeling of pain and produces shallow breathing. If the dose is too strong, the user can go into a coma.

But the main problem with heroin is the strong addiction that users develop. Heroin users develop a need for stronger doses. When the user gets no heroin or too little, he or she feels severe pain.

DID **YOU** KNOW?

Needles Are Dangerous
Users of heroin and other drugs that are injected by needle risk yet another danger. They may become infected by the AIDS virus. When a drug user who is infected by the virus shares a needle with another user, that person may inject the virus into his or her body. To learn more about AIDS, see Lesson 5 of Chapter 11.

Check Your Understanding

Conclusion Stimulants, depressants, and narcotics are drugs that can do a great deal of good when used properly. When they are misused or abused, they can do great harm. All are addictive drugs.

1. **Vocabulary** What is the difference between *drug misuse* and *drug abuse*?
2. **Recall** Define the term *addiction.*
3. **Recall** What are two stimulants that are most often misused and abused?
4. **Recall** What are two dangers of misusing or abusing depressants? Of misusing or abusing narcotics?
5. **Synthesize** What advice might you have for a friend who said she or he was just going to try crack once?

Teen Health
BULLETIN BOARD

TEEN
Q & A

Q: Some members of the football team use anabolic steroids. What are they? I've heard they can hurt you. Can they?

A: First things first — they are illegal. And anabolic steroids harm a person. They may even kill someone who uses them. For males, anabolic steroids cause the testicles to shrink and the breasts to grow. For females, they can deepen the voice and make hair grow on the face. In both sexes, steroids can raise the blood pressure, damage the liver, and cause violent mood changes.

And yet, some athletes use them. Anabolic steroids are the lab version of the male hormone. Athletes use them to build their muscles and increase their staying power, in spite of the risks.

But do they really work? Or do they just harm the body? Dr. Marcus Reidenberg, a professor at New York Hospital-Cornell Medical Center, says that some of their effect is in the mind. Steroids, he says, affect the brain to make an athlete train harder. "But... the best studies don't find real differences between steroids and sugar pills."

CAREERS

Wanted:

Drug Abuse Counselor

Specifics:

Provide counseling to enable former and current drug addicts to deal with practical problems, such as finding work.

Qualifications

Must work closely with people who have a difficult problem; must be able to accept frustrations and tensions of the job.

Preparation:

A high school diploma is usually needed, plus a training program lasting from 6 weeks to 2 years.

Contact:

American Hospital Association
840 North Lake Shore Drive
Chicago, IL 60611
or
National Health Council
70 West 40th Street
New York, NY 10018

HEALTH IN THE NEWS
No Pain, No Pain

Yes, there are strong painkillers around, and they give welcome relief to people who hurt badly. They are useful when they are taken by someone under a doctor's care. But many of them can get you hooked, and kicking a drug habit is one of the biggest pains around.

At the University of Rochester Center for Brain Research, scientists are studying the secrets of how painkillers work. They have found that a painkiller is like a key that opens a lock—the lock being certain proteins in the brain's cells. Drugs that get you addicted are one kind of "key." The scientists are now searching for ways to make similar "keys" that won't get people hooked. This research may also provide the "key" to help drug addicts unlock the chains of their addiction.

Lifestyle
No "Park"-ing

Some teens in New York City are angry about losing their play space to drug dealers, and they're not going to take it anymore. They call themselves "Take Back the Park." For the last few years, this group has been working to make city parks safe again.

"Take Back the Park" began when a group of youths found they were running out of safe places for afterschool sports. Working with the police and other concerned citizens, they have managed to clean up three of the city's more dangerous parks. "We want to give a message," says 13-year-old Tony Brown. "That message is, 'Look out, dealers...this community is fighting back!'" Judging from the group's success so far, that message is coming through loud and clear.

Sports and Recreation
Drugs Make Losers, Not Winners

Ben Johnson is a Canadian sprinter who, for 72 hours, was a world champ. His time of 9.72 seconds for the 100-meter dash in the 1988 Summer Olympics set a new world record! But when officials found traces of a steroid drug in his urine, Johnson's career screeched to a halt. He had to return his gold medal. He also lost $10 million in contracts, and he had to cancel plans to buy a million-dollar home outside of Toronto. On top of that, Johnson was barred from track events for 2 years.

"It's sad that people think a drug can make you a champion," says Florence Griffith-Joyner, who also ran in the 1988 Olympics and won a few gold medals herself. "Nothing replaces hard work, faith in God, and belief in yourself."

Hallucinogens and Inhalants

Words to Know

marijuana
hormones
hallucinogens
inhalants

This lesson contains a number of valuable facts and tips. Once you have studied them, you will be able to

- name the dangers of using marijuana.
- define the term *hallucinogens*.
- name the main hallucinogens.
- list some dangers of using inhalants.

Street Drugs

"If drugs do so much damage," some people have asked, "why not stop making them?" The answer is that many drugs also do much good. Drugs like amphetamines, when used carefully and under a doctor's direction, can help people who are ill.

Other drugs, however, have no medical benefits. They are used only by abusers and are bought and sold only on the streets. These "street drugs," as they are called, are against the law. When caught, users and sellers of them can be fined or sent to jail for a long time.

Teen Issue

Jury of Your Peers
Four out of five teens believe that current laws governing the sale and use of drugs should be stricter.

Marijuana

By far, the most commonly used street drug these days is **marijuana** (mehr·uh·WAHN·uh). This drug is *an illegal street drug that comes from the leaves of a plant.* Usually it is smoked as a cigarette. Sometimes it is eaten. Marijuana is known by several other names, including *pot* and *grass*.

Twenty years ago, some people argued that marijuana had some benefits. They claimed that it was safer than tobacco. They said that smoking it helped them think more clearly. Both claims have been proven false. Recent research has shown that marijuana fogs the brain. One study notes that marijuana cigarettes contain *four to five*

Learning from Photographs
The government seizes illegal drugs and destroys them after trials are completed. What other steps do you know of that the government takes to reduce the drug problem?

times as much of certain cancer-causing substances as tobacco cigarettes. Marijuana has more than 400 different chemicals. Many of these are dangerous.

The truth about marijuana is that it is a dangerous, addictive drug. Users develop a mental need for the drug. Knowing what it can do to your body can help you say "no" if it is ever offered to you.

Marijuana and the Body

Marijuana acts like both a stimulant and a depressant. The following box lists some of its effects.

Marijuana...

- makes the heart beat faster.
- lowers body temperature.
- increases hunger.
- slows down the ability to react.
- interferes with the proper working of the muscles.

The last two effects make marijuana very dangerous for users who are near machinery or traffic.

Marijuana's Long-Term Effects

Marijuana is very harmful. The drug poisons the structures that trigger cells to grow and replace themselves. Marijuana smokers also seem more likely to get sick than are people who stay away from the drug. It seems that the drug weakens the body's ability to fight germs.

DID **YOU** KNOW?

Marijuana and Personality
Marijuana users tend to have something in common. They have personality problems that include loss of mental energy, lack of interest in everyday things, loss of concentration, and difficulty in recalling events and actions.

Teen **I**ssue

Objects May Appear Closer...
Before you get into a car with someone who has been using marijuana or a hallucinogen, remember this. That person has a view of the road different from any other driver. That's really asking for trouble.

Street Drug Fact Sheet

Drug	What It's Called	How It Looks	How It's Taken	What It Can Do to You
Marijuana	Pot Grass Weed Reefer Dope Mary Jane Thai sticks Acapulco gold Sinsemilla	Dried greenish plant leaves	Smoked Eaten	• Increases heart rate and appetite, lowers body temperature • Interferes with proper working of muscles • Damages heart and lungs and causes memory loss • Interferes with normal body development in teens by changing hormone levels
PCP	Angel dust Lovely Loveboat Hog Killer weed	White powder Pills Capsules Liquid	Swallowed By needle Smoked when used with marijuana	• Causes loss of coordination, blocking of brain area that senses pain • Gives user false feeling of super powers • Dulls speech and causes memory loss • Leads to coma, heart and lung failure, bursting of blood vessels in brain
LSD	Acid White lightning Sugar cubes Green dragon Blue heaven Microdot	Tablets Liquid Squares soaked into paper	Swallowed Licked As eye drops	• Increases blood pressure and heart rate • Causes chills, nausea, tremors, and sleeplessness • Causes confusion and panic • Gives user false feeling of super powers

Many researchers fear that marijuana damages brain cells. Research into long-term effects of marijuana use is ongoing.

Because marijuana is usually inhaled and held in the lungs, repeated use can damage the lungs and heart. Heavy use of marijuana can also cause loss of memory and make it hard for the user to concentrate.

People who use marijuana regularly may lose interest in other parts of their lives. They may feel that they have no energy and lose interest in other people. A recent report stated that 40 percent of heavy users of the drug show these effects.

One damaging effect of regular marijuana use by teens is that it can slow down the body's rate of development. The teen years are a period of rapid growth. Right now, changes are taking place in your body as it prepares for adulthood. These changes are related to hormones. **Hormones** (HOR·mohnz) are *chemicals produced in the body that are responsible for rapid growth.*

DID **YOU** KNOW?

Hanging On

Marijuana can continue to harm the body for some time after it is used. The drug does not dissolve in water. Thus, it can stay in the body for as long as three weeks.

Using marijuana can lower the level of hormones the body produces. In boys, the drug can lower the level of the hormone that causes the voice to get deeper and the shoulders broader. In girls, marijuana smoking may affect the menstrual cycle.

Hallucinogens

One group of street drugs is **hallucinogens** (huh·LOOS·uhn·uh·juhnz). These are *drugs that cause the user's brain to form images of things that are not really there.* Like stimulants and depressants, hallucinogens affect the nervous system.

Hallucinogens have strong effects that sometimes last for a long time. Since they are street drugs, these drugs are not controlled by the government. Besides being illegal, they could be unsafe. There is no telling what chemicals or substances might be mixed in with them. This makes hallucinogens very dangerous.

PCP

Several years ago, a dangerous hallucinogen became known. Many young people died as a result of taking it. The drug, *phencyclidine* (fen·SIK·luh·deen), is known by several names. These include *PCP* and *angel dust.*

PCP comes in many forms. It is available as a liquid, as a white powder, in pills, and in capsules. Some users swallow the drug, while others mix the powder with marijuana and smoke it. Still others take liquid PCP by needle.

PCP's Effects on the Body

- PCP makes the user lose coordination. The user is unable to control the body's muscles.
- PCP removes the body's sense of pain. Pain signals us to do something to protect ourselves. By cutting off pain signals, PCP endangers the user.
- PCP gives the user a false feeling of super power. Teens high on PCP have tried dangerous stunts that killed them.

Unlike the effects of some other drugs, the effects of PCP last a long time. When the drug is used regularly, effects may come and go for as long as a year. When PCP is used in large amounts, it can lead to coma and to failure of the heart or lungs. It can also cause a blood vessel in the brain to burst, which results in death.

DID **YOU** KNOW?

Mescaline
Another hallucinogen that is used by some people is *mescaline* (MES·kuh·luhn). This drug is found naturally in a kind of cactus. Most mescaline sold today, however, is made from laboratory chemicals. The drug is illegal and dangerous. The effects can include nausea, cramps, and vomiting. Abuse of mescaline can make mental problems worse.

DID **YOU** KNOW?

A Flashback You Don't Want
When a person feels the effects of PCP on the body some time after taking the drug, the result is called a *flashback.*

LSD

Another hallucinogen known by its initials is *LSD*. Short for *lysergic* (luh·SER·jik) *acid diethylamide* (dy·eth·uh·LAM·yd), LSD is also known as *acid*. Acid is taken as a liquid or a tablet.

LSD and the Body

The many harmful effects of LSD on the body include an increase in heart rate and blood pressure. Some users get chills and lose their appetites. Others become sick to the stomach.

LSD's effects on the mind are like those of PCP. Mistaken beliefs about super strength caused by LSD have led to many needless deaths. Luckily, young people have learned about many of the dangers in the past 10 years. Use of the drug has dropped.

Learning from Photographs
There are countless ways that teens can have fun and expand their skills. Do drugs help or hinder teens as they learn or grow?

Inhalants

In recent years, some young people have come to use a very harmful group of drugs. These are the chemicals found in inhalants. **Inhalants** (in·HAY·luhnts) are *substances whose fumes are sniffed to give a hallucinogenic-like high.*

Inhalants include glue, spray paints, white out, and gasoline. These substances are not meant to be taken into the body. When they are, their harmful fumes go right to the brain.

Among the many effects inhalants cause in users are problems in talking and keeping their balance. Damage to the kidneys and liver is also common. Even worse, the fumes can kill brain cells and cause permanent brain damage or death.

Check Your Understanding

Conclusion Marijuana and the hallucinogens PCP and LSD are very addictive and very dangerous. Users of these street drugs lose the normal working of the body and mind. The same is true of inhalants.

1. **Vocabulary** Use the words *hallucinogen* and *inhalant* in an original sentence.
2. **Recall** What are three dangers of using marijuana?
3. **Recall** Name three widely used hallucinogens.
4. **Recall** What are three dangers of using inhalants?
5. **Analyze** Why is using marijuana especially dangerous for a teenager?

Choosing to Be Drug Free

Words to Know
peers
withdrawal

This lesson contains a number of valuable facts and tips. Once you have studied them, you will be able to

- list ways of saying "no" when offered drugs.
- list some better ways of spending time than taking drugs.
- name places where people with drug problems can turn for help.

Drugs and Teens

The teen years are filled with decisions. They are also filled with indecision. As you search for an answer to the question "Who am I?" you may find yourself feeling unsure about which way to turn. Pressure from **peers**—*people your age who are similar to you in many ways*—can be especially strong. The idea of trying new things to see if they are right for you may seem very exciting.

But if you decide to make one of those "new things" drugs, you will make a decision you will have to live with for the rest of your life. Teens who claim that "a little can't hurt" are wrong. Teens who say, "I can stop any time I want to" are just fooling themselves. Drugs are addictive, and they can kill. The damage that many drugs do to your mind and body is "for keeps."

Teen Issue

No Solution
Some teens begin taking drugs to escape problems. What they find out too late is that drugs don't solve problems. Drugs create problems. No matter how bad things seem, drugs are not the solution.

Learning from Photographs
These teens are enjoying themselves in a healthy way. How does having friends who don't do drugs help a teen stay away from drugs?

291

Saying "No" to Drugs

Ten years ago, 37 percent of the high school seniors in this country said they used marijuana. In a recent year, the number had shrunk to 21 percent. Teen cocaine use has also been going down steadily.

The reason for these changes is clear. More and more teens are becoming aware of the dangers of drug use. More and more are learning to say "no" to drugs. You can say "no," too. The following box shows you some ways.

Teen Issue

Once Is All It Takes

With drugs like crack, it takes only one experiment to get hooked. Keep this in mind when someone you know tries to persuade you to experiment with a drug "just once, out of curiosity."

Saying "No" Through Your Actions	Saying "No" Through Your Words
• Be friends with people who do not use or approve of drugs. • Stay away from situations where you think there may be drugs. • If you are at someone's house or party where people begin using drugs, leave.	When offered drugs, say: • "No, thanks. I get high on life." • "I don't do drugs." • "If you were really my friend, you'd lay off—I'm not interested." • "So long. I'll see you later."

You have a responsibility to yourself to be the best and healthiest *you* you can be. With that responsibility comes the right to make choices that will help you reach your goal of good health. Saying "no" to drugs or to anything else that can harm you is your right. Saying "no" to drugs protects your health.

Athletes and Drugs

More About

For more on the harm that can come to athletes who use steroids, see the "Teen Health Bulletin Board" on pages 284–285.

Some athletes take drugs illegally because they believe that the substances can improve their performance. Among the drugs these athletes may take are *anabolic* (an·uh·BAHL·ik) *steroids* (STIR·oyds), amphetamines, and cocaine. Some athletes think, wrongly, the steroids will build stronger muscles. The amphetamines and cocaine are incorrectly believed to provide energy.

These drugs—and many others—are banned by many of the groups that oversee athletics. Punishment to users is harsh. The National Collegiate Athletic Association (NCAA) tests athletes for these drugs. Professional sports leagues have plans to help athletes recover from cocaine addiction. If an athlete cannot kick the habit, he or she could be banned from playing in the league.

Healthy Alternatives to Drug Use

When you choose, like so many other teens, to be drug free, you open up a world of opportunities for getting "high" in a healthy way. The possibilities are limited only by your imagination. Here are a few.

- **Work at polishing up something you are good at.** Are you good at skateboarding? Spend your spare time becoming a great skateboarder. Or you can practice cooking, playing basketball, playing cards, using a computer, sewing, or scores of other activities.

- **Take up a new and challenging hobby.** Have you always wanted to paint? Ask the art teacher in your school what things you will need to start painting. Decorate your room at home with your own works of art.

- **Start a club with friends.** Find an interest that you share with friends, such as playing a particular board game or sport. Arrange to meet once a week for a game.

- **Break a world record.** Get a copy of the *Guinness Book of World Records*. Then set the world's record for the longest single unbroken apple peel. (The current record is 172 feet, 4 inches.) You could choose another record that interests you.

- **Start a business.** Let neighbors know that you are ready, willing, and able to do odd jobs such as baby-sitting, cleaning, or yard work.

SKILLS FOR LIVING

Stay Cool; Stay Clean
Don't let drug abuse mess up your life. Some famous entertainers and athletes have lost their careers because they used drugs. Baseball pitcher Steve Howe was an all-star until a cocaine habit drove him out of the pros. Comedian John Belushi was rich and famous. Drugs killed him. Show that you are smarter by staying free of drugs.

Teen Issue

Positive Peer Pressure
Be part of a campaign among teens in your school or community to get others to say "no" to drugs. Put on a little peer pressure of your own.

Kicking the Habit

Kicking the drug habit is a lot harder than fighting off pressure to start. The first step for the drug abuser is recognizing that a problem exists. From there, the road to recovery is an uphill one. It involves *a series of painful physical and mental symptoms* as the body slowly overcomes its need for the drug. **Withdrawal** (with·DRAW·uhl), as this series of symptoms is called, must occur whenever the body and mind have become addicted to a substance.

Often, a serious event, such as being hurt or arrested, must happen before a drug abuser is willing to seek help. All of these experiences may leave mental scars. In the end, however, the abuser is far better off being free of drugs.

Teen Issue

Where to Call
A number of toll-free hot lines give answers to questions about drug abuse.

- Drug Abuse Hotline: 1-800-662-HELP
- National Cocaine Hotline: 1-800-COCAINE
- National Federation of Parents for Drug-Free Youth: 1-800-554-KIDS

Help for the Abuser

There are many places in the community where the drug abuser can turn for help. These include special drug treatment centers, such as Day-Top Village. Many hospitals also run drug treatment programs such as Nar-Anon.

In all drug programs, trained people work with the abuser. These experts provide comfort and support. Some drug treatment programs bring in family members as well. This is very helpful when the abuser is a teenager. Family members who have been taught about the dangers of drugs and drug addiction can help an abuser return to health that much faster.

Check Your Understanding

Conclusion Saying "no" to drugs may be difficult for teens. Doing so, however, is a healthy, wise decision. Those who choose unwisely and develop a drug problem can find help in drug treatment centers and hospitals.

1. **Vocabulary** Use the words *peer* and *withdrawal*, each in a single original sentence.
2. **Recall** Give two ways of saying "no" through your actions. Give two ways of saying "no" through your words.
3. **Recall** What are two healthy alternatives to using drugs?
4. **Recall** Name two places in the community where people with drug problems can turn for help.
5. **Interpret** Why might a teen drug addict have a better chance of recovery if he or she has a close brother or sister who does not use drugs?

The Art of Saying "No" to Drugs

More and more young people are learning the dangers of using drugs. More and more are learning the importance of saying "no."

Yet, saying "no" is not always easy. This is especially true when the people you have to say "no" to are friends. First, you may be afraid that by turning them down you will lose their friendship. Second, friends can often be persuasive.

One way of overcoming this difficulty is by being prepared. By knowing the arguments you might hear, you can have an answer ready.

Recognizing the "Come-Ons"

The arguments people use to persuade others to try drugs take several forms.

- **The "good times" come-on.** The person claims that drugs make you "feel good." He or she never mentions the risks and dangers of drug abuse.
- **The "celebrities" come-on.** The person names stars or athletes who have admitted to using drugs. The message is: "If they do it, it must be okay." He or she never mentions the many public figures who have died from drug abuse or those who quit using drugs to save their careers.
- **The "for-the-sake-of-our-friendship" come-on.** The person tries to make you feel as though his or her feelings would be hurt if you said "no." He or she never mentions the greater harm you could do to *yourself* if you said "yes."
- **The "mass appeal" come-on.** The person plays on your fear of becoming unpopular by telling you that "everyone's doing it." He or she never mentions the many teens you both know who are *not* "doing it."

Using the Skill

Read the following stories. Then follow the instructions that come after the stories.

Case One

Elsa and Julie have been friends for years. Three days ago, Julie asked Elsa to smoke marijuana with her. Elsa has read that marijuana is a dangerous drug. Still, she is worried about disappointing her friend. She doesn't know what to do.

Case Two

Luis overheard some boys in his gym class talking about crack. Then he saw a news story on television about crack use. So when his buddy, Hal, told Luis that he was the only student left at Fairmont Junior High who hadn't tried crack, Luis figured maybe Hal was right. The idea of trying crack frightened Luis. But he didn't want to feel left out.

Case Three

Jason never had much fun. Every boring day seemed to be the same. But then this ninth-grader named Lee told Jason about "uppers." "They make life great," Lee had said. Jason remembered his teacher telling the class that drugs can hurt you. Still, Jason thought, maybe you have to take risks when you're in a rut.

Divide a separate sheet of paper into three columns. Label one column "Elsa," one "Luis," and one "Jason." For each teen, write the following: (1) The choices the teen faces. (2) The come-on the teen has heard. (3) The decision the teen should make.

Chapter 10 Review

Summary

- Drugs are substances that change the way the mind or body works. Drugs are helpful in preventing and curing diseases. To be safe and effective, drugs must be used as directed by doctors.
- Drug misuse and drug abuse are two ways of using drugs wrongly that can harm the body.
- Stimulants, depressants, and narcotics can cause harm, and even death, when misused or abused. All are highly addictive drugs.
- Street drugs like marijuana and hallucinogenics are against the law and are very dangerous. Inhalants, such as glue, have effects similar to those of street drugs.
- Learning to say "no" to all drugs is a healthy decision. This decision can be difficult, but it is also especially important for teens.
- People with drug abuse problems can find help in drug treatment centers and hospitals.

Reviewing Vocabulary and Concepts

On a separate sheet of paper, write the numbers 1–11. After each number, write the term from the list on the right that best completes each statement.

Lesson 1

1. _____ are drugs meant to cure or prevent diseases and other conditions.
2. Penicillin belongs to the group of drugs called _____ , which are produced by tiny living organisms.
3. When a person has a reaction to a drug other than one hoped for, that person has suffered a(n) _____ .
4. To make sure drugs are used safely, the FDA sees to it that certain drugs are _____ , available only with a doctor's written order.

Lesson 2

5. Changing the amount of a drug without first getting a doctor's approval is an example of _____ .
6. Using a drug for reasons other than intended ones is an example of _____ .
7. If a person continues to need more and more of a drug, that person can develop a(n) _____ , a physical or mental need.
8. The illegal stimulant _____ can lead to heart attack and death when used in large amounts.
9. It is possible to become addicted after one use of _____ , a more pure and very powerful form of cocaine.
10. Drugs that slow down the body's functions are known as _____ .
11. When some drugs are mixed, the user can fall into a(n) _____ , a deep unconscious state.

addiction

antibiotics

cocaine

coma

crack

depressants

drug abuse

drug misuse

medicines

prescription drugs

side effect

Write the numbers 12–20 on your paper. After each number, write the letter of the word or phrase in Column B that best matches the phrase in Column A.

Column A

Lesson 3

12. Drugs that cause the user's brain to form images of things that are not really there
13. The hallucinogen nicknamed *acid*
14. A street drug that is dangerous for teens because it affects hormone levels
15. A powerful drug that is dangerous because it blocks the sense of pain
16. Substances that are breathed in and have effects similar to hallucinogens

Lesson 4

17. The healthiest decision in regard to drugs
18. The first step in kicking a drug habit
19. A series of painful symptoms felt by a drug user while kicking a drug habit
20. A place where a drug addict can get help

Column B

a. LSD
b. marijuana
c. saying "no"
d. inhalants
e. withdrawal
f. recognizing that a problem exists
g. hallucinogens
h. drug treatment center
i. PCP

Thinking Critically About the Facts

Write your answers to the following questions on a separate sheet of paper.

21. **Synthesize** Suppose a classmate of yours told you he or she was going to try cocaine "just once, to see what it is like." What would you say to this person? Explain your answer.

22. **Summarize** Your class is holding a debate on whether or not marijuana should be made legal. You have been asked to head up the team arguing that marijuana should not be legalized. What reasons could you give your teammates to help your team win the debate?

23. **Analyze** While watching the small children who live next door you notice some cans of spray paint that are missing their caps. What might you say to your neighbors when they get home?

24. **Synthesize** Imagine that you are at a party where older teens are trying to get younger teens to try drugs. The older teens are saying such things as "PCP is the thing to do." What might you say or do?

Applying the Facts

25. Write a story about a teen your age who makes a new friend and then finds out that the friend uses drugs. Have the drug-using teen describe how she or he got started. Decide what the other teen does to help the new friend overcome her or his problem. Bring your finished story to class.

26. Make a book titled "How to Avoid the Drug Habit." In your book, include information on what certain drugs look like and what to do if someone offers them to you. Use the "Stimulant Fact Sheet" on page 280 and the "Street Drug Fact Sheet" on page 290 and add illustrations. Share your book with your classmates.

CHAPTER 11

Communicable Diseases

CHAPTER WARM-UP

Chapter Study Goals

After you have read this chapter, you will be able to

- explain what causes communicable diseases and how to prevent getting them.

- describe the workings of the immune system.

- identify some common communicable diseases.

- identify the best way to prevent infection from sexually transmitted diseases, including AIDS.

- describe what public health officials and the health-care system do to control the spread of sexually transmitted diseases, including AIDS.

Be on the lookout for information in the chapter that will help you reach these goals.

Getting Started

Many illnesses come from contact with tiny living germs that cause disease. Scientists can grow these germs in laboratories to find ways to fight them. But often these illnesses can be prevented. This is especially true of the diseases that result from sexual contact. An important part of living a healthy life is making choices that help you avoid these illnesses.

Study Tip

The chapter contains many suggestions on how to prevent catching diseases. Take notes and turn these suggestions into a list of tips for yourself.

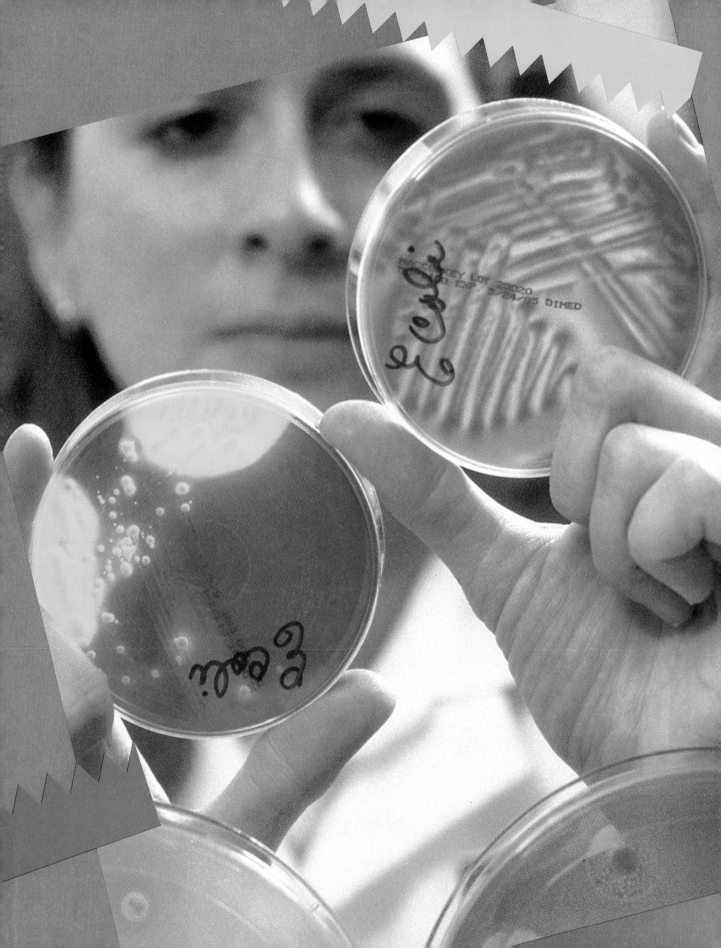

Preventing the Spread of Disease

This lesson contains a number of valuable facts and tips. Once you have studied them, you will be able to

- list the types of germs in the world around us.
- name the ways these germs can be spread.
- talk about how the spread of germs can be prevented.

More About

For more on noncom-municable diseases, see Chapter 12.

What Is Disease?

Being healthy means feeling good and being fit. It also means you can face your problems and work well with others. Sometimes disease gets in the way of health. A **disease** is *an illness that affects the body or mind.* Some diseases, like the common cold, come and go quickly. Others last longer. Some can even lead to death.

Some illnesses can be passed on from one person to another. These are called **communicable** (kuh·MYOO·ni·kuh·buhl) **diseases.** One way to stop the spread of these diseases is to fight the germs that cause them. Another way is to stop contact between people during the time that the disease can be passed on. *Other illnesses are caused by how people live, by conditions they are born with, or by hazards around them.* These are called **noncommunicable diseases.** To prevent these, people must try to change how they live or reduce the hazards around them.

DID **YOU** KNOW?

Medicines Against Disease

Some bacteria and viruses are changing to resist the medicines that used to destroy them. They reproduce so fast that the resistant types can spread quickly.

What Causes Communicable Diseases?

Communicable diseases are caused by germs. These tiny plants or animals are so small a person can only see them through a microscope. These *germs attack the body's cells and use them to grow and reproduce.* This is called an **infection** (in·FEK·shuhn). Through this attack, germs destroy or damage the body's cells.

Types of Germs

Among the germs that can cause disease are *bacteria, viruses, rickettsias, fungi,* and *protozoa.* Bacteria and viruses are the most common causes of illness in the United States.

Bacteria (bak·TIR·ee·uh) are *tiny one-celled organisms that grow everywhere.* There are countless bacteria in the world around you—and even inside you. Most bacteria do not cause disease. In fact, many are helpful. Bacteria that live in your intestines help you digest food. Others live in your mouth and skin without harming you. These harmless bacteria are called *resident bacteria.*

Bacteria are harmful when they go places they do not belong. Harmless bacteria from your mouth can enter your middle ear. Once there, they can cause an ear infection. Or bacteria from the soil can enter a cut and infect it. To grow, bacteria need a food supply, warmth, and moisture. The body provides an ideal home for them.

Viruses (VY·ruhs·uhs) are among the most common causes of communicable disease. These are *the smallest and simplest form of life.* Viruses are very specialized. Some attack only animals. Some attack only certain *kinds* of animals. And some attack only certain cells of animals' bodies. The rabies virus, for instance, only affects the nervous system.

There is also *a special kind of virus* called a **retrovirus** (re·troh·VY·ruhs). One retrovirus causes the disease AIDS, which attacks the body's defenses against disease. By studying this retrovirus, scientists are learning more about how viruses work.

DID YOU KNOW?

Bacteria
How tiny are bacteria? A single gram of soil can contain 100 *million* bacteria.

DID YOU KNOW?

Looking at Viruses
Viruses are so small people cannot even see them with a light microscope. Scientists must use a device called an *electron microscope.* No one saw viruses until 1932, when this tool was invented.

More About
For more on AIDS, see Lesson 5 of this chapter.

Learning from Photographs
The actions of the teens in these pictures may help prevent them from catching diseases. Can you explain how?

Spotting and Removing Ticks

Ticks attach themselves by embedding their heads under the skin. As they suck blood, their bodies grow. Anyone who spends time outdoors should check his or her body for ticks. If you find one, smother it by covering it with a thick substance like petroleum jelly or with rubbing alcohol. Once it dies, you can take it out. Be sure to remove the head.

DID YOU KNOW?

Water

Scientists estimate that 80 percent of all illness in Africa, Asia, and South America is caused by dirty water.

Learning from Photographs
This computer-created image shows how the flu virus has long projections. How do you think those spikes are used to attack the body's cells?

Rickettsias (rik·ET·see·uhs) are *disease-causing creatures that are passed on by insects.* They are found in lice, mites, and ticks. They enter the human body when one of these insects bites a person. Rocky Mountain spotted fever is one disease caused by rickettsias. People can get this disease when a tick that lives on a wild animal bites them. People who like to spend time in the woods camping, hiking, or hunting should guard against these ticks.

Fungi (FUHN·jy) are *simple life forms that cannot make their own food.* Mushrooms and yeasts are examples of fungi. Fungi that attack the body often live in the hair, nails, and skin. Athlete's foot and ringworm are two diseases caused by fungi. Athlete's foot affects the feet. Ringworm is an infection of the scalp.

Single-celled creatures that are larger and more complex than bacteria are **protozoa** (proht·uh·ZOH·uh). Most protozoa are harmless. Some, however, cause disease. This is especially true where the climate is hot and humid. Malaria is an example of such a disease.

How Germs Are Spread

Germs can be spread in one of four ways.

- **Close contact with a person who has the germ.** Colds and pneumonia are spread when a sick person coughs or sneezes. The germs travel through the air and enter another person's lungs. There they may cause the disease.

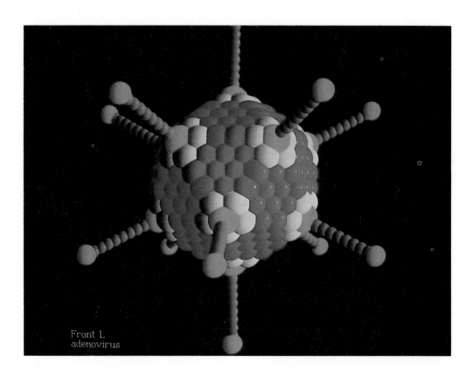

Front L adenovirus

- **Direct contact with a person who has the germ.** Some germs spread when the contact between the infected person and another person is more direct. Sexually transmitted diseases, including AIDS, work this way. The germs for these diseases are not carried through the air and cannot be passed with casual contact.

- **Contact with animals.** The bites of mosquitos may pass malaria to humans. Bites from infected animals can cause rabies.

- **Contact with nonliving things.** Some germs live for long periods of time in water or animal meat. If someone drinks this infected water or eats the meat, the germ enters the body.

Some diseases have *a period of time during which they can be passed to another person.* This is called the **contagious** (kuhn·TAY·juhs) **period.** The contagious period for chicken pox, for instance, lasts about a week after the disease first affects someone. The contagious period for many sexually transmitted diseases can last as long as the germ is in someone's body.

How to Prevent the Spread of Disease

Contact with a germ does not *always* cause a disease. Whether you catch a disease or not depends in part on how healthy you are in general. With the less serious diseases like the cold, your body can fight off the germs. With the more serious diseases, your body may not be able to resist the germs. That is why it is so important to take steps to avoid catching them.

Teen Issue

Myths About AIDS
People worry that shaking hands with someone with AIDS will pass on the disease. Some people wonder if they will get AIDS if they are bitten by a mosquito that bit someone who had AIDS. *These are myths.* The AIDS virus cannot enter your body in these ways.

Cooking for Health
The high temperatures used in cooking can kill bacteria that live in food or water. Someone who is going camping should take along clean water or boil any natural water before using it.

Learning from Photographs
By washing his hair, this teen is helping to prevent himself from getting a certain disease. Can you name it?

You can do three things to try to prevent yourself and others from getting communicable diseases.

- **Practice good health habits.** Bathe or shower every day to keep your skin and hair clean. Get plenty of rest and exercise, and eat a balanced diet. These habits keep you strong and better able to resist disease.

- **Practice good health behaviors to protect yourself.** Avoid using the same eating or drinking utensils as someone else. Store and prepare food in a safe way to prevent food poisoning. Avoid sexual contact to prevent sexually transmitted diseases. You can protect yourself from some diseases caused by viruses or bacteria by having a *vaccine.*

- **Practice good health behaviors to protect others.** If you know you are sick, avoid giving your illness to someone else. Get medical treatment so you can get over the illness. Many diseases can be cured with medicines. Stay home from school if you are in the contagious period. Cover your mouth when you cough or sneeze to prevent spreading the germs.

More About

*For more on **vaccines**, see Lesson 2 of this chapter.*

Check Your Understanding

Conclusion   Some diseases are passed from one person to another. These diseases are caused by germs, tiny creatures that enter the body and do damage to its cells. These diseases can often be prevented by taking healthy steps. A generally high level of health helps. So, too, does following good health practices.

1. **Vocabulary** What does the term *contagious period* mean?
2. **Recall** Name three types of germs that can cause disease and give an example of a disease caused by each type.
3. **Recall** What are the four ways that a communicable disease can be spread?
4. **Recall** What are the three ways you can help prevent the spread of a communicable disease?
5. **Identify** Read about the three diseases that follow. Tell whether each disease is communicable or noncommunicable.
   a. A disease that happens because a person eats spoiled food containing a germ
   b. A disease that happens because a person eats a diet high in fats and salt
   c. A disease that happens because an insect bites someone

The Body's Defenses Against Germs

Words to Know
immunity
immune system
phagocytosis
interferon
fever
lymphatic system
lymphocytes
lymph nodes
B-cells
T-cells
vaccines

This lesson contains a number of valuable facts and tips. Once you have studied them, you will be able to

- tell what the body's barriers against germs are.
- tell what the body's chemical defenses against germs are.
- tell how the immune system works.
- explain what the lymphatic system does.
- tell what vaccines are and why they are important.

The Body's Defenses

Sometimes germs attack even when you have taken steps to prevent infection. When that happens, your body has ways to fight those germs. The first line of defense takes two forms. First, body tissues form barriers to germs. Second, the body releases some chemicals to fight germs. Germs that pass these barriers reach the second line of defense, which is a set of germ-killing cells.

Your body also has a long-term defense against disease. Called **immunity** (im·YOO·nuht·ee), this is *the body's ability to remember how to fight certain germs.* It then "replays" the right defense if those germs ever enter the body again.

More About

*For more on **bacteria** and viruses, see Lesson 1 of this chapter.*

The First Line of Defense

Your body has two kinds of barriers against germs.

- **The skin's tough outer layer.** This layer protects you from germs as long as it remains unbroken. Germs can enter only when the skin is broken by a cut, burn, or scrape, or by cracking.

More About

*For more on the **skin**, see Chapter 2.*

Learning from Photographs
Each of these teens is protecting someone from the spread of germs. Explain who is being protected and how.

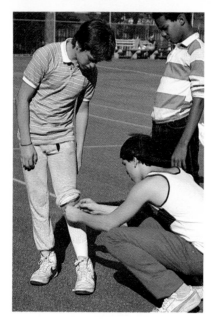

- **Mucous membranes** (MYOO·kuhs MEM·brayns) **in the mouth, nose, and throat.** All of these can trap dirt and germs. The germs are then sent out of the body when you cough.

Your body also uses chemicals to fight germs. Tears wash germs away from your eyes. The saliva in your mouth kills germs. So do the strong juices in your digestive system. Even the resident bacteria in your mouth and intestine help. They destroy harmful bacteria.

The Main Line of Defense

Sometimes harmful germs still get through your first defenses. Then your body's next line of defense takes over. It comes in two waves. First, invading germs are attacked by general reactions. These may include the actions of white blood cells, interferon, and fever.

The second wave of your body's main line of defense is your **immune** (im·YOON) **system.** This is *the group of organs and cells that fights germs and keeps a memory of how to destroy germs.* The immune system is one of the most important parts of your body.

The General Reactions

Suppose a germ enters your body. The blood vessels nearby release special white blood cells. These cells surround the harmful germ and destroy it. *The process in which white blood cells destroy germs* is called **phagocytosis** (fag·uh·suh·TOH·suhs). This word means "to eat up cells." Your body may take two other steps against a virus.

Good Fever or Bad Fever?

Sometimes fever is part of your body's fight against disease. Sometimes it is part of the disease. How do you know which is which? If the fever is below 102°F, it is probably helping you. Get plenty of rest and drink liquids to replace fluid lost from sweating. If your body aches, take a mild painkiller like acetaminophen. High fevers are signs of sickness. See a doctor.

Parts of the Body's General Reactions

- **The body releases interferon.** Cells attacked by germs release **interferon** (int·uh·FIR·ahn). This *chemical signals other cells to begin to fight the virus.* Interferon is like a messenger. When one part of your body learns how to fight a virus, interferon passes the word along to other parts. Then cells there are ready to fight the infection. Interferon is not released with all viruses.

- **The body produces a fever.** In a **fever,** *the body responds to infection by raising its temperature and taking other actions.* This higher temperature can kill some virus cells. One of the other responses of a fever is the release of more germ-killing cells. When the infection ends, the fever breaks. Body temperature returns to normal.

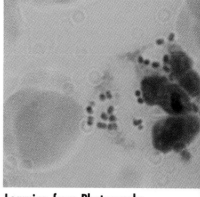

Learning from Photographs
These white blood cells are gathering near a clump of bacteria, just before destroying it. This response to germs is part of what system of the body?

The Lymphatic System

White blood cells travel in the bloodstream. They also use *a secondary circulatory* (SER·kyuh·luh·tohr·ee) *system* called the **lymphatic** (lim·FAT·ik) **system.** This system does not carry blood. Rather, it transports a special body fluid called *lymph.* Lymph is fluid that seeps out of the capillaries and collects in the vessels of the lymphatic system. These vessels move lymph to a vein near the heart, where it returns to the bloodstream. If the fluid were not returned to the bloodstream in this way, it would enter body tissues and make them swollen.

The lymphatic system plays a part in the immune system. It carries some *special white blood cells* called **lymphocytes** (LIM·fuh·syts). These germ fighters are in many parts of the body, including the **lymph nodes** (LIMF NOHDS). These are *glandlike structures located throughout the body which act as filters to screen out bacteria.*

The Immune System

The immune system is aimed at attacking specific diseases and remembering them in case they enter the body again. The lymphocytes are the main players in this defense. The two kinds of lymphocytes are *B-cells* and *T-cells.*

Many lymphocytes fight against specific diseases. Suppose the germs that cause a disease enter the body. The immune system searches the lymph nodes for the right B-cell and T-cell to fight that disease. When it finds the right B-cell and T-cell, the body begins to copy these cells. That way, many lymphocytes are on hand to attack the many germ cells.

DID **YOU** KNOW?

Trash Disposal
One of the jobs of the immune system is to eat up old red blood cells. Red blood cells become useless after about 4 months. Dead ones need to be cleaned out of the bloodstream.

Learning from Drawings
The lymphatic system carries the body fluid called lymph. The lymph nodes, also called *lymph glands,* filter the lymph and store the white blood cells called B-cells and T-cells. These special cells play a part in the body's defense against disease. What is the name for these two types of white blood cells?

The Lymphatic System

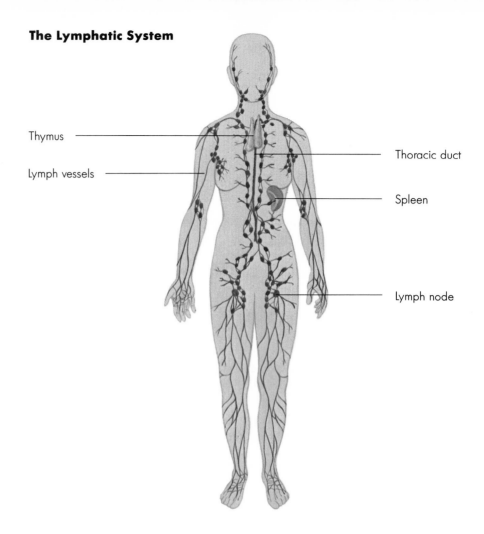

Thymus

Lymph vessels

Thoracic duct

Spleen

Lymph node

DID **YOU** KNOW?

What's in a Name?
B-cells are named that because they were first found in a part of birds called the *bursa.* T-cells are named after the thymus, which plays a role in producing them.

DID **YOU** KNOW?

Tonsils Today
In the past, scientists did not know what tonsils were for. Because tonsils often got infected, doctors removed them in surgery. Now that their role in making B-cells is known, doctors are less likely to take them out.

B-cells and T-cells fight germs in different ways.

- **B-cells.** *Lymphocytes that make a protein that attacks germ cells are called* **B-cells.** The protein is called an *antibody* (ANT·i·bahd·ee). Some antibodies destroy germ cells. Others force these cells to bunch together. Then other white-blood cells destroy these bunches. B-cells are made in the spleen, the intestines, the lymph nodes, the tonsils, and the appendix.

- **T-cells.** *Lymphocytes that fight germs in different ways are known as* **T-cells.** When the right T-cell for a disease is found, it makes four new T-cells. One kind helps B-cells. Another kind kills the body cells that have been harmed by the disease. The third kind shuts off these killer T-cells when the danger has passed. The fourth kind of T-cell "remembers" how to fight the particular disease. If that disease ever enters the body again, this T-cell starts the immune response right away. The AIDS virus harms the body by destroying T-cells. This opens the body to infection from other diseases.

Vaccines and Immunity

Is catching a disease the only way to become immune to it? No. Mothers pass immunity to disease to their newborn babies. But this immunity only lasts about 6 months. A second way to build up immunity is through **vaccines** (vak·SEENS). These are *preparations made of dead or weak germ cells put into the body so that antibodies will be made.* Then if you are ever infected by the germs for that disease, your body's immune system will be ready to act right away.

Vaccines can be given either by needle or orally. Vaccines contain germ cells that have been weakened or killed. These weak or dead germs are strong enough to lead the body to make antibodies. But they are not strong enough to cause the illness. The effects of vaccines made of dead germ cells wear off, so a new vaccine must be given. These later doses are called *boosters.*

Vaccines are, in general, safe. Sometimes a person has a mild reaction such as a slight fever or rash. On very rare occasions, the reaction can be stronger. The risk of having a reaction is almost always less than the risk of having the disease.

Many school systems require students to have certain vaccines before they may attend school. Other vaccines may be needed by someone who is about to travel to another country. Sometimes a disease like *influenza* (in·floo·EN·zuh) makes many people sick in one region or even around the nation. At such a time, the government could make a vaccine available to all people.

Check Your Understanding

Conclusion Your body defends itself against the germs that attack it. The key to this defense is the immune system, which can destroy germs and make you well again. The immune system remembers how to fight a disease so it cannot make you ill a second time. Vaccines also build this immunity.

1. **Vocabulary** Define the term *lymphatic system* and tell what this system does.
2. **Recall** What are the body's two barriers to disease?
3. **Recall** Name two chemical defenses against disease.
4. **Recall** Describe the two stages of the reaction of the immune system.
5. **Synthesize** Why do school systems require students to have vaccines for certain diseases before they may attend school?

DID **YOU** KNOW?

Vaccines: A Success Story
The first vaccine ever used was for smallpox. It was first used in 1796 by Edward Jenner, a British doctor. The World Health Organization (WHO) has given the smallpox vaccine to children throughout the world. Using a vaccine gun like the one shown below, WHO workers are able to vaccinate 1,000 children an hour. This program has all but wiped out smallpox. Polio and measles vaccines have almost wiped those diseases out of the United States and Canada.

Health Minute

Vaccinations and You
Find out what vaccinations you had when you were younger. Find out which ones your school requires for students.

Teen Health
BULLETIN BOARD

CAREERS

Wanted:

Microbiologist

Specifics:

Study causes and treatment of illness and epidemics; help maintain healthful food and water supplies.

Qualifications:

Need good eyesight, including depth and color perception. Good health and stamina a must to carry on research until complete. Must be disciplined and able to work alone in research. Irregular hours are common.

Preparation:

Concentration on science in high school, followed by college or university degree in biology or microbiology. Advanced study helpful.

Contact:

Registrar's office at college or university of your choice.

HEALTH IN THE NEWS

Donated Blood Is Safe but Scarce

Eight million people give blood each year. That sounds like a lot. However, *80* million people *could* give blood each year. In other words, there is a blood shortage. Hospitals need blood for people who have been in accidents. They also need blood for people who will have long operations. One reason that some people do not give blood is that they are afraid of getting AIDS. However, the AIDS virus is not passed on to anyone who gives blood. New needles are used, and there is no danger. The more people who understand this, the sooner the blood shortage will pass. Giving "the gift of life" is as safe as it ever was.

Q: I've heard a lot of confusing talk about AIDS. Can you get the disease from shaking hands?

A: You *cannot* get AIDS from casual contact. That includes shaking hands. AIDS is also not passed on from toilet seats, water fountains, saliva, or urine. You do not get AIDS if someone sneezes near you. You do not get AIDS if a mosquito bites you. You can only get AIDS if the virus is able to enter your bloodstream. It is important to protect yourself against AIDS. Knowing the facts will help you do this.

Q: A friend of mine has something called mono. Is it really catching?

A: Yes! Mono — or mononucleosis — is very contagious. And you don't want to get it. Mono is a virus that affects the liver and the lymph glands. People feel very tired when they have the disease. They feel run down for a while even after the disease goes away.

There is no vaccine against mono. Because mono is passed on through mucus or saliva, it is sometimes called "the kissing disease." To avoid it, you must stay away from your friend's drinking glasses, forks, knives, plates, and even makeup. Don't touch used tissues or napkins. Wash your hands carefully after each visit.

Do visit if you can, though. Long illnesses are *boring.* Your friend will be happy to have your company.

HEALTH IN THE NEWS

Legionnaires' Mystery Continues

Before 1976, Legionnaires' disease was practically unknown. Then, suddenly, 34 people died. All of them had been to the same convention in Philadelphia. Scientists have been studying the disease named for those victims since then.

The mechanism of how the disease is contracted is not completely understood yet, but *Legionella* bacteria live in water and have been found in some cooling systems. Scientists have found that exposure to the organism doesn't always cause the disease. Older people and people whose immune systems are suppressed seem to be the most susceptible.

Legionnaires' disease can strike any time, but occurs most commonly in late summer and fall. There are two forms. The milder one causes fever, headache, and muscle ache, and is not fatal. The other form causes chills, high fever, dry cough, and pneumonia. It lasts more than a week and can be fatal. Erythromycin and rifampin are antibiotics used to treat this disease.

Words to Know

Words to Know
symptoms
pneumonia
mononucleosis
hepatitis

Common Communicable Diseases

This lesson contains a number of valuable facts and tips. Once you have studied them, you will be able to

● tell how to spot, treat, and prevent the common cold.

● talk about how to treat and prevent some other common communicable diseases.

DID **YOU** KNOW?

Colds or Allergies

There are people who have *allergies*. This means that their bodies react when certain things are present. Someone could be allergic to cat hair or to milk. Most common are allergies to the pollen spread by plants each year. This type is called *hay fever*. The reactions look like colds. The person has a runny nose, watery eyes, and trouble breathing. Medicines can relieve these symptoms, but the best relief comes when pollen season ends.

The Most Common Problem

A cold is the most common communicable disease. Everyone gets colds. In fact, the average American has two or three every year. The cold is so common, you might think it would be easy to find a vaccine. This cannot be done because the common cold is not caused by just one virus. Over a hundred different viruses cause the cold.

Your body is always exposed to different cold viruses. They are spread through air and water and through contact with someone who is carrying one. The cold is contagious the first day after the symptoms appear. **Symptoms** (SIM·tuhms) are *the changes in the body that signal that a particular disease is present.* The symptoms of a cold include a mild fever, runny nose, itchy eyes, sneezing, a cough, a mild sore throat, and a headache.

Preventing Colds

You cannot completely prevent yourself from getting a cold. But you can do things to keep yourself healthy. That way you are more likely to resist coming down with the cold when the virus attacks you.

● **Get the proper amount of rest.** Teens your age should have 8 hours of sleep every night.

● **Eat healthfully.** Eat a balanced diet with regular meals every day.

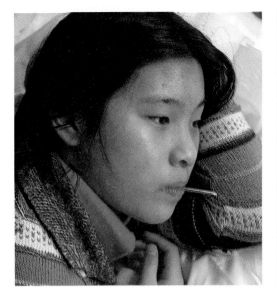
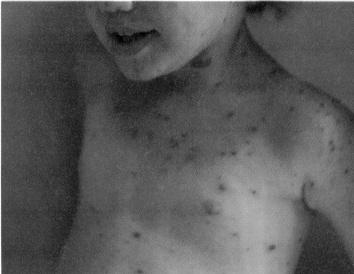

Learning from Photographs
The flu often brings a fever, which is a temperature of 100° or above. Can you identify the common communicable disease in the picture on the right?

- **Exercise regularly.** To keep your energy level and strength up, exercise on a regular basis.
- **Avoid smoking.** People who smoke get more colds, and those colds last longer than do the colds of nonsmokers.

You can also take steps to prevent infection by practicing good habits of cleanliness. Use your own eating and drinking utensils rather than those of someone else. This will protect you from cold germs the other person may have. Washing your hands helps, too.

Treating Colds

There is no cure for a cold. But you can do things to treat a cold so that it does not get worse. Once you have a cold, get plenty of rest and drink lots of liquids.

You can also take a cold medicine to relieve some of the symptoms, though these medicines can cause problems. One problem is that they can simply hide the symptoms. Even though you are still sick, you may feel well enough to go out. This puts your friends in danger of getting your cold. Be responsible for your friends. Stay home until you are really well.

Pneumonia

Pneumonia (noo·MOH·nyuh) is *a serious disease of the lungs that can be caused by either bacteria or viruses.* In either case, the victim of pneumonia finds it hard to breathe. The air sacs in the lungs fill with fluid and dead white-blood cells. That makes it hard for these sacs to fill with air.

Fighting Colds
There are pills, liquids, capsules, and sprays that can help you get rid of cold symptoms. You may have to try out a few to find the one that works best for you.

Some Common Communicable Diseases

Disease	Symptoms	Contagious Period	Vaccine
Chicken pox	Crusty rash, fever, headache, body ache	Day before first signs to 6 days after rash appears	No
Cold	Runny nose, sneezing, fever, body ache	First 24 hours	No
German measles (rubella)	Headache, swollen glands, cough, sore throat, rash	Seven days before rash starts to 5 days after	Yes
Influenza (flu)	Fever, chills, muscle aches	Day signs start to 7 days after	Some
Measles	Fever, runny nose, cough, red rash	Four days before rash starts to 5 days after	Yes
Mononucleosis	Sore throat, swollen glands, tiredness	Unknown	No
Mumps	Chills, headache, fever, swollen glands	Seven days before signs start to 9 days after	Yes
Polio	Fever, sore throat, muscle pain, possible paralysis	A few days before signs start to first week after	Yes
Scarlet fever	Sore throat, rash, fever, chills	Up to 5 days before signs appear to 2 to 3 weeks after	No

More About

*For more on the **lungs**, see Chapter 7.*

The kind of pneumonia caused by bacteria is less of a problem today than it was in the past. Now that doctors know of certain strong medicines, they can cure the disease fairly quickly.

There is no cure for the pneumonia caused by viruses. Doctors can give medicines to relieve symptoms. The ill person can also be cared for to make sure that the problem does not worsen. But the body has to rid itself of the disease. Since 1977, there has been a vaccine against this kind of pneumonia. However, it is not yet given to all people.

Mononucleosis

You have probably heard of "the kissing disease." This phrase refers to **mononucleosis** (mahn·uh·noo·klee·OH·suhs). This is *a disease common to young people caused by a virus that results in a high number of white-blood cells in the body.* It is passed on through direct contact, such as kissing. "Mono," as the disease is also called, looks like a cold at first. Doctors use a blood test to see whether mono is present.

More About

*For more on the **liver**, see Chapter 7.*

Treatment is complete bed rest for 3 to 6 weeks. The body may take that long to fight off the disease.

Hepatitis

Hepatitis (hep·uh·TYT·uhs) is *a disease that involves the swelling of the liver.* There are two main kinds of hepatitis.

Hepatitis A is caused by a virus that often enters the body in contaminated food or dirty water. Someone who get hepatitis A loses his or her appetite and feels weak and tired. Hepatitis A can also cause vomiting and turn the skin a yellowish color. These symptoms do not appear right away. They come 3 to 4 weeks after the germ enters the person's body. The disease lasts from 2 to 6 weeks.

Someone who comes in contact with a person who has hepatitis A can be protected from getting the disease. A shot of a protein called *gamma globulin* (GAM·uh GLAHB·yuh·luhn) gives this protection. He or she must have the shot within the first week of contact with the disease.

Hepatitis B is passed on through contact with an infected person. It can also be caused by using dirty needles to inject illegal drugs. Sharing these needles can pass the disease from one drug user to another. Its effects are similar to those of the other type. Treatment for both types is about the same. This treatment includes bed rest and drinking plenty of fluids.

Hepatitis B is much more dangerous than hepatitis A, however. It can cause long-term damage to the liver. It seems to be connected to liver cancer.

Check Your Understanding

Conclusion A number of common diseases can affect anyone. You can often take steps to prevent these diseases. With the cold, the most common disease of all, it is important to act responsibly to try to prevent others from catching it.

1. **Vocabulary** Which of the following diseases affects the lungs and which affects the liver? *hepatitis, pneumonia*

2. **Recall** What are two things you can do to treat the common cold? What are two things you can do to prevent the spread of a cold?

3. **Recall** What is the main treatment for mononucleosis?

4. **Identify** Look at the following list of symptoms and name the diseases described.
   a. red rash, fever, runny nose
   b. fever, chills, muscle aches and pains
   c. crusty rash, fever, body ache

DID YOU KNOW?

Neither A Nor B
A third type of hepatitis was discovered in 1975. It is called *non-A, non-B hepatitis* because traces of the other two viruses were not found in the blood of sufferers. This type is spread through sexual contact and through contact with infected blood. In the past, it was possible to get this type from infected blood received in a transfusion. Now, however, all blood is screened for this virus, making the blood supply safer. The symptoms of this disease are similar to the other two types, as is the treatment. It is somewhat more serious, however, in that it leads more often to chronic liver disease.

Words to Know
sexually transmitted
    disease (STD)
group date
chlamydia
pelvic inflammatory
    disease (PID)
nongonococcal
    urethritis (NGU)
gonorrhea
syphilis
herpes simplex II

Sexually Transmitted Diseases

This lesson contains a number of valuable facts and tips. Once you have studied them, you will be able to

- define the term *STD* and tell how these diseases are spread.
- tell how STDs can be prevented.
- tell how the family, the government, and the health-care system can help control the spread of STDs.
- tell how STDs affect the body and what is done to treat them.

More About

AIDS is also a sexually transmitted disease. For more on AIDS, see Lesson 5 of this chapter.

What Are STDs?

STD is a short form for **sexually** (SEKSH·wuh·lee) **transmitted disease.** STDs are *illnesses that pass from one person to another through sexual contact.* Another term for these diseases is *venereal* (vuh·NIR·ee·uhl) *disease, or VD.*

One important thing to remember about STDs is that they can be prevented very easily. By avoiding sexual contact, you can prevent yourself from getting almost all STDs. It's as simple as that.

Preventing STDs

One way to prevent STDs is to know the facts. You can then separate the truth from the myths. These are some facts about STDs.

- **STDs are dangerous.** They can damage the reproductive system and make the victim unable to have children. They can cause blindness, deafness, heart disease, and death.
- **STDs can be hidden.** These diseases may not always show symptoms. With some, the symptoms appear and then go away. It is important that anyone with an unusual sore or odor around the penis or vagina talk to a doctor. The same is true of anyone who

notices an unusual fluid coming from these organs or feels a burning or itching there.

- **Most STDs can be treated.** Early treatment gets the best results. But the body cannot build up an immunity to any STD. Someone can get any of these diseases more than once. And some STDs now have forms that can resist the medicines used to fight them.

- **The most serious STDs are spread only through sexual contact.** They cannot be passed on by using the same toilet seats as someone who has the disease. They cannot be passed on by casual touching like shaking hands.

Saying "No"

These diseases are scary. But you can prevent yourself from catching one of them in a basic way: say "no" to sexual contact. This can be one of the most important health decisions you make. By taking this step, though, you protect your health in a big way. Saying "no" to sex is one way of saying "yes" to good health.

As a teen, you may be pressured by others to have sex. Friends or dates may try to persuade you. Remember that they cannot decide *for* you. You must take responsibility for your own health. You have the right to decide for yourself, and your friends should respect that right.

Ways of Saying "No"

The pressure from others to have sex may be great. There are ways to prevent that pressure from arising, though.

Ways To Say "No"

- Avoid situations where the pressure may arise. Going out in groups is one way. A **group date** *is going out with a group of friends of both sexes.* When there is a group instead of just one couple, the chances of this pressure arising are less. Teens who do date as a couple can date in public places to reduce the pressure. Going to an isolated spot or being alone with a date in a house is a risky thing to do.

- **Make a deal with your date.** If you are dating someone, the two of you can agree ahead of time that sex is out. By setting limits together, you can help stick to them.

Sometimes these methods may not be enough, and a date may pressure you to have sex. Make clear that you don't want anything to do with it. If your date insists, explain your decision. The pressure may

Teen Issue

Who's "Doing It"?
You've heard the line—"everybody's doing it." But are they? Truth is, more teens don't "do it" than do. Besides, is this any kind of argument? If everybody you knew decided to be 20 pounds overweight, would that make you want to be 20 pounds overweight? Even if it were the fashion, being overweight would still be unhealthy. The same is true of sexual relations. Don't listen to myths about what everybody does. Take responsibility for your *own* health.

Teen Issue

"It Won't Happen to You"
Another argument that some teens use to persuade others is that "it won't happen to you." That's true if you say "no" to sex. Someone who says "yes" to sex, though, could become one of the 2 *million* cases of gonorrhea reported each year in the United States. Those 2 million people were *sure* that it "wouldn't happen to them." But they were wrong.

Learning from Photographs
Group dates like this picnic are a good way to have fun while eliminating the pressure to have sex. How does avoiding sex promote health?

Changing Scenes
Sometimes changing the scenery can be the best solution to a problem. If a date is pressuring you to have sexual relations, suggest that you go somewhere else. You could take in a movie or get a bite to eat. Choose something where lots of people will be around. That should change the subject. Of course, if your date puts this pressure on you all the time, you may need to find a new friend.

continue. Tell the person your decision is final and that any more arguments will just make you angry. If necessary, end the date. Leave or, if your date has the transportation, call a parent to come and get you. It is a good idea to have a quarter and your home phone number with you at all times.

You may hear various arguments that try to persuade you to have sex. You can answer these arguments if you are prepared for them.

- **Your date may say, "If you really loved me, you would have sex with me."** Point out that if your date really cared for you, he or she would respect your wishes.

- **Your date may say, "Everybody's doing it."** Remind your date that the majority of teens do *not* have sex. Point out, too, that you are concerned with *your* decision, not others'.

- **Your date may say that sex can be safe.** Remember that *the single best way to prevent catching an STD is to avoid sexual contact.*

A teen may feel that by not agreeing to have sex, he or she will lose the date to another person. Dating should be fun. If it is full of tension and unhappiness over the pressure to have sex, it is no longer fun. If a date won't stop the pressure, it may be best to end the relationship. This is a difficult decision to make, one that can hurt at the time. But the alternative will hurt more when agreeing to have sex goes against a teen's values. Afterward, he or she will feel guilty and unhappy. By sticking with the decision to say "no" to sex, the teen can live honestly and comfortably. He or she can still find company—and have fun without pressure—with other friends.

Help from Others

Remember that you are not alone. You can ask for help from a parent or some other trusted adult. He or she may be able to offer you good advice.

People in the government who are responsible for public health work hard to help control the spread of STDs. They prepare and pass out brochures that explain the diseases and how to prevent them. Some give talks at schools and community centers to answer teens' questions about these diseases. They place ads on television and in magazines to explain that the safest thing is to say "no" to sex.

The health-care system, too, acts to control the spread of STDs. People who go to a doctor or clinic are treated so that they cannot spread the disease to others. Patients with these diseases are also told how their behavior can affect other people. Much research is being done to try to understand how these diseases work and to find cures for them.

Teen Issue

Where to Go?
A teen who suspects that he or she has an STD needs medical help. The worst thing to do is to ignore the signs. STDs can devastate the body if left untreated. A teen in this situation should see an adult that he or she feels comfortable with. This could be a parent, counselor, or school nurse. The teen could also go to a clinic or call a hot line. The VD (STD) hot line number is 1-800-227-8922. The AIDS hot line number is 1-800-342-AIDS.

Types of STDs

There are a number of STDs. The most serious are *chlamydia*, *gonorrhea*, *syphilis*, *herpes simplex II*, and *AIDS*. Chlamydia and gonorrhea are two of the most common of all communicable diseases. In fact, only the cold is more common.

Signs of Some Common STDs	
Disease	**Sign**
Chlamydia	Males: pain and burning during urination; unusual fluid coming from penis
	Females: unusual liquid coming from vagina; pain in pelvis; painful urination
Gonorrhea	Males: whitish fluid coming from penis; burning during urination; swollen lymph glands in groin
	Females: fluid coming from vagina; burning in urination; menstrual cycles that are not normal; abdominal pain
Syphilis	First stage: a reddish painless sore appears where disease entered body
	Second stage: nonitching body rash (may be on outer edges of vagina in females); rash may turn into sores that give out clear liquid; fever, sore throat, body ache
	Third stage: damage to heart, blood vessels, and nervous system; effects can include blindness, insanity
Herpes simplex II	Painful, itchy sores on reproductive organs; fever; burning during urination

Learning from Photographs
Health classes are important places to learn the truth about sexually transmitted diseases like AIDS. What are other ways to get the facts?

Chlamydia

Chlamydia is the most common STD in the United States. It is also the hardest to spot. **Chlamydia** (kluh·MID·ee·uh) is *an STD that does great damage to the reproductive system.* The signs of chlamydia are shown in the chart "Signs of Some Common STDs." These signs do not always show up, however, until the disease is well advanced.

The presence of chlamydia is shown through a lab test. Medicine can be given to cure the disease. If the illness has already scarred body tissues, though, they cannot be repaired. That is why it is important for a person to learn early whether the disease is present.

If untreated, chlamydia can cause serious problems. In males, it can result in the urethra always being inflamed. It can also cause the person to become unable to have children. In females, it can cause **pelvic inflammatory** (PEL·vik in·FLAM·uh·tohr·ee) **disease (PID).** This is *a painful illness of the female reproductive organs.* Chlamydia can be passed on to babies by pregnant women.

Nongonococcal urethritis (nahn·gahn·uh·KAHK·uhl yur·i·THRYT·uhs) **(NGU)** is *an infection of the urethra in males and the cervix in females.* It is caused by chlamydia, among other factors. Its signs are the passing of unusual fluids from the penis or vagina. NGU can be treated and cured.

Gonorrhea

The next most common STD after chlamydia is **gonorrhea** (gahn·uh·REE·uh). This is *an STD, caused by bacteria, that does damage to the reproductive system and other parts of the body.* The bacteria live mostly in the male's urethra and in part of the female's uterus. These germs cannot live outside the body. For this reason, they cannot be passed from person to person by touching such things as toilet seats or towels.

DID **YOU** KNOW?

Chlamydia
About 75 percent of all females who have chlamydia show no signs until serious problems happen. This is true of about 15 to 20 percent of males with the disease.

The symptoms of gonorrhea are shown in the chart. Like chlamydia, gonorrhea does not always show itself with these signs. Sometimes it remains hidden. This is especially true for females.

The presence of gonorrhea is shown when doctors look at a sample discharge under a microscope. If they find the disease early, they can usually cure it. Some gonorrhea germs can now resist one of the medicines used, however.

If untreated, gonorrhea can make males or females unable to have children. This disease can also cause damage to body joints, the heart, and other organs. In females, PID can occur. Females with the disease can have problems when pregnant and can pass the disease to their babies.

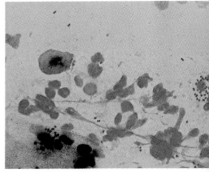

Learning from Photographs
The dots show gonorrhea bacteria. How common is gonorrhea?

Syphilis

Syphilis (SIF·luhs) is *an STD that can attack and do serious damage to the body.* It is one of the most dangerous STDs. Syphilis can cause blindness and insanity. It can damage the heart, the brain, the blood vessels, the liver, and the kidneys. And it can kill.

Syphilis has three stages. Each stage is shown in the chart "Signs of Some Common STDs." The symptoms of the first and second stages may go away, so that the person thinks he or she is healthy. There can be a long time between stages, too. The second stage may not happen for months after the first stage. The third stage, with its serious damage to the body, may not happen for up to 20 years. But even if the signs leave, the disease is still there.

The presence of syphilis can be found through a blood test. The disease is treated with the medicine *penicillin* (pen·uh·SIL·uhn). As with other STDs, the damage done by syphilis cannot be repaired, even if the person is cured of the illness. That is why early treatment is important.

Many states require that couples planning to get married take a blood test. The test shows the presence of syphilis in the blood.

Herpes Simplex II

Another name for **herpes simplex II** (HER·pees SIM·pleks) is *genital herpes.* This is *an STD that causes sores on the reproductive organs.* Like syphilis, the signs of this disease may go away even though the disease remains in the body.

Herpes II does not have a cure. Medicine can make the pain of the sores go away, but nothing can rid the body of the disease. It may show itself again, or it may not. In females, herpes II seems to be linked to cervical cancer. A woman with this disease should get regular Pap smears to test for this cancer.

DID **YOU** KNOW?

Herpes Simplex I
There is another disease caused by a herpes virus. This is *herpes simplex I*, which is less serious. Type I usually shows itself with cold sores around the mouth. Doctors no longer distinguish between the two types because type II can be found on the mouth and type I on the genitals. In this text, the virus is considered to be type II when it is transmitted by sexual contact.

Other Sexually Transmitted Problems

There are still other sexually transmitted problems. All these problems can be prevented by staying away from sex.

- **Vaginitis** (vaj·uh·NYT·uhs). This is an inflammation of the vagina. Males can give this problem to females. It can be treated and cured.

- **Genital** (JEN·uh·tuhl) **warts**. These are warts on the organs of reproduction. The warts can be treated. They are connected to cancer of the cervix.

- **Pubic lice** (PYOO·bik LYS). These are little animals that live on pubic hair and feed on tiny blood vessels. Special shampoos can remove them.

- **Scabies** (SKAY·bees). Scabies are tiny creatures that burrow under the skin. Hot baths and special creams can rid a person of scabies.

Staying Clean

Pubic lice and scabies can be passed from one person to another in ways other than through sexual contact. These small animals can live on clothes or towels for a short time. They can then infect another person who wears those clothes or uses the towel. It is important, then, not to use another person's towel, even just to dry your hands.

Check Your Understanding

Conclusion STDs are dangerous. They can do great damage to the body. They are also dangerous because they can be hidden. Early treatment can cure most STDs. But the most effective way to protect the body from STDs is to avoid sexual contact.

1. **Vocabulary** Why are the diseases discussed in this lesson called *sexually transmitted* diseases?

2. **Recall** What is the single best way to prevent the spread of STDs?

3. **Recall** Name one way that parents, public health officials, and health-care workers each help prevent the spread of STDs.

4. **Recall** What are three changes in the area of the penis or vagina that may be signs of an STD and that a doctor should look at?

5. **Recall** Answer these questions about chlamydia, gonorrhea, syphilis, and herpes simplex II.
   a. Which one has no cure?
   b. Which one can cause death?
   c. Which two may not show symptoms in females?

6. **Summarize** What are two ways to reduce the pressure to have sex on a date?

AIDS

Words to Know
acquired
    immunodeficiency
    syndrome (AIDS)
carriers
AIDS-related complex
    (ARC)
opportunistic infections
intravenous (IV)
    needles

This lesson contains a number of valuable facts and tips. Once you have studied them, you will be able to

- tell what AIDS is and how it affects the body.
- explain how AIDS is passed on and how it is *not* passed on.
- tell how AIDS can be prevented.
- tell what the government and the health-care system are doing to control AIDS.

What Is AIDS?

Few diseases are more frightening, less understood, and easier to prevent than AIDS. You probably have heard a lot about AIDS in the news. Two facts may stand out among all you have heard about AIDS.

- **AIDS is the most serious disease around.** There is no cure, and it leads to death.
- **AIDS can be prevented very easily.** People who avoid sex and who do not use drugs that are taken by needle probably will not get the disease.

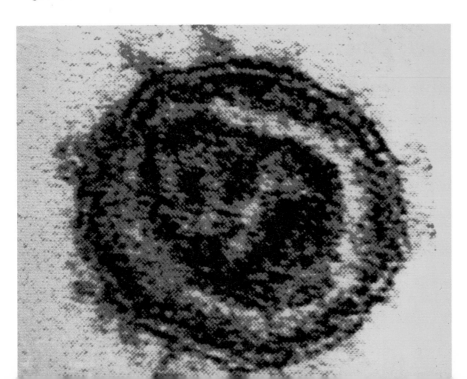

Learning from Photographs
This color-enhanced image shows the virus that causes the disease AIDS. Can infection by this virus be prevented? Explain your answer.

323

Each letter in the short form AIDS stands for something. *A* means *acquired*, meaning that the disease comes from outside the body. *I* means *immune*, meaning that the disease affects the immune system. *D* means *deficiency*, or the lack of something. *S* means *syndrome*, or a set of symptoms that are part of the disease.

More About

*For more on the **immune system**, see Lesson 2 of this chapter.*

DID **YOU** KNOW?

AIDS in Hiding
One of the problems with the AIDS virus, as with other sexually transmitted diseases, is that it can be in the body without there being any outward signs.

The word *AIDS* is short for the real name for this disease. That name is **acquired immunodeficiency syndrome** (uh·KWYRD im·yoo·noh·di·FISH·uhn·see SIN·drohm). This is *a deadly disease that attacks some of the body's white-blood cells.* AIDS opens the body to infections that can cause death. AIDS is caused by a kind of germ called a *retrovirus.* The name of the particular retrovirus is *human immunodeficiency virus,* or *HIV.* When we refer in this lesson to "the AIDS virus," we are speaking of this germ.

What the AIDS Virus Does to the Body

As you know from an earlier lesson in this chapter, your body has an immune system. This is the group of organs and cells that fight germs. The AIDS virus weakens the immune system. The system can then no longer protect the body. Other diseases can move in and attack the body. It is one of these other diseases that usually kills the person with AIDS. The AIDS virus itself can infect the brain and cause death sometimes.

How Does the AIDS Virus Weaken the Immune System?

When the AIDS virus enters the bloodstream, it infects one of the body's four kinds of T-cells. These are the white blood cells that help control the body's defenses against germs. The AIDS virus changes these T-cells.

When a germ enters the body, these T-cells normally signal other white blood cells to attack it. When germs enter the body of a person with the AIDS virus, though, these T-cells are unable to respond. The germs are not destroyed as they would normally be. They cause the person to become sick.

What Happens to the Body of Someone with the AIDS Virus?

The AIDS virus affects people in one of three ways.

- **Some people are carriers.** A **carrier** is *a person who has the virus and can pass it to other people but does not show the symptoms of the disease.* A carrier of the AIDS virus may develop the symptoms at a later time. It could be years later before the symptoms appear. In the meantime, this person could pass the virus on to many others.

- **Some people develop AIDS-related complex.** This set of early signs is often called *ARC.* Someone with **AIDS-related complex** *shows some of the symptoms of AIDS but cannot yet be said to* *have AIDS itself.* The symptoms of ARC include skin rashes, poor appetite and weight loss, swollen glands, tiredness, diarrhea, heavy sweating during sleep, and a fever that will not go away. People who have ARC may develop AIDS later.

- **Some people with the AIDS virus have the disease AIDS.** Once the disease appears, the person will probably die. This can happen in 6 months, or the person may live for 2 or 3 years or even longer. Some new medicines are being tested to save the lives of people with AIDS. So far, though, none has had success.

What Other Diseases Attack the Body?

With a weak immune system, the body is open to many different diseases. Some of these *diseases do not attack a body with a healthy immune system.* These are called **opportunistic** (ahp·er·too·NIS·tik) **infections.** The word *opportunistic* means that they take advantage of the weakness in the body that the AIDS virus causes.

Three of these diseases are common among persons with AIDS. One is a form of pneumonia. Another is a rare form of cancer. The third is a disease of the brain and nervous system called *AIDS dementia* (di·MEN·chuh).

Testing and Treating

The presence of the AIDS virus is shown by means of a blood test. But a person may not test positive until 6 months or so after being infected. Public health officials advise people who think they may have the disease to get tested again even if the first test shows no sign of infection by the AIDS virus.

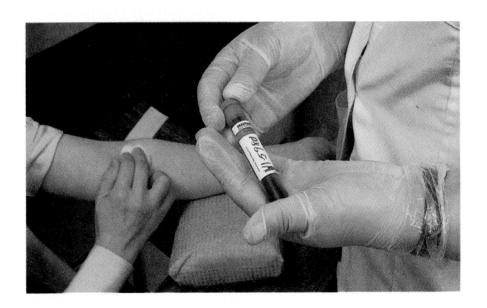

Teen Issue

Testing for the AIDS Virus
Many people feel that everyone should be required to take a blood test for the AIDS virus. They reason that public health officials could then know exactly how many people carry the virus. That would make them better able to prevent its spread. Others say that this kind of testing could be used to hurt the rights of people with the virus. What do you think?

Learning from Photographs
This blood sample will be used in a test for the presence of the AIDS virus. Are the results of the blood test always clear?

DID **YOU** KNOW?

A Cure for AIDS

In the late 1980s, Surgeon General C. Everett Koop predicted that a cure for AIDS would never be found. He said that a vaccine would probably not be found until after the year 2000.

DID **YOU** KNOW?

Babies with AIDS

Babies who get the AIDS virus from their mothers usually develop the disease. They rarely live past the age of 2.

There is no cure for AIDS. Scientists are doing research to find one, but the virus is hard to defeat. Some drugs are being used as a test. These do not cure the disease, but slow its effects on the body.

Researchers are also trying to find a vaccine to prevent infection by the AIDS virus. They have not found one yet.

How Is AIDS Spread?

The virus that causes AIDS is deadly. But it is also very fragile. It can only live in certain body fluids. These fluids are blood, semen from the male, and fluids in the female's vagina. To pass from one person to another, the virus must pass in one of these fluids.

How AIDS Is Spread

- **From an infected person.** A person with the virus can give it to another through sexual contact.
- **From an IV needle.** A person with the virus can give it to another through sharing an **intravenous** (in·truh·VEE·nuhs) **(IV) needle.** These needles are *used to inject illegal drugs into a person's veins.*
- **From infected blood.** A person can get it by receiving blood given by a person with the virus.
- **From an infected pregnant woman.** A pregnant woman with the virus may pass the virus to her baby.

The first two are the main ways that the virus is spread. The supply of blood used to give to people in emergencies and during surgery is now tested for the AIDS virus. Any blood with signs of the virus is disposed of. These signs may not show for 2 to 4 weeks, however. There is a chance, then, that infected blood may be used. This risk is very small, however. Someone who is going to have an operation can give his or her own blood in advance to avoid this risk.

How AIDS Is *Not* Spread

There are many myths about AIDS. Most of these myths are about how the disease is spread. The truth is as follows.

- **AIDS is not spread through the air.** You cannot get AIDS by breathing in the virus.
- **AIDS is not spread through saliva or tears.** Kissing does not spread AIDS.

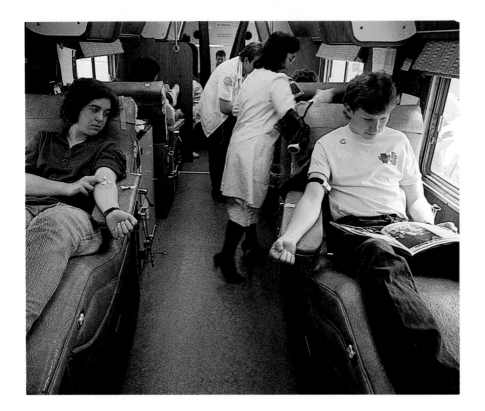

Learning from Photographs
These people are giving blood in a traveling blood donor unit called a bloodmobile. Are people safe from getting the AIDS virus when giving blood? Explain your answer.

- **AIDS is not spread by being bitten by a mosquito.** This is true even if the mosquito bit someone who has the virus.

- **AIDS is not spread by casual contact with someone who has the AIDS virus.** Shaking hands does not spread AIDS.

- **AIDS is not spread by using someone else's eating utensils.** The cups, plates, or silverware used by a person with the virus will not give you AIDS.

- **AIDS is not spread by giving blood.** Only clean needles are used when blood is taken.

How to Prevent the Spread of AIDS

The key to preventing the spread of AIDS is clear.

- **Avoid all sexual contact.** Saying "no" to sex will protect you better than anything else from getting this deadly disease.

- **Avoid illegal drugs taken by IV needle.** The needles are often dirty. Some may be infected by the AIDS virus. People who take illegal drugs risk addiction and the serious health problems caused by the drug. They also risk being arrested and put in jail. If they take those drugs by using an IV needle, they also risk getting AIDS.

Keeping Clean
It's true that you cannot get AIDS from using someone else's plate, cup, or fork. On the other hand, there are diseases that can be passed in this way. It simply isn't a good health habit to share plates, cups, or eating utensils.

More About
For more about saying "no" to sexual relations, see Lesson 4 of this chapter. For more on choosing to be drug free, see Chapter 10.

What Is Being Done About AIDS?

Millions of dollars are being spent on AIDS research and education. Public health officials have three main goals.

- Teach the public about the disease to prevent its spread
- Find a cure for the disease
- Find a vaccine that can be used to prevent the disease

The Centers for Disease Control (CDC), a part of the federal government, is at the center of the fight against AIDS. It keeps figures on the number of people who have the disease. It conducts research and holds conferences so that researchers can share what they have found. And the CDC leads the effort to educate people about AIDS.

The health-care system also plays a big part in the fight to control AIDS. When they treat AIDS patients, doctors and clinics may ask for the names of any sexual partners. That way those people can be informed and tested for the AIDS virus. These other people are contacted privately so that they can be tested for the presence of the virus. Counseling is available to help people who have AIDS understand and deal with the disease.

Teen **Issue**

AIDS and the Individual

Because AIDS is such a deadly disease, and because it seems to be spreading quickly, people are afraid of it. The government is trying to balance the necessity to protect the public with the need to protect the rights of each person. This means finding ways to test for the AIDS virus while respecting a person's right to privacy. It also means protecting the rights to work, housing, and health insurance of those who carry the virus. The debate over these issues is difficult and will probably continue for many years.

Check Your Understanding

Conclusion AIDS is a deadly disease that weakens the body's defenses to fight off other diseases. It can be prevented by avoiding sexual contact and by staying away from illegal drugs taken by needle. Both of these steps are healthy in many other ways. Both steps go far to protect you from this deadly disease.

1. **Vocabulary** Which of the following is (a) the name for someone who has the HIV virus but has not yet developed the disease? Which is (b) the name of a set of some signs of AIDS but not all of the symptoms? *AIDS-related complex, carrier*
2. **Recall** How does the HIV virus affect the body?
3. **Recall** Name the two main ways that the spread of AIDS can be prevented.
4. **Recall** Name three ways that AIDS is *not* spread.
5. **Recall** What are the three goals of public health officials in trying to control AIDS?
6. **Synthesize** Suppose you were going to have an operation. Would you be concerned about the safety of any blood you might get during the surgery? Why or why not?

Joining the "Cold" War

Who hasn't experienced the sore throat, sneezing, and runny nose of a cold? Every year students and parents lose school or work time because of colds. It can take from 2 to 7 days to recover from a cold.

Cold symptoms include a sore throat, sneezing, watery eyes, runny nose, and headache. By the time these symptoms appear, it may be too late to practice prevention. But when the cold season approaches each winter, you can take steps to prevent getting and giving a cold.

How to Declare War on the Common Cold

Here are some simple steps that everyone can follow to avoid getting and spreading the common cold.

- Cover your mouth when you cough and your nose when you sneeze.
- Do not share forks, knives, spoons, or drinking glasses with anyone.
- Wash your hands after sneezing or coughing and always before eating.

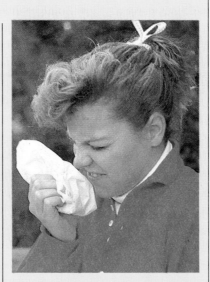

But the most important rule is this: stay away from people for the first 24 hours that you feel the signs of the cold. It is during this time that you are able to spread the disease to others. You can also get over the cold faster if you get plenty of rest. Staying home one day can help you get better so you can enjoy yourself more on another day.

Using the Skill

Sometimes staying home can be a tough choice to make. But it is the responsible choice — the choice that can help protect your friends from getting sick. Look at the following two stories. Then, on a separate sheet of paper, answer the questions that follow the stories.

Case One

Carlos feels lousy. His whole body aches, and his forehead feels hot. His head hurts and his nose is stuffy. He doesn't want to get out of bed. But today is practice, and the championship game is only a week away.

Case Two

As the day wears on, Helene feels worse and worse. She is constantly blowing her nose and sneezing all the time. She thought that she had been bothered by a cold the last 3 days, but this is worse. She thinks about staying home from school tomorrow. But if she does, she'll miss the tryouts for the Christmas show. She has practiced her song for a month. What will she do?

1. What would you do today if you were Carlos? How will his decision affect his teammates? How might it affect how well he plays at the game?

2. If you were Helene, would you decide to stay home from school tomorrow or to go in? What could she do between tonight and tomorrow to feel better?

Chapter 11 Review

Summary

- Communicable diseases are passed from person to person. We can help prevent the spread of these diseases.
- Your body has barriers and chemical defenses against the germs that cause disease. Vaccines can give immunity to some diseases.
- Keeping healthy can help your body resist disease.
- Some diseases are passed along through sexual contact. These are dangerous diseases, but they can be prevented by avoiding all sexual contact.
- AIDS is a deadly disease that is passed on by sexual contact and by sharing intravenous needles. Anyone who avoids these two actions can prevent AIDS from striking him or her.

Reviewing Vocabulary and Concepts

On a separate sheet of paper, write the numbers 1–12. Write the letter of the word or phrase in Column B that best matches the phrase in Column A.

Column A

Lesson 1

1. The smallest form of life, which can cause disease but someone can be vaccinated against
2. Illnesses that are passed from one person to another
3. Tiny organisms that may be harmless or may cause a disease
4. Getting plenty of rest, keeping clean, and eating a balanced diet
5. The time during which someone may pass on a disease to someone else

Lesson 2

6. The germ-killing cells that are part of the body's defenses
7. The organs and tissues that combine to fight disease
8. The first barrier against disease
9. The second circulatory system, which carries body fluids

Lesson 3

10. A disease common to young people that causes extreme tiredness
11. A serious disease that can affect the liver
12. A disease of the respiratory system that can be caused by bacteria or viruses

Column B

a. lymphocytes
b. contagious period
c. mononucleosis
d. virus
e. lymphatic system
f. good health habits
g. bacteria
h. hepatitis
i. skin
j. pneumonia
k. immune system
l. communicable diseases

Write the numbers 13–20 on your paper. After each number, write the letter of the answer that best completes each of the following statements.

Lesson 4

13. The sexually transmitted disease that comes in three stages and can cause death is
    a. chlamydia **b.** gonorrhea **c.** syphilis **d.** herpes II

14. The most common sexually transmitted disease is
    a. chlamydia **b.** gonorrhea **c.** syphilis **d.** herpes II

15. The sexually transmitted disease that has no cure is
    a. chlamydia **b.** gonorrhea **c.** syphilis **d.** herpes II

16. Each of the following is one of the ways public health officials try to control sexually transmitted diseases *except*
    a. publishing brochures **b.** giving talks **c.** jailing victims **d.** doing research

Lesson 5

17. Each of the following is a way that AIDS can be spread *except*
    a. having sexual relations **b.** shaking hands **c.** sharing dirty needles **d.** passing it on to baby by mother

18. Which of the following people have the AIDS virus?
    a. carriers of the virus **b.** people with ARC **c.** people with the disease **d.** all of these

19. AIDS is a deadly disease that weakens the victim's
    a. reproductive system **b.** immune system **c.** digestive system **d.** circulatory system

20. Persons with AIDS die not from the disease but from
    a. AIDS-related complex **b.** drug overdoses **c.** opportunistic infections **d.** blood transfusions

Thinking Critically About the Facts

Write your answers to the following questions on a separate sheet of paper.

21. **Sequence** What is the correct order for the following defenses against germs?
    a. Immune system attacks germs.
    b. Fever raises body temperature.
    c. Skin makes barrier to germs.
    d. Stomach juices attack germs.

22. **Compare and contrast** Compare how to protect yourself from getting a communicable disease with how you prevent yourself from getting a sexually transmitted disease.

23. **Summarize** What are three goals of public health officials in trying to prevent the spread of AIDS?

24. **Synthesize** To prevent yourself from catching AIDS, what two actions should you avoid?

Applying the Facts

25. Write or call your town or city public health agency for printed material it has on STDs or AIDS. Read the material and prepare a short talk describing one aspect of these diseases.

26. For a younger brother or sister, prepare a short talk explaining how the body acts to defend itself against the germs that can cause disease.

CHAPTER 12

Noncommunicable Diseases

CHAPTER WARM-UP

Chapter Study Goals

After you have read this chapter, you will be able to

- define *noncommunicable diseases* and give examples and tell how lifestyle leads to some.
- describe the two main types of heart disease and name steps that help to prevent them.
- define types of cancer and describe what people can do to reduce the risk of cancer.
- identify the two main types of diabetes and describe treatment for them.
- identify the two main types of arthritis and describe treatment for them.

Be on the lookout for information in the chapter that will help you reach these goals.

Getting Started

All through this book, you have learned that living an active, healthy life as a teen can have important results for you later in life. This is especially true of the diseases talked about in this chapter. Many of these diseases cause death. Many of them can be prevented. By exercising and following the other good health habits described in the text, you can help protect yourself from many of these diseases.

Study Tip

As you read this chapter, you will find many suggestions for healthy habits to follow. Can you adopt some of these habits to be healthier?

All About Noncommunicable Diseases

This lesson contains a number of valuable facts and tips. Once you have studied them, you will be able to

- define the term *noncommunicable disease.*
- tell what people can do to lessen their chances of getting lifestyle diseases.
- give examples of some noncommunicable diseases.

What Is a Noncommunicable Disease?

People get diseases in two ways. *Some illnesses can be passed on from one person to another.* These are called **communicable** (kuh·MYOO·ni·kuh·buhl) **diseases.** One way to stop the spread of these diseases is to fight the germs that cause them. Another way is to stop contact between people during the time the disease could be passed on. Examples of these diseases are colds and measles.

Other illnesses are caused by how people live, by conditions they are born with, or by hazards around them. These are called **noncommunicable diseases.** To prevent or control many of them, people must try to change how they live or reduce the hazards around them. Examples of these diseases are heart disease, cancer, diabetes, and arthritis. You will study each of them in one of the lessons in this chapter. The chart shows some other noncommunicable diseases.

Most noncommunicable diseases are present over a long time, often years. *Illnesses that last a long time* are called **chronic** (KRAHN·ik) **diseases.** Examples are heart disease, which takes a long time to develop, and diabetes, which cannot be cured.

Living Well

Some of these health conditions do not always make people sick. Someone who lives carefully can avoid more serious problems. Diabetes is an example. It can be controlled by eating a proper diet and injecting insulin. Once the person with diabetes takes those steps, she or he can lead a normal life.

Learning from Photographs
Some people with a noncommunicable disease are able to lead normal lives as long as they are careful to control the condition. Do you know of any such diseases?

Noncommunicable diseases result in the breakdown of the body's tissues. For that reason, they are said to be **degenerative** (di·JEN·uh·rayt·iv) **diseases.** Something that *degenerates* does the opposite of growing. It becomes unable to work normally. With arthritis, for example, the joints become swollen and painful to move. In muscular dystrophy, fat takes the place of muscle tissue.

Some Noncommunicable Diseases		
Disease	**What Causes It**	**What It Does**
Allergies	Immune system is too sensitive to some substance	Causes runny nose, itchy eyes, trouble breathing
Alzheimer's disease	Unknown	Leads to loss of muscle control, loss of memory
Cerebral palsy	Damage to part of brain	Causes poor muscle control, problems seeing, hearing, or speaking
Cystic fibrosis	Problem with genes	Affects glands related to sweat and mucus; may cause death
Malnutrition	Poor diet	Results in poor growth or body systems not working properly
Multiple sclerosis	Unknown	Leads to loss of control over muscles
Muscular dystrophy	Problem with genes	Causes fatty tissue to replace muscle
Obesity	Diet high in calories and too little exercise	Can cause heart disease
Stress	Unrelieved tension	Can result in high blood pressure, body pains, ulcers

What Causes Noncommunicable Diseases

Someone develops a noncommunicable disease in one of three ways.

- The person is born with the disease.
- The person develops the disease because of the way he or she lives.
- The person develops the disease because of a hazard around him or her.

More About

*For more on **cerebral palsy** and **muscular dystrophy**, see Chapter 7.*

Diseases Present from Birth

A baby may be born with a noncommunicable disease for one of two reasons. The baby may have *a disease or condition in which the body does not function normally because of a problem with his or her genes.* This is a **genetic** (juh·NET·ik) **disorder.** Sickle-cell anemia is one example. Cystic fibrosis is another. These diseases cannot be prevented.

The other cause of noncommunicable diseases in babies is **birth defects** (DEE·fekts). These are *disorders of the developing and newborn baby.* Birth defects may be caused by unhealthy habits of the mother-to-be. A pregnant woman who drinks alcohol, for example, may give her baby a problem called *fetal alcohol syndrome.* In other cases, something that happens during birth can lead to the problem. If the baby loses oxygen during birth, for instance, the brain may be damaged. The child might be born with cerebral palsy.

Learning from Photographs
Check-ups can help spot the signs of a lifestyle disease. What part of a physical exam is being done here?

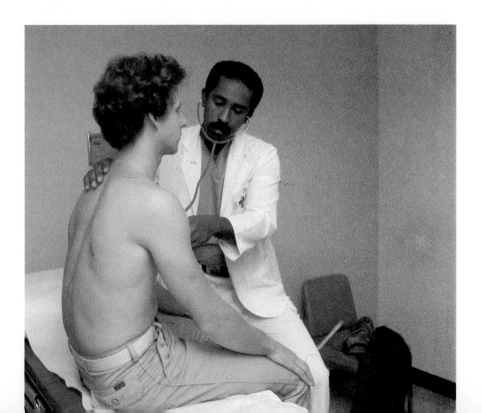

In general, there is no cure for either genetic disorders or birth defects. With some of these conditions, though, children may live a normal, healthy life. These people may be given **therapy** (THEHR·uh·pee), or *training to do certain tasks.* Therapy can help someone with cerebral palsy learn to walk, for instance.

Lifestyle Diseases

Diseases that are caused by our health habits are called **lifestyle diseases.** Heart disease and cancer are two lifestyle diseases. Others are the problems caused by using tobacco, alcohol, or drugs.

Many of these diseases do not appear until after the teen years. Some do not cause problems until the person is quite old. By then it may be too late to reverse the damage that has been done. By starting yourself off with healthy habits now, though, you can build yourself a healthy future.

Doctors say that these diseases have certain **risk factors.** These are *traits or habits that raise someone's chances of getting a disease.*

Family history is one risk factor. Scientists now believe that people inherit from their parents a greater or lesser chance of developing heart disease. A greater risk for high blood pressure and certain forms of cancer, too, seems to be passed on in families. But family history is only one factor, and it does not mean that someone will develop the disease for certain. You can reduce your risk of getting a lifestyle disease by following five health habits.

Five Good Health Habits

- **Eat a balanced diet.** Choose food from each of the four food groups. Be sure your diet is high in fiber and low in fat and salt.
- **Exercise regularly.** Regular vigorous exercise strengthens the heart and helps it to do its job better.
- **Maintain your ideal weight.** Keep your weight normal at the level for your height and body frame.
- **Lower your stress.** Learn to deal with stress in your daily life, and get plenty of rest.
- **Avoid using tobacco, alcohol, and drugs.** These substances harm the body.

Following these habits will not guarantee that you will be well, but consider this. Of the ten leading causes of death in the United States, seven are noncommunicable diseases. And all seven are affected at least in part by how you live.

Teen Issue

Health Can Be Habit Forming

Habits *are* hard to break. That's why it's a good idea to build good habits. Starting off right is the best way to live a long, healthy life. But saying that habits are hard to break does not mean that they are *impossible* to break. Someone who smokes can quit. Someone with a high-fat diet can change it to be low in fat. It's a matter of willpower and of getting help when you need it.

More About

*For more on a healthy diet, see Chapter 5. For more on **exercise**, see Chapter 1. For more on **stress**, see Chapter 3.*

More About

*For more on the health threats of **tobacco, alcohol, and drugs** see Chapters 8, 9, and 10.*

Learning from Photographs
The Special Olympics provide an opportunity for disabled people to show what they can do in athletics. How might involvement in this event help a disabled person's self-concept?

Leading Causes of Death	
Today	**1900**
1. **Heart disease**	1. Pneumonia and influenza
2. **Cancer**	2. Tuberculosis
3. **Stroke**	3. Diseases of the stomach and intestines
4. Accidents	4. **Heart disease**
5. **Lung disease**	5. **Stroke**
6. Pneumonia and influenza	6. Kidney disease
7. **Diabetes**	7. Accidents
8. Suicide	8. **Cancer**
9. **Liver disease**	9. Childhood diseases
10. **Atherosclerosis**	10. Diphtheria

Diseases in **boldface type** are lifestyle diseases.

Diseases Caused by Hazards Around Us

Some of these diseases can have other causes besides lifestyle. Cancer, for instance, is not just caused by smoking. It may be caused by chemicals in the air or water. While you cannot control what gets put in the air you breathe or the water you drink, you can take some action to protect yourself from these hazards. By being an active citizen, you can help keep the air and water clean and safe.

Check Your Understanding

Conclusion Noncommunicable diseases are not passed on from person to person. Many of these diseases are caused by how you live. Following healthy habits can prevent these diseases from affecting you.

1. **Vocabulary** Write definitions of the words *chronic* and *degenerative*.

2. **Recall** What is a noncommunicable disease?

3. **Recall** Give an example of one noncommunicable disease caused by genes and one caused by lifestyle.

4. **Recall** What are three healthy habits that you can follow to help prevent lifestyle diseases?

5. **Compare and contrast** Compare noncommunicable to communicable diseases.

All About Heart Disease

Words to Know
arteriosclerosis
atherosclerosis
heart attack
stroke
blood pressure
high blood pressure
bypass surgery
heart transplant
artificial pacemaker

This lesson contains a number of valuable facts and tips. Once you have studied them, you will be able to

● define the term *arteriosclerosis* and say what causes it.

● explain what high blood pressure is.

● tell how you can lower your risk of getting heart disease.

● discuss how doctors are now treating heart disease.

A Major Killer

The different kinds of heart disease are, together, the number one killer in the United States. The main kinds are hardening of the arteries and high blood pressure. Both conditions can cause major health problems, including heart attack. But you may prevent both of these diseases by following good health habits.

Learning from Photographs
Basketball is good aerobic exercise—and fun! Do you know how aerobic exercise helps the heart?

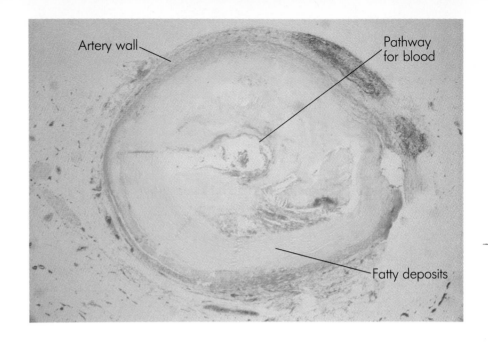

Artery wall

Pathway for blood

Fatty deposits

More About

*For more on the **heart**, see Chapter 7.*

Arteriosclerosis

The disease known as hardening of the arteries is called **arteriosclerosis** (ar·tir·ee·oh·skluh·ROH·suhs). It has a number of causes. One cause is high blood pressure, which makes the blood vessels tougher. The main cause of hardening of the arteries, though, is *the buildup of fatty deposits on the artery wall*. This condition is given the name **atherosclerosis** (ath·uh·roh·skluh·ROH·suhs).

The coronary arteries, which supply the heart itself with blood, are the ones most often damaged by atherosclerosis. This damage can produce two problems.

- **Chest pain.** If the arteries are partly, but not completely blocked, the person may feel pain in the chest. This is a warning sign that often leads people to get medical help.

- **Heart attack.** If the fatty buildup blocks the arteries completely, the flow of blood to the heart is cut off. A **heart attack** results. This means that *heart muscle tissue dies from lack of oxygen because of reduced blood flow.*

DID YOU KNOW?

Test Taking
Scientists are trying to create a blood test that can be used to see whether someone is likely to have a heart attack or not. The hope is to identify people who are at risk *before* the attack occurs.

Hardening of the arteries can also cause blood clots to form. Clots often attach to an artery wall. But if one breaks free, it can move throughout the body. When it reaches the small blood vessels in the head, *the clot can block the flow of blood to the brain*. This causes a **stroke.** In a stroke, some part of the brain dies. A stroke can cause the person to lose some feeling or the ability to move some part of the body. A serious stroke can cause death.

High Blood Pressure

Your heart pumps blood through the arteries that run throughout your body. *The force of the blood on the inside walls of these blood vessels* is called your **blood pressure.** Blood pressure is measured with two numbers. The higher number is the pressure put out when the heart pumps blood. The lower number is the lower pressure that happens in between heartbeats.

Your blood pressure is not the same at all times. When you are feeling stress, it may be higher than normal. When you are resting, it may be a bit lower. These changes are normal. *When blood pressure is higher than normal for a long time,* however, a health problem arises. **High blood pressure,** or *hypertension* (HY·per·ten·chuhn), is a major health problem. It can lead to arteriosclerosis, heart attack, stroke, and kidney failure.

What causes high blood pressure is not known. But doctors know that a few factors may raise your chance of having it.

- Eating large amounts of salt
- Being overweight
- Feeling extreme stress for long periods of time
- Having a family history of high blood pressure

Because there are often no outward signs of the disease until it is too late, high blood pressure is called the silent killer. A regular checkup can detect if blood pressure is too high.

Health Minute

Is the Pressure On?
You can check your blood pressure yourself. Many pharmacies and supermarkets have coin-operated blood pressure machines. Or you could see your doctor or go to a clinic. The range for normal blood pressure is between 110 and 140 for the higher number and between 70 and 90 for the lower.

Learning from Photographs
Exercise can help lower your blood pressure by helping you avoid one of the risk factors. Which one?

Health Minute

Feel Your Heart

Take your pulse for a minute. Then do some light exercise, such as touching your toes or running in place. Now take your pulse again. Notice the difference? When you exercise, your heart does, too. If you are in good shape, this workout won't bother it. If you are over-weight, the exercise puts added strain on your heart.

Not Worth the Salt

Take a test of how much salt you use. When you are home, take out a plate and pretend it's piled high with french fries. Get the salt-shaker and salt those imaginary fries as much as you normally do. Then take all the salt that col-lected on your plate and measure it with a tea-spoon—or maybe a table-spoon! That's how much salt you are putting in your body. Next time you eat those fries, keep yourself away from the saltshaker. (In fact, you should stay away from the french fries, too!)

Preventing Heart Disease

The way to try to prevent heart disease is to follow good health habits. Heart disease is a lifestyle disease—it results from how we live. Doctors have found nine different risk factors for heart disease. Four of them are beyond anyone's control. They are age, sex, race, and a family history of heart disease.

The other five risk factors, though, are very much in your control. It is up to you to choose healthy habits over unhealthy ones. The way to prevent heart disease is to make these choices.

Steps to Lower the Risk of Heart Disease

- **Maintain your ideal body weight.** Overweight people are more likely to have heart disease than people with normal weight.
- **Exercise regularly.** People who exercise keep their heart strong. Exercise also helps control weight.
- **Eat a healthy diet.** People who eat a balanced diet that is high in fiber and low in salt, fats, and cholesterol can reduce their risk of heart disease.
- **Manage stress in your life.** Stress touches all of us. Those who can manage stress are less likely to suffer heart disease than those who let stress overwhelm them.
- **Avoid cigarette smoking.** Smoking increases the risk for heart disease and stroke. People who smoke just one pack of cigarettes a day double their chances of having a heart attack.

Treating Heart Disease

Doctors have done much research into treating heart disease. Health-care leaders now feel that the best approach is prevention. But when people do get a form of heart disease, other steps are taken.

Treating Arteriosclerosis

Someone who has heart pain caused by arteriosclerosis is given medicines to relieve the pain. The doctor will also suggest a change in the person's habits to lower the chance of further damage.

Sometimes the damage caused by atherosclerosis is already too great. If so, the doctor may need to treat the arteries.

- **Cut down the blockage.** Doctors have come up with new ways to unclog a blocked artery. They may insert a balloon into the artery and then inflate the balloon. As the balloon grows, it

Learning from Photographs
Heart attacks are fatal 15 to 25 percent of the time. A heart attack victim can sometimes be saved by receiving CPR, which is being taught in this class. Do you know what the letters CPR stand for?

pushes the fat against the artery wall, opening a path for the blood to flow through. Another method uses lasers to burn off the fat. This technique was first used in Canada in 1987.

- **Go around the blockage.** In **bypass surgery,** doctors *create new paths for blood to flow so that it goes around the blocked artery.* A bypass begins by removing a vein from the patient's leg. Then one end of the healthy vein is attached below the blocked area and the other end above it. The newly attached vein forms a new path for the blood to follow.

Some treatments are aimed at helping the heart after it has been weakened by heart attacks. The most famous of these methods is the **heart transplant.** In this operation, *the patient's heart is removed and replaced with another from a donor.* The success rate of this operation has not been high. But some day heart transplants may be a more useful way of fighting heart disease. Doctors are now testing the use of an artificial or mechanical heart in transplants.

Treating High Blood Pressure

People with high blood pressure may be given medicines to lower the blood pressure. The secret to living with high blood pressure, though, is to change the habits that brought it on. Someone with high blood pressure must work to have a better diet, control his or her weight, exercise, and manage stress better. Quitting smoking may also be necessary if the person was a smoker.

DID **YOU** KNOW?

How Many?
About 70,000 bypass operations are done each year.

DID **YOU** KNOW?

Three Firsts
Bypasses and transplants are both types of *open-heart surgery,* which means that the doctor operates directly on the heart. The first surgery of this kind was done in 1952. The first heart transplant was done in 1967. The first time an artificial heart was given to someone was in 1982.

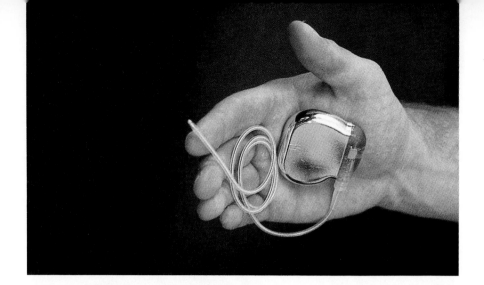

Learning from Photographs
Pacemakers come in many shapes and sizes. What other medical breakthroughs have helped save people with heart problems?

DID **YOU** KNOW?

The Rechargeable Heart
Pacemakers are battery operated. Earlier types had to be replaced every 5 years or so. Newer models use rechargeable batteries or nuclear batteries that do not run out.

Treating Other Heart Problems

Some people have problems with the valves in their hearts. The heart has four chambers that the blood moves through. The valves prevent blood from flowing back from one chamber into another. If a valve is not working correctly, doctors can operate to fix it. Or they may replace a bad valve with either the valve from a pig's heart or with a mechanical valve.

The heart beats at a strong regular pace. When a person's heartbeat is irregular or weak, doctors can put in an **artificial pacemaker** (art·uh·FISH·uhl PAY·smay·ker). This is *a small device that sends electrical pulses to the heart to make it beat regularly.* Pacemakers run on batteries.

DID **YOU** KNOW?

It's All Around
How widespread is high blood pressure? About one adult in six has it, and half of them probably don't know it.

Check Your Understanding

Conclusion   Heart disease is the number one killer in the United States. But you can prevent most forms of heart disease if you follow healthy habits.

1. **Vocabulary** What is the term for (a) hardening of the arteries? What is the term for (b) hardening of the arteries caused by the buildup of fatty deposits?
2. **Recall** What is high blood pressure? What can result from this condition?
3. **Recall** What are five health habits you can follow to prevent heart disease?
4. **Recall** Name two treatments for arteriosclerosis.
5. **Synthesize** Why would a regular check on your blood pressure be important?

All About Cancer

This lesson contains a number of valuable facts and tips. Once you have studied them, you will be able to

- explain how cancer develops.
- tell how you can reduce your risk of having cancer.
- name the seven warning signs of cancer.
- talk about how cancer is treated.

Words to Know
cancer
tumors
benign tumors
malignant tumors
metastasis
carcinogens
biopsy
chemotherapy
radiation

What Is Cancer?

Cancer is the second leading cause of death in the United States, after heart disease. It can harm the lungs, the blood, the skin, or the breast, among many other places. But wherever cancer appears, it starts the same way. **Cancer** is caused by *abnormal cells growing without control.*

Your body has hundreds of billions of cells. Billions of them die each minute and need to be replaced. Many thousands of the new cells are *abnormal,* or not as they should be. Most of these abnormal cells die, many are destroyed by the body's defenses. But sometimes one lives on and makes a copy of itself.

DID **YOU** KNOW?

Cancer Is Ancient
Cancer is not a new disease. Some skeletons from ancient Egypt show signs of bone cancer.

DID **YOU** KNOW?

Cancer Affects All Living Things
Cancer is not just a human disease. Plants and animals can have cancer, too.

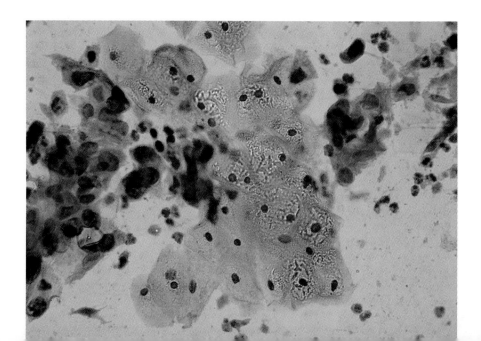

Learning from Photographs
The black cells in this photograph are cancer cells. How serious is cancer as a problem?

345

Where Tumors Grow

Tumors can grow almost anywhere in the body. They can form inside body organs, on the lips, and even on the fingers and toes.

The Forming of Tumors

Once they survive, these abnormal cells grow rapidly and without control. *Groups of these cells form in masses* called **tumors** (TOO·mers). Tumors can be either *benign* or *malignant*. **Benign** (bi·NYN) **tumors** are *masses of cells that are not cancerous.* **Malignant** (muh·LIG·nuhnt) **tumors** are *masses of cells that are cancerous.* Malignant tumors may *spread to other parts of the body.* The spreading is called **metastasis** (muh·TAS·tuh·suhs). They reach other parts of the body by moving along the blood vessels or through the lymph system. Benign tumors do not spread.

What Causes Cancer?

About 250 different kinds of cancer can attack the body. The chart "Most Common Cancers" lists the main cancers for both males and females and shows the chance of curing the disease.

Teen **Issue**

Food Additives and Cancer

Many people believe that it is healthful to stay away from chemicals added to food to color or preserve it. They argue that, although the government makes sure that the chemicals added to food are tested, tests for cancer take a long time to develop. They go on to say that it is safer to avoid these additives altogether. Others say that the food supply is quite safe and that even an additive like saccharine would need to be taken in huge amounts for cancer to develop. The decision, of course, is up to you.

Most Common Cancers		
Where It Occurs	**How Common It Is**	**How Curable It Is**
Skin	Most common	95 percent of treated persons recover
Colon and rectum	Second most common	About half of treated persons live 5 years or longer after treatment
Lungs	Mostly in men, but increasingly in women	Only about 10 percent of treated patients live
Breast	Mostly in women	About 70 percent of treated females recover
Reproductive organs	In males—prostate, testicles	More than 60 percent of patients treated live
	In females—cervix	About 85 percent of treated patients live
Bone marrow (leukemia) and lymphoma	Most common types in children	Rate of cures improving for leukemia; rate for lymphoma is 90 percent

What causes cancer is not known. Some causes seem to be *inherited*, or passed on by parents. Others are connected to habits. Smoking, as you probably know, is the main cause of lung cancer. Other cancers seem to result from things in the environment.

The *substances around us that cause cancer* are called **carcinogens** (kahr·SIN·uh·juhns). Some of these substances are found in nature. Prolonged exposure to the sun, for instance, can cause skin cancer. Some carcinogens are human-made. The smoke from factories or from cigarettes can cause cancer of the lungs. A human-made substitute for sugar called *saccharine* (SAK·ruhn) was found some years ago to cause cancer if eaten in very large amounts.

You can stay away from some carcinogens. You can choose not to smoke cigarettes or sunbathe. Others, such as the chemicals from factories, are more difficult to avoid. But the government works to lower the risk of cancer. It makes rules for clean air and water. The Food and Drug Administration (FDA) tries to make sure that the food we eat is free of carcinogens.

Preventing Cancer

Some factors that cause cancer are connected to choices you make. You can lower your own chances of developing cancer by making healthy choices.

- **Avoid tobacco.** By saying "no" to smoking and smokeless tobacco you lower your chances of getting cancer of the lung, bladder, mouth, and gums.

Sidestream Smoke
The smoke from someone else's cigarette can be dangerous for you. You are breathing in the same cancer-causing chemicals as the smoker. You can protect your health by learning to ask smokers to put out their cigarettes.

More About

For more on how to say "no" to tobacco, see Chapter 8. For tips on diet, see Chapter 5. Chapter 2 has more on protecting your skin from the sun.

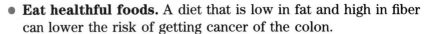

Testicular Self-Examination

Two or three times a month, a male should check himself for possible signs of testicular cancer. The test is simply a matter of feeling each testicle for any hard lumps. It can be done during the day's shower. Should he feel anything, he should contact a doctor.

• **Eat healthful foods.** A diet that is low in fat and high in fiber can lower the risk of getting cancer of the colon.

• **Limit the time you spend in the sun without protection.** Keep yourself covered or use sun-blocking agents.

Of course, taking any of these steps does not guarantee that you will not get cancer. But since smoking is the number one cause of lung cancer, for instance, you will certainly reduce your risk of getting cancer in a big way.

Spotting and Treating Cancer

Doctors can often spot different cancers during a routine physical exam. They can use tests to find others. A blood test, for instance, shows that the blood cancer leukemia is present. Females should have a Pap smear every year once they reach 18, to check for cancer of the uterus. The earlier the cancer is spotted, the better the chance of treating it.

If the doctor finds a tumor, he or she may do a **biopsy** (BY·ahp·see). In this test, *the doctor removes a small piece of the tumor for testing in a lab.* The test shows if the tumor is benign or malignant.

Warning Signs

A person can play an important part in spotting cancer. Females, for instance, can examine their breasts for the lumps that may be a sign of breast cancer. Males can give themselves a self-examination of the testicles. People of either sex can look for the seven warning signs of cancer that the American Cancer Society has identified.

Warning Signs of Cancer
- Change in bowel or bladder habits
- A sore that does not heal
- Unusual bleeding or discharge
- Thickening or lump in breast or elsewhere
- Indigestion or difficulty swallowing
- Obvious change in a wart or mole
- Nagging cough or hoarseness

Caution!

The first letters of the seven warning signs of cancer spell the word *caution*. Caution is certainly a good piece of advice with cancer. Anyone who notices any of these changes should see a doctor very soon.

Treating Cancer

The key to treating cancer is spotting it early. Once the cancer spreads through the blood or the lymph system to other parts of the body, treatment is difficult. The main ways to treat cancer are *surgery, chemotherapy,* and *radiation.* Often doctors use more than one of these methods for the same patient.

- **Surgery.** The goal of surgery is to remove the cancer cells. This method works best when the cancer has not spread. Surgery is used with good success for skin cancer and with some success for breast and colon cancers.
- **Chemotherapy.** *Using chemicals to destroy cancer cells* is called **chemotherapy** (kee·moh·THEHR·uh·pee). More than 50 drugs are used to fight cancer. The most success with this method has been with leukemia and lymphoma.
- **Radiation** (rayd·ee·AY·shuhn). *In this treatment, X rays or some other radiation are aimed at the tumor.* These rays destroy the cancer cells. This treatment is used for Hodgkin's disease, a cancer of the lymph nodes.

None of these treatments is perfect. Each can damage healthy cells as well as the cancer cells. The goal is to keep down the number of healthy cells that are harmed. Surgery and radiation are better with cancers that have not spread beyond one spot. Chemotherapy can be used to fight cancers that have spread throughout the body. But this method has the drawback of sometimes causing severe side affects such as nausea and hair loss.

Check Your Understanding

Conclusion   Cancer is one of the most serious diseases affecting people today. But anyone can reduce the risk of developing cancer by following good health habits. Anyone who notices any major change in how his or her body works should see a doctor. Early treatment of cancer has the best chance of success.

1. **Vocabulary** What is the name for (a) a tumor that is cancerous? What is the name for (b) a tumor that is not cancerous?
2. **Recall** How does cancer develop?
3. **Recall** What are three things you can do to try to prevent cancer?
4. **Recall** What are three of the warning signs of cancer?
5. **Recall** What are the three main treatments for cancer?
6. **Analyze** Why is metastasis such an important event for someone who has cancer?

SKILLS FOR LIVING

Breast Self-Examination

A female can protect herself from serious problems by checking herself every month for possible signs of breast cancer.

1. Look in the mirror to see anything unusual— a change in the size or shape of a breast, a discharge from the nipples, or any changes in the skin.
2. Feel for any possible lumps by pressing the flat part of the fingers on the outer edge of the breast and moving around in circles that slowly move closer to the nipple. Also feel the area between the breast and the armpit and the armpit itself.

You may do Step 2 while lying on your back.

Teen Health
BULLETIN BOARD

CAREERS

Wanted:
Occupational Therapist

Specifics:
Develop a therapy (job skills, physical recovery, recreation) to help patient deal with a disability.

Qualifications:
Must relate well to people and be able to contribute to team effort. Must take initiative for developing and applying therapy program.

Preparation:
High school education required. Bachelor's degree, or two-year college course, or master's after bachelor's in another field, are acceptable. Licensing required in some states.

Contact:
American Association for Rehabilitation Therapy
Box 93
North Little Rock, AR 72116
or
The American Occupational Therapy Association
1383 Piccard Drive
Rockville, MD 20850

HEALTH IN THE NEWS
I Can Do It Myself— With Your Help

Millions of Americans suffer from arthritis. It can make life very difficult. Now, a new kind of treatment is being tried. It is called "arthritis self-management."

With self-management, doctors still prescribe treatment for arthritis. However, the patient also learns new habits. Patients learn how to exercise and eat right. They learn how to relax. They learn about different kinds of treatments they can choose.

With self-management, patients often find that their arthritis gets somewhat better. This proves the theory that the patient can be an important part of the medical team.

CAREERS

Wanted:

Public Health Statistician

Specifics:

Provide charts or written reports summarizing data relating to disease, population growth, and other aspects of public health.

Qualifications:

Must be attentive to details and good at communicating results of research. Excellent math and writing skills required.

Preparation:

Bachelor's degree followed by master's or doctorate preferred, with training in computer science a plus.

Contact:

American Public Health Association
1015 Fifteenth Street, NW
Washington, DC 20005

or

American Statistical Association
806 Fifteenth Street, NW
Washington, DC 20005

Lifestyle
Another Plus for Exercise

A study at Stanford University Medical Center shows that some diabetics can use exercise to control their disease. These are people with Type II diabetes. Their bodies make the hormone insulin needed if the cells are to get enough glucose. Glucose is a form of sugar that cells use to make energy. However, people with Type II diabetes don't use the insulin they produce. This means their cells don't get the glucose they need.

Exercise helps the body use insulin. It also helps keep the glucose at the proper level, an important thing for diabetics. Exercise helps people with diabetes take better care of their condition. In fact, those who exercise regularly are probably in better shape than most people without diabetes who don't exercise.

Sports and Recreation

Horses Got Mikko Going Again

When she was 17, Mikko Mayeda developed multiple sclerosis. After the shock of the news wore off, she became depressed. But Mikko's mother urged her to learn horseback riding with other handicapped people.

Mikko's disease got worse, but her skill with horses got better. Mikko has won gold and silver medals for her riding. She also paints and has written the story of her life. Mikko believes that horseback riding helps her through life's hard times.

Rider Mikko Mayeda has overcome MS to become a champion rider.

All About Diabetes

Words to Know
diabetes
insulin
Type I diabetes
Type II diabetes
hypodermic needle

This lesson contains a number of valuable facts and tips. Once you have studied them, you will be able to

- define the term *diabetes* and tell what it does to the body.
- point out differences between the two types of diabetes.
- tell how diabetes is treated.

DID **YOU** KNOW?

The Quiet Condition
About half of the people who have diabetes don't even know it. Regular checkups can make sure that you are not one of those people.

What Is Diabetes?

Diabetes (dy·uh·BEET·eez) is *a disease that prevents the body from using food to make energy.* Today almost 12 million people in the United States have one of the two types of diabetes.

Diabetes is a major health problem. It is a leading cause of death and disability. People who have diabetes run a greater risk of having heart disease, stroke, blindness, and kidney failure. They also have a higher chance than normal of losing an arm or leg to amputation.

What Causes Diabetes?

The food you eat is changed into a sugar that your body's cells can use to make energy. The pancreas releases a hormone called **insulin** (IN·suh·luhn) to *control how the body uses this sugar for energy.* Some people do not make enough insulin. Other people make insulin but for some reason the body does not respond to it. Both these groups of people have diabetes.

Learning from Photographs
Some diabetics need to give themselves a dose of the hormone insulin every day. Do you know how this hormone helps them?

The causes of diabetes are not clearly understood. It is clear, however, that parents pass on a tendency to diabetes to their children. In one kind of diabetes, a germ or even the body's own defenses may destroy the cells that make insulin. With another form of diabetes, three factors are related to the disease. People with this form have a family history of diabetes, are older, and may be obese.

What Are the Types of Diabetes?

The two kinds of diabetes are based on how much insulin is in the body. *People whose bodies make little or no insulin* have **Type I diabetes.** About one in ten people with diabetes has this form. Until 1921, when insulin was first given to diabetics, most people with Type I diabetes died within a year or two of getting the disease. Type I most often appears in young people, but it can also begin when someone is an adult. It often shows itself quite suddenly.

Type I diabetes has five signs.

Signs of Type I Diabetes
- Urinating often and feeling very thirsty
- Feeling very hungry
- Losing a large amount of weight
- Vomiting and nausea
- Feeling weak and very tired

Someone who shows these signs and does not get help right away could die.

People whose bodies do not make enough insulin or make insulin but cannot use it correctly have **Type II diabetes.** This type often does not appear until later in life, when people are in their forties or beyond. It seems to be related to being overweight. This condition can sometimes be prevented by controlling weight and keeping physically active. Type II diabetes has five symptoms as well.

Signs of Type II Diabetes
- Loss of feeling in the hands and feet
- Skin infections and cuts that heal slowly
- Lack of energy
- Blurred vision
- Itching

DID **YOU** KNOW?

Human's Best Friend
The first insulin used for injections came from the pancreases of dogs. Now the hormone is created in labs, or insulin from pigs or cows is used.

More About

*For more on **digestion**, see Chapter 7.*

DID **YOU** KNOW?

Diabetes and Pregnancy
Pregnant women may develop *gestational* (jes·TAY·shuhn·uhl) diabetes. They need to be careful with their diet and how much weight they gain. Otherwise the baby could develop problems. This condition often goes away after they give birth.

Learning from Photographs
What steps can people take to lower their chances of having Type II diabetes?

If left untreated, diabetes can give a person serious health problems. The disease can lead to blindness, loss of feeling or severe pain in the feet and hands, kidney failure, and hardening of the arteries.

How Is Diabetes Treated?

Diabetes cannot be cured. With care, however, a person with diabetes can live a fairly normal life. People with Type I diabetes must take insulin every day. Most people with this type give themselves insulin one or more times a day. They inject it with a **hypodermic** (hy·poh·DER·mik) **needle.** The needle *puts the insulin under the skin.* They learn how to inject themselves and how to manage the disease.

Some people with Type II diabetes need to take a medicine to use the insulin that their bodies make. Others need to take insulin itself.

People with diabetes must also be very careful with what they eat. They often need to eat specific amounts of protein, fat, and carbohydrate. Someone with Type II diabetes can often control the disease by watching his or her diet and weight. The diet they must follow is most often a low-calorie diet.

If someone with Type I diabetes makes a mistake in how much insulin he or she takes, serious problems can result.

● **Too much insulin can cause insulin shock.** If the insulin works too well, all the sugar in the blood is used up. A person with low blood sugar may feel dizzy, irritable, and sweaty. He or she may even pass out. The solution is to eat a food high in

DID YOU KNOW?

Pumping Insulin
Insulin can also be given with a pump that is attached to the patient.

sugar, such as candy, fruit juice, or a soft drink. If the person is unconscious, he or she needs medical care. In that case, the person needs a shot of *glucagon* (GLOO·kuh·gahn) to raise the blood sugar level.

- **Too little insulin or a missed dose can cause high blood sugar.** A person may feel thirsty, urinate very often, vomit, and have a flushed skin. His or her breath may smell like fruit. If that person does not get treatment, he or she could pass out and eventually die. Someone with high blood sugar needs to be taken to a hospital.

Low blood sugar can also result from delaying or skipping meals or exercising too heavily. High blood sugar can also be caused by an injury or illness or from eating too much.

A major goal of care for someone with diabetes is to keep the blood sugar level as close to normal as possible. The best way to watch this level is to test the blood. A doctor or nurse can train the person with diabetes to test his or her blood at home. The results of these tests are useful for day-to-day control of the disease. The results are very helpful during illness or a period of heavy physical activity.

Check Your Understanding

Conclusion Diabetes is a serious disease that can be controlled with care. Someone with diabetes needs to watch his or her diet and level of activity. Most people with Type II diabetes develop the disease because they are overweight and have a family history of diabetes. If you maintain your weight and get plenty of exercise, you can help prevent yourself from getting this disease.

1. **Vocabulary** What role does insulin play in diabetes?

2. **Recall** What is diabetes?

3. **Recall** When do most people who have Type I diabetes develop the disease? When do most people who develop Type II diabetes develop the disease?

4. **Recall** What is the treatment for someone with Type I diabetes?

5. **Recall** How can a person prevent Type II diabetes?

6. **Analyze** You are in the middle of a long game of basketball with your friend, who has Type I diabetes. She is turning pale and becoming angry at you. She seems to move in an uncoordinated way. What may be happening? What can you do?

Watching What You Eat

A person with Type I diabetes must follow his or her diet carefully. The goal is to keep simple sugars out of the diet and to make sure that the daily changes in the amount of insulin needed are small. For more information on simple sugar, see Chapter 5.

Helping Out

If someone you know is having insulin shock, give him or her candy, fruit juice, or a soft drink. *Never* give a diet soda. It may be unclear whether the person is suffering from high blood sugar or low blood sugar. If you are not sure, try giving sugar. If the person doesn't look or feel better in about 10 minutes, get him or her to the hospital.

All About Arthritis

Words to Know
arthritis
rheumatoid arthritis
osteoarthritis
bone spurs

This lesson contains a number of valuable facts and tips. Once you have studied them, you will be able to

- describe the effects of the two main types of arthritis.
- tell how each type of arthritis is treated.

DID **YOU** KNOW?

How Many People?
About 31 million people in the United States are thought to have one form of arthritis or another.

A Crippling Disease

Arthritis is not one disease, but many. In fact, **arthritis** (ar·THRYT·uhs) is the term for *more than 100 conditions signaled by by pain and swelling in the joints.* About one person in seven suffers from one of these conditions. Many people think that only old people suffer from one of these diseases. But arthritis can affect people of any age, from infancy on.

While there are many kinds of arthritis, two types are the most common. They are *rheumatoid arthritis* and *osteoarthritis.*

Rheumatoid Arthritis

The more serious of the two main kinds of arthritis is **rheumatoid** (ROO·muh·toyd) **arthritis.** In this condition, *the joints become swollen and are destroyed.* The joints attacked are most often the wrists, knuckles, hips, legs, and feet. The disease may harm other joints as well, though. If it is not stopped, it can cause the joints to stiffen into deformed positions.

The disease can also spread to other tissues in the body. Then it can cause fever, tiredness, and swollen glands.

What It Does to the Body

The cause of rheumatoid arthritis is not known. Scientists believe it may be brought on by small organisms or by a problem in the immune system. It could be that the immune system, for some reason, begins to attack body tissue. Whatever the cause, the result is that tissue in

More About

For more on the skeletal system, see Chapter 7.

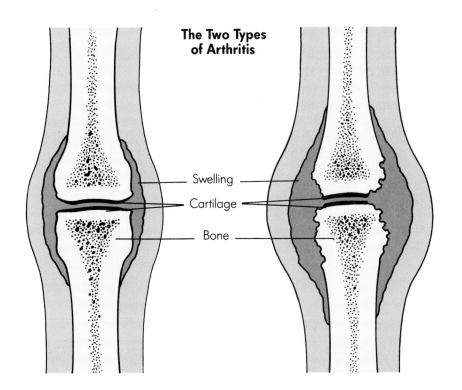

The Two Types of Arthritis

Swelling

Cartilage

Bone

Learning from Drawings
The left drawing shows the damage done by osteoarthritis. As cartilage breaks down, the two bones rub against each other. In rheumatoid arthritis (right), tissue in the joint swells. This swelling harms the cartilage and bone. Which of the two conditions is worse?

the joint swells. This swollen tissue then begins to eat away at bone and cartilage. That is where the real damage happens.

Most people who have rheumatoid arthritis got it when they were between 20 and 40. Children and older people can both get the disease, however. It may be that a greater chance to develop the disease is passed from parent to child.

Treating Rheumatoid Arthritis

There is no cure for rheumatoid arthritis. The goal of treatment is to relieve the pain and prevent the more serious effects. Treatment may include a number of steps. Rest is often one of them.

- **Medicine.** *Ibuprofen* (eye·byoo·PROH·fuhn) and aspirin are the medicines most often given to reduce the swelling and ease the pain.
- **Heat.** This is also used to lower the swelling.
- **Exercise, good posture, and therapy.** Each of these methods is aimed at keeping the joints movable and working properly.

When severe damage to the joints has taken place, surgery may be needed. Doctors can replace a damaged joint with a mechanical one.

DID **YOU** KNOW?

On Pins and Needles
Some people use the ancient Chinese method of *acupuncture* to relieve the pain of arthritis. With this method, long thin needles are inserted into the body in certain places. There they seem to have a pain-killing effect. No one knows exactly how acupuncture works, and it does not work for everyone.

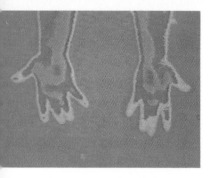

Learning from Photographs
This image shows a *thermograph,* a picture of the heat given off by the hand. The red areas show the presence of inflammation. How can doctors use this kind of imaging to help someone with arthritis?

Osteoarthritis

The more common kind of arthritis is **osteoarthritis** (ahs·tee·oh·ahr·THRYT·uhs). This condition *results from wearing away of the joints.* It affects the joints of the hip and knee most often. These are the joints that bear much of the body's weight.

The disease begins when cartilage at the end of a joint wears away. As the cartilage wears down, the bone ends grow thicker. The bones may even grow *little points or knobs at the end* called **bone spurs.** These spurs cause the tissue around them to grow. When this happens, the joint becomes deformed.

To treat osteoarthritis, doctors use ibuprofen and aspirin to ease the pain. They give their patients special exercises to prevent the damage from becoming too great. When the disease has damaged the joint too severely, doctors may operate to replace it with a mechanical joint.

Certain warning signs can tell a person that he or she may have this disease.

- Pain and stiffness in the morning
- Pain or swelling in a joint
- Pain and stiffness in the lower back or knees

Arthritis can affect people of all ages. Athletes may get this disease if a joint has been injured many times. Watching for these signs and seeing a doctor if they appear can help you stay healthy.

Check Your Understanding

Conclusion Arthritis is really a catchall term for more than 100 different diseases of the joints. The two most common forms involve swelling of the joints or their wearing down. Aches and pains in the joints may be signs of these conditions. They are certainly signals to have a doctor take a look at the condition.

1. **Vocabulary** What are bone spurs?
2. **Recall** What are the effects of rheumatoid arthritis?
3. **Recall** What are two treatments for rheumatoid arthritis?
4. **Recall** What is done to treat osteoarthritis?
5. **Analyze** Your brother is a football player who has had two knee injuries. Lately he's been waking up with pain in his knees. What should he do?

DID **YOU** KNOW?

Looking for Answers
Research into arthritis is being done at all times. Scientists are trying to find the cause so that the disease can be prevented.

Preventing Heart Disease

The major cause of death in the United States is heart disease. High blood pressure and hardening of the arteries are the two most common forms of this disease. Today medical care can save the lives of people with these conditions. Even more effective, though, is *preventing* these diseases. Four of the risk factors cannot be controlled.

- **Age.** The risk of heart disease goes up with age.
- **Sex.** Up to the age of 40, males have a higher risk for heart disease than females. Afterward, the rates are about the same.
- **Race.** Black Americans are more likely to have high blood pressure than are members of other races.
- **Family health history.** If your family has a history of heart disease, your chances of getting it are higher.

How to Keep Your Heart Healthy

While you cannot control any of these conditions, you can still keep your risk of having heart disease low. That's by controlling the other five risk factors.

- Maintain the correct body weight.
- Exercise regularly.
- Eat a healthy diet.
- Manage stress in your life.
- Avoid cigarette smoking.

Even someone who has one of the four uncontrolled risk factors can lower the chance of heart disease by working on these risks.

Using the Skill

Read the following situation. Think about what decisions these people can make to lower their risk for heart disease. Then answer the questions that follow.

Case

Mr. and Mrs. Daley looked over the menu as they smoked. Their daughter Sydney ordered a hamburger and french fries. Mr. Daley ordered fish and a salad. Mrs. Daley asked for a steak.

When the food came, Mrs. Daley and Sydney used lots of salt. As they ate, they talked about Mr. Daley's father, who had just had a heart attack. Mr. Daley had a checkup last week, and the doctor told him his blood pressure was good. Mrs. Daley said she hadn't had hers checked in a year or so.

Divide a separate sheet of paper into three columns. Label each column with the name of a Daley family member. For each person, answer these questions.

1. What does each member do that risks heart disease?
2. What could each decide to do differently to reduce his or her risk?

Chapter 12 Review

Summary

- Some diseases develop over time, either through age or because of the way people live. Many can be prevented.
- Heart disease is the most serious disease in the United States. But it can usually be prevented by following good health habits.
- Cancer is the second biggest killer of all the diseases in the United States. Some cancers can be prevented by following healthy habits.

- There are two types of diabetes, a condition that affects the way the body can use food to make energy. With proper care, the person with diabetes can live a normal life.
- Arthritis is a name for many diseases of the joints and bones. The two main types affect the victims with swelling or wearing away of the joints. Treatment aims at relieving the pain and reducing the damage.

Reviewing Vocabulary and Concepts

On a separate sheet of paper, write the numbers 1–15. After each number, write the letter of the answer that best completes each of the following statements.

Lesson 1

1. One noncommunicable disease is
   a. pneumonia   b. AIDS   c. measles   d. lung cancer

2. Each of the following is a lifestyle disease *except*
   a. hardening of the arteries   b. allergies   c. lung cancer   d. alcoholism

3. Each of the following is a way that a noncommunicable disease develops *except*
   a. being passed from person to person   b. being present at birth   c. as a result of habits   d. from hazards around us

Lesson 2

4. Each of the following is a condition that affects the heart *except*
   a. cancer   b. atherosclerosis   c. high blood pressure   d. a faulty valve

5. Each of the following is a treatment for atherosclerosis *except*
   a. bypass surgery   b. radiation   c. heart transplant   d. ballooning an artery

6. Which of the following parts of a diet helps keep the heart healthy?
   a. high fat   b. high cholesterol   c. low salt   d. low fiber

7. Which of the following is (are) often used to treat high blood pressure?
   a. weight loss and diet   b. surgery   c. weight loss and smoking   d. diet and surgery

Lesson 3

8. Which of the following types of tumor is cancerous?
   a. benign
   b. malignant
   c. both are
   d. neither is

9. The disease that results in the rapid and uncontrolled growth of cells is
   a. atherosclerosis
   b. diabetes
   c. arthritis
   d. cancer

10. The most common cancer is
    a. lung cancer
    b. breast cancer
    c. skin cancer
    d. colon cancer

11. The most deadly cancer is
    a. lung cancer
    b. breast cancer
    c. skin cancer
    d. colon cancer

Lesson 4

12. Someone who makes little or no insulin has which type of diabetes?
    a. Type I
    b. Type II
    c. neither
    d. both

13. Type II diabetes can sometimes be prevented by watching weight and
    a. smoking
    b. insulin injections
    c. drinking alcohol
    d. level of activity

Lesson 5

14. Each of the following is a treatment for rheumatoid arthritis *except*
    a. exercise
    b. radiation
    c. medicine
    d. surgery

15. The type of arthritis in which the joints wear down is
    a. rheumatoid arthritis
    b. osteoarthritis
    c. neither
    d. both

Thinking Critically About the Facts

Write your answers to the following questions on a separate sheet of paper.

16. **Compare and contrast** Compare noncommunicable diseases to communicable diseases.

17. **Synthesize** If people may inherit from their parents a tendency to a noncommunicable disease, why are health habits important?

18. **Draw conclusions** Stan eats a low-salt, high-fiber diet. His weight is normal. He does not exercise. He smokes a pack of cigarettes a day. Is Stan risking heart disease? What about his risk for cancer?

19. **Draw conclusions** Elise has given herself a breast self-examination. She has found a lump. What should she do?

20. **Analyze** Why is rheumatoid arthritis the more serious form?

Applying the Facts

21. Research your family's health history. Have any family members had any of the noncommunicable diseases covered in this chapter? Which disease did the person have and what happened to him or her? How can you use this information to build good health habits?

22. Form small groups in your class to research cancer. Each group can focus on one type. Find out what causes it, how many cases there are, what the treatment is, and what can be done to prevent it. Report your findings to the rest of the class.

361

Safety and Your Health

CHAPTER WARM-UP

Chapter Study Goals

After you have read this chapter, you will be able to

- explain how to break the accident chain.
- describe ways of preventing home accidents.
- explain how to act safely on the road and when outdoors.
- describe the basics of first aid and summarize how to act in common emergencies.
- explain how to save a choking victim.
- describe when CPR may be needed.

Be on the lookout for information in the chapter that will help you reach these goals.

Getting Started

"Accidents will happen," people say. But they need not happen if you act within your abilities and work to protect yourself. When accidents do occur, knowing how to help someone who is hurt—and when to call for medical help—may save a life. In this chapter, you will learn how to prevent accidents and act in emergencies.

Study Tip

As you read this chapter, pay attention to the numbered and bulleted lists. Many of these lists give safety strategies for you to follow.

362

Words to Know
safety conscious
risks
accident chain

Building Safe Habits

This lesson contains a number of valuable facts and tips. Once you have studied them, you will be able to

- tell why your attitude toward safety is important.
- give three guidelines for acting safely.
- suggest some reasons for making safe choices.
- tell how to prevent accidents.

Knowing Safety Rules

If you think about it, you probably know a number of safety rules. Cross with the green, not with the red. Do not play with matches. Never skate on thin ice. Don't run in the halls.

These rules are common sense. Their purpose is to protect you from harm. How well they work depends, to a large extent, on you.

When it comes to safety, knowing the rules is not enough. You need to *think that safety is important and act safely.* When you are **safety conscious,** you understand that safety rules help you prevent accidents. Then you put into practice the rules that you know.

Learning from Photographs
You already know a number of safety rules. What rule of car safety is this teen following?

Practicing Safety

Practicing safety means not taking needless **risks,** or *harmful chances.* Is that possible? Our world is full of risks. When you walk in the woods, you risk touching poison ivy. When you cross a street, you risk getting hit by a car. But avoiding risks does not mean staying out of the woods or off the streets. It means learning to spot poison ivy and walking on paths clear of it. It means following safe crossing rules.

The biggest risks come from being careless. To be safe, follow these guidelines.

- **Resist peer pressure.** Has someone ever talked you into doing something dangerous? Suppose you cannot swim well. What will you do if a group of friends wants you to dive into deep water? You may be tempted to take a needless risk to show off, to look important, or to fit in. In a situation like this, it takes strength to practice safety. Remember that your health is at stake.

- **Be careful when your feelings are strong.** When you are in a hurry or tired, you are more likely to get careless. When you are excited or depressed, you may not concentrate as well. Anytime you are not concentrating on what you are doing, you increase the chance of having an accident. Keep your mind on what you are doing, not the movie you want to see or the argument you just had.

- **Know your limits.** Skilled people in dangerous work or sports do not take needless risks. Skiers train for years before they take on the toughest slopes. You should prepare, too. Know how far or for how long you can swim in a lake. Don't take an unsafe risk if you do not have the skills or equipment you need.

Itchy Fingers

Spot poison ivy by looking for a vine covered with hairs. It has three heart-shaped leaves, a large middle one flanked by two smaller ones.

Haste Really *Does* Make Waste

It's funny how the more you hurry, the more time it takes. Doing something quickly doesn't save time if it's not done right. Take your time. Think ahead.

DID **YOU** KNOW?

Safety Pays

Drivers with poor driving records pay hundreds or even thousands of dollars more than safe drivers for car insurance.

Taking Risks

What can happen to you if you take unnecessary risks? Here is an example. Kevin was late for baseball practice. Racing to the field on his bike, he took a shortcut that made him ride against the traffic. As Kevin cut in front of a car, the driver swerved to avoid him and crashed into a fire hydrant. Kevin fell off his bike and got hurt. As you may guess, he never made it to practice.

By being in a hurry, Kevin did more than just miss a baseball practice. He needlessly put both his life and the driver's life in danger. While neither he nor the driver was seriously hurt, both were shaken up. Kevin broke his bike, and he damaged a car. Who pays for his risky action? He does, his family does, and so does the driver.

Playing It Safe

There are many benefits to making safe choices. By acting safely, you avoid the high costs of accidents like Kevin's. Acting safely avoids inconvenience, too. Because Kevin was careless, he lost the chance to go to practice. You save time and money. You avoid injury and emotional stress. You may even save lives.

The Accident Chain

Accidents like Kevin's do not just happen. They occur because of *the combination of a situation, an unsafe habit, and an unsafe act.* This pattern, the **accident chain,** is described on the next page.

Learning from Photographs
This teen is getting instruction in how to use tools properly. What other safety tip is she following?

- **The situation.** Kevin is late for practice and in a hurry. Because he is hurrying, he is not paying attention to traffic.
- **The unsafe habit.** The shortcut he usually takes means that he rides on the wrong side of the street, against the traffic.
- **The unsafe action.** Kevin cuts in front of an oncoming car.
- **The accident.** The car crashes into a fire hydrant, and Kevin falls.
- **The injuries and other results.** Kevin sprains his wrist. He has to miss baseball practice for 2 weeks. His bike is broken and needs repairs. And his parents must pay the driver for the damage to her car.

It would have been simple for Kevin to prevent this accident. There are three ways to break the accident chain.

- **Change the situation.** If Kevin had left for practice on time, he would have paid more attention to traffic.
- **Change the unsafe habit.** Kevin should have avoided the shortcut that made him ride against traffic. He should have followed the rules of bicycle safety.
- **Change the unsafe action.** Kevin should never have ridden his bike in front of an oncoming car.

If Kevin had done any of those three things differently, he would have broken the accident chain. His wrist would be fine, his bike would not need fixing, and the driver's car would not be damaged. Accidents do *not* have to happen.

Check Your Understanding

Conclusion Being safe is a mixture of knowing the rules, having the right attitude about safety, and acting safely. You can avoid accidents by not taking risks. Taking risks and getting hurt do not make sense. If you are hurt, you cannot do things you enjoy.

1. **Vocabulary** Write an original sentence defining the word *risk*.
2. **Recall** What are three rules for acting safely?
3. **Recall** Name two benefits of playing it safe.
4. **Recall** How can you break the accident chain?
5. **Interpret** There is an old saying that "an ounce of prevention is worth a pound of cure." How does this saying apply to being safety conscious?

Accident Prone?
Have you ever heard it said the someone is accident prone? Is it just bad luck? Remember that accidents don't *have* to happen. That streak of bad luck can be broken by just being more careful.

Caring for Infants
If you have an infant brother or sister, or if you ever baby-sit for an infant, you should always clear the play area of objects small enough for the child to swallow. If you see an infant playing with a small object, such as a marble or a pin, take it away immediately.

Words to Know

hazards
expiration date
smoke alarm
rape
date rape
rape treatment centers
neighborhood watch
  programs

Acting Safely at Home and at School

This lesson contains a number of valuable facts and tips. Once you have studied them, you will be able to

- tell how to prevent falls and home accidents that stem from poisons, electrical problems, fires, and guns.
- explain how to act safely at school.
- tell how to protect yourself from crime.

Safety at Home

Home is where you live, a happy and comfortable place. But your home also has many **hazards** (HAZ·erds), or *possible sources of harm.* These include such things as medicines, spills, slippery bathtubs, and objects left on stairs.

Most home accidents can be prevented. The hints that follow will help you prevent falls and injuries from poisons, electrical problems, fires, and guns.

Preventing Falls

Falls are common accidents. They are particularly dangerous in kitchens and bathrooms and on stairs. Falls can be prevented by taking some steps in advance.

- **Remove dangers.** Wipe up spills and pick up stray objects on the floor or stairs.
- **Act safely.** Do not run on a wet or waxed floor. Use a nonskid mat in your bathtub. If you need to reach a high object, stand on an indoor ladder or step stool, not on a chair or a counter.

Older people often have brittle bones. As a result, falls are especially dangerous to them. Help older family members avoid falls.

Learning from Photographs
This teen is making sure the stairs are not blocked by stray objects. What kind of home accident is he preventing?

Preventing Poisoning

Poisoning is a serious problem, especially for young children. Curious about all they see and unable to read labels, preschoolers may eat or drink a poison without knowing it. Many substances in the home are poisons. Soaps and other cleaning products are dangerous. Even a medicine can poison someone if he or she takes too much.

Poisoning can be prevented, though.

- **Placement.** Put all dangerous substances up high and out of children's reach. Locking them up is best.
- **Handling medicines.** Keep medicines in their childproof containers. Throw out drugs that have passed their **expiration date.** This is *a date stamped on the package that tells when a medicine is no longer useful.*

Using Electricity Safely

Electricity provides light, heat, cooking, and entertainment. But it can be dangerous if misused. Most electrical accidents come from problems with wires and outlets or from using electrical products in the wrong way.

- **Plugs and outlets.** Have any wires that are frayed replaced. Do not pull out a plug by its cord; pull on the plug. Put only two plugs into an outlet—do not overload with too many cords.
- **Electrical products.** Keep electrical products away from water, and never use a product when you are wet. If something seems to be wrong with an appliance, unplug it and have a service person look at it.

Teen Issue

Stay Dry
Some teens needlessly risk electrical shock in the bathroom. They use blow dryers or curling irons while still wet after bathing. Others listen to the radio in the tub. *Never* touch an electrical product while wet.

Learning from Photographs
Electrical hazards are common sources of fire. Which of these two pictures shows the safe use of electricity, and why?

Learning from Photographs
Fires are dangerous accidents. How is each teen helping protect his family from fire?

Making Your Home Safe from Fire

The main causes of fire in the home are cooking, problems with electrical products, smoking, and heating. Most fires, however, can be prevented. The rules are simple.

- Keep stoves clean and use care in cooking to avoid burns and grease fires.
- Make sure that electrical wires, outlets, and products are safe.
- Make sure that no one smokes in bed.
- Keep anything that will burn at least 3 feet from a portable heater.
- Throw out old newspapers, oil-soaked rags, and other materials that burn easily.
- Use matches properly. Persuade others not to play with them.

Even with these safe practices, fires can occur. But the risk of injury from fire can be reduced. A **smoke alarm** should be installed on each level of your home, especially outside bedroom areas. This *device makes a warning noise when it senses smoke.* The sound will warn your family to get to safety, even if everyone is asleep. Be sure to test the smoke alarm once a month and replace the battery if needed.

Another good idea is to join with your family in planning a fire escape route. Know a way to leave every room of the house. Have a second exit in mind in case the first is blocked by fire. Agree on a place everyone will meet when outside.

Fires are dangerous. Fire departments recommend that the best thing to do if a fire happens is to leave the house quickly and call the fire department. Leave fire fighting to the experts. If your clothes should catch on fire, do not run. Stop, drop to the ground, and roll to put the flames out. The greatest danger from fire is breathing in smoke. Stay low as you move, so you are below the smoke.

Oil and Water Don't Mix

Small kitchen fires are the only fires that fire officials say it is safe for people to put out. Most kitchen fires are grease fires. Do not try to put a grease fire out with water. Smother it with a metal lid, or cover it with baking soda.

Using Guns Safely

A gun is not a toy. Do not handle a gun unless an adult has taught you how to handle one safely and gives you permission to touch it. It is best not to handle a gun unless an adult is present. Guns should always be locked away and stored unloaded. Load a gun only when you are ready to use it. Keep the safety catch on until you are outdoors and ready to shoot. Carry a gun with the barrel downward.

There is one more rule, the most important of all—never point a gun at anyone.

Safety at School

Safety is always a concern in places where many people gather. For this reason, school buildings must meet certain safety standards. For example, new buildings must be fireproof. Fire exits must be clearly marked. Students, too, can help make school a safe place.

- Do not run in locker rooms or halls and obey hall monitors.
- Wear protective goggles in shop class.
- Learn what to do in a fire drill or other emergency.

Protecting Yourself from Crime

Sometimes your safety may be threatened by another person. The best way to protect yourself is to avoid situations that seem not to be safe. If you feel that a place can be dangerous, do not go near it. If you feel uncomfortable somewhere, leave. If you need help, find an adult or a police officer. Here are some other precautions to follow.

DO	*DON'T*
• Stay away from anyone you think may be a drug dealer.	• Walk alone in dark areas and deserted streets.
• Go places in groups.	• Open the door to anyone if you are home alone.
• Stay in well-lighted, public places at night.	• Get into a car with a stranger.
• Keep doors and windows locked when you are home alone.	• Give out any information over the telephone.

If a problem occurs, get to a phone and dial 911 or the local police department number. It is also a good idea always to carry with you the phone numbers of your home, your parents' work, and a neighbor.

Teen **Issue**

Do You Dare?
Three words — "I dare you" — cause many accidents. Teens take dares to prove they are tough. But the *really* tough teen is the one who stands up for what is safe. Resist pressure when you could get hurt. Say "no" to dares.

Teen **Issue**

You've Got a Friend
You'll be safer if you travel in a group or at least with one other friend. Avoid traveling alone. Stay with a buddy.

Preventing Rape

The crime of **rape** is *forcing another person to have sexual relations.* While most rape victims are young women, boys may also be attacked. Some people who commit rape choose their victims on the spur of the moment. Others have met their victims before. In the case of a **date rape,** *the victim is forced to have sexual relations by someone on a date.*

The best way to prevent rape is to try to avoid situations where you are open to attack. Going places in a group helps. Group dates can prevent date rape. Do not let anyone touch you in a way that makes you uncomfortable. Remember that you have the right to say "no." Try to leave or tell the other person to leave.

If someone is raped, she or he should get medical care right away and report the attack to the police. Many towns and cities have **rape treatment centers** in hospitals. These centers *give rape victims both medical care and counseling.* The people who work in these centers are very helpful. They respect the victim's feelings and privacy. They know that rape is *not* the victim's fault.

Neighborhood Watch Programs

Many areas have **neighborhood watch programs.** In these programs, *neighbors watch each other's homes to ensure safety.* The people are trained by the police to look for and report actions or people that look dangerous. In this way, the neighborhood helps reduce crime and protect itself.

Teen Issue

Reacting to Rape

Rape is a painful emotional experience. Rape victims can overcome that pain best if they seek help. Parents, priests or ministers, counselors, or rape crisis centers can provide understanding, suggestions for what to do, and good solid help. Don't go it alone.

Learning from Photographs
This sign shows that people are taking steps to keep their community safe. To whom do participants in a neighborhood watch program report problems?

Check Your Understanding

Conclusion   You can help protect yourself at home, in school, and in your neighborhood. By taking precautions, you can protect yourself and others.

1. **Vocabulary** What is another word for *hazard*?
2. **Recall** Name three kinds of home accidents and a way to prevent each one.
3. **Recall** Why is a smoke alarm a good device to have in your home?
4. **Recall** What are two things you can do to prevent accidents at school?
5. **Analyze** Kim and her friend Paul want to go to a concert in a downtown concert hall. What can they do to make sure they are safe?

Acting Safely on the Road

Words to Know
pedestrian
jaywalk
defensive driving

This lesson contains a number of valuable facts and tips. Once you have studied them, you will be able to

- list some important rules of pedestrian safety.
- list some important rules of safety on wheels.

Pedestrian Safety

A **pedestrian** (puh·DES·tree·uhn) is *anyone who travels on foot.* Injuries to young pedestrians happen. In fact, junior high school students are struck by cars and trucks twice as often as people in other age-groups. Drivers alone are not to blame. Many pedestrians cause such accidents.

Most of these accidents can be avoided. The pedestrian, like the driver, must always be alert to danger. Know how to walk safely near traffic and cross the street safely. It is no match when your body is struck by a car or truck. Joggers should follow these suggestions also.

DO	*DON'T*
• Cross streets at crosswalks and obey traffic lights.	• **Jaywalk,** or *cross the street in the middle of the block.*
• Before crossing, look both ways for traffic.	• Step out quickly from between parked cars.
• If parked cars block your view of traffic, move past them and check for oncoming traffic.	• Assume that a driver will see you.
• Wear bright-colored clothing in the daytime. At night, wear a jacket or belt that reflects light, and carry a lighted flashlight.	• Run into the street without stopping to look left, right, and left again.
• If there is no sidewalk, walk facing the traffic and keep as far to the left as possible.	

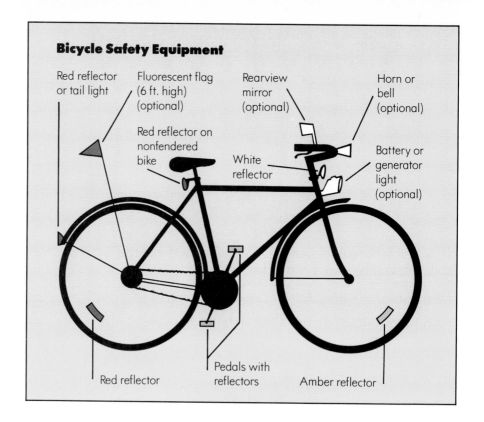

Bicycle Safety Equipment

Red reflector or tail light

Fluorescent flag (6 ft. high) (optional)

Red reflector on nonfendered bike

White reflector

Rearview mirror (optional)

Horn or bell (optional)

Battery or generator light (optional)

Red reflector

Pedals with reflectors

Amber reflector

Teen Issue

Loud and Clear

Some teens make the mistake of wearing earphones while riding a bike. This is dangerous because the music they hear can keep out the noise of traffic — noise that may tell them of approaching danger. Protect yourself from this risk.

Carrying a Load

If you need to carry a load on your bike, use a basket or a backpack. Keep your hands free for steering.

Bicycle Safety

The method of *obeying traffic laws and watching out for other road users* is called **defensive driving.** Users of cars, motorcycles, or bicycles can all act in this way. By riding your bike defensively, there are two ways you can reduce the chance that an accident will occur. First, because you obey the rules yourself, you will not do things to surprise drivers or other cyclists. Surprises can be dangerous. Second, because you watch what other road users are doing, you can react safely when someone else makes a mistake.

The safe bicyclist will...
- ride with traffic and not against it.
- stop before entering a street and check for traffic.
- obey traffic signs and lights.
- look back for oncoming traffic before turning left.
- use lights and reflective clothing if night riding is necessary.
- avoid baggy pants, which can get caught in the chain.
- keep the bike in good working order.

Learning from Photographs
This roller skater is getting ready to go skating. What safety equipment can you see?

Sometimes bike accidents do happen, though. It can be helpful to wear special clothing to prevent injury. The best protection against serious injury is a hard-shell helmet. Three out of four cyclists who die in bike crashes die from head injuries. A helmet could save your life.

Motorbike and Skateboard Safety

Like bicyclists, motorcyclists and moped riders must follow all safety rules on the road. They, too, should obey speed limits. They should also wear a safety helmet and protective clothing.

Skateboarders must also protect themselves and others. If you are doing stunts on your skateboard, be sure to wear wrist guards, elbow and knee pads, light gloves, and a helmet. Always keep your speed under control and watch out for pedestrians. Avoid using your skateboard in parking lots, in the street, or other areas with traffic. Practice falling properly before heading downhill.

Car Safety

Being safe in a car is as simple as buckling a safety belt. Studies prove that safety belts save lives. You can help the driver stay safe by not doing anything to distract him or her.

Check Your Understanding

Conclusion   Whether you are on wheels or on foot, it pays to be safety conscious. By knowing the rules of pedestrian and cycling safety, you can help ensure your well-being on the road.

1. **Vocabulary** Why is *defensive driving* safe?
2. **Recall** List two do's and two don'ts of pedestrian safety.
3. **Recall** Name two ways to prevent bicycle accidents.
4. **Recall** What can you do to use a skateboard safely?
5. **Analyze** A friend tells you that a passenger can do nothing about his or her own safety in a car. How would you convince your friend otherwise?

More About

*For more on **traffic safety**, see the Health Handbook.*

Acting Safely Outdoors

Words to Know
buddy system
hypothermia
drowning prevention
frostbite

This lesson contains a number of valuable facts and tips. Once you have studied them, you will be able to

- tell why it is helpful to have a "buddy" when you are playing outdoors.
- list the main points of water safety.
- tell what a person needs to know about safety when camping or hiking.
- give some safety tips for winter sports.

Safety Outdoors

You're not at home. You're not at school. You're not on the road. You're on vacation in the great outdoors. So you can enjoy yourself and forget about safety, right? Wrong! It doesn't pay to spoil a good time by taking risks. No matter what outdoor activity you prefer, it pays to have fun safely. Here are two guidelines for outdoor safety.

- **Use the buddy system.** The **buddy system** is *an agreement between two people to stay together and watch for each other's safety.* That way each can help the other in case of emergency.

- **Be aware of weather conditions and forecasts.** Use your common sense and try to avoid electrical storms, extreme heat, and extreme cold. If you are caught outdoors in an electrical storm, try to get into a car or house. If you cannot, take shelter under a group of bushes or squat and put your head down. Do not stand under a tall tree. Get out of and away from water. If you are outdoors on a very hot day, keep your head covered from the sun and drink lots of water. On very cold days, dress in layers and stay dry. That way you avoid **hypothermia** (hy·poh·THER·mee·uh), *a sudden drop in body temperature.* If you begin to shiver, it is important to get warmed up quickly.

If you plan on taking a long trip, it is a good idea to check in advance on what the weather will be. Remember if you are planning a vacation in the mountains that temperatures are lower in higher altitudes.

DID **YOU** KNOW?

The Great Conductor
Water conducts electricity. Protect yourself from lightning by getting out of the water.

Learning from Photographs
This teen is learning how to swim. Why is knowing how to swim the first step to water safety?

Water Safety

If your sport is swimming, diving, or boating, you will need to know about water safety. The main rule of water safety is not to enter the water unless you know how to swim. You can learn swimming in school or at community clubs. Swimming is a great skill to learn. It is fun, it is great exercise, and it can keep you safe.

The second most important rule is not to swim, dive, or boat alone. Use supervised pools or beaches, which have a trained lifeguard. Use the buddy system to have someone you can count on for help.

Learning from Photographs
These teens are kayaking. What safety clothing are they wearing?

A good technique to learn is **drowning prevention.** This is *a way of breathing slowly and treading water to prevent drowning.* The technique is shown in the Health Handbook. Should you ever feel yourself drowning, do not panic. Call for help, calm down, and try to get control. *Panicky thrashing in the water only makes your situation worse.*

It is best not to swim right after a heavy meal. Doing so could cause a *cramp*, or muscle tightening, so that you would not be able to swim easily. You should be well rested before swimming, too. If you are overtired, you could lose control.

Diving can be a great part of swimming. But do not try diving unless a qualified swim instructor has taught you how. And if you are going to dive, dive safely. Check the depth of the water and look for obstacles before diving in. Do not dive into shallow water or into aboveground pools. If you are not sure how deep the water is, jump in feet first the first time you go in. This prevents head injuries. Watch out for other swimmers and divers. Wait until the way is clear before diving in.

BUI
Operating a boat while under the influence of alcohol is just as dangerous as driving a car after drinking.

Health Minute

Guide to Field Guides
Handbooks called *field guides* tell about the plant and animal life in a region. You can find field guides in the library.

Boats are another form of water fun. Many parks provide canoes or rowboats that people can rent. Friends may own a sailboat or speedboat and invite you along. Always put on a life jacket before entering a boat. If you will be steering the boat, practice so you can handle it correctly. Avoid standing up and moving about if the boat is small. If you want to go out regularly on a boat, take a course in boating safety. Keep the boat safe by making sure it is in good condition and by not overloading it.

Hiking and Camping Safety

Hiking and camping are popular ways to enjoy the sights and sounds of nature. Good preparation is the key to success on a hiking or camping trip. Take the proper clothing and the proper equipment by planning carefully. Dress sensibly, according to the weather and the season of the year. Wear heavy shoes and socks to prevent getting blisters. Make sure you have a compass, a well-equipped first-aid kit, a flashlight with extra batteries, and a supply of fresh water. Let someone know where you will be and when you expect to return.

Campers must be ready for extremes in temperature and changes in weather. In some mountainous regions, you may be in danger of getting both sunburn during the day and frostbite at night. **Frostbite** is *freezing of the skin*. Be prepared with cold-weather, hot-weather, and wet-weather gear. Depending on where you will be, you may need to pack such items as sunscreen cream, mittens and ski mask, and waterproof boots.

Anyone walking in the outdoors must avoid poisonous plants, snakes, and insects. Know which ones to avoid. Know basic first-aid

Learning from Photographs
Good preparation is key to a safe camping or hiking trip. How does this family show good preparation?

techniques for treating reactions to poisonous plants, insect stings and bites, and snakebites.

Perhaps the most important rule of camping is to put out all campfires. Make sure that you are not responsible for a forest fire. *Drown* your campfire with water, continually stirring the fire as you add water. If no water is available, use dirt that is free of twigs, leaves, or paper. Make sure that the fire is out before leaving the area.

Winter Sports and Safety

Ice skating, sledding, and skiing are all healthy ways of enjoying winter weather. All carry the risks of cold and falls, but you can avoid these problems by wearing proper clothing and checking out the area for hazards.

Before gliding across a patch of ice, make sure that it is solid. It is safest to skate on supervised lakes or public rinks, where the ice has been tested. Before sledding down a hill, make sure that the way is clear. Use only hills that are free from traffic or streets that have been roped off. Be careful of other sledders and of pedestrians.

If you ski, wear proper clothing, boots, and goggles if it is snowing. Do not speed down a slope unless you know you can make it. Be sure to check the condition of the snow and to ski only in designated areas at your ability level. Take lessons before skiing. If you know what you're doing, you'll have more fun.

Winter Aerobics
Cross-country skiing does not require a hill. And it's one of the best forms of aerobic exercise.

Check Your Understanding

Conclusion You can enjoy the outdoors in many different ways. By following safety rules, you can avoid accidents that occur when you are having fun. You can make sure that your pleasure in outdoor sports activities is not ruined.

1. **Vocabulary** Which of the following terms is a way to prevent accidents and which are health problems? *hypothermia, frostbite, buddy system*
2. **Recall** What is the most important rule of water safety?
3. **Recall** Name two rules a person needs to know about camping or hiking safely.
4. **Recall** What are two basic rules for safety in winter sports?
5. **Synthesize** Why do you think it is important to take a first-aid kit when you go camping or hiking?

The Layered Look
Dress for the cold by using many layers of clothing. Layers keep you warmer by trapping air.

Teen Health
BULLETIN BOARD

CAREERS

Wanted:
Emergency Medical Technician

Specifics:
Determine and provide correct medical care to accident and illness victims. May drive ambulance.

Qualifications:
Must be able to bring physical and emotional strength to job; function well under stress. Shifts common.

Preparation:
High school diploma and driver's license required to enter any of four levels of EMT training—nonambulance, ambulance, intermediate, paramedic.

Contact:
National Association of
Emergency Medical Technicians
P.O. Box 334
Newton Highlands, MA 02161

Lifestyle

There's A Fire! Now What Do I Do?

Protecting yourself against fire means more than making sure there is a working battery in the smoke alarm. Every home needs a plan of escape in case of fire. Every family should hold fire drills every 6 months. The best way to find out how to plan your family's escape is to get in touch with your local fire fighters. They can give you full details about what you need to get and what you need to know. Knowing how to escape from a fire can keep your family from becoming just another fire statistic.

Families can protect themselves from injury in fires by planning an escape route—and practicing how to use it.

Sports and Recreation

The Scooter's Back!

In the summer of 1987, an old toy got a hot new look. Today's scooters go quickly and smoothly. They have hand brakes and rubber wheels. There are all kinds of ways to ride one. The basic way to ride is with a one-footed push. Just like riding a bicycle, teens who ride scooters need to wear safety helmets and observe traffic rules. They should also wear reflecting jackets if they are riding in the evening. The real goal is to have fun and to be safe doing it.

TEEN Q & A

Q: My older brother, who drives me to school, "hot dogs" sometimes to impress his friends. It scares me. What can I do?

A: The question is, what impresses your brother more, taking you to school or driving like a show-off? You have a right to get to school safely. More kids die in traffic-related accidents than for any other reason. Let your brother know that. Also let him know that you won't ride with him unless he begins driving safely. If you do take this stand, be prepared to back it up with action! Figure out another way to get to school before you make your stand.

Lifestyle
The "Kid Safe" System

What do you know about CPR? What happens when you dial 911? If you are baby-sitting, do you know how to call an ambulance for a sick child? The boys and girls who go to Kid Safe workshops come away knowing these and other facts about safety. Kid Safe workshops are held all over the country. Volunteer doctors, nurses, police officers, and fire fighters teach the children. The kids also get prizes and safety kits to take home. They have learned you are never too young to take good care of yourself and the people you love.

CAREERS

Wanted:
Ambulance Driver

Specifics:
Drive sick or injured people to hospital in ambulance. Give basic or advanced life-support care.

Qualifications:
Be prepared to work nights, weekends, holidays. Must be able to withstand stresses of constant medical crises. Job may require heavy lifting and carrying.

Preparation:
Driver's license and good driving record required. Training programs include those for emergency medical technician—ambulance, paramedic, or intermediate. Certification necessary.

Contact:
National Association of Emergency Medical Technicians
P.O. Box 334
Newton Highlands, MA 02161

Basic Principles of First Aid

Words to Know
first aid
rescue breathing
shock

This lesson contains a number of valuable facts and tips. Once you have studied them, you will be able to

- list the basic rules of first aid.
- tell how to help someone breathe again.
- outline the steps for controlled bleeding.

Helping Yourself and Others

Learning some basic first aid and keeping up with new methods should become a lifelong habit. Accidents occur frequently. If you learn first aid, you could help or even save the life of someone you know.

What Is First Aid?

First aid is *the care first given to a person who becomes injured or ill until regular medical care can be supplied.* Knowing what kind of care to provide can prevent serious and sometimes permanent damage to the victim. In some cases, first aid can even prevent death.

If you are around someone who is stricken by a sudden illness or injured in an accident, stay calm. Doing so will help the victim to remain calm, too. In most emergencies, you must give the proper first-aid care right away. Getting scared or excited can simply waste important time.

The First Things to Do

Once you realize that someone needs first aid, you must act quickly and carefully. Every second you save can help the victim. Take a deep breath, relax, and follow these steps, which are listed in order of importance.

1. Rescue the victim.

2. Check the victim's breathing.

3. Control severe bleeding.

4. Get help.

Learning from Photographs
Staying calm is important in an emergency. Why do you think this is true?

Rescue the Victim

Move the person only if he or she is not safe where he or she is. For example, move the victim if he or she is in danger from, say, a falling object or oncoming traffic. Move the victim as gently as possible. A person should *not* be moved if there is a broken bone or if there seems to be damage to the head, neck, or spine.

You should also be careful not to put your own life in danger. If you cannot swim, do not jump into a lake to save someone who is drowning. Try, instead, a different way of saving the person. You could throw the victim a life jacket, for instance.

Check the Victim's Breathing

Make sure the person is breathing normally. Even a few minutes without oxygen can cause brain damage. Four or five minutes can lead to death. First, check that nothing is blocking the victim's mouth and throat. Turning the person's head to the side can help prevent him or her from gagging on the tongue or choking. You should not move the person's head if the neck or spine may be injured.

If the victim has stopped breathing, you can use rescue breathing. **Rescue breathing** is *a substitute for normal breathing in which someone forces air into the victim's lungs.* Other terms for rescue breathing are *artificial* (ahrt·uh·FISH·uhl) *respiration* (res·puh·RAY·shuhn) and *mouth-to-mouth resuscitation* (ri·suhs·uh·TAY·shuhn).

- **Rescue breathing for adults and older children.** If an adult or older child is unconscious and not breathing, it is time to help. First, roll the person onto his or her back. Then check the person's breathing by taking three steps. *Look* to see if the chest is rising. *Listen* and *feel* for air leaving the lungs. If the victim is not breathing follow the steps shown in the drawing on this page.

Don't Add to the Trouble

Remember, there is no point in becoming a second victim. Only rescue a person if you are not in danger yourself.

Rescue Breathing for Adults and Older Children

1. Tilt the person's head back: place one hand under the chin and lift up while putting the other hand on the forehead and gently pressing down.

2. Pinch the person's nostrils shut. Take a deep breath and place your mouth over the person's mouth. Give two quick breaths.

3. Repeat, giving about 12 breaths per minute.

4. Keeping the head tilted, look, listen, and feel again. If necessary, repeat steps 2 and 3 until breathing resumes.

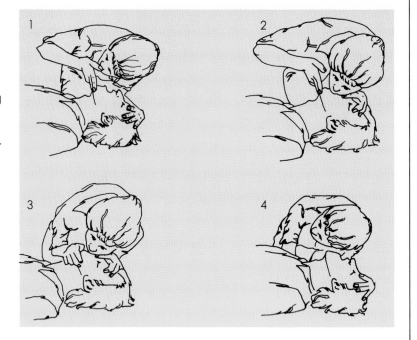

Learning from Drawings
This technique is to be used for adults and older children. What age must a child be to use this technique?

DID **YOU** KNOW?

Who Knows It
Rescue breathing is a valuable first-aid method that many professionals know. For instance, all lifeguards at pools and beaches are taught this skill.

- **Rescue breathing for infants and small children.** When giving rescue breathing to an infant or child aged 1 to 8, do not tilt the head back as far as you would an adult's. Gently support the infant's head. Do not pinch the child's nose. Instead, place your mouth over the infant's nose and mouth or over the child's mouth. Give one breath and count to three. Then give another. The breaths should be gentle or the child's lungs could be harmed. Repeat the procedure until normal breathing begins again or help arrives.

Control Severe Bleeding

The next step is to control any severe bleeding. To stop or slow the rapid loss of blood, you can use one of these three methods.

- **Apply direct and steady pressure to the wound.** Place a clean cloth over the wound and press on it firmly. Add more cloth if the blood soaks through, but do not remove the first piece.

- **Combine direct pressure with pressure to a main artery leading to the wound.** See the box on the bottom of the next page for a description of how to use pressure points.

- **Gently raise the bleeding body part above the level of the victim's heart.** This forces the blood to travel uphill, which slows its movement. However, if the victim has a broken bone, do *not* move the body part.

When the bleeding stops, cover the wound to prevent infection.

Severe bleeding can cause **shock.** This is *a serious condition in which the functions of the body are slowed down.* A person can also suffer shock from heart attack, electricity, and poisoning. You should look closely for these signs of shock.

- The victim's breathing is shallow and uneven.
- The skin is pale, cold, and moist.
- The pulse is weak or cannot be felt.
- The eyes are dull and sunken, and the pupils are wide open.

If you notice any of these signs, have the victim lie down on his or her back with the feet raised 8 to 12 inches. This position will allow blood to return to the heart. However, if there is any chance of a head injury, do *not* raise the feet. Cover the person with a blanket, coat, or other wrap to maintain body heat. Get help immediately.

Get Help

After you have taken care of the victim's first-aid needs, call the police, the fire department, or a hospital for medical help. A passerby may do this for you. Stay with the victim if you possibly can. Be sure to note the street address when you call for help. Remember, too, not to hang up until the emergency operator tells you that you can.

It Works for You, Too

You can use the methods for controlling bleeding on yourself, too. If you are badly cut, stay calm and use what you know.

Teen **Issue**

Should I Help?

Some people are afraid to help. They worry that if they try to rescue someone and fail, the victim — or the victim's family — may sue them. There's no need to fear. The *Good Samaritan Law* says that anyone who tries to help in an emergency cannot be sued unless he or she knowingly acted unsafely. So if you know what you're doing, don't hesitate to help.

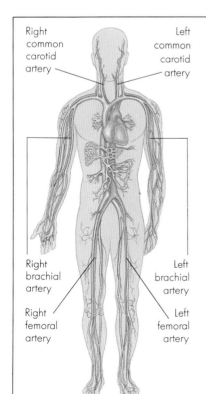

Right common carotid artery

Left common carotid artery

Right brachial artery

Left brachial artery

Right femoral artery

Left femoral artery

Pressure Points

The main pressure points are along the neck, on the upper arm, and the upper inside of the thighs. These are the *carotid* (kuh·RAHT·uhd), *brachial* (BRAY·kee·uhl), and *femoral* (FEM·uh·ruhl) arteries shown in the drawing. If direct pressure does not stop the bleeding, push on one of these pressure points until you feel the bone. Keep applying direct pressure to the wound as well. Slowly take your hand off the pressure point. If the bleeding has not stopped, apply pressure there again.

Learning from Drawings

Pressure on the arteries shown here can help stop severe bleeding. Why do you think that pressure here works?

First Aid for Poisoning

Many substances in our homes, such as cleaning fluids and soaps, should never be taken into the body. But sometimes they are, especially by infants and young children. To help someone who has swallowed a poison, follow these steps.

1. **Call the 24-hour poison control center or a doctor.** The number for the center usually appears on the inside front cover of the telephone book. Be prepared to give the victim's age and weight and where you are. Take the container that held the substance to the phone with you if possible. If you can, say how much the person swallowed and when. Ask for instructions and do what you are told.

2. **If you are advised by the poison control center to do so, call the 911 emergency telephone number and calmly explain the situation.** Soon an ambulance team will arrive to take over. While you wait for them, check to see that the victim is breathing properly. You may need to clear the person's airway. If the person is cold, put some kind of covering over him or her.

3. **Save the container of the poisonous substance you think the person swallowed.** Show it to the medical team when they arrive, and tell them all you know about what happened.

4. **Remove any extra bits of the poison from around the person's mouth.** Wrap a clean, damp cloth around your finger and wipe the person's mouth, lips, and tongue.

Teen Issue

Dumb Games

Some people think that drinking alcohol is "cool." Some are even foolish enough to have drinking contests to see who can drink the most in the shortest time. Such contests can result in alcohol poisoning. This is very serious and can lead to death. If you are ever around such a contest, warn the people of the dangers. If you suspect alcohol poisoning in someone you are with, get medical help immediately.

Check Your Understanding

Conclusion   When accidents occur, you must sometimes aid the victim before medical help can arrive. By staying calm and acting quickly and carefully, you can prevent serious injury and maybe save a life.

1. **Vocabulary** Write an original sentence defining *first aid.*

2. **Recall** List the four basic steps of first aid.

3. **Recall** What are the steps in rescue breathing for an adult or older child?

4. **Recall** Name three ways to stop severe bleeding.

5. **Interpret** You are baby-sitting, and you find the child unconscious in the kitchen alongside an open can of cleanser. What has probably happened? What should you do?

LESSON 6

Handling Common Emergencies

Words to Know
fainting
sprain
bruise
fracture
first-degree burn
second-degree burn
third-degree burn

This lesson contains a number of valuable facts and tips. Once you have studied them, you will be able to

- tell how to help someone who has fainted.
- explain what to do for a nosebleed.
- tell how to help someone who has a sprain, bruise, or broken bone.
- state what kind of first aid a person can use for an insect bite or sting.
- tell how to help someone who has a burn.

Fainting

Fainting is *a temporary loss of consciousness.* It occurs when the blood supply to the brain is cut off or reduced for a short time. Someone can faint while standing up or sitting down.

If you are around someone who faints, you can help with simple but valuable first aid. First, do not try to lift the person. Leave him or her lying down and raise the legs 8 to 12 inches. Loosen any tight clothing such as a buttoned collar. Check to see that the person is breathing in normal, even breaths. Keep the airway open.

Next, sponge the person's face and forehead with cool water. Never pour water over the face — the person could choke. If the person does not regain consciousness, get medical help.

Nosebleeds

Nosebleeds usually occur without warning. They can be caused by an injury, by being in a very dry place for a long time, or even by a cold. Nosebleeds are often not serious, but they should be stopped. Stopping a nosebleed is usually not difficult. You can help a person with a nosebleed.

Feeling Faint?

If someone you are with begins to feel faint, have the person sit down and place the head between the knees. Applying a cool wet rag or sponge to the back of the neck and face can also help keep the person from fainting.

Lesson 6: Handling Common Emergencies   **387**

More About

For more information on **sprains** *and* **broken bones**, *see Chapter 7.*

Learning from Photographs
The cold pack and the tight bandage are two steps that can be taken to help someone with a common injury. What should a person with an injury do if pain and swelling continue?

- Keep the person quiet. Make sure the person does not blow his or her nose.

- Have the person sit down and lean slightly forward. His or her head should be low. Then pinch the nose firmly for about 5 minutes. You can also hold a cold cloth to the person's nose while pinching it.

If these measures do not stop the bleeding, get medical help.

Sprains and Bruises

A **sprain** results when *a joint is suddenly and violently stretched.* The sprained part is usually painful and may become swollen.

The injured person should not use the sprained part. If an ankle is sprained, he or she should not walk on it. To prevent or reduce swelling, raise the sprained part and apply cold packs to the area. You can make a cold pack by wrapping ice in a towel. Do not apply ice or heat directly; either of these steps can *cause* swelling. Apply the cold pack for 20 or 30 minutes each hour for the first 24 hours.

If the pain and swelling do not stop, the person should see a doctor.

A **bruise** results from *a blow on a part of the body.* It is a very common injury and is usually not serious. Bruises can be painful, but a cold pack can help keep this pain at a minimum. It will also help to lessen the swelling.

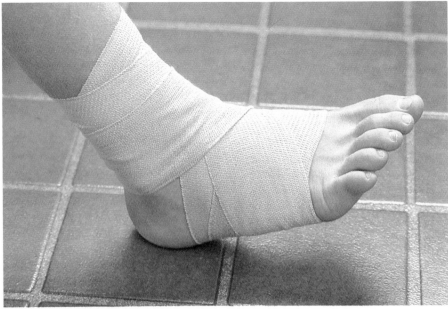

Broken Bones

People often break bones from falling or when playing contact sports. *A break in a bone*, called a **fracture,** is usually painful, more painful than a sprain. If someone around you gets hurt and you suspect a broken bone, tell the person not to move the injured part. Put a cold pack on the possible break and get medical help. If a leg is broken, it is best to have that help come to the person. If an arm is broken, the victim can travel to a doctor's office or clinic, but should be sure not to move the arm.

It is very important that you or the victim not try to straighten the broken bone. Doing so might force the broken bone to break through the skin. Leave the setting of the bone to a doctor.

Avoid Broken Bones
Broken bones frequently occur among people playing unsupervised sports after school or during the summer. Taking some safety precautions, such as wearing padding during a game of tackle football, can help prevent broken bones.

Insect Bites and Stings

Sometimes an insect hiding in a park or garden or in a corner that is being cleaned will bite a person. Such bites are usually not serious. They cause pain and swelling at the site of the bite, but nothing worse. To hold the swelling down, you can take these steps.

First Aid for Insect Bites and Stings

- Wash the bitten area with soap and water.
- Apply a cold wet cloth to the area.
- Apply an over-the-counter lotion for such bites.
- Cover the spot with a bandage or clean dressing.

Treating a bee or wasp sting is a bit more difficult than treating a common insect bite. When a bee stings you, it leaves its stinger in your skin along with an attached poison sac. You should not simply remove the stinger with tweezers. Doing so would force more poison from the poison sac into your skin. Instead, scrape against the stinger with your fingernail or the edge of a piece of cardboard. Doing this should push the poison sac free. Then wash the sting area with soap and water and apply a cold pack.

Some people have an *allergy* to insect bites or stings. They react to bites or stings strongly. They may develop a rash. They may show some of the signs of shock, becoming pale, sweaty, and faint. Breathing will be shallow. If this occurs, get medical help right away. This kind of reaction happens with bee or wasp stings more than with insect bites.

Learning from Photographs
Bees are common in spring and summer. Why are bee stings more complicated than insect bites?

There's Something in My Eye

You have probably felt an eyelash or particle of dirt drop or float into your eye. If this occurs, rubbing your eye is not the answer. Rubbing can scratch the eyeball. Instead, lift the upper lid over the lower lid and allow the eyelashes to brush the speck off the inside of the lid. Blink a few times and let the eye move the particle out.

If the tears do not wash the object out of the eye and if these steps do not work, get medical help.

DID **YOU** KNOW?

Don't Butter That Burn!
Do not use butter on a burn. Many people think that butter is a proper treatment, but they are wrong.

Burns

Burns are classified by the extent of damage done to the skin. The type of first aid you should give to a burn victim depends on the type of burn the person has. Never put ice on any burn.

A **first-degree burn** is *a burn in which only the outer layer of the skin is burned and turns red.* This type includes minor sunburn and burns resulting from hot water or touching hot objects. To treat first-degree burns, submerge the burned area in cold water to lower the skin temperature. Then wrap the burn loosely in a clean, dry dressing such as gauze.

A **second-degree burn** is *a more serious burn in which the burned area blisters.* Severe sunburn and scalding can be second-degree

Learning from Photographs
A sunburn is a first-degree burn. What kind of treatment is best for such a burn?

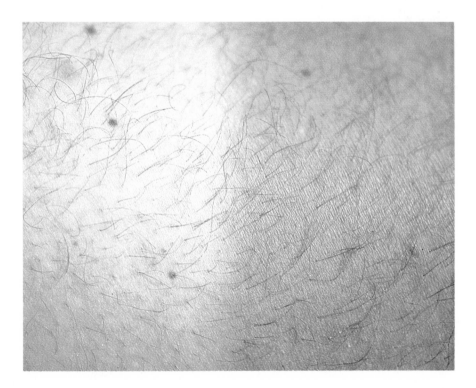

burns that lead to blistering or peeling. You can treat second-degree burns in this way.

1. Follow the procedure for first-degree burns. Submerge the burned area in cold water and wrap in a clean, dry dressing.

2. Do not pop blisters or peel any loose skin.

3. If possible, elevate the burned area.

A **third-degree burn** is *a very serious burn in which deeper layers of the skin and nerve endings are damaged.* The skin looks white and charred. Third-degree burns can result from exposure to fire or electricity. Burning clothing often causes these very serious burns also. A person with a third-degree burn needs medical help. Get him or her to an emergency room if possible. There are some other things you should be aware of with third-degree burns.

DO	DON'T
● cover the burned area with a clean dressing.	● remove burned clothing, because doing so can further damage burned skin.
● elevate the feet and arms.	
● have the person drink small amounts of fluid if he or she is conscious.	● apply cold water or ice to the burn, as this can lead to shock.

Check Your Understanding

Conclusion You can handle many common emergencies that arise by using simple first-aid techniques. Acting quickly, calmly, and carefully, you can solve some of these problems without the need for medical help. If the problem continues, or in the case of severe problems such as a broken bone or third-degree burn, the victim must have medical help.

1. **Vocabulary** What causes damage to the bone, a *sprain*, a *bruise*, or a *fracture*?

2. **Recall** How can you revive someone who has fainted?

3. **Recall** How do you stop a nosebleed?

4. **Recall** How do you remove an object from the eye?

5. **Recall** What is very dangerous about insect bites or stings for some people?

6. **Classify** One of your parents has a burn from being scalded by boiling water in the kitchen. A blister has developed on the arm. What kind of burn might it be? What would you do?

DID **YOU** KNOW?

Helping Burn Victims
To treat third-degree burns, doctors have in the past used skin from another part of the patient's body. They cut skin away and then put it in place over the burn in an operation called *grafting*. Doctors have now developed a new procedure. They remove a sheet of skin taken from another person, which has been kept in a skin bank. The skin is placed over the burned area to prevent infection. In the meantime, doctors remove some healthy skin cells from elsewhere on the patient's body. They grow these cells to produce more, until they finally have a sheet of new skin that can be grafted on.

First Aid for Choking and CPR

Words to Know
choking
abdominal thrusts
CPR (cardiopulmonary
    resuscitation)
carotid pulse

This lesson contains a number of valuable facts and tips. Once you have studied them, you will be able to

● describe what to do to help a choking person.

● explain when it is necessary to give CPR.

What Is Choking?

About 3,000 choking deaths occur each year in the United States. Luckily, death by choking can often be prevented.

Choking is *a condition that occurs when a person's airway becomes blocked.* When this happens, air cannot reach the lungs. If the object is not removed, the victim can die from lack of air.

There are several ways that you can recognize that someone is choking. The signal for choking that everyone knows is to grab the throat between the thumb and forefinger. Other signs are problems breathing or speaking, coughing, and turning reddish then bluish. Within seconds of showing these signs, a choking victim may faint.

Learning from Drawings
This is the universal sign of choking. What does it mean?

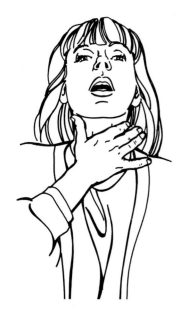

Some Basic First Aid for Choking

To help a choking victim, you need to remove the object blocking the airway. Because strong force is needed, practice the steps on a large doll, not on a person.

First Aid for Choking in Infants and Small Children

Two simple steps can help you save the life of a choking infant or child 1 to 8 years old. First try giving the child several blows with the heel of your hand between the shoulder blades. If that does not work, turn the child over on his or her back. Support the back of the neck

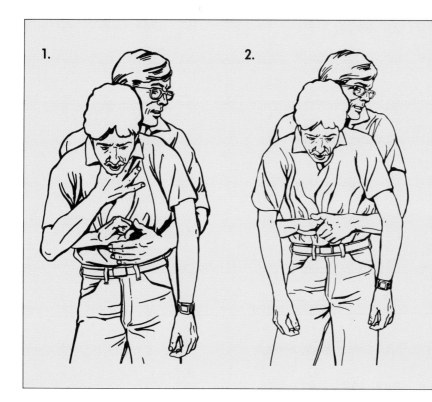

First Aid for Choking

1. Stand behind the victim, wrapping your arms around his or her chest. Put the thumb side of your wrist against the person's abdomen. Place your hand just above the navel.
2. Grab your fist with your other hand and press into the abdomen just above the navel with quick, upward thrusts until the person is no longer choking. Do not deliver the blows to the ribs, which could be broken. Once the object is dislodged, give rescue breathing if needed.

Learning from Drawings
The thrust should be delivered to the abdomen, but not the ribs. Why?

and shoulders with one of your hands. Press two fingers into the middle of the child's sternum. Repeat this action four times.

First Aid for Choking in Older Children and Adults

Ask the person, "Are you choking?" If you get no answer, move behind the person. You will then use the method called **abdominal thrusts.** This method uses *quick, upward pulls into the diaphragm to force out the substance blocking the airway.* The drawings on this page show what to do.

Learning from Drawings
To save yourself from choking, take this position. How can you *prevent* choking?

What to Do If You Are the Victim

If you are choking, alert someone around you to the emergency. Use the universal sign of choking.

If no one is around, you can use the steps just described on yourself. Simply make a fist and thrust it quickly into your upper abdomen to push free the object that is choking you.

You can avoid choking by not taking big bites of food and by chewing each bite thoroughly. Eat and drink slowly. Also, never talk or laugh with your mouth full. Finally, never go to sleep with chewing gum in your mouth.

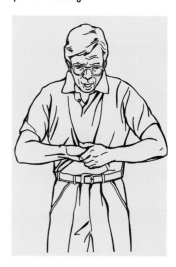

What Is CPR?

Learning from Photographs
The American Heart Association and the Red Cross give classes in CPR. Why can only people who are properly instructed do this procedure?

CPR, or **cardiopulmonary** (kard·ee·oh·PUL·muh·nehr·ee) **resuscitation** (ri·suhs·uh·TAY·shuhn), is *a first-aid procedure in which someone breathes for a victim while pushing on the heart.* You cannot do CPR unless you have taken and passed a special course that teaches it. CPR is dangerous. If done improperly, a person could crack one of the victim's ribs, puncture a lung, or cause internal bleeding.

How do you know when CPR is needed? If you see someone who has collapsed, you should ask if the person is all right. If you get no answer, the problem may be serious. If there are other people around, tell one of them to call 911, the emergency number. Then you need to see if CPR may be necessary. You begin by following the ABCs. Check the victim's airway, breathing, and circulation.

- **If the airway is blocked, it must be cleared.** Gently roll the person over on his or her back. Move the whole body at once, not the legs first and then the upper body. Do *not* move the body if there may be a neck injury.

- **If there is no breath, use rescue breathing.** Check the victim's **carotid** (kuh·RAHT·uhd) **pulse.** This is *the heartbeat you can feel on either side of the neck.* If there is a pulse, you can continue doing rescue breathing until the person revives.

- **If there is no pulse, the heart must be stimulated to work again.** This can only be done by someone who is trained in CPR. You can call to passersby to see if someone nearby has this skill. In the meantime, keep up the rescue breathing.

More About

The steps of CPR are shown in the Health Handbook.

More About — The steps of CPR are shown in the Health Handbook.

DID **YOU** KNOW?

Where Is the Stronger Pulse?
You check the carotid pulse rather than the wrist pulse because the carotid pulse is the stronger of the two.

Check Your Understanding

Conclusion Recognizing the signs of choking and acting quickly with the right first aid can save a life. In CPR, a trained person applies pressure to the victim's chest while giving breaths of air. You cannot give CPR unless you have been trained.

1. **Vocabulary** What is choking?
2. **Recall** What do you do to help a choking person?
3. **Recall** What does CPR stand for?
4. **Draw conclusions** You are at a recreational center. Suddenly an adult collapses. You think that CPR might be required, but you are not trained to perform it. What should you do?

Split-Second Decisions

When an emergency happens, the victim must rely on others for help. First aid — the treatment needed in an emergency — can provide that help. Acting right away can mean the difference between saving a life or not. In an emergency, you may feel that there is no time to think. But it is important to think clearly and act calmly.

Knowing What to Do

There are four basic steps of first aid.

- **Rescue the victim.** Get the victim out of any further danger. In doing so, you must be sure not to put yourself in danger.
- **Check breathing.** See if the victim is breathing. If not, try to revive him or her with rescue breathing.
- **Control bleeding.** If you see any heavy bleeding, you must try to stop it. You can apply pressure directly on the wound. Or you can cut off the blood supply to the wound by putting pressure on a main artery leading to it. Or you can raise the part of the body that is bleeding.
- **Get help.** You can call 911 for emergency medical help. You can also get help from another bystander. This would be a good choice if CPR is needed and you are not trained to give it.

Using the Skill

A good way to prepare yourself for handling an emergency is to think in advance about what you would do. Read the emergency situations that follow.

Case One

Lindsey is at the beach. She and her friend Terry begin to bodysurf. But when Lindsey comes out of the last wave, she doesn't see Terry. Moments later, Terry's body washes into the low water, face down.

Case Two

Gordon is standing at a bus stop with a group of people. Suddenly, a middle-aged man clutches his chest and falls to the ground. Gordon thinks the man is having a heart attack, but he is not trained in CPR.

Case Three

Marty and Jorge are walking home from school when they hear the screech of brakes and a crash. They turn to see a motorcyclist being thrown from his cycle onto the lawn. The car that struck the cycle has crashed into a telephone pole. The boys race to the cyclist, who is lying on his side, bleeding from the arm and leg. His head is at a funny angle.

Divide a separate sheet of paper into three columns. Label the columns "Lindsey," "Gordon," and "Marty and Jorge." Under the heading, write what you would do if you were the teen faced with this emergency.

Chapter 13 Review

Summary

- By thinking that safety is important and acting safely, you can prevent accidents. Not taking risks also helps prevent accidents.
- You can act safely at home, at school, on the road, and outdoors. Acting safely protects you.
- When injuries occur, you can often prevent serious problems by providing first aid.
- Many common problems do not need medical care. If they continue or are more serious, though, the victim needs medical help.
- You can save a choking victim by acting quickly to remove the object blocking the airway. A trained person can give CPR to save someone whose heart has stopped.

Reviewing Vocabulary and Concepts

On a separate sheet of paper, write the numbers 1–13. After each number, write the term from the list on the right that best completes each statement.

Lesson 1

1. Feeling that _____ is important and acting safely are as important as knowing the rules of safety.
2. An important way of not taking chances is to resist _____ because the influence of the group can lead you to do harmful things.
3. You can _____ the accident chain by changing the situation, changing the unsafe habit, or changing the unsafe action.

Lesson 2

4. Wiping up spills and picking up stray objects from the floor or stairs are two ways to prevent _____ .
5. _____ is a serious hazard at home, especially for young children.
6. You can protect your family from possible injury from fire by having a _____ installed to sound a warning.
7. Someone who has been raped can get medical help and _____ from a rape treatment center.

Lesson 3

8. The most important safety equipment for a bike rider is a hard-shell _____ .
9. Skateboarders can protect themselves from injury by wearing _____ clothing.
10. Something that all car passengers can do to ensure their own safety is to fasten their _____ .

break
buddy
counseling
falls
helmet
hypothermia
peer pressure
poisoning
protective
safety
safety belts
smoke alarm
swim

Lesson 4

11. Candace and Karin are going swimming together. This is an example of the _____ system.

12. Hikers and campers need to dress warmly to prevent _____ , which is the lowering of body temperature.

13. Anyone who plans on diving or boating should first learn to _____ .

Write the numbers 14–22 on your paper. After each number, write the letter of the word or phrase in Column B that best matches the phrase in Column A.

Column A

Lesson 5

14. Emergency help to someone who is injured
15. Used in controlling bleeding
16. Who to call if you see a fallen child next to an open bottle of pills

Lesson 6

17. The direction to move the head of someone with a nosebleed
18. A treatment for an insect bite or sting
19. A treatment for sunburn

Lesson 7

20. Grabbing the throat with thumbs and forefinger is the sign of
21. The technique for saving a choking victim
22. The rescue method needed by someone who has no pulse and is not breathing

Column B

a. poison control center
b. forward
c. choking
d. first aid
e. abdominal thrusts
f. pressure points
g. wash the area
h. CPR
i. cool water

Thinking Critically About the Facts

Write your answers to the following questions on a separate sheet of paper.

23. Synthesize Pedro is going to the beach with a group of friends, but he is anxious because they swim better than he does. What two guidelines of safety does Pedro need to follow?

24. Analyze Shawn hitchhiked a ride to see a movie at the shopping center. Was this safe? Explain your answer.

25. Interpret Natasha suffered an insect bite. Now she is turning pale and sweating and feeling faint. What is probably happening to her? What does she need?

26. Sequence Renumber the following steps to have the correct procedure for helping a choking victim. (1) Make a fist with one hand and place it above the person's navel, then grab your fist with your other hand. (2) Wrap your arms around the person's chest. (3) Give a quick thrust to the stomach with your hands. (4) Stand behind the person.

Applying the Facts

27. How would you "hazardproof" one room of your home? Write a list of things you could do to make sure that room was hazard free.

28. Prepare a fire-escape plan for your house or apartment. Draw a diagram that shows two escape routes from each room.

29. Go to your school or public library and find a book on health and first aid. Write down what supplies the book suggests each home should have to handle first-aid emergencies. Put a check next to the supplies your family has.

Consumer and Public Health

CHAPTER WARM-UP

Chapter Study Goals

After you have read this chapter, you will be able to

- identify the benefits of being a wise consumer.
- identify the rights of consumers.
- explain how to comparison shop.
- identify what influences your consumer choices.
- describe the dangers of fake health products.
- explain how to solve a consumer problem.
- describe the agencies that help protect consumers and promote public health.
- explain how to choose health services.

Be on the lookout for information in the chapter that will help you reach these goals.

Getting Started

Every day you make decisions that affect your health. Many of these decisions involve products or services that you buy and use.

You do not make these decisions alone. You have the help of a parent. You have the influence of your friends. You also feel the influence of ads that try to convince you to choose one brand over another. By reading this chapter, you will have some idea of how to make those choices healthy ones.

Study Tip

Make a list of all the headings in this chapter. This list will tell you about the main ideas of the chapter even before you read the text.

Words to Know
consumer
goods
services

Building Healthy Consumer Habits

This lesson contains a number of valuable facts and tips. Once you have studied them, you will be able to

- name some of the benefits of being a wise consumer.
- list the consumer's basic rights.
- name government groups that help consumers.

DID **YOU** KNOW?

Cold Cash
In a recent year, Americans spent over $1.2 billion on medicine to fight the common cold.

Just the Facts . . .
This textbook has many useful tips on how to buy such items as sunglasses, running shoes, contact lenses, and many other products. Take notes as you read. They may come in handy.

Where Does Your Money Go?

Who is a consumer? You are. All together, you and your friends and all other teens buy millions of dollars worth of products. A **consumer** (kuhn·SOO·mer) is *anybody who purchases goods or services.* Some of the things you buy, such as tapes, food, clothes, are **goods.** These are *products that are made and purchased to satisfy someone's wants.* You also buy services. You may pay to hear a concert or to have someone cut your hair. **Services** are *activities that are purchased to satisfy someone's wants.*

You are also a health consumer. The health goods you use may include cough drops, shampoos, and skin creams. If you join a swim club or visit a doctor, you are buying health services.

Some of the goods and services you buy are not as clearly related to your health, but they still affect it. Sunglasses are an example. You may think of sunglasses as a product you buy for their looks. But sunglasses are a health product. Some may protect your eyes from the sun's harmful ultraviolet rays, and others may not. To make healthy consumer decisions, you need to know which of these choices is better for your health. You can get information from many sources to help you learn the facts about sunglasses or other health products.

Being a consumer also means building your consumer skills. These help you choose health products and services wisely.

Learning from Photographs
When you buy grooming products, you are making health decisions. Can you think of other consumer decisions that affect your health?

Being a wise consumer means . . .

- using your money wisely to get the most out of what you spend.
- buying useful goods and services—ones that will help you maintain a high level of health.
- buying safe goods and services and staying away from those that will harm you.
- knowing what to do if you have a consumer problem.

Look at what happened to Margo. She bought a cream to help her get rid of acne but then got a rash when she used it. Was Margo a wise consumer? Margo knew that she was allergic to an ingredient in some face creams. She should have looked on the label for that ingredient. When she did not, she was not using good consumer skills. If she *had* looked, she might not have bought the cream. She would have saved herself some money—and spared herself the rash!

Why Be a Wise Consumer?

Being a wise consumer benefits you in four ways.

- **You can promote and protect your health.** When you purchase useful goods, you can improve your health. When you buy safe products, you lessen your risk of harm.
- **You can save time and money.** By shopping carefully, you can be sure that what you buy works for you. That means you won't

Don't Be Rash
Makers of cosmetics are required by law to list the ingredients on their packages. If you do have any allergies, you should always read these packages carefully. Some cosmetics are *hypoallergenic* (hy·poh·al·er·JEN·ik). That means they are made just for people who have sensitive skin.

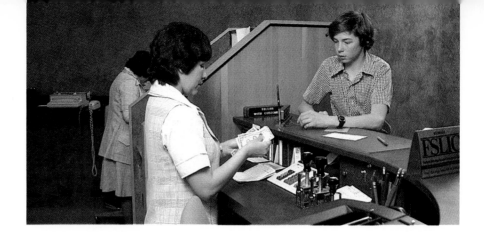

Learning from Photographs
This teen is putting money he saved in the bank. How can being a wise consumer help you save money?

waste your money on products that don't work, as Margo did. It can also mean that you won't have to spend more money later trying to fix a problem caused by an unwise purchase. Margo may now have to buy some medicine to clear up the rash.

- **You can build your self-confidence.** As you use your consumer skills well, you become more sure of yourself. This helps build your self-esteem. It can carry over to other areas of your life as well.

- **You protect your rights.** Each of us has certain rights as a consumer. Many groups work with consumers who have problems. You can turn to them for help and advice when you have a problem. But the best defender of your rights is you.

The Rights of Consumers

What are your consumer rights? Where do they come from? When John F. Kennedy was president, he stated that consumers have four basic rights. Since then, presidents Richard Nixon and Gerald Ford have added to the list.

- **The right to safety.** You have the right to purchase goods and services that will not harm you.

- **The right to choose.** You have the right to select from many goods and services at competitive prices.

- **The right to be informed.** You have the right to truthful information about goods and services.

- **The right to be heard.** You have the right to join in the making of laws about consumers.

- **The right to have problems corrected.** You have the right to complain about a supplier of goods or services when you have not been treated fairly. You also have the right for your problem to be solved.

- **The right to consumer education.** You have the right to learn the skills to help you make wise choices.

Teen Issue

Why Bother?

It may seem that being a wise consumer takes a lot of time. You need to compare brands and shop around at different stores. Why bother? It's your choice, really. But if you're like most people, you don't have an endless supply of money. You want to get the most out of the money you do have. *That's* why it's a good idea to shop around. It helps you get more for your money.

More About

For more on how to solve consumer problems, see Lesson 4.

Some Government Agencies	
Agency	**What It Does**
Consumer Product Safety Commission	Makes sure that products are safe Can order unsafe products taken off the market
Consumer Information Center	Distributes booklets published by other government agencies on consumer matters
Food and Drug Administration	Makes sure that food, drugs, and cosmetics are safe and pure Decides which medicines need prescriptions, and controls ads for them
Food Safety and Quality Service	Makes sure that meat and poultry are clean, safe, and correctly labeled
Federal Trade Commission	Makes sure that ads are not unfair, false, or misleading

Governments at all levels have agencies to protect these rights. Many city governments have a Consumer Affairs Office that has the job of protecting consumers. States have these offices, too. The national government includes a number of agencies that help consumers. Many do this work by preventing problems from happening. They make sure that products are safe. The chart on this page lists the main agencies of the federal government and their major concerns.

What happens if a consumer right is violated? Suppose a business sells you an unsafe product or does not fully inform you of what a

DID **YOU** KNOW?

Patient Rights
The American Hospital Association has listed the rights that hospital patients have. They include the right

- to good and considerate care.
- to have information about what treatments are being used.
- to refuse treatment.
- to privacy.
- to have records kept confidential.
- to have all costs explained.

Learning from Photographs
Being informed is one of your consumer rights. How might being informed help this teen make healthy food choices?

service might do to you. You have a chance to use the consumer laws to correct this problem.

Of course, consumer rights have another side. You also have consumer responsibilities. One of them is to exercise your rights. That starts with your right to consumer education. The educated consumer is the best-protected consumer.

Teen Issue

Shoplifting

One consumer responsibility is to pay for goods. Taking something out of a store without paying for it is a crime. Stealing is dangerous. A teen who is caught shoplifting can be put in jail. The arrest will stay on that person's record for life. Stealing is unfair to the store owner. And it raises prices for everybody—the store owner has to raise prices to cover the cost of a security system and of the lost merchandise.

Check Your Understanding

Conclusion   You are a consumer of health products and services. You can learn to be a wise consumer to get the most out of your money and to make yourself healthier. You have rights as a consumer that protect you. But the best protection is to be a wise consumer.

1. **Vocabulary** Which of the following health items are goods and which are services? *fast-food lunch, health magazine, running shoes, haircut, toothbrush, tooth cleaning, cough syrup, meeting with a family counselor*

2. **Recall** Name two benefits of being a wise consumer.

3. **Recall** Name three consumer rights.

4. **Recall** Name two agencies of the federal government that help consumers and explain what each does.

5. **Draw conclusions** Some people believe that the right to be an informed consumer is the most important right of all. Why would that be so?

What Influences Your Choices?

Words to Know
comparison shopping
warranty
discount stores
coupons
generic products
tradition
advertising
testimonial

This lesson contains a number of valuable facts and tips. Once you have studied them, you will be able to

- tell how to shop for a good.
- tell how to shop for a service.
- tell what influences you to buy the goods and services you buy.

Shopping Around

Roy, standing in a store that sells eyeglasses, is trying to choose frames. He is surrounded by hundreds of different styles. He sees metal frames and plastic frames, big and small ones, and round, square, and oval frames. His friend Lee says he should buy red ones. His mother told him to spend no more than the money she gave him. The salesperson says, "It's up to you." How can Roy decide?

Often, like Roy, you will need to choose from among more than one product or service that does the job. Getting information will help you choose. You can get some information by talking to family or friends. They can tell you how they like a certain store or a doctor. You can read books or magazines, too. They can tell you what to look for in a product or service and what questions to ask. Some magazines even publish ratings that say whether one product or service outperforms another.

Learning from Photographs
This teen is comparing prices in catalogs. What are other ways of getting information on products or services?

Shopping for Goods

This method of *judging the benefits of different goods or services* is called **comparison** (kuhm·PEHR·uh·suhn) **shopping.** It is a great way of getting the best value for your money. You can compare different products by looking at the following things.

Unit Pricing

One way to compare prices is to use unit pricing. Supermarkets have labels on the shelves showing how much each product costs by one unit of weight. Unit prices for items like tissues are given by a certain count—say, 100 tissues. With unit prices, you can compare the cost for two items that come in different sized packages. To calculate unit price, divide the price of the package by the number of units in the package.

Comparison Shopping

Compare products on more than price. Look at weight, freshness, quality, and warranties. Compare stores, too. What are their return policies? How helpful are the salespeople?

File It Away

Keep all the warranties you get in one spot so you can have them handy if a problem happens. You may need to keep the original packaging that a product came in, too. Read each warranty before you put it away.

By taking each of these factors into account, you can reach a decision. You can find out what product has the features you want and offers the best quality for the money.

Factors in Comparing Goods

- **Price.** Cost is always an important factor in making a purchase. Roy's mother told him how much he could spend on his glasses. He had to look for frames in that price range.

- **Features.** What a product includes is important. Roy has a few features to consider. Some lenses are clear and some are tinted. Some are coated to protect against breaking and scratching, but others are not. Some frames look better on his face than others do.

- **Quality.** Quality includes how well a product is made, how well it performs its job, and how long it will last. With health products, you don't always know enough to judge quality. In that case, ask for advice from someone whose job is to provide health care.

- **Convenience** (kuhn·VEEN·yuhns). Many purchases are made because one store or another is more convenient. Roy may go to the eyeglasses store that is nearest his home. Or he may go shopping at a store that he can easily reach by bus or that makes glasses in one hour.

- **Warranties.** The maker of a product may provide *a written promise to handle repairs if the product does not work.* This promise is a **warranty** (WAWR·uhnt·ee). Warranties usually last for a certain period of time after the purchase. This period might be 90 days or it might be a year. Some warranties cover the cost of new parts. Others include the cost of labor to do the fixing. Laws require stores to keep warranties on hand so that any consumer who is interested in a product can see them.

Shopping for Services

You can use four of the same factors to shop for services. Say Roy still needed to have his eyes tested. He could go to an *ophthalmologist* (ahf·thuh·MAHL·uh·juhst), a medical doctor who treats eyes. Or he could go to the glasses store, which has an *optometrist* (ahp·TAHM·uh·truhst), a health care worker who treats eyes, but is not a medical doctor. Which should he do?

- **Price.** Roy can call ahead to find out the cost of the exam.

- **Features.** He needs to find out what each exam includes. The optometrist at the store will check only his vision. The ophthalmologist will also check his eyes for certain diseases.

Learning from Photographs
This teen is trying on frames for new glasses. He learned he needed glasses when he used a health service—an eye exam. If you were shopping for a health service, what would you look for?

Guaranteed!
Some products come with money-back guarantees. If you are not happy with the product, you can return it. If a product you may buy has this kind of guarantee, find out all the details.

- How soon must you return it?
- What shape must the product be in?
- How do you have to show that you were not happy with it?

- **Quality.** Roy needs to make sure that both workers are licensed to give eye exams. He could also ask family, friends, or neighbors if they have been to either the store or the doctor. He could ask how happy they are with the service they got.

- **Convenience.** Roy needs to think about whether the store or the doctor is easier to get to and which has better hours for him.

Shopping for Price

Price is not the only thing to consider when shopping. But it sure is an important thing! Wise shoppers know there are ways to save money.

One way is to shop at **discount stores.** These are *stores that offer few services but have lower prices.* Most discount stores have fewer salespeople than full-price stores. They may look less fancy than a full-price store, too. Many shoppers find these to be small things to give up for the benefit of lower prices.

You can save money on many goods by using **coupons** (KOO·pahns). These *slips of paper offer savings on certain brands of goods.* Coupons can be used to buy many food products and over-the-counter medicines.

Another way to save is to buy **generic** (juh·NEHR·ik) **products.** These are *goods sold in plain packages and at lower prices than brand name goods.* Many foods are sold this way and many prescription drugs are as well. Buying a generic medicine saves money over buying a brand name drug.

Go Generic
Whenever you get a prescription from a doctor, ask if you can substitute a generic medicine. If the doctor allows it, make sure that the pharmacy gives you the generic drug.

Lesson 2: What Influences Your Choices? **407**

What Influences You to Buy?

Your consumer decisions are yours alone. *You* must decide which goods or service you want. But many factors influence you. Those influences include *tradition, advertising, peers,* and *salespeople.*

Tradition

Tradition (truh·DISH·uhn) is *the usual way of doing things.* Many consumer decisions are based on tradition. Your doctor, for instance, may be your parents' doctor. And your food choices are strongly influenced by the kind of food your family buys and eats.

Advertising

The strongest influence on your consumer choices is **advertising.** This is *sending out messages (or ads) meant to interest consumers in buying goods and services.* Billions of dollars are spent on ads, whether on radio, in magazines, or on billboards. They try to convince you that a product or service will make you healthier, happier, and more popular.

Ads give information. They tell you the name of a product, how much it costs, and where to buy it. But ads also try to influence you. A wise consumer uses ads to be informed, but sees through the ways that ads try to influence.

DID **YOU** KNOW?

It Ads Up
American companies spend over $100 billion each year on advertising.

DID **YOU** KNOW?

How Honest Are Testimonials?
Laws that cover ads say that a famous person must actually *use* a product before he or she can give a testimonial. But the law does not require that the person think the product is good. Companies pay these people thousands of dollars to say their products are good. A star may not really believe it, though.

Three Common Techniques Used in Ads

- **Testimonials.** As you may know, a **testimonial** (tes·tuh·MOH·nee·uhl) is *a famous person recommending a good or service.* The maker of the product hopes that you will buy a shampoo because a famous star tells you to. But ask yourself, is this star an expert on shampoo? Read what the *real* experts say before you buy.

- **Scientific test.** Ads for many over-the-counter drugs present the results of what seem to be scientific tests. They "prove" that the product is better than the rest. Such "tests" are hard to judge. Before you decide which product to buy, compare labels and talk to a druggist or your doctor.

- **Lifestyle.** Lifestyle ads say nothing about the good or service itself. They picture healthy, active people having fun and then show the product being promoted. They try to give you the idea that the product is the reason for the fun. Put aside the ad's message and decide for yourself. Will this product make you healthier?

Peers

Your friends and other teens can strongly influence your consumer decisions. You want to do things your friends are doing. This can mean wearing the latest styles or joining in their activities. But your health is affected by *your* health decisions—not anyone else's. If the group pressures you to do something that is not good for your health, you need to make your own decision.

Salespeople

Salespeople can give you good information about how a product works or what its features are. Sometimes, though, they pressure buyers. They may push for a certain brand. Or they may try to make you decide. Resist sales pressure in two ways.

- **Take as much time as you want to.** Don't be rushed into a decision. If you need time to think, ask the salesperson to leave you alone.
- **Ask questions.** If the salesperson is pushing one brand over another, ask about it. The answers may be useful. Or the salesperson may get tired of your questions and leave you alone.

Learning from Photographs
Salespeople may put pressure on you to make a purchase. How can you benefit from talking to a salesperson?

It's Up to You!
The key to resisting sales pressure is to remember that you are buying something for *you*, not the salesperson. It is your money, and you are the one who will have to live with your decision. Make sure purchases satisfy you, and not someone else.

Check Your Understanding

Conclusion Making a decision to purchase a good or service can be difficult. There are many goods and services to choose from and powerful influences, including your friends and ads, pushing and pulling you in different directions. You can make the best choices if you think carefully about what *you* want in a good or service.

1. **Vocabulary** Is a warranty the same thing as a guarantee? Explain.
2. **Recall** What are three factors you can use when shopping for a product?
3. **Recall** What ways can you shop to find the lowest possible price for a product?
4. **Recall** Name two factors you can use when shopping for a service.
5. **Recall** What are two influences on your consumer decisions?
6. **Interpret** Suppose you saw a commercial in which your favorite actor said that a certain cold remedy worked well. Is this testimonial useful? What might convince you more?

Teen Health
BULLETIN BOARD

CAREERS

Wanted:

Consumer Safety Officer

Specifics:

Work for Food and Drug Administration as an inspector of foods, drugs, and cosmetics to make sure that federal safety rules are being followed; suggest action to remedy problems.

Qualifications:

Must be detail-oriented and good at problem solving. Should be a good communicator. Must be willing to travel.

Preparation:

A college degree or three years of experience required for PACE exam. Training available at colleges or through the FDA.

Contact:

Food and Drug Administration
200 C Street, SW
Washington, DC 20204

HEALTH IN THE NEWS

Health Care Isn't Just Doctors Anymore

People can now choose from a wide variety of health-care options.

- **Adolescent health centers.** These clinics are usually in cities. They are formed specifically to provide health care to teens.

- **Holistic health centers.** These centers think of a person's total health. They develop a health plan that a person can follow to improve his or her overall health.

- **Neighborhood health centers.** These centers are located in neighborhoods or local areas, often to help people of one ethnic or social group.

- **Birthing centers.** These centers offer a more homelike atmosphere than hospitals for women who are going to have a baby.

- **Hospices.** These are centers that try to provide helpful, kind care for people who are dying of some disease.

Health care doesn't just come in doctor's offices or hospitals anymore.

TEEN Q & A

Q: I want to get a birthday present for a friend, but I don't have any money. What can I do?

A: The best idea, if you're strapped for cash, is to make a gift. Look through hobby or craft magazines for ideas. If you can cook, you could bake your friend a healthy loaf of bread. If you're a good artist, draw a picture. Or you and some other friends could perform a singing birthday message. You could also make a card. Your friend might keep the card forever because it is handmade. Most important is your attitude. Too many people make the mistake of thinking that the more money you spend, the more you like someone. It just isn't so.

HEALTH IN THE NEWS

What Do Advertisers Know About You?

If you watch television, you see ads every day. Did you know that advertisers also watch *you*? They care a lot about what you think and what you like. They know that American teenagers spend about $50 billion a year on the products they advertise. They watch you to find out how best to spend their money on ads for such products as shampoo, blue jeans, sunglasses, and soft drinks.

Lifestyle

Join the Crowd!

Many teens are finding a new way to add a sense of community to their lives. And they are building their self-esteem and their skills at the same time. These teens join a health campaign being organized by one of the major health organizations. Such groups use the effort of staff members and volunteer workers to promote the news of good health and to raise money for research into a disease or condition. There are many of these groups.

American Cancer Society
American Diabetes Association
American Foundation for the Blind
American Heart Association
American Lung Association
American Red Cross
Arthritis Foundation
Cystic Fibrosis Foundation

Epilepsy Foundation of America
Leukemia Society of America
Multiple Sclerosis Foundation
Muscular Dystrophy Association
National Council on Alcoholism
National Foundation—March of Dimes
United Cerebral Palsy Association

All About Quackery

Words to Know
quack
quackery
arthritis
placebo effect

This lesson contains a number of valuable facts and tips. Once you have studied them, you will be able to

- tell what quackery is.
- talk about some types of quacks and explain how to spot them.

Let the Buyer Beware

A centuries-old saying is "let the buyer beware." This phrase means that consumers have to watch out for goods and services that do not do what sellers claim they will do. Most products, in fact, do work, and most sellers are honest. But some businesses make a living out of selling useless products. Part of being a wise consumer is knowing how to spot them—and avoid them.

What Is a Quack?

A **quack** is a fake, *someone who pretends to have medical skills but in fact has none.* Quacks sell worthless products and treatments for diseases and other health problems. They take advantage of people who are ill to make money. *The dishonest actions of a quack are* called **quackery** (KWAK·ree). An example of quackery is someone selling a miracle "cure" that is not real for a disease such as cancer or arthritis. Selling weight reduction programs that are not healthy is also quackery.

It is against the law to make false claims about drugs and cosmetics. But quacks still make millions of dollars a year by selling cures that are not cures. Whenever you hear a health or beauty claim that sounds too good to be true, watch out. It probably *is* too good to be true.

Common Quackery

Quacks are most often found pushing products or services aimed at losing weight, improving people's appearance, or curing deadly or painful diseases.

Learning from Photographs
Medicines in the past often did some good, but many claimed to cure more diseases than they really could. Are any fake medicines sold nowadays?

AYER'S SARSAPARILLA
The DEACON. "Land sakes 'Liza, the very sight of that bottle makes me feel like another man."
A COMPOUND CONCENTRATED EXTRACT—THE STRONGEST-BEST-CHEAPEST BLOOD MEDICINE

Learning from Photographs
Many quack products aim to help people lose weight. What are the two basics of healthy weight loss?

Diet Aids

Many Americans are overweight. They know that it would be healthy to lose weight, but feel that doing so is hard work. The best way to reduce weight is to eat fewer calories and to exercise, but this takes time. Some people want results right away. That is where quacks come in. They promise fast, easy results.

Special wraps, pills, or fad diets are among the kinds of quackery aimed at people trying to lose weight. Most simply do not work. How can you tell a quack? A good weight-loss plan should be based on the idea of eating fewer calories and burning up more calories with exercise. Anything else is likely to be a waste of money. If the quack diet is not a balanced diet, it could even be unhealthy. Before spending money on a weight-loss plan, talk to a doctor or to the school dietitian.

Beauty Products

Quacks take advantage of people's desire to look better. They sell creams and lotions that offer beautiful skin or lovely hair. They promise to cure acne. Certainly there are skin products that can help people with skin problems. But no product can keep anyone's skin young forever. If the claims for a product seem to be too good to be true, what is being sold is probably quackery.

Miracle Cures

Perhaps the saddest kind of quackery is the kind that preys on people who suffer from diseases. Many people have **arthritis** (ar·THRYT·uhs), which makes their joints stiff and painful. Others have cancer, which in some forms can cause death. These people are often looking for cures, or at least for relief from their pain.

Quacks sell these people products that give absolutely no help at all. Worse, someone taking a quack "cure" may delay getting help from a

DID **YOU** KNOW?

Quacks and Teens
Some experts estimate that the average teen may spend up to $80 a month on personal products. Quacks want a part of that money. They prey on teens' desire to look better and be more popular.

Quack Techniques
Quacks may claim that their goods are a "medical breakthrough." If they can't show a medical school or scientific journal that sponsored the research, don't believe it. Quacks may also say that the health-care system is suppressing the news about their miracle cure because they don't want people to get well. Don't buy that line.

doctor. Such people could lose the chance to take medicines that could really help them.

Sometimes a person's health may improve soon after taking the quack's medicine. If this occurs, it is often due to something called the **placebo** (pluh·SEE·boh) **effect.** This means that *the person improves for natural reasons and not because of the substance that the quack provides.* The person gets better simply because the body is fighting the disease, not because the so-called medicine is any good.

How to Spot a Quack

Quacks tend to work alone, not with major drug companies or clinics. They tend to sell their products through the mail or door-to-door, so they are harder to catch. Some advertise on cable television. They often ask for cash and will not accept credit cards or checks. That way they do not have to worry that people who are not satisfied will stop payment.

If you have a question about some product or a person selling something, take care before you buy. Ask an expert—a doctor, a person at a clinic, or even someone in your local or state government. Cities and states have consumer protection agencies that will be happy to hear your questions and may be able to provide you with some help. Whatever you do, look before you pay money.

DID **YOU** KNOW?

The Placebo Effect
Scientists use the placebo effect to test new drugs. They give the new drug being tested and a *placebo* to two groups of patients. The placebo is nothing but a sugar pill. The number of people who take the placebo and still get well is compared to the number of people who took the actual medicine and improved. That way, researchers can find out exactly how effective the medicine is.

Check Your Understanding

Conclusion   Some dishonest people and businesses sell products or services that are worthless or even harmful. By keeping a sharp eye out, and by asking for help when you are not sure about an advertised claim, you can protect yourself from quacks.

1. **Vocabulary** What is the difference between a quack and quackery?
2. **Recall** What three kinds of goods and services do quacks often sell?
3. **Recall** Who can you ask about an advertisement if you think the product is worthless?
4. **Analyze** Suppose you saw an ad proclaiming "Lose 20 pounds in 2 weeks! The method that doctors won't let you know about. Read Dr. Smith's special book *Losing Weight the Easy Way.* Send $11.95 today." Does this sound like quackery or a good diet? What makes you think so? How could you check?

Handling Consumer Problems

Words to Know
consumer advocates
small-claims court
second opinion
license
malpractice

This lesson contains a number of valuable facts and tips. Once you have studied them, you will be able to

● tell how to solve a problem with a product.

● name some groups you can go to for help with consumer problems.

● tell how to solve a problem with a health service.

When Problems Occur with Products

Even the wisest consumer has a problem with a purchase from time to time. It happens to everybody once in a while. A soap gives you a rash, or an electric appliance breaks down. What can you do if this happens?

You can usually go to the store where you bought the product to have the problem solved. You can also write to the maker to get either a replacement or your money back. Remember that most businesses depend on their customers being satisfied. They will want to solve your problem so that you will come back again.

Step One: Go to the Source

The first thing to do if a product does not work properly is to make sure that you used it correctly. Read the instructions to see if you followed them.

If the product still does not work, you have a reason to complain. The product may have a warranty. Read it to see what responsibility the maker accepts if something should go wrong. You may need to mail the product to a service center or take it someplace for repairs. Follow the directions on the warranty or follow the steps on the next page.

Winning Through Communication
The key to handling a consumer problem is to communicate well. If you get the facts together, stay calm, and act reasonable, you have the best chance of getting your result. Screams and threats convince no one.

Letter Perfect

A basic skill is the ability to write an effective letter. Here are some tips.

- Keep it short.
- Be firm but polite.
- Include all the facts—the name of the product, when you bought it, how much you paid, how you used it, and what happened.
- Include copies of receipts, but keep the originals for yourself.
- Include a request for action—don't leave it up to the company to figure out what you want.
- Include your address and phone number.

One more thing: Make it neat.

Learning from Photographs
Sometimes a product does not work properly. Before complaining, what do you think is the first thing to do?

Actions for Solving a Consumer Problem

- **Pull together the papers you will need to back up your complaint.** You should have a sales receipt proving that you bought the product. Write down what you did, what happened, and why you are not satisfied.
- **Decide what you think would be a fair solution to the problem.** You could ask the store to replace the product or to give you your money back. Sometimes you may want to ask to be repaid for damage that the product caused.
- **Go back to the store where you bought the product and ask to talk to someone who can handle your complaint.** Tell your story calmly, show your evidence, and offer your solution.

The person you talk to may agree to your solution. Or he or she may say that what you suggest cannot be done. Ask the person to explain. If you agree to this explanation, that is the end of your complaint. If you do not accept this answer, though, continue to make your claim. Ask to see a manager and explain your story again.

If you bought the product through the mail or cannot get back to the store where you bought it, you can use the mail. Write to the mail-order house you bought from or to the maker of the product. Follow the suggestions above to explain your problem and suggest your solution. Be sure to include a copy of the sales receipt with your letter to prove ownership. Keep a copy of your letter. If an answer does not come in two weeks, call the company or write a follow-up letter.

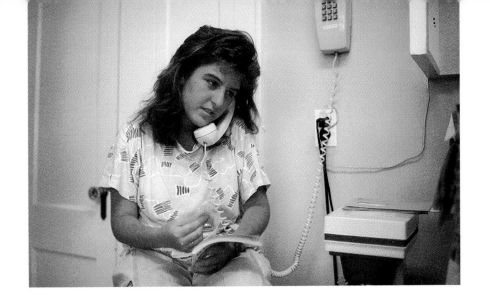

Step Two: Go for Help

The actions outlined in the first step should take care of most product problems. Sometimes, though, more action is required. Three different kinds of groups help consumers with problems if the first step does not work.

- **Special consumer groups.** *Some people or groups work just for the purpose of helping consumers with problems.* They are called **consumer advocates** (AD·vuh·kuhts). These include such groups as Consumers Union and local consumer groups. Another source of help is the consumer reporter for a local newspaper or television news show. Contact one of these people or groups and explain your problem. Store owners do not want people to hear news reports saying that customers are not happy. If a reporter calls a store manager about a problem, that manager will probably find a solution.

- **Business groups.** Businesses have formed many groups to help consumers with problems. Among the most useful are the Better Business Bureaus (BBB), which have offices in many cities across the country. You can go to one of these groups for help. They may contact the business to work out a solution.

- **Government agencies.** Governments of all levels have workers whose job is to make sure that consumers' rights are being upheld. They work in places like the Consumer Affairs Office.

You can find the addresses and phone numbers of any of these groups in your local library or in the telephone book. When you go to them for help, be prepared to tell the whole story. Describe your problem, how you tried to solve it yourself, and what happened. Many times one of these groups can get the problem solved. They know what to do and say.

DID **YOU** KNOW?

Help Is Out There
About 100 newspapers and 50 radio and television stations across the country help consumers with problems.

Tell It to the Judge

The way to win in small-claims court is to be persuasive. Remember that the judge will be deciding for you or for your opponent based on who presents the best argument. To be your persuasive best, keep these guidelines in mind.

• **Be organized.** Gather all the papers you need. Put them in the right order so you can refer to them if necessary.

• **Be prepared.** Know in advance what you will say. Make notes so you can refer to them as the hearing goes on. You could even act out the event. Have someone pretend to be the judge, and tell you how your argument sounds.

• **Be calm.** Stick to your facts and avoid name-calling or shouting matches. Loud or rude behavior persuades no one.

• **Be fair.** Accept the judge's decision, whatever it is.

Step Three: Take Legal Action

Sometimes both the first and second steps simply do not work. You try everything, but get no results. When that happens, you may want to consider going to court.

You could hire a lawyer and sue the company. The lawyer will charge a fee. This fee may be based on how much money is won from the company—if you win. You could ask for legal help from the legal aid society. The lawyers in these offices provide legal help for free or for a smaller fee than private lawyers charge.

You could also sue the company yourself in **small-claims court.** These *state courts handle cases with problems involving amounts under $3,000.* In small-claims court, you present your own case. So does the person or store you are suing. A judge hears both sides and decides who wins. To win, you must be well organized and persuasive.

What About Health Services?

Problems may arise with health services as well as with products. Some are solved simply by changing the person who provides health care. Someone who feels that a certain doctor does not spend enough time answering questions can change doctors.

Sometimes, though, the question is over the quality of the health care given. Someone may feel that a doctor did not identify an illness early enough. Or a patient may think that recommended surgery is not really needed.

The first step is to get a **second opinion.** This is *a statement from another doctor giving his or her view of what should be done.* This doctor may say that the first doctor made a mistake. Or the second doctor might say that the first doctor is correct.

If the surgery has already been done but the patient thinks it was not needed, he or she can take a second step. The patient can complain to the state's licensing board. These agencies give licenses to such health workers as doctors and dentists, among others. A **license** *gives a person the right to provide health care but holds that person to certain standards.* If the licensing board gets a complaint, it will look into the matter. It may find that the worker did something wrong. Or it may say that what the worker did was reasonable.

After taking these steps, the patient must decide whether to sue the doctor for **malpractice** (mal·PRAK·tuhs). This is *a failure to provide an acceptable degree of quality health care.* Someone making a decision to sue needs the help of a lawyer. If the case is taken to a trial, a judge or jury will decide the case.

Learning from Photographs
If you are not happy with the health care you are getting, you could talk to another health-care provider. What resources could you use to find one?

Check Your Understanding

Conclusion   Sometimes purchases go wrong. If that happens, you can take steps to solve the problem. First go to the company that sold you the good or service. If that does not work, try getting help from a consumer group, business group, or government agency. If you still are not satisfied, you can take legal action.

1. **Vocabulary** What is a consumer advocate?
2. **Recall** What are the three steps for resolving product problems?
3. **Recall** Where can you find the names and addresses of groups that help consumers?
4. **Recall** What government group can a consumer go to if he or she has a complaint about the care provided by a doctor?
5. **Analyze** Jeff bought a wrap to put around his sprained wrist. When he used it, though, he could not get the hooks to hold well enough to keep the bandage tight on his wrist. What should he do?

DID **YOU** KNOW?

Insurance for Doctors
Doctors buy a kind of insurance against malpractice suits. If they are sued and lose, then the insurance company pays the claim.

Choosing Health Services

Words to Know
family doctor
specialist
health maintenance
organization (HMO)
health insurance
Medicare
Medicaid

This lesson contains a number of valuable facts and tips. Once you have studied them, you will be able to

- name some of the different types of jobs health-care workers perform.
- tell how to shop for health services.
- define the term *health insurance.*
- tell what government agencies do to promote good health.

Who Provides Health Care?

Doctors are often thought of as the main providers of health care. They are important parts of the health-care system. But a wide range of people and groups can provide this care. Nurses, dentists, and other people who work in hospitals or clinics give health care. So do social workers who help people with their mental health. Health teachers who help explain how to build healthy habits are part of the health-care system, too.

Health care has three main goals.

- **Prevent health problems.** The work of a diet counselor helps you prevent weight problems. A teacher helps people learn how to live healthy lives.
- **Maintain good health.** Working with a physical fitness teacher or visiting a dentist regularly helps you stay healthy.
- **Treat problems that arise.** Doctors, nurses, clinics, social workers, and pharmacists all treat illness or other conditions.

Many health workers meet all these goals. The work of a doctor is a good example. A doctor prevents illness by giving you a vaccine. He or she maintains health by giving you a checkup. And the doctor treats you when you are sick.

You can receive health care in many different places. You can get many services in a doctor's office. Some health care takes place in clinics or in hospitals. You buy medicines from drugstores. Drug abuse treatment centers or halfway houses also provide important health care. Some treatment by nurses or therapists takes place in the home.

Learning from Photographs
You often need the services of a health-care worker, but can also act to contribute to your own health care. How is this teen doing so?

These different settings are grouped in one of two categories.

- **Inpatient care.** Someone who must stay overnight at a hospital or nursing home is an *inpatient.*
- **Outpatient care.** Someone who comes to a health-care unit, gets health care, and then leaves all in the same day is an *outpatient.*

Where you go depends on the kind of care you need. Inpatient care is needed when the patient must be treated for a long time or closely watched. This can include treatment for serious conditions and many kinds of surgery. But some simple operations can be done in a doctor's office or in a clinic.

Some facilities provide services for a wide range of health problems. A hospital that does so is called a *general hospital.* Other facilities specialize in certain kinds of health care. Nursing homes give health care mainly to older people. A poison control center helps people who have been poisoned.

Choosing a Health Service

When choosing a health service, you need to use the same standards you use for choosing any other service. These include price, quality, and convenience. You want the best health care you can find at the most convenient place for the best possible price. Because choosing health care is such an important decision, a parent will probably help you. To find good health care, you can follow these steps.

Steps for Choosing a Health-Care Provider

- **Ask people you know for a person or facility they recommend.** You could ask friends, neighbors, or others in your family. You could talk to the school nurse or to a doctor you already use.
- **Call the local medical society or public health department.** The medical society can give you the names of doctors near you. The public health department can tell you about other kinds of health-care workers you may need.
- **Prepare a checklist of questions, and call places to get answers.** You can ask about the charges for various services and how they are billed. You can ask about the hours of service. You should ask whether a doctor or a dentist has a license. Never get health care from a doctor or dentist who is not licensed.

Be sure that you feel comfortable with the person. Buying health services is buying your well-being. If one health-care worker does not listen to your questions, you may want to look for another.

Hospital Rights

Not all doctors can treat patients at a hospital. If you are looking for a doctor, ask whether the doctor has that right. If so, find out where the hospital is. If the doctor doesn't have the right, and you have to go to the hospital for some reason, you will need to be treated by another doctor during your stay there.

Got You Covered?

Doctors agree with other doctors to *cover* for each other. That means that when one doctor is not available, the other will see his or her patients. Doctors in a group practice often cover for each other. If you are considering going to a doctor who practices alone, ask who covers for him or her.

Don't Practice Without a License

Whatever you do, make sure that you only get health care from doctors who are licensed.

Learning from Photographs
Many health care procedures can be handled in a doctor's office or in a clinic. What is being done in this picture?

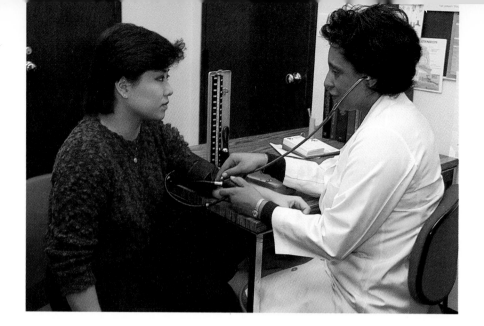

DID YOU KNOW?

We Specialize
The following lists several common medical specialists.

- **Allergist.** Treats asthma, hay fever, and other allergies.
- **Cardiologist.** Treats the heart.
- **Dermatologist.** Treats skin diseases and conditions.
- **Gynecologist.** Treats the female reproductive system.
- **Neurologist.** Treats the nervous system.
- **Obstetrician.** Treats females who are pregnant.
- **Ophthalmologist.** Treats eyes.
- **Orthopedist.** Treats bones.
- **Otolaryngologist.** Treats ears, nose, and throat.
- **Pediatrician.** Treats children.
- **Podiatrist.** Treats feet.
- **Psychiatrist.** Treats mental and emotional problems.
- **Surgeon.** Along with any other specialty, is trained to perform operations.
- **Urologist.** Treats the urinary system.

Options to Choose From

When you are looking for a doctor, you need to choose what kind of doctor you want. Many people get their main health care from a **family doctor.** This *kind of doctor provides basic health care to people.*

Someone with special needs must go to a doctor who is trained to meet those needs. Such a doctor is called a **specialist** (SPESH· uh·luhst). This *kind of doctor is trained to handle particular kinds of patients or health matters.* A family doctor will often suggest two or three specialists you can go to if you need one.

Some doctors have their own offices. They are working in *private practices.* Sometimes two or more doctors join together to offer health care. They are working in a *group practice.* Groups may include a number of doctors with different specialties.

Some people buy health care by joining a **health maintenance** (MAYNT·nuhns) **organization (HMO).** This is a group like a clinic. It includes *many different types of doctors who give health care to members.* The members pay a yearly fee for the health care instead of paying a bill each time they visit.

Insuring Your Health

Health care is costly. This is very true of hospital stays. Many people protect themselves from the cost of health care by buying **health insurance** (in·SHUR·uhns). This is *a program in which a person pays a yearly fee to a company that agrees to pay certain health-care costs.* Most workers get health insurance from the company they work for.

People who do not have insurance through work can buy it on their own.

The national government has two health insurance programs. **Medicare** (MED·i·kehr) gives *health insurance to people 65 years old or older*. The other program is called **Medicaid** (MED·i·kayd). It gives *health insurance to people who are poor*.

Government Health Departments

You can also receive health care from many parts of the government. Local, state, and federal governments all give people information on health and even give health services.

Local and State Health Departments

Most cities and counties have a health department and all states do. The jobs that these agencies do differ from place to place. Generally, though, all help to prevent disease. Some care for the poor and the aged. Different parts of local and state governments do the following tasks.

Tasks of Local and State Health Departments

- They make sure that restaurant and hotel kitchens are clean and safe.
- They pick up garbage and take it away.
- They make sure that local water is clean.
- They offer health education programs.
- They enforce laws aimed at controlling disease.
- They make sure that buildings are clean.
- They keep birth and death records and records of diseases.

Federal Health Departments

Many agencies of the federal government provide services related to health care. They belong to the Department of Health and Human Services. This department has four main groups.

- The *Health Care Financing Administration* runs Medicare and Medicaid.
- The *Office of Human Development Services* helps people with special needs. These include handicapped people, American Indians, and people who live in rural areas.

Know Your Coverage

Over 1,500 companies provide health insurance. Policies cover a range of health-care services. Policies may include doctor's fees, the cost of medicine, the cost of special equipment, and the cost of hospitalization and supplies required in inpatient care. Some—but not all—cover dental fees. In many insurance programs, the insured person pays, then submits the bills to claim re-payment from the insurance company. You must fill out a form to file a claim. Some doctors are willing to bill the insurance company directly. Always ask a doctor what the rules about insurance claims are.

More About

*For more on how governments work to control **AIDS** and other **sexually transmitted diseases**, see Chapter 11.*

DID **YOU** KNOW?

The Public Health Service

The Public Health Service, a branch of the federal government, includes the following units.

- *Health Services Administration.* Runs community health and family planning services.
- *Health Resources Administration.* Runs education and training programs for health workers. Does research into health services.
- *Food and Drug Administration.* Makes sure that food, drugs, and cosmetics are safe and pure. Decides which medications need subscriptions, and controls ads for them.
- *Alcohol, Drug Abuse, and Mental Health Administration.* Runs programs for the prevention and treatment of alcohol, drug, and mental health problems.
- *National Institutes of Health.* Conducts research into health conditions such as aging, cancer, and child health; there are 12 areas of research in all.
- *Centers for Disease Control.* Runs a national program to control the spread of disease.

- The *Social Security Administration* is mostly known for the payments it sends to retirees. However, it also makes payments each month to workers who cannot work because of serious illness or injury.

- The *Public Health Service* has a number of important agencies. They are listed on this page. The Food and Drug Administration, which ensures the safety of all medicines, is a well-known agency that is part of the Public Health Service.

Voluntary Health Groups

An important source of health services is the work of voluntary health groups. Groups like the American Heart Association and the American Cancer Society do many useful jobs. They pay for research into ways to prevent and cure serious diseases. They help people who suffer from these diseases. They even teach the public about these diseases and how to avoid them.

These groups need people's help. They are not businesses that make money by selling goods or services. They are not governments that get money from taxes. They can only do their work if they receive money from people. Many people also give their time to help these groups do their jobs.

Check Your Understanding

Conclusion   There are many sources of health services. Some are part of the local, state, or federal government. Whatever the source, wise consumers know what is available to them and choose carefully. By doing so, they help protect their own health.

1. **Vocabulary** Name the two health insurance programs run by the national government.
2. **Recall** What are the three goals of health care?
3. **Recall** Name three different providers of health care.
4. **Recall** What are the steps to follow in shopping for health care?
5. **Recall** What is health insurance?
6. **Recall** Name two health services provided by local or state government.
7. **Analyze** Why is it important to make sure that a health-care provider has a license if one is necessary?

Visiting the Doctor

One part of growing up is taking more responsibility. That can include becoming responsible for your own health. Making sure that you get regular health checkups is part of meeting that responsibility. Preparing for those visits and understanding what the doctor says are another part.

How to Visit the Doctor

Visiting the doctor may seem easy—you just walk in and the doctor knows what to do. Taking that approach to health care is unhealthy. You may not get a good checkup, and you may not understand what the doctor tells you. You'll do more for your health if you prepare yourself for the visit. Try following these steps.

1. **Make a date.** Call the doctor's office to make an appointment for a time that suits your schedule. Tell the person you talk to what the office visit is for. If you are not feeling well and want the problem checked out, the person will make the appointment sooner than if you just want a checkup. Write down the date and time of the visit, and show up on time.

2. **Prepare yourself.** If you are feeling ill, write down notes of how you are feeling and when the problem started. That way you can clearly describe your symptoms. If you are seeing the doctor for the first time, take along information on your medical history. Find out what diseases you have had, whether you have taken any medicines before, and whether you have any allergies. Prepare a list of questions you may have.

3. **Take notes.** As the doctor gives you the checkup and talks about any tests or treatments, write down what he or she says. This will help you remember it later.

4. **Ask questions.** If the doctor says anything that is not clear to you, ask questions until you understand it. If you have any questions later, call the office and ask.

5. **Make a list and follow up.** Write the doctor's directions on a list and check them off as you do them. Be sure you follow them exactly. If the doctor says you are to call after a few days or return in a week for a recheck, do it. Don't take these decisions into your own hands.

Using the Skill

Read the situation below and then answer the questions that follow.

Case

Ramon had a sore throat, a fever, and a runny nose. He was tired all the time. After feeling bad for 2 weeks, he finally went to the doctor who said he might have a cold or might have mononucleosis. The doctor took a blood test and told Ramon to rest for a couple of days. Ramon got a prescription and was told to call back in 2 days. Ramon took the medicine and rested. After the second day he felt great. His friend Pat came by and suggested they go to a movie. Ramon remembered that he should call the doctor, but thought it was a waste of time since he felt better.

1. What bad decision did Ramon make early in this situation?
2. What should he do now?

Chapter 14 Review

Summary

- By being a wise consumer, you can improve your health and get the most out of your money. You can also protect your rights.
- Wise consumers comparison shop to get the best quality they can for the money.
- Tradition, peers, advertising, and salespeople all influence consumer decisions. Wise consumers know how to resist these influences and make the choice that is right for them.
- Some people and companies sell fake health aids. They take advantage of people's desire to be beautiful, lose weight, or be healthy.
- When problems arise, consumers can often solve them by going back to the business where they bought the goods or service. If that does not work, consumers can get help from business groups or agencies of the government. Or they can take the problem to court.
- The health-care system is set up to prevent health problems, maintain good health, and treat health problems that arise. Consumers can get help for some health-care needs from the government.

Reviewing Vocabulary and Concepts

On a separate sheet of paper, write the numbers 1–12. After each number, write the letter of the word or phrase in Column B that best matches the phrase in Column A.

Column A

Lesson 1

1. Products that satisfy your wants
2. The right to be told about products and services for sale
3. What buying safe products does to your health
4. One of the benefits of being a wise health consumer

Lesson 2

5. The right to select from competing goods
6. How well a product is made
7. How much a product costs
8. A person who has a strong influence on purchases at the time they are made
9. A common advertising technique

Lesson 3

10. A person who pretends to have medical training but has none
11. Who should you talk to before buying a diet plan
12. The form of payment a quack may insist on

Column B

a. protects
b. salesperson
c. right to choose
d. quack
e. goods
f. testimonial
g. quality
h. cash
i. right to be informed
j. doctor
k. price
l. saves time and money

Write the numbers 13–20 on your paper. After each number, write the letter of the answer that best completes each of the following statements.

426

Lesson 4

13. The first thing to do if you have a consumer problem is to
    a. make sure you used the product correctly
    b. call the police
    c. call a lawyer
    d. go back to the store where you bought it

14. After pulling together what you will need to present your problem, you should
    a. go to the store
    b. write a letter
    c. decide on a fair solution
    d. call a lawyer

15. The Better Business Bureau is an example of what kind of group that helps consumers?
    a. consumer group
    b. government agency
    c. business group
    d. none — it helps businesses, not consumers

16. If you have a problem with a doctor, you can go for help to
    a. your parent
    b. another doctor
    c. the licensing board
    d. No one can help.

Lesson 5

17. Each of the following is a purpose of the health-care system *except*
    a. to prevent health problems
    b. to maintain good health
    c. to ensure health forever
    d. to treat health problems

18. The protection that people get from the high cost of health care is called
    a. health insurance
    b. a specialist
    c. a health maintenance organization
    d. a clinic

19. The kind of doctor consumers go to for particular problems is called a
    a. license
    b. family doctor
    c. specialist
    d. health service

20. Health services are provided by which level of government?
    a. local
    b. state
    c. federal
    d. all of these

Thinking Critically About the Facts

Write your answers to the following questions on a separate sheet of paper.

21. **Analyze** Think of a purchase that you made this week. Were you a wise consumer when you bought it? If not, what could you have done differently?

22. **Interpret** Suppose you saw an ad showing a group of teens playing volleyball and enjoying a cola drink. What is the ad trying to tell you about the drink? Do you believe it?

23. **Draw conclusions** On the basis of your reading of Lesson 4, do you think it is true that being prepared and acting calmly are two important things about handling a complaint? Why or why not?

Applying the Facts

24. Clip out a newspaper or magazine ad for a health product or service that you are thinking about buying. Write an essay that tells what kind of technique the advertiser is using to convince you to buy the good or service. Why do you think the advertiser is using this technique?

25. Some health and beauty products have warnings about possible harm on their labels. Find three household products that have such a warning. Write the name of the product and its use on a sheet of paper. Copy down the warning underneath. Why is the warning needed?

The Environment and Your Health

Lesson 1	**Building a Healthier Environment**	Lesson 2	**The Weather and Your Health**

CHAPTER WARM-UP

Chapter Study Goals

After you have read this chapter, you will be able to

- state the causes of different kinds of pollution.
- explain the importance of clean air and water.
- explain the importance of finding safe ways of disposing of waste.
- describe what can be done to protect the environment.
- describe ways to conserve energy.
- describe several dangerous weather conditions.
- explain how to be safe in dangerous weather.

Be on the lookout for information in the chapter that will help you to reach these goals.

Getting Started

"No doubt about it," said Steve, who was in the lead. "This spot is fantastic! And smell how fresh the air is!"

Steve and his family were enjoying one of our country's many national parks. Many people use state and national parks as places for healthy recreation. They like the change of pace and the scenery. They understand that the world around us is a special place.

In this chapter, you will read about some damage being done to that world. You will also learn what you can do to keep your environment healthy.

Study Tip

Use the headings and subheadings in this chapter to make an outline of the topics that are covered.

Building a Healthier Environment

Words to Know

environment
pollution
fossil fuels
ozone
acid rain
sewage
biodegradable
conservation
recycled
hazardous waste
nuclear waste

This lesson contains a number of valuable facts and tips. Once you have studied them, you will be able to

- define the term *environment.*
- tell what causes air, water, and solid-waste pollution and how they affect health.
- explain what you can do to make the environment healthy.

Health and Your Environment

You live in the context of your *environment.* The **environment** (in·VY·ruhn·muhnt) is *you and all the living and nonliving things around you.* It includes things people make such as buildings, roads, parks, and cars. It includes the rivers that flow through many towns and the lakes that other towns are built alongside. The environment also includes the trees, flowers, birds, and animals that share space with people.

You depend on some things in your environment to live. Air and water are essential for life. Good soil is needed to grow food. That is why the health of your environment has such a large effect on your health. As a side effect of how we live, we *make parts of our environment become dirty and unhealthy.* This is called **pollution** (puh·LOO·shuhn). Pollution can harm your health.

DID YOU KNOW?

Past Polluters

Pollution is not new. People have been dirtying water for centuries because they flushed raw human waste into rivers and oceans. But with more people alive today, there is more waste. And the cars and smokestacks we have give off more pollution than anything in the past.

The Air You Breathe

The main causes of air pollution are smoke and exhaust. They come mostly from the burning of **fossil** (FAHS·uhl) **fuels.** These are *the coal, oil, and natural gas used to power the engines of motor vehicles and factories.*

More About

*For more on your **lungs** and **respiratory system,** see Chapter 7.*

There are other sources of air pollution. Smoke from burning cigarettes and from the burning of trash makes the air dirty. So do chemicals that are used to kill insects.

What Does Air Pollution Do?

Air pollution harms people in a number of ways. Dirty air can make your eyes water. One gas in car exhaust, carbon monoxide, can cause headaches, tiredness, and dizziness. More serious is the damage that pollution can do to your lungs. Scientists have linked dirty air to diseases such as *emphysema* (em·fuh·SEE·muh). Pollution makes breathing hard for people who have *asthma* (AS·muh).

The smoke and exhaust may build up and stay in the air for a long time. This happens mainly above cities, where the large number of cars people drive creates great amounts of exhaust. When this dirty air sits over a city for many days, people may have trouble breathing. This problem is quite hard on young children, elderly people, and anyone with respiratory problems.

Some scientists think that dirty air has three other dangerous results.

- **The greenhouse effect.** By putting more carbon dioxide in the air, pollution may make the world warmer. The carbon dioxide acts as a blanket that keeps warmth near the earth. If this goes on, some scientists believe, some of the ice in the north and south poles may melt. This new water will cause the oceans to rise, which may cause some coastal cities to become flooded. The rise in temperatures may also make crops grow less well.

- **The ozone layer.** High above the earth is a layer of *a kind of oxygen* called **ozone** (OH·zohn). This layer protects us from the sun's harmful ultraviolet rays. Air pollution, however, may be damaging this protective layer. Some scientists believe they have found a hole in the ozone layer. They worry that the hole may allow more ultraviolet rays to reach the earth's surface.

The Pollution Count
The Environmental Protection Agency (EPA) is the government agency that works for a clean environment. The EPA has made a number system to show how dirty the air is at any given time. This is called the *Pollutant Standards Index* or PSI. You may hear the PSI number on a weather report. A PSI of 100 or more is unhealthful.

Learning from Photographs
These teens are walking to school. How does walking help the environment?

- **Acid rain.** The chemicals and dirt pumped into the air in smoke and exhaust stay there. When rain comes, this pollution is washed to the ground. *The rain that contains pollution* is called **acid rain.** Acid rain may kill trees and plants along with fish and other water life. It also eats away at the stone used in buildings.

Not all scientists agree about these effects of pollution. Some say that the problems are not great. Others, though, are very concerned about what the pollution may do.

What Can You Do for Cleaner Air?

Cars are one of the major causes of air pollution. People can make the air cleaner by putting fewer cars on the road.

- **Use public transportation.** People can cut down on car use by taking public buses, trains, or subways, by walking, and by biking.
- **Form car pools.** People can give rides to other people.

When you are old enough to drive, you can take these steps. In the meantime, you can suggest these steps to adults you know.

Some pollution depends on how much fuel is burned to make energy. You can help lower pollution by using less energy. The chart "How to Save Energy" shows some steps you can take.

How to Save Energy

- Close off air leaks in your home around the attic and doors or windows.
- Keep doors and windows closed if heat or air-conditioning is on.
- Put insulation in the roof and outside walls.
- Run appliances at off-peak hours.
- Keep the heat or air-conditioning low when no one is at home and at night.
- Turn off hot water when it is not being used.
- Fix leaky faucets, and use flow controllers to avoid wasting water.
- Let dishes air dry rather than using a dishwasher to dry them.

Water: A Vital Resource

All living things need water. Many plants and animals live in the rivers, lakes, and oceans of the world. They depend on each other to live. Humans, in turn, depend on many of them for food. Water is also

Health Minute

Car Pooling
Many cities offer cars with more than one person in them a special lane on the highway so they can pass the slow rush hour traffic. Find out what rules your community has about car pooling.

DID **YOU** KNOW?

Water, Water Everywhere?
Almost 70 percent of the earth's surface is water. But only *3* percent of that water is free of salt and drinkable. And almost all of that fresh water is frozen in polar ice.

a source of recreation. Imagine not having water for swimming, fishing, or boating.

What Pollutes Water?

A number of things make water dirty. Chemicals spill from factories into water. Other chemicals that enter water come from fertilizers washed out of farm fields. The **sewage** (SOO·ij) produced in cities and towns may be flushed into water. This includes *food, human waste, detergents, and other products washed down people's drains.*

These wastes can kill the plants and animals that live in water. If humans eat the fish that eat the chemicals, the humans, too, may be harmed. Water full of human wastes can lead to disease.

What Can You Do for Cleaner Water?

You can play a part in keeping water clean. Avoid putting strong detergents in the water supply. Some *products have chemicals that can break down in water without causing a problem.* They are said to be **biodegradable** (by·oh·di·GRAYD·i·buhl). You can use those brands. Another way to keep water clean is to put trash where it belongs and not dump it in the water.

A good way to protect water is to use less of it. **Conservation** (kahn·ser·VAY·shuhn) is *the saving of resources.*

- **Take shorter showers.** Also, use flow controllers to use less water when taking showers.
- **Repair leaky faucets.** Doing this can save gallons of water every month.
- **Buy grasses and plants that need little water.** Also, sweep driveways and walks rather than hosing them.

Health Minute

Unlucky Leak

If you have a leaky faucet, find out how much water is being wasted. Put a measuring cup or other container below the faucet and catch the water. See how much water the container collects in half an hour. Multiply that by 48 and you know how much water is wasted each day.

Lesson 1: Building a Healthier Environment   **433**

Solid Waste: The Leftovers

Every year we throw out enough trash to fill 5 million large truck trailers. We spend millions of dollars a year just to pick it up.

Sometimes people just throw this waste anywhere. Paper bags, plastic wrappers, newspaper, or empty soft drink cans can clutter parks or roadsides. This waste is called *litter*. Litter makes public places and communities look unattractive. People who use trash cans to hold solid waste help prevent litter.

Some of this trash is burned, but the amount is not large. Burning is not used often because it increases air pollution. Most of the trash is dumped into sanitary landfills. These are places where waste is collected and buried under soil. Much of this waste, though, could be **recycled** (ree·SY· kuhld). This means that it could be *changed in some way and used again.* Paper can be broken down and made into new paper. Aluminum cans and glass bottles can be crushed and used to make new cans and bottles.

What Are Hazardous Wastes?

Some wastes cannot be recycled easily or safely. *A waste product that may cause illness* is a **hazardous** (HAZ·erd·uhs) **waste.** Plastics, paints, and the chemicals used to kill insects are examples.

These wastes are dangerous in a number of ways. Some easily catch fire and can produce dangerous smoke. Some are so powerful they can eat away at the containers that hold them. The chemicals then enter the water supply and harm plants, animals, and even people. Some can sit in the soil for years and poison the food supply.

A special kind of hazardous waste is **nuclear** (NOO·klee·er) **waste.** This is *the dangerous products left over by an atomic power plant.* Nuclear waste is linked to cancer. It is a big problem because it stays dangerous for hundreds of years.

The government has rules about how to get rid of hazardous waste and nuclear waste. The EPA has the job of making sure that chemicals being thrown out do not poison the environment. The Nuclear Regulatory Commission, or NRC, watches how nuclear waste is handled.

Working for a Cleaner Environment

You have read of a number of steps you can take to make the environment cleaner. Cutting down on the use of energy helps the air. Using less water helps preserve the water supply. Recycling can cut down on the amount of waste that must be handled.

Teen Issue

Round and Round

It is estimated that 80 percent of the solid waste that is thrown out could be recycled. If the newspapers thrown out in a medium-sized city in a month were recycled, 34,000 pine trees would be saved. Is there a recycling center in your community?

Teen Issue

Writing Letters

It is true that young teens are not yet voters. But political leaders listen to groups of teens who make themselves heard. If you are concerned about the environment, you can do something. Write to a local leader like the mayor, a state representative, or a member of Congress. Tell that leader what you are concerned about and what you think should be done. Or you could write to find out what programs are being used and how you can help.

Learning from Photographs
This teen is making a nicer environment in a creative and attractive way. What other steps can you think of to make your community a more healthful place to live?

You can also join with others to protect the environment. Many students form groups to clean rivers or lakes and make that water healthy to use. A class can collect trash from the neighborhood and separate out the paper, cans, and bottles that can be recycled.

Government plays an important role in controlling pollution. Laws control what is done with waste. Other rules set standards for clean air and water. People who are concerned about having a clean environment can work with local and national leaders. They can use their power as citizens to get laws passed.

Check Your Understanding

Conclusion Your health depends on clean air and water. The trash that we dump on the land or in water can be a danger to health, too. You can help to control pollution. You can take steps to use less energy, conserve water, and recycle trash.

1. **Vocabulary** What does the word *environment* mean?
2. **Recall** What are two health dangers of air pollution?
3. **Recall** Name three causes of water pollution.
4. **Recall** What one step can you take to reduce the amount of solid waste?
5. **Analyze** What do you think is a greater danger to people in the long run, the warming of the earth or the problem of disposing of hazardous waste? Explain your answer.

DID **YOU** KNOW?

Save the Ears!
There is another kind of pollution—*noise* pollution. Loud radios and televisions, honking cars and trucks, and jet airplanes are just a few causes. Too much noise can hurt your hearing. About half of all young people lose some hearing because of noise. Loud noise makes you blink, your muslces tense, your heart beat faster, and your blood pressure rises.

You can control noise.

- **Turn it down.** Keep the volume on radios, stereos, and televisions low.
- **Speak softly.** Talk to others in a soft tone.
- **Use earplugs.** If you cannot avoid loud noises, wear earplugs.
- **Check on noise-control laws.** See what you can do to get stricter laws passed.

Teen Health
BULLETIN BOARD

CAREERS

Wanted:
Sanitarian

Specifics:
Inspect water treatment plants, waste disposal actions; alert public to health hazards; prevent damage to environment.

Qualifications:
Must be willing to travel, work outdoors, put in overtime. Must be good in science and able to communicate well.

Preparation:
College degree in environmental health, biology, or chemistry. Advanced degree helpful. Licensing may be needed.

Contact:
American Public Health Association
1015 Fifteenth Street, NW
Washington, DC 20005

HEALTH IN THE NEWS
You Can't See It, but It Can Hurt You

Many homes in America have too much radon in them. Radon is a natural gas that comes up from the soil. But you would never know when radon is entering your home—it has no smell and no color. What radon *does* have is danger. Radon can increase the risk of lung cancer. Radon is widespread. The government recently said that every home in the country should be tested for radon.

Testing is fairly simple. You can buy a testing kit at a hardware store for about $10. Or you can ask a professional service to come in and test for radon. Be careful to use someone honest. Some people are making money by taking advantage of people's fear of radon. If radon is found, it can be removed by putting in a fan and by sealing cracks. The steps are simple—and the benefit to your lungs is great!

Lifestyle

Something to Sneeze At

What do the numbers 12, 41, and 73 mean to you? If you have hay fever, they mean a lot. These are "pollen count" numbers. The pollen count reports how much pollen is in the air on a given day. Pollen is what drives people with hay fever straight to the tissue box. A pollen count of 10 is low. A count above 50 is very high. When does the pollen strike? It depends on where you live and what kind of pollen there is.

Region	Tree Pollen	Grass Pollen	Weed Pollen
East and Midwest	Mid-March to June	Mid-May to mid-July	Aug. to frost
South	Feb. to May	Mid-Feb. to mid-Oct.	June to mid-Oct.
Southwest	Mid-Jan. to May	Late Feb. to Oct.	April to May, Aug. to Oct.
Northwest	Late Feb. to May	Late April to Sept.	Mid-July to Oct.
West Coast	Mid-Jan. to June	April to Sept.	May to Oct.

TEEN Q & A

Q: What causes allergies?

A: Some people are more sensitive than others to things in the environment. Dust, pet hair, pollen, and certain foods make these people sneeze and itch. Most people develop these allergies when they are children. If you think you have an allergy, you should see an allergist. He or she can test you. If you are allergic to something, the allergist can tell you how to care for yourself.

Lifestyle

Garbage Power!

People are trying very hard to figure out what to do with their garbage. There aren't many more places to dump it. One answer is to burn it and use the heat to make energy. Almost 100 power plants in the United States are powered by burning trash. They use special smokestacks that clean the smoke before it gets into the air. Many cities are planning on building plants like this in the future. After all, there will always be garbage!

The Weather and Your Health

Words to Know
tornado
tornado watch
tornado warning
hurricane
earthquake
blizzard
frostbite

This lesson contains a number of valuable facts and tips. Once you have studied them, you will be able to

- talk about some of the dangers made by tornadoes, hurricanes, earthquakes, and blizzards.
- tell how to prepare for each of these weather dangers.

Learning from Photographs
This black funnel-shaped windstorm is a tornado. Do you know where tornadoes are most common?

Keeping Safe in Hazardous Weather

You have probably heard news reports about hazardous weather. Some storms are so severe that they damage property and may even take lives. But people can protect themselves from injury.

Tornadoes

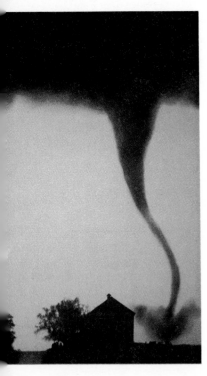

A **tornado** (tor·NAYD·oh) is *a whirling, funnel-shaped windstorm that drops from the sky to the ground.* The winds of a tornado can travel at speeds up to 300 miles an hour. Tornadoes occur mostly in the central part of the United States. They may also happen along the coasts following a hurricane.

Because tornadoes have such high winds, they can be very dangerous. The National Weather Service watches the weather to see when a tornado may form. When *the weather conditions are right for a tornado,* the Weather Service issues a **tornado watch.** This news is sent to radio and television stations, which tell viewers and listeners. If conditions change, the watch is removed.

When *a tornado is in a certain area and people are in danger,* the Weather Service issues a **tornado warning** for that area. When that happens, people need to take steps to protect themselves. The safest thing to do is to go to a cellar or basement that has no windows and stay there until the storm passes. If you cannot do that, you can take other steps.

What To Do in a Tornado

- **Avoid places with windows.** Go into a hallway or other place that has no windows.
- **Cover yourself.** Duck down and cover your head. Use a mattress, blanket, or clothing to protect yourself from flying objects.
- **Lie down.** If you are outside, get into a ditch or other low ground and lie down.

Hurricanes

Another kind of dangerous storm is a **hurricane** (HER·uh·kayn). This is *a strong windstorm with driving rain.* Hurricanes usually happen on the eastern and southern coasts of our country. They occur most often in late summer and early fall. The National Weather Service also makes hurricane watches and warnings. Sometimes a tornado directly follows a hurricane, adding to the damage.

What To Do in a Hurricane

- **Board up the doors and windows of your house.** Otherwise, the force of the storm may blow them in.
- **Take inside any objects that may be blown away.** These include bicycles, lawn furniture, and garbage cans.
- **Leave the area.** If you live on the coast, go inland.

Earthquakes

An **earthquake** occurs where *the ground may shake as the rock below the surface moves.* Some quakes are minor. In others the earth shakes so strongly that it can topple buildings. Most injuries from earthquakes happen when people are hit by falling objects.

What To Do in an Earthquake

- **Stay inside.** If you are at home, stay there. Stand in a strong doorway or in a hallway or lie under a bed. Stay away from objects that could fall or cave in.
- **If you are outdoors, stand in the open.** Stay away from telephone poles, electric wires, and buildings.

It's a good idea to take certain steps for any of these hazardous conditions.

- Make sure you have a battery-operated radio so you can hear news if the power goes off.
- Keep a working flashlight or two on hand so you can have light if power is lost.
- Know the local emergency phone number—911—so you can call for help if you need it.

The main things to remember if a severe storm hits are these.

- Stay calm.
- Follow the directions of the officials.
- Stay with your parents or an adult.
- Never leave your safe position until you hear official word that the danger is over.

Blizzards

A very heavy snowstorm with high wind is a **blizzard.** In a blizzard, winds may reach 45 miles an hour. You can see less than 500 feet in front of you. The best thing to do in a blizzard is to stay indoors. If you are caught outdoors, though, protect yourself in these ways.

- **Keep your nose and mouth covered and keep moving.** These actions can keep you from freezing.
- **Avoid getting lost.** Find a fence or other landmark and walk along it.
- **Wear clothing that will protect you.** Woolen underwear and outer clothes that keep out wind and moisture are best. Extra socks and warm boots along with gloves will protect your hands and feet.

When you are in extreme cold, your body tries to save heat for your heart, lungs, and brain. It does this by sending less blood to the hands and feet. If these *body parts freeze,* you have **frostbite.**

Frostbite needs to be treated right away so that the damaged parts do not die. Get the person who has frostbite to a doctor as quickly as possible. In the meantime, get the person indoors and covered with a blanket. Give him or her a warm drink like hot chocolate or warm cider. Place the frozen area in *warm w*water—not hot water—or wrap it in blankets. Do not rub the frozen part; rubbing may damage it.

Learning from Photographs
Severe cold can damage exposed skin. What can you do to protect yourself from this danger?

Dressing for Winter
A good way to protect yourself from the cold is to dress in layers. Wearing two or three sweaters and then a coat is better than just wearing a heavy coat. The layers trap warm air near your body, which keeps you warm.

Check Your Understanding

Conclusion   Some serious weather conditions can create dangers for people. Knowing what to do and acting safely can protect you from those dangers. With tornadoes, hurricanes, and blizzards, there is usually some warning that the weather is coming. In that case, follow the directions of your local officials.

1. **Vocabulary** What is frostbite?
2. **Recall** Where is the safest place to be when a tornado strikes?
3. **Recall** What three things should you do when a hurricane comes to your area?
4. **Recall** What causes the most injuries in an earthquake?
5. **Recall** Name two ways you can protect yourself in a blizzard.
6. **Compare and contrast** What is the difference between a tornado watch and a tornado warning?

Protecting the Environment

Jane's class decided to have a Spot the Pollution Day. Each student took a notepad and pencil to the town's streets to look for examples of pollution. Jane noted these examples.

3:30 P.M. Man and woman throw paper lunch bags into trash bin. Man does nothing when his bag falls out of the bin.

3:36 P.M. Tour bus driver leaves bus engine running while she waits for passengers.

3:39 P.M. Jackhammer runs for 20 minutes while people walk by.

3:45 P.M. Traffic jam caused when a car is double-parked and its engine is running.

3:50 P.M. Car drives past with black smoke trailing from tailpipe.

3:52 P.M. Group of teens walks past with portable radio playing loudly. Dogs start to bark.

3:55 P.M. Group of teens plays in park with beach ball. Ball loses air, and teens throw it into pond.

How We All Can Protect the Environment

Jane saw many examples of things that cause pollution. Litter, car exhaust, and loud noise all make the environment a less pleasant place to live. Keeping the environment clean is something that we all can do.

- Use fewer cars and conserve energy.
- Keep water clean and conserve water.
- Recycle paper, cans, and bottles and dispose of trash properly.
- Keep the noise down and remind others to do so.

Using the Skill

Read the description below. Number your paper from 1 to 3 and write down what decisions each person could make that would help the environment.

Case One
Mark will be starting a new job next week and needs to decide how to get there. It is 2 miles from his home. He can walk, take a bus, or get a ride from his mother on the way to work. What would you do if you were Mark?

Case Two
Joan and her friends are riding on the bus with about 20 other passengers. The teens are sitting in the middle of the bus and begin to sing. One member of the group starts playing a radio. If you were one of the other passengers, what would you say to the teens?

Case Three
Karen takes a shower every morning. She runs the water for a few minutes before she gets in to get the temperature right. During the shower, she often finds that the water is getting colder. She has to turn the hot water higher to make the temperature right. If you were Karen, what would you do?

Chapter 15 Review

Summary

- Your health depends on the health of the environment. Pollution of the air and water can cause disease. Long-term effects such as the warming of the earth and acid rain may endanger life. The disposal of solid waste and hazardous waste is an important health issue. Even noise pollution can make you unwell.
- You can help to make the environment cleaner. By cutting down on the amount of fossil fuels that you burn, you help the air. By using water carefully, you can conserve it. By recycling paper, cans, and bottles, you cut down on the amount of waste.
- You can take action to influence government leaders to work for a cleaner environment, too.
- Severe weather like tornadoes, hurricanes, and blizzards cause dangers to health. Earthquakes also are a threat to safety.
- Knowing what to do when severe weather strikes can protect you from harm. Public officials alert people to the dangers of severe weather. It is wise to follow their instructions in such a situation.

Reviewing Vocabulary and Concepts

On a separate sheet of paper, write the numbers 1–16. After each number, write the letter of the answer that best completes each of the following statements.

Lesson 1

1. Which of the following is a way to protect fresh water?
   a. recycling
   b. conservation
   c. saving energy
   d. using fewer cars

2. Which of the following is a way to protect the air from pollution?
   a. recycling
   b. conserving water
   c. using fewer cars
   d. eliminating toxic waste

3. All the living and nonliving things around you make up the
   a. conservation
   b. pollution
   c. recycling
   d. environment

4. Glass, cans, and newspapers are all kinds of solid waste that can be
   a. recycled
   b. conserved
   c. polluted
   d. burned

5. The gradual warming of the Earth is called
   a. pollution
   b. the greenhouse effect
   c. the ozone layer
   d. acid rain

6. Loud sounds from people and machines are
   a. air pollution
   b. water pollution
   c. noise pollution
   d. waste pollution

7. One cause of water pollution is
   a. noise
   b. sewage
   c. trash
   d. energy use

8. Chemicals and nuclear waste are
   a. toxic
   b. air pollution
   c. recyclable
   d. biodegradable

9. A product that includes chemicals that can break down in water is
   a. recyclable   **b.** a pollutant   **c.** biodegradable   **d.** dangerous

10. We are protected from the sun's ultraviolet rays by
    a. the ozone layer   **b.** acid rain   **c.** the greenhouse effect   **d.** conservation

Lesson 2

11. When the weather conditions are right for a funnel-shaped storm, the Weather Service gives a
    a. hurricane watch   **b.** hurricane warning   **c.** tornado watch   **d.** tornado warning

12. A snowstorm with winds up to 45 miles an hour is a
    a. tornado   **b.** hurricane   **c.** cyclone   **d.** blizzard

13. To treat frostbite, you make the skin
    a. warm   **b.** hot   **c.** wet   **d.** cold

14. The best place to be in an earthquake is
    a. anywhere indoors   **b.** indoors away from windows   **c.** anywhere outdoors   **d.** outdoors away from power lines

15. A rainstorm with heavy winds is called a
    a. tornado   **b.** hurricane   **c.** cyclone   **d.** blizzard

16. When the Weather Service sees a severe wind- and rainstorm in your area, it will issue a
    a. hurricane watch   **b.** hurricane warning   **c.** tornado watch   **d.** tornado warning

Thinking Critically About the Facts

Write your answers to the following questions on a separate sheet of paper.

17. **Organize** Make a list that shows what you could do in your own home to conserve energy.

18. **Synthesize** Explain why clean air and water are so important.

19. **Analyze** What pollution problems are there in your community? What are two things you and others could do for each problem to make the environment cleaner?

20. **Summarize** Suppose you had to explain how to protect yourself from hazardous weather to a class of fourth-graders. Write out what you would say.

21. **Analyze** Why do you think that people are advised to be indoors, in a basement, and away from windows during tornadoes and hurricanes?

Applying the Facts

22. Do some research in the library to find out what sources of energy experts are looking into to replace fossil fuels. Report to the class on what you learn about the benefits and drawbacks of one of those alternative sources of energy.

23. Write a letter to your local newspaper telling why you think it is important for your town to set up a recycling center if one does not exist. If your town *has* a recycling center, write a letter urging people to use it.

24. Check to see what supplies you have at home in case of hazardous weather. Make a list of what your family has and what your family needs to get.

443

Health Handbook

1. Basic Good Health Habits

Use with Chapters 1, 5, and 7.

There are many things you can do to care for all your body systems. But following these basic habits will help you have good health.

- **Get plenty of rest.** You should get 8 or 9 hours of sleep every night.

- **Eat a balanced diet.** Eat nutritious foods that are low in fat, cholesterol, and sugar. Eat plenty of fiber and drink lots of water. Eat from all four food groups.

- **Eat regular meals spaced out throughout the day.** Eat three meals a day, including breakfast. If you snack, snack on healthy foods.

- **Stay at the recommended weight for your sex, height, and body type.** Eating a balanced diet and exercising will help you do so.

- **Exercise regularly and include aerobic exercise in your routine.** You should exercise vigorously at least three or four times a week.

- **Lower the amount of stress you feel.** Use stress-management techniques to stay relaxed.

- **Act safely to avoid accidents.** Accidents cause injury. They can be avoided by thinking about what you are doing. When you are doing some activity that may be dangerous, give yourself any protection that you may need.

- **Avoid using tobacco, alcohol, and drugs.** These substances are addictive and harmful. Alcohol and drugs are also illegal.

- **Have a clear self-concept.** Know your strengths and your weaknesses. Develop a sure sense of who you are and what you can do.

- **Communicate well.** Speak clearly to others to get your messages across. Listen to others so you can understand what they are saying.

- **Cooperate with others.** Remember that living with other people involves working together.

- **Compromise with others when it does not violate your principles.** Part of working with other people is compromise, in which each person gives up a little of what he or she wants but gets something in return. But you don't have to compromise when others are trying to pressure you into doing something against your beliefs. That's when it's time to say "no."

2. 12 Suggestions for a Safe Workout

Use with Chapter 1.

1. **Begin by warming up and end by cooling down.** Start out slowly and cool down slowly. These steps will get your muscles ready to work out vigorously and prevent injury.

2. **Set realistic goals.** Make yourself a short-term goal rather than something that will take a long time to reach. If you are starting a swimming program, for instance, make your first goal swimming the length of the pool one time. Once you have mastered that goal, you can increase the distance.

3. **Watch your body for signals of pain.** As you begin exercising muscles in a new way, you will probably feel some discomfort in those muscles. This is nothing to be alarmed about. If you feel pain, however, you should stop. Keeping up exercise when you feel pain could lead to injury or permanent damage. If you feel pain whenever you exercise, see a doctor.

4. **Wear loose-fitting clothing.** The looseness helps your skin breathe. This allows you to stay cool and avoid overheating.

5. **Wear light-colored clothing and reflective coverings if you exercise outside at night.** The light-colored clothes and the reflective coverings will make you visible to drivers.

6. **When exercising in the heat, work out less than you normally do.** Hot, humid weather puts an extra strain on your body. You could dehydrate, or dry out, or become exhausted if you work too hard in such weather. On hot, humid days, it helps to exercise during the cooler parts of the day, such as early morning or dusk.

7. **When exercising in cold weather, wear one layer less of clothing than you would otherwise wear.** Because you will be generating heat when you work out, you do not need as much covering as you would normally. Dress in layers rather than wearing one heavier coat.

8. **Drink plenty of fluids, especially water, if you are exercising regularly.** When you work out, your sweat removes water from your body. This needs to be replaced by drinking fluids. In addition to water, fruit juices are healthy drinks for a person who exercises regularly.

9. **Wait about two hours after eating a meal before exercising strenuously.** This wait will prevent cramps.

10. **Exercise on soft, even surfaces, such as a track, grass, or dirt.** The evenness reduces the risk of injury. A soft surface is better for a runner's knees than a hard surface.

11. **If you move about during exercise, try to land on your heels rather than the balls of your feet.** Doing this prevents injury to the feet and legs.

12. **Don't shortcut in the equipment or footwear you use.** Be sure to get shoes that fit comfortably and have well-cushioned soles. If you need other equipment, such as pads or a helmet for bicycling, try to get the best that you can. Good equipment can protect you from injury.

3. Testing Flexibility

Use with Chapter 1.

The flexibility, or freedom of movement, of your body differs from joint to joint. This fact makes it hard to measure the flexibility of your whole body. Still, the following test will give you a general sense of how flexible you are.

Before you begin, remember two things.

- **Warm up.** Begin by doing some light stretching. This will help you avoid hurting yourself.
- **Move smoothly.** Avoid quick, jerking motions during the test. Your reach should be gradual and slow.

The test for flexibility consists of three steps.

1. Sit on the floor with your legs straight in front of you. Your heels should touch a tape on the floor and be about five inches apart.
2. Place a yardstick on the floor between your legs. The 36-inch end of the stick should point away from your body. The 15-inch mark should be even with your heels. It may be helpful to tape the stick in place.
3. Slowly reach with both hands as far forward as possible and hold this position. See how many inches your fingers reach.

The chart below shows the rating for different scores on this test. You should repeat the test three times and use your longest reach to determine your flexibility.

Scoring (in inches)		
Males	**Females**	**Rating**
22 +	23 +	Excellent
16–22	19–23	Good
12–16	16–19	Average
9–12	14–16	Fair
less than 9	less than 14	Poor

4. Testing Leg Muscle Strength

Use with Chapter 1.

You can measure leg muscle strength by doing the standing broad jump. The test has two steps.

1. Put a piece of tape on the floor and stand behind it with your toes touching the back of the tape.
2. Bend your knees and jump forward as far as you can, landing with your weight on both feet. Mark where you land.

Use a yardstick or tape measure to measure your jump from the starting tape to your landing point. Your muscle strength is found by comparing the distance you jumped to your height.

Scoring (distance compared to height)	
Distance Jumped	**Rating**
About 5.9 inches (8.75 centimeters) more than your height	Excellent
Between 2 and 4 inches (3 to 6 centimeters) more than your height	Good
Equal to your height	Fair
Less than your height	Poor

5. Testing Muscle Endurance

Use with Chapter 1.

You test your muscle endurance by seeing how many sit-ups you can do in one minute. You will need a stopwatch and a partner. During the test, remember to breathe freely. Do not hold your breath. Your partner should keep the time and count your sit-ups.

1. Start by lying on your back with your knees slightly bent and your hands behind your head. Have your partner hold your ankles for support.

2. Do as many sit-ups as you can in one minute. Raise your upper body from the floor to a point where you touch one elbow to the knee on the opposite side.

Return to the full starting position and repeat.

Your score depends on how many sit-ups you did in a minute.

Scoring (number of sit-ups per minute)		
Male	**Female**	**Rating**
40+	30+	Excellent
33–39	24–29	Good
29–32	18–23	Average
21–28	11–17	Fair
20 or less	10 or less	Poor

6. Testing Your Heart and Lung Endurance

Use with Chapter 1.

To test the condition of your heart and lungs, take this 3-minute test. To do the test, you need a sturdy bench such as in a locker room. You will also need a watch.

1. Stand in front of the bench. Begin the test when the second hand is on the 12 mark of the watch. For the next 3 minutes, step up and down on the bench repeatedly. Step up with the right foot, then the left. Be sure to extend each leg fully. Then step down with the right foot and then the left. Step at the rate of 24 steps per minute.

2. When 3 minutes are done, sit down and relax without talking.

Your score depends on your pulse rate after the test is complete. Find your pulse, either on your wrist or on the side of your neck, and count the number of beats in a minute.

Scoring (number of heartbeats in 1 minute)	
Heartbeats	**Rating**
70–80	Excellent
81–105	Good
106–119	Average
120–130	Fair
131+	Poor

7. Finding Your Target Pulse Rate

Use with Chapter 1.

Your target pulse rate is the number of heartbeats per minute that will give you the most benefit out of exercise. It is *not* your normal or resting pulse, but your pulse at the peak of aerobic exercise.

To find your target pulse rate, you first need to find your *maximum pulse rate.* This is the most your heart should beat each minute. Exercising at this pulse rate is dangerous. The target pulse rate is *less* than the maximum pulse rate.

Your maximum pulse rate is the number 220 minus your age. Your target pulse rate is a range that is found by multiplying the maximum pulse rate by 70 percent and by 85 percent. When you exercise at your peak, your pulse should be somewhere between these two numbers.

Pulse Rates		
Age	Maximum Pulse Rate	Target Pulse Rate
11	209	146–178
12	208	146–177
13	207	145–176
14	206	144–175
15	205	143–174
16	204	142–173

8. Basic Warm-Up Body Movements

Use with Chapter 1.

The first component of physical fitness is flexibility. As you improve your flexibility, you improve your efficiency of movement. This means you do not have as much wasted movement. More efficient movement means more efficient use of energy. Warm-up exercises are excellent for improving basic body movements because they involve stretching the muscles. Movements should be long and slow stretching with very gentle bouncing. Avoid quick, hard bouncing because you risk injuring a muscle.

When warming up, begin slowly, repeating each of your exercises twice. Add to repetitions each week until you have built up to a maximum of 30. This is a critical part of any exercise program. Too many people start out overenthusiastically and attempt 30 repetitions the first day. The results are usually very sore muscles and a discouraged person. Begin slowly, giving your body time to adjust.

Warm-Ups for the Leg Muscles

1. **Sitting Toe Touches.** Sit with legs extended in front of you. Feet together and legs flat on the floor. Reach for toes with hands, bringing forehead as close to knees as possible.

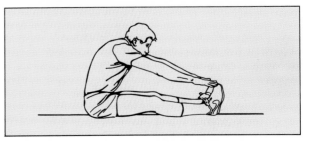

2. **Calf Tendon Stretcher.** Stand two to three feet from a wall. Lean forward, body straight. Place palms against the wall at eye level. Step backward. Continue to support your weight with your hands. Remain flat-footed until you feel your calf muscles stretching.

3. **Calf Stretch.** Assume a stride position with right leg forward. Place hands on hips. Lean upper body forward. Simultaneously bend your right leg at the knee to a 130° angle. Extend your left leg so that it is in line with the upper body. Your left foot should be flat on the floor. Return to starting position. Repeat with left foot forward.

4. **Sprinter.** Assume a squatting position with hands on the floor. Extend right leg backward as far as possible. The left leg should be bent at your knee and kept under your chest. Stretch slowly and then hold for a slow count of six. Then return to the squatting position and repeat the stretch, this time with the left leg back and the right leg under your chest.

5. **Standing Leg Stretcher.** Find a chair or table 2½ to 3 feet in height. Place left foot on the chair or table. Keep this leg straight and parallel to the floor. Your right leg should be firmly planted on the floor. From this position, slowly extend fingertips toward your outstretched leg on the chair. Hold and return. Repeat with other leg.

As you become more flexible from this and other stretching exercises, you should eventually be able to get your forehead to your knees.

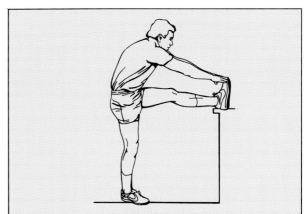

6. **Side Stretch.** Stand erect with hands on hips, feet spread wider than shoulder width. Lean to the right, bending the right leg, keeping the left leg extended. Return to starting position and repeat on opposite side. This firms thighs, hips, and buttocks.

7. **Leg Crossover.** Lie on back, legs together, arms extended sideward for balance. Raise the left leg to a vertical position. Keeping the left leg straight, lower it to the floor on right side. Return to starting position. Repeat with right leg. Leg crossovers firm hip muscles and stretch muscles on the back of the leg.

Warm-Ups for the Abdominal Muscles

1. **Bicycle Pumps.** Sit with legs extended and hands resting on the floor on or beside the hips. Lift right leg slightly off the floor and bend it so that it almost touches the buttocks, then return it. As you return the right leg, start to bring the left leg forward. Repeat in a rapid manner. This exercise is good for both the abdominal muscles and the thighs.

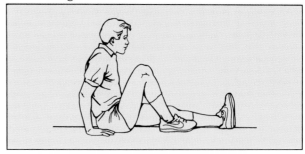

2. **Abdominal Curls.** Lie flat on your back with the lower back touching the floor, knees bent. Curl the head and upper part of the body upward and forward to about a 45° angle. At the same time, contract your abdominal muscles. Return slowly to the starting position. Repeat. Abdominal curls tone the abdomen.

3. **Curl-Down—45° Angle.** Start from a sitting position with knees bent and hands placed behind head. Lower the upper body to a 45° angle. Hold that position and return. Repeat. This also tones the abdominal muscles.

Warm-Ups for the Torso and Shoulders

1. **Side Stretch.** Stand with feet shoulder-width apart, legs straight. Place one hand on hip and extend the other hand up and over your head. Bend to the side on which the hand is placed. Move slowly. Hold. Repeat on the other side.

2. **Shoulder Stretch.** With arms over your head, hold the elbow of one arm with the hand of the other. Slowly pull the elbow behind your head. Do not force. Hold. Repeat on the other side.

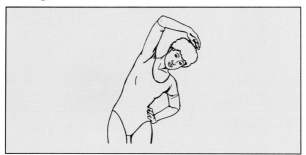

9. An Exercise Program Using Walking or Jogging

Use with Chapter 1.

Walking or Jogging Program

Day		1	2	3	4	5	Totals
Week 1	Distance	W 2 mi	W 2 mi	W/J 2 mi J total ½ mi	W/J 2 mi J total ½ mi	W/J 2½ mi J total ¾ mi	12.25
	Time	36 min	36 min	34 min	34 min	32 min	172
	Calories burned	195	195	218	218	225	1051
Week 2	Distance	W/J 2½ mi J ¾ mi	W/J 3 mi J ¾ mi	W/J 3 mi J 1 mi	W/J 3 mi J 1 mi	W/J 3 mi J 1 mi	17
	Time	32 min	50 min	48 min	48 min	48 min	226
	Calories burned	225	274	290	290	290	1369
Week 3	Distance	W/J 3 mi J 1¼ mi	W/J 3 mi J 1¼ mi	W/J 3 mi J 1½ mi	W/J 3 mi J 1½ mi	W/J 3 mi J 1½ mi	22
	Time	45 min	45 min	42 min	42 min	42 min	216
	Calories burned	300	300	310	310	310	1530

Key: W = Walk
J = Jog
mi = miles
min = minutes

Note: Continue adding about ¼ to ½ mile to the distance you jog, subtracting the distance you walk. Then, depending on your goal, you can add more total distance or increase your speed. Remember to monitor your pulse rate. Also begin each activity with a warm-up and end it with a cool down.

10. An Exercise Program Using Bicycling

Use with Chapter 1.

Bicycling Program							
	Day	1	2	3	4	5	Total
Week 1	Distance	5 mi	5 mi	5.5 mi	5.5 mi	6 mi	27
	Time	30 min	30 min	33 min	33 min	36 min	162
	Calories burned	185	185	195	195	205	965
Week 2	Distance	6 mi	6.5 mi	6.5 mi	7 mi	7 mi	33
	Time	36 min	39 min	39 min	42 min	42 min	198
	Calories burned	205	215	215	225	225	1085
Week 3	Distance	7.5 mi	7.5 mi	8 mi	8 mi	8.5 mi	39.5
	Time	45 min	45 min	48 min	48 min	51 min	237
	Calories burned	235	235	245	245	245	1205

11. Avoiding Back Problems

Use with Chapter 2.

Exercises That Can Help

Three exercises can help give you good posture by strengthening your back and stomach muscles. These exercises should be done for a short while every day. Descriptions of each exercise follow.

Knee-to-Chest Raise

Begin by lying on the floor with your legs bent and your arms at your sides. Keep your head straight and your back as straight as possible—it should not be curved. Take one knee with your two hands and lift it toward your chest. Hold it there for a count of four, then let the leg return to its original place. Do the same with the other leg, then do the same taking both legs in your hands. Repeat all three movements eight to ten times.

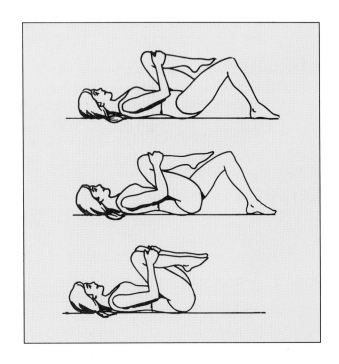

Stomach Curl

This exercise begins the same way as the knee-to-chest raise. You should be lying on the floor with head looking up, back as flat as possible, and knees slightly bent. Your arms should be resting at your sides with your hands on your stomach. To do the exercise, lift your upper body so that your back makes approximately a 45° angle. At the same time, stretch your arms so that your fingers touch your knees. Be sure to keep your back straight as you move. Return to the starting position and then repeat the exercise 10 to 15 times.

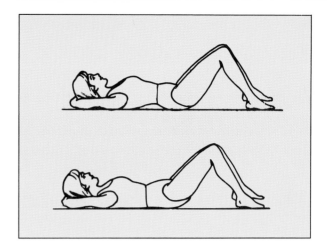

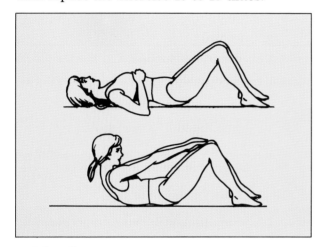

Pelvic Tilt

The key to good posture—and to preventing back problems—is keeping your back straight. By standing, sitting, and walking using the pelvic tilt, you can meet that goal. Begin by lying on the floor with your hands behind your head, your head looking up, and your knees bent. Take one hand out and feel under the lower part of your back. There is probably space between it and the floor. To do the exercise, rotate your hips forward so that your buttocks moves slightly in the direction of your feet. At the same time tighten your stomach muscles. These motions should straighten your lower back so that it pushes against the floor. Use your hand to feel there again. When the tilt is done correctly, there will be no space between your back and the floor. Repeat the exercise.

Help Through Good Habits

Sitting

- Sit in a firm chair with a back that provides support. Do not sit in very deep or well-stuffed chairs or sofas.

- When sitting, keep your knees about one-half to one inch higher than your hips.

- Avoid sitting in one position for long periods. Get up and move around every 20 minutes.

Standing

- Do not stand in one position for longer than a few minutes. Shift your weight from one foot to another.

- Females should use low heels if they will be standing for a long period of time.

- Stand with one leg bent and with that foot resting on a 6-inch high box or step.

Sleeping

- When sleeping, lie on either side and draw one or both knees toward your chin.

- Sleep on a flat, firm mattress or use a bed board one-half to three-quarters of an inch thick placed between the bed's spring and mattress.

A11

Lifting

- Bend at the knees, not at the waist. Let your legs, not your back, do the work.
- Carry packages as close to your body as possible.
- If you must carry a heavy load, divide it into two parts.

- Don't bend over furniture to open or close windows.

Pushing and Reaching

- When moving a large object, push it, don't pull it.
- Use a step stool for reaching high objects.

12. A Guide to Your Mental Health

Use with Chapter 3.

The following 26 questions offer a brief guide to mental health. The number of questions that are true of someone *most of the time* provide a rough idea of that person's strengths and weaknesses. Keep in mind that there is not a perfect score of 26. Everyone's level of mental health varies. Most of us have some areas that need work.

1. Feeling Comfortable About Myself

   - I can express my thoughts and feelings.
   - I can express my emotions and am not overcome or immobilized by them.
   - I can cope with both disappointment and success.
   - I recognize personal shortcomings.
   - I can laugh at myself.
   - I am optimistic.
   - I am generally cheerful and active.
   - I know my limits as well as my abilities.
   - I live by a set of standards and know what is important to me.
   - I like who I am.

2. Feeling Right About Other People

   - I enjoy spending some time alone.
   - I get along well with others.
   - I can interact with people and work with a group.

   - I continue to participate when I do not get my way.
   - I do not try to dominate.
   - I can accept differences in other people.
   - I feel I am a part of a group.
   - I am interested in and enjoy being with others.
   - I have several satisfying relationships.

3. Meeting the Demands of Life

   - I face my problems rather than avoid them.
   - I can ask for help when it is needed.
   - I do not make excuses for my actions.
   - I set realistic personal goals and have a plan for working toward them.
   - I give my best effort in whatever I do.
   - I can cope with change.
   - I see challenges and experiences as opportunities for growth.

   Scoring: The highest possible score is 24. A score of between 18 and 24 is *good*, 10 to 17 *fair*, 9 to 0 *poor*. A person should look at the statements not checked to make some generalizations about an area in which improvement is needed. That person could then make a plan for working on that area. He or she is likely to see the benefits quickly.

13. Setting Goals

Use with Chapter 3.

One of the most important skills to learn is how to set goals. This skill can be used in all areas of your life as a way of getting things done. The key to setting goals is to make them realistic—to set goals that are possible for you to achieve.

1. **Decide on one thing you want to work on.** Trying to do too many things at once can make it harder for you to meet your goals. If you are most concerned about, say, making yourself a better piano player, you may not have enough time to become a better tennis player too. Be realistic about the time and energy you have available.

2. **Make your goal specific.** Wanting to be a better piano player is not specific enough. You need a way to measure your success. Your goal could be to play a certain piece without mistakes at the recital or to learn a new technique.

3. **List what you can do to reach your goal.** Often something you want in the future can be broken down into a few smaller goals. One way to learn a new technique in three months is to set the goal of practicing that technique every day for half an hour. Sometimes this step involves getting help from others. You might need instruction from a piano teacher, for instance.

4. **Give yourself a set period of time in which to meet the goal.** Say that you want to be ready for the recital in three months. Be sure to set a number of checkpoints that will come sooner so that you can measure your progress as you work toward your goal.

5. **Reward yourself for reaching your goal.** Once you have reached your goal, give yourself a healthy reward. It could be getting something you wanted, like a new sweater. Or you could simply make yourself a medal to recognize your success. Either way, find a healthy way to congratulate yourself.

14. Making Decisions

Use with Chapter 3.

You will have to make decisions all your life. Some are simple, such as what to wear to school or what movie to see. But others are more complex, and often they are more important to your overall level of health. By following a step-by-step process, you can help yourself make these decisions.

1. **Identify the problem.** Be sure that you understand exactly what the problem is. Try to put aside your emotions and look at the situation logically.

2. **Make a list of all the choices available to you.** Think of as many different ways as you can to solve the problem. It could help to get ideas from someone else.

3. **Carefully examine the consequences of each possible solution.** Before you make a choice, you need to know what the results will be. Ask yourself what would happen in each possible solution. Ask what the results will be now *and* in the future. Ask how it will affect others, too. Remember that all choices have some negative results, or drawbacks, as well.

4. **Determine which solution seems to be the best and act on it.** Choose the

solution that has the best results and the fewest drawbacks.

5. **Check the results.** See whether your solution worked or whether the problem still remains. If the problem has not been solved, go back over the steps and find a new solution. If the solution didn't work, try to find out why. Were there factors you didn't take into account? Is there something you learned so that you can use this process better next time? If your solution *did* work, what does that tell you about how good you can become at making decisions?

15. Toll-Free Information

Use with Chapters 3, 4, 6, 8, 9, and 10.

Many groups provide toll-free numbers that allow people to call long distance for information or help. Some—labeled *(hot line)*—provide immediate help.

AIDS Hotline *(hot line)*	1-800-342-AIDS
Better Hearing Institute—Hearing Helpline	1-800-424-8576 (except AK, DC)
Cancer Information Service	1-800-422-6237 (except AK, MD)
Chemical Referral Center	1-800-262-8200 (except AK, DC)
Conservation and Renewable Energy Inquiry and Referral Service	1-800-233-3071 (except PA) 1-800-462-4983 (in PA)
Drug Abuse Hotline *(hot line)*	1-800-662-HELP
Dyslexia Society	1-800-222-3123
Epilepsy Information Line	1-800-426-0660 (except WA) 1-800-542-7054 (in WA)
International Juvenile Diabetes Foundation	1-800-223-1138 (except AK, NY)
Missing Children Help Center	1-800-872-5437 (except AK, FL)
Missing Children Network	1-800-235-3535
National Adolescent Suicide Hotline *(hot line)*	1-800-621-4000
National Child Abuse Hotline *(hot line)*	1-800-442-4453
National Cocaine Hotline *(hot line)*	1-800-COCAINE
National Federation of Parents for Drug-Free Youth	1-800-554-KIDS
National Hotline for Missing Children *(hot line)*	1-800-843-5678 (except DC)
National Runaway Switchboard *(hot line)*	1-800-621-4000
Runaway Hotline *(hot line)*	1-800-231-6946 (except AK, TX) 1-800-392-3352 (in TX)
Skin Care Hotline *(hot line)*	1-800-527-5448 (except AK, TX)
Spinal Cord Injury Hotline *(hot line)*	1-800-526-3456 (except MD) 1-800-638-1733 (in MD)
United States Consumer Product Safety Commission	1-800-638-8270
Venereal Disease Hotline *(hot line)*	1-800-227-8922

16. Building Good Communication Skills

Use with Chapters 3 and 4.

Give Positive Messages

One key to good communication is to give positive messages. You will find that others will be more willing to cooperate and be more friendly if they hear positive things from you. Some examples will give you an idea of how to make your messages more positive. Suppose another member of your group suggests going to a movie that you would rather not see.

- You could say, "I've heard about that one. Pete said it wasn't very good. How about seeing something else?"

- You could say, "George has already seen it, and he may not want to see it again."

- You could say, "I'm not in the mood for a comedy today. Is there something else you'd like to see?"

Use Good Listening Skills

An important part of good communicating is listening to what the other person has to say. Here are some guidelines for good listening.

- Keep an open mind. Someone who assumes that he or she knows what the other person is going to say cannot listen well.

- Give the other person a chance to talk. Interrupting is not good listening.

- Stop doing anything else so you can listen well and concentrate on what the person is saying. Trying to do something and listen at the same time means that you aren't doing either thing well. Thinking in advance about what you will say gets in the way of listening.

- Listen carefully. Hear everything the person is saying so he or she won't have to repeat it.

- Ask questions if you are not sure what was said. You can prevent many misunderstandings if you check to make sure you got the message right.

17. The Alphabet in Sign Language

Use with Chapter 2.

One way that deaf people learn to communicate is by *signing*. This is the practice of using finger shapes and movements to form words. The agreed-upon signs are called *Ameslan*, which comes from the words *American Sign Language*. Some words cannot be conveyed with these signs. These words are spelled out using the American Manual Alphabet.

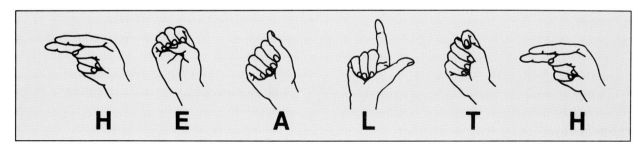

H E A L T H

18. Managing Your Time
Use with Chapter 3.

One of the best tools for living a stress-free life is to manage your time well. By controlling how you use your time, you can reduce the number of times that conflicting demands put stress on you. You can also be sure to complete tasks before they are due to be finished. Being prepared is a great way to lower stress.

1. **Start by keeping a log of your activities for one day.** Identify the amount of time you spend on each activity. Analyze your time chart to see how much of your time is useful and how much is wasted.

2. **Set goals for yourself.** Think of what you would like to have accomplished at the end of a day or a week that will make you feel proud of yourself. This will help you to identify what you want to do. Write

down what you must do to achieve those goals and try to estimate how long you must work at those activities.

3. **Make a list of all the things you must do.** Write down the things you are responsible for. This includes eating and sleeping, homework, and any chores or jobs you have around the house. Be sure to write down how long each responsibility takes.

4. **Combine the two lists.** Put the two lists together and then rank the items in terms of the ones that are most important.

5. **Plan your day to get your highest priority items accomplished.** Don't plan every minute of your day—leave some extra time for interruptions and for the unexpected. Leave time for relaxing, too.

19. Acting Cooperatively in a Group
Use with Chapter 4.

Part of getting along with others is learning how to cooperate in groups. Here are some suggestions for working in groups.

- **Give everybody a chance to participate.** In discussions, each member of the group should have a chance to speak his or her mind. When jobs are given out, find something for everyone to do.

- **Take turns.** Vary the jobs that people in the group do from time to time so that each member gets a chance to do different things.

- **Stay calm.** In group discussions, especially when there is a disagreement, people sometimes get excited and begin to speak loudly and harshly. Remembering to keep emotions tamed can help prevent the discussion from getting out of hand.

- **Speak to the issue, not the person.** When commenting on an idea, talk about the merits of the idea itself. Don't call the other person names or give insults. The result is only to make the other person angry.

- **Pay attention to others.** Listen to what other people have to say and give their ideas a chance.

- **Be ready to compromise.** Everybody will not always be convinced by one person's opinion. It is often necessary to reach an agreement that includes parts of a number of different suggestions. Be flexible and ready to adjust to a compromise.

- **Let the majority rule.** Group members are usually willing to go along with the idea that the largest number of people favors.

20. Finding Your Desired Weight

Use with Chapter 5.

Recommended Weight for Females and Males							
Female				**Male**			
Hgt.	**Small Frame**	**Medium Frame**	**Large Frame**	**Hgt.**	**Small Frame**	**Medium Frame**	**Large Frame**
4' 8"	88– 94	92–103	100–115	5' 0"	101-109	107–117	115–130
9	90– 97	94–106	102–118	1	104–112	110–121	118–133
10	92–100	97–109	105–121	2	107–115	113–125	121–136
11	95–103	100–112	108–124	3	110–118	116–128	124–140
5' 0"	98–106	103–115	111–127	4	113–121	119–131	127–144
1	101–109	106–118	114–130	5	116–125	122–135	130–148
2	104–112	109–122	117–134	6	120–129	126–139	134–153
3	107–115	112–126	121–138	7	124–133	130–144	139–158
4	110–119	116–131	125–142	8	128–137	134–148	143–162
5	114–123	120–135	129–146	9	132–142	138–152	147–166
6	118–127	124–139	133–150	10	136–146	142–157	151–171
7	122–131	128–143	137–154	11	140–150	146–162	156–176
8	126–136	132–147	141–157	6' 0"	144–154	150–167	160–181
9	130–140	136–151	145–164	1	148–158	154–172	165–186
10	134–144	140–155	149–169	2	152–162	159–177	170–191
11	138–148	144–159	153–174	3	156–167	164–182	174–196
6' 0"	142–152	149–163	157–179	4	160–171	169–187	178–201

Adapted from Metropolitan Life Insurance chart on weight of males and females.

21. Eating Manners

Use with Chapter 5.

Meals can be more relaxed and pleasant occasions if you eat following the rules of good manners. Here are some hints.

- Wash your hands and make yourself look nice before sitting down for a meal.
- If you spill anything on yourself, go to the washroom to clean it off.
- Put your napkin on your lap before the meal begins. Use it to clean bits of food off your mouth and hands.
- Rest your forearms on the edge of the table, but do not lean on your elbows.

- Take one bite of food at a time. Chew thoroughly, with your mouth closed.
- Speak when you do not have food in your mouth. Speak in a normal tone, not loudly.
- Use smaller forks for salad and larger forks for the main dish. Large spoons are meant for soup, and smaller spoons for dessert.
- Make a point of trying every dish that has been prepared. Refuse something only if you have an allergy to the food.
- Compliment the cook on his or her effort and good results.

A17

22. Recommended Daily Dietary Allowances

Use with Chapter 5.

Food and Nutrition Board, National Academy of Sciences—
  National Research Council
*Designed for the maintenance of good nutrition of practically
  all healthy people in the U.S.A.*

	Age (years)	Weight (kg)	Weight (lb)	Height (cm)	Height (in)	Protein (g)	Water-Soluble Vitamins				
							C (mg)	Thiamin (mg)	Riboflavin (mg)	Niacin (mg NE)[b]	B-6 (mg)
Infants	0.0–0.5	6	13	60	24	kg x 2.2	35	0.3	0.4	6	0.3
	0.5–1.0	9	20	71	28	kg x 2.0	35	0.5	0.6	8	0.6
Children	1–3	13	29	90	35	23	45	0.7	0.8	9	0.9
	4–6	20	44	112	44	30	45	0.9	1.0	11	1.3
	7–10	28	62	132	52	34	45	1.2	1.4	16	1.6
Males	11–14	45	99	157	62	45	50	1.4	1.6	18	1.8
	15–18	66	145	176	69	56	60	1.4	1.7	18	2.0
	19–22	70	154	177	70	56	60	1.5	1.7	19	2.2
	23–50	70	154	178	70	56	60	1.4	1.6	18	2.2
	51 +	70	154	178	70	56	60	1.2	1.4	16	2.2
Females	11–14	46	101	157	62	46	50	1.1	1.3	15	1.8
	15–18	55	120	163	64	46	60	1.1	1.3	14	2.0
	19–22	55	120	163	64	44	60	1.1	1.3	14	2.0
	23–50	55	120	163	64	44	60	1.0	1.2	13	2.0
	51 +	55	120	163	64	44	60	1.0	1.2	13	2.0
Pregnant						+30	+20	+0.4	+0.3	+2	+0.6
Lactating						+20	+40	+0.5	+0.5	+5	+0.5

Note: The Recommended Daily Dietary Allowances are revised every 5 years. The 1985 revision has been postponed pending further research into the advisability of certain changes.

[a] The allowances are intended to provide for individual variations among most normal persons as they live in the United States under usual environmental stresses. Diets should be based on a variety of common foods in order to provide other nutrients for which human requirements have been less well defined. See text for detailed discussion of allowance and of nutrients not tabulated.

[b] 1 NE (niacin equivalent) is equal to 1 mg of niacin or 60 mg of dietary tryptophan.

[c] The folacin allowances refer to dietary sources as determined by *Lactobacillus casei* assay after treatment with enzymes (conjugases) to make polyglutamyl forms of the vitamin available to the test organism.

Folacin[c]	B-12[d]	A[e]	D[f] (μg)	E[g]	Calcium (mg)	Phosphorous (mg)	Magnesium (mg)	Iron (mg)	Zinc (mg)	Iodine[h]
		Fat-Soluble Vitamins			**Minerals**					
30	0.5[g]	420	10	3	360	240	50	10	3	40
45	1.5	400	10	4	540	360	70	15	5	50
100	2.0	400	10	5	800	800	150	15	10	70
200	2.5	500	10	6	800	800	200	10	10	90
300	3.0	700	10	7	800	800	250	10	10	120
400	3.0	1000	10	8	1200	1200	350	18	15	150
400	3.0	1000	10	10	1200	1200	400	18	15	150
400	3.0	1000	7.5	10	800	800	350	10	15	150
400	3.0	1000	5	10	800	800	350	10	15	150
400	3.0	1000	5	10	800	800	350	10	15	150
400	3.0	800	10	8	1200	1200	300	18	15	150
400	3.0	800	10	8	1200	1200	300	18	15	150
400	3.0	800	7.5	8	800	800	300	18	15	150
400	3.0	800	5	8	800	800	300	18	15	150
400	3.0	800	5	8	800	800	300	10	15	150
+400	+1.0	+200	+5	+2	+400	+400	+150	h	+5	+25
+100	+1.0	+400	+5	+3	+400	+400	+150	h	+10	+50

[d] The recommended dietary allowance for vitamin B-12 in infants is based on average concentration of the vitamin in human milk. The allowances after weaning are based on energy intake (as recommended by the American Academy of Pediatrics) and consideration of other factors, such as intestinal absorption.

[e] Retinol equivalents. 1 retinol equivalent = 1 microgram retinol or 6 microgram beta-carotene.

[f] As cholecalciferol. 10 microgram cholecalciferol = 400 IU of vitamin D.

[g] alpha-tocopherol equivalents. 1 mg d-alpha-tocopherol = 1 microgram-TE.

[h] Measured in micrograms. The increased requirement during pregnancy cannot be met by the iron content of habitual American diets nor by the existing iron stores of many women; therefore the use of 30–60 mg of supplemental iron is recommended. Iron needs during lactation are not substantially different from those of nonpregnant women, but continued supplementation of the mother for 2–3 months after parturition is advisable in order to replenish stores depleted by pregnancy.

23. Table of Food Values for Selected Foods

Use with Chapter 5.

Table of Food Values

Food Group	Amount	Calories	Carbohydrates (g)	Fat (g)	Protein (g)	Calcium (mg)	Iron (mg)	Vitamin A (IU)	Thiamin (mg)	Riboflavin (mg)	Niacin (mg)	Vitamin C (mg)
Milk and Milk Products Group												
Cheese, American, process	1 oz/28 g	105	Tr	9	6	174	.1	340	.01	.10	Tr	0
Cheese, Cheddar	1 oz/28 g	115	Tr	9	7	204	.2	300	.01	.11	Tr	0
Cheese, cottage, creamed	½ c/120 ml	117	.1	5	14	67.5	.15	185	.025	.185	.135	Tr
Cheese, cottage, dry	½ c/120 ml	62.5	.5	Tr	12.5	238	.15	20	.02	.10	.1	0
Cheese, cream	1 oz/28 g	100	.2	10	2	23	.3	400	Tr	.06	Tr	0
Chocolate milk	1 c/240 ml	210	26	8	8	280	.6	300	.09	.41	.3	2
Cream, heavy	1 T/15 ml	80	.1	6	Tr	10	Tr	220	Tr	.02	Tr	Tr
Cream, light	1 T/15 ml	30	1	3	Tr	14	Tr	110	Tr	.02	Tr	Tr
Cream, sour	1 T/15 ml	25	1	3	Tr	14	Tr	90	Tr	.02	Tr	Tr
Ice cream 16% fat	½ c/120 ml	175	16	12	2	75.5	.05	445	.02	.14	.5	5
Milk	1 c/240 ml	150	11	8	8	291	.1	310	.09	.4	.2	2
Milk, low fat 2%	1 c/240 ml	121	12	5	8	297	.1	500	.1	.4	.2	2
Milk, skim	1 c/240 ml	85	12	Tr	8	302	.1	500	.09	.34	.2	2
Yogurt, fruit	1 c/240 ml	230	42	3	10	343	.2	120	.08	.4	.2	21
Yogurt, plain, skim milk	1 c/240 ml	125	17	Tr	13	452	.2	20	.11	.53	.3	2
Yogurt, plain, whole milk	1 c/240 ml	140	11	7	8	274	.1	280	.07	.32	.2	1
Meat, Poultry, Eggs, Fish, and Legumes Group												
Beef, lean (roasted)	3 oz/85 g	165	0	7	25	11	3.2	10	.06	.19	4.5	—
Beef, hamburger, 21% fat	3 oz/85 g	235	0	17	20	9	2.6	30	.07	.17	4.4	—
Chicken (broiled)	3 oz/85 g	120	0	3.5	21	3	1.5	30	.05	.17	7.8	—
Chicken (fried)	3 oz/85 g	160	1	5	26	9	1.3	70	.04	.17	11.6	—
Eggs (hard cooked)	1	80	1	6	6	28	1	260	.04	.13	Tr	0
Fish, bluefish (baked)	3½ oz/100 g	135	0	4	22	25	0.6	40	.09	.08	31.6	—
Ham, boiled	1 oz/28 g	65	0	5	5	3	.8	0	.12	.04	.7	—
Kidney beans (red beans)	1 c/240 ml	230	42	1	15	74	4.6	10	.13	.10	1.5	—
Lamb shoulder (roasted)	3 oz/85 g	285	0	18	23	9	1.0	—	.11	.2	4.0	—

Food	Serving											
Lentils	1 c/240 ml	210	39	Tr	16	50	4.2	40	.14	.12	1.2	0
Peanut butter	2 T/30 ml	190	6	16	8	20	.6	0	.04	.04	4.8	0
Peas, dried, split	1 c/240 ml	230	42	1	16	22	3.4	80	.3	.18	1.8	—
Pork (roast)	3 oz/85 g	310	0	20	26	9	2.6	0	.46	.21	4.1	—
Sardines	3 oz/85 g	175	0	9	20	372	2.5	190	.02	.17	4.6	—
Tuna, canned in oil	3 oz/85 g	170	0	7	24	7	1.6	70	.04	.1	10.1	—
Turkey, dark meat (roasted)	3 oz/85 g	175	0	7	26	—	2.0	—	.03	.2	3.6	—
Veal cutlet	3 oz/85 g	185	0	9	23	9	2.7	—	.06	.21	4.6	—

Fruits and Vegetables Group

Food	Serving											
Apple	1 (2¾"/63 mm)	80	20	1	Tr	10	.4	120	.04	.03	.1	6
Apricots	3 med	55	14	Tr	1	18	.5	2,890	.03	.04	.6	11
Banana	1 med	100	26	Tr	2	10	.8	230	.06	.07	.8	12
Beans, green	1 c/240 ml	30	7	Tr	2	63	.8	680	.07	.11	.6	15
Bean sprouts	1 c/240 ml	35	7	Tr	4	20	1.4	20	.14	.14	.8	20
Blueberries	1 c/240 ml	90	22	1	1	22	1.5	150	.04	.09	.7	20
Broccoli	1 c/240 ml	40	7	Tr	5	136	1.2	3,880	.14	.31	1.2	140
Cabbage, shredded	1 c/240 ml	15	4	Tr	1	34	.03	90	.04	.04	.2	33
Cabbage, red, shredded, raw	1 c/240 ml	20	5	Tr	1	29	.6	30	.06	.04	.3	43
Cantaloupe	½ melon	80	20	Tr	2	38	1.1	9,240	.11	.08	1.6	90
Carrots	1	30	7	Tr	1	27	.5	7,930	.04	.04	.4	6
Celery, raw	3 stalks	15	6	Tr	Tr	48	.3	330	.03	.03	.3	12
Corn, sweet kernels	1 c/240 ml	130	31	1	5	5	.3	580	.15	.10	2.5	8
Cranberry sauce	½ c/120 ml	202.5	52	Tr	.5	8.5	.3	30	.015	.015	.5	3
Dates	10	220	58	Tr	2	47	2.4	40	.07	.08	1.8	0
Grapefruit juice a	¼ c/60 ml	25	6	Tr	.25	6	.05	5	.01	.01	.1	24
Grapes, seedless	10	81	9	Tr	Tr	6	.2	50	.03	.02	.2	2
Lettuce, iceberg, raw	¼ head	17.5	2.6	Tr	.8	18	.45	297	.05	.05	.3	5
Mustard greens	1 c/240 ml	30	6	1	3	193	2.5	8,120	.11	.20	.8	67
Onions, boiled	½ c/120 ml	30	7	Tr	1.5	25	.4	Tr	.03	.03	.2	7.5
Orange	1 (3"/76 mm)	65	16	Tr	1	54	.5	260	.13	.05	.5	66

Note: Although ice cream is a good source of calcium, it also contains many calories, and may lead to weight problems.
Key: Tr—Nutrient present in trace amounts. ªMade from concentrate.

23. Table of Food Values for Selected Foods (continued)

Use with Chapter 5.

Table of Food Values (cont.)

Food Group	Amount	Calories	Carbohydrates (g)	Fat (g)	Protein (g)	Calcium (mg)	Iron (mg)	Vitamin A (IU)	Thiamin (mg)	Riboflavin (mg)	Niacin (mg)	Vitamin C (mg)
Fruits and Vegetables Group												
Orange juice[a]	¼ c/60 ml	30	7.25	Tr	.5	6.25	.1	135	.05	.001	.22	30
Peaches, peeled	1 (2½"/63 mm)	40	10	Tr	1	9	.5	1,330	.02	.05	1.0	7
Pear, Bartlett	1 (2½"/63 mm)	100	25	1	1	13	.5	30	.03	.07	.2	7
Peas, green, frozen	1 c/240 ml	110	19	Tr	.8	30	2.3	960	.43	.14	2.7	21
Pepper, green sweet, raw	1 med	15	4	Tr	1	7	.5	310	.06	.06	.4	94
Peach, peeled	1 (2½"/63 mm)	40	10	Tr	1	9	.5	1,330	.02	.05	1.0	7
Pineapple, cubed	1 c/240 ml	80	21	Tr	1	26	.5	110	.14	.05	.3	26
Potato, baked	1 med	145	33	Tr	4	14	1.1	Tr	.15	.07	2.7	31
Potatoes, French fried	10 pieces	155	18	7	2	9	.7	Tr	.07	.04	1.8	12
Prunes, dried	4 med	110	29	Tr	1	22	1.7	690	.04	.07	.7	1
Raisins (snack package)	½ oz/14 g	40	11	Tr	Tr	9	.5	Tr	.02	.01	.1	Tr
Spinach	1 c/240 ml	40	6	1	5	167	4	14,580	.13	.25	.9	50
Tomatoes, canned	1 c/240 ml	50	10	Tr	2	14	1.2	2,170	.12	.07	1.7	41
Tomato, raw	1 med	25	6	Tr	1	16	.6	1,110	.07	.05	.9	28
Tomato juice	6 oz/170 g	35	8	Tr	2	13	1.6	1,460	.09	.05	1.5	29
Bread and Cereals Group												
Bread, white enriched	1 slice	70	13	1	2	21	.6	Tr	.08	.06	.8	Tr
Bread, whole wheat	1 slice	65	14	1	3	24	.8	0	.07	.03	.8	Tr
Bread, pumpernickel (⅔% rye)	1 slice	80	17	Tr	3	27	.8	0	.09	.07	.6	0
Corn flakes, fortified (25% RDA)	1 c/240 ml	95	21	Tr	2	V	V	V	V	V	V	13
Crackers, saltines	4	50	8	1	1	2	.5	0	.05	.05	.4	0
Egg noodles, enriched	1 c/240 ml	200	37	2	7	16	1.4	110	.22	.13	1.9	0
Pasta, enriched, (macaroni cooked, etc.)	1 c/240 ml	190	39	1	7	14	1.4	0	.23	.13	1.8	0
Rice, instant, enriched	1 c/240 ml	180	40	Tr	4	5	1.3	0	.21	V	1.7	0
Rice, enriched	1 c/240 ml	185	41	Tr	4	33	1.4	0	.19	.02	2.1	0
Rice, puffed, whole grain	1 c/240 ml	60	13	Tr	1	3	.3	0	.07	.01	.7	0

Food	Measure											
Wheat, farina, quick	1 c/240 ml	105	22	Tr	3	147	V	0	.12	.07	1	0
Wheat flakes, fortified, 25% U.S. RDA	¾ c/180 ml	105	24	Tr	3	12	4.8	1,320	.40	.45	5.3	16
Wheat puffed, whole grain	1 c/240 ml	55	12	Tr	2	4	.6	0	.08	.03	1.2	0
Wheat, shredded, whole grain	1 large biscuit	90	20	1	2	11	.9	0	.06	.03	1.1	0
Wheat, whole grain cereal	1 c/240 ml	110	23	1	4	17	1.2	0	.15	.05	1.5	0
Other												
Bacon, fried crisp	2 slices	85	Tr	8	4	2	.5	0	.08	.05	.8	—
Butter	1 T/14 g	100	Tr	12	Tr	3	Tr	430	Tr	Tr	Tr	0
Doughnuts, glazed	1	205	22	11	3	16	.6	25	.1	.1	.8	0
Honey	1 T/21 g	65	17	0	Tr	1	.1	0	Tr	.01	.1	Tr
Margarine, regular	1 T/15 g	100	Tr	12	Tr	3	Tr	470	Tr	Tr	Tr	0
Mayonnaise	1 T/15 ml	100	Tr	11	Tr	3	.1	40	Tr	.01	Tr	—
Nuts, peanuts, salted	1 c/240 ml	840	27	72	37	107	3	—	.46	.19	24.8	0
Nuts, walnuts	1 c/240 ml	785	19	74	26	Tr	7.5	380	.28	.14	.9	—
Oil, corn	1 T/15 ml	120	0	14	0	0	0	—	0	0	0	0
Pizza, cheese	1 slice	145	22	4	6	86	1.1	230	.16	.18	1.6	4
Popcorn, plain	1 c/240 ml	25	5	Tr	1	1	.2	—	—	.01	.1	0
Salad dressing, Italian	1 T/15 ml	85	1	9	Tr	2	Tr	Tr	Tr	Tr	Tr	—
Salad dressing, Italian low calorie	1 T/15 ml	10	Tr	1	Tr	Tr	Tr	Tr	Tr	Tr	Tr	—
Seeds, sunflower	½ c/120 g	405	14.5	34.5	17.5	87	5.15	35	1.42	.17	3.9	—
Sugar	1 T/12 g	45	12	0	0	0	Tr	0	0	0	0	0

Note: All fruits and vegetables fresh unless noted. Vegetables fresh cooked unless noted.

Key: [a] Made from concentrate. Tr—Nutrient present in trace amounts. V—Varies by brand; consult label.

24. Fast Food and the Basic Food Groups

Use with Chapter 5.

Analysis of Fast Foods						
Fast Food Item	Estimated Number of Calories	Milk Group	Meat Group	Fruit Vegetable Group	Grain Group	Other
Main Dishes						
Hamburger	560–675		Hamburger	Onions, lettuce, tomato	Roll	Ketchup, pickles, mayonnaise
Beef taco	190	Cheese	Beef	Lettuce	Taco Shell	
Bean burrito	345	Cheese	Refried beans	Onions	Flour tortilla	Sauce
Fish dinner	840–900		Fish	French fries, coleslaw	Muffins	
Chicken dinner	650		Chicken	Mashed potatoes, coleslaw	Roll	Gravy
Meat and mushroom pizza	380–450	Cheese	Beef	Mushrooms, tomato sauce	Crust	
Other Dishes (calories)				French fries (220), coleslaw (121), corn on the cob (169), mashed potatoes (64)	Roll (61), hush puppies (153)	Onion rings (270), gravy (23)
Beverages (calories)		Whole milk (150), 2% milk (120), chocolate shake (390)	Orange juice (80)		Soft drinks, coffee (2)	

25. Dangerous Chemicals in Tobacco

Use with Chapter 8.

Tobacco contains a number of dangerous chemicals. The list that follows shows the chemicals released by cigarette smoke. These chemicals affect the nonsmoker as much as they do the smoker. These chemicals are the ones that create the most danger for non-smokers. They are listed in order of most to least dangerous.

1. **Acrolein.** A toxic, colorless liquid with irritating vapors.

2. **Carbon Monoxide.** A highly toxic, flammable gas used in the manufacture of numerous chemical products. Inhalation of carbon monoxide interferes with the transportation of oxygen from the lungs to the tissues in which it is required.

3. **Nicotine.** A poisonous alkaloid; also used as an insecticide, and to kill parasitic worms in animals.

4. **Ammonia.** A gaseous alkaline compound of nitrogen and hydrogen used as a coolant in refrigeration and air-conditioning equipment, and in explosives, artificial fertilizers, and disinfectants.

5. **Formic Acid.** A liquid acid used in processing textiles and leather. Exposure to the acid irritates the mucous membranes and causes blistering.

6. **Hydrogen Cyanide.** An extremely poisonous liquid used in many chemical processes, including fumigation.

7. **Nitrous Oxides.** A group of irritating and sometimes poisonous gases which combine with hydrocarbons to produce smog. Nitrogen dioxide can weaken bodily tissues and increase susceptibility to respiratory ailments.

8. **Formaldehyde.** A pungent gas used primarily as a disinfectant and preser-vative. It is extremely irritating to the mucous membranes.

9. **Phenol.** A caustic, poisonous acidic compound present in coal and wood tar, which is used as a disinfectant.

10. **Acetaldehyde.** A highly toxic, flammable liquid, which irritates the eyes and mucous membranes and accelerates the action of the heart. Prolonged exposure causes blood pressure to rise and decreases the number of blood cells.

11. **Hydrogen Sulfide.** A poisonous gas that is produced naturally from decomposing matter and which is used extensively in chemical laboratories.

12. **Pyridine.** A flammable liquid used in pharmaceuticals, water repellents, bactericides, and herbicides.

13. **Methyl Chloride.** A toxic gas used in the production of rubber, in paint remover, and as an antiknock agent in gasoline.

14. **Acetonitrile.** A toxic compound found in coal tar and molasses residue and used in the production of plastics, rubber, acrylic fiber, insecticide, and perfumery.

15. **Propionaldehyde.** A colorless liquid with a suffocating odor used in chemical disinfectant and preservative, as well as in plastic and rubber production.

16. **Methanol.** A poisonous liquid alcohol used in automotive antifreezes, rocket fuels, synthetic dyestuffs, resins, drugs, and perfumes.

26. Reading Cautions on Prescription Drugs

Use with Chapter 10.

Cautions on Prescription Drugs	
Caution	**What It Means**
Shake well before using	Be sure to shake the bottle to mix the medicine thoroughly before measuring out the dosage
Take with food or milk	Take the medicine with a meal
A great deal of water should be taken with this medication	Drink plenty of water as long as the medicine is being used
For external use only	Only apply to the skin; eating this medicine will cause illness
Refrigerate; Shake well	Keep the medicine in the refrigerator or it will spoil; the medicine separates or settles when it sits, so it must be shaken to be effective
May cause drowsiness	Taking the medicine may make the person sleepy
This prescription may be refilled	The person can get more of the medicine from the pharmacy without needing a new prescription
No refills	The person needs a new prescription before getting any more of the medicine

27. Saying "No" to Peer Pressure

Use with Chapters 4, 6, 8, 9, 10, and 13.

As you grow, you will find yourself in situations where friends put pressure on you to do things you do not wish to do. It could be a dare to do something dangerous. The pressure could be to use tobacco, alcohol, or drugs. Or it could be pressure to have sexual relations. Whatever the cause, it is important to know how to resist this pressure.

Below are some steps you can take.

- **Avoid situations where the pressure will arise.** The first thing to remember is to try to prevent the problem from occurring. Staying away from parties where you think there will be alcohol or drugs helps. Going out on group dates can reduce the pressure to have sex.

- **Get support from others you can rely on.** Talk to a parent, an older brother or sister, a teacher, counselor, or coach, or a religious leader. Spending time with friends who don't put this pressure on you helps, too.

- **Know what to say if the pressure arises.** Plan ahead about how you might respond to such pressure. Know what your reasons are so that you can state them if you must.

- **Say "no."** While it's good to have your reasons stored away, you should not have to use them. Simply say "no." It is your decision, and you do not have to justify it to others. Still, if you must, state your reasons.

- **If the pressure is too great, walk away.** Don't stay around if you can't get rid of the pressure. The best thing to do is to leave.

28. Immunization Schedule

Use with Chapter 11.

The American Medical Association recommends that each person receive the following vaccines in childhood. Check with your parent or family doctor to see if you have had the needed vaccines.

Age	Vaccinations		Age	Vaccinations
2 months	Diphtheria (1st of 5)[a] Pertussis (1st of 5)[a] Tetanus (1st of 5)[a]	} DPT	15 months	Measles[a, c] Mumps[a, d] Rubella[a]
	Trivalent oral polio[b] (1st of 4)		18 months	Diphtheria (4th of 5) Pertussis (4th of 5) Tetanus (4th of 5) Polio (3rd of 4)
4 months	Diphtheria (2nd of 5) Pertussis (2nd of 5) Tetanus (2nd of 5) Polio (2nd of 4)		At school entry (4 through 6 years)	Diphtheria (5th of 5) Pertussis (5th of 5) Tetanus (5th of 5) Polio (4th of 4)

6 months	Diphtheria (3rd of 5)
	Pertussis (3rd of 5)
	Tetanus (3rd of 5)
	Polio (optional, but
	   some physicians give
	   this additional dose)
			14 through 16
			and every 10
			years thereafter[e]
				Diphtheria booster
				Tetanus booster

[a]Usually combined into one shot.
[b]**Trivalent** means that it *protects against all strains of polio.* A child gets three doses of trivalent oral polio vaccine (at 3, 6, and 8 months), followed by boosters.
[c]A measles injection usually gives lifetime immunity.
[d]Immunity from mumps is known to last for six years.
[e]People in their teens can become quite ill from pertussis vaccine, so they are given a special adult vaccine, called DT vaccine.

29. Lowering the Risk of Heart Disease

Use with Chapter 12.

There are nine factors that can increase the risk of heart disease. The first four are beyond your control.

- **Age.** As you become older, your risk increases.

- **Sex.** Up until age 40, males have a greater risk than females. Afterwards, the risks are about the same.

- **Race.** Black Americans have a greater risk than other groups.

- **Family history.** Someone with a family history of heart disease has a greater risk than someone without such a history.

The other five factors, however, are related to lifestyle. Your level of risk can be controlled by following these healthy habits.

A27

- **Maintain the correct body weight.** Being at the correct weight for your age, sex, and body type keeps your risk down.
- **Exercise regularly.** Exercising keeps your circulatory system healthy. Doing aerobic exercise three or four times a week is especially healthy.
- **Eat a healthy diet.** Eating a diet that is low in fat and salt and high in fiber keeps your risk low.
- **Manage stress in your life.** Keeping stress to a minimum helps lower your risk.
- **Avoid cigarette smoking.** Saying "no" to smoking is a healthy decision.

30. Drowning Prevention

Use with Chapter 13.

Drowning is a constant danger for anyone who is in or near the water. Someone who falls overboard or is left alone in the water for some reason can use the technique called *drowning prevention* to save his or her life. Even a non-swimmer can use this technique. Staying calm and not panicking are key to this technique.

1. **Relax.** After taking a deep breath, sink vertically beneath the surface of the water with only the back of your head above the surface. Allow your arms and legs to relax until your fingers touch your knees. Keep your neck relaxed.

2. **Get ready.** Raise your arms gently—without thrashing about—to a crossed position until the backs of your wrists touch your forehead. Step forward with one leg and back with the other at the same time.

3. **Raise your head.** Raise your head quickly but smoothly above the water and exhale through your nose. You should keep your arms and legs in the position described in step 2.

4. **Breathe in.** Keep your head above the surface by gently sweeping your arms down and out and by stepping downward with both feet. While doing this, breathe in through your mouth.

5. **Drop below the surface.** Go below the surface again by putting your head down. Press downward with your arms and hands to prevent yourself from descending too far.

6. **Rest.** Repeat step 1 again for 6 to 10 seconds. Be sure that you relax completely. Then repeat steps 2 through 5.

Continue this procedure until help arrives. If you stay calm and breathe carefully, you can keep yourself afloat for some time.

31. Uniform Traffic Controls

Use with Chapter 13.

Knowing—and obeying—traffic signals, signs, and pavement markings is just as important to pedestrians and cyclists as it is to drivers of motor vehicles. The purpose of these traffic controls is to regulate the movement of all people who use streets and highways. By obeying these traffic controls, each person helps prevent accidents from happening.

Traffic Signals

There are two main kinds of traffic signals. Traffic lights use green, amber, and red lights to control how traffic moves.

- **Green light.** The green light signals that traffic can proceed through an intersection if it is clear.
- **Yellow light.** The yellow light warns that a red light will soon follow. Anyone approaching an intersection that shows a yellow light should stop unless it is not safe to do so.
- **Red light.** A red light signals that the person approaching an intersection must stop. Unless there is a sign posted otherwise, a cyclist could turn right when facing a red light if the way is clear.

The other kind of traffic signal that you may encounter is a **WALK/DON'T WALK** sign. This is positioned at pedestrian crossings and controls pedestrian movement.

Traffic Signs

There are many different kinds of traffic signs, but they can all be grouped into one of three types.

- **Regulatory signs.** These control the flow of traffic. Examples are **STOP** signs, **YIELD** signs, and **ONE WAY** signs.

- **Warning signs.** These alert drivers, pedestrians, and cyclists to upcoming changes that they must bear in mind.
- **Guide signs.** These signs notify drivers, pedestrians, or cyclists of the roadway that they are on or will be meeting up with.

The **STOP** sign has the same function as a red traffic light. It tells the road user to stop. Whereas a user must stay at the traffic light until it changes to green, someone at a **STOP** sign can proceed once the intersection is clear. He or she should look both ways before proceeding.

The **YIELD** sign signals that whoever is using the other road at an intersection has the right of way. This means that oncoming traffic must be allowed to pass before a pedestrian, cyclist, or driver can proceed through the intersection.

The **ONE WAY** sign shows that all traffic on the road must go in the direction in which the arrow is pointing.

Road users are warned not to enter a one-way street incorrectly by a **DO NOT ENTER** sign.

Another common kind of regulatory sign is the **directional sign.** It is a white rectangle with black arrows showing the direction that traffic in a given lane must take.

A common warning sign is the **school crossing sign** posted near schools. It tells cyclists and drivers to slow until they have passed the school zone.

Some warning signs are orange colored and diamond shaped. They give notice about **construction work** that affects traffic.

Pavement Markings

Various markings are painted on the pavement to show road users what movement is or is not allowed.

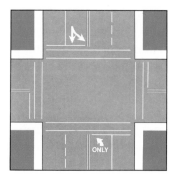

- **White lines.** Solid white lines may not be crossed. They mark off lanes that are set aside for special traffic movement. At some intersections, arrows within the lane marked by a solid white line indicate that movement is only allowed in certain directions. A pair of solid white lines is used from one corner to another at an intersection to show where pedestrians may cross. All pedestrians should cross within those lines and not elsewhere.

- **Dashed white lines.** Dashed white lines show that movement is allowed from one lane to another. A cyclist or driver should never move into another lane without looking back to see that the way is clear of oncoming traffic.

- **Yellow lines.** Yellow lines mark the boundary between lanes of traffic moving in two different directions. Solid yellow lines should never be crossed. Broken yellow lines may be crossed by a driver who is passing another vehicle if the way is clear.

32. The Steps in CPR

Use with Chapter 13.

Giving CPR to Adults

Cardiopulmonary resuscitation (CPR) is a life-saving procedure that should only be given by someone who has been properly taught. The American Heart Association and the American Red Cross give courses in CPR.

When using CPR on an unconscious victim, you follow a fixed order of steps. You can think of these steps as the ABCs. A stands for *airway*, B for *breathing*, and C for *circulation*.

A Is for Airway

If you are around a person who has fainted, or collapsed, first shake the person gently and ask in a loud voice if he or she is all right. If the person is unconscious, you must act quickly.

(1) Gently roll the person over on his or her back. Do not, however, move the person if you think the neck is injured. When turning the person over, try to move the whole body at once. Do not turn the upper part first, then the legs.

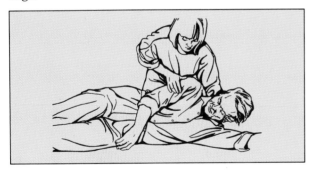

B Is for Breathing

Next, see if the person is breathing. To do so, see if the person's chest is rising and falling. Or you can listen at the mouth and nose for the sounds of breathing. You can also lean close to the person to feel on your cheek any breath being exhaled. (2) If the victim is not breathing, give rescue breathing.

C Is for Circulation

Next, find out if the person's heart is beating. You can do this by feeling for the carotid pulse. This is *the heartbeat you can feel on either side of the neck* by placing your index and middle fingers on the carotid artery just below the ear.

If you cannot find a pulse, the victim's heart has stopped. You must then start the victim's heart pumping again by giving CPR. Remember, you must have a certificate in CPR to perform the following procedure.

(3) Place the first two fingers of your hand closest to the person's legs on the person's lowest rib. Then move this hand up along the rib until you come to the point at which the rib joins the breastbone. Keep your two fingers resting at this point and place the heel of the other hand just above them on the person's chest. Then lift the hand that you used to find the breastbone and put it on top of the hand whose heel is resting on the chest. Interlock the fingers of your two hands so that only the heel of the bottom hand touches the person's chest.

(4) Once you have correctly placed your hands, kneel over the person's chest. Keep your arms straight and slowly push in the person's breastbone about *one to two inches*. Then ease up, but do not lift the heel of your hand off the person's chest. Repeat this procedure *fifteen times*.

After applying and relaxing pressure to the victim's chest fifteen times, give the person two breaths of air. To do so, push the victim's head back. Then lean over and breathe into the victim's mouth. Then repeat the procedure for placing the hands and again apply and relax pressure fifteen times. Continue this process until medical help arrives. You should apply and relax pressure to the person's chest at a rate of about eighty to a hundred times each minute. This is much faster than once a second. Be sure to give the person two breaths every fifteen pushes.

Giving CPR to Infants and Small Children

Opening the Child's Airway. (1) Tilt the child's head back slightly. (2) If the child is not breathing, cover the mouth and nose with your mouth. Then give the child one breath of air every three seconds.

Placing Your Hand and Applying Pressure. (3) Turn the child on his or her back. Support the neck and shoulders with one of your hands. (4) Next, place your first two fingers on the child's breastbone just below where an imaginary line would run connecting the nipples. Press the breastbone *one-half to one inch*, then relax the pressure. Repeat this procedure *five times*, then give the child a breath. Continue at a rate of eighty to a hundred times per minute, with one breath every five pushes until help arrives.

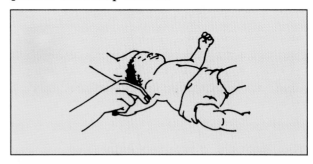

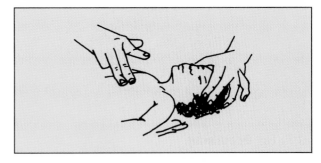

33. Giving Rescue Breathing

Use with Chapter 13.

Adults and Older Children

1. Check to see if the victim is conscious. Shake the person gently and ask, "Are you all right?"

2. If there is no response, lift the chin with the fingers, place one hand on the forehead and tilt the victim's head back, pointing the chin upward. This moves the jaw and tongue forward, opening the airway.

3. Place your ear and cheek close to the victim's mouth and nose. *Look, listen,* and *feel. Look* at the chest to see if it is rising and falling; *listen* and *feel* for air that is being exhaled.

4. If there is no breathing, pinch the victim's nostrils shut with your index finger and thumb.

5. Place your mouth over the victim's mouth, forming a seal.

6. Give the person two full breaths.

7. Keep the head tilted. Then *look, listen,* and *feel* again. Check the pulse. If there is a pulse but no breathing, begin giving the victim one breath every five seconds.

8. Watch the chest to see whether it is rising and falling. If it is, you know that air is getting into the lungs.

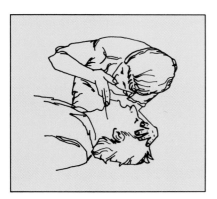  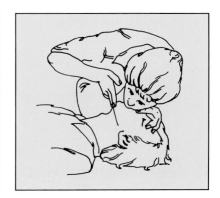

Infants and Small Children

For children (ages 1 to 8) and infants (up to 1 year of age), do not tilt the head as far back. Your mouth will cover and form a seal around an infant's mouth and nose. Gently puff into the infant's mouth and count to three. Then give another puff. Continue until breathing resumes.

34. Choosing a Health Care Professional

Use with Chapter 14.

When looking around to find a health care professional, use the following checklist.

1. **Basic information.** Name; address; office phone; office hours.

2. **Type of professional.** What kind of professional are you? (Examples are family doctor, pediatrician, obstetrician/gynecologist, etc.)

3. **Type of practice.** Is it a solo or group practice or an HMO?

4. **Professional affiliations.** What medical societies does the provider belong to? What are the requirements for membership?

5. **Use of paramedical professionals.** Does the professional use the services of nurse-practitioners, physicians' assistants, or nurse midwives?

6. **Services provided.** What services does the professional provide? How much time is allowed for visits? How far in advance must routine visits be scheduled? What provision is made for urgent or emergency visits? What is done for weekend or nighttime care? What kind of care is given on the phone? Are medical records open to the patient? Is the professional affiliated with any hospitals?

7. **Coverage.** When the professional is ill or on vacation, who covers the patients? Describe the professional who gives coverage.

8. **Special services.** What equipment is in the office and what special services are offered?

9. **Billing information.** How are bills handled? Is payment required when services are provided? Does the professional accept Medicare or Medicaid? Is any help given with filling out insurance forms?

10. **Accessibility.** How easy is it to get to the office?

11. **Medical philosophy.** What is the professional's attitude to self-care, exercise, nutrition, second opinions, or any other topics you are concerned about?

Glossary

The Glossary contains all the important terms used throughout the text. It includes the **boldfaced** terms listed in the "Words to Know" lists at the beginning of each lesson and all the *italicized* words that appear in text, captions, and features.

The Glossary lists the term, the pronunciation (in the case of difficult terms), the definition, and all page numbers on which the term appears. The pronunciations here and in the text follow the system outlined below. The column headed "symbol" shows the spelling used in this book to represent the appropriate method.

Pronunciation Key

Sound	As in	Symbol	Example
ă	h*a*t, m*a*p	a	abscess (AB·sess)
ā	*a*ge, f*a*ce	ay	atrium (AY·tree·uhm)
a	c*a*re, th*eir*	ehr	capillaries (KAP·uh·lehr·ees)
ä, ŏ	f*a*ther, h*o*t	ah	biopsy (BY·ahp·see)
ar	f*ar*	ar	cardiac (KARD·ee·ak)
ch	*ch*ild, mu*ch*	ch	barbiturate (bahr·BICH·uh·ruht)
ĕ	l*e*t, b*e*st	e	vessels (VES·uhls)
ē	b*ea*t, s*ee*, cit*y*	ee	acne (AK·nee)
er	t*er*m, st*ir*, p*urr*	er	nuclear (NOO·klee·er)
ĭ	*i*t, h*y*mn	i	bacteria (bak·TIR·ee·uh)
ī	*i*ce, f*i*ve	y	benign (bi·NYN)
		eye	iris (EYE·ruhs)
k	*c*oat, loo*k*, *ch*orus	k	defect (DEE·fekt)
ō	*o*pen, c*o*at, gr*ow*	oh	aerobic (ehr·OH·bik)
ô	*or*der	or	organ (OR·guhn)
ȯ	fl*aw*, *a*ll	aw	palsy (PAWL·zee)
oi	v*oi*ce	oy	goiter (GOYT·er)
ou	*ou*t	ow	fountain (FOWN·tuhn)
s	*s*ay, ri*c*e	s	dermis (DER·muhs)
sh	*sh*e, atten*tion*	sh	conservation (kahn·ser·VAY·shuhn)
ŭ	c*u*p, fl*oo*d	uh	bunion (BUHN·yuhn)
u	p*u*t, w*oo*d, c*ou*ld	u	compulsive (kuhm·PUL·siv)
ü	r*u*le, m*o*ve, y*ou*	oo	attitudes (AT·uh·toodz)
zh	plea*s*ure	zh	transfusion (trans·FYOO·zhuhn)
ə	*a*bout, tak*e*n	uh	asthma (AS·muh)

A

Abdominal thrusts. Quick, upward pulls into the diaphragm to force out a substance blocking the airway when someone is choking. (page 393)

Abnormal. Not normal. (page 345)

Abscess (AB·sess). A painful tooth condition in which pus collects in the bone sockets around a tooth. (page 40)

Abuse (uh·BYOOS). Physical or mental mistreatment of another person. (page 109)

Accident chain. The combination of a situation, an unsafe habit, and an unsafe act leading to an accident. (page 366)

Acetaminophen (uh·seet·uh·MIN·uh·fuhn). A medicine that reduces pain and fever. (page 183)

Acid rain. Rain that contains pollution. (page 432)

Acne (AK·nee). A clogging of the pores with oil. (page 30)

Acquired immunodeficiency syndrome (uh·KWYRD im·yoo·noh·di·FISH·uhn·see SIN·drohm) (AIDS). A deadly disease that attacks some of the body's white-blood cells. (page 324)

Acupuncture. An ancient Chinese method of relieving pain by inserting long thin needles into the body in certain places. (page 357)

Addiction (uh·DIK·shuhn). A physical or mental need for a drug or other substance. (pages 158, 236, 255, 279)

Adolescence (ad·uhl·ES·uhns). The time of life between childhood and adulthood. (pages 114, 162)

Adrenal (uh·DREEN·uhl) **glands.** The glands that control the stress response and the amount of salt and water in the body. (page 217)

Adrenaline (uh·DREN·uhl·uhn. A chemical that makes the heart beat faster and speeds up blood flow in response to stress. (pages 79, 219)

Advertising. Sending out messages (or ads) meant to interest consumers in buying goods and services. (page 408)

Aerobic (ehr·OH·bik) **exercise.** Rhythmic, nonstop, vigorous activity that aids the heart. (pages 18, 206)

AIDS. See *Acquired immunodeficiency syndrome.*

AIDS dementia (di·MEN·chuh). A disease of the brain and nervous system that can affect someone with AIDS. (page 325)

AIDS-related complex (ARC). A set of early signs of AIDS but not yet the disease itself. (page 324)

Al-Anon. A group that helps the husbands, wives, and friends of alcoholics. (page 260)

Alateen. A group that helps children of alcoholic parents. (page 260)

Alcohol (AL·kuh·hawl). A drug that is produced by a chemical reaction in some foods and that has powerful effects on the body. (page 250)

Alcoholic. A person who cannot keep from drinking alcohol. (page 258)

Alcoholics Anonymous (uh·NAHN·uh·muhs) **(AA).** A support group for alcoholics. (page 259)

Alcoholism. A disease caused by a physical and mental need for alcohol. (page 258)

Allergy. Extreme sensitivity to a substance. (pages 312, 389)

Alternative (ahl·TER·nuht·iv). Another way of thinking or acting. (page 265)

Alveoli (al·VEE·oh·ly). Tiny air sacs at the end of the bronchi that perform the work of exchanging gases with the blood. (pages 194, 234)

Alzheimer's (AHLTS·hy·merz) **disease.** A form of mental slowdown. (page 170)

Amino (uh·MEE·noh) **acids.** Chains of building blocks that make up proteins. (page 126)

Amphetamine (am·FET·uh·meen). A drug prescribed to stimulate the central nervous system to make a person feel less tired or to reduce a person's appetite. (page 280)

Anabolic steroids (an·uh·BAHL·ik STIR·oyds). Drugs that some athletes take illegally because they believe the drugs will build stronger muscles. (page 292)

Anemia (uh·NEE·mee·uh). A condition in which a person does not have enough red-blood cells. (page 191)

Anorexia nervosa (an·uh·REK·see·uh nuhr·VOH·suh). A serious eating disorder in which the victim has an unreasonable fear of being overweight that often leads to extreme weight loss from self-starvation. (pages 85, 145)

Antibiotic (an·ti·by·AHT·ik). A drug produced by a tiny living organism that is used to fight germs. (page 273)

Antiperspirant. A product that contains chemicals to help a body area remain dry and that covers up a body odor with a pleasant scent. (page 29)

Anus (AY·nuhs). Opening through which the feces pass out of the body. (page 213)

Anvil. A small bone behind the eardrum. (page 48)

Appendicular (ap·uhn·DIK·yuh·ler) **skeleton.** The shoulders, arms, hips, and legs. (page 199)

Arteries. The largest blood vessels, which take blood away from the heart. (page 188)

Arteriosclerosis (ar·tir·ee·oh·skluh·ROH·suhs). Hardening of the arteries. See also Atherosclerosis. (pages 192, 340)

Arthritis (ar·THRYT·uhs). Any of more than 100 conditions caused by a painful swelling in the joints caused by the breakdown of bones or connective tissue. (pages 202, 356, 413)

Artificial pacemaker (art·uh·FISH·uhl PAY·smay·ker). A small device that sends electrical pulses to the heart to make it beat regularly. (page 344)

Artificial respiration. See *Rescue breathing.*

Asthma (AS·muh). A respiratory condition in which the bronchi swell and close up. (pages 197, 431)

Astigmatism (uh·STIG·muh·tiz·uhm). An eye condition in which images are distorted. (page 46)

Atherosclerosis (ath·uh·roh·skluh·ROH·suhs). A condition in which fatty acid deposits build up on the artery wall. See also Arteriosclerosis. (page 340)

Athlete's foot. A problem caused by fungi growing in the warm, damp areas of the foot. (page 52)

Atrium (AY·tree·uhm). The top chamber on each side of the heart. (page 189)

Attitudes (AT·uh·toodz). Feelings and beliefs. (page 9)

Auditory (AWD·uh·tor·ee) **nerve.** A network of nerves in the cochlea that carry messages to the brain. (page 49)

Axial (AK·see·uhl) **skeleton.** The skull and spine. (page 199)

B

Baby teeth. The teeth that come in late in the first year of life. (page 39)

Bacteria (bak·TIR·ee·uh). Tiny one-celled organisms that grow everywhere. (page 301)

Balance. A feeling of stability and control over the body. (page 49)

Barbiturate (bahr·BICH·uh·ruht). A depressant to help a person relax; often used as a sleeping aid. (page 282)

Basic food group. One of four groups in which the foods within each group supply similar nutrients. (page 130)

B-cell. A lymphocyte that makes a protein that attacks germ cells. (page 308)

Behavior. The way you act in the many different situations and events in your life. (pages 7, 62)

Benign (bi·NYN) **tumor.** A mass of cells that is not cancerous. (page 346)

Bile. A substance the liver produces to help digest fat. (page 213)

Biodegradable (by·oh·di·GRAYD·i·buhl). A quality of certain products that have chemicals that can break down in water without polluting the water. (page 433)

Biological (by·uh·LAHJ·i·kuhl) **age.** Age measured by how well various body parts are working. (page 169)

Biopsy (BY·ahp·see). The removal by a doctor of a small piece of a tumor for testing in a lab for cancer. (page 348)

Birth defect (DEE·fekt). A disorder of a developing and newborn baby. (pages 157, 336)

Blackhead. An oil-plugged pore that is exposed to the air and darkens. (page 30)

Bladder. The part of the body that stores urine before it is pushed out of the body. (page 213)

Blended family. The type of family composed of a remarried parent, a stepparent, and the children of one or both parents. (page 106)

Blister. A fluid-filled mark on the skin. (page 52)

Blizzard. A very heavy snowstorm with high winds. (page 440)

Blood alcohol level (BAL). The percentage of alcohol in the blood. (page 253)

Blood bank. A place where blood is given and stored. (page 190)

Blood pressure. The force of the blood on the inside walls of the blood vessels. (pages 189, 341)

Blood transfusion (trans·FYOO·zhuhn). Putting one person's blood into another person's body. (page 190)

Blood vessels (VES·uhls). Tubes that carry blood throughout the body. (page 188)

Body language. Messages passed on through body movements. (page 70)

Body odor. The unpleasant smell that occurs when bacteria feed on sweat that builds up in certain body areas. (page 29)

Boils. An infection of the skin accompanied by swelling, redness, and a buildup of pus. (page 31)

Bone spur. A little point or knob at the end of a bone. (page 358)

Booster. A later dose of vaccine given after the effects of the first one wears off. (page 309)

Braces. Small wires that are applied to the teeth to remedy malocclusion. (page 41)

Brain. The organ that commands all the body's actions and allows a person to think. (page 182)

Brain death. The result when oxygen is cut off from all the brain cells. (page 172)

Brain stem. The part of the brain that controls such body actions as breathing, the heartbeat, and digestion. (page 183)

Brain tumor (TOO·mer). A mass of cells in the brain that grows out of control. (page 185)

Breast self-examination. An examination that females should do to check themselves for breast cancer. (pages 224, 349)

Bronchi (BRAHN·ky). The two passages through which air enters the lungs. (pages 194, 234)

Bronchitis (brahn·KYT·uhs). A swelling of the bronchi. (page 197)

Bruise. The result of a blow on a part of the body. (page 388)

Buddy system. An agreement between two people to stay together and watch for each other's safety. (page 376)

Bulimia (byoo·LIM·ee·uh). A serious eating disorder in which the victim has an unreasonable fear of being overweight and eats large amounts of food and then tries to get rid of the food. (pages 85, 145)

Bunion (BUHN·yuhn). A swelling in the first joint of the big toe. (page 52)

Bursa. A saclike space located between joints. (page 308)

Bypass surgery. Surgery in which doctors create new paths for blood to flow so that it goes around a blocked artery. (page 343)

C

Caffeine (ka·FEEN). A chemical found in some plants that can make the heart beat faster. (pages 136, 280)

Calculus. Hardened plaque formed on the teeth; also called *tartar*. (page 40)

Callus. A hard, thickened part of the skin on the foot. (page 52)

Calorie (KAL·uh·ree). A unit of heat that measures the energy available in different foods or used up in exercise. (page 139)

Cancer. A serious disease caused by the uncontrolled growth of cells. (pages 234, 345)

Canine (KAY·nyn). One of the four pointed teeth next to the incisors. (page 39)

Capillaries (KAP·uh·lehr·ees). The smallest blood vessels, which carry blood from the arteries to the body's cells and from those cells to the veins. (page 189)

Carbohydrates (kahr·boh·HY·drayts). Sugars and starches that provide energy. (page 126)

Carbon monoxide (KAR·buhn·muh·NAHK·syd). A poisonous gas produced when tobacco burns. (page 233)

Carcinogen (kahr·SIN·uh·juhn). Any substance in the environment that causes cancer. (page 347)

Cardiac (KARD·ee·ak) **muscle.** The muscle that makes the heart work. (page 205)

Cardiopulmonary resuscitation. See *CPR*.

Carotid (kuh·RAHT·uhd) **pulse.** The heartbeat you can feel on either side of the neck. (page 394)

Carrier. Someone who has a virus and can pass it to other people but does not show the symptoms of the disease himself or herself. (page 324)

Cartilage (KAHRT·uhl·ij). A strong elastic material on the ends of bones. (page 200)

Cell. The basic unit, or building block, of life. (page 152)

Cementum (si·MEN·tuhm). Thin bonelike material covering the root of a tooth. (page 39)

Central nervous system (CNS). The control center of the body, which tells all body parts what to do. (page 182)

Cerebellum (ser·uh·BEL·uhm). The part of the brain that controls balance, posture, and coordination. (page 182)

Cerebral palsy (suh·REE·bruhl PAWL·zee). A condition in which the cerebrum is damaged. (page 186)

Cerebrum (suh·REE·bruhm). The part of the brain that controls the five senses, the sensation of pain or temperature, and muscle control, thought, and speech. (page 182)

Cervix (SER·viks). The neck of the uterus. (page 153)

Chemotherapy (kee·moh·THEHR·uh·pee). The use of chemicals to kill cancer cells. (page 349)

Child abuse. The mistreatment of a child. (page 109)

Chlamydia (kluh·MID·ee·uh). An STD that does great damage to the reproductive system. (page 320)

Choking. A condition that occurs when a person's airway becomes blocked by food or some other object. (page 392)

Cholesterol (kuh·LES·tuh·rawl). A fatty, waxlike substance that helps the body produce substances it needs. (page 134)

Chromosome (KROH·muh·sohm). A tiny structure within cells that determines the specific type of creature an organism turns out to be. (page 156)

Chronic (KRAHN·ik) **disease.** An illness that lasts a long time. (page 334)

Chronological (krahn·uhl·AHJ·i·kuhl) **age.** Age measured in years. (page 169)

Circulatory (SER·kyuh·luh·tohr·ee) **system.** The group of body parts that carries the blood throughout the body to keep the body working well. (page 187)

Cirrhosis (suh·ROH·suhs). Scarring of the liver. (pages 215, 251)

Clinical (KLIN·i·kuhl) **death.** The result when a person's body systems shut down. (page 172)

Clot. A lump of blood. (page 192)

Cocaine (koh·KAYN). An illegal stimulant. (page 281)

Cochlea (KOK·lee·uh). A structure of the inner ear made up of three ducts filled with fluid and more than 15,000 hair cells. (page 49)

Codeine (KOH·deen). A narcotic used in cough medicine. (page 283)

Colon (KOH·luhn). The large intestine. (page 213)

Coma (KOH·muh). A deep unconscious state. (page 283)

Commitment (kuh·MIT·muhnt). A pledge or a promise. (page 116)

Communicable (kuh·MYOO·ni·kuh·buhl) **disease.** An illness that can be passed on from one person to another. (pages 300, 334)

Communication. The exchange of thoughts, ideas, and beliefs between two or more people. (page 98)

Comparison (kuhm·PEHR·uh·suhn) **shopping.** Judging the benefits of different goods or services. (page 405)

Complete proteins. Protein foods that contain all eight essential amino acids. (page 126)

Compromise (KAHM·pruh·myz). The result of each person's giving up something in order to reach a solution that satisfies everyone. (page 99)

Cones. Nerve endings in the eye that distinguish the colors red, blue, and green and their different shadings. (page 44)

Connecting neuron. A nerve that sends a message from a sensory neuron to a motor neuron. (page 182)

Conservation (kahn·ser·VAY·shuhn). The saving of resources. (page 433)

Consumer (kuhn·SOO·mer). Anybody who purchases goods or services. (page 400)

Consumer advocate (AD·vuh·kuht). A person or group whose main purpose is helping consumers with problems. (page 417)

Contagious (kuhn·TAY·juhs) **period.** A period during which some diseases can be passed to another person. (page 303)

Contract. Shorten. (page 203)

Contraction (kuhn·TRAK·shuhn). A sudden tightening in the muscles of the uterus that is part of the birth process. (page 153)

Cooling down. Slowly winding down an activity; an essential part of an exercise session. (page 20)

Cooperation. Working together for the good of all; teamwork. (page 99)

Coping strategy. A way of dealing with the sense of loss people feel at the death of someone close. (page 174)

Corn. An overgrowth of the skin at some point on a toe. (page 52)

Cornea (KOR·nee·uh). A clear, almost round structure that serves as the window of the eye. (page 43)

Coupon (KOO·pahn). A slip of paper that offers savings on certain brands of goods. (page 407)

CPR or **Cardiopulmonary resuscitation** (kard·ee·oh·PUL·muh·nehr·ee ri·suhs·uh·TAY·shuhn). A first-aid procedure for restoring a person's breathing and forcing the heart to pump blood. (page 394)

Crack. A more pure and very powerful form of cocaine. (page 281)

Cretinism (KREET·uhn·is·uhm). A condition of little growth and, sometimes, mental retardation caused by under-production of hormones by the thyroid. (page 219)

Crown. The part of a tooth visible to the eye. (page 38)

Cuticle (KYOOT·i·kuhl). A non-living band of epidermis. (page 35)

D

Dandruff. Flaking of the outer layer of dead skin cells. (page 35)

Date rape. The situation in which a victim is forced to have sexual relations with someone on a date. (pages 116, 372)

Deafness. The loss of hearing. (page 50)

Decision making. Problem solving. (page 74)

Defense mechanism (duh·FENS MEK·uh·nizm). A way by which people, without being aware of what they are doing, temporarily escape from their problems. (page 83)

Defensive driving. Obeying traffic laws and watching out for other road users. (page 374)

Deficiency. A lack of something. (page 324)

Degenerative (di·JEN·uh·rayt·iv) **disease.** A noncommunicable disease that results in the breakdown of the body's tissues. (page 335)

Dehydration (dee·hy·DRAY·shuhn). Serious drying out of the body. (pages 145, 251)

Dementia (di·MEN·chuh). A disease that interferes with the normal working of the mind. (page 170)

Denial. An inability to see reality. (page 83)

Dentin (DEN·tuhn). Bonelike material surrounding the pulp of a tooth. (page 39)

Deodorant. A product that covers up body odor with a pleasant scent. (page 29)

Depressant (di·PRES·uhnt). A drug that tends to slow down the working of the brain and other parts of the nervous system. (pages 251, 282)

Depression (di·PRESH·uhn). A medical condition marked by not being able to eat or sleep, feeling bored, and losing interest in life. (page 84)

Dermatologist (DER·muh·TAHL·uh·juhst). A doctor who treats skin disorders. (page 30)

Dermis (DER·muhs). Broad inner layer of skin. (page 28)

Desired weight. The weight that is best for a person based on his or her sex, height, and body frame. (page 137)

Developmental (di·vel·uhp·MENT·uhl) **task.** Something that needs to happen in order for a person to continue growing toward becoming a healthy, mature adult. (page 165)

Diabetes (dy·uh·BEET·eez). A disease in which the body cannot properly use food to make energy. (pages 219, 352)

Diaphragm (DY·uh·fram). A large muscle that separates the chest from the abdomen. (page 195)

Diet. The food and drink that a person regularly eats. (page 124)

Digestion (dy·JES·chuhn). The breaking down of food into small particles that can pass through the bloodstream. (page 210)

Digestive (dy·JES·tiv) **system.** The group of body parts that takes in food and puts it in a form that can be used to create energy. (page 210)

Discount store. A store that offers few services but has lower prices. (page 407)

Disease. An illness that affects the body or mind. (page 300)

Dislocation (dis·loh·KAY·shuhn). A condition in which the end of a bone is pushed out of its joint. (page 201)

Displacement. Having bad feelings toward someone not really related to the problem. (page 83)

Distress. Negative stress that can hold a person back. (page 79)

Drowning prevention. A way of breathing slowly and deeply and floating on your back to prevent drowning. (page 377)

Drug. A substance other than food that changes the structure or function of the body or mind. (page 273)

Drug abuse. Using substances that are against the law or not supposed to be taken into the human body. (page 279)

Drug misuse. Using a drug in a way other than how it is supposed to be used. (page 279)

E

Earache. Pain in the ear. (page 50)

Eardrum. A thin piece of tissue that separates the outer ear from the middle ear. (page 48)

Earthquake. The shaking of the ground as the rock below the surface moves. (page 439)

Eating disorder. An extreme and damaging eating behavior that can lead to sickness and even death. (page 144)

Egg cell. The cell from the mother that plays a part in fertilization. (page 152)

Ejaculation (i·jak·yuh·LAY·shuhn). The process in which sperm leave the male body. (page 221)

Electron microscope. A high-powered instrument capable of providing views of objects or structures too small to be seen using a light microscope. (page 301)

Emotionally mature. The state of a person who can make sound decisions, who is sympathetic to others' needs, sets and reaches goals, and knows and accepts his or her own strengths and weaknesses. (page 116)

Emotional need. A need that affects a person's feelings and sense of well-being. (page 67)

Emotions. Feelings. (page 69)

Emphysema (em·fuh·SEE·muh). A severe disease in which the alveoli are damaged or destroyed. (pages 197, 234, 431)

Enamel (ee·NAM·uhl). The hard material that covers the crown of a tooth. (page 39)

Endocrine (EN·duh·kruhn) **system.** The group of body parts that uses chemicals to control some of the body's actions. (page 216)

Environment (in·VY·ruhn·muhnt). The sum total of your surroundings, including yourself and all living and nonliving things. (pages 6, 62, 157, 430)

Epidermis (ep·uh·DER·muhs). Outermost layer of the skin. (page 27)

Epididymis (ep·uh·DID·uh·muhs). A tube in which sperm are stored in the male body. (page 221)

Epiglottis (ep·uh·GLAHT·uhs). A small flap of skin that closes over the top of the trachea to make sure that no food enters there. (page 194)

Epilepsy (EP·uh·lep·see). A brain disorder that results from a sudden burst of nerve action. (page 185)

Esophagus (i·SAHF·uh·guhs). The back part of the throat through which food and drink travel to the stomach. (page 194)

Essential (i·SEN·chuhl) **amino acids.** The eight amino acids that must come from the food people eat. (page 126)

Essential (i·SEN·chuhl) **fatty acids.** Fats that are needed in the diet. (page 126)

Eustachian (yoo·STAY·shuhn) **tube.** The tube that allows air to pass from the nose to the middle ear. (page 48)

Excretory (EK·skruh·tohr·ee) **system.** The group of body parts that removes wastes from the body. (page 210)

Exhale. To breathe out. (page 195)

Expiration date. A date stamped on a package that tells when a medicine is no longer useful. (pages 279, 369)

Extend. Stretch. (page 203)

Extended family. A nuclear family plus other relatives. (page 106)

Extensor (ik·STEN·ser). A muscle that straightens an arm or a leg. (page 205)

F

Fainting. A temporary loss of consciousness. (page 387)

Fallen arches. A condition caused by flatness in the bottom of the foot. (page 52)

Fallopian (fuh·LOH·pee·uhn) **tube.** A tube through which a mature egg passes and in which fertilization occurs if a sperm is present. (page 222)

Family. The basic unit of society. (page 106)

Family doctor. A doctor who provides basic health care to people. (page 422)

Fantasy. Something imagined or a daydream. (page 83)

Farsightedness. A condition in which close objects appear blurred. (page 46)

Fatigue. Extreme tiredness. (page 80)

Fats. Fatty acids that provide energy. (page 126)

Fat-soluble (SOL·yuh·buhl) **vitamins.** Vitamins that can be stored in the body. (page 126)

Faulty thinking. To approach an event or situation without thinking through all the possible consequences. (page 119)

Feces (FEE·sees). An almost solid waste that passes out of the body. (page 213)

Feminine (FEM·uh·nuhn). Qualities usually associated with a female. (page 165)

Fertilization (fert·uhl·uh·ZAY·shuhn). The joining together of two special cells, one from each parent. (pages 152, 222)

Fetal (FEET·uhl) **alcohol syndrome** (SIN·drohm). A group of physical and mental problems in a developing baby caused by the mother-to-be drinking alcohol. (pages 158, 252, 336)

Fever. The body's response to infection by raising its temperature and taking other actions. (page 307)

Fiber (FY·ber). The part of fruits, vegetables, grains, and beans that the body cannot digest. (page 133)

Field guide. A handbook that discusses the plant or animal life in a region. (page 378)

First aid. The care given to a person when injury occurs or when he or she becomes ill. (page 382)

First-degree burn. A burn in which only the outer layer of the skin is burned and turns red. (page 390)

Fit. Ready to handle whatever comes your way from day to day. (page 16)

Flashback. The experience of feeling the effects of a drug some time after taking the drug. (page 289)

Flexibility (fleks·uh·BIL·uh·tee). The ability to move body joints in certain ways. (page 17)

Flexor (FLEK·ser). A muscle that bends an arm or leg. (page 205)

Fluoride. A substance added to the water in many communities and to some toothpastes to reduce tooth decay. (page 41)

Follicle (FAHL·i·kuhl). A small pocket in the skin in which hair grows. (page 34)

Fossil (FAHS·uhl) **fuels.** The coal, oil, and natural gas used to power the engines of motor vehicles and factories. (page 430)

Fracture. A break in a bone. (pages 201, 389)

Fraternal (fruh·TERN·uhl) **twins.** Non-identical twins that develop from two eggs and two sperm cells. (page 153)

Freebasing. A method of using cocaine by mixing it with an explosive liquid. (page 281)

Freely movable joint. A joint that allows movement in all directions. (page 201)

Frostbite. Freezing of the skin. (pages 378, 438)

Fungi (FUHN·jy). Simple life forms which cannot make their own food and which can cause disease. (page 302)

G

Gallbladder (GAWL·blad·er). The part of the body where bile is stored until the small intestine is ready for it. (page 212)

Gall stones. Small, hardened crystals of bile which block the passage from the gallbladder to the small intestine. (page 215)

Gamma globulin (GAM·uh GLAHB·yuh·luhn). A protein given in the form of a shot to protect someone from getting hepatitis A. (page 315)

Gene (JEEN). A tiny bit of matter that controls which traits of your parents get passed along to you. (page 156)

General hospital. A hospital that provides services for a wide range of health problems. (page 421)

Generic (juh·NEHR·ik) **product.** A good sold in a plain package and at a lower price than a brand name good. (page 407)

Genetic (juh·NET·ik) **disorder.** A disease or condition in which the body does not function normally because of a problem with genes. (page 156, 336)

Genital herpes (HER·pees). Another name for the STD herpes simplex II. (page 321)

Genital (JEN·uh·tuhl) **warts.** Warts on the reproductive organs; an STD. (page 322)

Gestational (jes·TAY·shuhn·uhl) **diabetes.** A form of diabetes contracted by some pregnant women that usually lasts for the term of the pregnancy. (page 353)

Gigantism (jy·GAN·tis·uhm). A condition of extreme growth caused by too much growth hormone being produced by the pituitary gland. (page 218)

Gingivitis (JIN·juh·VY·tuhs). A gum disease caused by plaque or decaying food caught between the teeth. (page 40)

Gland. A part of the body that releases a substance. (page 216)

Glucagon (GLOO·kuh·gahn). A hormone that raises the blood sugar level. (page 355)

Gluteus maximus. The largest muscle in your body, which covers your buttocks. (page 207)

Going steady. Dating only one other person. (page 115)

Goiter (GOYT·er). A condition of the thyroid caused by too little iodine in the diet. (page 219)

Gonorrhea (gahn·uh·REE· uh). An STD caused by bacteria, that does great damage to the reproductive system and other parts of the body. (page 320)

Goods. Products that are made and purchased to satisfy someone's wants. (page 400)

Good Samaritan Law. A law which states that anyone who tries to help in an emergency cannot be sued unless he or she knowingly acted unsafely. (page 385)

Grief. The sum total of feelings caused by the death of a loved one. (page 173)

Grooming. Taking care of one's appearance. (page 25)

Group date. Going out with a group of friends of both sexes. (pages 115, 317)

Group practice. Two or more doctors who join together to offer health care. (page 422)

Gynecologist (gyn·uh·KAHL· uh·juhst). A doctor who handles health care of the female reproductive system. (page 224)

H

Hallucinogen (huh·LOOS·uhn· uh·juhn). A drug that causes the user's brain to form images of things that are not really there. (page 289)

Hammer. A small bone behind the eardrum. (page 48)

Hangnail. A split in the cuticle along the edge of the nail. (page 36)

Hay fever. An allergy to the pollen spread by plants. (page 312)

Hazard (HAZ·erd). A possible source of harm. (page 368)

Hazardous (HAZ·erd·uhs) **waste.** A waste product that may cause illness. (page 434)

Head lice. Insects that live in the hair. (page 35)

Health. A combination of physical, mental, and social well-being. (page 3)

Health insurance (in· SHUR·uhns). A program in which a person pays a yearly fee to a company that agrees to pay certain health-care costs. (page 422)

Health maintenance (MAYNT· nuhns) **organization (HMO).** A group of many different types of doctors who give health care to members. (page 422)

Hearing impairment. Partial hearing loss. (page 50)

Heart. The muscle that pumps blood throughout the body. (page 187)

Heart and lung endurance. How well the heart and lungs get oxygen to the body during exercise and how quickly they return to normal. (page 17)

Heart attack. The condition in which a part of the heart fails to work because it is not getting enough blood. (pages 192, 340)

Heart transplant. An operation in which doctors remove the patient's heart and replace it with another. (page 343)

Hemisphere (HEM·uh·sfeer). One half of the brain. (page 183)

Hemophilia (hee·muh·FIL· ee·uh). A disease in which the blood clots little or not at all. (page 191)

Hepatitis (hep·uh·TYT·uhs). A disease that involves the swelling of the liver. (page 315)

Hepatitis A. A form of hepatitis in which infection often results from eating contaminated food or drinking dirty water. (page 314)

Hepatitis B. A form of hepatitis in which infection often results from contact with an infected person or by using dirty needles to inject drugs; can result in long-term damage to the liver. (page 314)

Heredity (huh·RED·uh·tee). The passing on of traits from your parents. (pages 6, 62, 156)

Heroin (HEHR·uh·wuhn). An illegal narcotic that is strongly addictive. (page 283)

Herpes simplex I. A virus that causes a cold sore or fever blister; a small sore on or near the lips. (page 31)

Herpes simplex II (HER· pees SIM·pleks). An STD that causes sores on the reproductive organs; also called genital herpes. (page 321)

High blood pressure. The serious condition that occurs when blood pressure is higher than normal for long periods of time; also called hypertension. (pages 192, 341)

Hormone (HOR·mohn). A chemical produced in the body. (pages 30, 69, 162, 216, 290)

Human immunodeficiency virus. The retrovirus that causes AIDS. (page 324)

Hurricane (HER·uh·kayn). A strong windstorm with driving rain. (page 439)

Hypertension. See *High blood pressure.*

Hypnotic (hip·NAHT·ik). A very strong depressant that brings on sleep. (page 282)

Hypoallergenic (hy·poh·al·er·JEN·ik). A cosmetic made for people who have sensitive skin. (page 401)

Hypodermic (hy·poh·DER·mik) **needle.** The kind of needle one uses to put insulin under the skin. (page 354)

Hypothalamus (hy·poh·THAL·uh·muhs). The part of the brain that stimulates the pituitary gland. (page 183)

Hypothermia (hy·poh·THER·mee·uh). A sudden drop in body temperature. (page 376)

I

Ibuprofen (eye·byoo·PROH·fuhn). A medicine that eases pain and reduces swelling. (page 357).

Immovable joint. A joint that allows no movement at all. (page 201)

Immune (im·YOON) **system.** The group of organs and cells that fights germs and keeps a memory of how to destroy germs. (page 306)

Immunity (im·YOO·nuht·ee). The body's ability to remember how to fight certain germs. (page 305)

Incisor (in·SY·ser). One of the front or center teeth. (page 39)

Incomplete proteins. Protein foods that do not have all eight essential amino acids. (page 126)

Infancy (IN·fuhn·see). The first year of life. (page 159)

Infection (in·FEK·shuhn). A condition that occurs when germs attack the body's cells and use them to grow and reproduce. (pages 184, 300)

Influenza (in·floo·EN·zuh). A serious and very contagious disease caused by viruses. (page 309)

Ingrown toenail. A condition in which the nail pushes into the skin on the side of the toe. (page 36)

Inguinal hernia (IN·gwuhn·uhl HER·nee·uh). The condition that results when a hole opens in the abdominal wall through which a piece of intestine pushes into the scrotum. (page 221)

Inhalant (in·HAY·luhnt). A substance whose fumes are sniffed to give a hallucinogenic-like high. (page 290)

Inhale. To breathe in. (page 195)

Inherited. Passed along to someone by her or his parents. (pages 34, 347)

Inner ear. The part of the ear that is made up of the vestibule, the semicircular canals, and the cochlea. (page 48)

Inpatient. Someone who must stay overnight at a hospital or nursing home. (page 421)

Insulin (IN·suh·luhn). A hormone that is released by the pancreas and controls how the body uses glucose for energy. (pages 218, 352)

Interferon (int·uh·FIR·ahn). A chemical that signals other cells to fight a virus. (page 307)

Intravenous (in·truh·VEE·nuhs) **(IV) needle.** A needle used to inject drugs into a person's veins. (page 326)

Involuntary (in·VAHL·uhn·ter·ee) **muscle.** A muscle that works without the person's being aware of it. (page 205)

Iodized. A substance that has iodine added to it. (page 218)

Iris (EYE·ruhs). The color of the eye that is seen from the outside. (page 43)

Islets of Langerhans (EYE·luhts uhv LAHNG·er·hahnz). Groups of cells located in the pancreas that are important in the control of sugar in the blood. (page 217)

J

Jaywalk. Cross the street in the middle of the block. (page 373)

Joint. The point at which two bones meet. (page 200)

K

Keratin (KEHR·uh·tuhn). A substance that makes nails hard. (page 36)

Kidneys. The two bean-shaped organs that remove the body's waste products that can be dissolved in water. (page 213)

L

Large intestine. The colon. (page 213)

Laxative (LAKS·uh·tiv). A medicine that makes foods speed through the digestive system with little time to release their nutrients. (page 145)

Leader nutrients. The main nutrients in each of the four food groups. (page 130)

Lens (LENZ). A structure behind the pupil that allows the light to come together in the inner part of the eye. (page 44)

Leukemia (loo·KEE·mee·uh). A disease of both the bones and the blood caused by too many white blood cells. (page 191)

Leukoplakia (loo·koh·PLAY·kee·uh). White spots on the gums and on the inside of the cheeks. (page 237)

License. A permit that gives a person the right to provide health care but holds that person to certain standards. (page 419)

Lifestyle disease. A disease that is caused by a person's health habits. (page 337)

Lifestyle factor. A life-related habit. (page 15)

Lifetime sport. A physical activity that can be enjoyed throughout life. (page 18)

Ligament (LIG·uh·muhnt). A cord of tissue that joins bones or keeps an organ in place. (page 200)

Liver. The largest gland in the body. (page 212)

Lobe. Section of the brain. (page 183)

Love. A strong emotional attachment to another person. (page 116)

LSD. See *Lysergic acid diethylamide.*

Lung cancer. A disease in which cancer cells grow out of control and destroy the alveoli. (page 197)

Lungs. The two main organs of breathing. (page 194)

Lymph. Body fluid that must be removed from cells and recycled so that the cells do not swell. (page 307)

Lymphatic (lim·FAT·ik) **system.** A secondary circulatory system. (page 307)

Lymph nodes. (LIMF NOHDS). Glandlike structures located throughout the body to store white blood cells. (page 307)

Lymphocyte (LIM·fuh·syt). A special white-blood cell. (page 307)

Lysergic (luh·SER·jik) **acid diethylamide** (dy·eth·uh·LAM·yd) **(LSD).** A hallucinogen that has many harmful effects on the body. (page 290)

M

Malignant (muh·LIG·nuhnt) **tumor.** A mass of cells that is cancerous. (page 346)

Malnutrition (mal·noo·TRISH·uhn). A condition in which the body does not get the nutrients it needs to grow and function well. (page 145)

Malocclusion (MAL·uh·KLOO·zhuhn). A condition in which teeth fail to line up properly. (page 40)

Malpractice (mal·PRAK·tuhs). A failure to provide an acceptable degree of quality health care. (page 419)

Marijuana (mehr·uh·WAHN·uh). An illegal hallucinogen that comes from the leaves of a plant. (page 286)

Masculine (MAS·kyuh·luhn). Qualities usually associated with a male. (page 165)

Medicaid (MED·i·kayd). A government program that gives health insurance to people who are poor. (page 423)

Medicare (MED·i·kehr). A government program that gives

health insurance to people 65 years old or older. (page 423)

Medicine. A drug meant to cure or prevent diseases or other conditions. (page 273)

Melanin (MEL·uh·nuhn). An agent that gives the skin most of its color. (page 27)

Menstrual (MEN·struhl) **cycle.** The time from one menstruation to the next. (page 223)

Menstruation (men·struh·WAY·shuhn). The action in which the lining of the uterus walls breaks down and passes out of the body. (page 223)

Mental health. The ability to like and accept oneself. (pages 2, 60)

Mental imaging. Picturing oneself succeeding in a situation before the situation arises; a form of preparation for upcoming challenges. (page 73)

Mescaline (MES·kuh·luhn). An illegal hallucinogenic drug found naturally in a cactus but most often made in a laboratory. (page 289)

Metastasis (muh·TAS·tuh·suhs). The spread of a tumor to other parts of the body. (page 346)

Middle ear. The part of the ear that contains the eardrum. (page 48)

Minerals (MIN·uh·ruhls). Nonliving substances the body needs in small amounts to work properly. (page 127)

Molar (MOH·ler). One of the shorter, stubbier teeth to the sides and back of the mouth. (page 39)

Mononucleosis (mahn·uh·noo·klee·OH·suhs). A disease common to young people that is caused by a virus that results

A45

in a high number of white blood cells in the body. (page 314)

Morphine (MOR·feen). A narcotic used to control pain. (page 283)

Motion sickness. The feeling of dizziness and nausea some people have when riding in a car, boat, or airplane. (page 49)

Motor neuron. A neuron that tells a muscle what to do. (page 182)

Mouth-to-mouth resuscitation. See *Rescue breathing*.

Mucous membrane (MYOO·kuhs MEM·brayn). A soft substance that keeps the inside of the nose and other body parts moist and traps dirt. (pages 193, 306)

Multiple sclerosis (skluh·ROH·suhs) **(MS).** A disease in which the outer coating that protects some nerves is destroyed. (page 186)

Muscle endurance (in·DER·uhns). How well a muscle group can perform over a given time without becoming overly tired. (page 17)

Muscle strength. The most work someone's muscles can do at any given time. (page 17)

Muscle tone. The firmness that muscles have at all times. (page 207)

Muscular dystrophy (DIS·truh·fee). A disease in which a skeletal muscle tissue wastes away. (page 207)

Muscular (MUHS·kyuh·ler) **system.** A group of tough tissues that makes body parts move. (page 203)

N

Narcotic (nahr·KAHT·ik). A highly addictive drug meant to bring on sleep or a loss of feeling. (page 283)

Nearsightedness. A condition in which distant objects appear blurred. (page 46).

Neck. The part of a tooth between the crown and the root. (page 38)

Negative peer pressure. What a person feels when others who are the same age try to persuade him or her to try something he or she does not want to do. (page 102)

Negative stress. Stress that can hold people back; also known as distress. (page 79)

Neighborhood watch program. A program in which neighbors watch each other's homes to ensure safety. (page 372)

Nerve ending. A sensitive part of the body that reacts to forces outside the body. (page 27)

Nervous system. The group of body parts that makes and sends the commands that control all the body's actions. (page 180)

Neuron (NOO·rahn). A special nerve cell. (page 180)

Neurosis (noo·ROH·sis). A condition in which fear gets in the way of a person's ability to function in daily life. (page 83)

Nicotine (NIK·uh·teen). A drug in tobacco that speeds up the heartbeat. (pages 158, 233)

Noncommunicable disease. An illness that is caused by how people live, conditions they are born with, or by

hazards around them. (pages 300, 334)

Nongonococcal urethritis (nahn·gahn·uh·KAHK·uhl yur·i·THRYT·uhs) **(NGU).** An STD; an infection of the urethra in males and the cervix in females. (page 320)

Nuclear (NOO·klee·er) **family.** The type of family composed of a mother, father, and children, or any combination of the three. (page 106)

Nuclear (NOO·klee·er) **waste.** The dangerous products left over by the reactions that take place in an atomic power plant. (page 434)

Nutrient (NOO·tree·uhnt). One of six types of substances in food that the body needs. (page 125)

Nutrient density (DEN·suht·ee). In foods, a large number of nutrients compared with the calories they provide. (page 139)

Nutrition (noo·TRISH·uhn). Eating the foods the body needs to grow, to develop, and to work properly. (page 124)

O

Obesity (oh·BEE·suh·tee). The condition in which there is too much fat in the body. (page 138)

Obsessive-compulsive (uhb·SES·iv kuhm·PUL·siv) **behavior.** A type of neurosis characterized by certain activities being done repeatedly. (page 83)

Obstetrician (ahb·stuh·TRISH·uhn). A doctor who specializes in the care of a woman and her baby. (page 157)

Oil gland. A gland which produces oil that keeps the skin soft and waterproof. (page 28)

Open-heart surgery. A surgical procedure during which a doctor operates directly on the heart. (page 343)

Ophthalmologist (ahf·thuh·MAHL·uh·juhst). A doctor who treats eyes. (page 406)

Opportunistic (ahp·er·too·NIS·tik) **infection.** An infection that attacks a body with a weakened immune system. (page 325)

Optic (AHP·tik) **nerve.** A cord of nerve fibers that carries electrical messages to the brain. (page 44)

Optometrist (ahp·TAHM·uh·truhst). A health care worker who treats eyes, but is not a doctor. (page 406)

Organ. A body part such as the brain or heart. (page 152)

Orthodontist (or·thuh·DAHNT·ist). A dentist who specializes in treating malocclusion. (page 41)

Osteoarthritis (ahs·tee·oh·ar·THRYT·uhs). The condition that results from a wearing away of the joints. (page 358)

Osteomyelitis (ahs·tee·oh·my·uh·LYT·uhs). A disease marked by an infection of the bone caused by a germ. (page 202)

Osteoporosis (ahs·tee·oh·puh·ROH·suhs). A condition in which the body does not have enough calcium for bones to stay strong and flexible. (page 202)

Outer ear. The fleshy, curved part of the ear attached to each side of the head. (page 48)

Outpatient. Someone who goes to a health-care unit, gets care, and then leaves all in the same day. (page 421)

Oval window. An opening between the middle ear and inner ear. (page 49)

Ovaries (OHV·uh·rees). The glands in the female reproductive system that store egg cells. (page 217, 222)

Over-the-counter (OTC) drug. A drug that is safe enough to be taken without a written order from a doctor. (page 276)

Overweight. More than the desired weight for a person's sex, height, and body type. (page 138)

Ovulation (ahv·yuh·LAY·shuhn). The release of egg cells every month or so. (page 222)

Oxidize (AHK·suh·dyz). To change alcohol into water and the gas carbon dioxide. (page

Ozone (OH·zohn). A kind of oxygen. (page 431)

P

Pancreas (PAN·kree·uhs). The body part that releases chemicals to break down carbohydrates, proteins, and fats in the small intestine. (page 212)

Pap smear. A test to detect cancer of the cervix. (page 224)

Paregoric (pehr·uh·GAWR·ik). A narcotic used to control diarrhea and relieve pain from teething in infants. (page 283)

Partially movable joint. A joint that allows movement in only one or two directions, such as the elbow. (page 201)

Pedestrian (puh·DES·tree·uhn). Anyone who travels on foot. (page 373)

Peer. A person of the same age. (pages 102, 289)

Peer pressure. Pressure to go along with others' beliefs and to try new things. (page 102)

Pelvic inflammatory (PEL·vik in·FLAM·uh·tohr·ee) **disease (PID).** A painful illness of the female reproductive organs. (page 320)

Penicillin (pen·uh·SIL·uhn). A very effective antibiotic used to destroy germs that cause infections. (pages 273, 321)

Penis (PEE·nuhs). An organ like a tube that hangs outside the male body; used in urination and reproduction. (page 220)

Periodontium (pehr·ree·oh·DAHN·shee·um). A structure made up of the jawbone, the gums, and connectors called ligaments. (page 38)

Peripheral (puh·RIF·uh·ruhl) **nervous system (PNS).** The system made up of many nerves that connect the CNS to all parts of the body. (page 183)

Permanent teeth. The teeth that come in by the fifth year of life and, usually, last a lifetime. (page 39)

Personality. The sum total of a person's feelings, attitudes, and habits. (page 61)

Personality disorder. A condition in which a person has trouble getting along with others or getting along in certain situations. (page 85)

Perspiration. A combination of body wastes and water. (page 28)

Phagocytosis (fag·uh·suh·TOH·suhs). A process in which white blood cells destroy germs. (page 306)

Phencyclidine (fen·SIK·luh·deen). A dangerous hallucinogen also known as PCP and angel dust. (page 291)

Phobia. A form of neurosis in which the fear of an object or situation is so great that it interferes with reasonable action. (page 85)

Physical addiction. A type of addiction where the body itself feels a direct need for a drug. (page 255)

Physical fatigue. Extreme tiredness of the body as a whole. (page 80)

Physical health. Total care of the body and meeting the demands of life each day. (page 3)

Pimple. A clogged pore that has become infected and filled with pus. (page 30)

Pinched nerve. An injury that occurs when one part of the spine becomes displaced after a sudden movement or blow. (page 184)

Pineal (PI·nee·uhl) **gland.** A gland in the brain that regulates sexual development. (page 183)

Pituitary (puh·TOO·uh·tehr·ee) **gland.** A gland that does many jobs to control body actions. (page 183, 216)

Placebo (pluh·SEE·boh) **effect.** Improvement for natural reasons and not because of the substance that a quack provides. (page 414)

Placenta (pluh·ENT·uh). A thick, rich lining of tissue that builds up along the walls of the uterus and connects the mother to the baby. (page 153)

Plaque (PLAK). A sticky film constantly forming on the teeth. (page 40)

Pneumonia (noo·MOH·nyuh). A serious disease of the lungs that can be caused by either bacteria or viruses. (pages 196, 313)

Polio (POH·lee·oh). A serious disease that can make the victim unable to move the legs. (page 185)

Pollutant Standards Index. A number system that shows how dirty the air is at any given time. (page 431)

Pollution (puh·LOO·shuhn). What is created when parts of the environment are made to be dirty and unhealthy. (page 430)

Pore. A tiny hole in the skin. (page 28)

Positive peer pressure. What a person feels when others who are the same age inspire him or her to do something worthwhile. (page 102)

Positive stress. Stress that helps people reach goals. (page 79)

Posture. The way people carry themselves. (page 53)

Premenstrual syndrome (pree·MEN·struhl SIN·drohm). **(PMS).** A set of symptoms some females feel just before menstruation. (page 224)

Premolar (PREE·moh·ler). One of the shorter, stubbier teeth to the sides and back of the mouth. (page 39)

Prenatal (pree·NAYT·uhl) **care.** A number of steps taken to provide for the health of a pregnant woman and her unborn baby. (page 157)

Prescription (pri·SKRIP·shuhn) **drug.** A drug to be sold only with a written order from a doctor. (page 275)

Private practice. A doctor who has his or her own office. (page 422)

Projection. Unknowingly blaming someone else for a problem. (page 83)

Proteins (PROH·teens). Nutrients that help build cells and make them work properly. (page 126)

Protozoa (proht·uh·ZOH·uh). Single-celled creatures that are larger and more complex than bacteria. (page 302)

Psychological addiction. An addiction where the mind sends the body the message that it needs more of a drug. (page 255)

Psychological (SY·kuh·LAHJ·uh·kuhl) **fatigue.** Extreme tiredness caused by a person's mental state. (page 80)

Psychosis (sy·KOH·sis). A condition in which a person is not able to function in the real world. (page 84)

Puberty (PYOO·bert·ee). The time when a person begins to develop certain traits of his or her sex. (pages 162, 220)

Pubic lice (PYOO·bik LYS). Little animals that live on pubic hair and feed on tiny blood vessels. (page 322)

Pulmonary (PUL·muh·ner·ee) **artery.** The artery that carries blood from the heart to the lung. (page 194)

Pulmonary (PUL·muh·nehr·ee) **vein.** The vein that carries blood full of oxygen from the lung to the heart. (page 194)

Pulp. Soft sensitive tissue containing nerves and blood vessels deep within the root of a tooth. (page 39)

Pulse. The number of times the heart pumps blood, or beats, per minute. (pages 20, 188)

Pupil (PYOO·puhl). The dark opening in the center of the iris of the eye. (page 43)

Q

Quack. Someone who pretends to have medical skills but in fact has none. (page 412)

Quackery (KWAK·ree). The dishonest actions of a quack. (page 412)

R

Rabies (RAY·bees). A disease that enters the nervous system from a bite by an infected animal. (page 185)

Radiation (rayd·ee·AY·shuhn). An x-ray treatment used for cancer. (page 349)

Rape. Forcing another person to have sexual relations. (page 372)

Rape treatment center. A place where rape victims can get medical treatment and counseling. (page 372)

Recommended (rek·uh·MEND·uhd) **Dietary Allowance (RDA).** A guideline for the amount of each nutrient to be eaten each day. (page 128)

Recycle (ree·SY·kuhl). Change in some way and use again. (page 434)

Red bone marrow (MAR·oh). Substance in the center of bone which is made of blood vessels, connecting tissues, and cells. (page 200)

Reinforce. Back up. (page 65)

Relationship (rih·LAY·shuhn·ship). The connection you have with another person or group in your life; based on how you relate to, or act to-ward, another. (page 97)

Relative abuse. The mistreat-ment of a relative. (page 109)

Reliable. Able to be counted on. (page 102)

Reproductive (ree·pruh·DUHK·tiv) **system.** The group of body parts that is used to produce children. (page 220)

Rescue breathing. A way of restoring normal breathing by forcing air into the victim's lungs; also known as *artificial respiration* or *mouth-to-mouth resuscitation.* (page 383)

Resident bacteria. Harmless bacteria that live in the human body. (page 301)

Respiratory (res·puh·ruh·TOHR·ee) **system.** The group of body parts that changes gases in order for the body to work properly. (page 193)

Retina (RET·uh·nuh). A net-work of nerves that absorbs the light rays after they pass through the lens of the eye. (page 44)

Retrovirus (re·troh·VY·ruhs). A kind of virus that is more complex. (page 301)

Rheumatoid (ROO·muh·toyd) **arthritis.** The kind of arthritis in which the joints become swollen and are destroyed. (page 356)

Rickettsia (rik·ET·see·uh). A disease-causing creature that is passed on by insects. (page 302)

Risk factor. A trait or habit that raises a person's chances of getting a disease. (page 337)

Risks. Harmful chances. (page 365)

Rods. Nerve endings in the eye that distinguish objects in shades of black, white, and gray. (page 44)

Root. The part of a tooth inside the gum. (page 38)

Rubella (roo·BEL·uh). The dis-ease also called German mea-sles. (page 158)

S

Saccharine (SAK·ruhn). A human-made substitute for sugar identified as a cancer-causing substance when taken in large amounts. (page 347)

Safety conscious. Think that safety is important and act safely. (page 364)

Saliva (suh·LY·vuh). The liquid used to soften food so that it can be swallowed. (page 211)

Salivary (SAL·uh·ver·ee) **glands.** Three bodies in the mouth that send out saliva. (page 211)

Scabies (SKAY·bees). Tiny creatures that burrow under the skin; a sexually transmitted problem. (page 322)

Scale. To scrape the teeth with a dental instrument. (page 42)

Schizophrenia (skit·zoh·FREE·nee·uh). A serious disor-der in which people turn in-ward and often lose touch with reality completely. (page 84)

Sclera (SKLEHR·uh). The tough outer covering of the eye. (page 43)

Scrotum (SKROHT·uhm). A bag that hangs outside the male body between the legs and holds the testes. (page 220)

Seasonal affective disorder. A form of depression related to seasons. (page 73)

Sebum (SEE·buhm). An oily substance. (page 30)

Second-degree burn. A serious burn in which the burned area blisters. (page 390)

Second opinion. A statement from another doctor giving his or her view of what should be done. (page 419)

Seizure (SEE·zher). A physical reaction brought on by epilepsy which can be mild or severe. (page 185)

Self-concept. The picture you have of yourself and the way you believe you are seen by others. (page 64)

Semen (SEE·muhn). A mixture of liquids produced in the male reproductive system. (page 221)

Semicircular (SEM·i·SER·kyuh·ler) **canals.** Structures of the inner ear that contain hair cells and nerve fibers responsible for balance. (page 48)

Sensory (SENS·ree) **neuron.** A nerve that feels something. (page 182)

Services. Activities that are purchased to satisfy someone's wants. (page 400)

Sewage (SOO·ij). Food, human waste, detergents, and other products washed down people's drains. (page 433)

Sexual abuse. Any sexual act between an adult and a child. (page 110)

Sexually (SEKSH·wuh·lee) **transmitted disease (STD).** An illness that passes from one person to another through sexual contact. (page 316)

Shock. A serious condition in which the functions of the body are slowed down. (page 385)

Sickle-cell anemia. A condi-

tion passed on from parents that results in red-blood cells that are not correctly shaped. (page 191)

Side effect. Any reaction to a drug other than the one intended. (page 274)

Sidestream smoke. The smoke coming from the burning tip of another person's cigarette. (page 243)

Single-parent family. The type of a family in which only one parent lives with the child or children. (page 106)

Skeletal (SKEL·uht·uhl) **muscles.** The muscles that make the body move. (page 205)

Skeletal (SKEL·uht·uhl) **system.** The joints, connecting tissue, and bones of the body. (page 198)

Small-claims court. State courts that handle cases with problems involving amounts under $3,000. (page 418)

Small intestine (in·TES·tuhn). A 20-foot-long tube in which most of digestion occurs. (page 212)

Smoke alarm. A device that makes a warning noise when it senses smoke. (page 370)

Smooth muscles. The muscles in the digestive system and the blood vessels. (page 205)

Snuff (SNUHF). Finely ground tobacco. (page 236)

Social age. Age measured by a person's lifestyle. (page 169)

Social health. Your ability to get along with the people around you. (pages 2, 96)

Socializing (SOH·shuh·ly·zing). Getting along and communicating with other people. (page 114)

Sodium (SOHD·ee·uhm). A nutrient in salt that the body needs in small amounts. (page 135)

Sound waves. Vibrations in the air caused by anything that moves. (page 49)

Specialist (SPESH·uh·luhst). A doctor who is trained to handle particular kinds of patients or health matters. (page 422)

Sperm cell. The cell from the male that joins with the female egg in fertilization to start a new life. (pages 152, 220)

Spinal (SPYN·uhl) **cord.** A long stalk that carries messages from the body to the brain and from the brain to the body. (page 182)

Spouse (SPOWS) **abuse.** The mistreatment of a husband or wife. (page 109)

Sprain. The result of a joint being suddenly and violently stretched. (pages 201, 388)

STD. See *Sexually transmitted disease.*

Stepparent. Someone who marries a child's mother or father. (page 106)

Stimulant (STIM·yuh·luhnt). A drug that speeds up the body's function. (page 279)

Stirrup. A small bone behind the eardrum. (page 48)

Stomach. A j-shaped organ that has many layers of muscle. (page 212)

Stress. The body's response to changes around it. (page 77)

Stressor. A trigger of stress. (page 79)

Stroke. The condition that occurs when the blood supply to part of the brain is cut off because of a clot. (pages 184, 340)

Strychnine (STRIK·nyn). A poison often mixed into heroin. (page 283)

Sulfa (SUHL·fuh) **drugs.** A family of germ killers made from certain chemicals. (page 273)

Sun-blocking agent. A product that contains chemicals that prevent harmful sun rays from reaching the skin. (page 29)

Sun lotion. A product that gives some protection from the sun. (page 29)

Sun protection factor (SPF). A number between 2 and 40 that tells how many times the body's natural protection from the sun a product provides. (page 29)

Sunscreen. A product that slows down the tanning process. (page 29)

Support group. A group in which people have a chance to talk with and listen to others with problems like their own. (page 88)

Suppression (suh·PRESH·uhn). The blocking out of unpleasant thoughts. (page 83)

Sweat gland. A pouch in the skin that holds a combination of body wastes and water. (page 28)

Sympathetic (sim·puh·THET·ik). Aware of how another is feeling at a given moment. (page 102)

Symptom (SIM·tuhm). A change in the body that signals that a particular disease is present. (page 312)

Syndrome. A set of symptoms that are part of a disease. (page 324)

Syphilis (SIF·luhs). An STD that can attack and do serious damage to the body. (page 321)

System. A group of organs that work together in the body. (page 152)

T

Tar. A thick, dark liquid formed when tobacco burns. (page 233)

Target pulse rate. The level at which the heart and lungs receive the most benefit from a workout. (page 20)

Tartar (TAR·ter). Hardened plaque formed on the teeth; also called *calculus.* (page 40)

Taste buds. A sensitive area of the tongue. (page 38)

T-cell. A lymphocyte that fights germs in a different way than B-cells do. (page 308)

Teen hot line. A special telephone service that teens can call when feeling stress. (page 89)

Tendon. A cord of fibers that joins skeletal muscles to other parts of the body. (page 205)

Testes (TES·tees). The glands in the male reproductive system that produce sperm. (pages 217, 220)

Testicular self-examination. An examination that males should do to check themselves for cancer of the testes. (page 348)

Testimonial (tes·tuh·MOH·nee·uhl). A famous person recommending a good or service. (page 408)

Thalamus (THAL·uh·muhs). The part of the brain that handles incoming sensory messages. (page 183)

Therapy (THEHR·uh·pee). Training to do certain tasks. (pages 186, 337)

Thermograph. An image of the heat given off by a part of the body to detect inflammation. (page 358)

Third-degree burn. A very serious burn in which deep layers of the skin and nerve endings are damaged. (page 391)

Thyroid (THY·royd) **gland.** A gland that releases the hormone that controls how fast the body uses food for energy. (page 216)

Tissue. Groups of cells that join together and do similar jobs. (pages 39, 152)

Tolerance (TAHL·uh·ruhns). A condition that occurs when a person's body becomes used to a drug's effect. (page 274)

Tornado (tor·NAYD·oh). A whirling, funnel-shaped windstorm that drops from the sky to the ground. (page 438)

Tornado warning. A warning the National Weather Service puts out when a tornado is in a certain area and people are in danger. (page 438)

Tornado watch. A message issued by the National Weather Service that says weather conditions are right for a tornado. (page 438)

Toxic shock syndrome. A condition caused by the misuse of tampons. (page 223)

Trachea (TRAY·kee·uh). Windpipe. (page 193)

Tradition (truh·DISH·uhn). The usual way of doing things. (page 408)

Tranquilizer (tran·kwuh·LY·zer). A type of depressant that can calm a person without making him or her less alert. (page 282)

Tumor (TOO·mer). A group of cells that form in a mass. (page 346)

Type I diabetes. The kind of diabetes in which the person's body makes little or no insulin. (page 353)

Type II diabetes. The kind of diabetes in which the person's body does not make enough insulin or makes insulin but cannot use it correctly. (page 353)

U

Ulcer. A sore in the stomach or small intestine. (pages 215, 237, 251)

Ultraviolet rays. Light rays that come from the sun which, in the case of prolonged exposure, may cause skin cancer. (page 29)

Umbilical (uhm·BIL·i·kuhl) **cord.** A tube that grows out of the placenta and attaches to what will become the baby's navel through which food and oxygen pass to the baby. (page 153)

Universal donor. A person with blood type O, who can give blood to people with all other types. (page 190)

Universal recipient. A person with type AB blood, who can receive blood of all other types. (page 190)

Urethra (yoo·REE·thruh). A tube that runs down the center of the penis. (page 221)

Urine (YUR·uhn). Liquid waste made by the body's cells. (page 213)

Uterus (YOOT·uh·ruhs). A pear-shaped female organ in which a

baby grows and develops until it is ready to be born. (pages 153, 222)

Uvula (YOO·vyuh·luh). A flap of skin in the back of the throat that closes the airway to the nose. (page 212)

V

Vaccine (vak·SEEN). A preparation made of dead or weak germ cells that is put into the body so that antibodies will be made. (pages 185, 273, 309)

Vagina (vuh·JY·nuh). The female canal leading from the uterus to the outside of the body. (page 222)

Vaginitis (vaj·uh·NYT·uhs). An infection of the vagina. (pages 224, 322)

Vegetarians. People whose diet includes no meat. (page 126)

Veins (VAYNS). Blood vessels that take blood from the body back to the heart. (page 189)

Venereal (vuh·NIR·ee·uhl) **disease (VD).** Another name for a sexually transmitted disease. (page 316)

Ventricle (VEN·tri·kuhl). The bottom chamber on each side of the heart. (page 189)

Vestibule. A baglike structure of the inner ear, lined with hair cells that are essential to hearing. (page 48)

Villi. Fingerlike points inside the small intestine which help the food be absorbed into the bloodstream. (page 212)

Virus (VY·ruhs). The smallest and simplest form of life. (pages 196, 301)

Vitamins (VYT·uh·muhns). Nutrients the body needs in small amounts to work properly. (page 126)

Voluntary muscle. A muscle whose movement is controlled. (page 205)

W

Warming up. Doing activities and movements that stretch the muscles before exercising; an essential part of an exercise session. (page 20)

Warranty (WAWR·uhnt·ee). A written promise to handle repairs if a product does not work. (page 406)

Wart. A small growth on the skin caused by a virus. (page 31)

Water. The most common nutrient the body needs for many tasks. (page 127)

Water-soluble (SOL·yuh·buhl) **vitamins.** Vitamins that dissolve in water and must be replaced in the body every day. (page 126)

Weight control. Reaching the weight that is best for you and then staying there. (page 137)

Well-balanced diet. A nutrition routine that includes food from the four basic food groups. (page 30)

Wellness. Actively making choices and decisions that promote good health. (page 5)

Whitehead. The result of oil becoming trapped in a pore. (page 30)

Withdrawal (with·DRAW·uhl). A series of painful physical and mental symptoms. (page 294)

Y

Yellow bone marrow (MAR·oh). The substance in the center of a bone that is mostly fat. (page 200)

Index

Photo Credits

Chapter 1. Page 1: Comstock; page 3, all: Tom Dunham; page 4: Tom Dunham; page 7: David W. Hamilton/The Image Bank; page 8: Four By Five Inc.; page 11: Win McNamee/Duomo; page 12: Mel Di-Giacomo/The Image Bank; page 13: Tom Dunham; page 15: Larry Mulvehill/Photo Researchers Inc.; page 17: Tony Freeman/PhotoEdit; page 18, left: Dan McCoy/Rainbow; page 18, right: Alvis Upitis/The Image Bank; page 19: Melchior DiGiacomo/The Image Bank; page 20: Richard Choy/Peter Arnold, Inc.

Chapter 2. Page 25: Richard Hutchings; page 26: Four By Five Inc.; page 27: Jon Riley/Medichrome; page 28: Mieke Maas/The Image Bank; page 29: Sara Matthews; page 32: Courtesy Dennis Pelli; page 35, left: Richard Hutchings/Info Edit; page 35, middle: Joseph Nettis/Stock, Boston; page 35, right: Fritz Henle/Photo Researchers, Inc.; page 37, left: Four By Five Inc.; page 37, right: Stephen McBrady/PhotoEdit; page 38: Tom Dunham; page 40, all: Courtesy of the American Dental Association; page 41, all: Courtesy of the American Dental Association; page 42: Gerard Champlong/The Image Bank; page 46: Larry Gatz/The Image Bank; page 47: E.M. Bordis/The Stock Shop; page 50: Bob Taylor/The Stock Shop; page 51: David Falconer/West Stock, Inc.; page 54, left: Richard Hutchings/Photo Researchers, Inc.; page 54, right: Tom Dunham.

Chapter 3. Page 59: Mark Snyder/Journalism Services; page 61: Elaine Wicks/Taurus Photos; page 62: Charles Marden Fitch; page 63: Michal Heron/Woodfin Camp & Associates; page 64: Richard Hutchings/Photo Researchers, Inc.; page 65: Clyde H. Smith/Peter Arnold, Inc.; page 66: Cliff Fuelner/The Image Bank; page 67: Ray Ellis/Photo Researchers, Inc.; page 69: Four By Five Inc.; page 70: Alan Oddie/PhotoEdit; page 74: Horst Fenchel/The Image Bank; page 76: A. Boccaccio/The Image Bank; page 77, left: Dan Helms/Duomo; page 77, right: David Madison/Duomo; page 79, left: Four By Five Inc.; page 79, right: Tom Dunham; page 80: Richard Hutchings/Photo Researchers, Inc.; page 81: Norris Taylor/

Photo Researchers, Inc.; page 82: Suzanne Szasz/Photo Researchers, Inc.; page 83: Jonathan Taylor/The Stock Shop; page 84: Tom Dunham; page 85: The Stock Shop; page 86: Nancy Brown/The Image Bank; page 88: Bob Daemmrich/Stock, Boston; page 89: Lester Sloan/Woodfin Camp & Associates; page 90: Tony Freeman/PhotoEdit.

Chapter 4. Page 95: Bob Daemmrich/Stock, Boston: page 97, all: Tom Dunham; page 98: Richard Hutchings/Photo Researchers, Inc.; page 99: Jim Witmer/Nawrocki Stock Photo; page 101: Louis Fernandez/Black Star; page 103: Mary Kate Denny/PhotoEdit; page 104: Diana Walker/Gamma-Liaison; page 105: Tony Freeman/PhotoEdit; page 107: Comstock; page 108, left: Lawrence Fried/The Image Bank; page 108, right: Mary Kate Denny/PhotoEdit; page 109, left: Wayne Sproul/International Stock Photo; page 109, right: Michael Salas/The Image Bank; page 110: C. L. Chryslin/The Image Bank; page 113: David S. Strickler/Monkmeyer Press; page 115: Naoki Okamoto/Black Star; page 117: David Frazier; page 118: Tony Freeman/PhotoEdit.

Chapter 5. Page 123: Don Smetzer/TSW/Click/Chicago; page 125, left: Pat Lanza/Bruce Coleman Inc.; page 125, top right: Mike Yamashita/Woodfin Camp & Associates; page 125, bottom: Alan Oddie/PhotoEdit; page 126: Bob Daemmrich/Stock, Boston; page 128: G. M. Smith/The Image Bank; page 131, all: Impact Communications; page 132: M. Skott/The Image Bank; page 133, right: Michel Tcheverkoff/The Image Bank; page 133, left: Tom Raymond/The Stock Shop; page 134: Michel Tcheverkoff/The Image Bank; page 138, left: P. H. Curran-Miller/The Stock Shop; page 138, right: Nancy Brown/The Image Bank; page 143: Audrey Gottlieb/Monkmeyer Press; page 144: Don and Pat Valenti/Taurus Photos; page 145: Tom Dunham.

Chapter 6. Page 151: Janeart Ltd./The Image Bank; page 153, left: Petit Format/Nestle/Photo Researchers, Inc.; page 153, right: C. Edelmann/La Villette/Photo Researchers, Inc.; page 155, left: Suzanne

Szasz/Photo Researchers, Inc.; page 155, right: Margaret W. Peterson/The Image Bank; page 156: Stephen McBrady/PhotoEdit; page 158: Mel DiGiacomo/The Image Bank; page 159: Jon Riley/The Stock Shop; page 160, top right: Ed Bock/West Stock, Inc.; page 160, top left: Jeff Thiebauth/Lightwave; page 160, bottom right: Edward Lettau/FPG International; page 160, bottom left: Myrleen Ferguson/PhotoEdit; page 161, left: B. Bakalian/Gamma-Liaison; page 161, middle: Kevin Horan/Picture Group; page 161, right: Myrleen Ferguson/PhotoEdit; page 162: Four By Five Inc.; page 165: Will & Deni McIntyre/Photo Researchers, Inc.; page 167: Rick Friedman/Black Star; page 168: Bill Stanton/International Stock Photo; page 169: Edward Lettau/FPG International; page 170: William Thompson III/The Image Bank; page 171: Blair Seitz/Photo Researchers, Inc.; page 173: Tom Dunham; page 174: Jeff Thompson/Gamma-Liaison.

Chapter 7. Page 179: Howard Sochurek/Medichrome; page 185: Michal Heron; page 191: D. M. Phillips/Taurus Photos; page 192: Walter Iooss/The Image Bank; page 196: Tom Dunham; page 198: Richard Hutchings/Photo Researchers, Inc.; page 206: Richard Hutchings/Photo Researchers, Inc.; page 208: Romano Cagnoni/Black Star; page 214: Frank Cezus/TSW/Click/Chicago; page 219: David R. Frazier; page 225: Richard Hutchings/Photo Researchers, Inc.

Chapter 8. Page 231: Courtesy of the American Lung Association; page 232: Scanlon/Comstock; page 235, all: Martin M. Rotker/Taurus Photos; page 236: Tom Dunham; page 240: Maria Taglient/The Image Bank; page 242: John Zimmerman/FPG International; page 243: Richard Hutchings/Info Edit.

Chapter 9. Page 249: © 1985 Bobby Holland/Poster reprinted by permission of Reader's Digest Foundation; page 250: Four By Five Inc.; page 252: David York/Medichrome; page 255, left: Audrey Gottlieb/Monkmeyer Press; page 255, right: Comstock; page 257: David Falconer/West Stock, Inc.; page 259: Myrleen Ferguson/PhotoEdit; page 260: Daemmrich/ Uniphoto Picture Agency; page 263: Daemmrich/Uniphoto Picture Agency; page 264: Richard Hutchings/Info Edit; page 265, left: Michal Heron; page 265, right: Bruce Byers/FPG International.

Chapter 10. Page 271: Tom Dunham; page 272: Tom Dunham; page 274: Paul Fry/ Peter Arnold, Inc.; page 278: Rhoda Sidney/Monkmeyer Press; page 281: Eric Roth/The Picture Cube; page 285, left: Steven E. Sutton/Duomo; page 285, right: Duomo; page 287: Shahn Kermani/ Gamma-Liaison; page 290: Richard Hutchings/Photo Researchers, Inc.; page 291: Comstock; page 293: Richard Hutchings/Info Edit.

Chapter 11. Page 300: Alvis Upitis/The Image Bank; page 301, left: Paul Conklin/ Monkmeyer Press; page 301, right: Ellis Herwig/Taurus Photos; page 302: R. Feldmann & D. McCoy/Rainbow; page 303: Four By Five Inc.; page 304: Tony Freeman/PhotoEdit; page 306, top left: Lenore Weber/Taurus Photos; page 306, top right: D. & J. McClurg/Bruce Coleman Inc.; page 306, bottom left: LeBeau/ Biological Photo Service; page 309: S. Niedorf/The Image Bank; page 313, top left: Michal Heron; page 313, top right: Don Spiro/Medichrome; page 318: Four By Five Inc.; page 320: Mario Ruiz/Picture Group; page 321: Mary Brown/Medichrome; page 323: Alfred Pasieka/Taurus Photos; page 325: Doug Menuez/Picture Group; page 327: Bob Daemmrich/Stock, Boston; page 329: Myrleen Ferguson/ PhotoEdit.

Chapter 12. Page 334: Frank Cezus/FPG International; page 335: Dan McCoy/ Rainbow; page 336: Grace Moore/Medichrome; page 338: Bob Daemmrich/ Stock, Boston; page 339: Paul Light/Lightwave; page 340: M. Rotker/Taurus Photos; page 341: Jerry Cooke/Photo Researchers, Inc.; page 343: Don & Pat Valenti/Tom Stack & Associates; page 344: Gary Bistram/The Image Bank; page 345: Kay Chernush/The Image Bank; page 347, top left: Earl Roberge/West Stock, Inc.; page 347, top right: Tony Freeman/ PhotoEdit; page 351: Courtesy of the National Multiple Sclerosis Society; page 352: Tom Dunham; page 354: Craig Sherburne/West Stock, Inc.; page 358: B. Montrose, M.D./Custom Medical Stock Photo; page 359: Bobbie Kingsley/Photo Researchers, Inc.

Chapter 13. Page 363: Alan Carey/Photo Researchers, Inc.; page 364: Sara Matthews; page 365: Richard Hutchings/ Photo Researchers, Inc.; page 366: Will & Deni McIntyre/Photo Researchers, Inc.; page 368: Tom Dunham; page 369, bottom left: Tom Dunham; page 369, bottom right: Richard Hutchings; page 370, top left: Charles E. Schmidt/Taurus Photos; page 370, top right: Tony Freeman/PhotoEdit; page 372: Tom Dunham; page 375: Richard Hutchings; page 377, top: John Terence Turner/FPG International; page 377, bottom: Momatiuk/Eastcott/Woodfin

Camp & Associates; page 378: David Stoecklein/Uniphoto Picture Agency; page 380: Richard Hutchings; page 383: Tony Freeman/PhotoEdit; page 388, left:

Tom Raymond/Medichrome; page 388, right: Tom Dunham; page 389: Rod Planck/Tom Stack & Associates; page 390: Joyce Photographics/Photo Researchers, Inc.; page 394: Vladimir Lange/ The Image Bank; page 395: Tom Dunham.

Chapter 14. Page 400: Tom Dunham; page 401: Cathlyn Melloan/TSW/Click/Chicago Ltd.; page 402: Michal Heron; page 403: Tom Raymond/The Stock Shop; page 404: Jon Feingersh/Tom Stack & Associates; page 405: Michal Heron; page 407: Tom Dunham; page 409: Mary Kate Denny/ PhotoEdit; page 412: The Granger Collection; page 413: Bob Daemmrich/Stock, Boston; page 416: Tom Dunham; page 417: Rick Kopstein/Monkmeyer Press; page 418: Bob Daemmrich/Stock, Boston; page 419: Jeff Dunn/The Picture Cube; page 420: J. L. Barkan/The Picture Cube; page 422: R. Capece/Monkmeyer Press.

Chapter 15. Page 430: Spencer Swanger/ Tom Stack & Associates; page 431: Four By Five Inc.; page 433: Ed Resnick/TSW/ Click/Chicago, Ltd.; page 435: Yada Claassen/Stock, Boston; page 438: Cliff Feulner/The Image Bank; page 439: Martin Rogers/Stock, Boston; page 440: Martha Bates/Stock, Boston; page 441: Eric Anderson/Stock, Boston.

Front Cover. Chuck O'Rear/Westlight
Back Cover. All Sport/Westlight

Health Handbook. Page A2: Margaret W. Peterson/The Image Bank.